T0305370

Our professionals develop lasting client relationships by delivering the superior banking capabilities, creative ideas, and capital markets resources clients need to succeed.

We customize innovative financing for real estate investors, funds, operating companies, homebuilders, REITS, mortgage banking, and lodging companies.

Clients benefit from our track record and expertise, which are at the forefront of the industry—dominating in number of relationships, dollars committed, and products and services provided.

The Handbook of Nonagency Mortgage-Backed Securities

Second Edition

Edited by

Frank J. Fabozzi, Ph.D., CFA
Adjunct Professor of Finance
School of Management
Yale University

Chuck Ramsey
CEO
Mortgage Risk Assessment Corporation

Michael Marz
Vice Chairman
First Southwest Company

Published by Frank J. Fabozzi Associates

ISBN: 1-883249-68-6

TABLE OF CONTENTS

CONTRIBUTING AUTHORS

Steven Abrahams	Freddie Mac
Steve Banerjee	Prudential Securities Incorporated
Douglas L. Bendt	Mortgage Risk Assessment Corporation
Eric Bruskin	Office of Federal Housing Enterprise Oversight
Da Cheng	Wall Street Analytics, Inc.
Manus J. Clancy	The Trepp Group
Michael Constantino, III	The Trepp Group
Adrian R. Cooper	Wall Street Analytics, Inc.
Glenn T. Costello	Fitch IBCA
Akiva Dickstein	Lehman Brothers
Michael A. Ervolini	Charter Research Corporation
Howard Esaki	Morgan Stanley Dean Witter
Frank J. Fabozzi	Yale University
Mark Feldman	Bear Stearns & Co.
Abner Figueroa	Duff & Phelps Credit Rating Company
Thomas Gillis	Standard and Poor's
Laurie Goodman	PaineWebber, Inc.
Harold J. A. Haig	Charter Research Corporation
Ted C.H. Hong	Capital America
Oliver Hsiang	Morgan Stanley Dean Witter
Jason Huang	Wall Street Analytics, Inc.
David P. Jacob	Capital America
Hedi T. Katz	Fitch IBCA
Brian P. Lancaster	Bear Stearns & Co. Inc.
Laurence H. Lee	Warburg Dillon Reed LLC
Linda Lowell	Credit Suisse First Boston
Michael Marz	First Southwest Company
John N. McElravey	Banc One Capital Markets
Michael A. Megliola	Bear Stearns & Co.
Errol Mustafa	Prudential Securities Incorporated
Frank Raiter	Standard & Poor's
Chuck Ramsey	Mortgage Risk Assessment Corporation
Robert Restrick	Pentalpha Capital Group Llc
W. Alexander Roever	Banc One Capital Markets
Anthony B. Sanders	The Ohio State University
Charles Schorin	Morgan Stanley Dean Witter
Glenn M. Schultz	Banc One Capital Markets
V.S. Srinivasan	Bear Stearns & Co.
David Sykes	Consultant
Edward L. Toy	Teachers Insurance and Annuity Association
Steven Weinreich	Morgan Stanley Dean Witter
Dale Westhoff	Bear Stearns & Co.
Michael Youngblood	Banc of America Securities LLC
Thomas Zimmerman	PaineWebber, Inc.

Section I

Residential Real Estate-Backed Securities

A. Products and Their Structure

Chapter 1

The Nonagency Mortgage Market: Background and Overview

Eric Bruskin, Ph.D.*
Manager, Economic and Financial Research
Office of Federal Housing Enterprise Oversight

Anthony B. Sanders, Ph.D.
Galbreath Distinguished Scholar and Professor of Finance
The Ohio State University

David Sykes, Ph.D.
Consultant

INTRODUCTION: NONCONFORMING LOANS AND NONAGENCY SECURITIES

The three U.S. government-chartered mortgage agencies are the foundation on which the entire mortgage-backed securities (MBS) market is based: the Federal National Mortgage Association (FNMA or "Fannie Mae," now its official corporate designation), the Federal Home Loan Mortgage Corporation (FHLMC or "Freddie Mac"), and the Government National Mortgage Association (GNMA or "Ginnie Mae"). The constituencies they serve and the nature of their government sponsorship may differ somewhat, but the end result is the same. By issuing securities with their implicit (Fannie Mae and Freddie Mac) or explicit (Ginnie Mae) government guarantee, the agencies promote the availability of mortgage funding at the lowest possible cost to all qualified American home buyers. However, this policy-driven "agency advantage" applies only to loans that meet certain criteria, most significantly with respect to loan size and underwriting standards.

Only conforming loans are eligible to be purchased and/or guaranteed by one or more of the agencies; these are the loans that back (or "collateralize") agency

---

* The views expressed in this chapter are those of Dr. Bruskin and do not represent policies or positions of the Office of Federal Housing Enterprise Oversight or any other officials or agencies of the U.S. Government.

MBSs, which are guaranteed against credit losses by the agency that issues them. As a part of the Department of Housing and Urban Development, Ginnie Mae securitizes government-sponsored mortgages, primarily FHA-insured or VA-guaranteed mortgage loans. Fannie Mae and Freddie Mac securitize conventional mortgage loans that conform to their loan size and underwriting standards. Nonconforming conventional loans are securitized and traded in a parallel nonagency market which, to investors, primarily means that the mortgages do not carry an agency guarantee against credit losses. (The nonagency sector is also alternately referred to as the private-label market.) Thus, in order to qualify for a rating, securities backed by nonagency mortgages must carry alternative forms of credit enhancement.

Loan Size

To qualify for agency securitization or purchase programs, a conventional mortgage loan must have a "conforming balance." The maximum in 1999 was $240,000 for both Fannie Mae and Freddie Mac. Each agency decides independently, but historically their limits have been the same. Higher limits apply to 2-to-4 family properties, and lower limits apply to the FHA/VA mortgages collateralizing Ginnie Mae securities. Mortgage loans that exceed the conforming limits, generally termed "jumbos," comprise a substantial portion of the assets underlying nonagency securities. These loans tend to be concentrated in metropolitan areas with high-cost housing: the Boston-to-Washington corridor on the East Coast, and the San Diego-to-Los Angeles and San Francisco regions on the west coast. Thus, a pool of jumbo loans will usually be more regionally concentrated than a conforming pool. For example, it is not uncommon for a jumbo pool to have a California concentration in excess of 50% as compared with a typical conforming pool's concentration of around 25%.

The conforming limit is based on the year-over-year average house price change as reported by the Federal Housing Finance Board (FHFB); however, it is reset based only on the value reported in October, which could represent a short-term spike. The agencies may, but are not required to, raise the loan limit if the index increases, and historically they have not lowered it in response to declines in the index. For example, between 1993 and 1995 the FHFB index declined nearly 5%, yet Fannie Mae and Freddie Mac held the loan limits fixed at $203,150. A flurry of controversy ensued, as "jumbo" lenders and conduits have seen their market eaten away in small slices as Fannie Mae and Freddie Mac have continued to raised their limits over time (see Exhibit 1).

Exhibit 1: Conforming Loan Limits

Year	Loan Limit ($)	Year	Loan Limit ($)	Year	Loan Limit ($)
1985	115,300	1990	187,450	1995	203,150
1986	133,250	1991	191,250	1996	207,000
1987	153,100	1992	202,300	1997	214,600
1988	168,700	1993	203,150	1998	227,150
1989	187,600	1994	203,150	1999	240,000

The controversy surrounding conforming loan limits intensified briefly in October 1996, when the FHFB index surged nearly 10%, potentially enabling a loan limit increase of almost $18,000. Members of Congress joined mortgage industry trade groups in calling for Fannie Mae and Freddie Mac to voluntarily limit their 1997 loan limit increases consistent with the spirit of their legal mandate: to serve low and moderate income housing needs. Fannie Mae and Freddie Mac conceded and increased their 1997 conforming loan limits to only $214,600, about $10,000 less than the legal limit, effectively netting out the prior decreases in the FHFB Index. However, over the next two years the limit was raised another 12%, to $240,000, apparently making up for lost time.

Underwriting Standards

The second major source of nonconforming loans is so-called "B/C quality" or "subprime" originations, which fail to meet agency standards with respect to borrower characteristics (such as debt-to-income ratio and credit history) or loan characteristics (such as loan-to-value ratio). "B/C" refers to a grading scale that classifies loan credit quality on a scale from A (fully underwritten with a strong borrower) to D (equity-based lending without regard to borrower income or credit history). This subprime category of nonconforming loans also includes "low-doc" and "no-doc" originations where the borrower's income and/or other credit information are inadequately documented, i.e. either unreported or unverified. These borrowers would most likely not qualify for the loan under the more stringent agency guidelines.

Typically a weak borrower is required to make a larger down payment: thus, most B/C loans have lower loan-to-value ratios. On the other hand, a stronger borrower may be granted a loan with a very low down payment. This is often the case with first-time homebuyers who may be cash-poor but starting out in a career that pays well. The agencies increased their involvement with high-LTV loans in 1994 when origination volume dropped significantly after a nearly 3-year refinancing boom, during which lenders easily maintained more restrictive underwriting standards. Similarly, jumbo originators have dramatically increased their activity in the B/C sector to maintain origination volume and broaden their customer base.

Thus a conventional loan backing a nonagency MBS may be nonconforming with respect to balance, underwriting standards, or both. A new loan with a conforming balance in a nonagency pool almost invariably signals nonconforming underwriting. Loans conforming with respect to both will naturally be securitized through the agencies because the price execution is better. Jumbo loans have no other securitization outlet to siphon off the highest quality product; thus nonagency MBS issuance should reflect the industry's overall underwriting mix, which is still predominantly "A" level. In response to investor preference, however, nonagency issuers rarely mix underwriting categories within a single MBS and several even use a different issuing entity for their subprime loans.

Risks in Nonagency Securities

Credit risk is the major difference between agency-backed and nonagency MBSs. Agency securities are 100% guaranteed against credit losses by the U.S. government (explicitly or implicitly, as described above). Nonagency MBSs almost always carry more limited loss protection, in a form that is less robust than a U.S. government guarantee. As a result, there are several ways in which credit problems on the underlying mortgage loans could affect investors. If enough borrowers default, and property losses are sufficiently high, aggregate losses could exceed the amount of the limited guarantee. Alternatively, severe economic stress could render third-party guarantors unable to pay claims. The rating agencies have established various criteria — loss coverage requirements and legal/structural requirements for the mechanism that delivers this loss coverage — intended to render these possibilities sufficiently remote to merit the high credit ratings that investors demand.

Many structural options are available to protect investors against mortgage default risk, event risk, and cash flow timing risk. Throughout the 1980s, third-party supports such as pool insurance, bond insurance, letters of credit (LOCs), and corporate guarantees were most frequently used. However, investors' heightened awareness of event risk (mostly due to bank and insurance company downgrades), combined with the withdrawal of many third-party credit enhancement providers from the mortgage business in the aftermath of the Texas, New England, and California real estate debacles, resulted in a decisive turn towards subordination and other "standalone" (as opposed to external or third party) credit enhancement techniques that are internal to the structure itself. We outline the mechanics of these techniques below in a discussion of the structuring process.

Callability, due to prepayments of the underlying mortgages, has also become an extremely important consideration for both agency and nonagency MBSs during the past several years. The main issue here is whether nonconforming loans prepay differently from conforming loans. But call risk (generally called "prepayment risk" in the MBS literature) can be mitigated or exacerbated by the structure of an MBS transaction — specifically, in the way that principal is allocated among different classes of a multiclass security. Most of these structural techniques are familiar from agency REMICs or CMOs, but two mechanisms ("shifting interest" and "stepdown triggers," which are related to each other) are unique to nonagency securities. As detailed in our section on the structuring process, these structural mechanisms are creatures of the rating agencies: they respond to credit events, not prepayments, and need to be analyzed differently.

HISTORICAL HIGHLIGHTS

The Early Years: 1977-1986

The first rated publicly issued nonagency MBS was issued by Bank of America in 1977. For the next several years, until the mid-1980s, nonagency issuance was sparse and inconsistent. During this period, the dominant nonconforming loan originators were savings and loan institutions, whose traditional business was originating 30-year fixed-rate mortgages funded by retail deposits and other short term financing. As the yield curve inverted and competition for deposits intensified, the spread of mortgage rates over funding costs disappeared and then turned negative. In response, some of the more agile institutions (especially in California) turned to the secondary market to dispose of their fixed-rate mortgage loans and shifted their focus to adjustable-rate lending. At least one conduit was also established during this period to purchase nonconforming loans from institutions that lacked the "critical mass" to issue their own MBS. At that time, a $50-$100 million issue was pretty respectable for a public security, but many private transactions were less than $25 million. Most issues were rated double-A by Standard and Poor's (then the only rating agency active in the nonagency MBS sector) on the basis of credit support provided, in most cases, by pool insurance or a letter of credit (LOC) from a double-A or triple-A rated institution.

The nonagency market got off to a slow start primarily because of high interest rates, which resulted in low mortgage production and an ill tempered bond market. Issuers who wanted to reach the public market were also inconvenienced by the need to register each new MBS separately. In fact, many early nonagency MBSs were private placements, but "pipeline" originators would eventually require the size and liquidity of the public securities market to absorb the supply. The nonagency MBS market thus received a considerable boost from the Secondary Mortgage Market Enhancement Act of 1984 (SMMEA), which permitted shelf registration of nonagency MBSs rated double-A or higher. (Agency securities have always been exempt from SEC registration requirements.)

The vast majority of nonconforming mortgages, however, were still traded as unsecuritized "whole loans." In some of these transactions, the buyer had recourse to the seller for reimbursement of credit losses in the form of a 10% subordinated interest retained by the seller, who was generally the servicer as well. This prototypical senior/subordinated structure improved upon traditional recourse arrangements in one significant respect: the buyer had recourse to asset cash flow instead of the unsecured credit of the seller. Most mortgage seller/servicers were unrated or noninvestment grade entities, especially in the aftermath of a nationwide recession and real estate debacles in Texas, the "oil patch" and the southwest.

The Advent of Senior/Subordinated MBSs: Mid 1980s

In the early 1980s, an attempt was made to use a senior/subordinated (or "A/B") structure in a publicly issued MBS, but the securities were never issued because of the unfavorable tax treatment then accorded to multiclass mortgage-backed securities. The IRS removed this obstacle with an interim rule in 1986 and Congress followed up with the REMIC (Real Estate Mortgage Investment Conduit) legislation in 1987. As a credit enhancement technique, subordination could be applied to any type of mortgage including those which, for whatever reason, were rejected by pool insurers; and subordination could be used by any issuer to create highly rated securities, regardless of the issuer's own credit rating (which in the late 1980s was not likely to be very strong) or even the quality of the mortgages themselves. (Weaker assets would simply require a larger subordinated interest.) The rating agencies developed extensive criteria for senior/subordinated structures, and over the next few years a flood of senior/subordinated issuers entered the market, starting with Home Savings of America in July 1986. These issuers fell into one of three categories:

1. Banks and thrifts that were either "testing the market" or selling assets to raise capital (recall that the late 1980s saw the final phase of the thrift crisis). These were not a steady source of MBS supply.
2. Larger originators of nonconforming loans who found third-party loss coverage to be uneconomical (in the case of ARM loans, which pool insurers were reluctant to cover) or unavailable (especially in California following the 1989 earthquake). These were a steady source of MBS supply as long as the loans could be securitized at a profit.
3. Mortgage banking and conduit operations that funded their nonconforming originations and loan purchases through securitization. These organizations depended on the securitization market for their very existence, and provided a steady supply of MBS product that did the most to fuel the market's growth.

Origins of the "B-Piece" Market: Late 1980s

Issuers of senior/subordinated MBSs under the pre-REMIC tax rule were required to retain the subordinated interest (or "B-piece"). REMIC issuers were permitted to sell the subordinated interest, although most chose initially to retain it, for three reasons: (1) they believed that their credit losses would be small; (2) the regulatory treatment was lenient, not yet fully recognizing the highly leveraged nature of a subordinated MBS; and (3) nobody believed that investors would buy a subordinated MBS. Agency MBS investors were unaccustomed to credit risk, corporate high yield investors were unfamiliar with mortgage risk, and the size of the bonds was too small to entice either group to invest the time required to understand this new product.

A few issuers did begin to sell their B pieces as soon as the REMIC legislation permitted them to: the first such sale was by the Residential Funding Corporation (RFC) in the first half of 1987. In general, the early sellers of subordinated interests were conduits and mortgage banks, who unlike banks and thrifts were not portfolio originators and thus were uninterested in retaining their subordinated interests. However, the advent of various risk-based capital regulations and accounting rules in 1989 and the early 1990s made it much less attractive for regulated institutions to hold subordinated interests, and they too began to release them into the market.

Early B-piece valuation was relatively crude. The securities were usually untranched "shifting-interest" subordinated classes (described more fully in the discussion of structure below), sized to provide double-A levels of credit support: at the time, generally 6% to 8% for fixed-rate loans and 8% to 12% for ARMs. Because they were in a first loss position (and thus essentially certain to suffer some losses), the B-pieces were unrated; but they were also large enough that if the losses remained at hitherto historical levels they might represent only a small portion of the security's face amount. At the time, however, investors had little or no historical data on anything other than the Great Depression and early reports from the developing debacle in Texas. Thus, most investors initially valued B pieces too conservatively for the sale to make economic sense for most issuers.

Pricing aside, the investor base for unrated subordinated securities, which typically had average lives in excess of 15 years (with 30-year mortgages), was vanishingly small. But it was soon realized that if the B piece was itself tiered into a senior "fast pay" and a junior "slow pay" class, the senior-subordinated (or "mezzanine") class could merit an investment-grade rating. Moody's was the first to rate such classes, in late 1988. The resulting Baa-rated security had an average life of less than 10 years, which increased its investor appeal somewhat, although many MBS investors were still restricted to double- and triple-A securities. However, the first-loss class that remained was more highly levered and extremely long, essentially unsalable and less appealing to retain. Thus, for many issuers, the triple-B mezzanine structure didn't significantly improve the economics of the overall transaction.

The Thrift Crisis and The Resolution Trust Corporation: Early 1990s

In response to the massive collapse of savings and loans in the late 1980s, Congress created the Resolution Trust Corporation (RTC) in 1989 as a corporation wholly owned by the U.S. government. Its primary function was to oversee the liquidation of the assets in thrift institutions seized by regulatory authorities. In this capacity, the RTC was the largest issuer of nonagency residential MBSs in 1991 and 1992. After depleting its inventory of performing residential loans, the RTC pioneered the securitization of nonperforming mortgages with its "N-series" transactions in 1993. With the abatement of the thrift crisis, the RTC was merged into the FDIC at the end of 1995. Nevertheless, in its heyday the RTC's frequent issuance and large transaction size helped consolidate the nonagency MBS investor base and transform the nonagency MBS market into a major mortgage market sector.

Another of the RTC's important contributions to the development of the nonagency MBS market was its focus on investor reporting. Prior to 1991, most private issuers were unwilling or unable to provide detailed information on the mortgages backing their nonagency MBSs, primarily because of the amount of information processing involved. Notable exceptions at the time were the Prudential Home Mortgage Company (since acquired by Norwest) which provided loan-level updates on its nonagency pools in electronic form, and Citicorp Mortgage

Securities which provided summary updates on its MBS issues in a well-designed quarterly digest. The RTC worked actively with its Wall Street dealers to assure the marketability and liquidity of its securities. Part of its strategy was the coordinated distribution of information, raising the prevailing market standards for investor reporting. Standardization was limited because many RTC transactions involved unusual or unique collateral. Nevertheless, the efforts of the RTC in providing collateral information effectively prodded the private issuers to provide detailed and updated data regarding collateral composition and performance.

Explosive Growth and Structural Evolution: 1991-1993

As discussed above, nonagency issuance increased significantly with the advent of the senior/subordinated structure in 1986 (Exhibit 2), but the most dramatic growth came with the 1991-1993 rally in the bond market. Annual issuance quadrupled between 1990 and 1993. As interest rates dropped more nonconforming loans were being originated, and a higher percentage of them were being securitized. As shown in Exhibit 4, in 1990 only about 27% of nonconforming loans went into MBSs; by 1993, this number had risen to about 46%, a record high. Nonagency MBS issuance grew from 3% of all MBSs issued in 1986 to 16% in 1992. In terms of total mortgage securities outstanding (see Exhibit 3), nonagency securities have grown from 4% in 1987 to 18% in 1998. This is especially impressive given the agencies' steady encroachment upon the nonagency market via increases in their conforming loan limit requirements by more than 80% during this period, from $133,250 in 1986 to $240,000 in 1999 (see Exhibit 1 above).

Exhibit 2: Nonagency Issuance ($ Million)

Year	REMICs	ARMs	Total Whole Loan Issuance
1982	NA	NA	$253
1983	NA	NA	1,585
1984	NA	NA	236
1985	NA	NA	1,956
1986	NA	NA	6,993
1987	$9,043	$2,057	11,100
1988	3,341	12,118	15,459
1989	7,812	6,426	14,238
1990	16,811	7,619	24,430
1991	30,599	18,750	49,349
1992	63,448	26,018	89,466
1993	77,759	20,734	98,493
1994	47,583	15,280	62,863
1995	23,691	11,135	34,826
1996	32,510	5,959	38,469
1997	53,340	10,133	63,473
1998	128,106	6,368	134,474

Source: *Inside MBS & ABS, Inside Mortgage Finance*, Mortgage Market Statistical Annual. Copyright 1999, Bethesda, MD, 301.951.1240

Exhibit 3: Securities Outstanding: Nonagency Versus Agency ($ Million)

Year	Agency ($)	% Total	Whole Loan ($)	% Total	Total ($)
1987	$653,771	96	$27,800	4	$681,571
1988	723,576	95	34,865	5	758,441
1989	843,779	95	43,325	5	887,104
1990	991,068	95	55,408	5	1,046,476
1991	1,130,340	92	100,110	8	1,230,450
1992	1,248,179	89	151,933	11	1,400,112
1993	1,334,280	88	184,796	12	1,519,076
1994	1,449,686	87	208,500	13	1,658,186
1995	1,543,400	87	227,800	13	1,771,200
1996	1,678,881	87	261,900	13	1,940,781
1997	1,787,983	85	318,000	15	2,105,983
1998	1,970,153	82	425,836	18	2,395,989

Source: *Inside MBS & ABS* Copyright 1999, Bethesda, MD, 301.951.1240

Exhibit 4: Securitization Rates: Whole Loans Versus Agency ($ Million)

	Agency		Whole Loans	
Year	Originations ($)	Securitized (%)	Originations ($)	Securitized (%)
1990	$367,820	64	$90,620	27
1991	449,660	60	112,410	35
1992	714,940	64	178,730	42
1993	818,000	70	201,860	48
1994	610,760	59	162,360	39
1995	489,540	54	146,230	24
1996	604,700	60	180,630	21
1997	661,330	54	197,600	32
1998	1,101,100	66	328,900	41

Source: *Inside MBS & ABS* Copyright 1999, Bethesda, MD, 301.951.1240

Investors willingly absorbed this increased issuance for several reasons:

1. A massive educational blitz by Wall Street dealers and the four rating agencies now rating nonagency MBSs significantly raised investors' awareness of the product, their comfort level with its credit quality, and their understanding of the various cash flow structures involved.
2. More frequent issuance, larger deal sizes and greater uniformity in the credit enhancement structures from one deal to the next also improved the product's liquidity.
3. Most nonagency MBSs were now being issued as CMOs rather than as single-class passthroughs, thus accessing a much broader spectrum of fixed income investors.

This shift to CMO issuance was itself the outward manifestation of several underlying trends that were changing the structure of the entire nonagency MBS market:

1. A shift from adjustable-rate to fixed-rate originations in the nonconforming loan sector;
2. The related shift in loan origination market share from thrifts and other portfolio originators to secondary-market driven mortgage banks and conduits;
3. Increased attention to nonagency loan prepayment trends (although with varying degrees of success), which facilitated investor acceptance of increasingly prepayment-sensitive principal allocation structures.

The shift to CMOs was also responsible for a change in the predominant rating level of new issue nonagency MBSs from double A (which was customary for single-class passthroughs) to triple-A (which is customary in the CMO sector). This in turn helped to establish subordination as the dominant credit enhancement technique, for several reasons:

1. By 1992, the traditional LOC banks had all been downgraded below triple-A, precluding them from playing a primary role in a triple-A rated transaction;
2. By 1992, only one pool insurance provider was still rated triple-A, and it was strictly limiting its exposure to California loans;
3. The triple-A bond insurers' pricing levels were uncompetitive for generic nonconforming mortgages (although they did play a significant role in transactions backed by difficult or unusual collateral);
4. The larger subordinated classes required to support a triple-A rated senior class were readily divisible into various subclasses with intermediate ratings, particularly in the double A to triple B range, thus accessing a much broader spectrum of fixed income investors — who, it should be recalled, were desperately searching for yield in the face of declining interest rates in the bond rally that sparked this entire phase of the nonagency market.

The B-Piece Market Comes Into Its Own

The successive tiering (differential allocation of credit risk) and tranching (differential allocation of prepayment risk) of residential subordinated classes thus continued — spurred on by parallel innovations in the RTC's commercial MBS sector with its large (and thus readily divisible) subordinated classes — and in 1992 a number of favorable trends combined to jump-start what could finally be called the B-piece market:

1. A move towards triple-A senior classes (for reasons discussed above) resulted in larger subordinated classes which could be divided into more

different credit tiers — everything from double-A down to single-B on top of an unrated first loss class. Larger subordinated classes also increased the importance of favorable B-piece pricing to the economics of the overall securitization.

2. Credit portents were turning favorable: delinquency rates on residential fixed-rate mortgages and consumer credit lines were declining noticeably, and, with the exception of California, home prices had demonstrably bottomed out in the southwest and the northeast. (The California experience in the early-to-mid 1990s represented more of a speed bump than a genuine obstacle in the path of the securitized mortgage credit markets.)

3. The bond market rally began to force investors to seek out new sources of yield enhancement. Double-A and even triple-A rated mezzanine classes enabled more conservative investors to get comfortable with subordinated MBSs (although ERISA regulations continued to prevent pension funds — significant buyers of long-maturity securities — from investing in subordinated MBSs regardless of the rating).

4. A number of large issuers had settled on a standard structure that included multi-tiered subordinated classes, enhancing the prospects for continued supply and liquidity. This was important because the structure and analysis had become quite complex, requiring a lengthy education process that could be justified only if the product was to remain available in significant amounts.

As a result, yield spreads on rated subordinated MBSs tightened dramatically during 1992 — by about 100 basis points (bps) for triple-B classes and 200 400 bps for noninvestment grade classes.

The MBS Tidal Wave

Throughout 1992 and 1993, the nonagency MBS market was running on all cylinders. Loan origination and MBS issuance hit unprecedented levels, as did the ever-tightening offering spreads of most credit-sensitive tranches. Investors continued to absorb the ongoing supply, despite growing disenchantment with the extremely high prepayment speeds being experienced by new issues. (However, this did increase the appeal of the longer, quite heavily call-protected subordinated classes.) These speeds were very far above the rates forecasted by Wall Street prepayment models, largely because the mortgage origination market had undergone a structural change that went undetected by the model-fitters: balloon mortgages (fixed-rate loans priced off of the shorter end of the yield curve) and no-point refinancings (which made it cheaper and easier to refinance a loan at the drop of a half-point).

On the other hand, there seemed to be few worries about credit quality, apart from California, where foreclosures were beginning to rise in response to a powerful recession that had begun in 1991. The traditional "A quality" lenders could pick and choose among the huge volume of mortgage applicants, and fully underwritten loans once again became the rule after several years of "limited doc" and "no-doc" lending aimed at preserving market share. According to the rating agencies' loss curves, the newly originated loans backing new-issue MBSs would not be at significant risk of default for several years. In fact, even seasoned MBSs were expected to benefit from the avalanche of prepayments, which prematurely depleted those pools of many loans which, although still performing at the time, could nevertheless be expected (on statistical grounds) to default at some future time. The massive rally had apparently "cleansed" the national mortgage pool of much of its credit risk, further enhancing the appeal of subordinated classes from newly issued MBSs and seasoned deals with low California concentrations.

Retrenchment: 1994-1996

But then the music stopped. During the first six months of 1994 interest rates increased by more than 200 basis points (bps), an abrupt end to a remarkable 3-year rally. Refinancing activity dried up, causing total originations to drop by 36% from 1993 to 1995. Moreover, many investors lost confidence in some of the more recent structural innovations. For example, investors who had purchased prepayment-protected CMO classes saw their structural protection eroded by the massive prepayments of 1991-1993. Then in 1994, these same bonds that had experienced an unanticipated shortening came under threat of a dramatic extension as prepayments rates dropped precipitously. Several highly publicized interest-rate derivatives related failures such as Orange County (California) and the Askin (Granite) funds also shook investor confidence in structured fixed-income products. On the supply side, CMO issuance became less profitable as the yield curve flattened by 155 bps: the spread between the 10-year and the 1-year Treasury dropped from 220 bps at the beginning of 1994 to 65 bps by year-end. Consequently, agency CMO issuance collapsed from $324 billion in 1993 to $23 billion in 1995.

Over the next couple of years, MBS investors assimilated the lessons to be gleaned from the 1993-1994 turn in the market. Although the yield curve as of this writing is still relatively flat relative to 1992-1993, renewed investor confidence and better understanding of the risks substantially restored the demand for mortgage securities in general, and CMO products in particular.

Alternative Lending Programs: 1996-1998

When interest rates backed up in 1994, mortgage originators scrambled to find ways to offset the dramatic drop in refinancing applications. Most originators broadened their market base by developing or expanding not only the subprime (B/C) credit programs mentioned above, but also more specialized B/C programs involving high LTV mortgages (some known informally as "125s," referring to the maximum LTV percentage these lenders would offer), and other programs designed to accommodate "alternative" A-quality borrowers who for whatever reason did not fit either the agency conforming or standard jumbo underwriting criteria.

Exhibit 5: B/C Mortgage-Backed Issuance (millions)

Year	Issuance
1994	$11,051
1995	$18,466
1996	$38,031
1997	$66,191
1998	$82,580

Source: *Inside MBS & ABS, Inside Mortgage Finance*, Mortgage Market Statistical Annual, Copyright 1999, Bethesda, MD, 301.951.1240

B/C-Credit Programs

Many B/C credit programs have had considerable success. As illustrated in Exhibit 5, B/C issuance increased from $11 billion in 1994 to $82 billion in 1998. Much of this growth springs from the increased packaging of B/C mortgages as home equity loan-backed securities (HELs) which trade in the asset-backed securities market, despite their undeniable mortgage-like nature (long-term, fully amortizing, first liens).

This peculiar state of affairs turns on a prepayment story: B/C borrowers take mortgage loans with high interest rates because they cannot qualify for anything else, and their loan amounts are typically lower than for A quality loans. Thus, these borrowers are expected to be less sensitive to interest rates because of the restricted opportunities to refinance and the limited dollar reduction in their debt service. On the other hand, overall B/C prepayment speeds (it is further claimed) are secularly fast because these borrowers are motivated to refinance into an A quality loan as soon as their credit position improves. Under these prepayment assumptions, securities backed by B/C loans should be shorter and yet less callable — precisely the characteristics sought by ABS investors. However, these assumptions were untested by experience, and could unravel, as conforming MBS assumptions did, if future product innovation provides appealing alternative financing for credit-impaired borrowers. For the present, though, established B/C lenders increasingly focus their B/C mortgage production on HELs that are funneled into the ABS market. In 1994, HELs backed 56% of B/C MBSs; by the third quarter of 1996, HELs accounted for 75% of all B/C issuance.

High LTV ("125") Programs

Given the partially unsecured, consumer loan-like nature of 125% LTV loans, most originators restricted their 125 lending to borrowers with at least A quality credit. (The increased use of credit scores in screening potential borrowers, although not foolproof, has enabled borrower credit quality to be quantified more precisely than ever before.) With LTVs above 100%, the usual protection afforded by borrower equity is no longer present; thus, the integrity of these loans depends entirely on the creditworthiness of the borrower. Consequently, borrowers in these programs typically pay consumer loan level interest rates that are approximately 500-600 bps over conforming mortgage rates. Nevertheless, at least some of this debt (the portion representing up to 100% of the home's value) is tax deductible, making this one of the cheaper consumer borrowing alternatives on an after-tax basis. Given the tremendous increase in higher rate and non-tax deductible credit card borrowings, it is not surprising that 125 lending volume skyrocketed. Citing the huge size of consumer debt (over $1.7 trillion), many believe the 125 loan market still has tremendous growth potential.

Another reason for the rapid growth of 125 LTV lending has been the strong housing market. As housing prices increase, homeowners can increase their borrowing using the 125 LTV product. Also, as housing prices increase, 125 LTV loans are more likely to be refinanced as their LTV drops. However, if the economy declines and housing prices decline with it, defaults will likely increase on 125 loans as homeowners lose their jobs or suffer a reduction in wages, making it difficult to maintain the high debt levels. As can be seen in Exhibit 6a, the 125 LTV loan adds additional debt burden for the borrower so that in the case of default on the first mortgage and the 125 LTV (second) mortgage, a decline in housing prices will have a greater negative impact on the 125 LTV mortgage. The severity of loss due to a correction in the residential housing market is depicted in Exhibit 6b. While a decline in housing prices is not likely to trigger default in isolation, a decline in housing prices can be symptomatic of a local or national recession, where job loss or earnings curtailment can lead to default.

Event Risk Redux — A Speed Bump from Overseas

After two years of heady growth in the "B/C" sector of the nonagency MBS market, the August 1998 credit scare precipitated by Russia's default on some of its debt wreaked havoc in many credit sensitive market sectors, from emerging markets to commercial mortgage-backed securities; but the relatively new 125 LTV sector was hit especially hard — probably excessively so. Secondary market participants substantially discounted the price of the securitized offerings after the middle of 1998, despite demonstrably low prepayment speeds (compared with other nonagency loan products) and delinquencies (compared with other home equity loan products). As buyers pulled back, the originators who relied on securitization to finance their lending operations were unable to survive this devastating blow from "left field." Larger banks have since acquired many of these firms and some have declared bankruptcy, most notably FirstPlus Financial, the (until then) undisputed market leader.

Investor Viewpoint: A Tale of Three Mortgages

One of the selling points of the 125 LTV loan product to investors is that prepayment speeds should be lower than prepayment speeds on other home-equity loans and nonconforming whole loans. In Exhibit 7, we compare the historical prepayment speeds (CPRs) on the 1997-1 FirstPlus 125 loan deal, The Money Store 1996-D home-equity loan deal and the Residential Funding RFMSI 8% 1997-S5 whole loan deal.

Exhibit 6: The Relationship Between a First Mortgage Loan, a 125 LTV Loan, and the Underlying House Price

(a)

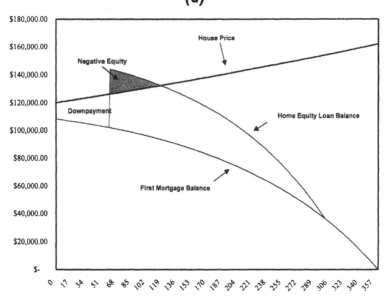

(b)

Assuming a Price Correction in the Residential Housing Market at Month 100

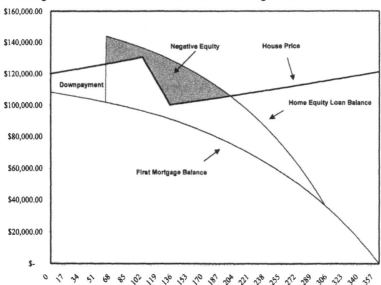

Exhibit 7: Historical Prepayments for Comparable Vintage Whole Loans, Home Equity Loans, and 125 LTV Loans

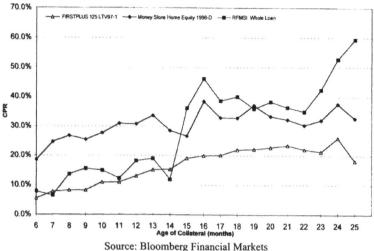

Source: Bloomberg Financial Markets

The prepayment speeds on the Residential Funding whole loan pool approached 60% CPR after two years. (The dramatic increase in the prepayment speed on the whole loans in month 14 was caused by a sudden decline in mortgage rates). The Money Store home-equity loan pool is in the 30-40% CPR range after two years while the FirstPlus 125 LTV loan portfolio has settled in the low 20% CPR range. While the historical prepayment speeds on the 125 LTV pool are higher than the 14% that some analysts expected after two years, the speeds are considerably less than those of whole loans and traditional home equity loans. (Also, the 125 loans showed almost no response to the drop in interest rates that caused the other two pools to accelerate noticeably.)

A Note on Credit Risk in Alternative Lending Programs

Standardization of loan programs nationwide has been a key element facilitating the development and evolution of today's massive MBS market. However, as we have seen, in their search to preserve market share and fully utilize existing servicing capability when loan originations slow down, lenders need to unearth borrowers who were previously undetected, underserved, or underqualified. In the jumbo loan sector, these have generally been borrowers who fail to satisfy one or more of the standard underwriting guidelines. In the 1980s, these borrowers were attracted to the "limited doc" or "no doc" programs in which the lenders waived most of the documentation required to demonstrate the borrower's financial strength (in other words, "don't ask, don't tell") in return for a large down payment. "No doc" programs were also known as "equity lending" because the loan quality depended entirely on the value of the underlying real estate. Lenders believed that increased borrower equity would reduce the probability of default and mitigate losses in the actual event of default.

Unfortunately, the lenders had miscalculated. "Limited doc" loans rapidly became the worst-performing sector of the nonagency MBS market. The most spectacular failures were due to borrower fraud, particularly fraudulent appraisals (which misrepresented the LTV ratio) and "silent second" mortgages (i.e., second mortgages taken out simultaneously with the first mortgage, unbeknownst to the first mortgage lender, thus misrepresenting the borrower's debt ratios). However, even mainstream lenders experienced much higher-than-anticipated losses on their limited doc portfolios, for several reasons:

1. *Adverse selection:* The near-total lack of borrower disclosure attracted genuinely weak borrowers, rather than creditworthy ones who failed to qualify on a technicality.
2. *Payment-induced borrower default:* Most limited doc loans were ARMs because they were more likely to have to remain in the lender's portfolio; and the combination of deep teaser rates and rising interest rates caused payments to increase dramatically through the late 1980s.
3. *Vanishing equity:* When the real estate market turned sour, prices on distressed properties dropped much faster than the overall average, which rapidly deflated the enhanced equity cushion.

The mid 1990s vintage alternative lending programs described above — high LTV loans and loans to borrowers with poor credit histories — are admittedly risky, but they do avoid most of the errors of the 1980s' "limited doc" programs. All borrower information is fully disclosed, so lenders are dealing with "the devil they know."

The Recent Experience on High LTV Loans

As pointed out previously, the 125 LTV loan portfolios have a lower prepayment speed than whole loans and other lower LTV home equity loan products. We might also expect that high LTV loan-backed transactions would have the highest default rates and that standard "A quality" jumbo MBSs would have the lowest. Unfortunately, default data are somewhat difficult to obtain for these products; however, we can use historical 90-day delinquencies as a proxy for default.

In Exhibit 8, we compare the historical 90-day delinquencies on whole loan, lower LTV home equity loans, and 125 LTV loans. As expected, the "A"-quality jumbo delinquencies are very low. What is somewhat surprising is that the lower LTV home equity loans from The Money Store have almost a linear growth in delinquencies that reach 12% after two years. The FirstPlus 125 LTV loans have a 90-day delinquency rate that is increasing with time as well; however, it is just above 2% of the portfolio after two years which is substantially less than The Money Store's experience. This appears to support the wisdom of lending larger amounts to high-quality borrowers, and points up the risks in lending even small amounts at lower LTVs to lower-quality borrowers.

Exhibit 8: Historical 90-Day Delinquency for Comparable Vintage Whole Loans, Home Equity Loans, and 125 LTV Loans

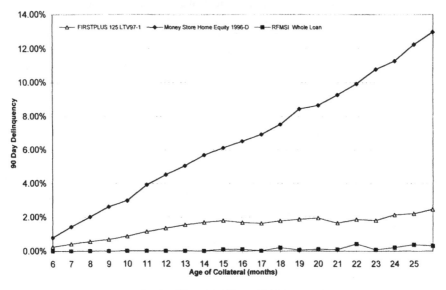

Source: Bloomberg Financial Markets

Subperforming and Nonperforming Loans

What might seem like the final frontier in mortgage securitization has now been reached with the development of an active market for the securitization and sale of delinquent and defaulted loans. This growing market sector was initially spawned by the leftovers from the RTC's securitizations, and the key to its acceptance was the practice (also initiated by the RTC) of structuring the transactions around a "special servicer" with specific expertise in working out and disposing of troubled loans. In the RTC transactions, the special servicer was also required to take an equity interest in the transaction.

More recently, the main sources of product have been HUD and large institutional lenders looking to cleanse their balance sheets. If the securitization's purpose is to finance the acquisition of the loans, it will generally employ a "liquidating structure" in which the bonds are paid down by the proceeds from sale of the loans as they are resolved — either through foreclosure or a return to performing status. Otherwise, the loans are securitized after they are worked out using more traditional CMO structures. All of these securitizations were nonagency transactions until late 1996 when Freddie Mac guaranteed a large pool of reperforming loans from a HUD auction. However, a controversy has arisen (unresolved as of this writing) as to whether this type of transaction is consistent with the U.S. government's goal in the HUD auctions of disposing of troubled assets, because Freddie Mac is itself a government-sponsored enterprise.

The Lessons of History: The View From 1999

It seems, then, that the nonagency MBS market has "been around the block a few times" since the early 1980s. Interest rates have rallied and backed up three times (bond market crashes in early 1987, 1994, and 1998), with corresponding flows and ebbs in issuance volume.

Underwriting standards have gone from agency-conforming down to no documentation, back up to agency conforming, and now perhaps have made a sideways extension to riskier borrowers (but smaller, lower-LTV loans) and riskier loans (higher LTVs, but only for the strongest borrowers) — but in both cases generally with full documentation.

Home prices peaked and troughed first in the southwest, then the northeast, and then in California, while continuing (so far) to advance more moderately in the Midwest and Southeast. In 1997 and 1998, even California joined the party.

Delinquency and default rates for nonagency mortgages deteriorated and then recovered strongly, with early indications of another moderate downturn as high-LTV and other "alternative" loans season.

Hundreds of insolvent savings and loan institutions went through a final spasm of loan activity before being flushed through the system by the RTC. In their wake, bank capital regulations fostered a more conservative attitude towards risk assessment that drastically reduced weaker borrowers' access to funding. As a result, more aggressive lending is now the province of specialized mortgage bankers and conduits that are, at this writing, amply funded by the capital markets, largely through securitization.

Nonagency MBS structures underwent an efflorescence from simple passthrough to CMOs with 40 classes distributed among 6 or 7 rating levels, and then pulled back to somewhat simpler structures after the derivatives debacle of 1994 before resuming the trend towards customized bonds.

If the nonagency market can be said to have "seen it all," or at least to have shaken out most of the kinks, then nonagency MBSs are well on their way to becoming commoditized portfolio staples, with adventurous yield seekers advised to set their sights elsewhere. However, if history is any guide, surprising developments are always lying in wait, creating the best opportunities for swift learners.

THE SECURITIZATION PROCESS

The process of securitizing residential whole loans can involve either seasoned or newly originated loans. The overwhelming majority of nonagency MBSs, however, are backed by newly originated mortgages. The process for securitizing new originations is outlined in Exhibit 9. In general, the primary components are:

1. Mortgage originator: mortgage brokers or loan origination offices or bank branches
2. Seller/servicer (usually the same party)

Exhibit 9: The Securitization Process

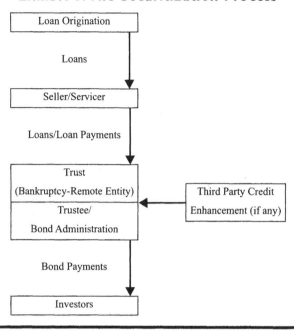

3. Issuer (a special-purpose, bankruptcy-remote entity)
4. REMIC or grantor trust
5. Master servicer (usually different from the servicer if securitized by a conduit)
6. Trustee/bond administrator
7. Investors

Mortgage conduits monitor both the lender and investor sides of the market, compiling a daily pricing sheet that informs the participating mortgage bankers and brokers of the levels at which new loans will be purchased. As the mortgage banks sell into the "warehouse," the individual loans are accumulated into pools that are deposited into a special purpose, bankruptcy-remote entity. The special-purpose entity is a wholly owned subsidiary of the issuer, essentially a legal vehicle that shields the integrity of the MBS from any future economic difficulties of the issuer's parent company. The master servicer often acts as the on going servicer of the loans once they are securitized. When the issuer is an independent conduit, the master servicing is usually performed in-house, whereas investment bank conduits generally contract out the master servicing to an outside party.

The trustee acts on behalf of the investors. Its primary responsibilities include monitoring the integrity of the overall transaction and the monthly bond administration. This generally includes overseeing the servicing activity, receiving monthly cash payments from the servicer, forwarding the cash flows (as paying agent) to the investors, and maintaining any reserve accounts called for by the bond structure. In some instances, the trustee may subcontract with a separate party to carry out all or part of the bond administrative process. In any case, these details are transparent to the investor, just as they are with agency deals.

THE STRUCTURING PROCESS

Credit Structuring: General Principles

Rating agencies determine the level of credit support required for a structured MBS based upon the collateral characteristics, the rating of any parties who play a significant role in the ongoing transaction, and the rating desired for the security itself. In general, the required levels and how they are allowed to vary over time are independent of how the credit support is provided (e.g., whether through a reserve fund, third-party guarantees, subordination, etc.). Until the early 1990s, triple-A rated MBSs generally required 4% to 5% loss coverage for 15-year fixed-rate collateral, 6% to 8% for 30-year fixed-rate collateral, and 10% to 12% for ARM collateral. In recent years, these levels have come down somewhat due to a combination of tighter underwriting standards and increased historical experience which has increased the rating agencies' confidence in their ability to predict credit losses on mortgage pools.

The full amount of credit support must be available at or soon after the start of the transaction (the *Cut-Off Date*), and the initial requirement remains in force for an extended period of time: it is not reduced as the pool balance declines over time — at least for the first several years. Initially, the pool balance is reduced almost exclusively by prepayments (as opposed to amortization). However, the rating agencies take a conservative view (which is now generally accepted) that only good loans prepay early, because weaker borrowers cannot qualify for a refinancing. Thus, although the pool balance has declined, the pool's credit risk has not. To counteract the effects of this adverse selection, rating agencies require that the initial loss coverage be maintained until the pools are sufficiently seasoned to ascertain their performance character. This period is generally 5 years for fixed-rate loans, 10 years for ARMs, and 15 years for negatively amortizing ARMs.

During this period, the credit support grows as a percentage of the outstanding pool balance. After this period, the loss coverage requirement "steps down" over the next few years, provided that the delinquency and loss experience of the pool does not exceed certain levels, known as "triggers." During the stepdown period, the amount of credit support is gradually reduced, but may continue to grow as a percentage of the pool balance — it just grows at a slower rate. The stepdown schedule generally runs for 4 years, after which the credit enhancement requirement becomes simply a fixed percentage of the outstanding pool balance, which number varies depending on the structure and, in most structures currently in use, on the historical paydown experience of the pool.

Coverage for short-term delinquencies, also known as liquidity coverage, is now generally provided by the servicer's agreement to advance delinquent payments to investors, backed by a highly rated entity — most commonly the master servicer or trustee — who provides this service for a fee. In older transactions or when the assets are particularly unconventional, this coverage is more often included with the loss coverage, which is sized appropriately to include the liquidity requirement. The rating agencies generally require that any third party providing delinquency coverage be assessed no lower than one level below the desired rating on the security or alternatively, have a sufficiently high short-term credit rating.

Although the rating agencies vary in the methods in which they assign security ratings, all of their methodologies are based on a review of the risk characteristics of the underlying mortgage collateral and the security's structure.

Collateral Quality

The rating agencies review the aggregate pool characteristics in addition to each loan's individual characteristics. At the loan level, the contractual features of the loan and the underlying property securing each loan are examined. At the pool level, aggregate characteristics such as the number of loans in the pool and their geographic concentration are taken into consideration.

Loan-to-Value Ratio

The loan-to-value (LTV) ratio is the ratio of the loan balance to the lesser of the purchase price and the appraised value of the property. LTV is an important indicator of default potential because a financially troubled borrower should not need to default if the property can be sold to repay the mortgage, i.e. if the current LTV ratio (based on a realistic appraisal and adjusted for selling costs) is less than 100%.

Prospectuses report the LTV at origination of the loan, which loses meaning over time as the loan seasons and property values change. Also, LTVs can be artificially lowered by inflated appraisals. Investors in seasoned transactions (particularly the subordinate classes) use brokers' price opinions (BPOs) or home price indexes to obtain a current LTV. Loan amortization also affects the LTV, but amortization is negligible throughout the period when a loan is at highest risk of default. (This is less true of 15-year fully amortizing loans.) A high original LTV indicates a low down payment, which usually reflects poorly on a borrower's credit quality. As mentioned in the historical survey, however, high-LTV lending (even over 100%) is currently an area of intense focus by loan originators.

Mortgage Type

Fixed-rate loans default less often than loans with variable payments. Rating agencies assign higher risk weightings for adjustable rate mortgages (ARMs) as well as buydown loans, tiered payment mortgages (TPMs), and other mortgages with contractual payment increases because of the risk of "payment shock" when the increase occurs. This risk is particularly high for borrowers who qualified for the loan on the basis of a discounted initial rate ("teaser"). ARMs with a more volatile underlying index, less restrictive interest rate caps, or payment caps that cause negative amortization or provide for periodic unlimited payment resets are especially at risk.

Mortgage Term and Coupon

Shorter amortizing terms and lower coupons cause a faster buildup in equity. Shorter terms result in larger monthly payments, which only a relatively strong borrower will voluntarily assume. Note that balloon loans have short maturities but longer amortizing terms, resulting in a lump sum payment due at maturity, making default highly likely if the borrower cannot refinance.

By itself, mortgage coupon is not a strong indicator of risk within a given lending grade. Clearly B/C loans carry higher rates than A-quality mortgages (see the Historical Overview above for further discussion of these terms). But within the A category, borrowers can to some extent choose their own mortgage rate by paying more or fewer origination "points" upon assumption of the mortgage loan. This is commonly referred to as "buying down" the rate. For example, if a borrower qualifies for a 7% mortgage loan with no "points," the rate can be reduced to 6.75% if the borrower pays 1% of the loan balance "up front" as an origination fee. This sliding scale commonly extends to two or three points. Therefore, the actual mortgage coupon is not completely observable: some of it may have been "bought down" in this way. This makes prepayment studies more difficult because they typically rely quite heavily on the observed mortgage rate to measure prepayment incentive.

Recently the concept of "risk-based pricing" has come under discussion, in which riskier borrowers pay a higher mortgage rate than borrowers with stronger economic credentials (often measured by credit scoring). While not yet a prevalent practice, if it does become more common then mortgage coupon may merit closer scrutiny as an indicator of borrower credit quality.

Documentation Standards

Full documentation standards for conforming loans require verification of income (VOI), verification of employment (VOE), verification of deposits (VOD) as the source of the down payment, credit reports, and property appraisals. The VOD and the property appraisal are especially important to the integrity of the LTV ratio, and the VOI validates the borrower debt-to-income ratio. Many loans are nonconforming simply because of inadequate ("limited") documentation.

Loan Purpose

Financing the purchase of a vacation home or investment property is riskier than financing the purchase of a primary home, because the borrower can default on the second home and still have a place to live. Investment properties are particularly risky because the borrower is less committed to maintaining a property that he does not personally occupy and may depend on rental income to maintain the mortgage payments. Refinancing to a lower rate improves loan quality because it accelerates loan amortization and reduces the borrower's debt service. However, equity take-out (or "cash-out") refinancings increase the LTV ratio and, therefore, the risk of default.

Loan Seasoning

According to Standard & Poor's (S&P), about two-thirds of mortgage losses generally occur by the seventh year of a pool's life, and 90% by the tenth year. By that time, the expectation is that property appreciation and loan amortization will have produced substantial borrower equity, and the borrower's long occupancy indicates financial stability. However, the record low mortgage rates in 1993 and the consequent wave of refinancings may actually have increased the risk in older mortgage pools because the loans that remain are presumably those that were unable to refinance because of poor credit, i.e. they have been adversely selected. On the other hand, Moody's has observed that many of the loans that were refinanced at a very early age would have defaulted later on; therefore, the refinancing wave actually removed some credit risk from the then existing pools. Thus, the credit performance of MBSs backed by loans originated in 1991 and 1992 were generally better than originally expected.

Property Type

The default risk is lower for loans secured by owner-occupied, detached single-family properties than those secured by multifamily dwellings, planned unit developments (PUD), condominiums, and townhouses. Although housing prices usually decline during a recession, there is more sustained demand for single-family detached homes. Townhouses, PUDs, condominiums, and especially 2-4 family dwellings generally experience sharper declines. As the property value declines, the LTV ratio increases and thus the risk of default increases.

Geographic Diversification

Economic diversification and regional special hazards must be considered when analyzing the default risk of a loan. More credit support is required when more than a few percent of the loans are in one zip code, or as little as 1% per zip code in an area prone to special hazards like earthquakes. Loans originated in an area dominated by one industry are more susceptible to troubles in that industry, as demonstrated by the debacle in Texas and the surrounding "oil patch" states precipitated by the collapse of oil prices in the mid 1980s. On the other hand, special hazard related fears failed to materialize in the aftermath of two serious earthquakes in California in 1989 (Loma Prieta, near San Francisco) and 1994 (Northridge in Los Angeles' San Fernando Valley), although the 1994 quake did temporarily exacerbate existing mortgage credit problems. Simple probabilistic arguments show that earthquake-related losses should not exceed rating agency-mandates for special hazard coverage unless the frequency and severity of property damage approach levels far in excess of anything observed even near the epicenters of the two recent California quakes.

Structural Issues

Once the quality of the collateral has been established, the rating agencies verify that the collateral cash flow adequately supports the deal structure. Scrutiny of the deal structure provides the final element in assessing the credit enhancement required for a security.

Soundness of the Servicer and Trustee

Many of the servicer's functions are critical to the credit quality of a transaction. In addition to collecting the monthly payments and passing the cash flows to the trustee, the servicer handles delinquent loans, initiates foreclosure procedures, and liquidates properties when necessary. To maintain the timely payment of principal and interest to investors, the servicer typically advances missed payments due to delinquency and foreclosure, and is reimbursed as loans cure and properties are liquidated. If the servicer is rated (generally) more than one grade lower than the transaction, a backup servicer is required. Generally, however, trustees are rated at least double A for any issue.

Interest Shortfall

Investors expect to receive interest based on a full 30-day month. However, borrowers who prepay between monthly payments only pay interest through the prepayment date. In most nonagency MBSs the servicer is required to pay compensating interest to cover the shortfall, but only up to a specified percentage of the monthly servicing fee. In the event that the interest shortfall is not fully compensated, the loss is shared on a pro-rata basis by all classes, regardless of their credit priority. As investors realized in 1992-1993, structures that do not pay compensating interest can result in significant yield impairment in a high prepayment environment.

Credit Enhancement Techniques

As we have seen, mortgage credit risk encompasses short-term delinquencies as well as unrecoverable losses due to borrower default. The government agencies eliminate mortgage credit risk from the securities they issue by guaranteeing the timely payment of principal and interest (or ultimate payment of principal for Freddie Mac non-Gold PCs). Nonagency MBSs rely on a variety of credit enhancement techniques, which can be categorized according to whether they are internal or external to the security structure. External credit enhancement techniques are provided by either the issuer or a third party; internal credit enhancement techniques rely on reallocation of cash flow within the structure, thus avoiding "event risk" associated with third parties which can result in the downgrade of a MBS whose mortgage loans are performing flawlessly.

External Credit Enhancements

Prior to any structural considerations — before any decision is made as to whether a loan is to be retained, sold or securitized — all lenders require the borrower to provide standard hazard insurance, and most require primary mortgage insurance (PMI) if the LTV ratio is above 80%. PMI is usually written to cover 20% to 25% of the original loan balance. Normally, when the LTV ratio falls below 80%, PMI insurance is no longer required. Flood insurance is required in government-designated flood plains, but earthquake insurance is not required in seismic risk areas.

Pool Insurance Pool insurance normally covers losses due to borrowers' economic circumstances, but specifically excludes ("carves out") losses that result from bankruptcy, origination fraud, and special hazards. The amount of pool insurance purchased for a transaction is determined by the rating agencies as described in the previous section.

A bankruptcy bond provides coverage against a court order that modifies the mortgage debt by decreasing the interest rate or reducing the unpaid principal balance. Such a reduction in mortgage debt is known as a "cramdown." Individuals can file for bankruptcy under Chapter 13 and Chapter 7 of the Internal Revenue Code. Chapter 13 bankruptcy filings allow individuals to retain their assets while restructuring or forgiving debts. Under Chapter 7 bankruptcy filings, personal assets are liquidated to pay debts; cramdowns are not allowed. In the 1993 case of Nobleman versus American Savings, the U.S. Supreme Court disallowed cramdowns under Chapter 13 filings as well. While cramdowns are allowed under Chapter 11 bankruptcy filings, Chapter 11 is primarily used by businesses. Thus, given the relatively unlikely event of bankruptcy, most rating agencies would normally require as little as $100,000 to $150,000 of loss coverage on a $250 million pool of high quality mortgages.

Because pool insurers will not cover losses stemming from fraud during the loan application process, rating agencies require fraud coverage of 1% to 3% of the original pool balance. Fraud coverage is allowed to decrease over the first six years of a transaction, because the risk of losses due to fraud declines as the loans season.

Sources of special hazard insurance have largely dried up since the 1989 and 1994 earthquakes in California. This has become more or less moot, however, as subordination has now almost universally supplanted pool insurance in nonagency MBS transactions. In the period after 1989, however, many pool-insured transactions included a small subordinated class specifically for special hazard loss coverage. These classes found a few willing buyers (and mostly did very well in the wake of the 1994 quake), and were thus arguably the first securitization of earthquake risk, predating the currently popular "earthquake bonds."

Letters of Credit The issuer of a whole-loan security or a third party with a sufficient rating can provide a LOC in the amount required by the rating agencies to enhance the entire deal or in a lesser amount designed to complement or upgrade other forms of credit enhancement. To protect the investor from event risks, some LOCs are designed to convert to cash if the LOC provider is downgraded.

Bond Insurance ("Surety Bonds") Traditionally insurers of municipal bonds, Capital Markets Assurance Corporation (CapMAC), Financial Guarantee Insurance Corporation (FGIC), Financial Security Assurance (FSA), and Municipal Bond Insurance Association (MBIA) are also active in the mortgage-backed securities arena. Typically, bond insurers will not take the first-loss position in the credit support structure and thus require at least one other form of credit support, usually subordination, to bring the underlying assets up to an investment-grade (usually triple-B) rating. Since surety bonds generally provide 100% coverage for all types of losses unconditionally, they are often used to "wrap" existing transactions that are extremely novel or otherwise off-putting to investors regardless of their structural enhancements. For a time in the early 1990s, several extremely conservative investors would demand (and pay for) a "surety wrap" around an already triple-A transaction.

Corporate Guarantees Corporate guarantees cover all types of losses and can be used as stand-alone credit support or in conjunction with other forms of credit enhancement to provide the loss coverage required to obtain a particular rating. However, if the primary credit support is provided by a rated entity, the security is subject to reevaluation, and potentially downgrade, if that entity is downgraded. For example, when Citibank was downgraded in the early 1990s, all but the most highly seasoned of the MBSs guaranteed by Citibank were downgraded as well.

Because of concerns about the ratings of third-party credit support providers, and because of the more stringent capital treatment of issuer recourse for financial institutions, the use of external credit enhancement techniques has declined substantially since the 1980s. For example, in 1987 70% of nonagency MBSs were externally credit enhanced. As shown in Exhibit 10, this figure dropped as low as 8% in 1994 but revived briefly as a result of the rapid growth in subprime and home equity loan-backed security issuance, which (as described above) traded as asset-backed securities, a market more accustomed to bond insurance. In the traditional A-quality jumbo market, however, the senior/subordinated structure has long been by far the most widely used credit enhancement technique.

Internal Credit Enhancement

Internal credit enhancement techniques allocate a portion of the collateral cash flow to provide the credit support needed to obtain a desired rating for the security. This eliminates the event risks associated with external credit enhancement methods. The most popular form of internal credit enhancement is the senior/subordinated structure. Other internal structures include reserve funds and spread accounts, both of which are normally used in addition to a subordinate class.

Exhibit 10: Private Label Issuance by Credit Enhancement Type

	1998	1997	1996	1995	1994	1993	1992	1991	1990
Total Issuance (Dollars in Billions)		$63.5	$38.4	$37.0	$63.2	$98.5	$89.5	$49.7	$24.4
Internal Credit Enhancement: (%):									
Subordination	84	78	72	61	92	83	48	70	49
Reserve Fund	—	—	—	5	1	1	17	—	—
Super-Senior	—	—	—	—	—	2	3	11	—
External Credit Enhancement (%):									
Pool Insurance	—	—	1	2	2	11	28	10	23
Surety Bonds	9	8	18	21	4	2	2	<1	5
Letter of Credit	—	—	—	—	—	—	1	5	15
Corporate Guaranty	—	—	—	—	—	1	1	4	5
Multiple Support	6	1	4	2	—	1	1	4	5
Other/Resecuritization	1	13	4	9	2	1	—	—	—

Source: *Inside MBS & ABS, Inside Mortgage Finance*, Mortgage Market Statistical Annual, Copyright 1999, Bethesda, MD, 301.951.1240

Senior/Subordinated Structures In this structure, one or more subordinate classes are created to protect the senior classes from the risks associated with whole-loan mortgages. The original senior/subordinated structures were composed of two classes. The senior ("A") class is protected against credit loss by the subordinate ("B" or "junior") class that assumes a first-loss position. If a loss is experienced on an underlying mortgage loan, funds that would normally be allocated to the subordinate class are redirected to the senior class. If these funds are insufficient to cover the loss and if no funds are available from a reserve fund, spread account or other form of credit enhancement, payments otherwise due to the subordinated class are diverted in subsequent months until the shortfall is paid off. It is important to note, however, that the specific allocation of cash flow to accomplish this can vary considerably in different versions of the structure.

In current structures, the senior class is protected from losses until the subordinated B class is exhausted. In early senior/subordinated transactions, however, protection was limited to a prespecified "subordinated amount" which applied to the actual cash amount diverted from the subordinated to the senior class. In either case, prepayment makes the total amount of available interest cash flow uncertain, so the rating agencies have required the total amount of loss coverage in the form of principal. Thus the subordinate class size must be at least as large as the initial required coverage amount. For example, a $100 million pool which requires an initial 8% loss coverage would need a subordinate class of size $8 million to provide sufficient loss coverage to receive a triple-A rating on the senior class. In structures that exhaust the subordinated class, the total amount of credit support will equal the principal balance plus all interest payments diverted to the senior class, thus providing more than the required 8%.

In the early senior/subordinated transactions (as discussed in greater detail in the Historical Overview above), the issuer was required by tax regulations to hold the subordinate class. This requirement was eliminated in 1987 by the REMIC regulations, but investors were not sufficiently comfortable with mortgage credit risk to take even a mildly leveraged first-loss position in a mortgage pool. In 1989 a three class senior/ subordinated structure appeared, which divided the subordinated class into a "senior subordinated" or "mezzanine" class which was investment grade (generally triple-B) and an unrated "junior subordinated" first-loss class. In 1991, in response to conservative investors' concerns about mortgage credit in a generally weak economic environment, the senior class was divided in the same way to produce a "super-senior" class on top of a regular triple-A senior class. This "belt and suspenders" structure was short-lived, however, and (as discussed above) the market soon settled on a structure with triple-A senior classes, double-A "mezzanine" classes, and a series of tiered subordinate classes rated from single-A down to single-B. The senior class is further structured into a variety of tranches familiar from agency CMOs, such as PAC-support structures or floater-inverse floater structures, suiting the needs of a diverse investor population.

The senior/subordinated concept can be implemented in many different specific forms, and for a while it seemed as if issuers and Wall Street dealers were intent on trying every one at least once. However, all of the structures can be understood in terms of a single general principle: the structure must preserve the availability of sufficient credit support to satisfy the general loss coverage requirements described under "Credit Structuring" above. This can be done with a subordinated class alone or in combination with a reserve fund or spread account, third-party guaranties, etc. The earliest senior/subordinated transactions used a specific type of "reserve fund" structure, but since about 1989 the structure of choice has been the so-called "shifting interest" structure. An alternative structure that is increasingly used with high-margin (i.e., the spread between the mortgage interest rate and the MBS interest rate) collateral combines a subordinated class with a spread account that provides a measure of first-loss protection.

Reserve Fund Structure Recall that (1) in all MBS transactions, the initial level of loss coverage must be maintained for the first 5 or 10 years for fixed-rate or adjustable-rate loans respectively; and (2) the rating agencies require credit support from a subordinated class to be available in the form of principal, because prepayments render the total amount of interest cash flow uncertain. Any principal amounts distributed to a subordinate class reduces its principal balance and thus reduces available credit support. For this reason, during the initial "fixed" period of the credit support requirement, the subordinate class' share of principal is directed to a reserve fund. Thus, the sum of the subordinated class balance and the reserve fund balance will satisfy the credit support requirement. As actually implemented, the subordinated class' share of both principal and interest are diverted to the reserve fund until an initial targeted balance is attained, because under normal conditions both amortization and prepayments are minimal at the outset of a transaction, and a certain amount of liquidity is desirable to cover early delinquencies or even losses. This requirement is relaxed as the pool seasons, in accordance with the "stepdown" principles outlined above. If the pool performs well, the accumulated funds in the reserve fund are released incrementally to the subordinated class starting at the beginning of the "stepdown" phase of the transaction.

Historically, the delinquency portion of the credit support requirement was deposited into the reserve fund by the issuer at the outset of the transaction. Once the reserve fund reached the initial required target, the issuer was reimbursed. The structure becomes fully self-insured once the issuer has been reimbursed.

The rating agencies require that amounts in the reserve fund can be invested only in short-term high-quality securities. Thus the owner of the subordinate class experiences a decline in yield without a corresponding decline in risk. This disadvantage led to the development of a structure without a reserve fund.

Shifting Interest Structure Instead of diverting subordinate cash flows to a reserve fund, the shifting interest structure diverts subordinate cash flows to the senior class — in particular, during the initial phase of the credit support requirement, the subordinated class' share of prepayment principal is reallocated to the senior class instead.[1] Since the senior class receives more than its pro rata share of principal, it is paid down disproportionately quickly and over time will constitute a progressively smaller percentage of the total ownership interest in the mortgage pool.

During this initial period, the subordinate class receives only its pro rata share of principal amortization, which is practically nothing at all in the early years of a transaction. Its balance remains nearly constant (near enough to satisfy the rating agencies), thus preserving the required amount of credit support. As the pool pays down but the subordinated class does not, its ownership interest in the pool increases over time. Thus, the ownership interest gradually "shifts" from the senior class to the subordinated class — hence the name "shifting interest."[2]

As with any MBS structure, the loss coverage requirement will eventually be allowed to decline if the pool seasons well. In the shifting interest structure, this is accomplished by reducing the percentage of the subordinated class' prepayment entitlement that is diverted to the senior class. For the first 5 or 10 years of the transaction, 100% of the subordinated class' share of prepayments is diverted to the senior class. During the next 4 years, this percentage is allowed to gradually "step down" to zero, at which point no further diversions are made and the two classes receive principal on a pro rata basis. From then on, the respective

---

[1] The adverse selection theory can be used to argue that only the percentage of prepayments due to the subordinated class needs to be diverted to the senior class, since only prepayments reduce the pool balance without reducing the latent credit risk.

[2] Note that this reallocation of principal cash flows within a multiclass structure was not possible until the REMIC legislation took effect in 1987; thus, pre-1987 senior/subordinated transactions were required to use the reserve fund structure, as did many post-1987 transactions until the early issuers revised their legal documents accordingly.

senior and subordinate percentages (i.e. their proportionate ownership interests in the pool) remain constant.

Because the senior class receives prepayments otherwise due to the subordinate class, the senior class has a higher effective prepayment rate than the collateral, while the subordinate class has a lower effective prepayment rate. In fact, during the initial phase of the credit support requirement, the subordinated class' effective prepayment rate is zero (unless the collateral prepays so quickly that the senior class is retired completely during this period). This causes the subordinate class to have the average life stability of a PAC or super PAC. (In fact, some senior classes are structured this way as well precisely to achieve this degree of cash flow stability. These are known as "non-accelerated senior" or "NAS bonds.")

Although reserve funds are occasionally used for delinquency coverage, the whole point of the shifting interest structure was to eliminate the need for the reserve fund. Thus, delinquency coverage is usually external to the shifting interest structure, and has been customarily provided by the master servicer or trustee.

Spread Accounts "Excess servicing" or "spread," i.e. mortgage interest in excess of that required to pay investors, the servicer or other fees, can be used to pay down bonds or deposited into a spread account. (Otherwise, it is returned to the issuer or residual holder and plays no part in the structure.) If the spread is used to pay down bonds, the result is a buildup of "overcollateralization." If the spread is deposited into a spread account, then the subordinated class can be paid down as the spread account builds up, so that the sum of the subordinated class balance plus the spread account satisfies the total credit support requirement. Of course, the subordinated class cannot be paid down by the spread itself! Instead, the subordinated class is permitted to receive appropriate amounts of principal which, in the absence of the spread account, would be diverted to the senior class as described above. In MBS transactions, spread accounts must be supplemented by another form of credit enhancement because (1) excess servicing is typically insufficient to provide the required levels of credit support by itself, and (2) even if it were, prepayments render unpredictable the ultimate amount of excess spread that will be collected over time.

Spread accounts are most often used to help support a senior/subordinated structure with high margin collateral such as ARMs or B/C loans, and are generally used to enhance the appeal of subordinated classes by providing first-loss protection.

PREPAYMENTS

Fannie Mae's and Freddie Mac's securitization programs require loans to meet guidelines that limit servicing fees, loan size, weighted average maturity (WAM) dispersion, and underwriting criteria. The homogenous nature of the collateral and an abundance of historical data have facilitated the creation of relatively sophisticated prepayment models for agency-conforming mortgages. However, nonagency prepayment rates are more difficult to model because the collateral is much less homogeneous than conforming loans.

In general, historical data on prepayments, defaults, and foreclosures are more difficult to come by; fortunately, however, many of the larger nonagency issuers have been providing some of this information to investors and dealers. Most of them provide the necessary prepayment information, and many also provide monthly loss and delinquency levels aggregated at the deal level. The current state of the art in this area is probably Norwest Mortgage's SecuritiesLink, which provides deal-level information on prepayments, delinquencies, losses, prepayment interest shortfalls and all other information pertinent to investor distributions, free to investors through various electronic media. Also available by subscription is complete loan-level payment histories on every nonagency loan ever securitized through Prudential Home Mortgage, SASI, and NASCOR. This is especially valuable for studying prepayments and defaults because it includes loans that are no longer active, thus avoiding the statistical censoring problem.

When attempting to forecast nonagency prepayment rates, investors must consider the variables (loan rate, age, and seasonal effects) as well as the geographic concentration, term, LTV ratios, origination standards, and the loan sizes, and types comprising the pool. As with conforming loans, whole-loan prepayment rates tend to increase when interest rates decline, and as the loans season. Typically, a greater variance in loan types results in higher prepayment rates for nonagency MBSs relative to similar coupon agency MBSs because pools with a given net coupon will include some mortgages with higher mortgage interest rates.

Since nonagency securities are frequently backed by a large number of jumbo loans, the collateral often has a relatively high regional concentration. Hence, the prepayment performance of a whole loan security is often tied to a particular region's economic circumstances. The earliest conventional wisdom was that jumbo borrowers were wealthier and thus more mobile and more likely to be "trading up" to larger homes; they were also more financially sophisticated, hence more likely to take advantage of refinancing opportunities. Recent prepayment theories frame the prepayment incentive more systematically, in terms of dollar savings in the monthly payment rather than rate reductions in the mortgage contract; in this view, even a small rate reduction can still produce substantial monthly savings on a high balance loan, which should result in faster prepayment speeds for nonconforming loans. More recently, however, with the collapse of most high-priced real estate markets and the advent of mortgage products for distressed borrowers, nonconforming loans are sometimes observed to prepay more slowly than their conforming counterparts.

DEFAULTS

Default research on nonagency MBSs has been more sporadic than prepayment research because (1) detailed mortgage credit analysis under expected conditions (as opposed to the rating agency stress scenarios) wasn't critically important to investors until they began to look at lower rated subordinated classes, and (2) even when investors began to clamor for this information, it wasn't generally available from issuers. Academic research in the field has focused almost exclusively on conforming loans, and has produced little that can be usefully applied to investment analysis of nonagency MBSs.

Most research has focused on the option theory of mortgage default, which views default as the borrower's exercise of an option to put the property to the issuer at a price equal to the unpaid mortgage balance. In this view, the option is "in the money" if the property value is less than the mortgage balance. However, people don't default on a mortgage simply because it is "under water." Clearly factors such as the legal, social, and transactional costs of default, the preservation of a good credit record, and the cost of alternative housing affect the borrower's decision. These are variously accounted for in the theory as "transaction costs," but there is no agreement as to exactly how to do this to obtain successful predictions. Arguably, a pure or "ruthless" option-based theory of default is a failing paradigm.

Perhaps the biggest problem with the "ruthless" default model is that homeowners are often uninformed as to the value of their residence. Traders and investors who use option-pricing models can continuously observe the value of the underlying asset (e.g., stock price). With a residence, the borrower cannot observe house prices on a continual basis, and house prices are much more subjective than stock prices. Usually, something else other than house price declines triggers the actual default on a residential mortgage.

A competing theory of mortgage default is the "ability to pay" theory, which focuses on the borrower's cash flow. Eclipsed for a while by the option theory, it is now in effect being revived by the recent focus on using borrower credit scores and credit reports as predictors of borrower default. In this view, a borrower will default if he cannot afford to pay the mortgage. However, it is clear that if the property value exceeds the mortgage balance (i.e. the option is "out of the money"), the distressed borrower should be able to sell the property and pay off the mortgage. Thus, default should only occur if both circumstances hold: insufficient cash flow and an "in the money" option. As with most economic processes, however, individual psychology acts as a source of "friction" or "inertia" that can result in "irrational" borrower behavior that doesn't obey the theory.

A few dealers and data vendors have constructed "default models," but these are primarily statistical fits of the rather sparse data that are actually available, not descriptive models. They involve more parameters than prepayment models do, and are based on far fewer observations. For that reason alone, on statistical grounds their predictions will be much less reliable than those of the prepayment models that have been around for years. Standard errors and out-of-sample historical validations are rarely reported, and in general the research, because of its proprietary nature, is not subject to the type of review typical of academic research. In addition, even when default is a certainty, loss severities are extremely sensitive to servicer practice, including workout strategies, short sales and, if all else fails, the efficacy of their foreclosure and REO departments. Thus, investors need to closely scrutinize the underlying data, assumptions, and methodologies to ascertain whether the "credit adjusted spreads" from the current generation of default models are as useful to valuation of MBS credit risk as OASs have proved to be for prepayment risk.

SUMMARY AND OUTLOOK

In summary, nonagency MBSs afford a wide range of yield opportunities to investors willing to take structured mortgage credit risk. Investors can take simple mortgage credit risk by purchasing whole loans. Structured securities are created with ratings from triple-A to single-B (and occasionally lower), depending on leverage and credit support levels. Unrated securities generally exhibit extreme leverage and equity-like risk profiles. The underlying mortgages comprise familiar products such as 15- and 30-year fixed-rate jumbo loans with well-characterized risk profiles, and newer, relatively untested products such as "B/C" mortgages. Credit risk is unique to nonagency MBSs; prepayment risk is common to the agency and nonagency sectors, and operates in much the same way in both. Historically, the nonagency sector has richly repaid investors who were willing to take the time to familiarize themselves with something new and "unconventional" (to coin a phrase). We expect this to continue to be the case as the market continues to mature and broaden its investor appeal.

Chapter 2

Understanding Shifting Interest Subordination

Manus J. Clancy
Vice President
The Trepp Group

Michael Constantino, III
Assistant Vice President
The Trepp Group

INTRODUCTION

During the early years of the evolution of the collateralized mortgage obligation market, the challenge of securitizing pools of residential mortgages focused on providing greater average life stability to investors eager to reduce prepayment exposure. In fact, since the majority of securitizations of residential mortgages involved the packaging of government agency mortgage-backed securities, issuers and underwriters rarely had to concern themselves with credit risk at that time. Those issuers that did securitize "whole loans" (those not guaranteed by FNMA, FHLMC, or GNMA) used a potpourri of bond structures to mitigate credit risk. Letters of credit, pool insurance, corporate guarantees, and reserve funds were all used periodically to reduce credit risk from these issues.

Over time, the agency CMO and whole loan CMO markets became both more competitive and, not surprisingly, more efficient. In the pursuit of alleviating call risk and creating tranches that were appealing to investors, agency CMOs became increasingly complex. Seemingly, with each new issue came more intricate principal repayment rules and diverse bond types, all aimed at meeting the average life demands of the marketplace and providing greater prepayment certainty. Likewise, the whole loan CMO market evolved. Gradually, the whole loan market moved away from third-party guarantees and gave way to bond structures that could "stand alone." The result was the senior/subordinate bond structure combined with the shifting interest mechanism. This structure sought to combine the tranching common in agency CMOs with the creation of senior tranches, mezzanine tranches, and subordinate tranches to isolate and manage the risks arising from mortgage defaults and delinquencies. Today, the vast majority of whole loan CMOs utilize the senior/subordinate structure with shifting interest.

The introduction of "credit tranching" to bond structures added substantially to the complexity of securitization (as if the 128-tranche agency CMO was not complex enough). As mentioned earlier, the securitization of whole loans relies on the creation of senior and subordinate classes within the bond structure. Often these classes are paid principal and interest simultaneously over time. The percentage of principal each subordination level receives changes periodically based upon the credit history of the loans backing the CMO causing the subordination percentages to "shift" over time (hence "shifting interest"). This chapter will examine the intricacies of whole loan CMO senior/subordinate bond structures focusing primarily on the shifting interest rules of such structures. First, the differences between bond structures of agency CMOs and whole loan CMOs will be reviewed in greater detail. Second, shifting interest itself will be explained more thoroughly. Third, the various methods that are utilized to determine how principal is paid each period will be discussed. Finally, it will be demonstrated that the presence of these rules can have a significant effect on the yield and average life of a security.

COMPARING BOND STRUCTURES

Clearly, there are substantial differences between the bond structures that have emerged from issues backed by agency MBS and those of deals backed by whole loans. For agency CMOs in which prepayment or "call" risk has been the only concern, the structures have relied entirely on "horizontal" slicing and dicing: carving out different tranche types to meet certain average life demands by the marketplace and providing more prepayment stability. This involves the use of payment rules to allocate principal in different directions over time. The result has often been 30 or 40 tranche issues with PACs, TACs, VADMs, accrual bonds, and so forth. For traditional CMOs backed by whole loans in which both prepayment risk and credit risk are concerns, issuers must combine horizontal tranching to alleviate call risk with "vertical" credit support structuring. This has meant carving out senior tranches, mezzanine tranches, and subordinate tranches to isolate the risks arising from mortgage defaults and delinquencies. Exhibits 1 and 2 illustrate the differences between agency CMOs and whole loan CMOs.

Exhibit 1: Principal Distribution for Agency CMOs

A-1 PAC	A-2 PAC	A-3 PAC	A-4 PAC	A-5 COMPANION / A-6 COMPANION	A-7 COMPANION	A-4	A-3	A-2	A-1

Exhibit 2: Principal Distribution for Whole Loan CMOs

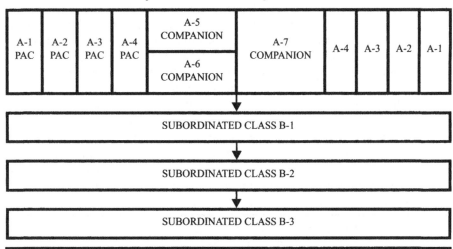

DEFINING SHIFTING INTEREST

The vast majority of whole loan CMOs that have been issued since 1992 utilize the senior/subordinate structure with shifting interest. The protection afforded to the senior classes of bonds against losses arising from mortgage defaults in these structures is the result of three features of the bond structure: (1) each period the senior bonds are given their allocation of principal and interest before any distributions are made to the subordinate bonds, (2) the losses from the liquidation of defaulted mortgage loans are first allocated to the subordinate bonds until they are retired before any losses are allocated to the senior bonds, and (3) the constantly changing allocation of prepayments and certain liquidation proceeds is disproportionately weighted toward the senior classes in the early years of the issue. The focus of this chapter is on the third component which will be referred to henceforth as shifting interest, so called because the disproportionate allocation of principal causes senior and subordinate percentages to shift over time.

The purpose of shifting interest is to manage, over the life of the CMO, the amount of subordinate bonds that remain outstanding each period to "absorb" losses and protect the senior bonds. The weaker the credit history of the loans backing a whole loan CMO, the greater the level of subordination that will be required to remain outstanding over time. Conversely the stronger the credit history, the lower the subordination requirement each period. In addition, because historical default rates are lower for newly originated mortgages, the level of protection that is needed at closing is usually less than the level of protection that is needed as a mortgage pool seasons. The percentage of subordination is managed by manipulating the amount of principal paid to the senior bonds versus the subordinate bonds each period according to a set of rules outlined in the prospectus. Generally, if the collateral backing a whole loan CMO has a weak credit history, these rules will direct a greater percentage of principal flows to the senior bonds so that a higher subordination percentage remains. Alternatively, the payment rules will "reward" strong credit history by allowing a greater percentage of the principal flows to go to the subordinate tranches. It is important to note that even for those whole loan CMOs with the strongest collateral history, principal will generally be allocated disproportionately to the senior bonds, causing the subordination percentage to grow over time.

The following examples demonstrate the effects on the subordination level of "manipulating" the amount of principal paid to the senior bonds each period for Prudential Home Mortgage Securities Company, Inc., Series 1995-7. Exhibits 3, 4, and 5 show the level of subordination (the "subordinate interest") for the first 15 years of the issue at various prepayment speeds assuming no defaults. As Exhibits 4 and 5 indicate, the subordination level grows over time providing greater "cushion" for the senior bonds.

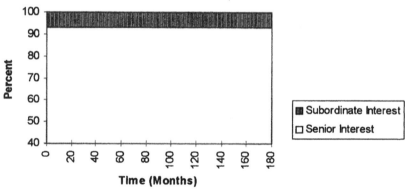

Exhibit 3: The Effects of Shifting Interest
0% PSA, No Defaults

Exhibit 4: The Effects of Shifting Interest
250% PSA, No Defaults

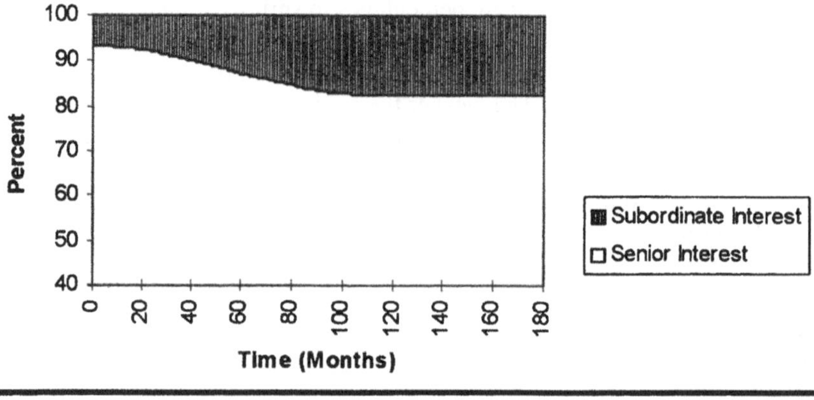

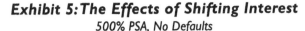

Exhibit 5: The Effects of Shifting Interest
500% PSA, No Defaults

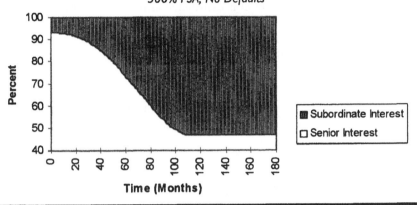

The percentages of the aggregate principal balance of the mortgage loans represented by the senior and subordinate bonds will, in all likelihood, fluctuate over time for two reasons. First, losses that are incurred on defaulted mortgages are allocated to the subordinate bonds prior to being allocated to the senior bonds. Because losses are allocated to the subordinate bonds first, the outstanding balance of the subordinate bonds is reduced thereby decreasing the subordinate percentage and increasing the senior percentage. Second, prepayments and other unscheduled payments on the mortgages are disproportionately allocated to the senior bonds for a defined period of time. Because prepayments and certain recoveries are disproportionately allocated to the senior bonds, the amortization of the senior bonds is accelerated thereby decreasing the senior percentage and increasing the subordinate percentage. Although the rules that govern the allocation of both losses and prepayments each alter the percentages of the classes, shifting interest refers to the mechanism that determines the ratio of the distributions of prepayments and other unscheduled payments of principal to the senior and subordinate bonds.

COMPARING PRINCIPAL ALLOCATION FROM ISSUE TO ISSUE

Payments of principal that are available to pay bonds are usually classified in the following categories: (1) scheduled principal, (2) prepayment principal, (3) recovery principal of liquidated loans, and (4) repurchase principal (the difference in the principal balance of loans that were repurchased due to substitution). In the principal payment rules of whole loan CMOs, the percentage of each category that is allocated to the senior bonds can differ significantly. The four categories listed above are all "cash flow items" (i.e., amounts that are part of available cash). In addition to these amounts, the senior bonds are sometimes allocated a portion of the "loss" amount. The loss amount is the difference between the balance of a defaulted loan and the amount recovered through the sale of the property which is categorized as "recovery principal." Clearly this is not a cash flow item. To the extent the loss amount is distributed as principal to the senior bonds, it must come from cash that would otherwise be paid to the subordinate bonds.

The following examples demonstrate two of the most common sets of principal distribution rules that are found in whole loan CMO bond structures:

Prudential Home Mortgage Securities Company, Inc., Series 1993-39

Principal Type	Percentage Allocated to Senior Bonds
1. Scheduled Principal	Senior Percentage (or "Senior Interest")
2. Prepayment Principal	
(Full and Partial)	Senior Prepayment Percentage
3. Repurchase Principal	Senior Prepayment Percentage
4. Recovery Principal	Senior Prepayment Percentage
5. Realized Losses	
(Principal Portion)	Senior Prepayment Percentage

Residential Funding Mortgage Securities, Inc., Series 1994-S13

Principal Type	Percentage Allocated to Senior Bonds
1. Scheduled Principal	Senior Percentage
2. Prepayment Principal	
(Full and Partial)	Senior Accelerated Distribution Percentage
3. Repurchase Principal	Senior Percentage
4. The lesser of	
a) Recovery Principal	Senior Accelerated Distribution Percentage
or	
b) Recovery Principal	
plus	Senior Percentage
Realized Losses	
(Principal Portion)	

The senior percentage is defined as the ratio of the balance of the senior bonds to the balance of the mortgage loans. This is also referred to in some transactions as the senior interest. If the mortgage loans experience neither prepayments nor defaults, the senior bonds will be paid their proportionate share of principal and the initial percentages that were evidenced by the senior and subordinate bonds at deal closing will remain constant throughout the life of the issue. In other words, since only scheduled principal payments are made by the mortgagors and because the senior bonds are entitled to only their pro rata share of these amounts, the senior percentage will never change. Exhibit 3 illustrates this point.

The senior prepayment percentage (or the senior accelerated distribution percentage as it is referred to in Residential 1994-S13) is defined as the senior percentage plus the product of (1) a declining percentage (the "shifting interest vector" for purposes of this chapter) and (2) the subordinate percentage, where the subordinate percentage is equal to the difference between 100% and the senior percentage. By allocating a portion (the shifting interest vector) of the subordinate bonds' pro rata share of certain types of principal to the senior classes, the senior classes will amortize more quickly and the subordinate interest in the mortgage loans will increase as a result.

The shifting interest vector normally equals 100% at deal closing and reduces over time according to a schedule of percentages specified in the prospectus (the vector specified in the prospectus will be referred to as the "base vector" — it will be described in greater detail below). In other words, in the early years of the transaction, the senior bonds will receive 100% of certain principal receipts that would otherwise go to the subordinate tranches if the deal was paying *pari passu*. As mentioned above, the presence of losses decreases the protection afforded to the senior classes by reducing the subordinate bonds, while the presence of prepayments has the effect of offsetting those losses by increasing the protection afforded to the senior classes by increasing the subordinate percentage. Normally, the base vector percentages diminish over time until reaching a point at which the senior and subordinate bonds begin paying pro rata based on their outstanding balances. However, because the future performance of a given portfolio of mortgage loans cannot be known with certainty at issuance, performance "triggers" are built into the principal payment rules which, if activated, will cause the shifting interest vector to vary from the base vector if certain criteria are not satisfied. These triggers will be referred to henceforth as shifting interest tests. In such cases, the shifting interest vector percentages may not reduce and the senior bonds will continue to receive a disproportionately high share of principal.

The analysis of how the shifting interest vector can vary from the base vector and the effect that changes to the shifting interest vector have on the performance of the bonds is one of the most difficult, as well as one of the most widely overlooked, challenges in analyzing whole loan CMOs. There is a multitude of different types of triggers as well as a host of differing methods for calculating each trigger. Furthermore, each type of test has a different effect on the shifting interest vector and can alter the yield on a given bond significantly. The following section will examine the structural nuances of shifting interest.

Base Vector

To help clarify the analysis of this topic, the term "base vector" will be used to distinguish the shifting interest percentages that are established in the prospectus at issuance from that which is calculated each period. The actual vector of percentages that is used each period for the purpose of calculating the principal distribution amount is referred to as the "shifting interest vector." It is important to remember that the base vector and the shifting interest vector will be identical each period unless the loans backing an issue fail to meet certain criteria. In such cases the shifting interest vector will vary from the base vector.

There are two base vectors that are commonly used in the payment rules of whole loan CMOs, one for issues backed by fixed-rate mortgages and one for issues backed by adjustable-rate mortgages. These vectors are shown below.

Issues Collateralized with Fixed Rate Mortgages		Issues Collateralized with Adjustable Rate Mortgages	
Base Vector	Period After Issuance	Base Vector	Period After Issuance
100%	First Five Years	100%	First Ten Years
70%	Sixth Year	70%	Eleventh Year
60%	Seventh Year	60%	Twelfth Year
40%	Eighth Year	40%	Thirteenth Year
20%	Ninth Year	20%	Fourteenth Year
0%	Thereafter	0%	Thereafter

It is important to add that the base vector for issues that are collateralized by loans that are not fully amortizing (i.e., balloon loans) always equals 100%. Moreover, some of these issues collateralized by balloon mortgages treat the balloon amount as scheduled principal while others treat it as a prepayment of principal.

Recall that these figures represent the percentage of the subordinate bonds' pro rata share of certain principal flows that will be redirected to the senior bonds. For example, assume that an issue is in its sixth year and is backed by fixed-rate mortgages. At closing, the ratio of senior to subordinate bonds was 94% to 6%. Assume further that losses have been modest and prepayments have been relatively high and as a result, the current ratio of senior bonds to subordinate bonds is 78% to 22%. In a particular month in the sixth year, scheduled principal flows equal $200,000 and prepayments total $500,000. In this example, assuming no triggers have been activated that would cause the shifting interest vector to differ from the base vector, the senior bonds would receive the following:

78% of $200,000   or $156,000

plus

78% of $500,000   or $390,000

plus

70% of 22% of $500,000   or $77,000

In the example above, 78% represents the senior percentage, 22% represents the subordinate percentage, and 70% represents the value of the shifting interest vector in the sixth year.

SHIFTING INTEREST TESTS

The base vector will be applicable for as long as the performance of the mortgage pool satisfies certain criteria. This criteria is evaluated through the use of a web of complex tests that are required to be completed at the beginning of each payment period before principal is distributed. Although there are many different tests that are used in the whole loan CMO universe of transactions, the majority of them can fit into three broad categories: balance tests, principal loss tests, and delinquency tests.

Balance Tests

The *balance test* is the most universally applied and homogeneous of all the shifting interest tests. Balance tests directly evaluate the current subordinate interest available to protect the senior bonds. In a deal with shifting interest, losses are allocated to the subordinate bonds first and thus have the effect of reducing the subordinate interest or percentage. However, if prepayment activity has existed at a sufficiently high rate, the senior interest may decrease since prepayments are allocated to the senior bonds in an accelerated manner. Even though losses may have taken place, the senior bonds may have more protection in percentage terms than they did at closing. The purpose of the balance test is to evaluate this ongoing relationship.

For example, assume that at bond issuance a deal has the following characteristics: the aggregate principal balance of the mortgage pool is $100 million, the principal balance of the senior bonds is $95.5 million, and the principal balance of the subordinate bonds is $4.5 million. If, at the end of five years, $19.5 million in principal has been prepaid and $500,000 of losses has been allocated to the bonds, are the senior bonds more at risk than they were at bond issuance? In other words, do the remaining senior bonds have as much protection (in percentage terms) as they did at issuance?

The balance test compares the current senior interest to the senior interest at closing. In the example above, the senior interest or senior percentage equals 95.5% at closing. If the test reveals that the current senior percentage is greater than 95.5%, it will evidence the fact that losses on the portfolio are outweighing the benefits to the senior bonds of prepayments. In such an event, the balance test trigger will be activated and the shifting interest vector will recalibrate to give the senior bonds an even larger share of certain principal revenues than called for in the base vector.

In our example, the principal balance of the senior bonds at the end of the fifth year is $76 million (assuming all principal paid, $19.5 million, is "prepayment" principal) and the principal balance of the subordinate bonds is $4 million. The senior percentage is 95% while the subordinate percentage equals 5%. Therefore, the subordinate interest has increased from 4.5% to 5% meaning the protection afforded to the senior bonds has increased as a percentage of the issue. In this case, the balance test is not triggered and the shifting interest vector will continue to mirror the base vector. If losses on the pool had been $1.5 million instead of $500,000, the senior and subordinate bonds would have been $76 million and $3 million, respectively. Thus, the senior percentage would have been approximately 96.2% and the test would have "failed." In such an event, the shifting interest vector would no longer mirror the base vector. Instead of reducing from 100% to

70%, this hypothetical issue would see its shifting interest vector continue to give 100% of all prepayments to the senior bonds.

Another type of balance test compares the current subordinate percentage with a different threshold percentage. Although the majority of issues have tests that only seek to identify a poor credit history for the pool, this balance test is intended to signify a strong history. If the current subordinate interest is greater than a multiple (usually two) of the subordinate interest at issuance, the balance test trigger will be activated and the shifting interest vector will begin to differ from the base vector. However, unlike the change to the base vector that would accompany a senior percentage trigger event, the change to the base vector that would accompany a subordinate percentage trigger event would increase the principal flows to the subordinate bonds rather than decrease them.

Principal Loss Tests

As a mortgage pool seasons, it will inevitably experience unscheduled events such as prepayments and liquidations, the latter being the focus of *principal loss tests*. Loans can be classified as either *performing*, those currently remitting scheduled payments each month, or *non-performing*, those that are not currently remitting scheduled payments each month. A loan that is delinquent may return to performing status. However, a delinquent loan that never begins remitting payments will enter the foreclosure process and will ultimately be liquidated.

The majority of whole loan CMOs are structured with liquidity provisions that require the servicer to make advances of scheduled principal and interest. Therefore, during the delinquency and foreclosure period, the cash flows to the bondholders are not interrupted. Upon the sale of a foreclosed property, the liquidation proceeds minus foreclosure costs and servicer reimbursements will most likely be less than the principal balance of the mortgage loan and thus will affect the cash flow to the bondholders. This amount represents the total loss on the property and, depending on the deal structure, is a close approximation of the loss that will be allocated to the bonds. A principal loss test trigger will be activated if the historical dollar amount of principal losses on the collateral exceeds certain threshold levels. Such an event would result in the shifting interest vector being altered.

There are two basic types of principal loss tests: a fixed structure and a variable structure. In a fixed structure, the principal losses of the mortgage pool that have been experienced up to and including the current period are compared with a fixed threshold balance that is defined in the prospectus. The fixed threshold balance is usually equal to the product of a given percentage and the initial principal balance of the subordinate bonds. Using the earlier example in which the principal balance of the subordinate bonds is $4,500,000, assume the principal loss test establishes that the shifting interest vector will be altered if losses exceed 10% of the original subordinate bond balance. In this case, the trigger event of the principal loss test will be activated as soon as cumulative losses exceed $450,000 (i.e., 10% of $4,500,000). If losses are less than $450,000, the event will not be triggered and the shifting interest vector will mirror the base vector (unless some other test has been triggered). If losses exceed $450,000, the trigger event will be activated and the two vectors will diverge.

In a variable structure, the principal losses of the mortgage pool that have been experienced up to and including the current period are compared with a threshold balance that increases over time. The computation of the balance is the same as under the fixed structure, however, the given percentage varies as the issue seasons. Using the previous example and a variable structure, the trigger event of the principal loss test will be activated as soon as cumulative losses exceed the threshold balance for the corresponding period. For instance, if cumulative losses equal $1,400,000 in the 65th period (the sixth year), the trigger event of the principal loss test will be activated as illustrated in the table below.

Loss Percentage	Period After Issuance	Threshold Balance
30%	Sixth Year	$1,350,000
35%	Seventh Year	$1,575,000
40%	Eighth Year	$1,800,000
45%	Ninth Year	$2,025,000
50%	Thereafter	$2,250,000

Delinquency Tests

Delinquency tests are by far the most complicated and have the most variations of all shifting interest tests. Delinquency tests, like principal loss tests, are created to evaluate the credit history of the mortgage pool. However, delinquency tests serve a purpose that is slightly different than principal loss tests. Principal loss tests track the severity of losses from the date of issuance through the current period, which provides the context for evaluating the entire history of the mortgage pool. In contrast, delinquency tests aim to evaluate the recent payment history of the mortgage pool (which, in turn, can be used to predict how the pool will behave in the future). Because a significant number of loans that are delinquent will ultimately be liquidated, the monitoring of delinquency levels helps to estimate the number of liquidations that will take place in the near future.

Unlike the two tests described earlier which are very similar from issue to issue, delinquency tests differ from one issue to the next. Although there are numerous variations in these tests, the basic structure is relatively consistent. Most delinquency tests compare, over a certain period of time, the average percentage of loans in the mortgage pool that have a specified delinquency status to a threshold percentage stated in the prospectus.

The basic structure of a typical delinquency test consists of four components:

1. Period of time tested
2. Severity of delinquency (*delinquency range*)
3. Delinquency calculation (*delinquency level*)
4. Threshold percentage

The period of time that is considered "recent" delinquency history is the most widely altered component from issue to issue. The "window" that is tested can vary from three months to a year. For instance, a prospectus may state that the test will fail if, during the previous six months, the average aggregate balance of loans that have been delinquent for 60 days or more each month exceeds 2% of the average aggregate loan balance during that same six month period. Alternatively, some issues use the same parameters but test a 12-month period.

Another component that is varied is the severity of the loan delinquencies that are tested. The delinquency severity refers to the length of time since a particular loan has last remitted a scheduled payment. For example, one delinquency test may consider, as a starting point, all loans that have been delinquent for 60 days or more. That subset, which would include loans 60, 90, 120 days, etc. delinquent, is the delinquency range. The most common delinquency range includes loans that are 60 days delinquent and beyond. However, 30-day and 90-day severities have been used as starting points for these calculations in certain issues. (Some variations of this test exclude delinquent loans that are classified as REO while others include loans that are classified as REO.)

The first component designates the period of time that will be analyzed while the second component designates the subset of loans that will be analyzed. The third component designates the formula that will be used to calculate the percentage that will be compared to the threshold percentage. Because the test compares the current delinquency level to a threshold percentage, the calculation must convert real numbers into percentage form.

The first step of the calculation is aggregating the balance (or payment) of the loans that are within the delinquency range each period (which will be used in the numerator), and aggregating the balance (or payment) of all loans each period (which will be used in the denominator). The ratio that will be calculated represents the *delinquency level* for each period. As alluded to above, there are two methods that are used to calculate this ratio: a balance method and a payment method. The *balance method* uses the sum of the individual balances of those loans that meet the specified criteria (delinquency range and period of time tested) for each month. For example, if the test is written to compare the average balance of loans that were delinquent for 60 days or more during the previous 12 months, the aggregate balance of loans that meet that criteria in each of the 12 months will be used in the numerator and the aggregate balance of all loans in each of the 12 months will be used in the denominator. In contrast, the *payment method* uses the sum of the individual scheduled payments of those loans that meet the criteria that would have been received on each loan had they not been delinquent and the sum of the individual scheduled payments of all loans.

Because the test evaluates a period of time rather than a single period, there is a delinquency level for each period. Delinquency tests compare the average delinquency level during this period of time to the threshold percentage. To determine the average delinquency level that will be compared to the threshold level, there are two methods. For example, suppose that the period of time tested is three months (i.e., the delinquency range includes loans that are delinquent for 60 days or more), and the balances of all loans and delinquent loans are as follows:

Time	Aggregate Balance of All Loans	Balance of Loans 60 days or More Delinquent
−3	$100,000,000	$9,000,000
−2	$98,000,000	$1,850,000
−1	$93,000,000	$1,000,000

Assuming that the balance method is utilized, some issues specify that the calculation should be as follows:

$$\frac{(d_3 + d_2 + d_1)}{3} \div \frac{(b_3 + b_2 + b_1)}{3}$$

$$\left[\frac{9,000,000 + 1,850,000 + 1,000,000}{3}\right]$$

$$\div \left[\frac{100,000,000 + 98,000,000 + 93,000,000}{3}\right] = 4.07\%$$

In contrast, other issues state that the calculation should be as follows:

$$\left[\frac{d_3}{b_3} + \frac{d_2}{b_2} + \frac{d_1}{b_1}\right] \div 3$$

$$\left[\frac{9,000,000}{100,000,000} + \frac{1,850,000}{98,000,000} + \frac{1,000,000}{93,000,000}\right] \div 3 = 3.99\%$$

Assuming that the threshold delinquency percentage equals 4.0%, it would be important to perform the calculation using the correct method. One method calculates the average delinquency level to be greater than 4% (which would cause the shifting interest vector to change) while the other method calculates the average delinquency level to be less than 4% (in which case there would be no change).

How the Shifting Interest Vector Changes

It has been mentioned throughout the chapter that the base vector is established at closing as a set of declining percentages that are used for the calculation of principal payment distributions. If a trigger from any performance test or group of performance tests is activated, the shifting interest vector will deviate from the base vector. The question is, how does it deviate? Each test or group of performance tests specifies how the shifting interest vector will change if the particular test fails. These changes are not necessarily the same from test to test. For instance, the triggering of one type of test may cause the shifting interest vector to "revert" to the original base vector value of 100%. The balance test, which is the most widely used test, normally uses this method. Other tests, by comparison, will hold the shifting interest vector as well as the senior prepayment percentage constant at the value that was registered in the period the trigger event of a test was first activated rather than reducing the percentages as scheduled in the base vector. The delinquency test and the principal loss test normally use this method.

EFFECT OF SHIFTING INTEREST TESTS ON YIELDS AND AVERAGE LIVES

A decline in the credit quality of a portfolio of loans collateralizing a whole loan CMO and the consequent triggering of shifting interest performance tests can have a dramatic effect on the yield and average life of a security. Residential Funding Mortgage Securities I, 94-S13 illustrates this effect. Cash flows were projected for this deal at issuance using summary collateral and prepayment speeds of 0%, 250%, and 500% PSA. Exhibit 6 shows the yields and average lives for Tranches A-4 and B-1 at those three speeds *assuming no shifting interest tests are triggered.*

Cash flows were then projected a second time for the same tranches using the same prepayment speeds. In the second projection, however, it was assumed that the shifting interest vector never reduces below 100%. The results of the second scenario can be seen in Exhibit 7.

Exhibit 6: Residential Funding, 94-513 Assuming No Shifting Interest Tests are Triggered

Tranche	Average Lives			Yields		
Prepayment Speed	0	250	500	0	250	500
A-4						
Price 98	23.63	10.88	5.89	7.18	7.27	7.39
B-1						
Price 94	20.04	11.91	9.63	7.69	7.87	7.97

Exhibit 7: Residential Funding, 94-513 Assuming the Shifting Interest Vector Never Falls below 100%

Tranche	Average Lives			Yields		
Prepayment Speed	0	250	500	0	250	500
A-4						
Price 98	23.63	9.76	5.51	7.18	7.28	7.40
B-1						
Price 94	20.04	18.14	10.79	7.69	7.71	7.91

In the first example, since no tests were triggered, the actual shifting interest vector mimicked the base vector (i.e., 100%-70%-60%-40%-20%-0%). In the second hypothetical example, the shifting interest vector remained locked at 100% and the subordinate tranches were not entitled to any of the prepayment principal received on the loans until all senior bonds (with the exception of the PO tranche) were retired. The results indicate sharp average life differences between the two examples, particularly at 250 PSA. Specifically, the average life on Tranche A-4 diminishes by over a year while the average life on Tranche B-1 increases by over six years.

As one would expect, the results assuming no prepayments are identical from one example to the next. Although the vector itself changes between the two scenarios, each vector is being multiplied by zero (the amount of prepayments) and, therefore, there is no effect.

To further illustrate the potential for average life and yield differences, cash flows were projected for the same issue using actual collateral, a settlement date of August 25, 1996, a prepayment speed assumption of 200% PSA, and a default speed assumption of 500% SDA with a loss severity of 50%. Prepayments have the effect of decreasing the senior interest and liquidations have the effect of increasing the senior interest. If the performance tests were ignored, prepayments and certain unscheduled collections of principal would be distributed according to the base vector. However, if the performance tests were modeled, the trigger of senior percentage test (balance test) would be activated and 100% of prepayments and other unscheduled collections of principal would be distributed to the senior classes as opposed to the percentages set by the base vector. The following table displays the difference in yield that would result if the performance tests were ignored versus if the performance tests were modeled.

Class	Price	Yield Modeling Performance Tests	Yield Ignoring Performance Tests
M-1	93.67	1.33	−0.47

CONCLUSION

Throughout the history of the CMO market, clearly the lion's share of research has been devoted to determining principal repayment expectations. The process of determining the value of a CMO security has evolved from simply choosing a prepayment speed based on historical data to the development of complex interest rate generators, prepayment models, and OAS. Not surprisingly, relatively little effort has been devoted to the understanding of how modest changes to the credit history of a set of loans backing a whole loan CMO can alter a security's cash flow. However, as demonstrated earlier, this element of analyzing whole loan CMOs cannot be overlooked. Significant yield and average life differences can result from changes to the credit characteristics of a portfolio of loans collateralizing a whole loan CMO using a senior/subordinate bond structure once the intricate shifting interest rules are taken into consideration.

Chapter 3

Understanding Compensating Interest

Laurie Goodman, Ph.D.
Managing Director
Mortgage Strategy Group
PaineWebber, Inc.

Thomas Zimmerman
Senior Vice President
Mortgage Strategy Group
PaineWebber, Inc.

In this chapter, we will explain the "compensating interest" features on whole loan securities and home equity securities. We show that in most new whole loan structures, there's little impact from standard compensating interest features. Only in a minority of securities — those that are very seasoned without compensating interest provisions — does it really deserve consideration. In our world of substantial uncertainty regarding prepayment and average life, compensating interest is, at best, a footnote. It will rarely impact a decision to buy or not to buy a bond. We cover the few situations where it should be a factor. We also show that in most home equity deals, the compensating interest provisions are even more generous, and hence even the likelihood of an interest rate shortfall is even smaller.

COMPENSATING INTEREST DEFINED

Mortgage interest accrues from the first of the month, payable on the first day of the following month. When a borrower prepays a mortgage, accrued interest is collected for the period that the loan was outstanding (since the last payment). That means the servicer generally collects less than a full month's interest on a prepaid loan to pass on to bondholders. Bond investors justifiably expect to receive a full month's interest on the beginning principal balance. At this point, all MBS issuers arrange to make up accrued income foregone due to prepayments

55

— but only up to some limit. That amount of shortfall made up is called "compensating interest." In short, compensating interest is monies paid by the servicer out of servicing fees to compensate for the fact that less than a full 30 days of interest is received on a loan because it was prepaid during the month.

COMPENSATING INTEREST ON WHOLE LOAN SECURITIES

To show the importance of this subject, assume an issuer agreed to pay compensating interest up to a level of 12.5 basis points/year. Assume furthermore the beginning principal balance is $300,000,000; the investor's coupon is 6.75%; and the security has a WAM of 357. As can be seen in Exhibit 1, assuming 25% CPR, or 2.3688% SMM (single monthly mortality), prepayments would be $7,100,438.28. Interest shortfall to the investor before "compensating interest" would be 15 days interest on the $7,100,438.28 prepaid, or $19,969.98 (15/30 × 1/12 × 6.75/100 × 7,100,438.18). The maximum amount of compensating interest available is $30,880.19 (12.5 basis points on the outstanding balance). The difference is positive. Thus, there is more than sufficient compensating interest to cover this interest shortfall.

In Exhibit 2 we look at a more severe prepayment scenario. Assuming 50% CPR (5.6126% SMM), prepayments for the month would be $16,813,279.38. Here, interest shortfall to the bondholder would be the same 15 days interest on this higher prepaid amount, but now totals $47,315.47 (15/30 × 1/12 × 6.75/100 × 16,823,279.03). The maximum compensating interest available (again, at 12.5 basis points) is $30,373.79. Thus bondholders would experience an interest shortfall of $16,941.69, even after full compensating interest is paid.

Exhibit 1: Calculation of Accrued and Compensating Interest

Beginning Principal Balance:	$300,000,000
Accrued Bondholder Interest:	1,687,500
Scheduled Amortization:	257,044.75
Prepayments at 25% CPR, 2.3688% SMM:	7,100,438.28

Interest Shortfall to Bondholder before Compensating Interest:

$$= \frac{15}{30} \times \frac{1}{12} \times \frac{6.75}{100} \times 7,100,438.28 = 19,969.98$$

Maximum Compensating Interest Available:

$$= \frac{0.125}{100} \times \frac{1}{12} \times (300,000,000 - 7,100,438.28)$$
$$+ \frac{0.125}{100} \times \frac{15}{30} \times \frac{1}{12} \times 7,100,438.28 = 30,880.19$$

Difference = 30,880.19 − 19,969.98 = 10,910.20

Note: Coupon = 6.75%, WAM = 357, Servicing = 0.125%

Exhibit 2: Calculation of Accrued and Compensating Interest

Beginning Principal Balance:	$300,000,000
Accrued Bondholder Interest:	1,687,500
Scheduled Amortization:	257,044.75
Prepayments at 50% CPR, 5.6126% SMM:	16,823,279.38

Interest Shortfall to Bondholder before Compensating Interest:

$$= \frac{15}{30} \times \frac{1}{12} \times \frac{6.75}{100} \times 16,823,279.38 = 47,315.47$$

Maximum Compensating Interest Available:

$$= \frac{0.125}{100} \times \frac{1}{12} \times (300,000,000 - 16,823,279.38)$$

$$+ \frac{0.125}{100} \times \frac{15}{30} \times \frac{1}{12} \times 16,823,279.38 = 30,373.79$$

Difference = 30,373.79 − 47,315.47 = −16,941.69

Note: Coupon = 6.75%, WAM = 357, Servicing = 0.125%

To get a feel for how big a deal this is, we first discuss typical compensating interest arrangements. We then look at how high prepayments must be in order to induce any shortfall. Finally, we look at the foregone yield in different deal tranches under different compensating interest structures.

What Arrangements are Customary?

Exhibit 3 shows the compensating interest policies for major nonagency issuers. Note from the exhibit that all issuers now provide at least 12.5 basis points of compensating interest on prepayment interest shortfalls. In the 1992-93 rally, lost interest was much more material, as many issuers did not provide compensating interest at all, and prepayment speeds held much higher. But as we will see below, 12.5 basis points is sufficient for most bonds, even under most scenarios.

Exhibit 3 also shows minor differences between issuers, both in the maximum amount of compensating interest paid out, as well as the types of prepayments covered. Most issuers pay a maximum of 12.5 basis points out of servicing revenues. Only NASCOR pays 20 basis points. Another difference is whether issuers pay compensating interest on prepayments in full as well as on curtailments, or only on prepayments in full. CMSI (Citibank), Chase, Countrywide, and GE pay compensating interest on both prepayments in full and curtailments. NASCOR and RFC pay compensating interest only on prepayments in full. However, in NASCOR deals, the subordinate bond covers foregone loss due to curtailments.

The maximum number of basis points to be paid as compensating interest may actually understate protection provided by some originators. By altering the payment remittance cycle, protection can be even greater. In our example, all prepayments received in the previous month are passed through in the current month.

However, Countrywide, GE, and NASCOR pass through prepayments received from the middle of the previous month to the middle of the current month. Thus, prepayments made before the middle of the current month do not cause interest shortfalls, because the principal is passed through on the current remittance date. If prepayments are made evenly throughout the month, having a mid-month to mid-month payment remittance cycle cuts the average number of days during which the servicer must make up interest from 15 down to 7.5. That's because the servicer "hot potatoes" the principal back to the bondholder all that much earlier, eliminating the need to pay compensating interest on payments received during the first half of the month. That acceleration, due to a mid-month to mid-month remittance cycle, allows a given amount of compensating interest to go much further.

Breakeven Speeds on Whole Loans Before Compensating Interest Becomes an Issue

Now that we have established the general parameters of how much protection is provided, we can determine how high speeds must rise before an interest shortfall costs the bondholders anything. We refer to this as the "breakeven speed." Results of this analysis are shown in Exhibit 4. As can be seen, assuming a maximum of 12.5 basis points basis points in compensating interest, and, on average, 15 days of foregone interest, the breakeven CPR is in the 30%-36% CPR range. For example, with a 6.75% coupon, 357 WAM security, the breakeven CPR is 35.91%. For an 8.0% coupon, 330 WAM, the breakeven CPR is 31.29%. Thus, at all speeds less than this breakeven number, the bondholder does not loss a single penny due to interest shortfalls.

There are several additional noteworthy points. First, WAM of a mortgage pool makes only a marginal difference in determining breakeven CPR. Had we done breakeven PSAs, WAM could have made a difference. We chose breakeven CPRs, as interest shortfalls come into play mostly in low interest rate environments, and we know the PSA ramp is misleading for refinanceable collateral. Second, coupon does matter in determining breakeven CPR. The breakeven is clearly lower on an 8% coupon than on a 6.75% coupon, as interest shortfall will be larger.

Exhibit 3: Compensating Interest Policies for Major Nonagency Issuers

	Chase	CMSI	Countrywide	GE	NASCOR	RFC
Max Compensating Interest Paid Annually (bps)	12.5	12.5	12.5	12.5	20	12.5
Type of Prepayments Covered:						
Prepayments in Full	Yes	Yes	Yes	Yes	Yes	Yes
Curtailments	Yes	Yes	Yes	Yes	No	No
Prepayment Remittance Cycle	Previous month	Previous month	Mid-month to Mid-month	Mid-month to Mid-month	Mid-month to Mid-month	Previous month

Exhibit 4: Breakeven CPRs for
Various Compensating Interest Arrangements

		Breakeven CPR			
		15 days foregone		7.5 days foregone	
Coupon	WAM	12.5*	20*	12.5*	20*
6.75	357	35.91	50.93	58.27	74.94
6.75	300	35.92	50.95	58.28	74.96
7.00	357	34.88	49.66	56.97	73.71
7.00	300	34.89	49.68	56.98	73.72
7.50	330	32.99	47.31	54.52	71.32
7.50	270	33.01	47.33	54.54	71.34
8.00	330	31.29	45.15	52.26	69.05
8.00	270	31.31	45.17	52.27	69.06

* Basis points of servicing that can be used to pay compensating interest.

Note that the breakevens we have discussed are for the least generous set of arrangements — 12.5 basis points maximum compensating interest, with a 15-day interest shortfall. At 20 basis points of compensating interest, breakeven CPRs are considerably higher — about 45%-51%. Assuming the mid-month to mid-month remittance cycle discussed above, breakeven CPRs are even higher (also shown in Exhibit 4). For a 6.75% coupon, 357 WAM security, with 12.5 basis points maximum compensating interest, shortening the average interest shortfall from 15 days to 7.5 raises the breakeven to 58.27% (up from 35.91%) assuming the traditional remittance cycle. In general, note that with a mid-month to mid-month remittance cycle, breakeven CPRs are above 50%, regardless of the coupon.

Cost to Various Tranches

We have shown that under the most unfavorable set of compensating interest arrangements, it takes minimum speeds in the 30% CPR area to impact yield at all. For most issuers, speeds have to approximate 50% CPR before yields are impacted. The question is, "If yield on the collateral is affected, does it differentially affect the bondholders of different tranches?"

The answer can be found in Exhibits 5 and 6. Exhibit 5 shows the cost to the bondholder of various compensating interest arrangements with prepayments expressed in CPR; Exhibit 6 shows bondholder's costs of various compensating interest arrangements with prepayments expressed in PSA. We set up a representative new deal (6.75% coupon, priced at 275% PSA). The deal contains a 3-year sequential (3.49 years at 275% PSA), a 10-year security (10.99 years at 275% PSA), a long security, and a 10% NAS bond. This is very typical of deals as of this writing. We assume 357 WAM on the collateral. We first calculated the yield on the security assuming that interest rate shortfalls never occur (top section of Exhibits 5 and 6). Actually, we ran the analysis assuming 100 basis points of compensating interest, a high enough amount such that shortfalls will never be generated. In the bottom section of the exhibits, we look at various levels of compensating interest to determine foregone yield. For example, at 40% CPR and 12.5 basis points compensating interest, assuming a 15-day interest shortfall, the foregone yield is just under 2 basis points on all tranches. This is the most stingy set of compensating interest arrangements prevailing as of this writing.

Exhibit 5: Effect of Different Levels of Compensating Interest at Different CPRs
(6.75% Coupon, 357 WAM*)

	Yield at CPR Level (If full accrued interest is paid)			
	10	25	40	50
3-yr	6.55	6.15	5.69	5.32
10-yr	6.90	6.96	7.04	7.10
Long	6.97	7.11	7.30	7.44
NAS	6.71	6.68	6.56	6.48

	Foregone Yield at CPR Level											
	10% CPR			25% CPR			40% CPR			50% CPR		
Comp Int.	0	12.5	20	0	12.5	20	0	12.5	20	0	12.5	20
3-yr	2.9	0.0	0.0	7.8	0.0	0.0	13.2	1.7	0.0	17.3	6.2	0.0
10-yr	3.0	0.0	0.0	8.1	0.0	0.0	14.1	1.8	0.0	18.8	6.7	0.0
Long	3.0	0.0	0.0	8.2	0.0	0.0	14.3	1.8	0.0	19.1	6.8	0.0
NAS	3.0	0.0	0.0	8.1	0.0	0.0	14.1	1.8	0.0	18.9	6.8	0.0

*Assumes 15 days foregone interest.

Exhibit 6: Effect of Different Levels of Compensating Interest at Different PSAs
(6.75% Coupon, 357 WAM*)

	Yield at PSA Level (If full accrued interest is paid)			
	100	275	500	1000
3-yr	6.66	6.50	6.35	6.10
10-yr	6.89	6.91	6.96	7.03
Long	6.96	6.99	7.12	7.34
NAS	6.72	6.69	6.67	6.51

	Foregone Yield at PSA Level											
	100% PSA			275% PSA			500% PSA			1000% PSA		
Comp Int.	0	12.5	20	0	12.5	20	0	12.5	20	0	12.5	20
3-yr	1.5	0.0	0.0	3.5	0.0	0.0	5.5	0.0	0.0	8.8	1.2	0.2
10-yr	1.6	0.0	0.0	4.4	0.0	0.0	7.6	0.0	0.0	13.9	4.3	1.3
Long	1.7	0.0	0.0	4.7	0.0	0.0	8.2	0.0	0.0	15.5	5.4	1.9
NAS	1.6	0.0	0.0	4.4	0.0	0.0	8.5	0.0	0.0	16.9	6.6	2.5

*Assumes 15 days foregone interest.

For slower speeds, there is no foregone yield. At 50% CPR, the foregone yield is 6-7 basis points, depending on the tranche. Had we allowed a mid-month remittance cycle, producing only 7.5 days, on average, of foregone interest, the cost would have been zero. This is clear from Exhibit 4 showing breakeven CPRs.

Compensating interest arrangements have become more generous through the years. In 1993 a number of issuers did not pay out compensating interest. With no compensating interest, assuming 50% CPR, the cost on each bond was 17-19 basis points. That's quite a significant amount, which would be slightly greater for higher coupons. Investors considering the purchase of a seasoned bond will want to make sure that compensating interest arrangements are in place, or bid the security accordingly.

Exhibit 6 shows foregone interest expressed in PSA terms. Note that here, the difference is greater for longer bonds. This reflects the fact that a given PSA will translate into a lower lifetime CPR for a bond still on the ramp than a bond off the ramp. Because longer bonds spend a lower percent of their life on the ramp, lifetime CPRs will be greater at a given PSA for longer bonds. Thus, the basis point effect will be more substantial for those longer bonds. So at 1000% PSA, assuming 12.5 basis points compensating interest, the cost on the 3-year bond is just over 1 basis point, while it is 5.4 basis points on the long sequential, and 6.6 basis points on the NAS bond.

COMPENSATING INTEREST IN HOME EQUITIES

Compensating interest has always been an important consideration in the whole loan market, but has received less attention within the home equity and 125 arenas. As we discussed above, in the whole loan market, servicers are usually responsible for paying compensating interest up to a prospectus-specified amount. Frequently that is 50% of the servicing fee, or 12.5 basis points. In the home equity market, the servicer is typically responsible for an amount equal to the entire servicing fee of around 50 basis points. Unlike advances for delinquent payments, compensating interest is not recoverable by the servicer from excess spread or any other source.

Exhibit 7 contrasts the magnitude (at several speeds) of the servicer's maximum compensating interest with interest rate shortfalls for whole loans and home equities. The whole loan specified has a 6.75% coupon and a maximum compensating interest of 12.5 basis points ($1.04/(100) \times 2$ on a decimal, monthly basis). The home equity has an 11.00% coupon rate and a maximum compensating interest of 50 basis points ($4.17/(100) \times 2$ on a decimal, monthly basis). We assumed that prepayments take place after 15 days, i.e., in the middle of the month. For the whole loan, the maximum servicer's compensating interest falls about halfway between the interest shortfall for speeds of 25% and 50% CPR. (It can be shown that the breakeven speed is about 36% CPR.) For home equities, the maximum compensating interest of 50 basis points covers speeds well above 50% CPR. The breakeven speed is at 68% CPR.

Exhibit 7: Interest Shortfalls Due to Prepayments and Maximum Compensating Interest

Whole Loans

Maximum Servicer Payments	$\frac{1}{12} \times \frac{0.125}{100} \times Bal = \frac{1.04}{100^2} \times Bal$

Interest Shortfall:

at 25% CPR (2.37% SMM)	$\frac{15}{30} \times \left(\frac{1}{12} \times \frac{6.75}{100}\right) \times \frac{2.37}{100} \times Bal = \frac{0.666}{100^2} \times Bal$
at 50% CPR (5.61% SMM)	$\frac{15}{30} \times \left(\frac{1}{12} \times \frac{6.75}{100}\right) \times \frac{5.61}{100} \times Bal = \frac{1.578}{100^2} \times Bal$

B&C Home Equities

Maximum Servicer Payments	$\frac{1}{12} \times \frac{0.50}{100} \times Bal = \frac{4.17}{100^2} \times Bal$

Interest Shortfall:

at 25% CPR (2.37% SMM)	$\frac{15}{30} \times \left(\frac{1}{12} \times \frac{11.00}{100}\right) \times \frac{2.37}{100} \times Bal = \frac{1.086}{100^2} \times Bal$
at 50% CPR (5.61% SMM)	$\frac{15}{30} \times \left(\frac{1}{12} \times \frac{11.00}{100}\right) \times \frac{5.61}{100} \times Bal = \frac{2.571}{100^2} \times Bal$
at 70% CPR (9.55% SMM)	$\frac{15}{30} \times \left(\frac{1}{12} \times \frac{11.00}{100}\right) \times \frac{9.55}{100} \times Bal = \frac{4.375}{100^2} \times Bal$

The coupons on home equities are roughly twice those on whole loans, which will lead to about twice the interest shortfall for the same prepayment rate. However, the maximum compensating interest in home equities is around four times as large as in whole loans, which means it will cover the interest shortfalls at much higher speeds, even with a higher coupon.

If the servicer's compensating interest does not cover the shortfall caused by prepayments, the remaining shortfall is covered by excess spread in the deal. If shortfall is greater than the maximum compensating interest from the servicer plus the excess spread, then on a wrapped deal, the bond insurer is responsible for any remaining interest shortfall. This second line of responsibility is not spelled out explicitly in the prospectus, nor in the pooling or servicing agreement. However, since payment of this interest is not specifically carved out (i.e., specifically excluded), the bond insurer is responsible under its guarantee of timely payment of interest.

In a senior/sub home equity deal, if the servicer's compensating interest and excess spread are exhausted, any remaining interest shortfall must be covered by a write-down of the subordinate bonds.

Compensating interest is not required in 125 deals. (Just as advancing delinquent interest payments is not required.) Thus, interest shortfalls stemming from prepayments are covered solely by excess spread in the deal. One of the reasons that advances and compensating interest are handled differently in 125 deals than in home equity deals is the manner in which float (i.e. interest earned on prepayment before they are passed to the deal) is handled. In a home equity deal, the float is usually retained by the servicer. In the 125 market, the float is not retained by the servicer but is passed through to the deal. More broadly, because 125s have many attributes similar to those on credit cards, it is not surprising that some of their structuring details differ from the more traditional mortgage-related ABS securities.

CONCLUSION

Investors are better off focusing on how their whole loan securities will behave in a rally or a sell-off, and worrying less about compensating interest arrangements. Except for older securities which pay no compensating interest, the yield impact of compensating interest arrangements will generally be a second order effect. Meanwhile in the home equity market, compensating interest arrangements are even more generous to investors. Speeds must reach extremely high levels before investors are impacted at all.

Chapter 4

RALI Alternative-A Mortgages

Steve Banerjee
Vice President
Prudential Securities Incorporated

Errol Mustafa, Ph. D.
Senior Vice President
Prudential Securities Incorporated

INTRODUCTION

This chapter describes the characteristics of the alternative-A (alt-A) sector of the mortgage market in general, with special emphasis on RALI alt-A mortgages. A discussion of the important differences in prepayment characteristics between RALI alt-A collateral and agency conforming collateral follows. In particular, it is noted that RALI collateral exhibits improved convexity characteristics relative to conventional mortgages due to its lower prepayment sensitivity to interest-rate changes. RALI securities also have less extension risk as a result of higher base-case prepayments. We also analyze RALI alt-A loan characteristics based on conforming and non-conforming balances and examine the implications of continuing improvements in the credit performance of RALI alt-A securities in recent years. A discussion of the future growth prospects and the potential impact of government-sponsored enterprise (GSE) participation in the alt-A sector is also included.

As the U.S. homeownership rate has continued to reach new highs, so too has the proliferation of mortgage debt. The overall mortgage securitization rate, as measured by the percentage of new originations funneled into securities, has ranged from 47.4% in 1995 to 65.6% in the first nine months of 1998. Mortgages that fall within the conforming or FNMA and FHLMC guidelines are at the top of the lending credit spectrum, followed by the private-label market, which can be further divided into four major categories: jumbos, alt-As, 125-LTVs, and B&C mortgages (mainly home-equity and manufactured-housing loans). There is no line that clearly defines where A-

The authors would like to thank John Collins, Tim Johnson, and Warren Loken of the Residential Funding Corporation for their assistance. Gratitude is also due to Shrikant Ramamurthy, Inna Koren, Steve Bernhardt, Bill Chesner, Limin Zhang, and Mike Valente of Prudential Securities Incorporated.

credit ends and B-credit begins, and there are no precise standards in the industry to differentiate between B, C, and lower credits. Exhibit 1 outlines some of the loan characteristics associated with various mortgage sectors. These include borrower credit, average loan size, loan rate, loan-to-value (LTV), property type, and lien status.

Residential mortgage product is becoming increasingly diverse, and loans such as alt-As are becoming popular with originators. The need for alt-A mortgages was primarily driven by demand from borrowers who were unable or unwilling to provide full documentation as required by GSEs like Fannie Mae and Freddie Mac. Nevertheless, these borrowers were still considered A-quality borrowers as measured by FICO or other credit scores. In spite of their A-quality credit, these prospective borrowers were usually turned down by the agencies due to their lack of full documentation. Private-label mortgage issuers moved in to service them, giving birth to alt-A loans.

CHARACTERISTICS OF ALTERNATIVE-A LOANS

The alt-A sector encompasses both conforming and non-conforming loan balances, though the average balance on the typical alt-A loan is more in line with the agency average of around $114,000. Alt-A borrowers usually have an A-rated quality credit history and the loans have the following characteristics:

Exhibit 1: Loan Characteristics of Mortgage Sectors

Collateral	Agency	Alt-A	Jumbo	125-LTV	Home Equity (trad. B/C)	MH
Borrower Credit (%)						
A-Credit	100	100	100	100	0	0
Finance Company A/A-					20-50	10-40
Finance Company B/C					5-55	30-60
Loan Characteristics						
Loan Limit ($ in 000s)	<240	none	>240	none	none	none
Avg. Loan Size ($ in 000s)	114	100-130	300	35	50-70	37
Loan Rate above Agy. (BPs)	0	+100	+50	+440/600	+220/400	+250/400
Avg. LTV (%)	75-85	75-85	70-80	113	65-80	83-88
Property Type (%)						
Single Family	95-100	60-80	75-95	80-100	80-95	90-100
PUD/Condominium	0-5	20-40	5-15	N/A	0-10	N/A
Occupancy (%)						
Primary	100	60-75	85-100	N/A	90-100	90-100
Investment		15-35	0-10		0-15	0-10
Secondary		0-5	0-5		0-2	0-5
Lien Status (%)						
First	100	100	100	90-100	75-95	100
Second				0-10	10-30	
Avg. FICO Scores		High 600	High 600	660-680	580-640	N/A

Note: Figures are approximations

Source: Prudential Securities

- *Expanded underwriting criteria* Alt-A product can include loans from borrowers whose income information is omitted or not verified.
- *High LTVs* LTV ratios are often above 80%, though generally below 95%. In contrast, agency LTVs are in the 75% to 85% range.
- *Expanded debt-to-income (DTI) ratios* DTIs often approach 40%, compared to the higher end of 36% for most conforming loans.
- *Loans carry higher rates* As a result of higher LTVs and DTIs (among other things), alt-A loans carry interest rates that are, on average, 100 basis points higher than those of conforming loans.
- *High percentage of loans are for investment purposes* Alt-A pools carry a high percentage of investment loans (see Exhibit 1). Those who borrow for investment purposes often prefer alt-A mortgages for their competitive pricing versus other sources of financing, like privately placed mortgages.

While the alt-A sector only represents around 3% of total mortgage lending, the pace of alt-A growth has been very strong. The sector has been securitized since 1994 and at year-end 1998 had about $25 billion in bonds outstanding. Issuance has jumped from a little over $2 billion in 1994 to around $18 billion in 1998.

KEY ISSUERS

Residential Accredit Loan, Incorporated (RALI), one of the shelf registrations of the Residential Funding Corporation (RFC), and Residential Asset Securitization Trust (RAST) of the Independent National Mortgage Corporation (Indy Mac) are the major issuers of alt-As. Together, they account for some three-quarters of all issuance in the alt-A sector. Other originators/issuers include Headland Mortgage Company, ICI Funding (ICI), North American Mortgage Company (NAMC), and Norwest Integrated Structured Assets, Inc. (NISTR). This chapter confines itself to the discussion of RALI-issued alt-A product.

PREPAYMENT CHARACTERISTICS OF RALI ALT-A SECURITIES

Exhibit 2 presents the aggregate collateral characteristics of RALI deals, all of which are backed by purely A-credit loans. As mentioned earlier, a large percentage of alt-A borrowers provide limited documentation — in the case of RALI, it equates to 47.2%. Limited documentation leaves borrowers with fewer refinancing options. In addition, the low loan balance on a large percentage of RALI loans reduces the potential savings from refinancings. Both traits have the effect of lowering prepayments.

Exhibit 2: RFC's RALI Shelf, Fixed-Rate Alternative-A Mortgages
Aggregate Composition (%) as of September 1998

Vintage	All	1998	1997	1996	1995
Loan-to-Value (LTV) Ratio	76.0	75.6	76.6	75.0	73.7
Limited Documentation	47.2	50.1	46.6	38.5	43.3
California Borrowers	20.8	23.0	18.1	20.2	18.0
Purchase Money Loans	59.0	52.6	65.6	63.2	67.4
Cash-Out Refinance Loans	23.2	26.6	19.5	21.2	20.1
Rate Refinance Loans	17.8	20.8	14.9	15.6	12.5
Single-Family Borrowers	61.3	62.7	59.6	60.7	59.6
Multifamily (2-4) Borrowers	15.4	13.6	16.3	18.5	21.8
Condominium Borrowers	7.9	7.8	8.4	7.8	5.9
PUD Borrowers	14.0	14.5	14.1	11.9	11.5
Owner-Occupied Properties	63.2	66.7	61.2	57.5	50.9
Investor Properties	32.3	29.1	34.2	37.2	45.0

Aggregate Prepayments (% CPR) as of September 1998

Vintage	All	1998	1997	1996	1995
1-Month Speed	20.4	10.0	27.3	33.7	32.8
6-Month Speed	25.9	15.7	23.6	35.1	37.9
12-Month Speed	25.4	N/A	22.6	28.8	30.4
Life Speed	13.9	8.4	17.2	20.8	20.7

Source: Residential Funding Corporation, Prudential Securities

The first critical test of RALI prepayments came during the refinancing wave of March and April 1998, which was precipitated by conforming mortgage rates moving below the psychologically important 7.0% level. Exhibit 3 compares monthly prepayment speeds for the RALI 1996-QS3 1 (with a WAC of 8.78%) with those of 30-year, 1996-production FNMA 8.00% and 8.50% passthroughs (with WACs of 8.53% and 8.94%, respectively). The peak prepayment speeds for the RALI issue were well below the FNMA speeds during the peak refi months of March and April 1998, and RALI speeds took more time to respond to the lower rates. Similar prepayment patterns exist for other vintages. This points to the lower interest-rate sensitivity of RALI loans relative to conventional loans in a bullish-rate environment. Exhibits 4 through 6 show the seasoning characteristics of RALI alt-A collateral for similar WAC groupings. The groupings are for observations where the WACs are 100 basis points, 150 basis points, and 200 basis points above the FHLMC mortgage rate.

RALI prepayments result in paydowns that are much less volatile, and hence more predictable than those of conventional mortgages. This is illustrated in Exhibit 7, which shows the aggregate 1-month CPRs for all RALI deals and all FNMA 30-year collateral over the 12-month period ending November 1998. The standard deviation of the monthly percentage changes in prepayment speeds is 11.3% for RALI deals and 26.4% for 30-year FNMAs. Thus, the month-to-month prepayment changes are smaller for RALI deals than they are for conventional collateral, at least on an aggregate basis.

Exhibit 3: RALI and FNMA 30-Year Prepayments

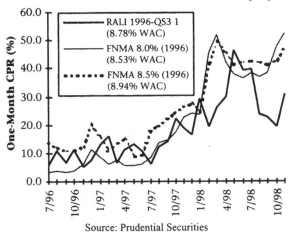

Source: Prudential Securities

Exhibit 4: Seasoning of RALI and 30-Year FNMA Passthroughs: WAC 100 Basis Points over FHLMC Mortgage Rate

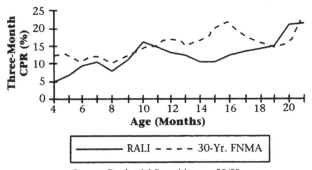

Source: Prudential Securities as of 9/98

Exhibit 5: Seasoning of RALI and 30-Year FNMA Passthroughs: WAC 150 Basis Points over FHLMC Mortgage Rate

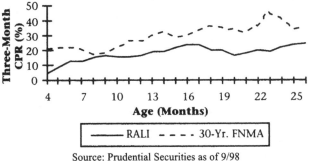

Source: Prudential Securities as of 9/98

Exhibit 6: Seasoning of RALI and 30-Year FNMA Passthroughs: WAC 200 Basis Points over FHLMC Mortgage Rate

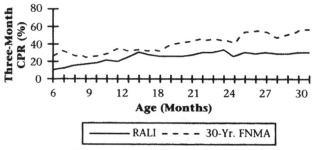

Source: Prudential Securities as of 9/98

Exhibit 7: Aggregate Prepayments and Volatility of RALI and FNMA 30-Year Passthroughs

	1-Mo. CPR (%)		% Change in 1-Mo. CPR (%)	
	All RALI	All FNMA 30-Yr.	RALI	FNMA 30-Yr.
11/97	15.19	12.40	−7.55	5.08
12/97	14.23	13.70	−6.32	10.48
1/98	15.98	12.80	12.30	−6.57
2/98	16.76	23.70	4.88	85.16
3/98	20.15	28.00	20.23	18.14
4/98	24.63	23.20	22.23	−17.14
5/98	22.70	20.20	−7.84	−12.93
6/98	21.31	20.40	−6.12	0.99
7/98	20.58	20.70	−3.43	1.47
8/98	20.79	20.10	1.02	−2.90
9/98	19.86	20.10	−4.47	0.00
10/98	19.28	27.40	−2.92	36.32
11/98	22.79	30.40	18.21	10.95

Source: Prudential Securities

RALI loans clearly tend to prepay more slowly than conventional collateral in a bullish-rate environment when compared on a similar-WAC basis.

Exhibit 8 shows the historical spread between RALI weighted-average coupons and the FHLMC 30-year fixed conforming mortgage rate. As the alt-A market has matured, the difference in coupon between alt-A loans and conforming loans has stabilized, and has ranged between 90 and 120 basis points since mid-1997.

BETTER CONVEXITY OF RALI ALT-A SECURITIES

The convexity characteristics of RALI and conventional mortgage collateral are a function of the prevailing interest-rate incentive. One difficulty in comparing the

rate refi incentive of RALI securities with that of conventional MBSs is the identification of a proper alt-A mortgage rate. The Freddie Mac 30-year fixed-rate
mortgage survey is generally used as the benchmark against which the refi incentive of conforming collateral is measured. However, the refinancing alternative of
a RALI fixed-rate borrower is situated somewhere between the conforming mortgage rate (for those refinancing into agency conforming mortgages) and the RALI
fixed mortgage rate (for those refinancing into another alt-A product). For the
purposes of this analysis, we assume that the RALI fixed mortgage-rate refi incentive is measured relative to the average of RALI and FHLMC mortgage rates.
However, our conclusions stated herein are fairly insensitive to the precise measure of the RALI refi incentive.

Exhibit 9 compares the performance of RALI and FNMA 30-year collateral when the rate refi incentive is approximately 100 basis points. RALI sensitivity to interest-rate changes is much lower than comparable 30-year FNMA
collateral. This is displayed in Exhibit 10, which shows RALI and 30-year FNMA
prepayments for incentives of 50 basis points, 100 basis points, and 150 basis
points at 10 months and 20 months of seasoning. In both cases the slope of the
RALI prepayment curve is flatter than that of the FNMA 30-year curve. Based on
these curves, for a 100-basis-point incentive, we estimate that RALI collateral is
approximately 30% less negatively convex than comparable agency securities.

In addition, our analysis shows that RALI loans have higher base-case
(zero refi incentive) prepayments compared to conforming loans. In the base case,
at 18 months of seasoning, RALI speeds are around 12% CPR compared to 6.5%
CPR for conforming loans. Thus, at lower incentives, there is less extension risk
in RALI loans.

Exhibit 8: RALI Fixed-Rate WAC Spread to FHLMC Mortgage Rate

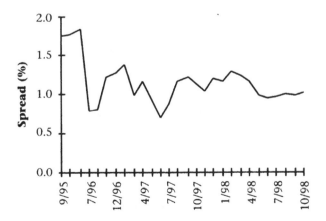

Source: Prudential Securities

Exhibit 9: Seasoning of 30-Year RALIs and 30-Year FNMAs: 100-Basis Point Incentive*

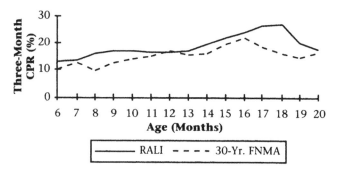

* Approximate

Source: Prudential Securities as of 9/98

Exhibit 10: Prepay S-Curves: RALI and 30-Year FNMA

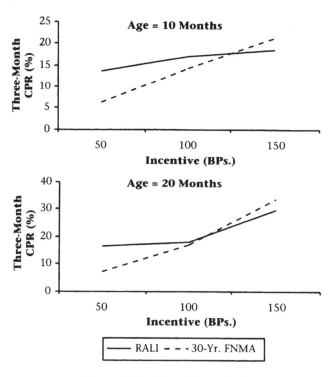

Source: Prudential Securities as of 9/98

Exhibit 11: RALI Seasoning by Origination Year

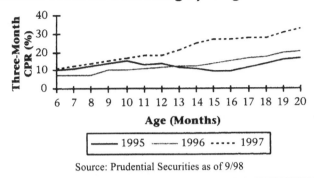

Source: Prudential Securities as of 9/98

It is our observation that RALI issues have better convexity than conventional collateral, while they have reduced extension risk for out-of-the-money incentives.

FUTURE TRENDS IN RALI PREPAYMENTS

Exhibit 11 shows the effect of vintage on RALI alt-A seasoning. The higher prepayment level of 1997-vintage loans is most likely a reflection of the extraordinary refi opportunities available in 1998, rather than of any inherent bias in 1997 originations. By contrast, 1995 and 1996 originations experienced a much more benign prepayment environment during the seasoning process.

We believe that RALI prepayments will be dictated mainly by the level of mortgage rates (both conforming and alt-A rates) and the extent to which GSEs penetrate the alt-A sector. Historically, after a refi wave has ended and rates stabilize, RALI mortgages are more greatly impacted by the "burnout" effect (i.e., lowered refinancibility of the remaining collateral) than conventional mortgages. Thus, if rates remain stable at year-end 1998 levels, we expect RALI prepayments to slow considerably more than conventional prepayments. Additionally, the seasoning ramp at 25 to 30 months should peak at around 25% CPR. A bearish-rate scenario would likely peg the seasoning ramp at around 20% CPR. In contrast, a bullish-rate environment will likely raise the ramp to around 30% CPR. While GSE participation in the alt-A market is likely to put near-term, upward pressure on these levels, the extent of this pressure will further depend on a number of factors, like mortgage rates, the percentage of owner-occupied properties, the amount of documentation acceptable to GSEs, loan-balance distribution, etc.

DELINQUENCY AND LOSS IN RALI ALT-A SECURITIES

Exhibit 12 presents the 90+ day delinquency experience of RALI alt-A securities. The worst performers were of 1995 vintage, which is in line with the default experience of conforming loans. However, there was only one RALI alt-A deal issued in 1995, which accounts for the volatile nature of the 1995 delinquency profile. Exhibit 13 includes loans that are in foreclosure and real-estate owned (REO), and profiles the RALI loans that are in serious trouble at any given time.

RALI alt-A mortgages have displayed improved credit performance in recent years. RALI delinquencies have been improving since 1995.

Exhibit 12: RALI 90+ Day Delinquencies*

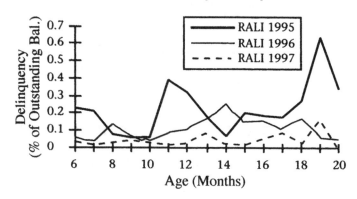

* 1995 data based on one deal

Source: Prudential Securities as of 9/98

Exhibit 13: Seriously Troubled RALI Loans: 90+ Day Delinquency, Foreclosure, and REO*

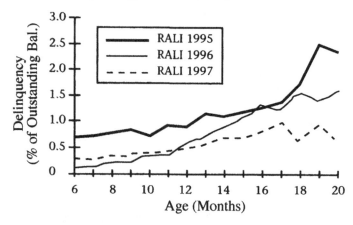

* 1995 data based on one deal

Source: Prudential Securities as of 9/98

Exhibit 14: RALI Loan Characteristics by Conforming/Non-Conforming Balance (as of 8/98)

All Originations	WAC (%)	WAM (Mos.)	Out. Bal. ($BB)	Org. Bal. ($BB)	Factor	CPR (%)	Avg. Loan Size ($)	LTV (%)	FICO	Seriously Troubled Loans* (%)
Non-conforming	8.21	319	1.658	2.210	0.78	28.8	328,447	75.8	714	0.5
Conforming	8.50	328	4.682	5.484	0.85	18.0	93,717	77.7	714	0.4

Breakdown by Origination Year

	Orig. Year	WAC (%)	WAM (Mos.)	Out. Bal. ($BB)	Org. Bal. ($BB)	Factor	CPR (%)	Avg. Loan Size ($)	LTV (%)	FICO	Seriously Troubled Loans* (%)
Non-conforming	1996	8.71	293	0.174	0.350	0.50	46.6	324,244	77.6	710	2.9
	1997	8.44	302	0.521	0.706	0.74	30.9	317,293	76.6	718	0.5
	1998	7.97	334	0.927	0.967	0.96	20.3	332,699	75.0	714	0.1
Conforming	1996	9.03	303	0.614	0.917	0.67	27.6	82,805	77.4	710	1.4
	1997	8.65	322	1.890	2.236	0.85	20.5	91,521	78.4	718	0.4
	1998	8.16	344	2.054	2.105	0.98	8.9	100,457	77.1	714	0.1

* Includes REO, loans in foreclosure, and 90+ day delinquencies.
Source: Residential Funding Corp.

Along with delinquency information, the RFC provides actual loss data once a property is sold. As of December 1998 loss information is available on all 1995, all 1996, and some 1997 originations. The gross losses on individual deals have ranged between 3 and 40 basis points (RFC's Mortgage Data Report of December 1998). According to RFC estimates, the loss-severity level on seriously delinquent RALI loans at year-end 1998 was around 24%.

RALI COLLATERAL AND CONFORMING/NON-CONFORMING BALANCE

Overall, RALI loans have an average loan balance of around $113,000, which is well within the conforming-loan limit. A detailed look at the collateral shows that roughly 26% of RALI outstanding balances fall outside of conforming limits, averaging $328,447 (see Exhibit 14). The average balance on three-quarters of the loans that do fall into the conforming category is approximately $93,717. As shown in Exhibit 14, prepays on the conforming segment are almost 11% CPR slower than the non-conforming pay-downs. Clearly, loan size plays a crucial role in determining prepayment sensitivity, as larger loans exhibit higher prepayment volatility.

Exhibit 14 also shows that FICO scores are similar for conforming and non-conforming balances. RALI conforming loans have slightly higher WACs due to special features, like the preponderance of investor loans in a RALI pool. Non-conforming mortgages, as expected, have a slightly higher percentage of loans that are seriously delinquent. As of August 1998, RALI loans that were in serious trouble (REO, foreclosed, and 90+ day delinquency) constituted 0.5% (50 basis points) of the non-conforming outstanding balance, while around 0.4% of conforming loans fell into this category. In comparison, recent data available for agency conforming, 30-year, fixed-rate mortgages show that some 0.72% were seriously delinquent, while the corresponding level for 30-year, fixed-rate, jumbo loans was 0.52%.[1]

The low conforming RALI loss numbers reflect a conscious effort by the RFC to tighten credit requirements. Among other measures, the RFC increased the minimum required FICO score from 620 to 680 for reduced-documentation loans. Underwriting guidelines require zero delinquencies in the last 12 months and a 7-year bankruptcy window. As a result of these changes, the percentage of loans in the overall pool with FICO scores above 680 increased from 59.9% in 1996 to 76.2% in 1998. In addition, better loss-mitigation techniques, like the frequent use of "short payoff disposition" (versus REO), have decreased loss severity.

GSES AND ALT-A MORTGAGES

The GSEs have become the primary influence in the mortgage industry. They are the two largest purchasers of residential mortgages in the United States, and at the end of 1998 accounted for over 35% of overall mortgage-market debt (through guarantees). Their combined mortgage-portfolio holdings surpassed $670 billion in December 1998, having grown 38% during 1998.

The agencies' participation in the mortgage industry continues to broaden. In order to increase their share of the mortgage market, both agencies have expanded their underwriting criteria. For example, Fannie Mae introduced the Desktop Underwriter 4.0 in September 1997. The new system allows for 80% LTV cash-out refis (up from 75%) on owner-occupied, single-family homes, while the maximum LTV limit for investor properties has been relaxed — increasing from 70% to 80%. Also in the summer of 1997, Fannie Mae introduced Flex-97, which allows LTV to go as high as 97% for good-credit borrowers, while reducing private mortgage insurance (PMI) to only 18% from 30%. Clearly, this system gives the lender a fair degree of latitude to qualify a potential alt-A candidate into Fannie Mae's conforming category. For instance, a borrower with a good payment history may be allowed to qualify under a low-documentation scheme. Reportedly, more than $1.8 billion of Flex-97 mortgages have been underwritten nationwide.

In contrast to Fannie Mae, Freddie Mac has been a late entrant into the alt-A arena. However, it is hoping to gain ground with an upgrade to Loan Prospector, its desktop refinancing system, which should offer more flexibility to originators qualifying alt-A type borrowers. Freddie Mac officials indicated that they expect to issue around $10 billion in alt-A and A-minus rated product in 1999.

---

[1] The source for this data is Mortgage Information Corporation, *The Market Pulse* (Winter 1999).

In addition, the agencies have increased the loan limits for single-family homes to $240,000 in 1999 from $227,150. According to Fannie Mae, the increase in the loan-size limit should enable about 200,000 more families to obtain a Fannie Mae mortgage.

GSE initiatives are likely to increase competition in the alt-A sector, potentially lowering alt-A mortgage rates. Initially, this may lead to faster prepayment speeds. In the long run, however, the GSEs are likely to attract the more nimble refinancers, leaving behind a pool of homeowners that should exhibit less prepayment sensitivity to interest rates. Ultimately, this could enhance the convexity of alt-A collateral.

At this point, it is difficult to quantify these changes. It must be remembered that the flexibility of the agencies is limited by their mandate to aggregate the best-quality conforming mortgages into TBA-deliverable pools; this is likely to curb their potential penetration into the alt-A sector.

CONCLUSION

Securitization of alt-A mortgages has come a long way in the past few years. Our analysis reveals that RALI alt-A mortgages, with their predominantly conforming balances, provide better convexity than conventional mortgages. Furthermore, the credit performance of RALI alt-A mortgages continues to improve. Though the GSEs may take some business away from traditional alt-A originators, eventually such action actually may enhance the convexity of alt-A mortgages.

Chapter 5

Home Equity Loans

Charles Schorin
Principal
Director of ABS Research
Morgan Stanley Dean Witter

Steven Weinreich
Associate
Morgan Stanley Dean Witter

Oliver Hsiang
Analyst
Morgan Stanley Dean Witter

INTRODUCTION

This chapter provides a background to the home equity loan asset backed securities market. In order to have a firm grasp on securities backed by home equity loans, it is necessary to understand fundamental aspects of the loans themselves: loan attributes, borrower characteristics, loan purposes, underwriting criteria and loan performance. With a knowledge of the loan collateral, investors must then understand the structures of securities that are backed by these loans, as well as the differences in the lenders that originate loans and issue securities. With this knowledge, investors would be well suited to ascertain both relative value within the home equity loan ABS sector and between various fixed income markets.

The term "home equity loan" covers a broad array of products. While this includes the traditional second lien mortgage, it more commonly today refers to first liens to borrowers with impaired credit histories and/or debt-to-income ratios that exceed the agency guidelines. Referred to as B and C borrowers, these mortgagors would not qualify for a conventional mortgage loan and must seek an alternative source of funds. The primary loan purpose is to consolidate consumer debt and is rarely to purchase a home.

Exhibit 1: The HEL Market Has Moved Toward First Liens, Longer Maturities and Larger Loan Balances

Characteristic	Advanta 91-1		Advanta 98-1*	
	Average	Range	Average	Range
Loan Size	$41,116	$4,499-$260,508	$59,344	$3,840 - $700,000
Remaining Term	173 mos.	32-180 mos.	252 mos.	18-360 mos.
Original Term	180 mos.	180 mos.	256 mos.	256 mos.
First Lien	24%		93%	

* Fixed-rate collateral pool

Source: Advanta prospectuses, Morgan Stanley

Home equity loans can take several forms. Most are *closed-end home equity loans* (HEL), where the loan amount and term to maturity are set at origination. Closed-end HELs may be either fixed or adjustable rate. Adjustable-rate HELs (called HEL ARMs) usually have both periodic and lifetime caps. There also are open-end, revolving loans, where the borrower receives a *home equity line of credit* (HELOC) that can be (partially or completely) drawn down and (partially or completely) paid back over time. HELOCs carry floating rates, usually with very high lifetime caps and no interim caps.

MARKET OVERVIEW

The home equity sector is now one of the single largest asset classes in the ABS market. The top five issuers of HEL ABS in 1998 and the first nine months of 1999 were GreenTree Financial, Residential Funding Corporation, ContiMortgage, Advanta, and EquiCredit Corporation.

Evolution of the Home Equity Market

Through the late 1980s and early 1990s, the home equity loan market was characterized by relatively small balance, second lien loans. The market, however, has evolved dramatically in the past few years toward larger loans that are first liens and with longer maturities. The changed nature of the home equity market is indicated in Exhibit 1 by a comparison of collateral characteristics for Advanta 91-1 and 98-1. The tendency toward first liens, longer maturities and larger loan balances is clear.

The market's evolution and growth have been fueled by several factors, including

- a generally lower interest rate environment
- an increase in the use of home equity loans as debt consolidation instruments
- an increase in the number and volume of B and C lending programs

• a change in tax laws making mortgage debt the only remaining tax deductible form of consumer debt.

Low rates allow homeowners to refinance their first lien and take out equity or consolidate debt more cheaply than with a non-mortgage consumer loan. The cost effectiveness of mortgage versus non-mortgage consumer debt has increased since tax laws changed to make mortgage debt the only tax deductible form of consumer debt. The acceptance by homeowners of using equity in their home to increase their financial flexibility and consolidate debt has grown tremendously. As homeowners have sought to consolidate debt and as A quality conventional lenders saw their traditional lines of business diminish, they developed B and C programs to fill the void.

B and C grade home equity borrowers tend either to have had some blemishes on their credit records that prevent them from qualifying for A quality conventional mortgages or else have debt-to-income ratios (or some other loan parameters) that disqualify them from conventional loans. Tapping the equity in their homes provides their readiest access to credit, which often is used to consolidate other consumer debt (such as credit card or automobile debt), or for home improvements, medical or education expenditures. Borrower classification by lenders into various credit grades is discussed in the next section.

Home Equity Loan Underwriting

Lenders classify borrowers by their credit quality. Specific criteria for a credit grade sometimes differ among lenders, so that one lender's B applicant may be another's C candidate. Within the home equity arena, however, A quality finance company borrowers either do not generally possess as strong personal credit profiles, or do not meet certain loan parameters, such as debt-to-income ratio, as required for standard conventional mortgages.

Exhibit 2 shows guidelines that ContiMortgage uses when evaluating its borrowing applicants. The difference between credit grades can result in substantially different mortgage rates offered to borrowers (Exhibit 3).

Borrower credit grades have significant implications for home equity loan prepayments. Less-than-A quality borrowers can achieve considerable reductions in their mortgage rates if they can cure their impaired credit record and achieve a personal credit "upgrade". They may be able to obtain an upgrade by being current on their mortgage for 12 months. As indicated in Exhibit 3, moving from grade C to B could lower a borrower's rate by 100-200 bp. Note that this savings would occur with no change in market interest rates. The prepayment implications of the different credit grades will be discussed in detail in the section below on prepayments.

A broad summary of the types of issuers is presented in Exhibit 4. While any particular issuer or product may not fit precisely into the table, it nonetheless provides a general illustration of lenders' guidelines.

Exhibit 2: ContiMortgage Underwriting Guidelines Matrix

Grade	Credit History and Rating
A	• Good overall credit, perhaps some minor delinquencies; current on mortgage, with maximum two 30-day delinquencies in past 12 months; major debt should be current, but could have some minor 30-day delinquency; minor credit may have some minor delinquency • No former bankruptcies, charge-offs, judgments or liens are acceptable • Debt-to-income ratio maximum 45%; Loan-to-value ratio maximum generally 80%
B	• Pays majority of accounts on time, but some 30- and/or 60-day delinquency; current on mortgage, with maximum three 30-day delinquencies in past 12 months; major credit debt may have some minor 30- and 60-day delinquency, minor debt may have up to 90-day delinquency • Bankruptcy permitted, if discharged more than two years ago and major re-established credit • Debt-to-income ratio maximum 45%; Loan-to-value ratio maximum generally 80%
C	• Marginal credit history which is offset by other positive attributes; mortgage cannot exceed four 30-day or one 60-day delinquency in past 12 months; major credit may have some minor 60- and or 90-day delinquency; minor credit may have some more serious delinquency • Bankruptcy permitted, if discharged more than two years ago and major re-established credit • Debt-to-income ratio maximum 45%; Loan-to-value ratio maximum generally 75%
D	• Designed to provide borrower with poor credit history opportunity to lower monthly payments; mortgage must be paid in full from loan proceeds and not more than 119 days delinquent; major and minor credit delinquencies acceptable, but must demonstrate some regularity • Bankruptcies permitted, but must be discharged prior to closing • Debt-to-income ratio maximum 50%; Loan-to-value ratio maximum generally 65%

Source: ContiMortgage

Exhibit 3: Mortgage Rate Differentials by Borrower Credit Grade: ContiMortgage

First and Third Quartile Mortgage Rates for Indicated Credit Grade

	1997 Originations	
	1st Quartile	3rd Quartile
A	9.85%	11.39%
B	10.77	12.50
C	11.75	13.99
D	13.00	15.19

Source: ContiMortgage

Exhibit 4: Home Equity Loan Issuer Summary

Banks	Finance Companies	"Hard Money" Lenders
Excellent credit quality: A/B credits	Good to average credit quality: B/C credits	Poor or riskier credit quality: C/D credits
Lending on ability to repay	Lending on ability to repay and equity	Lending primarily on homeowner equity
Low delinquency and loss experience	Average level of delinquencies and losses	Highest level of delinquencies and losses
Relatively low interest rates	Moderately high interest rates	Relatively high interest rates
Relatively high CLTV	Moderate CLTV	Relatively low CLTV

Source: Morgan Stanley

Credit Scoring

Mortgage lenders have increasingly used credit scores to evaluate their loan applicants. Credit scoring attaches a quantitative measure to candidates based upon their personal credit history. It is used by many home equity lenders as an additional piece of information to that in the underwriting matrix in Exhibit 2.

Some home equity lenders will not lend to applicants who score below a particular numerical threshold.[1] Other lenders use the score as an additional piece of information — which could offset other borrower data that are either positive or negative — in determining the overall quality of the borrower and affecting the credit decision.

Loan Servicing

Servicing loans to subprime borrowers requires markedly more attention than servicing loans to A quality conventional borrowers. B and C borrowers generally require active attention by servicers to maximize the likelihood of payment. The quality and effectiveness of servicing can have a substantial impact on the performance of a home equity loan pool.

Loan servicers who have extensive experience with A borrowers have found that their expertise in that arena does not necessarily, or even generally, carry over into the B and C sector. The cost of servicing B and C loans could easily be double that of servicing A loans.

Some of the larger lender/servicers, such as Advanta, perform servicing for other lenders on a contract basis. These large operations allow servicers to achieve scale economies. When loans are serviced on a contract basis, the servicer may not give a preference in servicing to either its owned portfolio or its contracted servicing.

Recent Developments in the HEL Sector

The subprime sector has been characterized over the past two years by increasing competition and, more recently, by the consolidation seen in the financial services industry generally. In 1998, for example, the following mergers and acquisitions involving subprime lenders have included:

- First Union purchased The Money Store
- NationsBank purchased Barnett Banks, parent of EquiCredit
- Fleet Bank bought the credit card operation of Advanta
- Conseco bought GreenTree Financial
- Household and Beneficial merged
- Coast-to-Coast Mortgage conditionally agreed to infuse capital to First-Plus.

In addition, as we go to print this chapter, several subprime lenders, such as United Companies Financial Corporation, Southern Pacific, Cityscape, and

---

[1] On the other hand, borrowers with credit scores above a given level probably are not applicants for finance company loans.

FirstPlus filed for bankruptcy, and the sector in general had to endure a severe liquidity squeeze in 1998. The result of this activity is likely to be a weeding out of the weaker performing firms and the solidification of fewer, but stronger, entities. In the long term, a reduction in competition is likely to lead to higher quality loan originations, as lenders will not feel compelled to lower their lending standards in order to compete for business.

In terms of securitization, the biggest development has been the blurring of the boundaries between the mortgage-backed securities (MBS) and asset-backed securities (ABS) markets. The introduction to the home equity market of the senior/subordinate structure in ContiMortgage 1997-1 resulted in a flood of cross-over buying by traditional and, in many cases, very sophisticated MBS investors of home equity loan product. Even if they were not completely comfortable with the home equity product, these traditional mortgage investors understood cash flows, prepayments and subordination, but were less comfortable taking on the corporate credit risk of a monoline insurer. The senior/subordinate structure brought an increasing number of MBS investors to the ABS market, so that now, most mortgage investors view MBS and ABS as competing products, and will purchase in the sector that they deem contains the better relative value.

In addition to the senior/subordinate structure, the home equity loan sector has borrowed other structural features from the CMO market. ContiMortgage 1997-4 introduced the PAC (planned amortization class)/companion structure to the home equity sector, while IMC Mortgage 1997-5 contained the first TAC (targeted amortization class) bond. We expect that the blurring of structural boundaries between the mortgage and home equity sectors will continue, as developments occur in both sectors.

PREPAYMENTS ON HOME EQUITY COLLATERAL

ContiMortgage provided Morgan Stanley with loan level data on its fixed rate home equity loan originations that allow us to investigate quantitatively the impacts of various factors on prepayment behavior. Voluntary prepayments may be classified as due to either interest rate refinancing opportunities or loan seasoning. The seasoning may result from borrowers who improve their credit records — the "credit curing" or "personal credit upgrade" described in the introduction to this chapter — so that they qualify for lower rate loans, even without a change in market interest rates. Seasoning also occurs as borrowers — many of whom may be more dollar-payment, than interest rate, sensitive — seek to extend the term of their loans to lower their monthly payments, even perhaps at the expense of a higher interest rate. In addition, after a period of time, borrowers may accumulate more debt and want to re-consolidate debt. Prepayments may also be involuntary, as the result of borrower defaults.

The prepayment behavior of home equity loans is closely related to the characteristics of the borrower. Home equity loans are typically used to

• Consolidate consumer debt in a lower rate, tax deductible form
• Reduce a homeowner's monthly mortgage payment by extending the loan's term
• Finance home improvements
• Monetize equity in the home
• Finance temporary liquidity needs, such as for education or medical expenses

Accessing equity in the home is typically the least expensive and most readily available means of financing for the borrowers. In many cases, most of the borrower's wealth is the equity in his home. Aside from credit card lines — which usually charge interest at rates that are several hundred basis points higher than home equity note rates and that is not tax deductible — home equity borrowers generally do not have access to other forms of credit. Borrowers who have consolidated debt or taken cash out to meet an expense frequently consolidate again after their debt burden re-accumulates. This behavior is especially achievable if home values rise over time. This pattern of reconsolidation keeps the life of these loans considerably shorter than their maturity.

Seasoning

Prepayments on home equity collateral tend to reach a plateau, or a fully seasoned level, much faster and at a higher level than do A quality conventional loans. The reasons for this behavior are the credit curing, re-consolidating and term extending processes described above.

Even within the sub-prime sector, the lower quality loans — those to C and D borrowers — tend to season faster and to a higher prepayment rate than the higher quality A and B loans. This is because the weaker borrowers face an opportunity to achieve a credit upgrade, say from C to B, which could significantly lower their monthly payments. The A quality home equity borrowers are already at the top credit grade within the sub-prime sector and an upgrade for them would mean going into a conventional mortgage. The leap from sub-prime to conventional mortgage, however, is very difficult, as even the best sub-prime borrowers are unlikely to satisfy the mortgage agencies' debt-to-income ratios.

In addition to the credit curing effect, the weaker borrowers in the sub-prime sector also are likely to be in greater need of debt re-consolidation or term extension than the stronger borrowers. All of these effects result in the following general conclusion: the weaker is the borrower, the faster we should expect to be base case prepayments and seasoning. In contrast, as we will see below, the higher quality loans tend to respond to an interest rate refinancing incentive to a greater degree than the lower quality loans.

Exhibit 5 compares the seasoning patterns on A, B and C/D quality loans. C and D quality loans are grouped together because of the paucity of D loans in the Conti portfolio. The prepayments displayed in Exhibit 5 are purely voluntary; prepayments due to defaults are not incorporated in these curves. The curves show that the lower the quality of the loan, the faster it seasons and the higher its prepayment rate at the fully seasoned, plateau level.

Interest Rate Sensitivity

Exhibit 6 shows a spectrum of refinancing sensitivity to interest rate movements of various mortgage products. Large balance (jumbo) conventional loans have the strongest response, followed by agency conforming mortgages. After this are home equity loans, with loans to A borrowers the most responsive and those to D borrowers the least responsive. One of the reasons that home equity loans display less interest rate refinancing sensitivity than conventional loans is that home equities typically have smaller loan balances. The smaller home equity loan balances means that it requires a larger interest rate movement for the borrower to achieve a substantial monthly dollar savings from refinancing.[2] Small balances also make these loans less of a target to lenders that solicit refinancings, for which larger loans are more profitable.

Exhibit 5: HEL Seasoning: Lower Grade Loans Season Faster than Higher Quality Loans

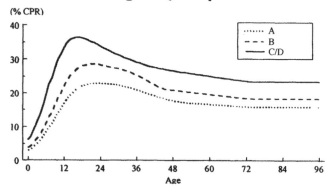

Source: ContiMortgage, Morgan Stanley

Exhibit 6: Mortgage Products Interest Rate Sensitivity Spectrum

Most Sensitive					Least Sensitive
Jumbo Mortgages	Agency Conforming Mortgages	"A" Quality Home Equity	"B" Quality Home Equity	"C" Quality Home Equity	"D" Quality Home Equity

Source: Morgan Stanley

---

[2] As an example, consider a $50,000 home equity loan. It may require points and origination fees of perhaps 5%, which typically would be financed. At an 11% note rate on a 30-year loan, the borrower's monthly payment would be $499.97 (assuming points are financed). If, after this loan has been outstanding for 3 years, rates fall 100 bp, the borrower could refinance his $51,705.85 loan balance and pay $476.44 per month (assuming origination fees and points are financed). This 100 bp reduction in rates would save the borrower only $23.53 per month. By comparison, a 100 bp reduction in rates after 3 years from 8.50% to 7.50% for a $300,000 non-conforming loan would reduce the borrower's monthly payments by $261.00 per month.

Exhibit 7: Home Equity Loans Have Less Interest Rate Sensitivity Than Conventional Mortgages

(% CPR)

	10-Yr. UST (Right Axis)
- - -	FN 8.5
——	FN 8.0
——	Conti

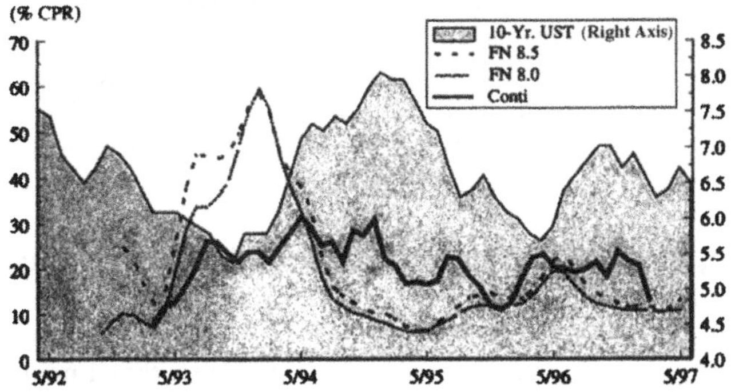

Source: ContiMortgage, Morgan Stanley

As an illustration of the limited interest rate sensitivity of home equity loans, Exhibit 7 compares home equity prepayments to those on conventional mortgages. The home equity prepayment rates in Exhibit 7 are derived from loan level data from ContiMortgage. The Conti loans are 15-year closed-end, fixed-rate, fully amortizing first liens originated in 1992. The conventionals are represented by 15-year FNMA 8% and 8.5% pass-through coupons that also were originated in 1992.[3] Exhibit 7 displays prepayments on a 3-month average basis to smooth volatility in the 1-month CPR series.

It is clear from Exhibit 7 that when interest rates fell dramatically in 1993, conventional pass-throughs responded with prepayment speeds in the neighborhood of 60% CPR, whereas home equity prepayments — as represented by ContiMortgage — on a 3-month average basis barely pierced half that level. Moreover, when the 1994 bear market arrived, home equity prepayment speeds declined less than the conventional loans: the FNMA 8s in Exhibit 7 prepaid on a 3-month average basis between 6% and 10% CPR in the fourth quarter of 1994 and the first half of 1995, whereas the home equity loans prepaid between 10% and 23% CPR over this period.[4]

We will see later in this chapter exhibits that incorporate the more recent competitive environment under which newer loans were originated; these will show that home equities still clearly display markedly less interest rate sensitivity than conventional mortgages. Securities backed by home equity loans, then, have less optionality than those backed by conventional mortgages.

We saw above that the seasoning patterns of home equity loans vary depending upon whether the loans are to A, B or C/D borrowers. The lower the quality of the loan, the faster the seasoning process and the higher the prepayment

---

[3] The FNMA pass-throughs are collateralized by 15-year, fixed rate, fully amortizing first liens.

[4] The FNMA 8.5s prepaid between 6% and 13% CPR over this period, and between 6% and 10% CPR for the first half of 1995.

speed that is attained. This is because lower quality borrowers have the opportunity to take advantage of a credit upgrade, are more likely to re-consolidate debt at some future point and may desire to extend the term of their loan to reduce monthly payments. In contrast to their relative seasoning patterns, the higher quality borrowers have a greater refinancing response than the lower quality borrowers. This is because, being of better quality, the A borrowers have more opportunities to refinance than B or C/D borrowers. This stronger refinancing response by the higher quality borrowers is shown in Exhibit 8.

Prepayment Effects of Various Loan Attributes

While seasoning and interest rate sensitivity can be used to explain home equity prepayments, knowledge of other loan attributes can be used to marginally adjust our estimate of prepayments. For example, if we know that a pool of A quality borrowers is predominantly second liens, we would expect prepayments to be higher than if the pool consisted mostly of first liens. In this section, we consider several loan attributes and examine their affect on home equity prepayments at the margin. These loan attributes are the following:

- Lien position
- Owner occupancy
- Prepayment penalty
- Documentation level
- Original loan-to-value ratio
- Current balance
- Loan purpose

Exhibit 8: Lower Credit Grade Borrowers Have Less Interest Rate Sensitivity than Higher Grade Borrowers

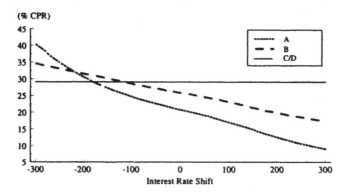

Source: ContiMortgage, Morgan Stanley

Exhibit 9: Second Liens Season Faster Than First Liens for A Quality Borrowers

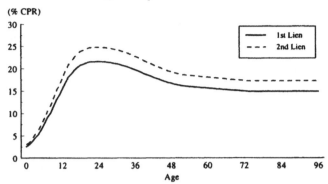

Source: ContiMortgage, Morgan Stanley

Exhibit 10: Second Liens Season More Slowly Than First Liens for C Borrowers

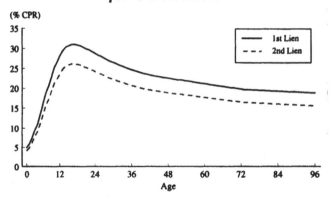

Source: ContiMortgage, Morgan Stanley

We first consider the affect of lien position on seasoning. We found that second liens season faster than first liens for A quality borrowers (Exhibit 9), but no faster than first liens for lower quality borrowers. (Exhibit 10 shows this for C quality borrowers.) First and second liens season similarly for B borrowers.

Homes that are owner occupied tend to prepay their respective mortgages faster than those that are investor properties (Exhibit 11). This relationship holds across borrower credit grades. Exhibit 11 shows this relative behavior for A quality borrowers.

The influence of prepayment penalties is shown in Exhibit 12 as leading to slower seasoning, all else equal. When considering prepayment penalties and their effects, we have to be a little bit careful, because prepayment penalties are determined on a state-by-state basis. States differ in the amount and duration of prepayment penalties that they permit, with some states' penalties being practically non-constraining. This said, Exhibit 12 shows the marginal effect of a penalty without regard to its severity.

The other important caveat in dealing with prepayment penalties is that with increased competition, some lenders may be willing to waive or finance the penalties in order to retain the borrower. From an entire portfolio standpoint the lender is left whole, but the affects of the prepayment would be felt in the securitized transaction (or transactions, if the residual from the original securitization collateralizes a net interest margin, or NIM, transaction). With these warnings in hand, it appears that loans with prepayment penalties season on the order of only 90% as fast as those without penalties.

Exhibit 11: Owner Occupied Homes Season Faster Than Investor Properties

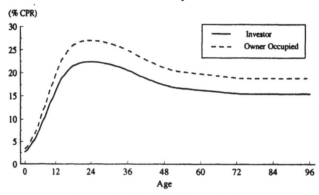

Source: ContiMortgage, Morgan Stanley

Exhibit 12: Loans with Prepayment Penalties Season More Slowly Than Loans Without Penalties

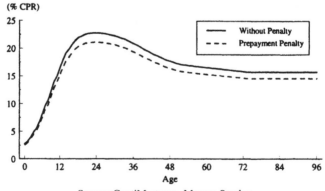

Source: ContiMortgage, Morgan Stanley

Exhibit 13: Limited Documentation Loans Season Faster Than Full Documentation Loans

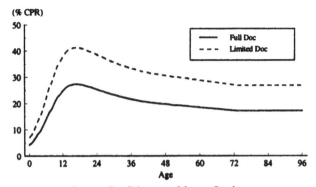

Source: ContiMortgage, Morgan Stanley

Exhibit 14: Higher Loan-to-Value Loans Season More Slowly Than Lower LTV Loans

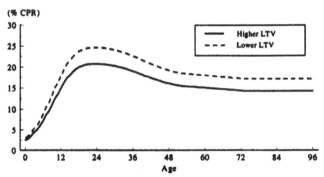

Source: ContiMortgage, Morgan Stanley

The degree of loan documentation also influences prepayments. "Limited doc" loans tend to prepay faster than "full doc" loans. (See Exhibit 13.) This is likely because limited doc loans may partly have the characteristic of being bridge loans, being completed without full documentation to get the loan processed, albeit at a higher note rate. Some of these bridge loan borrowers ultimately compile documentation, prepay the limited doc loan and take out another mortgage. Other limited doc borrowers are undoubtedly those for whom documentation may not provide full verification of their cash flow and ability to service the loan; these borrowers are likely, then, to remain in the pool.

Loans with higher loan-to-value (LTV) ratios tend to prepay slower than those with lower LTVs. (See Exhibit 14.) This is to be expected, as lower LTVs provide more equity against which borrowers can reconsolidate debt in the future, as well as making them more attractive borrowing candidates to lenders.

Exhibit 15: Higher Balance Loans Season More Slowly Than Lower Balance Loans

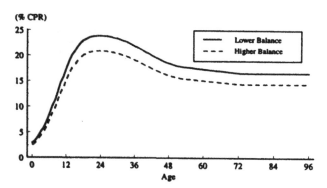

Source: ContiMortgage, Morgan Stanley

Exhibit 16: Higher Balance Loans Display a Greater Response to a Refinancing Incentive Than Lower Balance Loans

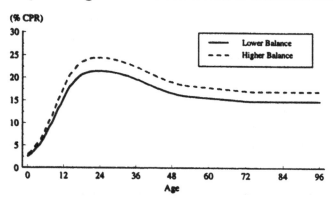

Source: ContiMortgage, Morgan Stanley

In terms of loan balance, there is an interesting relationship relative to prepayments. When not presented with a refinancing opportunity, higher balance loans actually prepay more slowly than lower balance loans (Exhibit 15), but when the loans are in-the-money, the higher balance loans refinance about 15% faster than lower balance loans (Exhibit 16). The latter results from the greater dollar savings for the larger balance loans when presented with a refinancing opportunity.

We also found that debt consolidation loans prepay about 10% faster than loans for other purposes. (See Exhibit 17.) This result is probably because borrowers who already have tapped the equity in their homes to consolidate debt may be more likely to need to do so in the future, or in any event, are already aware that this type of financial flexibility is available.

Exhibit 17: Debt Consolidation Loans Season Faster than Loans for Other Purposes

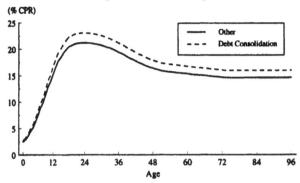

Source: ContiMortgage, Morgan Stanley

Exhibit 18: Lower Quality Borrowers Have Higher Default Rates than A Borrowers

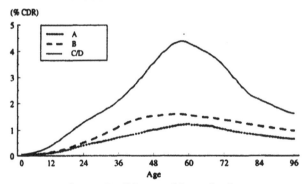

Source: ContiMortgage, Morgan Stanley

Defaults

We have so far focused on voluntary prepayments, but prepayments in securitized transactions may also be the result of defaults. When a borrower defaults, his loan is essentially "bought out" from the pool, either by the monoline insurer or by the internal credit enhancement. Exhibit 18 shows the default pattern of A, B and C/D quality loans from ContiMortgage's portfolio. Not surprisingly, the lower the credit quality of the borrower, the higher is the expected level of defaults.

Similar to the effects of loan attributes on voluntary prepayments, we can examine the affect of various loan characteristics on defaults, or involuntary prepayments. Here we consider the following:

- Lien position
- Documentation level

Exhibit 19: Second Liens Imply Greater Defaults for A Quality Borrowers

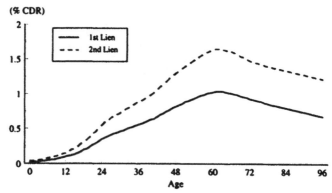

Source: ContiMortgage, Morgan Stanley

Exhibit 20: Lower Defaults for C/D Borrowers

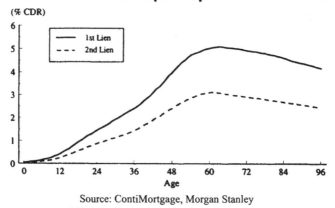

Source: ContiMortgage, Morgan Stanley

- Original loan-to-value
- Marginal credit quality

Second liens are more likely to experience defaults than first liens for A quality borrowers (Exhibit 19), but less likely to default for C/D borrowers (Exhibit 20). This is probably because lenders are less willing to provide second liens to C and D quality borrowers unless there is substantial offsetting criteria to indicate that the loans will be paid. This extra care probably results in less defaults on second liens to the lower quality borrowers.

Documentation levels are strongly related to default likelihood (Exhibit 21). Low doc borrowers qualify for loans based on providing less information than full doc loans, and it appears that the lack of information indicates a weaker quality borrower, all else equal.

Exhibit 21: Lower Documentation Loans Have Higher Default Rates than Full Doc Loans

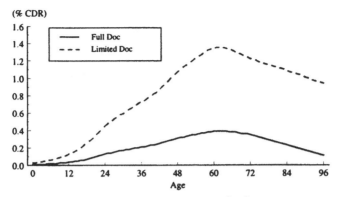

Source: ContiMortgage, Morgan Stanley

Exhibit 22: Higher LTV Loans Default More Frequently Than Lower LTVs

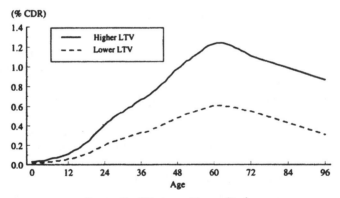

Source: ContiMortgage, Morgan Stanley

Loan-to-value ratios on mortgages have always been strongly correlated with default rates, and the subprime sector is no exception. Clearly, borrowers with lower LTVs have more equity at stake in their homes – and therefore, more to lose – and would be less likely to walk away from the loan in the event of a problem. Exhibit 22 shows the differential addition to default likelihood due to an 80% LTV vs. 60% LTV.

We saw in Exhibit 18 that lower quality loans, not surprisingly, have greater default likelihood than higher quality loans. In that graph, we compared Λ and B loans with the combination of C and D loans. The differential impact in moving from a C to D loan is a fairly substantial increase in default probability (Exhibit 23).

Exhibit 23: D Credits Default More Than C Quality Loans

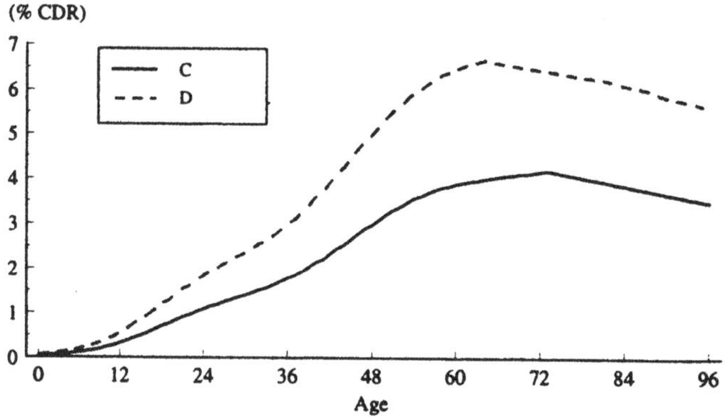

(% CDR)

Source: ContiMortgage, Morgan Stanley

PREPAYMENTS ON HOME EQUITY TRANSACTIONS

Cash flows on securities backed by fixed-rate home equity loans are heavily dependent on the prepayment characteristics of the underlying loans. In the previous section, we examined the determinants of loan level prepayments, and saw that home equities display less interest rate sensitivity than mortgages that collateralize agency mortgage pass-throughs. In the present section, we examine the recent history of prepayments on home equity loan securitizations.

The Treasury market began rallying in April 1997, and continued to trend higher through early 1999. As interest rates fell, prepayments on agency conventional mortgage pools began to spike fairly dramatically. As shown in Exhibit 24, prepayments on some large coupon/year class cohorts reached as high as 60% CPR. As mortgage prepayments surged, ABS market participants questioned the ability of the home equities to avoid prepayments. As it turned out, home equity prepayment speeds did increase due to the combination of a low interest rate environment and increased competition. With rates low, it is easier for competitive lenders to solicit borrowers to refinance their loans from other lenders. Nonetheless, home equity loan prepayments did not increase anywhere nearly to the levels of agency mortgages.

When examining home equity prepayments, it is important to note that there is considerable month-to-month variability in the transaction level prepayment data for home equity loan issuers, as well as for the issuers' year class aggregates. This is because of the relatively small size of the individual deals. Note that prior to 1997, the average HEL transaction for Advanta, Amresco, ContiMortgage, EquiCredit, IMC Mortgage, The Money Store, and United Companies was on the order of $228 million in size, with an average issuance of $713 million per year. For 1997 and 1998, the average transaction size was $566 million, with an average issuance of $2 billion per year for these issuers. This compares to the agencies, where current coupon/year class aggregates are typically on the order of $10-30 billion. The larger size over which the agency prepayment data are aggregated smooths over much of the month-to-month variability seen at the individual pool level.

Exhibit 24: Home Equity Loan ABS have Less Interest Rate Sensitivity than Conventional MBS

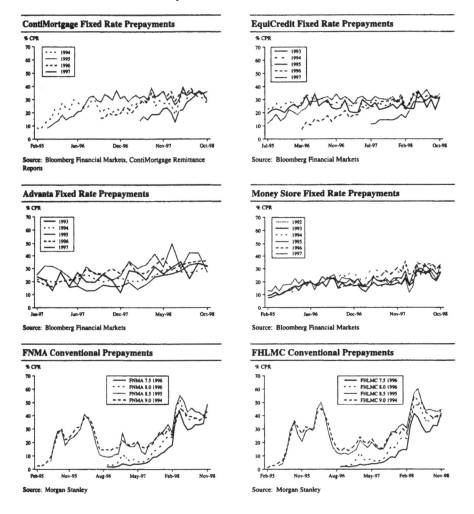

In addition to the relatively small size of the home equity year class aggregates, the relatively fast prepayment speeds on home equity collateral — even when not in-the-money — means that the deal factors decline fairly rapidly. At the time Exhibit 24 was computed, the factor for 1996 issuance for Advanta, Amresco, ContiMortgage, EquiCredit, IMC Mortgage, The Money Store, and United Companies was in the area of 0.55, while factors for 1995 and 1994 issuance were about 0.35 and 0.30, respectively. In contrast, factors on FNMA and FHLMC issuance in 1996, 1995 and 1994 were about 0.75, 0.70 and 0.65, respectively. As the factors decline, the significance of individual loans prepaying is magnified and month-to-month prepayment rates display greater variability.

We believe that home equity prepayments will continue to display less interest rate sensitivity than agency mortgage product. The reasons for our conclusions are

- Despite increased competition among lenders over the past few years, borrowers in the B and C HEL sector still are credit impaired and have less refinancing opportunities than true A quality borrowers.
- With an opportunity to refinance jumbo and other conventional mortgages, we believe that mortgage bankers will solicit large balance loans and resort to soliciting refinancings of the relatively low balance B and C loans only after exhausting their jumbo rolodex.
- As the sub-prime home equity sector continues to experience consolidation by both acquisition and evaporation, there will be fewer lenders cannibalizing each others' customers. This should reduce competition and result in slower and more stable prepayment behavior, as well as improved loan underwriting.

Chapter 6

Home Equity Loan Transaction Structures

Charles Schorin
Principal
Director of ABS Research
Morgan Stanley Dean Witter

Steven Weinreich
Associate
Morgan Stanley Dean Witter

Oliver Hsiang
Analyst
Morgan Stanley Dean Witter

INTRODUCTION

This chapter highlights some of the newer structures that have been introduced to the home equity loan ABS market. These structures were developed in and borrowed from the mortgage-backed securities market.

NAS BONDS

Non-accelerating senior (NAS) bonds have gained in popularity and are found in almost every home equity loan ABS transaction. They are attractive because of their average life stability over a range of prepayment scenarios. In this section, we discuss more fully their cash flow characteristics.

NAS Cash Flow Rules

Recent home equity NAS bonds typically receive principal payments according to the schedule in Exhibit 1. The NAS bond is locked out for the first three years, after which it receives an increasing amount of its pro rata principal. The lockout up front, plus the receipt of 300% of its pro rata principal at the back end, provide the NAS bond with an extremely stable average life over a wide range of prepayment scenarios.

Average Life Stability of NAS Bonds

Home equity loan ABS transactions typically are priced at a percentage of the prepayment prospectus curve, or PPC. The PPC defines a seasoning ramp for home equity loan prepayments, similar to the PSA curve used in the mortgage market, except that the PPC is deal specific. For example, 100% PPC is defined for ContiMortgage Home Equity Loan Trust 1997-2 as prepayments of 4% CPR in month 1, increasing linearly to 20% CPR in month 12. This transaction was priced at 120% PPC, defining a vector of prepayment speeds beginning with 4.8% CPR in month 1, increasing linearly to 24% CPR in month 12.

Exhibit 2 shows the average life shortly after new issue for Conti 1997-2 Class A9, the NAS bond in that transaction. Its average life variability is compared to that of Conti 1997-2 A7, a non-NAS sequential with similar average life. Also calculated is the average life differential over the wide range of 75% PPC to 200% PPC. These correspond to plateau speeds of 15% and 40% CPR, respectively. We believe that it is unlikely that prepayment speeds on fixed-rate home equity ABS would display long-term speeds outside of this range.

Exhibit 2 shows that even over the wide range of 75% to 200% PPC, the average life of the NAS bond differs by only 1.09 years. Over the more likely range of 100% to 150% PPC, the NAS bond's average life differs by only 0.52 year. These compare to 9.35 and 4.11 years, respectively, for the similar average life non-NAS sequential.

Exhibit 1: Typical Principal Schedule of NAS Bond

Months	Share of Pro Rata Principal (%)
1 through 36	0
37 through 60	45
61 through 72	80
73 through 84	100
After month 84	300

Source: Morgan Stanley

Exhibit 2: NAS Bonds Display Average Life Stability Over a Range of Prepayment Speeds

	% PPC												Avg Life Difference
	0	50	75	100	120	150	200	250	300	350	400	500	
Plateau CPR	0	10	15	20	24	30	40	50	60	70	80	100	75% to
Avg Life													200% PPC
NAS Bond	11.71	7.81	7.06	6.58	6.30	6.06	5.97	3.98	2.17	1.73	1.38	0.67	1.09 yrs
Non-NAS Bond	21.93	14.54	11.94	8.82	6.73	4.71	2.59	1.96	1.55	1.25	1.03	0.58	9.35

Source: Bloomberg Financial Markets

Exhibit 3: Average Life Profile of PAC Bond: PAC Provides Constant Average Life Over Range of Prepayment Scenarios
ContiMortgage 98-2 A6 at new issue

	Percent PPC*											
	75	100	110	125	130	140	150	160	175	180	185	190	200
Avg Life (yrs)	6.89	5.36	5.10	5.10	5.10	5.10	5.10	5.10	5.10	5.10	5.09	4.96	4.72

* For this table, the indicated PPC applies the fixed rate ramp PPCF to the fixed rate collateral, but uses a constant 100% PPCA for the ARMs collateral. In the table, therefore, 140% PPC means a ramp from 5.6% CPR (1.4 × 4% CPR) to 28% CPR (1.4 × 20% CPR) over 12 months for the fixed rate collateral, but 100% PPCA for the ARMs. This is done for simplicity and illustrative purposes.

Source: Morgan Stanley

PAC BONDS

The home equity market borrowed the PAC (or *planned amortization class*) bond structure from the mortgage backed securities market. PAC bonds are shielded from prepayment risk within certain defined ranges of prepayment speeds. For any *constant* prepayment rate within this range of prepayment speeds, the PAC bond will pay principal according to its predefined schedule.

It is important to note that the collateral can temporarily prepay outside of the PAC range and still have the PAC pay principal on schedule. It also is important to understand that as actual prepayments are realized on the collateral, the effective PAC range that provides the bond with the same average life can — and generally does — change over time.

Exhibit 3 shows the average life profile of ContiMortgage 1998-2 A6, a 5.10-year average life PAC within its PAC bands. The PAC bands for this bond are defined separately for both fixed-rate and adjustable-rate collateral:

- Fixed-rate collateral: 125%-175% of fixed-rate collateral PPC[1]
- ARMs collateral: 95%-130% of adjustable-rate collateral PPC

For notational convenience, let PPCF represent the fixed-rate collateral PPC, and let PPCA denote the ARMs collateral PPC. Then for ContiMortgage 98-2, the PPCs are defined as follows:

- PPCF is a prepayment ramp beginning at 4% CPR in month 1 and increasing linearly by 1.45455% CPR per month until month 12, at which point it is 20% CPR.
- PPCA is a prepayment ramp beginning at 4% CPR in month 1 and increasing linearly by 1.82353% CPR per month until month 18, at which point it is 35% CPR.

---

[1] Home equity PAC bonds have been structured with floating-rate companion bonds that absorb average life volatility. To quote a PAC range for these transactions requires an assumption on the prepayment speed of both the fixed and the floating rate collateral.

Exhibit 4: Average Life Profile of PAC Bond: Short PACs Have Greater Call Protection than Stated Range

ContiMortgage 98-2 A3 at new issue

	Percent PPC*												
	75	100	110	125	130	140	150	160	175	180	185	190	200
Avg Life (yrs)	2.93	2.36	2.19	2.02	2.02	2.02	2.02	2.02	2.02	2.02	2.02	2.01	1.86

* For this table, the indicated PPC applies the fixed rate ramp PPCF to the fixed rate collateral, but uses a constant 100% PPCA for the ARMs collateral. In the table, therefore, 140% PPC means a ramp from 5.6% CPR (1.4 × 4% CPR) to 28% CPR (1.4 × 20% CPR) over 12 months for the fixed rate collateral, but 100% PPCA for the ARMs. This is done for simplicity and illustrative purposes.

Source: Morgan Stanley

The pricing speed that was actually used for the transaction was the combination of 130% PPCF and 100% PPCA.

Effective PAC Bands

The PAC range is often quoted as the range of constant speeds for which the last PAC class (that is, the longest average life PAC after time tranching) would pay on its schedule. In fact, the shorter PACs actually have higher effective upper PAC bands than the longer classes from the same transaction, for a given quoted PAC range on a deal. An example of this is shown in Exhibit 4, which shows the average life profile from ContiMortgage 98-2 A3, the 2.02 year average life PAC from the same transaction as the 5.10-year PAC shown in Exhibit 3.

Note that it meets its schedule up to at least 185 PPC, whereas the 5.10 year Class A6 from the same transaction breaks down above 180 PPC.

The reason that shorter PACs have higher effective upper bands is that at fast prepayment speeds, shorter PACs are more likely than longer PACs to continue to have companions remaining over their life. The longer that prepayments are fast, the more likely that companions will be paid down, exposing the PAC to call risk. Clearly, this risk is lower for shorter tranches.

The longer PACs, however, have more protection against slow speeds — i.e., lower, lower bands — than the shorter PACs. The reason for this is that the principal cash flow schedule for PACs is defined as the minimum of the principal generated by the lower and upper bands. In the earlier months, the lower band is the binding constraint and there is insufficient cash generated by the collateral at slow speeds to keep the PACs on schedule.

On the other hand, there is a crossover point in the later months, after which the principal cash flow generated by the upper band is binding. After this point, prepayments slower than the lower band are still sufficient to keep the PAC on schedule. Longer bonds, then, defined as those receiving principal cash flow after the crossover point, enjoy this extra protection at slower speeds, whereas shorter classes find the lower band is a binding constraint. The extra protection afforded the longer PACs at slower speeds is seen by comparing Exhibits 3 and 4 at the slower speed ranges.

Exhibit 5: PAC Bands May Drift Over Time as Actual Collateral Prepayments are Realized

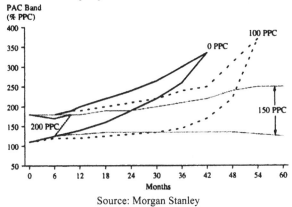

Source: Morgan Stanley

PAC Band Drift

Over time, as the PAC bond is outstanding and prepayments are realized on the collateral, the PAC bands in general will drift over time. This means that the range of prepayment speeds going forward that will provide the same average life on the bond will generally change. Whether the bands narrow, widen or break altogether depends upon actual realized prepayments on the transaction's collateral.

An example of PAC band drift is shown in Exhibit 5 for ContiMortgage 98-2 A6, the 5.10 year bond profiled in Exhibit 3. We can interpret PAC band drift from Exhibit 5. For illustrative purposes, the analysis in Exhibit 5 is as of the settlement date of the transaction.

First, let's discuss how to examine Exhibit 5.

- Consider, for example, the two lines marked 150% PPC.[2] This means that — given the collateral prepayment history to date[3] — if the collateral were to prepay at a constant rate of 150% PPC for every month going forward, then after 36 months, the PAC band at that point going forward would be 135-210% PPC.

---

[2] For illustrative purposes and the sake of simplicity, the indicated PPC for Exhibit 5 applies the fixed rate ramp PPCF to *both* the fixed and ARM collateral. Therefore, 150% PPC means a ramp from 6% CPR (1.5 × 4% CPR) to 30% CPR (1.5 × 20% CPR) over 12 months for *both* the fixed and ARM collateral. Clearly, any combination of fixed and ARM PPCs can be run for the analysis, but we chose the current definition to keep the exposition as simple as possible. Note that our application of the fixed rate ramp PPCF to both the fixed and ARM collateral differs from the definition of PPC in the price/yield tables on Bloomberg, which uses a percentage of the *pricing* PPC. Therefore, on Bloomberg, 100% PPC means the combination of 130% PPCF and 100% PPCA.

[3] In Exhibit 5, we are analyzing the bond as of the new issue settlement, so there is no collateral prepayment history in this example. The analysis is prospective and, of course, could be done at any point in the bond's life.

- Consider now the lines marked 200% PPC. This means that, if the collateral were to prepay at the constant speed of 200% PPC, then after 10 months, there would be no range of constant prepayment speeds going forward that would result in a constant average life for the PAC bond. At this point (or possibly sooner),[4] the companions would have paid down, and what was structured as a PAC bond would now behave like a sequential pay bond. This is referred to as a broken PAC.

Analysis

While home equity PAC bonds have been *structured* similarly to mortgage CMO PACs, the home equities have employed a collateral pool that contains both fixed-rate and adjustable-rate loans and produced floating-rate companion bonds. In the mortgage market, a fixed-rate collateral pool is used to create PAC bonds and their companions. The companions absorb the prepayment risk, and accompanying average life volatility, from which the PACs are protected. The result is usually fixed-rate companion bonds with average lives that may vary from perhaps 2 years in a rally to 20 years in a bear market. This is because if prepayments are fast, the companions absorb the cash flow in excess of that needed to keep the PACs on schedule. This shortens the average lives of the companions. If prepayments are very slow, the cash flow is diverted from the companions to the PACs to permit the PACs to maintain their scheduled principal payments. This would cause the average lives of the companions to extend.

While the concept of companions providing average life protection to the PACs is the same in the home equity sector as in mortgage CMOs, the HEL PAC/companion structure has thus far differed by producing floating-rate companions. The home equity sector has used a mixed fixed rate/ARM collateral pool and structured fixed rate PACs supported by floating-rate companions. The benefit of this structure is that the average life uncertainty is contained in bonds that are floating rate, and thus are limited in their price volatility. While the average life of the home equity companions can fluctuate, their duration, duration drift and spread duration are dramatically lower than those of fixed-rate mortgage companions.

Another difference between mortgage CMO and HEL PAC/companions is with the home equities' rate of overcollateralization (O/C) acceleration and stepdowns. These will influence the construction of the PACs and the ability of the pool to meet the PAC schedules. For the ContiMortgage PACs that have been constructed to-date, the O/C targets have been relatively low, so the affects of these are less than for other issuers that would have higher O/C targets. ContiMortgage, however, is the only HEL issuer thus far to employ the PAC/companion structure.

---

[4] We say "or possibly sooner" because it is conceivable that the companions could be completely eroded, and yet there could be a constant range of prepayment speeds for which the PAC will have the same average life. This is most likely to be the case for longer broken PACs, for which the shorter broken PACs will have to pay down sequentially before the longer broken PACs absorb principal.

Exhibit 6: Average Life Profile of TAC Bond: TAC Provides Call Protection

Advanta 98-1 A4 at new issue

	Percent PPC*									
	75	100	115	125	130	140	150	160	180	190	200
Avg Life (yrs)	6.21	4.62	4.00	4.01	4.01	4.03	3.87	3.59	3.12	2.94	2.77

* For this table, the indicated PPC applies the fixed rate ramp to the fixed rate collateral, but uses a constant 25% CPR for the ARMs collateral. In the table, therefore, 140% PPC means a ramp from 4.2% CPR (1.4 x 3% CPR) to 28% CPR (1.4 x 20% CPR) over 12 months for the fixed rate collateral, but 25% CPR for the ARMs. This is done for simplicity and illustrative purposes.

Source: Morgan Stanley

TAC BONDS

The home equity loan market also adopted the TAC (or *targeted amortization class*) bond structure from the mortgage market. TAC bonds provide investors with protection against call risk, although the investor still is exposed to extension risk. This is in contrast to PAC bonds, which provide protection against both call and extension risk.

Similar to PAC bonds, however,

- the TAC can *temporarily* prepay off of its schedule and still have the TAC pay principal on schedule
- as actual prepayments are realized, the effective TAC schedule that provides the bond with the same average life can — and generally does — change over time.

Exhibit 6 shows the average life profile of Advanta 1998-1 A4, a 4.0-year average life TAC bond. The pricing speed for this transaction is 115% PPC for the fixed rate collateral and 25% CPR for the ARMs collateral. For this transaction, 100% PPC is defined as prepayments beginning at 3% CPR in month 1, and increasing by 1.545% per month until month 12, at which point it remains at 20% CPR. The TAC schedule is defined as the cash flows at the pricing speed.

A few items from Exhibit 6 are of note. First, we see that the TAC provides only call protection for a range of speeds above the pricing TAC schedule. At speeds below 115% PPC, the TAC bond faces extension.

Note also that the TAC is protected from call risk to prepayment speeds as high as 140% to 150% PPC. In fact, for prepayment speeds in a range above the TAC schedule, the average life actually extends marginally. This is shown in Exhibit 6 by average lives slightly longer than 4.00 years for prepayments between 125% and 140% PPC. The reason for this modest extension is that at prepayment speeds above that required to meet the TAC schedule (i.e., 115% PPC), cash flow is diverted from the TAC to the companion bonds. As speeds get increasingly faster, increasing amounts of excess cash get sent to the companion bonds, marginally extending the TACs. After the companion bonds are paid down, cash beyond that necessary to meet the TAC schedule is used to pay down the TACs, causing a shortening of average life (at speeds of 150% PPC and higher in Exhibit 6).

TAC Drift

As the TAC bond is outstanding and prepayments are realized over time, the prepayment rate up to which call protection is still provided to the TAC changes over time. An example of this is shown in Exhibit 7 for Advanta 98-1 A4, the TAC bond profiled in Exhibit 6. For illustrative purposes, the analysis in Exhibit 7 is as of the settlement date of the transaction.

We first explain how to interpret Exhibit 7.

- Consider, for example, the line labeled 150 PPC.[5] This means that — given the collateral prepayment history to date[6] — if the collateral were to prepay at a constant rate of 150% PPC for every month going forward, then after 30 months, the average life of the TAC would still be maintained at prepayment speeds as high as 138% PPC.

Exhibit 7: The TAC Speed May Drift Over Time as Actual Collateral Prepayments are Realized

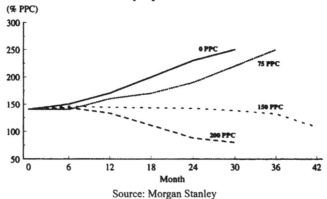

Source: Morgan Stanley

[5] For illustrative purposes and the sake of simplicity, the indicated PPC for Exhibit 7 applies the fixed rate ramp to both the fixed and ARM collateral. Therefore, 150% PPC means a ramp from 4.5% CPR (1.5 × 3% CPR) to 30% CPR (1.5 × 20% CPR) over 12 months for *both* the fixed and ARM collateral. Certainly, any combination of fixed and ARM prepayment assumptions can be run for the analysis, but we chose the current definition to keep the exposition as simple as possible. Note that our application of the fixed rate prepayment ramp to both the fixed and ARM collateral is consistent with the definition of PPC in the price/yield calculator for this transaction on Bloomberg. Also note that Bloomberg's treatment of the PPC for this transaction differs from its treatment of the PPC on ContiMortgage 1998-2. For a comparison, see Footnote 2 above in our explanation of PAC bonds.

[6] In Exhibit 7, we are analyzing the bond as of the new issue settlement, so there is no collateral prepayment history in this example. The analysis is prospective and, of course, could be conducted at any point in the bond's life.

- If prepayments were to continue at 150% PPC for another 12 months till month 42, however, then the average life of the TAC could withstand shortening at speeds only as high as 108% PPC.
- The opposite occurs for slow speeds, as seen in the line labeled 75 PPC. If prepayments were to come in at 75% PPC for 24 months, then the TAC could withstand prepayments going forward as fast as 190% PPC without facing shortening.

Analysis

Whereas home equity loan PAC structures have employed a combined fixed rate and ARM collateral pool to produce fixed rate PAC bonds and floating rate companions, home equity loan TACs have been structured from collateral pools that were solely fixed rate, as well as combined fixed rate/ARM pools. In IMC 1997-5, only fixed rate collateral was employed and most of the companion bonds were sequential pay fixed rate classes, although there was a floating rate companion class backed by fixed rate loans.

By paying a floating rate coupon to the more volatile bonds, the companions are limited in their price volatility. Despite potential fluctuation in their average lives, floating rate companions will have lower duration and exhibit less duration drift and spread duration than fixed rate companions. In the IMC 97-5 transaction with both a floating rate companion and a series of fixed rate companions, the average life volatility of the fixed rate supports is ameliorated by having tranched, sequential pay, tight window bonds.

SENIOR/SUBORDINATE STRUCTURE

Since the first senior/subordinate structure was introduced into the home equity ABS market by ContiMortgage 1997-1, the senior/sub structure has alternated with monoline insurance wrappers as the preferred method of credit enhancement for home equity loan ABS depending upon prevailing market conditions and credit concerns. This section describes and attempts to clarify the often confusing and somewhat elusive cash flow rules for this home equity loan ABS structure.

It is important to note that specific features of the senior/sub cash flow rules differ from issuer to issuer and from transaction to transaction. Nonetheless, we provide an example to generalize the senior/sub structure to provide investors with the basic concepts of the cash flow rules seen in recent home equity loan ABS transactions (Exhibit 8).

The Initial Period: O/C Stepdown and the Two-Times Test

Most senior/sub structures provide for overcollateralization (O/C) to build up over time. After a specified number of months — usually 36 — and assuming certain loss and delinquency triggers are not breached (see below), the dollar amount of O/C is allowed to step down to the lesser of the given percentage of the deal's original balance or some multiple (generally two times) that percentage of the pool's current balance.

In our example, we build O/C to 2.00% of the original fixed rate pool balance. After the 36th month, if loss and delinquency performance tests are satisfied, the O/C can step down to the lesser of 2.00% of the original loan balance and 4.00% (2 × 2.00%) of the current loan balance (Exhibit 9). If the pricing speed is realized, then half of the fixed rate pool will have paid down by the 36th month. In this case, 2.00% of the original balance would equal 4.00% of the current loan balance in the month that the current pool balance has a factor of 0.5.

Fixed rate O/C targets have ranged from 80 bp to 250 bp. For ARM HELs, O/C targets have ranged from 100 bp to 400 bp. O/C targets have varied for individual issuers over their brief history, with trade-offs between O/C and subordination levels.

Until the stepdown date, all principal is directed to the most senior classes in order of rating. There are two common methods for determining the stepdown date. Both methods typically utilize the later of a date (e.g., 36 months) and a percentage collateral pool reduction (e.g., 50%) in determining when pro rata stepdowns may commence provided certain enhancement targets are achieved. One method begins the stepdown period early if the AAA classes are retired. The other method continues paying the classes in order of rating until the stepdown date.

Unless prepayment rates are extremely fast — i.e., fast enough to pay down the entire senior AAA bond classes — the mezzanine and subordinate classes will be locked out from principal payments over the initial period prior to the stepdown date.

Exhibit 8: Generic Senior/Sub HEL ABS Structure

Class	Type
AAA-Rated Classes	Sequential Pay
AAA-Rated Class	NAS Bond
AA-Rated Class M-1	Mezzanine
A-Rated Class M-2	Mezzanine
BBB-Rated Class B-1	Subordinate

Source: Morgan Stanley

Exhibit 9: Overcollateralization Targets for Example Structure

Stepdown Date	O/C Target	
	Pre-Stepdown	Post-Stepdown
36 months	2.00% of original balance	4.00% of current balance

Source: Morgan Stanley

Exhibit 10: Principal Pay Pattern of Senior/Sub Structure Assuming Triggers Are Not Breached

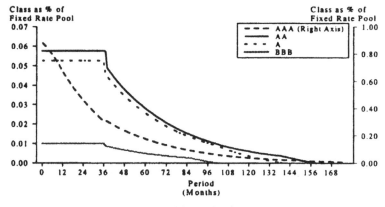

Source: Morgan Stanley

After the Stepdown Date: Loss and Delinquency Triggers

After the stepdown date, loss and/or delinquency trigger tests are performed each month. There are two possibilities:

- *Triggers are not hit:* in this case, principal payments are made on the senior-most classes until they have achieved a given targeted enhancement level (called the *senior target enhancement percentage*). This process is repeated to the next most-senior level, etc., until all ratings classes have achieved their respective target enhancement percentages. By paying down senior classes prior to more subordinate classes, their enhancement increases.
- *Triggers are hit:* depending upon which trigger is breached, O/C targets and/or senior enhancement percentages may be increased.

It is important to note that trigger tests are performed each month. If a trigger is breached one month, for example, then the mezzanine and subordinate classes may switch from receiving principal to getting in line behind the senior classes; if the trigger test is satisfied the next month, the mezzanines and subordinate may return to receiving principal.

Cash Flow for Example Structure

Exhibit 10 shows the principal payment pattern for AAA, AA, A and BBB rated classes for our example, assuming a base case where losses are able to be absorbed by excess spread and O/C without causing a writedown of any bond classes. After the stepdown date, the AAA, mezzanine and subordinates all receive principal such that their enhancement percentages match those in Exhibit 11.

Exhibit 11: Senior Target Enhancement Percentages for Example Structure

Ratings Class	Actual % of Pool	Initial % Credit Enhancement*	Targeted % Credit Enhancement**
AAA	88.00	14.00	28.00
AA	5.75	8.25	16.50
A	5.25	3.00	6.00
BBB	1.00	2.00	4.00
O/C	target 2.00	NA	NA

* Includes 2% O/C.
** Two times initial % credit enhancement.

Source: Morgan Stanley

Exhibit 12: Principal Pay Pattern Assuming Delinquency and Loss Triggers Are Breached

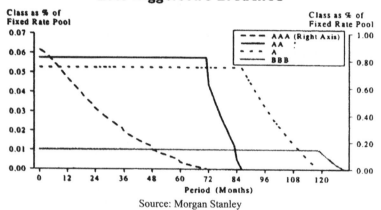

Source: Morgan Stanley

Exhibit 12 shows the principal payment pattern for these ratings classes, assuming an extreme stress scenario similar to a rating agency stress test that causes both loss and delinquency triggers to be breached. In this example, cash flows are reordered from the previous example, but the subordinate bond classes experience no writedowns; losses are absorbed by excess spread and O/C.

In this case, the delinquency triggers cause 100% of the principal to go to the AAAs (see the cash flow rules in Exhibit 13), and the mezzanines and subordinate to pay sequentially behind the AAA class. The average life of the AAA class shortens, while that of the mezzanines and subordinate lengthen. In reality, what is more likely is that the mezzanines and subordinate will flip back and forth between sequential and pro rata pay with the AAA class, as the rapid retirement of the AAA class results in the satisfaction of the increased senior enhancement percentage even at extreme delinquency levels. Upon the retirement of the AAA, the senior enhancement test is passed down to the AA, and so on. The payment window and average life implications of the two scenarios presented here are compared in Exhibit 14.

Exhibit 13: Delinquency and Loss Triggers for Example Structure

Delinquency Trigger	Cash Flow Implications
• The 3-month average of 60+ day delinquencies is at least one-half the senior target enhancement percentage (14%)	• The most senior ratings class outstanding receives 100% of principal distributions until its subordination percentage increases to 2 x 60+ day delinquencies • Once achieved, principal distribution is made available to the subordinate classes in original manner, except that the senior-most ratings class must maintain the new target
Net Loss Trigger	Cash Flow Implications
• Cumulative net losses as a % of original balance breach a pre-determined loss schedule	• O/C has to step up to a higher percentage of the original balance • As in many cases, if trigger is cured, O/C can step down to original enhancement level

Source: Morgan Stanley

Exhibit 14: Comparison of Principal Windows and Average Lives Under "Trigger Hit" and "Trigger Not Hit" Scenarios

Ratings Class	No Trigger Hit (from Exhibit 10)		Trigger Hit (from Exhibit 12)	
	Principal Window (months)	Average Life (yrs)	Principal Window (months)	Average Life (yrs)
AAA	178	3.2	72	2.4
AA	124	5.8	16	6.5
A	104	5.7	33	8.4
BBB	66	5.3	12	10.3

Source: Morgan Stanley

This section attempted to remove some of the fog surrounding the implications of cash flow rules of senior/sub home equity ABS structures. Investors need to understand scenarios that can cause cash flow priorities to switch, and the extent of the reprioritization. With this understanding, investors can assign probabilities to these scenarios and get a better feel for the likely performance of their securities. The next section conducts some thought experiments on the levels of defaults that might cause a deterioration in the integrity of the subordinate class.

Credit Protection in Subordinate HELs

The senior/subordinate structure is one of most important innovations to be introduced in the home equity loan ABS market. While this structure has been embraced by many investors, others are reluctant to partake of this sector due to the relative lack of information available on the portfolio performance histories of home equity lenders.

We present here a framework for examining subordinate HEL tranches. Despite the lack of information, this framework presents a reasonableness check on the level of losses that would be required to eat through the subordinates' protection.

Exhibit 15: Excess Spreads Should be Sufficient to Absorb Even Relatively High CDRs

CDR (%)	Monthly CDR (%)	Monthly Excess Spread (in bp) for Various Annual Excess Spreads			
		300	350	400	450
1	0.0837	25.0	29.2	33.3	37.5
2	0.1682	25.0	29.2	33.3	37.5
3	0.2535	25.0	29.2	33.3	37.5
4	0.3396	25.0	29.2	33.3	37.5
5	0.4265	25.0	29.2	33.3	37.5
6	0.5143	25.0	29.2	33.3	37.5

We show that, in general:

- subordinate HELs have sufficient enhancement to protect against even severe loss scenarios, and
- high *levels* of defaults and losses, per se, are less of a problem than *spikes* in losses.

Excess Spread Should Provide Sufficient Protection Even in High Loss Scenarios

Excess spread in most home equity transactions is in the range of 300 to 450 bp annually. This corresponds to a monthly range of 25 to 37.5 bp.

Exhibit 15 shows the *monthly* default rate or *monthly* CDR corresponding to annual CDRs from 1% to 6%, and how these relate to monthly excess spreads. The boxed values in Exhibit 15 identify the excess spread/CDR combinations for which excess spread would be breached.

The next question is: what do the CDRs in Exhibit 15 translate into in terms of cumulative defaults? Then, given the cumulative default rate, we can determine our subjective probability of defaults actually reaching those levels.

This question is answered in Exhibit 16, which shows the cumulative default rate as a share of original pool balance (over the life of the pool) for various combinations of CDR and prepayment rate (as depicted by the PPC). CDRs as high as 5% or 6% imply that about ⅕ to ⅙ of the original pool balance would be in default for most likely prepayment scenarios. These would be extremely high default rates.

In addition, note that we are not distinguishing between defaults and losses; we would expect that the *severity of losses* on home equity loans should be considerably below 100%, so even defaults as high as ⅕ or ⅙ of a pool would be expected to results in losses that are considerably lower. To provide a benchmark, note that Moody's index of closed end home equity ABS losses as a percentage of original pool balances is just above 6% for 1990 origination loans and 2.19% for 1989 originations.[7]

---

[7] See Moody's Investors Service, *Home Equity Index Update,* Structured Finance Credit Index, March 7, 1997.

Exhibit 16: Cumulative Default Rates as % of Original Balance for Combinations of CDR and PPC

CDR	PPC* (%)					
(%)	75	100	120	125	130	140
1	5.2	4.1	3.4	3.3	3.2	2.9
2	10.4	8.2	6.9	6.6	6.3	5.9
3	15.7	12.3	10.4	9.9	9.6	8.8
4	21.1	16.5	13.9	13.3	12.8	11.8
5	26.5	20.7	17.4	16.7	16.1	14.9
6	31.9	25.0	21.0	20.2	19.4	17.9

*PPC defines a deal-specific prepayment seasoning ramp. Here we take 100% PPC to define prepayments beginning at 4% CPR in month 1, increasing linearly to 20% CPR in month 12 and remaining at 20% CPR thereafter. Table assumes collateral has 11.5% coupon and 240 months original term.

Exhibit 17: CDRs Would Have to Be Huge to Eat Through Overcollateralization

CDRs Required to Deplete Overcollateralization

	Typical Range of Overcollateralization						
	1.0%	1.5%	2.0%	2.5%	3.0%	3.5%	4.0%
CDR	11.4%	16.6%	21.5%	26.2%	30.6%	34.8%	38.7%

Suppose, however, that defaults and losses are high enough to eat through excess spread. In that case, overcollateralization comes into play.

Overcollateralization Steps in if Excess Spread Not Enough

In most home equity deals, overcollateralization (O/C) is funded from excess spread and builds up to a target level as a share of original balance. Usually, after 36 months, as long as losses and delinquencies are not too severe, the O/C steps down to a minimum of the original percentage of the original balance, or two times that percentage of the current balance.

We want to ask: What level of CDR would be required to deplete the O/C? For the O/C to be eaten up would require a huge CDR (with high loss severity). Exhibit 17 shows, for various typical levels of overcollateralization, the CDR that would be required to deplete the O/C (assuming 100% loss severity) in one month.

Putting together Exhibits 15, 16 and 17 result in the following conclusions:

- Excess spread on home equity transactions generally is sufficient to cover most levels of default
- Levels of default that are not supported by excess spread would correspond to extremely high levels of cumulative defaults
- For those levels of default for which excess spread is insufficient to cover, overcollateralization appears likely to cover

- This analysis dealt only with *defaults* and *not* losses. If we were explicitly to include losses, then excess spread and overcollateralization would be able to absorb even greater levels of default.
- This analysis also dealt only with exposure of the BBB subordinates to defaults. Default and loss rates would have to be even larger to interrupt cash flow to mezzanine classes.

Even without having detailed historical information about the performance of home equity loan portfolios, we nonetheless can analyze default rates relative to credit enhancement levels and conclude that the levels of default required to deplete excess spread and overcollateralization are much larger than are likely to result in most circumstances.

Chapter 7

Home Equity Line of Credit (HELOC) Securitizations

W. Alexander Roever, CFA
Managing Director, ABS Research
Banc One Capital Markets

John N. McElravey
Director, ABS Research
Banc One Capital Markets

Glenn M. Schultz, CFA
Director, ABS Research
Banc One Capital Markets

INTRODUCTION

As housing values have appreciated over the past decade, homeowners have borrowed large amounts of money against the equity in their homes. Outstanding home equity debt totaled $420 billion as of year-end 1997 according to the Federal Reserve. This borrowing generally is used as a substitute for other types of consumer credit, either to finance new consumption or to pay down other outstanding consumer credit balances. The securitization of home equity debt has created one of the largest segments of the asset-backed securities (ABS) market. In 1998, residential loan backed ABS accounted for 37% of total new issuance in the public market.

Several factors make home equity borrowing attractive to consumers. One is tax deductibility. The Tax Reform Act of 1986 phased out federal tax deductions for nonmortgage consumer debt, such as credit cards and auto loans, and increased their after-tax cost. Home equity borrowing allows the funds to be used for just about any reason, but maintains its privileged tax status. Another attractive aspect is that home equity lending allows borrowers to access the equity accumulated in their homes. Homeowners' equity represents one of the largest components of household wealth in the United States.[1] Home equity borrowing

---

[1] Glenn B. Canner, *et. al.*, "Recent Developments in Home Equity Lending," *Federal Reserve Bulletin* (April 1998), pp. 241-251.

provides a means for homeowners to monetize the equity in their homes that would otherwise be relatively illiquid.

HOME EQUITY LINES OF CREDIT

When ABS investors, analysts, and traders mention the home equity market, they generally are referring to securities backed by closed-end loans, which are the primary type of collateral in this sector. However, another class of home equity credit exists that receives comparatively little attention. Home equity lines of credit (HELOCs) are revolving lines of credit available to homeowners that can be drawn and repaid based on the equity in their homes. While HELOCs represent only about 4% of total home equity securitizations outstanding, they do represent a potentially large source of collateral for future transactions. Over the last ten years, HELOCs represented between 20% and 25% of total home equity originations (see Exhibit 1). The majority of HELOCs that have been originated are still held on the balance sheets of commercial banks, thrifts, and credit unions (see Exhibit 2). Depository institutions hold 80% to 85% of all outstanding lines, and this market share has been relatively stable over the past ten years. Finance companies hold about 8% of outstanding HELOCs. Meanwhile, only 7% of lines outstanding have been securitized.

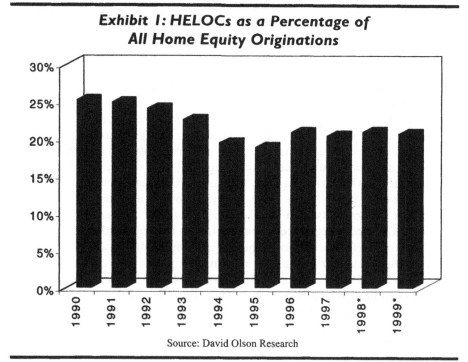

Exhibit 1: HELOCs as a Percentage of All Home Equity Originations

Source: David Olson Research

Exhibit 2: Estimated Share of HELOCs Outstanding by Institutional Holder

Institution	1990	1991	1992	1993	1994	1995	1996	1997	1998
Commercial Banks	59%	56%	57%	58%	62%	61%	62%	63%	61%
Thrift Institutions	14%	16%	17%	14%	14%	14%	13%	11%	13%
Credit Unions	10%	10%	9%	9%	9%	9%	9%	9%	9%
Finance Companies	12%	11%	11%	11%	6%	7%	8%	8%	8%
Securitized Pools	5%	6%	6%	7%	8%	9%	7%	7%	8%
Other	1%	1%	1%	1%	1%	1%	0%	1%	1%
Total	100%	100%	100%	100%	100%	100%	100%	100%	100%
Total Amount (billion$)	113.9	124.7	129.5	125.7	123.7	129.4	137.0	153.4	172.0

Source: David Olson Research, Banc One Capital Markets, Inc.

Depository institutions seem to predominate this area of lending for several reasons. First, lines of credit are generally more complex to administer, and more costly to originate and service, than traditional closed-end loans. As a result, larger banks are more likely than smaller banks or finance companies to offer this product. Second, because the loan is a revolving account, a relationship between borrower and lender can give a competitive advantage over specialty finance firms. A bank or thrift, for example, should have better information about the credit quality of a customer because of other loan or deposit accounts held at that institution. Third, home equity lines provide another cross-selling opportunity for the bank. Finally, HELOCs may be accessed several times per year, primarily through drafts or checking accounts, or by personal withdrawals. Depository institutions already have an infrastructure in place to facilitate customers to make withdrawals and deposits.

CHARACTERISTICS OF HELOCS AND BORROWERS

The characteristics of the collateral and the borrower profile would make HELOCs attractive for securitization. Typically, the revolving period for HELOCs extends for 10 to 15 years. At the end of the revolving period, the loans provide for an amortization period, extending for as much as 10 years, or a balloon payment at maturity. According to the 1998 Home Equity Loan Study from the Consumer Bankers Association (CBA), nearly all HELOCs carry variable rates.[2] Closed-end loans are predominantly fixed rate with only 9% of closed-end loans carrying variable rates. About three-quarters of all lines reset monthly using the Prime Rate reported in *The Wall Street Journal* (see Exhibit 3). The average spread over *The Wall Street Journal* Prime Rate declined over the last few years, falling to 127 basis points over prime in 1997.

[2] Richard F. DeMong and John H. Lindgren, *1998 Home Equity Loan Study*, Consumer Bankers Association, 1998.

Exhibit 3: HELOC Characteristics
Variable Rate Index

	1997	1996
The Wall Street Journal Prime Rate	78%	90%
Bank Prime Rate	6%	2%
90 Day Treasury Bill	2%	2%
180 Day Treasury Bill	4%	0%
Federal Reserve Treasury Bill Discount Rate	2%	2%
Other	10%	5%
Total	100%	100%

Average HELOC Spread Over The Wall Street Journal Prime Rate (Basis Points)

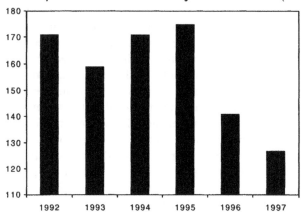

Variable Rate Adjustment Period

	1997	1996
Daily	20%	11%
Weekly	0%	3%
Monthly	78%	81%
Quarterly	2%	5%
Total	100%	100%

Source: CBA 1998 Home Equity Loan Study

Exhibit 4 provides a graphical description of the uses of home equity lines. The primary reason for home equity borrowing is debt consolidation, which represented 40% of HELOC borrowing in 1997. Many consumers replaced higher interest rate credit card debt with lower interest rate home equity borrowing that has the added benefit of being tax deductible. Prior to 1992, the primary reason for home equity borrowing was home improvement, which in 1997 accounted for 23% of the lines extended. Other uses of home equity lines include automobile purchases (7%), education (6%), and other major purchases (6%). The uses of closed-end loans are broadly similar to the responses given for lines of credit. Overall, the shift from home improvement, where the underlying real estate is being upgraded, to debt consolidation suggests that the risk profile associated with home equity lending has increased somewhat over time.

As they have on closed-end home equity loans, average loan-to-value ratios (LTVs) have been rising on HELOCs. LTVs reached an average of 77% in 1997, up from 72% in 1995. These levels are comparable to the LTVs on closed-end loans. At the same time, the number of lenders that offer at least some high LTV HELOCs has increased. According to the CBA survey, 25% of lenders offer at least some lines with LTVs greater than 100%. (See Exhibit 5.)

Given the shift to debt consolidation and higher LTVs, it appears that the level of risk may have increased somewhat in the home equity sector. However, the superior demographic characteristics and financial circumstances of HELOC borrowers relative to traditional closed-end loan borrowers provide some additional credit support. According to the results from the 1997 Surveys of Consumers conducted by the University of Michigan's Survey Research Center and the Federal Reserve Board, HELOC borrowers were older, had more expensive homes, more home equity, higher household incomes, and more education than closed-end loan borrowers.[3] These same characteristics are found in the CBA survey.[4] The relative affluence, and corresponding credit quality, of the HELOC borrowers may be one reason that many banks and thrifts prefer to keep these lines on balance sheet rather than securitize them.

Delinquency and charge-off rates are generally superior to other types of consumer credit. Average delinquencies on HELOCs from the CBA Survey were 1.11% in 1997. This compares to non-credit card consumer debt delinquencies of about 3% and credit card delinquencies of nearly 5% for the same period. The story for charge-offs is similar. Average charge-offs on HELOCs were 0.11% in 1997 compared to about 1% for non-credit card consumer debt and more than 5% for credit cards. Given the credit performance of collateral and borrower demographics, the ABS market would welcome more HELOC issuance.

Exhibit 4: Uses of Home Equity Loans

	Percent
Debt Consolidation	40
Home Improvement	23
Automobile	7
Major Purchase	6
Education	6
Business Expenses & Investment	5
Other or Don't Know	13
Total	100

Source: CBA 1998 Home Equity Loan Study

---

[3] Canner, *et. al.*, "Recent Developments in Home Equity Lending," pp. 244-246.
[4] DeMong and Lindgren, *1998 Home Equity Loan Study*, p. 13.

Exhibit 5: HELOC LTVs and Percent of Institutions Offering High LTV HELOCs

Industry Average HELOC LTVs

1995	72%
1996	73%
1997	77%

Percent of Institutions Offering High LTV HELOCs

Maximum LTV	
<100%	63%
101% - 124%	10%
125%	10%
> 125%	5%

Source: CBA 1998 Home Equity Loan Study

Exhibit 6: HELOC Pricing History

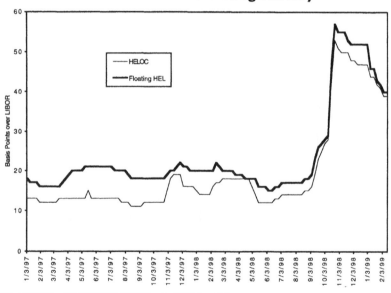

HELOC STRUCTURES

HELOC ABS are structured as floating-rate certificates, and are priced at a spread above 1-month LIBOR. For this reason they are often compared to floating-rate tranches of closed-end home equity transactions. Exhibit 6 illustrates recent pricing spread history for both products. These two assets have historically priced comparably to one another; however, HELOCs have generally commanded a slight premium versus a closed-end product because of better obligor quality and stronger servicer profiles.

But, because HELOC loans more closely resemble credit card accounts than mortgage loans, the structures used to securitize these loans differ dramatically from those employed in the closed-end home equity market. Due to the open-ended nature of the collateral, HELOC transactions usually rely on revolving trust structures. Unlike the static issuance vehicles used to securitize closed-end loan pools, a revolving trust allows for the securitization of outstanding principal amounts while providing obligors the ability to draw against their lines of credit.

To achieve this, a HELOC trust is generally divided into two interests: a certificate, or investor interest, and a seller interest. This multiple interest structure is common to most types of revolving ABS transactions. The certificate interest is the portion of the trust assets that collateralize the HELOC certificates sold in the term ABS market. The seller interest is the difference between the collateral pool balance and the certificate interest balance. The size of the seller interest will fluctuate over time since the investor interest will either remain constant or decline, depending on whether the certificates are in a revolving or amortization phase, while the pool balance will increase or decrease, depending on the relative amount of draws or paydowns during a given month. Typically, there is a required minimum level for the seller interest that is often sized to 2% of the initial pool balance, and then may decline as the investor interest amortizes.

Principal Repayment

Given the similarities between HELOC and revolving ABS structures, it should not be surprising that HELOC certificates repay principal in a manner that is more akin to a revolving ABS than to a typical MBS. As such, the life of HELOC can be divided into three phases: a revolving period, a managed amortization period, and a rapid amortization period. While not all HELOC transactions feature revolving periods, most feature some combination of managed and rapid amortization periods.

Revolving Period

During a revolving period, the certificates are typically locked out from receiving principal payments. Instead, principal collected on the underlying loans, in excess of new draws, can be captured in a trust funding account. This cash can then be used to fund future draws or purchase new loans. At the end of the revolving period, cash remaining in the funding account may be used to paydown outstanding certificate balances.

Managed Amortization Period

Most transactions provide for a managed amortization period of five years. During the managed amortization period, principal payments are equal to some fraction of principal paid on the loans, net of all new draws. Principal paid may include both scheduled and unscheduled payments. If new draws exceed principal collections during a given month, there may be no principal payment for that month.

When evaluating prepayment risk during the managed amortization period it is helpful to understand the cash flow conventions used in the HELOC sector. The rate at which additional balances are created is referred to as the *constant draw rate* (CDR) and the rate at which balances are paid down is the *constant payment rate* (CPR). The formulas for both the CDR and the CPR are given below:

$$CDR = 1 - (1 - \text{Single monthly draw rate})^{12}$$

$$CPR = 1 - (1 - \text{Single monthly mortality rate})^{12}$$

where

$$\text{Single monthly draw rate} = 1 - \frac{\text{Total \$ amount drawn during month}}{\text{Beginning monthly pool balance}}$$

$$\text{Single monthly mortality rate} = 1 - \frac{\text{Total \$ amount paid down}}{\text{Beginning monthly pool balance}}$$

The *single monthly draw rate* (SMD) is the increase in pool balance expressed as a percentage of the pool balance at the beginning of the month. Conversely, the *single monthly mortality rate* (SMM) is the decrease the pool balance expressed as a percentage of the pool balance at the beginning of the month. Finally, both the CDR and CPR are annualized expressions of the monthly draw and payment rates. The annualized prepayment rate realized by the investor during the managed amortization period is given by the following:

$$\text{Max} \{0, 1 - (1 - [(SMM - SMD)/\text{Beginning monthly pool balance}])^{12}\}$$

Rapid Amortization Period

A rapid amortization can occur either as a normal phase late in the life of a HELOC, or can be triggered by a decline in credit quality or other event. Normally, a rapid amortization period will follow a revolving or managed amortization period, and is characterized by the distribution of a high fixed percentage of gross principal collections (*not* net of draws) to certificate holders.

During rapid amortization, the rate of principal repayment can be affected by the trust's historical draw experience and the size of the seller's interest. If borrowers make more draws than principal payments during the life of a transaction, the seller interest will grow relative to the investor's interest. Because certificate holders are allocated a fixed percentage of all principal collections, HELOC ABS issued from trusts with larger seller interests will experience faster repayment during rapid amortization than those certificates issued by trusts with smaller seller interests. This implies that the utilization rate of the underlying loans affects the rate at which investors will receive principal payments, and that higher utilization rates at the time of securitization may be correlated with slower repayment rates.

Rapid amortization can also be used as a protective structural device for investors and third party credit enhancers. Rapid amortization can be triggered by a number of events, typically including:

- Failure on the part of the servicer to make timely payments or deposits under the pool and servicing agreement, or to observe or perform in a material respect the covenants or agreements set forth in the transaction documentation;
- Breach of representations or warranties made by the seller or servicer;
- The occurrence of certain events of bankruptcy, insolvency or receivership relating to the seller;
- Violation of certain collateral performance related either in the transaction documentation or surety agreement.

Credit Enhancement

The most common form of credit enhancement for HELOCs consists of a mono-line insurance policy. Other structural tools like overcollateralization, spread accounts, and excess spread are often used in conjunction with a wrapped structure. However, in wrapped transactions these devices are sized and exist primarily for the benefit of the insurer. Investors should look to the insurance provider as their primary source of enhancement.

Overcollateralization can be created by allocating principal payments to the certificates using a fixed allocation percentage method. Certificate holders are allocated a fixed percentage of collections, which reduces the size of the investor interest relative to the size of the overall collateral pool, thereby growing the amount of collateral relative to the certificates. Once the desired overcollateralization target is achieved, some principal collections may be redirected to the holder of the seller interest.

Spread accounts build to a predetermined level by capturing the excess spread in the transaction and depositing the funds into an trust account. To the extent that the investor interest and principal collection amounts are insufficient to pay the certificate holders, the spread account will be drawn upon. In the event that the spread account is drawn down below its target level, excess spread will again be captured to fund the spread account back to targeted levels.

Available Funds Caps

HELOCs, like floaters structured from closed-end adjustable rate HELs, are subject to basis risk in the form of both index risk and reset risk. Index risk arises when the coupon on the underlying collateral is tied to an index other than that of the certificate. While HELOC certificates almost always pay a coupon spread over 1-month LIBOR, the underlying loans are more likely tied to the prime rate or some other index.

Reset risk is the difference between the frequency of the investor coupon resets and the frequency of the resets of the underlying collateral. Reset risk is often mitigated in HELOC structures since approximately 80% of HELOC loans reset their coupons monthly.

Thus, index risk is responsible for most of the basis risk present in HELOC transactions. The combination of basis risk with available funds caps embedded in a structure can potentially cause problems for investors, and should be closely examined. An available funds cap can limit the coupon payment on a structured security, if the dollar amount of the coupon to be paid exceeds the dollar amount of funds available from collections. A mismatch between the index used to reprice the collateral and the index used to reprice the security potentially increases the risk of an available funds cap being triggered. To mitigate this risk, many — but not all — transactions have interest carryover provisions that allow for the carryover of the previous period's interest shortfall. These provisions generally specify that any carryover will earn interest at the then-current coupon rate.

To evaluate the likelihood of hitting an available funds cap, investors must compute both the available funds margin and the available funds cap.[5] Also, when considering the likelihood of hitting the available funds cap and the subsequent interest carryover provisions, it is important to bear in mind several facts, including:

- That the monoline wrap does not apply to interest carried over from one period to the next;
- The interest carryover is paid from the excess spread in the transactions and often subordinate in the waterfall, and therefore is likely to persist for more than one period; and
- The payment of the interest carryover may not be mandatory, and in the event of an interest carryover balance upon the maturity of the transaction, the investor will forego the carryover balance to the extent that funds are insufficient to pay the balance in full.

SUMMARY

The securitization of revolving home equity lines of credit has been relatively limited compared to the outstanding supply of HELOCs and the growth in securitization of closed-end home equity loans. This shortage is due more to financial institutions deciding to carry them on the balance sheet than it is to any lack of

---

[5] The available funds margin (AFM) is the amount available to pay the bondholders coupon and the servicing and surety fees as well as other fees. The available funds margin is calculated as follows:

AFM = Gross coupon − Servicing fees − Surety fees − Other fees − (Coupon index − Margin)

The available funds cap (AFC) is the maximum amount available to pay the bondholders coupon. The available funds cap is calculated as follows:

AFC = Gross coupon − Servicing spread − Surety fees − Other fees

investor demand for the product. In general, the credit quality of the collateral, the demographics of the borrowers, and a lack of supply have led to HELOCs commanding a slight pricing premium to floating rate closed-end product. Given the solid collateral performance and floating rate nature of the collateral, we believe that ABS investors would welcome additional issuance from this market niche.

Chapter 8

Securitization of
125 LTV Mortgages

Hedi T. Katz
Senior Director
Fitch IBCA

Glenn T. Costello
Managing Director
Fitch IBCA

INTRODUCTION

Securitization of low- and no-equity debt consolidation second liens has grown from $1.7 billion in 1995 to $8 billion in 1997 and close to $9 billion in 1998 (see Exhibit 1). The 1998 figure reflects the significant interruption in growth caused by the liquidity crisis experienced by major lenders in late 1998, but the product type is expected to continue to develop.[1] These low- and no-equity loans, referred to as "125 LTV" or "high LTV" loans, represent a significant departure from the existing conventions of home equity lending, which dictate that a mortgagor must have some equity in the home to provide incentive to the mortgagor to repay the mortgage as well as to increase the likelihood of the lender recovering some por-

---

[1] No-equity mortgage lending experienced double digit growth from the mid-1990s through the first half of 1998. However the sharp sell-off of risk in the fixed income markets during the liquidity crisis in the fall of 1998 had a substantial impact on the 125 LTV market.

Reduced demand for subordinate securities contributed to a deepening of the negative cash flow positions of finance companies dependent on securitization. Combined with the pending issues surrounding gain-on-sale accounting, these conditions heightened concerns regarding the credit-worthiness of these finance companies. This led to decreased accessibility of the financing required to continue buying loans on a wholesale basis.

The deepening liquidity crisis culminated in an announcement by FirstPlus Financial, the dominant lender in the 125 LTV market, of an intent to seek a partner, and a subsequent announcement that FirstPlus would cease purchasing loans wholesale. Empire Financial Corp., another major lender also shut down its wholesale lending division. The ensuing reduction in 125 LTV origination volumes and continued risk aversion in the capital markets have greatly reduced the volume of 125 LTV securitization.

tion of the loan in the event of foreclosure. By offering second liens with a combined loan-to-value ratio (CLTV) of more than 100%, 125 LTV lenders have turned away from traditional mortgage lending standards in favor of a lending model similar to unsecured lending products. This model puts substantial emphasis on the mortgagor's demonstrated credit performance, particularly regarding the existing first-lien mortgage. Most 125 LTV lenders also employ credit scoring technology in their underwriting guidelines.

In this chapter we describe the evolution and nature of 125 LTV lending, with an examination of securitization structures and Fitch IBCA's approach to rating 125 LTV HEL-backed bonds. The demographic and credit characteristics of 125 LTV borrowers are described and a set of sample underwriting guidelines is provided. 125 LTV lending shares many common characteristics with other more established debt products, but also presents distinct challenges to the credit analyst, not the least of which is the unseasoned, untested nature of the product as of this writing. Investors should carefully consider all the points discussed in this chapter when considering this sector.

MARKET OVERVIEW AND PRODUCT EVOLUTION

Lenders have developed their 125 LTV product lines as a result of increasing competition among home equity and mortgage lenders, general product expansion efforts, and greater comfort with the no equity concept. Many of these lenders began in the Federal Housing Administration (FHA) Title I or other home improvement loan program and moved primarily into debt consolidation/cash out 125 LTV mortgages.

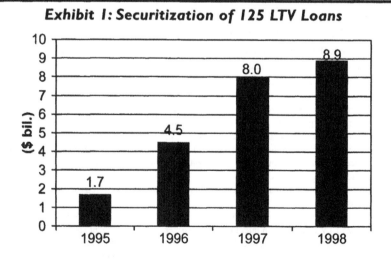

Exhibit 1: Securitization of 125 LTV Loans

FHA Title I

The predecessor to most 125 LTV programs is the FHA Title I loan program. FHA Title I loans are originated under the National Housing Act of 1934 and are used for specific purposes, such as home improvement. The originators of these loans benefit from FHA insurance, which protects the lender against limited losses. These loans are characterized by an exclusive use of proceeds for home improvement and a maximum size, but no CLTV limit. They require a good deal of paperwork for the application procedure and the processing of claims. Because the loans are made in the context of a government program, the borrowers' credit quality is mixed.

Lender Home Improvement Loan Programs

Private lender home improvement loan programs were created by lenders to take advantage of the value associated with home improvement versus other types of home equity loans, without the size limitations or paperwork involved with the FHA Title I program. These loans generally permit CLTVs of up to 125% and require that funds be disbursed directly to the vendors.

Second Lien Debt Consolidation

The next stage of 125 LTV product evolution was the introduction of the junior lien debt consolidation loan. The typical borrower for this loan has fair to good credit and a relatively high LTV first lien mortgage outstanding, usually in the 85%-90% range, but has a substantial amount of revolving and/or installment debt. This borrower wants to take advantage of the more attractive rates and potential tax benefit offered by mortgage debt[2] by converting consumer debt into a debt consolidation mortgage loan that brings the borrower's CLTV up to a maximum of 125%. In addition, this type of loan allows lenders to break away from the follow-up work associated with home improvement loans and concentrate on underwriting. The funds are usually disbursed directly to the creditors.

Combination

The fourth category of 125 LTV product consists of a combination of debt consolidation and a limited amount of cashout. This category represents the bulk of 125 LTV product securitized today.

---

[2] The Internal Revenue Service defines two types of mortgage debt (interest on both types of debt is fully deductible):

Home Acquisition: Debt used to buy, build, improve, or refinance a home up to the home's cost plus the cost of improvements.

Maximum Allowable: $1,000,000

Home Equity: Debt used for any other purpose not to exceed the fair market value of the home plus the cost of improvements less any home acquisition debt, or debt used to buy, build, or substantially improve the home to the extent it exceeds the home acquisition debt limit.

Maximum Allowable: $100,000

Cashout

The most recent type of 125 LTV loan product to appear is a pure cashout loan of as much as $150,000. These loans require a relatively high minimum credit score and good prior mortgage performance.

BORROWER DEMOGRAPHICS

No-equity lending is a controversial topic. Critics of 125 LTV lenders characterize it as a particularly dangerous form of subprime lending. These critics argue that providing essentially unsecured loans to "B/C" quality borrowers will result in extremely high default rates. Advocates of 125 LTV lending argue that weighted average credit scores (discussed below) in the 670-680 range show that these pools are composed of "A" quality credits, which will benefit from a debt consolidation loan. Fitch IBCA's analysis suggests an accurate assessment is somewhere between these extremes.

The attributes of 125 LTV borrowers are reflective of "A"/"A–" borrowers. The weighted average credit score falls in the 670-680 range, the average age is in the late 30s to early 40s, residency is established for an average of four to five years, and borrowers are employed in the same position for five years or more. In addition, household income averages about $60,000, with some portfolios in the $70,000 range. Most pools consist primarily (95%-97%) of salaried versus self-employed borrowers, with back-end debt-to-income ratios after the 125 LTV loan of 35%-40%.

These attributes compare favorably to the respective attributes for subprime portfolios. Credit scores for "A–"/"B" subprime pools tend to average in the high 500 to low 600 range and median household income for all subprime borrowers is approximately $34,000. In addition, subprime borrowers have, on average, less than two years in their current residence or occupation.

Negative considerations include the loan purpose and some degree of permissible poor credit performance. A debt consolidation loan by definition implies that the borrower has a sufficiently high debt burden that converting revolving debt into a long-term second lien is an attractive alternative. Given that these borrowers are also commonly taking significant cash out, causing a net increase in total debt, a potential for overextension exists. Moreover, given the unseasoned nature of the product, information on "reloading" is not yet available.[3]

UNDERWRITING

High LTV underwriting guidelines tend to be notably different from those of typical subprime programs in two key ways. First, the primary determinant of a borrower's grade is the repository credit score. Second, the credit grading systems of

---

[3] We discuss this further later in this chapter.

125 LTV issuers generally require uniform mortgage performance across grades. In addition, debt-to-income ratios and other measures of the borrower's ability to pay take on a special significance as erosion in ability of the borrower to pay is likely to be the primary cause of default in an economic downturn.

Credit Scores

Credit scoring is a mechanism for uniformly assessing borrowers by assigning numerical values to various borrower attributes that have been observed to positively or negatively correlate with credit behavior. Credit scores are generated by three major repositories: Experian, Trans Union, and Equifax. Each repository score was designed by Fair, Issac and has comparable scales, with 900 being the best obtainable score and "A" credit quality associated with scores above 660. High LTV lenders typically select a credit score either from the preferred repository for a particular state or by using a middle-of-three approach. The reliance on credit scores, while common in consumer finance, is notable in mortgage lending, which has been slower to adopt scoring technology in place of direct assessment of credit bureau information.

Fitch IBCA has researched the use of credit scores in-depth, particularly in the jumbo prime mortgage area. Specifically, Fitch IBCA examined the impact of bureau scores and sound mortgage underwriting guidelines on the degree and distribution of default rates. Fitch IBCA research has provided compelling evidence of the statistical power of scoring technology as an underwriting tool.[4]

Fitch IBCA emphasizes that scores be used in conjunction with a sound set of underwriting guidelines. Mortgage lenders are in a position to obtain a great deal of valuable information that might not otherwise be available on a credit report. For example, credit scores do not always adequately reflect mortgage performance due to inconsistent reporting to the repositories by mortgage lenders. High LTV issuers and other mortgage lenders address this concern through a mortgage history component of underwriting guidelines. The historical performance on the prior or first-lien mortgage should be verified as part of the customary practices of the 125 LTV lender.

Grading System

For subprime and alternative mortgage loan products, such as 125 LTV, the most important attribute of the analysis is the borrower's credit profile, as evidenced through a grade assigned by the originator in accordance with published underwriting guidelines. Most 125 LTV issuers initially establish their grading systems based on a credit score range, as well as performance categories, such as late mortgage and revolving debt payments, debt-to-income ratios, and bankruptcy history. These guidelines typically specify permissible loan sizes, amount of cash-out, and interest rates in each credit score range.

---

[4] See *Fitch IBCA Residential Mortgage Backed Securities Criteria*, December 16, 1998.

Exhibit 2: Sample Underwriting Guidelines

Qualifying Parameters	A+	A	B+	B	C+
Credit Score	700+	680-699	660-679	640-659	630-639
Mortgage History (Last 12 Months)	1 × 30	1 × 30	1 × 30	1 × 30	1 × 30
Consumer Debt (Last 12 Months)	No Limit	No Limit	2 × 60; 1 × 90	2 × 60; 1 × 90	No 60 or 90 day lates
Bankruptcy	3 years	3 years	3 years	None	None
Foreclosures, NOD, Deed in Lieu, Forbearances, Repossessions	None	None	None	None	None
Max Debt to Income	50%	50%	50%	45%	40%
Min Disposable Income	$1,500	$1,500	$1,500	$1,000	$1,000
Max Cashout	$35,000	$25,000	$15,000	$5,00	$1,000
Max Loan Amount	$100,000	$75,000	$65,000	$45,000	$30,000

The second significant departure from convention in 125 LTV guidelines is the difference in requirements at the lower grades. In a typical subprime lending grade system, an "A" borrower might be permitted one 30-day delinquency in the past year, whereas a "C" borrower might be permitted up to three 30-day or one 60-day delinquencies. Lower grades are associated with worse credit performance. Some of the larger 125 LTV lenders' grades require more uniform mortgage performance in all grades. Therefore, whether a borrower has a 680 or a 600 credit score, no 30-day or, perhaps, one 30-day delinquency is permitted in the mortgage history. These delinquency levels correspond to Fitch IBCA "A" and "A-" mortgage credit grades, respectively. Other elements of credit history, such as credit card debt, might reflect requirements that would be more characteristic of a "B" credit. This makes sense in light of the nature of the 125 LTV product, the purpose of which is to offer good mortgage payers an opportunity to alleviate their credit card burdens by reducing overall monthly payments.

FirstPlus Financial, Inc., one of the first of the 125 LTV issuers, actually takes this concept one step further. Not only is mortgage performance uniform across all credit grades, but tolerance for poor performance decreases as the credit score and respective grade decreases. Therefore, lower grades are associated primarily with lower credit scores and the determinants of lower scores are less a function of the borrowers' credit performance than of the degree of credit utilization. In addition, a well designed 125 LTV grading system would impose more stringent cashout limitations on the lower credit score ranges, resulting in post-loan debt-to-income ratios similar to those for the higher credit grades. The following sample set of underwriting guidelines illustrates these points. Sample underwriting guidelines are provided in Exhibit 2.

Ability to Pay

Although debt-to-income ratio has been a significant factor in mortgage underwriting for some time, recent experience has shown that measures of the borrower's ability to pay are particularly important in 125 LTV lending, where there is generally no recovery from the sale of property. Some 125 LTV lenders have responded to these early indications and have created additional parameters in their underwriting guidelines that emphasize the borrower's ability to pay. These are usually in the form of disposable income requirements which establish minimum disposable incomes particularly at the higher debt-to-income ratios for the different credit grades (see Exhibit 2). Some lenders have also developed more stringent guidelines for the calculation of income.

Loan Performance

Delinquencies

Although the 125 LTV product is still relatively new, and true performance is yet to be determined, it is helpful to compare some available performance data with that of similar asset types. Exhibit 3 shows November 1998 average subprime and home equity mortgage pool delinquency and loss statistics for pools issued in September 1997 versus average statistics for 125 LTV pools of the same period. As can be seen in from the exhibit, 90-day plus delinquencies of the traditional home equity pools are approximately twice those of 125 LTV 90-day plus delinquencies. Some of this difference may be accounted for by the lag in the liquidation of properties of defaulted home equity loans which can take between one and two years. A better proxy might be all delinquencies from the 30-day through 90-day categories not including foreclosure and REO. By this measure, home equity delinquencies are approximately 1.3 times that of high LTV delinquencies.

Since Fitch IBCA's due diligence has shown adequate servicing capabilities on the part of the home equity issuers, these numbers should reflect the differentiation between the two product types rather than specific servicers.

Exhibit 3: Average One Year Performance for Fixed Rate Home Equity and High LTV Securitizations
(as of November, 1998)

	Home Equity	High LTV
Original Balance	$448,144,750.08	$379,231,466.00
Current Balance	$323,803,914.15	$320,263,795.29
Delinquency:		
30 days	3.26%	1.58%
60 days	1.11%	0.81%
90 days	2.07%	2.44%
Sum 30-90 days	6.44%	4.83%
F/C	2.73%	0.09%
REO	0.44%	0.00%
90+Total	5.24%	2.52%
Cum Losses	$800,649.92	$5,675,696.29
As % of Original	0.21%	1.51%

Exhibit 4: Cumulative Losses as a Percent of Original Balance

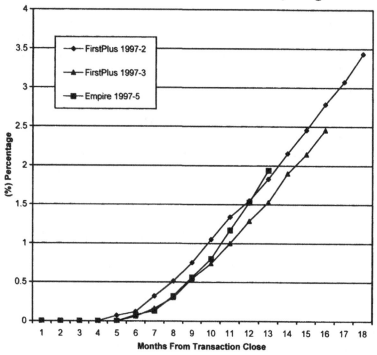

Losses

The data used for the comparative delinquency analysis show that losses in the first year are higher for the 125 LTV pools. This is to be expected, since defaulted 125 LTV loans are rarely taken through the foreclosure process, but are written off after six months.

Exhibit 4 shows the relative trends of the three most seasoned high LTV transactions rated by Fitch IBCA, FirstPlus 97-2, 97-3, and Empire 97-5. As can be seen from the exhibit, losses started their upward trend at about month 6 when charge-offs begin. This upward trend should continue into the first few years of seasoning.

Deal Structures

Most 125 LTV transactions to date were executed as senior/subordinate structures, with excess interest available to cover losses and build overcollateralization. They tend to be issued through owner trusts due to the lack of real estate mortgage investment conduit eligibility of most underlying loans.

In the typical senior/subordinate structure, all payments of principal are allocated to the class A notes until a stepdown date has been reached. The stepdown date is defined as the later of three years or the point at which the senior credit enhancement percentage equals twice its initial percentage. After the step-down date, principal payments will be distributed to the subordinate notes as long as the amount of principal allocated to any subordinate class does not reduce the credit enhancement level below two times its initial percentage. Like many HEL transactions, the lowest rated subordinate tranche is usually "BBB" or "BB".

Triggers
Once the stepdown date has been reached and principal begins to be allocated to the subordinate tranches, a test is performed each month to ensure that credit enhancement remains at twice its initial percentage (by current balance) for each rating level. In addition, most 125 LTV transactions have a mechanism in place that acts as an overcollateralization "step up." This mechanism forces overcollateralization to always be maintained at a certain minimum requirement as a function of 60-day plus delinquencies and available excess spread. This mechanism, called the "net delinquency calculation amount," is calculated as follows: [multiplier × 60-day+ delinquency six-month average] – preceding three-month excess spread.

Although the multiplier varies by transaction, multipliers usually range from 1.7-2.5. Fitch IBCA requires that sufficiently conservative trigger mechanisms be in place for every transaction to ensure that subordinate certificates or overcollateralization are not being paid down if the deal is performing poorly.

NAS/IO Bonds
A non-accelerated senior (NAS) bond is an "AAA" rated tranche of securities for which all principal payments are locked out for a specified period, usually about three years. These bonds are similar to the prepayment lockout classes that have been used in collateralized mortgage obligations (CMOs) and other prime mortgage transactions for several years. By increasing the principal pro rata shares of the other senior tranches, the NAS bond offers more payment stability and protection from prepayment risk. However, the creation of an NAS bond also has the effect of increasing the volatility and sensitivity to prepayments of the other senior bonds in a transaction.

Because of the payment stability of the NAS bond, interest-only (IO) classes are created to take advantage of the steady interest payment stream. As with any IO class, Fitch IBCA reduces the spread available to cover losses by the size of the IO class. In the case of NAS/IO bonds, this reduction is applied only for the life of the bond.[5]

Premium Bonds
It is not uncommon to see 125 LTV deals containing premium senior bonds. This reflects the relatively low prepayment rates exhibited by 125 LTV pools.

---

[5] This is discussed further below when we cover structural analysis.

Exhibit 5: Summary of Fitch IBCA Mortgage Credit Grade Matrix

	A+	A	A-	B	B-	C	C-	D
Credit History								
Mortgage History	0 × 30	0 × 30	1 × 30	2 × 30	3 × 30	4 × 30	5 × 30	6 × 30
(Last 12 Months)	0 × 60	0 × 60	0 × 60	0 × 60	0 × 60	1 × 60	2 × 60	1 × 90
Installment Debt (Last 24 Months)	0 × 30	0 × 30	1 × 30	1 × 60	2 × 60	1 × 90	2 × 90	>2 × 90
Revolving Debt (Last 24 Months)	1 × 30	1 × 30	2 × 30	Max. 60	Max. 60	Max. 90	Max. 90	> 90
Bankruptcy	None	Past 5 Years	Past 3 Years	Past 3 Years	Past 2 Years	Past 2 Years	Past Year	Within 1 Year

RATING APPROACH

Despite the uncertainties associated with the 125 LTV product, Fitch IBCA has developed a rating approach that conservatively assigns credit enhancement levels for the various rating categories of 125 LTV pools. Ratings incorporate analysis of the credit characteristics of the specific collateral pool and the financial and legal structures of the proposed transaction, an on-site inspection of the seller's underwriting and servicing operations, and a review of the historical performance of the seller's production.

Collateral Analysis

When analyzing the credit characteristics of a mortgage pool, Fitch IBCA models the pool on a loan-by-loan basis, assigning a probability of default to each loan, as well as an estimated recovery value for stress scenarios corresponding to each rating level, where the most severe scenarios are associated with an "AAA" rating. Default probability is a function of three elements of the borrower's willingness and ability to pay: the borrower's credit score; a Fitch IBCA-assigned credit grade based on elements of traditional mortgage underwriting, such as past mortgage and credit payment histories (see Exhibit 5); and ability to pay as measured by debt-to-income ratio.

To determine a borrower's credit grade, the issuer's underwriting guidelines are reviewed and compared to the underwriting matrix established by Fitch IBCA. Within each credit grade, Fitch IBCA assigns frequency of foreclosure (FOF) probabilities based on credit score and debt-to-income ratio in the context of CLTVs of 100%-125%. Additional FOF adjustments are then made based on loan type, occupancy status, and documentation requirements.

Exhibit 6: Comparison of High LTV Securitizations

Deal	First Plus 1997-4	Empire 1997-5	Master Financial 97-1	PSB 1997-4	Mego 1997-4
Weighted Avg FICO	684	672	671	669	671
Weighted Avg LTV	112.42%	117.09%	114.49%	115.00%	112.86%
Loan WAC	13.75%	14.28%	13.97%	13.91%	13.90%
% Largest State	29.29% (CA)	29.8% (CA)	38.02% (CA)	47.60% (CA)	13.40% (FL)
AAA C/E					
Subordination	22.50%	32.00%	30.75%	35.25%	26.75%
OC Target	3.50%	4.00%	3.25%	3.25%	7.50%
Total AAA C/E	26.00%	36.00%	34.00%	38.50%	34.25%

FICO – Fair, Issac & Co. CLTV – Combined loan-to-value ratio.
WAC – Weighted average coupon. C/E – Credit enhancement.

Another important aspect of Fitch IBCA's pool analysis is geographic concentration. To capture credit for geographic diversification and penalize for geographic concentration, particularly at the non-investment-grade stress scenarios, Fitch IBCA uses the capabilities of its regionally based mortgage default model for 125 LTV mortgage pools. Fitch IBCA has divided the United States into 75 distinct metropolitan, state, and multistate regions. This segmentation reflects the similarity of the underlying economies, the proximity of the regions to each other, and the geographic distribution of the housing markets. The economic projections incorporated into the model provide a reliable forecast of how regional economic trends affect default rates.

The loss severity for a particular loan is determined by the property's market value decline, foreclosure and interest carrying costs, and borrower lien position. However, if the CLTV is greater than 100%, no recoveries are assumed and the loss severity is equal to or greater than 100%.

Credit enhancement levels for 125 LTV securitizations are relatively conservative to account for the uncertainties of product performance. Typical 125 LTV credit enhancement levels indicate that the "AAA" tranche could withstand gross losses of 30%-40% of the pool. This is approximately three times greater than the losses implied by "AAA" credit enhancement levels for a typical subprime pool. However, part of this differential is accounted for by the lack of recoveries for 125 LTV product versus subprime mortgages. Exhibit 6 outlines the salient features, including "AAA" credit enhancement levels, for several 125 LTV securitizations.

Structural Analysis

As part of its analysis, Fitch IBCA determines the value of excess spread as credit enhancement through a series of prepayment and loss scenarios simulated over the life of the bonds using Fitch IBCA's expected default curve for 125 LTV loans. The prepayment speeds assumed for 125 LTV collateral are lower than those for typical subprime product, reflecting the characteristics of these loans.

Pricing speeds usually ramp from a conditional prepayment rate (CPR) of two to four to between 12 and 14 CPR over a 12-month period. This prepayment speed reflects defaults, moveout turnover, and a certain degree of refinancing activity. The lower speeds are a function of the limited refinancing incentives normally available to borrowers with equity in their homes. However, since the 125 LTV product is unseasoned, long-term prepayment levels are unknown. Therefore, Fitch IBCA remains relatively conservative in its prepayment assumptions.

Another important aspect of Fitch IBCA's analysis of 125 LTV cash flows is that losses are projected to occur earlier in the seasoning curve than for other mortgage-related products. This is due to the fact that since the 125 LTV lender will be in a junior lien position with little potential to realize recoveries from foreclosure, chargeoffs will occur earlier after a default than would be the case if the foreclosure process is pursued. This limits the degree of benefit Fitch IBCA's model assigns to an overcollateralization target, as the ability of reaching the target under the high investment-grade stress scenarios is weakened. However, there is also more excess spread in 125 LTV transactions compared to traditional home equity deals because of the higher rates offered on the loans. Because this spread is available to cover losses, it is reflected in the credit enhancement levels. Fitch IBCA's analysis also accounts for the impact on excess interest of the non-advancing nature of most 125 LTV deal structures.

Due Diligence

Loan File Review

An important aspect of Fitch IBCA's analysis for a 125 LTV loan transaction is the review of a lender's underwriting guidelines and philosophy. This is supplemented by a loan file audit of a random sample of loans to establish the data integrity of the loan level information provided by the lender and to confirm that the lender is underwriting according to its established guidelines.

Operations/Servicing

Although the 125 LTV product is considered a prime-based product in the aggregate, it represents a distribution across a range of borrowers. Those borrowers with lower credit scores and high levels of debt burden will need to be aggressively serviced if overall pool performance is to be maintained. Therefore, Fitch IBCA looks for a relatively high degree of sophistication and experience in its due diligence of servicing and operations. Servicers should demonstrate sufficient servicing capability to address a degree of delinquency and default behavior that currently may not be exhibited, but that will occur as the pool becomes more seasoned.

Historical Performance

As is the case with evaluating the risk of any particular transaction or asset type, a lender's historical performance and experience are important. Although extensive historical pool performance is a rarity in the 125 LTV loan market, the lender's performance and experience in other related areas, such as FHA Title I loans, consumer loans, credit cards, or other types of mortgages can help to mitigate the lack of direct historical experience.

FUTURE RESEARCH FOCUS

Reloading

As discussed, to date, 125 LTV pool delinquencies have been lower than those of typical home equity and subprime mortgage pools. However, a number of considerations remain to be addressed as this collateral becomes more seasoned. One of the most relevant questions is to what extent and how quickly borrowers will subsequently "reload" on revolving credit lines once their overall payments have been reduced through 125 LTV loans. In this situation, a borrower's overall debt burden relative to income could rise, which would erode the borrower's credit profile.

High FICO scores mitigate this risk, as someone who has demonstrated their ability to manage debt is less likely to be tempted to reload. Some lenders have elected to periodically rescore portfolios and use the revised credit scores to determine the direction in which the credit profiles of the borrowers are moving. To date, credit scores have generally risen for rescored pools; however, the product is not sufficiently seasoned to draw any conclusions about potential credit erosion from reloading. The credit score of a heavily debt-burdened borrower who converted his or her consumer debt into lower rate/payment mortgage debt would be expected to increase. Fitch IBCA monitors future rescorings of portfolios as part of its surveillance of 125 LTV product.

Economic Stress

Another consideration of 125 LTV product is that it has not been subjected to a downturn in the economic cycle and its performance under a stress scenario is unknown. Although most 125 LTV lenders are prudent in their estimates of income, Fitch IBCA expects that the greatest impact of an economic downturn will result from decreased income or the borrowers' ability to make monthly payments. Since income is measured by household, should a member of the household become unemployed during a recession, the household income is reduced. Therefore, the debt-to-income ratio of the household increases.

Churning by Lenders

Although the industry consolidation and current market environment discourage lender churning, it is important to understand the added risks associated with this practice should market conditions begin to favor increased competition. When a borrower takes out a junior lien debt consolidation loan to pay off consumer debt, that borrower's credit score increases as a result of the reduction in revolving debt outstanding. Since credit scores represent a significant component of 125 LTV loan underwriting, the refinancing of such a loan, if it is processed shortly after the original loan, would likely contain inflated credit scores as part of its underwriting package.

For example, in January 1997, Mr. Jones had a credit score of 660 and took out a 125 LTV loan for $50,000, bringing his LTV up to 110%. Of the loan amount, $40,000 was used to pay off credit card bills and the rest was cash, paid directly to Mr. Jones. As a result, Mr. Jones' overall monthly payment decreased from $600 per month to $470 per month and his credit score increased to 710. In March 1997, another 125 LTV lender offered Mr. Jones the opportunity to refinance his loan and decrease his monthly payment to $430 per month. The lender was able to offer the lower rate because of the higher credit score.

Although this scenario may seem to be a result of fair competition, it is worrisome not only because of the increased prepayment rates that would be seen industrywide, but because the refinanced 125 LTV loan underwriter did not take into consideration the fact that the borrower had recently paid off a substantial amount of debt. This borrower is not as strong as one who has a 710 credit score strictly on the basis of consumer and mortgage credit performance prior to debt consolidation. Some lenders have addressed this problem by applying a downward adjustment to the credit scores of potential borrowers who show recent junior lien debt consolidation activity that is not reflected on their credit reports. To the extent an underwriter does not enforce such a policy, Fitch IBCA will require an identifying flag for such loans and apply its own downward adjustment to the credit score for purposes of rating transactions.

SUMMARY

Following is a summary of the highlights discussed in this chapter:

- The product type that represented the greatest area of growth in the 125 LTV sector was the combination debt consolidation/cashout junior lien mortgage loan.

- Borrower demographics are similar to those of "A"/"A-" mortgage pools, while other attributes, such as high debt burden, suggest elements of subprime mortgage lending. Fitch IBCA's analysis suggests that the actual credit profile is somewhere in between the two.

- Although the product is not seasoned enough to draw conclusions relative to overall performance, early indications show that home equity loan delinquencies are higher than those of high LTV loans.

- Default probability is based on three elements of the borrower's willingness and ability to pay: credit score; a Fitch IBCA-assigned credit grade reflecting prior mortgage and consumer credit history; and debt-to-income ratio.

- Loss severity is equal to or greater than 100%.

- Typical 125 LTV "AAA" credit enhancement levels can withstand approximately three times greater losses than those implied by comparable "AAA" levels for conventional home equity loan pools.

- Servicers should demonstrate sufficient capabilities to address a degree of delinquency and default behavior that currently may not be exhibited, but that will occur as the pool seasons.

- Future industry considerations include reloading of credit lines by 125 LTV borrowers, economic stress with regard to household income, and potential churning by lenders.

- The liquidity crisis of fall 1998 should result in consolidation of players, tightening of underwriting guidelines, and lower prepayments.

Chapter 9

Manufactured Housing: Overview, Securitization, and Prepayments

Steven Abrahams*
Director of Portfolio Analysis
Single Family Portfolio Management Division
Freddie Mac

Howard Esaki
Principal
Securitized Products Group
Morgan Stanley Dean Witter

Robert Restrick*
Vice President
Pentalpha Capital Group Llc

INTRODUCTION

Securitization of manufactured housing loans has grown dramatically in recent years. The purpose of this chapter is to discuss this sector of the market. Specifically, we will cover the following topics: (1) the market for manufactured housing; (2) the market for the securitized loans; (3) credit risk; and, (4) prepayment risk.

THE MARKET FOR MANUFACTURED HOUSING

Manufactured homes are single-family detached homes constructed off-site and transported to an individual plot of land or to a manufactured housing community. There are eight million manufactured homes in the United States, representing about 7% of all homes and more than 10% of the housing stock in some southern states. About one-third of manufactured homes are located in manufactured housing communities,[1] with the remainder located on individually owned or rented

---

[1] See for example, Howard Esaki and Robert Restrick, "Manufactured Housing Communities: Outlook and Risk Assessment," *Morgan Stanley Mortgage Research*, October 1995 and Eric Hemel and Steve Sakura, "Manufactured Housing REITs," *Morgan Stanley U.S. Investment Research* (May 26, 1995).

---

* This chapter was written when these authors were employed by Morgan Stanley Dean Witter.

plots of land. According to the Census Bureau, manufactured homes are the fastest growing type of housing, increasing by 57% in the 1980s. In the same period, the number of one-family houses increased by 13%.

Although manufactured homes are sometimes called "mobile homes," most are moved infrequently and are expensive to transport. For example, the average homeowner stay in a manufactured housing community is seven years. The home is likely to stay in the community for a much longer period. Costs of transporting a manufactured home range from $2,000 to $6,000, depending on the size of the home and location. In recent years, manufactured housing has come to more closely resemble site-built housing, containing many of the amenities of standard single-family detached homes. Newer "double-wide" homes are twice the size of older manufactured homes and are similar in size to standard homes with an average of 1,525 square feet of living space. In addition, federal government standards established in 1976 for manufactured homes have helped to improve the overall quality of this housing type.

Size, Cost and Buyer Demographics

Exhibits 1 and 2 provide cost and demographic characteristics for manufactured homes. On average, manufactured housing is less expensive and smaller than site-built housing. In 1993, the average sales price of a manufactured home was about one-fourth the cost of a site-built home, excluding land cost. The average manufactured home is about 60% of the size of the average site-built home. Since 1980, the average sales price of a manufactured home has fallen by 10% in real terms, while the price of a site-built home has risen by 13% in real terms. Manufactured housing occupants are, on average, younger and have lower incomes than site-built housing residents.

Exhibit 1: Cost Comparison: Manufactured Homes versus Site-Built Homes

	1980	1993
Manufactured Homes:		
Average sales price*	$33,900	$30,500
Average square footage	1,050	1,295
Average cost/square foot*	$32.29	$23.55
Site-Built Homes:		
Average sales price*	$130,900	$147,700
Land sales price	$26,200	$36,925
Sales price without land	$104,700	$110,775
Average square footage	1,740	2,095
Average cost/square foot*	$60.17	$52.88

*in 1993 dollars

Source: U.S Department of Commerce and Bureau of the Census cited in Daniel Friedman "Manufactured Housing: It Just Keeps Rolling Along," Balcor Consulting Group.

Exhibit 2: Demographic Characteristics: Manufactured Housing versus Non-Manufactured Housing
(in percent, except for income)

	Manufactured	Non-Manufactured*
Median Household Income	$21,052	$36,785
Age:		
Under 25	5.2	0.8
25-34	22.2	13.9
35-54	33.4	42.2
55-74	28.2	32.5
Over 75	11.0	10.6
Race:		
White	92.1	89.8
Non-White	7.9	10.2

*includes multifamily housing
Source: U.S Department of Commerce and Bureau of the Census cited in Daniel Friedman, "Manufactured Housing: It Just Keeps Rolling Along," Balcor Consulting Group.

Exhibit 3: Top 10 Growth States for Manufactured Homes, 1980 to 1990

State	Percent Growth (in units)
South Carolina	91.2
Georgia	87.9
North Carolina	80.6
Texas	80.5
Alabama	75.4
Rhode Island	75.4
Mississippi	75.3
Louisiana	75.3
Oklahoma	73.9
Arkansas	70.6

Source: Bureau of the Census

Geographic Location

Almost 60% of all manufactured homes in the US are located in the South Atlantic and South Central geographical census regions. Florida alone accounts for 10% of all units nationwide. The top three growth states for manufactured housing are also in the South Atlantic, with more than 80% growth from 1980 to 1990. Exhibit 3 lists the top ten growth states for manufactured housing. Exhibit 4 shows the top ten metropolitan areas for manufactured housing, by number of units. Most of these areas are in the Sunbelt, with the exception of the Seattle and Detroit metropolitan areas.

Exhibit 4: Top 10 Metro Areas by Number of Manufactured Homes (thousands of units), 1990

Los Angeles-Anaheim-Riverside, CA	217.3
Tampa-St. Petersburg-Clearwater, FL	147.0
Phoenix, AZ	86.0
Houston-Galveston-Brazoria, TX	68.8
San Francisco-Oakland-San Jose, CA	68.1
Dallas-Ft. Worth, TX	61.8
Seattle-Tacoma, WA	59.2
Detroit-Ann Arbor, MI	58.0
Lakeland-Winter Haven, FL	51.8
Miami-Ft. Lauderdale, FL	46.5

Source: American Demographics, January 1993

Exhibit 5: Total Issuance of Manufactured Housing Securities, 1987 to 1995

Issuer	Issues	Original Balance ($ Millions)	Market Share (%)
CFAC Grantor Trust	1	306	2
CIT Group Securitization Corporation	2	279	1
Green Tree Financial Corporation	25	9,961	52
Merrill Lynch Mortgage Investors, Inc.	41	5,774	30
Oakwood Mortgage Investors, Inc.	3	468	2
RTC	3	616	3
Security Pacific Acceptance Corp.	6	919	5
USWFS Manufactured Housing Contract	1	214	1
Vanderbilt Mortgage Finance	3	539	3
Total	85	19,076	100

Source: Bloomberg

THE MARKET FOR SECURITIES BACKED BY MANUFACTURED HOUSING LOANS

Over $19 billion of securities backed by manufactured housing loans have been issued since 1987. Exhibit 5 lists the total issuance of manufactured housing securities from 1987 to 1995. About 90% of these loans are on the value of the manufactured home itself, with 10% to 20% including the land. Green Tree Financial Corporation, through Merrill Lynch Mortgage Investors, Inc. and its own shelf, accounts for about two-thirds of total issuance.

With the exception of a few early deals, the majority of manufactured housing loan asset-backed securities (ABS) are composed of AAA-rated, sequential-pay classes. Credit enhancement is usually provided by excess servicing and subordination. The excess servicing strip, which represents the difference between the weighted average coupon on the bonds and the higher coupons on the mortgages, may be 350 basis points per year or more at issue. This strip covers losses first, and allows the rating agencies to assign investment grade ratings to 100% of the bonds issued. Mezzanine and subordinate classes, rated AA, A, and BBB, or some combination thereof, provide additional enhancement for the AAA classes. The mezzanine classes are typically locked out from receiving any principal for four or more years. Many recent manufactured housing loan ABS now pay principal pro rata to the senior classes and to certain of the mezzanine classes after the initial 4-year lockout period.

Exhibit 6 shows the characteristics of the ten most recent Green Tree manufactured housing loan transactions. The average size of the Green Tree transactions was $454 million, backed by an average of more than 15,000 loans. More than 80% of the loans are on new manufactured homes. The weighted average loan-to-value ratio was 87.2%. About 42% of the loans were on single-wide homes; the remainder were on double-wides or other sizes. About one-third of the loans were on homes located in manufactured housing communities. The largest state concentrations were North Carolina (9.6%), Texas (9.5%), and Florida (6.7%). Credit support for the senior classes has averaged 19.7%. Exhibit 7 shows the characteristics of the two CIT manufactured housing loan transactions.

Indicative spread to Treasury levels as of October 15, 1995 for the asset-backed securities issued in a sample Green Tree transaction, 1995-8, are shown in Exhibit 8. Spread levels on manufactured housing loan ABS have been fairly constant over the prior year.

RATING AGENCY VIEW OF MANUFACTURED HOUSING

Rating agencies have a generally favorable view of the manufactured housing industry and securities backed by manufactured housing loans. For example, Moody's recently wrote that "the recent favorable operating environment for the manufactured housing industry — along with an improved product line and new financing options — should provide for continued growth for the industry over the short-to-intermediate term." [2]

The credit performance of securities backed by manufactured housing loans is among the best of any type of mortgage- or asset-backed security. As can be seen from Exhibit 9, of the 70 asset-backed classes upgraded by Moody's since 1986, 38 are on deals backed by manufactured housing loans. Twenty-four of the manufactured housing upgrades were based on collateral performance and 14 were because of upgrades of third-party credit enhancers or Green Tree Financial Corporation.

---

[2] Mark Stancher, "Manufactured Housing Collateral and Structural Aspects: A Solid Foundation," *Moody's Investors Service*, January 27, 1995.

Exhibit 6: Characteristics of the Ten Mid-1990s Green Tree Issues

Series	1994-6	1994-7	1994-8	1995-1
Issue Date	Sep-94	Nov-94	Dec-94	Feb-95
Original Balance ($ mil.)	463.9	353.5	523.2	378.3
Number of Loans	17,515	12,723	18,430	12,805
Average Balance ($)	26,485	27,784	28,388	29,546
WAM (Years)	18.1	18.6	18.8	19.9
WAC	11.48	11.46	11.57	11.91
Ratings (Moody's/S&P/Fitch)				
Seniors	Aaa/AAA/NR	Aaa/AAA/NR	Aaa/AAA/NR	Aaa/AAA/NR
Subordinates				
Class M-1	Aa3/AA+/NR	Aa3/AA/NR	Aa3/AA/NR	AA/Aa3/NR
Class B-1	Baa1/A-/NR	Baa1/BBB+/NR	Baa1/BBB+/NR	Baa1/BBB+/NR
Class B-2	Baa1/A/NR	Baa1/A/NR	Baa1/A/NR	Baa1/A/NR
Credit Support (%)				
Seniors	21.0	21.0	21.0	19.0
Subordinates (%)				
Class M-1	12.0	11.5	11.5	10.0
Class B-1	6.5	6.0	6.0	6.0
Class B-2	Limited Guarantee from Green Tree Financial Corporation			
Sep-95 CPR (MHP)				
1mo	7.6 (156)	6.5 (144)	7.4 (161)	6.9 (157)
3mo	7.7 (161)	7.0 (150)	6.0 (133)	6.3 (146)
Life	4.8 (111)	5.2 (122)	n/a	6.2 (149)
Loan to Value (%)				
<80	16.1	16.2	18.9	11.2
80-85	11.8	12.2	12.9	11.4
85-90	42.7	41.9	39.3	35.5
90-95	28.8	29.2	28.2	32.1
95-100	0.7	0.6	0.7	9.8
Est. Wtd Avg.	87.3	87.2	86.4	85.2
Manufactured Homes (%)				
New	82	83	83	84
Single-Wide	45	41	39	37
Double-Wide/Other	55	59	61	63
Location (%)				
Park Property	33	32	29	27
Privately Owned	51	52	55	56
Nonpark Rental	16	16	16	17
State Percentage>5%				
Texas	10.3	8.9	8.3	8.7
Florida	6.3	6.1	6.8	7.5
North Carolina	9.0	9.0	9.6	10.8
Michigan	—	6.9	5.8	6.2
Georgia	5.6	5.2	5.5	6.9
South Carolina	—	—	5.3	—
Alabama	—	—	5.2	—

Source: Morgan Stanley, Fitch, Bloomberg

Exhibit 6 (Continued)

Series	1995-2	1995-3	1995-4	1995-5
Issue Date	Mar-95	May-95	Jun-95	Jul-95
Original Balance ($ mil.)	328.3	502.2	320.0	451.2
Number of Loans	11,738	18,112	11,138	14,283
Average Balance ($)	27,966	27,727	28,730	31,593
WAM (Years)	20.5	20.8	21.2	22.3
WAC	12.10	11.67	11.19	10.65
Ratings (Moody's/S&P/Fitch)				
Seniors	Aaa/AAA/AAA	Aaa/AAA/AAA	Aaa/AAA/AAA	Aaa/AAA/AAA
Subordinates				
Class M-1	Aa2/AA–/AA–	Aa2/AA–/AA–	Aa3/AA–/AA–	Aa3/AA–/AA–
Class B-1	Baa1/BBB+/BBB	Baa1/BBB+/BBB+	Baa1/BBB+/BBB+	Baa1/BBB+/BBB+
Class B-2	Baa1/A–/A	Baa1/A–/A	Baa1/A–/A	Baa1/A–/A
Credit Support (%)				
Seniors	18.0	18.0	17.0	17.0
Subordinates (%)				
Class M-1	9.0	9.0	8.0	8.0
Class B-1	5.0	4.5	4.0	4.0
Class B-2	Limited Guarantee from Green Tree Financial Corporation			
Sep-95 CPR (MHP)				
1mo	5.3 (123)	4.8 (118)	2.7 (68)	7.5 (191)
3mo	5.4 (129)	4.6 (114)	4.5 (116)	4.0 (106)
Life	5.5 (135)	4.5 (113)	4.5 (116)	6.5 (166)
Loan to Value (%)				
<80	13.8	13.0	15.1	16.7
80-85	12.5	11.3	11.0	10.9
85-90	35.9	30.3	29.0	26.6
90-95	36.3	43.4	42.7	43.9
95-100	1.5	2.1	2.2	2.0
Est. Wtd Avg.	88.1	88.8	88.2	87.7
Manufactured Homes (%)				
New	81	80	81	83
Single-Wide	43	45	44	39
Double-Wide/Other	57	55	56	61
Location (%)				
Park Property	34	36	36	31
Privately Owned	49	45	45	54
Nonpark Rental	17	19	19	15
State Percentage>5%				
Texas	10.8	10.1	9.1	7.9
Florida	6.9	6.7	6.9	6.9
North Carolina	9.5	10.0	9.0	8.2
Michigan	5.2	—	—	7.0
Georgia	6.1	5.9	6.1	5.0
South Carolina	6.2	6.2	5.9	5.4
Alabama	5.1	—	5.1	—

Source: Morgan Stanley, Fitch, Bloomberg

Exhibit 6 (Continued)

Series	1995-6	1995-7	1995-8	Average
Issue Date	Aug-95	Sep-95	Oct-95	
Original Balance ($ mil.)	396.7	347.8	479.9	424.9
Number of Loans	12,591	10,785	14,708	15,221
Average Balance ($)	31,506	32,244	32,628	27,916
WAM (Years)	22.4	22.6	22.9	19.4
WAC	10.27	10.12	10.11	11.7
Ratings (Moody's/S&P/Fitch)				
Seniors	Aaa/AAA/AAA	Aaa/AAA/AAA	Aaa/AAA/AAA	
Subordinates				
Class M-1	Aa3/AA-/AA	Aa3/AA-/AA	Aa3/AA-/AA	
Class B-1	Baa2/BBB+/BBB+	Baa1/BBB+/BBB+	Baa1/BBB+/BBB+	
Class B-2	Baa1/A-/A	Baa1/A-/A	Baa1/A-/A	
Credit Support (%)				
Seniors	17.0	17.0	17.0	19.7
Subordinates (%)				
Class M-1	9.5	9.5	9.5	10.6
Class B-1	4.5	4.0	4.0	5.7
Class B-2	Limited Guarantee from Green Tree Financial Corporation			
Sep-95 CPR (MHP)				
1mo	7.8 (205)	—	—	
3mo	—	—	—	
Life	7.8 (205)	—	—	
Loan to Value (%)				
<80	16.5	16.7	17.4	15.0
80-85	11.3	11.2	10.8	12.0
85-90	26.8	26.5	26.3	37.5
90-95	43.8	43.7	43.9	33.0
95-100	1.6	1.9	1.6	2.4
Est. Wtd Avg.	87.7	87.6	87.6	87.2
Manufactured Homes (%)				
New	82	83	82	82
Single-Wide	39	39	37	42
Double-Wide/Other	61	61	63	58
Location (%)				
Park Property	32	31	32	32
Privately Owned	52	53	52	51
Nonpark Rental	16	16	16	17
State Percentage >5%				
Texas	7.0	6.5	5.9	9.5
Florida	6.4	5.6	6.1	6.7
North Carolina	9.1	8.3	9.3	9.6
Michigan	6.4	7.2	7.5	3.7
Georgia	5.3	5.3	—	5.8
South Carolina	5.9	6.3	5.6	3.1
Alabama	—	—	—	1.7

Source: Morgan Stanley, Fitch, Bloomberg

Exhibit 7: Characteristics of CIT Issues

Series	1993-1	1995-1*
Issue Date	Jul-93	Feb-95
Original Balance ($ mil.)	155.0	84.6
Number of Loans	4,598	2,152
Average Balance ($)	33,719	39,297
WAM (Years)	17.1	19.9
WAC	10.61	11.32
Ratings (Moody's/S&P/Fitch)		
Seniors	NR/AAA/NR	Aaa/NR/NR
Subordinates		
Mezzanine	NA	Aa3/NR/NR
Subordinate	NR/BBB+/NR	Aa3/NR/NR
Credit Support (%)		
Seniors	15.8	16.5
Subordinates (%)		
Mezzanine	NA	8.5
Subordinate	1.8	Limited Guarantee
Aug-95 CPR (MHP)		
1mo	12.8 (213)	7.6 (176)
3mo	10.6 (177)	7.5 (179)
Life	12.5 (210)	5.8 (143)
Loan to Value (%)		
<80	30.0	12.4
80-85	30.8	10.6
85-90	29.2	24.5
90-95	9.1	32.4
95-100	0.9	19.2
Manufactured Homes (%)		
New	84	93
Double-Wide/Other	—	74
State Percentage>5%		
Texas	—	26.4
Arizona	—	10.8
Washington	6.8	—
California	18.8	—
Nevada	6.7	—
Oregon	7.3	—

*Based on initial contracts sold to the Trust.

Source: Morgan Stanley, Fitch, Bloomberg

Only two classes of ABS backed by manufactured housing have been downgraded by Moody's, both related to downgrades of third-party credit enhancement providers. The upgrade to downgrade ratio for manufactured housing transactions (19 to 1) is greater than for any other type of ABS. As a comparison, the residential MBS upgrade downgrade ratio is about 2 to 1 for 1995. Fitch and Duff and Phelps have also upgraded several manufactured housing transactions.

Exhibit 8: Pricing Spread Levels on Green Tree 1995-8

Class	Average Life (years)	Nominal Spread (bp) Over Benchmark	Benchmark U.S. Treasury
A-1	1.05	45	5.27% of 10/17/96
A-2	3.05	45	3 year
A-3	5.05	55	5 year
A-4	7.08	70	6 3/8% of 8/02
A-5	10.29	92	10 year
A-6	17.07	140	10 year
M-1	13.35	135	10 year
B-1	8.75	135	10 year
B-2	17.44	168	10 year

Source: *Asset Sales Report*, Morgan Stanley, yields as of October 15, 1995

Exhibit 9: ABS Rating Changes by Moody's, 1986-1995

Asset Type	Upgrades		Downgrades	
	#	$ (Mil)	#	$ (Mil)
Autos	17	1,087	27	14,416
Credit Cards	7	372	14	4,750
Home Equity	4	359	7	21,607
Manufactured Housing	38	3,149	2	413
Other	4	216	6	1,139
Total	70	5,182	56	42,324

Source: Moody's

Going forward, we believe credit performance will remain strong as the rating agencies continue to maintain strict standards for ratings of manufactured housing securities. Moody's notes, "..since most securities in the asset-backed market are rated Aaa initially (and therefore cannot be upgraded), we expect that there will be relatively more downgrades in this market than in the total corporate bond market." The average rating in the corporate bond market is close to BBB/Baa, leaving more opportunities for upgrades. However, Moody's also points out that, "...given the predominance of high initial ratings and the relatively short maturities, ...relatively few of [manufactured housing] securities will end in default."[3]

PREPAYMENT RISKS

Prepayments in manufactured housing arise from the same major sources as in other mortgage-backed bonds: refinancings, housing turnover, and defaults. Because of their smaller average loan balance, manufactured housing prepayment

---

[3] Andrew Silver, "A Historical Review of Rating Changes in the Public Asset-Backed Securities Market, 1986-1995," *Moody's Investors Service*, October 20, 1995.

speeds, nonetheless, tend to be lower and much more stable than speeds on mortgages on site-build homes. In fact, prepayments on manufactured housing loans are arguably more stable than prepayments on higher-balance home equity loans.

Refinancings

As in other mortgage-backed securities, refinancing of manufactured housing loans represents the most volatile component of prepayments. Refinancings can double or triple prepayments on manufactured homes within a few months, sending speeds from 6% CPR to 18% CPR. Refinancings in site-built homes, however, can generate a tenfold jump in speeds from 6% CPR to 60% CPR.

A handful of factors drive the refinancings of most manufactured housing loans:

Primary
- Interest rate incentives
- Loan size

Secondary
- Loan age
- Seasonality

Tertiary
- The economy
- Competition among lenders

Exhibit 10 summarizes the factors driving refinancing on manufactured housing loans.

Exhibit 10: Factors Driving Refinancings in Manufactured Housing Loans

Factor	Factor Levels	Proportional Prepayment Impact (% CPR)				
		Interest Rates Shift (bp from loan mortgage rate)				
		0	−50	−100	−200	−300
Refinancing	$18,000 balance (< avg size loan)	6	7	9	12	14
Incentive	$24,000 balance (avg size loan)	6	8	10	13	16
and Loan Size	$30,000 balance (> avg size loan)	6	9	12	14	17
Loan Age	< 24 Months	80% of average life speed				
	> 24 Months	105% of average life speed				
Seasonality	January, February	80% of average life speed				
	Other Months	105% of average life speed				
The	0.8 Million New Home Sales	Slower				
Economy	1.0 Million New Home Sales	Average				
	1.2 Million New Home Sales	Faster				
Lender	More	Raises prepayments				
Competition	Less	Lowers prepayment				

Source: Morgan Stanley

Exhibit 11: Savings from Refinancing

Monthly Payment At:	Loan Size	
	$24,400	$118,160
9% Interest Rate	$247	$1,198
8% Interest Rate	$233	$1,129
7% Interest Rate	$219	$1,062
6% Interest Rate	$205	$997
Monthly Savings From Refinancing A 9% Interest Rate Loan to a:		
8% Interest Rate	$14.30	$69.26
7% Interest Rate	$28.17	$136.41
6% Interest Rate	$41.58	$201.36

Source: Morgan Stanley

Primary Refinancing Risks

Falling interest rates represent the single most important driver of prepayments. Lower rates create opportunities for borrowers to refinance their loans and capture a stream of future monthly savings. The greater the drop in financing rates below the borrower's rate, the larger the absolute stream of potential savings. Monthly savings are also directly proportional to loan size, with small and large loans producing correspondingly small and large savings. (See Exhibit 11.)

As an example, take the savings from refinancing the average 80% LTV, 15-year manufactured housing loan of $24,400. If the borrower starts with a 9% interest rate, refinancing into an 8% interest rate only saves $14.30 a month. Refinancing into a 6% interest rate only saves $41.58 a month.

Refinancing the average 80% LTV, 15-year loan on a site-built home and land, by contrast, would save much more. With an average balance of $118,160, refinancing a site-built's loan from a 9% interest rate to an 8% rate saves $69.26 a month, and refinancing to a 6% rate saves $201.36 a month — nearly five times the potential savings from refinancing the smaller manufactured housing loan.

Because mortgages on manufactured homes are roughly one-fifth the size of conventional loans for site-built homes and land, the manufactured housing loans show much less interest-rate sensitivity. For small manufactured housing loans, monthly savings from refinancing may seem small against the upfront, fixed costs of attorney's fees, title searches, and the like. Prepayments from 1992-93 suggest that prepayment rates on seasoned par manufactured housing loans would rise from 6% to 10% CPR-to-life to 16% to 20% CPR-to-life if rates dropped 300 bp. In contrast, CPR-to-life speeds on conventional par 30-year agency mortgages could rise from 6% CPR to 49% CPR, according to Morgan Stanley prepayment models.

Secondary Refinancing Risks

Even in the event of falling interest rates, refinancing risk falls in the first two years of a loan made on a new manufactured home. During these two years, the underlying home typically depreciates, raising its loan-to-value ratio to levels unacceptable to many lenders. Refinancings in the first 24 months of a loan run slowly relative to their long-run average.

Seasonality influences refinancings as well. Refinancings on manufactured housing loans typically fall in January and February to 80% of their annual average. Conventional agency mortgages show the same pattern. Refinancings typically slow in January and February as borrowers recover from year-end holiday spending.

Tertiary Refinancing Risks

The economy and employment also shape prepayment risk. Robust economies with more jobs allow more applicants to build the job histories, credit, and assets to qualify for refinancing or upgrade to another home. A bad economy brings the opposite. Using new single-family home sales as an economic benchmark, an annualized pace of 1.2 million sales has coincided with refinancings running above their long-run average. A 0.8 million sales pace has coincided with speeds running well below their long-run average, and a 1.0 million sales pace typically has kept refinancings at their long-run mean.

Finally, competition among lenders can influence refinancing activity as well. To the extent that lenders get more aggressive either through lower rates or their efforts to inform borrowers of refinancing options, prepayments could become more interest-rate sensitive.

Housing Turnover

For borrowers holding mortgages with below-market rates of interest, housing turnover drives prepayments. Most of that turnover reflects borrowers trading up to larger manufactured housing units or into site-built homes, or moving out of the home to another area altogether.

A handful of factors again predict most of the pattern of turnover:

Primary
- Loan age
- Economic conditions
Secondary
- Seasonality
- Setting for the manufactured home

Exhibit 12 shows the factors driving turnover in manufactured housing loans.

Primary Turnover Risks

As in mortgages on traditional homes, prepayments on manufactured homes rise with age. Some investors have settled on a standard *manufactured housing pre-*

payment curve (MHP) to describe the rising speeds. The 100% MHP curve starts at 3.7% CPR in the first month after origination and rises 0.1% CPR monthly to 6.0% CPR in the 24th month, remaining constant thereafter. This is depicted in Exhibit 13. Manufactured housing prepayment speeds can be described as multiples of the MHP curve, the same way that other sectors of the mortgage market use the PSA curve. Like the PSA curve, the MHP curve is a yardstick for prepayments rather than a forecast or a predictor. Actual seasoning can differ from 100% MHP due to changing rates of home depreciation, economic conditions, interest rates, and other factors.

Exhibit 12: Factors Driving Turnover in Manufactured Housing Loans

Factor	Factor Levels	Prepayment Impact
Loan Age	Month 1	3.7% CPR
	Months 2-23	Increases 0.1% CPR a month
	Months 24 and beyond	6.0% CPR
The Economy	0.8 Million New Home Sales	Slower
	1.0 Million New Home Sales	Average
	1.2 Million New Home Sales	Faster
Seasonality	January Low	80% of average annual speed
	July High	120% of average annual speed
Setting	On Borrower-Owned Land	Seasons over 36 Months
	In an MH Park	Seasons over 24 Months

Source: Morgan Stanley

Exhibit 13: 100% MHP

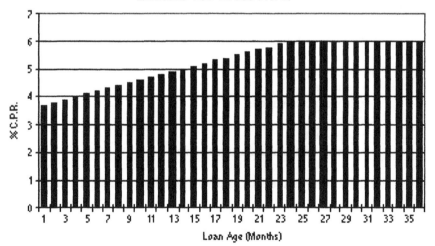

Source: Morgan Stanley

The economy can have a significant influence on rates of manufactured housing turnover, beyond its already important impact on refinancing. Robust economies with strong employment tend to draw migration, raising demand for all housing. In addition, improving employment prospects for existing homeowners allow them to move easily and trade up to better homes.

Secondary Turnover Risks

Borrowers' tendency to move at the end of the school year, and with the arrival of summer weather, drives turnover toward an annual high in July, and a low in January. July's pace typically runs at 120% of its annual average, with January coming in at 80%, the same pattern as other mortgages.

The physical location of the manufactured home also helps predict turnover. Homes located on the borrower's own property turnover more slowly than homes in manufactured housing parks. The homes on owned property take roughly 36 months to fully season, rather than the normal 24. Presumably, borrowers located on owned property have a longer-term commitment to living in that area.

Defaults

Defaults constitute a larger component of manufactured housings' prepayments than of prepayments in site-built homes. Defaulted loans eventually become prepayments when the financed property is liquidated and principal returned to the investor. However, they show limited month-to-month variability. In many manufactured housing securitizations, monthly defaults constitute a steady 0.1% to 0.2% of original principal, roughly equivalent to 2% to 3% CPR a year.

CONCLUSION

The recent growth in securitized manufactured housing loans and current investor appetite for less negatively convex securities makes manufactured housing loans an attractive alternative. The small loan size, at least relative to conventional mortgage-backed securities, historically has made borrowers less sensitive to refinancing opportunities. Moreover, credit support in securitized deals has proven to be more than adequate historically, and should continue to cover reasonable credit risk.

Chapter 10

Securities Backed by CRA Loans

Dale Westhoff
Senior Managing Director
Bear Stearns & Co.

V.S. Srinivasan
Associate Director
Bear Stearns & Co.

INTRODUCTION

CRA loans are loans targeted to low and moderate income borrowers within a lender's assessment area under the Community Reinvestment Act (CRA) of 1977. The CRA ensures that a lending institution meets the credit needs of its entire community. CRA securities represent a unique investment vehicle for mortgage- and asset-backed investors for two reasons. First, institutions that purchase CRA-backed securities will generally receive favorable CRA consideration under the "qualified investment" provisions of the act. Second, the borrower population defined under CRA guidelines exhibits very stable prepayment behavior (analogous to VA Vendee loans) enhancing the performance profile of CRA securities.

Institutions often originate CRA loans under special "affordable housing" lending programs that typically offer favorable financing terms, including: below market interest rates, no private mortgage insurance requirements, and/or less stringent debt ratio limits.[1] As a result, these borrowers tend to be "locked" into their loans since the universe of lenders able or willing to refinance them if rates decline is limited. (Many CRA loans do not meet current agency conforming guidelines — see Exhibit 1.) In addition, CRA loans possess many of the well-recognized loan and borrower attributes that tend to reduce prepayment sensitivity, including: low loan balances, high loan-to-value ratios, and a demographic profile characterized by low and moderate income borrowers with limited liquid assets. Therefore, we would expect CRA loan prepayments to be slow but very stable, making CRA-backed securities more positively convex than traditional agency conforming MBS and many home equity securities.

---

[1] CRA data provided by First Union.

Exhibit 1: Underwriting and Loan Attribute Comparison
CRA* versus Agency Conforming, Home Equity, and VA Vendee Loans

	Typical CRA (Affordable Housing) Program	Agency Conforming (FH/FN)	HEL	VA Vendee
Loan Pricing	50-100 basis points BELOW conforming rate	Conforming Rate	350-400 bp above effective conforming rate	FHA Rate
PMI	Usually not required	Required above 80% LTV LTV / MI Coverage: 80-85% 12%, >85-90% 25%, >90% 30%	Not required	PMI not required. Until August 1997, borrower paid an upfront funding fee between 0.50% and 1.25%, depending on LTV. After August 1997, fee is 2.25% for all borrowers.
Borrower Income Levels	Located in low income census tract and/or less than 50% (low income) or 80% (moderate income) of median income for assessment area	≈ Median	Below median	Defaulted property; may be located in depressed area.
Average Original LTV	≈85%-90%	≈75%-80%	75%	95%-100%
Average Balance	$65,000-$75,000	≈$105,000-$110,000	$45,000-$65,000	$65,000
Typical Borrowers	Predominantly first time purchase	Combination of purchase/refi/cash-out/second home	Primarily debt consolidation and rate/term refis	Purchase only.
Ratios: Housing Expense-to-Income Debt-to-Income	31-33% of monthly income 38-40%	25%-28% of monthly income 33%-36%	28%-60% depending on credit grade	No strict adherence to ratios.
FICO	≈685-690	FHLMC recommends extra review when FICO is less than 660 (single family) Review Type / FICO Basic >660, Comprehensive 620-660, Cautious <620	580	Not available.
Other	Borrowers not penalized for frequent job changes		Statistics apply primarily to B/C HEL sector	Generally, standards equal to VA Loan Guaranty Program.

Source: First Union

*Individual programs may vary.

This view is supported by an analysis of $1.9 billion CRA loans originated between 1990 and 1996. The data confirmed that despite substantial fluctuations in interest rates during the observation period, CRA loan prepayments deviated little from their slow baseline prepayment speed. We also found that this prepayment behavior was analogous to that found in loans originated under the VA Vendee program where comparable borrower demographics, low average loan sizes, and high LTVs produce similar slow and stable prepayment profiles.

WHAT CONSTITUTES A CRA LOAN?

The Community Reinvestment Act of 1977 is intended to encourage commercial banks and savings institutions to help meet the credit needs of the local communities in which they are chartered. CRA provisions are administered by four federal agencies: the Board of Governors at the Federal Reserve System, the OCC, the FDIC, and the OTS. These agencies ensure that an institution meets the credit needs of its entire community including the low and moderate income neighborhoods.

To enforce the CRA provisions, the regulatory agencies conduct regular CRA examinations and evaluate CRA performance during the process of bank acquisitions and mergers. The CRA focuses on the distribution and level of an institution's lending, investments, and services within its assessment area. Both quantitative and qualitative measures are used to determine the compliance of a particular institution with the CRA. A heavy emphasis is placed on the institution's lending distribution across low, moderate, middle, and upper income borrowers in relation to the actual distribution of borrowers within their communities across these same classifications. This evaluation may be done on a geographic basis or on a borrower basis (i.e., a low income borrower in a high income area could still be considered favorably under CRA guidelines).

A low income area is defined as an area where the median family income is less than 50% of the median for the entire area. Similarly, a moderate income area has a median income that is at least 50% and less than 80% of the entire area. As a reference, we provide the median family incomes by state followed by the low and moderate income limits as defined under the CRA guidelines in Exhibit 2.

Institutions that are found not to be in compliance with CRA provisions may be given a "substantial noncompliance" rating by the agencies which will negatively impact future applications for charters, deposit insurance, branch expansion, mergers, or acquisitions. To meet CRA requirements, lenders often establish very specific origination programs targeting the low and moderate income borrower segments within their communities. These low income lending programs (often called "affordable housing" programs) ensure that the institution maintains compliance with CRA provisions. In general, the loans backing CRA securities come from these targeted lending programs.

Exhibit 2: 1994 Median Income by State and Aug. 1997 State Prepayment Index

State	State Prepayment Index	1994 Median Income ($)	50% of Median	80% of Median
AK	167	$45,367	$22,684	$36,294
AL	143	$27,196	$13,598	$21,757
AR	123	$25,565	$12,783	$20,452
AZ	153	$31,293	$15,647	$25,034
CA	84	$35,331	$17,666	$28,265
CO	166	$37,833	$18,917	$30,266
CT	89	$41,097	$20,549	$32,878
DC	88	$30,116	$15,058	$24,093
DE	126	$35,873	$17,937	$28,698
FL	117	$29,294	$14,647	$23,435
GA	114	$31,467	$15,734	$25,174
HI	45	$42,255	$21,128	$33,804
IA	140	$33,079	$16,540	$26,463
ID	164	$31,536	$15,768	$25,229
IL	119	$35,081	$17,541	$28,065
IN	126	$27,858	$13,929	$22,286
KS	143	$28,322	$14,161	$22,658
KY	148	$26,595	$13,298	$21,276
LA	120	$25,676	$12,838	$20,541
MA	99	$40,500	$20,250	$32,400
MD	107	$39,198	$19,599	$31,358
ME	118	$30,316	$15,158	$24,253
MI	124	$35,284	$17,642	$28,227
MN	109	$33,644	$16,822	$26,915
MO	124	$30,190	$15,095	$24,152
MS	144	$25,400	$12,700	$20,320

State	State Prepayment Index	1994 Median Income ($)	50% of Median	80% of Median
MT	126	$27,631	$13,816	$22,105
NC	114	$30,114	$15,057	$24,091
ND	216	$28,278	$14,139	$22,622
NE	128	$31,794	$15,897	$25,435
NH	167	$35,245	$17,623	$28,196
NJ	97	$42,280	$21,140	$33,824
NM	126	$26,905	$13,453	$21,524
NV	132	$35,871	$17,936	$28,697
NY	84	$31,899	$15,950	$25,519
OH	121	$31,855	$15,928	$25,484
OK	117	$26,991	$13,496	$21,593
OR	150	$31,456	$15,728	$25,165
PA	87	$32,066	$16,033	$25,653
RI	128	$31,928	$15,964	$25,542
SC	100	$29,846	$14,923	$23,877
SD	93	$29,733	$14,867	$23,786
TN	135	$28,639	$14,320	$22,911
TX	118	$30,755	$15,378	$24,604
UT	151	$35,716	$17,858	$28,573
VA	113	$37,647	$18,824	$30,118
VT	110	$35,802	$17,901	$28,642
WA	104	$33,533	$16,767	$26,826
WI	121	$35,388	$17,694	$28,310
WV	134	$23,564	$11,782	$18,851
WY	90	$33,140	$16,570	$26,512

Source: 1995 US Census, Bear, Stearns & Co. Inc.

INVESTING IN CRA-BACKED SECURITIES

Securities backed by residential loans made primarily to low and moderate income borrowers are considered qualified investments and will receive favorable treatment under the investment test provisions of the act. Qualified investments must benefit the institution's assessment area or a broader statewide or regional area that includes the institution's assessment area in order to receive favorable CRA consideration. Examiners will consider the size of the region and the actual or potential benefit to the institution's assessment area when evaluating qualified investments. In general, the larger the regional area the more diffuse the benefit will be to the institution's assessment area. In addition, the fact that a security is backed by some loans from individuals earning above 80% of the area median does not, by itself, disqualify it as a qualified investment under CRA.

The degree of favorable treatment an institution receives for an investment in CRA-backed securities is contingent on a number of variables, including the number of loans within an institution's assessment area in the trust (as determined by the regulators), the scope of the institution's strategic plan to meet CRA guidelines, and the extent to which it has satisfied plan objectives. An institution considering an investment in CRA securities should consult with its officers responsible for compliance with CRA regulations, and with CRA regulators.

A COMPARISON OF CRA ORIGINATION PROGRAMS TO OTHER PROGRAMS

Because CRA loan programs are targeted to meet the special needs of low and moderate income borrowers, loan attributes and prepayment behavior reflect the unique characteristics of this demographic segment of the community. Exhibit 1 compares the typical underwriting criteria and loan attributes of loans from CRA programs to those for agency conforming, home equity, and VA Vendee loans.

It is clear from Exhibit 1 that CRA loans differ from other programs in three important respects:

1. *Low/moderate Income Borrower Demographics:* By definition, CRA borrowers come from the low/moderate income segment of a community; consequently, they are often first-time home buyers with relatively few liquid assets. In general, they tend to be more payment sensitive than interest rate sensitive. In addition, relatively high FICO scores suggest that targeted CRA borrowers strive to meet their monthly debt obligations.

2. *Favorable Underwriting Standards:* The most obvious difference between CRA and conforming loans is that CRA borrowers tend to receive favorable financing rates with no PMI obligation. Exhibit 3 compares the aver-

age CRA mortgage rate[2] to the conforming rate since 1990. In our sample, the average CRA loan was originated at a 72 basis point discount to conforming rates during that time. In addition, debt-to-income ratio limits are higher than agency conforming guidelines.

3. *Loan Attributes Reflect the Low and Moderate Income Borrower Population:* CRA loans tend to have small balances, high LTVs, and be primarily for first-time purchase transactions. All of these attributes tend to slow prepayments and make the borrowers less sensitive to refinancing opportunities.

CRA HISTORICAL PREPAYMENT ANALYSIS

We have analyzed the historical prepayment experience of $1.88 billion CRA loans originated between 1990 and 1996 over an observation window extending from April 1996 to July 1997. Summary statistics on the loan sample can be found in Exhibit 4.

For reference purposes we compared the CRA experience from our data sample to equivalent conventional conforming prepayments over the same observation window. A summary of our findings follows.

The Baseline CRA Speed

We found that the baseline seasoning ramp[3] for CRA loans was 24% below that of agency conforming collateral (see Exhibits 5 and 6). We believe the following two underlying factors are responsible for this behavior:

Exhibit 3: CRA versus Agency Mortgage Rates

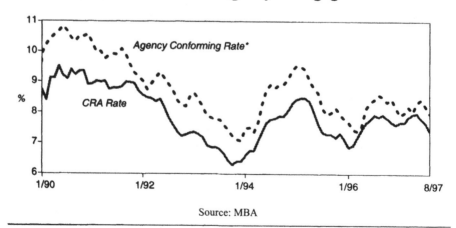

Source: MBA

---

[2] A CRA mortgage rate series was derived from an historical sample of 28,932 CRA loans provided by First Union.

[3] The average CRA prepayment for near current coupon loans conditional on the age of the loan.

Exhibit 4: CRA Loan Sample Statistics

Number of Loans		28,932
Average Original Balance		$64,878
Original LTV		83%
WAC		7.72%
Avg. Rate Subsidy		0.72%
Geography	Florida:	39%
	New Jersey:	13%
	North Carolina:	13%
	Pennsylvania:	7%
	Virginia:	6%
Total Sample Size		$1.88 billion

Source: First Union

Exhibit 5: CRA Baseline Seasoning Ramp

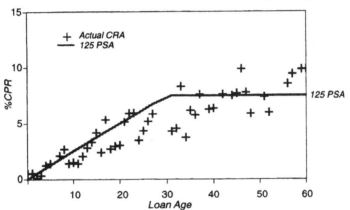

Exhibit 6: CRA versus Agency Conforming

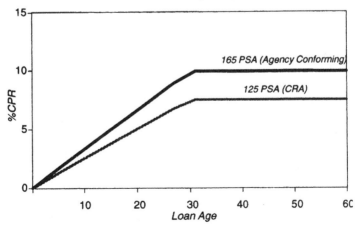

Exhibit 7: Actual Prepayments Conditional on Refinancing Incentive (April 1996-July 1997)

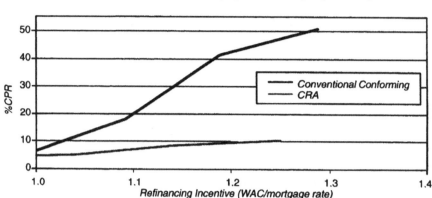

1. The mobility rates of low income borrowers are substantially below those of high income borrowers.
2. Borrowers with less equity in their properties are less likely to move or "trade-up" to another property.

Although we would expect regional economic conditions to influence the slope of the seasoning ramp, the loans in our sample are located in states that approximate the national average prepayment rate on conventional conforming loans. Thus, the difference in baseline seasoning ramps (prepayments caused by housing turnover only) between the CRA sample and the agency conforming loans is primarily a function of borrower demographics (low/moderate income versus high income prepayment behavior).

Sensitivity to Refinancing Opportunities

Exhibit 7 compares the average prepayment rate of CRA and agency loans conditional on the economic incentive to refinance (data from April 1996-July 1997). Clearly, CRA borrowers were less sensitive than agency borrowers given equivalent refinancing opportunities over the observation window. In fact no significant premium coupon/origination year cohort of CRA loans exhibited a single month prepayment rate above 20 CPR during the observation period despite sometimes large economic incentives to refinance.

The structural and behavioral characteristics of CRA loans/borrowers that are responsible for this finding are highlighted below.

1. *Favorable Loan Terms "Lock" Borrowers Into Their Loans and Limit Refinancing Alternatives.* An important feature of CRA origination programs is that

they provide very favorable financing terms for low and moderate income borrowers. In our CRA sample, 64% of the loans had LTVs above 80% with no private mortgage insurance, a combination that is not acceptable under normal FHLMC/FNMA underwriting guidelines. In addition, the average CRA loan rate was 72 basis points below the conforming rate. Although there is no structural impediment to refinancing (like a prepayment penalty) CRA borrowers do not have access to the liquid refinancing market available to most conforming borrowers. In addition, because of their unique financing terms and low average balances, they are less likely to be solicited by lenders to refinance.

While lenders are generally committed to providing refinancing choices to CRA borrowers, it is important to note that they have no additional incentive to refinance a CRA loan in their own portfolio, since that action constitutes the replacement of an existing CRA loan and does not change their lending distribution to the low/moderate income borrower segment. In conversations with several institutions, CRA lenders indicated that there was no systematic solicitation of these borrowers to refinance when interest rates decline. In practice, CRA lending programs focus on lending to new purchase borrowers in order to meet CRA requirements. As a result, CRA borrowers face the same refinancing transaction costs that most other borrowers face. Historical results confirm that CRA loans are predominantly purchase originations. Exhibit 8 compares the refinancing portion of originations in our CRA sample to that of FHLMC originations from 1991 to 1995. During the refinancing boom of 1993 the refinancing share of FHLMC originations mushroomed to a 12-month average of 58% while the CRA refinancing share peaked at only 20% of originations.

Exhibit 8: Refinancing Share of Originations

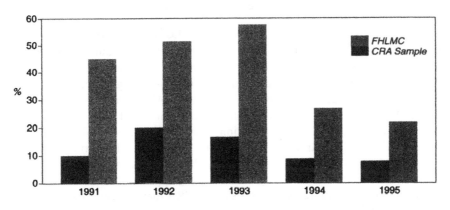

2. *Small Balances and High LTVs Reduce the Borrower's Economic Gain in a Refinancing Transaction.* The impact of loan size on prepayments is well recognized in the MBS markets. Our empirical studies have shown that agency pools with small average loan sizes tend to be much less prepayment sensitive (less negatively convex) than equivalent pools with large loan sizes. The reasoning is straightforward: the economics of refinancing a small balance are less attractive when rates fall assuming all borrowers face fixed refinancing transaction costs. The average loan size of our CRA sample was $64,878, 38% below the average conforming loan size of approximately $105,000. In addition, high LTVs limit cash-out refinancing transactions since there is generally little equity in the property. One notable difference between our CRA sample and newly originated CRA loans is that LTVs on new loans tend to be about 7% higher (our data sample LTV averaged 83% while new CRA loans tend to average closer to 90% LTVs).

3. *Low and Moderate Income Borrowers are More Payment Sensitive than Interest Rate Sensitive.* The low income borrower population is much more likely to have limited access to funds and/or have limited desire or ability to pay the out-of-pocket expenses associated with a refinancing transaction. CRA lenders indicated that because "affordable" housing programs were purchase-oriented programs, borrowers looking to refinance faced similar refinancing transaction costs as their conforming counterparts (CRA closing costs run in the 2% to 3% range). We suspect that a similar but less concentrated demographic effect in FNMA/FHLMC Low Loan Balance pools contributes to the stable prepayment behavior in that sector (loan size and income are highly correlated). The advantage of CRA securities is that investors know with complete certainty that the loans are originated to low and moderate income borrowers either on an income basis or a census tract basis. Investors also know the exact distribution of loan sizes in the pool and the exact terms under which the loans were originated. This should give investors added comfort with respect to future prepayment behavior.

CRA Prepayments Compared to VA Vendee Loans

The most comparable existing sector within the ABS/MBS universe in terms of borrower characteristics and historical prepayment experience can be found in VA Vendee loans. The VA Vendee program provides financing for properties it has acquired from defaulted borrowers under the VA's Loan Guarantee and VA Vendee Loan programs. Like CRA loans, these loans tend to be located in low/moderate income census tracts, in regions with low borrower mobility rates, and have small average loan balances ($65,000) and high LTV ratios. Like CRA loans, Vendee loans have exhibited a slow baseline prepayment rate (housing turnover rate) and little sensitivity to refinancing opportunities. However, Vendee loans tend to exhibit more extension risk than CRA loans because they are assumable. Exhibit 9 compares the historical prepayment experience of VNMA 922 (Vendee) to comparable 30-year GNMA issues through the severe 1992/93 refinancing cycle; it highlights the strong call protection exhibited by Vendee loans.

Exhibit 9: GNMA versus VA-Vendee Prepayments (1991 Issues)

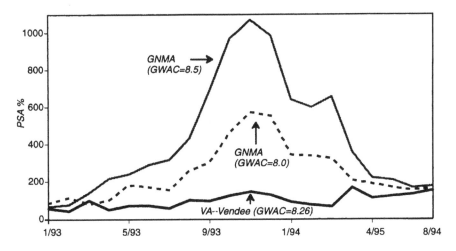

Exhibit 10: Cross-Sector Sensitivities

	Projected Prepayment Speeds (PSA)						
	−200	−100	−50	0	+50	+100	+200
CRA	264	172	142	120	108	103	100
VA Vendee	250	160	130	110	100	85	60
Conventional Conform-ing	844	401	232	165	144	134	113

CRA VALUATION RESULTS

From the investor's perspective, the most attractive feature of CRA-backed securities is that they are less negatively convex than agency conforming mortgages and many home equity securities. CRA securities tend to benefit from limited extension risk (they are priced to a slow base prepayment speed) and less call risk because of limited refinancing alternatives for the borrowers. To evaluate CRA-backed securities, we calibrated our agency conforming prepayment model in two ways. First, we slowed the housing turnover component of the model to be consistent with the slow baseline speed of CRA loans. Second, we tempered the CRA refinancing function to account for the CRA's lower sensitivity to interest rates.

Exhibit 10 compares the projected prepayment sensitivity profiles of CRA loans to agency conforming and VA Vendee loans (assuming current coupon collateral). The CRA prepayment profile is most similar to that of Vendee collateral, offering similar call protection in down interest rate scenarios. However, in up scenarios Vendee collateral extends more because VA Vendee loans are assumable.

Exhibit 11: Cross-Sector Nominal Spread Matrix

	Nominal Spread						
	1-Yr.	2-Yr.	3-Yr.	4-Yr.	5-Yr.	7-Yr.	10-Yr.
CRA	50	60	62	72	82	86	95
VA Vendee	45	57	62	69	75	85	95
Home Equities	55	53	58	64	75	90	98
Agency Plain Vanilla	60	65	70	85	90	100	108

Exhibit 12: Cross-Sector OAS Matrix

	Option Adjusted Spread*					
	2-Yr.	3-Yr.	4-Yr.	5-Yr.	7-Yr.	10-Yr.
CRA	48	39	45	54	55	57
Agency Plain Vanilla	20	21	22	25	35	38
Home Equities	43	34	28	40	60	77

* Pricing Date: 9/24/97
  Volatility: 15.96%
  Straight sequentials, near par pricing.

Using the CRA adjusted model, we can then compare CRA nominal and option-adjusted spreads to other sectors in the mortgage- and asset-backed markets as shown in Exhibits 11 and 12. The results shown in the exhibits suggest that on a nominal spread basis CRA securities tend to fall between home equities and agency plain vanillas and are comparable to VA Vendee spreads. However, on an option-adjusted spread basis, the stable prepayment characteristics of CRA loans reduce the convexity costs of CRA securities, benefiting their OAS results. CRA OAS's compare favorably to both home equities and agency plain vanillas in the 2- to 5-year part of the curve and fall between agency plain vanillas and home equities in the 7-year to 10-year part of the curve.[4]

---

[4] Home equities in the 7- to 10-year part of the curve benefit from limited extension due to shorter loan terms (15-20 years).

Chapter 11

Single Family Mortgage Revenue Bonds

Michael Marz
Vice Chairman
First Southwest Company

Frank J. Fabozzi, Ph.D., CFA
Adjunct Professor of Finance
School of Management
Yale University

INTRODUCTION

In 1968, Congress passed legislation permitting the use of tax-exempt bonds to obtain proceeds that would finance low- and moderate-cost housing. To obtain funding, most states created state housing finance agencies to issue tax-exempt housing bonds. The first issuance of housing bonds by state agencies was done in the early 1970s. In 1978, local governments began issuing housing bonds. Local government issuers include counties, cities, towns, and villages. These bonds are called *single family mortgage revenue bonds*, although they have been issued under other names such as residential mortgage revenue bonds, home ownership development bonds, and single family mortgage purchase bonds.

Historically, single family mortgage revenue bonds have been structured as either a mortgage purchase bond or a loans-to-lender bond. In the former structure, the proceeds from the bond issue are used to buy mortgages from lenders who have agreed to originate loans on behalf of the issuer. In a loans-to-lender bond, the proceeds from the issue are used to make collateralized loans to approved lending institutions that must use the borrowed funds to make mortgage loans. Today, a mortgage purchase bond is the most common structure used by state housing finance agencies and local issuers.

An *official statement* describing the issue and the issuer is prepared for new offerings. Municipal securities have legal opinions which are summarized in the official statement. The importance of the legal opinion is twofold. First, bond counsel determines if the issuer is indeed legally able to issue the securities. Second, bond counsel verifies that the issuer has properly prepared for the bond sale

171

by having enacted various required ordinances, resolutions, and trust indentures and without violating any other laws and regulations.

When market participants first attempt to evaluate mortgage revenue bonds, it is common to try to use the extensive research available from the taxable mortgage-backed securities market. Investors should resist this temptation. Although it is common for tax-exempt "qualified mortgage bonds" to be backed by Ginnie Mae, Fannie Mae or Freddie Mac, there are a lot of basic tax issues which make the analysis of these securities quite difficult. Because of their structural complexity and because much of the information needed for analysis of these securities is unavailable, the evaluation of mortgage revenue bonds even today is more art than science. In this chapter we will discuss the structure of these bonds and the difficulties associated with analyzing their cash flows.

THE COLLATERAL

First, let's review the collateral which backs these bond issues. The basic requirements of qualified mortgage bonds fall under Section 143 of the Internal Revenue Code. To be a "qualified bond" a single family bond must: (1) be a "qualified mortgage bond," (2) obtain a volume cap allocation under Section 146, which includes "private activity bonds," and (3) meet certain other requirements including a public approval process.

In qualified mortgage revenue bond issues, the individual loans must satisfy two types of requirements. First they must satisfy mortgage eligibility requirements. These include the residence requirement, first time home buyer requirement, the purchase price limitation, mortgagor income limitation, and the new mortgage and assumption requirement. Second, the individual loans must satisfy non-mortgage eligibility requirements. These are the special arbitrage rules for qualified mortgage bonds, the targeted area requirement, and the mortgage subsidiary recapture provisions.

Mortgage eligibility for these types of bond issues requires that in addition to real property, a residence may include stock in cooperative housing and mobile homes if they are permanently affixed to real property. The "principal" residence requirements may normally be satisfied by the execution of an affidavit by the mortgagor to the effect that the borrower intends to use the residence as a principal residence within at least 60 days after closing of the mortgage. The first time home buyer requirement generally states that mortgages under the bond program may not have had a mortgage interest deduction on their tax return in a principal residence within a 3-year period prior to the date the mortgage (for the bond program) is executed. Certain exceptions may exist for targeted areas which fulfill a special public purpose and for certain qualified home improvement or rehabilitation loans.

Virtually all single family mortgage revenue bonds provide that the "acquisition cost" of a residence may not exceed 90% of the "average area purchase price." The total costs are included in this consideration, and applied against the "statistical area" during the last 12 months for which such data exist. Mortgages under Section 143 programs have income limitations which state that family income may not exceed a certain percentage of an areas "applicable median family income." This is specific to any geographical region and thus can extenuate the regional aspects of the prepayment rate of all mortgages financed under an issuer's indenture.

The last point to be made in respect to mortgage eligibility requirements for tax-exempt bond issues is the most powerful. The IRS Code requires that a portion of the "subsidy" provided to mortgagors through qualified mortgage bond programs be "recaptured." A basic generalization of this requirement is that the mortgagor must rebate to the Treasury up to 50% of the gain, if any, realized on the disposition of the bond-financed residence for up to nine years or as a result of the mortgagor's death. The bond issuer is required to provide notice to the borrower at the closing settlement and within 90 days following the loan closing notifying the mortgagor of the federally subsidized amount of the loan.

The loans purchased by an housing agency will consist of loans insured by the Federal Housing Administration (FHA), Veterans Administration (VA), or Rural Housing Service (RHS), or conventional loans (i.e., those not insured by one of these entities). For conventional loans, there may be private mortgage insurance. For example, to be included in the mortgage loan portfolio of the Texas Department of Housing and Community Affairs, the trust indenture requires: "Mortgage Loans must (i) be federally insured or guaranteed, (ii) have a principal balance not exceeding 80% of the lower of the appraised value of the purchase price of the property securing the Mortgage Loan (the "Value"), or (iii) be insured by a private mortgage insurer approved by the Department in an amount by which the loan exceeds 80% of the Value."

The composition of the mortgage loan portfolio for the Texas Department of Housing and Community Affairs as of 1996 was:

Loan type	No. of prior loans	Outstanding principal amount	Percent of total (%)
Conventional	3,045	$134,711,226	44.02
FHA	2,967	155,907,174	50.94
VA	333	14,792,645	4.83
RHS	9	641,573	0.21
Total	6,354	$306,052,618	100.00%

EMBEDDED CALL OPTIONS

The non-mortgage eligibility requirements relate more to issuers than to bondholders. As investors attempt to analyze the properties of single family mortgage revenue bonds, the primary consideration usually relates to the wide variety of call options embedded in a given structure. Mortgage revenue bonds can be more complex than some of the most complicated classes of collateralized mortgage obligations. Unlike a generic passthrough security, mortgage revenue bonds tend to have serial maturities. Thus, based on stated final maturities, bonds are redeemed first from scheduled principal payments on the underlying mortgages and then usually called with the proceeds of prepayments. The effect of this serialization of maturities means that most of these bond structures resemble sequential CMOs. For total-rate-of-return investors, option adjusting the duration and convexity of these type bonds is particularly difficult because of the large uncertainty in the speed of prepayments on the underlying collateral.

Prepayments

It is a widely accepted practice to use the GNMA market as a starting point for making a prepayment assumption. It is important to remember that the unpredictability of this class of mortgages is due to their relatively small size and the significant geographical bias inherent to an issuer. Investors will find that the lag in prepayments to corresponding levels of interest rate movements are greater in tax-exempt mortgage bonds than in their taxable counterparts. Primarily the difference is the true passthrough nature of typical taxable mortgage bond structures. Single family mortgage revenue bonds commonly have semiannual redemption cycles, as well as provisions which require notice of call redemptions as far as 30 to 60 days in advance. The lengthy intervals between prepayment calls also has a smoothing effect on prepayment redemption activity. Market participants can attempt to translate information about how many bonds from a given issue have been called into an estimate of what the prepayment rate on the underlying mortgages has been.

The use of municipal prepayment indexes can be a good relative value analysis tool for investors. Using an index can be an easy measure of estimating prepayments and will help rule out the trends of small pools which may exhibit random aberrations. Geographic bias is a significant factor in any mortgage pool. Insight into state prepayment differentials are provided in the *Kenny Housing Call Report* published by J.J. Kenny and the *Merrill Lynch Municipal Prepayment Redemption Index*. Prepayment differentials among various bond structures are often not reflected in municipal bond pricing. The use of index analysis can aid in active management and help portfolio managers exploit opportunities.

Conclusions drawn from this type of analysis must take into account the specific structure of each bond issue and each indenture under which a specific issuer operates.

Other Call Features

Aside from prepayments, other call options which may be specific to single family mortgage revenue bonds are unused proceeds calls, surplus calls, cross calls, and optional redemptions.

Unused Proceeds Call

Since 1989, federal law has required a mandatory redemption of any unused bond proceeds within 42 months of the date of issuance. Once a new money bond issue is priced the mortgage origination period is limited and any unspent proceeds must be used to redeem a corresponding amount of bonds.

The conventional market assumption is that unused proceeds calls are unavoidable consequences of interest rate declines which might follow the issuance of a mortgage revenue bond. Investors should review the program's underwriting guidelines, who the specific mortgage originators are, and what the historical issuer originations have been. Although the market does not consistently discriminate between different bond issues based on unused proceeds call risk, investors may find value in the substantial differences which do in fact exist due to the wide range of issuer origination efficiency. Municipal bond pricing does not distinguish between single family mortgage revenue bonds on the basis of unused proceeds call risk. Historically, redemptions have exhibited interest rate cyclical behavior. These calls reached record levels following the sharp decline in interest rates in 1993.

Although interest rate declines following the issuance of a single family mortgage revenue bond are virtually a prerequisite for an unused proceeds call to exist, it does not explain the disparate levels of call that have been made. Issue size, continuous origination pipeline, and ability to warehouse loans in advance of bond sales will produce results which can be contrary to conventional wisdom.

Surplus Calls

Under Section 143, a primary rule which applies to the mortgages originated under the bond program is that the "effective rate of interest" may not exceed the yield (true interest cost) on the bond issue by more than 1.125%. The result of this allowable excess is surplus calls. Surplus exists from the spread between the net mortgage rate and the bond rate. Other structural items such as over-collateralization, interest earnings, and excess reserve funds can provide the dollars to trigger surplus calls.

Cross Calls

Another element which exists as a call option on single family mortgage revenue bonds is the *cross call option*. Cross calling is a practice followed by some state housing finance agencies, in which repayments from lower interest rate loans financed by one "issue" are applied to pay bonds of a different "issue." The appendix to this chapter provides an example of this option from the official statement of the Department of Housing and Community Affairs Single Family Mortgage Revenue Bonds 1996 Series D and Series E.

Here again is where investors are forced to do all their homework. Although it is more common for state issuers than local housing agencies, an authority with bonds issued under the same master bond indenture or resolution, commonly referred to as "open indentures," will cross call their bonds. That results in more interest savings to the issuer than if it had called a lower interest rate bond of the issue that originated such lower interest rate mortgages. Thus, investors should initially assume that the issuer will use or not use its cross call option in the worst possible way from the bond buyer's point of view. Under an open indenture, although unlikely in the market environment at the time of this writing, issuers sometimes retain the right to "recycle" funds by making new mortgage loans with the proceeds of prepayments. Recycling works only if new mortgages will pay a high enough rate to service outstanding bonds. Given all these uncertainties, bondholders dealing with bonds issued under open indentures would be wise to make very conservative assumptions in estimating effective redemption dates.

Optional Redemption

The last major call option generic to single family mortgage bonds is optional redemption. The municipal market standard is that housing bonds are sold with 10-year 102 calls against optional redemption. Over the last 20 years, the bulk of the outstanding housing bond new issue volume was created between 1980 through 1985. It was not until the bulk of outstanding single family mortgage revenue bonds reached their optional call date and became eligible for current refundings that empirical evidence could evaluate the importance of optional call behavior. A variety of motives can exist for the exercise of an optional refunding, some of which are not particularly sensitive to the levels of interest rates.

An overview of what some mortgage revenue bondholders have experienced reveals a wide array of justifications, all of which have caused rapid amortizations of their bonds. Issuers often are motivated to provide deeply discounted loans which can be achieved by blending these loans with higher coupon mortgages to pay the debt service on a refunding bond while remaining within legal arbitrage limits. Another reason for optional redemption is transferring mortgages to restructure new indentures and bolster asset/liability ratios. Restructuring can also allow outdated indenture language to be removed. Needless to say, buyers of single family mortgage revenue bonds cannot focus solely on prepayment options. In fact, the list of characteristics and considerations may seem unbearable. Invariably, proper analysis will tend to produce an even shorter average life than an estimate which is based upon any single embedded call.

CREDIT RISK

While municipal bonds at one time were considered second in safety only to U.S. Treasury securities, today there are concerns about the credit risks of municipal securities. Concern about credit risk came out of the New York City billion-dollar financial crisis in 1975. On February 25, 1975, the state of New York's Urban

Development Corporation defaulted on a $100 million note issue that was the obligation of New York City; many market participants had been convinced that the state of New York would not allow the issue to default. Although New York City was able later to obtain a $140 million revolving credit from banks to cure the default, lenders became concerned that the city would face difficulties in repaying its accumulated debt, which stood at $14 billion on March 31, 1975. This financial crisis sent a loud and clear warning to market participants in general — regardless of supposedly ironclad protection for the bondholder, when issuers such as large cities have severe financial difficulties, the financial stakes of public employee unions, vendors, and community groups may be dominant forces in balancing budgets. This reality was reinforced by the federal bankruptcy law that took effect in October 1979, which made it easier for the issuer of a municipal security to go into bankruptcy.

The nationally recognized statistical rating organizations assign ratings to single family mortgage revenue bonds. In addition, to the guarantees by the insurers of individual mortgages, these bonds can be credit enhanced — municipal bond insurance or state appropriation provision.

Insured Bonds

Insured bonds, in addition to being secured by the issuer's revenue, are also backed by insurance policies written by commercial insurance companies. Insurance on a municipal bond is an agreement by an insurance company to pay the bondholder any bond principal and/or coupon interest that is due on a stated maturity date but that has not been paid by the bond issuer. Once issued, this municipal bond insurance usually extends for the term of the bond issue, and it cannot be canceled by the insurance company.

Most insured municipal bonds are insured by one of the following insurance companies that are primarily in the business of insuring municipal bonds: AMBAC Indemnity Corporation; Capital Guaranty Insurance Company; Connie Lee Insurance Company; Financial Guaranty Insurance Company; Financial Security Assurance, Inc.; and, Municipal Bond Investors Insurance Corporation.

Appropriation-Backed Obligations

Housing agencies or authorities of several states have issued single family mortgage revenue bonds that carry a potential state liability for making up shortfalls in the issuing entities obligation. The appropriation of funds from the state's general tax revenue must be approved by the state legislation. However, the state's pledge is not binding. A debt obligation with this nonbinding pledge of tax revenue is called a *moral obligation bond*. Because a moral obligation bond requires legislative approval to appropriate the funds, it is classified as an *appropriation-backed obligation*.

An example of the legal language describing the procedure for a moral obligation bond that is enacted into legislation is as follows:

In order to further assure the maintenance of each such debt reserve fund, there shall be annually apportioned and paid to the agency for deposit in each debt reserve fund such sum, if any, as shall be certified by the chairman of the agency to the governor and director of the budget as necessary to restore such reserve fund to an amount equal to the debt reserve fund requirement. The chairman of the agency shall annually, on or before December I, make and deliver to the governor and director of the budget his certificate stating the sum or sums, if any, required to restore each such debt reserve fund to the amount aforesaid, and the sum so certified, if any, shall be apportioned and paid to the agency during the then current state fiscal year.

The purpose of the moral obligation pledge is to enhance the creditworthiness of the issuing entity. The first moral obligation bond was issued by the Housing Finance Agency of the state of New York. Historically, most moral obligation debt has been self supporting; that is, it has not been necessary for the state of the issuing entity to make an appropriation. In those cases in which state legislatures have been called upon to make an appropriation, they have. For example, the states of New York and Pennsylvania did this for bonds issued by their Housing Finance Agency.

Moody's and Standard & Poor's appear to have a different view of moral obligation bonds. Moody's appears to view the moral obligation feature as more literary than legal. Therefore, it does not consider this feature a credit strength or enhancement. Standard & Poor's appears to view moral obligation bonds as being no lower than one rating category below a state's own general obligation bonds. Its rationale is based upon the implied state support for the bonds and the marked implications for that state's own general obligation bonds should it ever fail to honor its moral obligations.

ALTERNATIVE MINIMUM TAX

Tax-exempt municipal bonds are not treated uniformly with respect to federal income taxes. *Taxable income* is the amount on which the tax liability is determined. For an individual, it is found by subtracting the personal exemption allowance and itemized deductions (other than those deductible in arriving at adjusted gross income) from adjusted gross income. The *alternative minimum taxable income* (AMTI) is a taxpayer's taxable income with certain adjustments for specified tax preferences designed to cause AMTI to approximate economic income. For both individuals and corporations, a taxpayer's tax liability is the greater of (1) the tax computed at regular tax rates on taxable income and (2) the tax computed at a lower rate on AMTI. This parallel tax system, the *alternative minimum tax* (AMT), is designed to prevent taxpayers from avoiding significant tax liability as a result of taking advantage of exclusions from gross income, deductions, and tax credits otherwise allowed under the Internal Revenue Code.

Some municipal issues are subject to the AMT, while others are not. Those issues subject to the AMT will trade at a higher yield to compensate for the tax effect. For the Texas Department of Housing and Community Affairs Single Family Mortgage Revenue Bonds, the 1996 Series D was subject to the AMT while the 1996 Series E was not.

CONCLUSION

Local governments have been issuing single family mortgages revenue bonds since 1978. Traditionally, single family mortgage revenue bonds have taken one of two forms: loans-to-lender bond structures and mortgage purchase bond structures. Mortgage purchase bonds are the prevalent form today. Single family mortgage revenue bonds are usually secured by the mortgages and mortgage loan repayments on single-family homes.

Collateral for single family mortgage revenue bonds must meet both mortgage and non-mortgage eligibility requirements. Along with having both personal income and residential cost limitations, mortgage eligibility requires not only a first time home buyer, but that this first home be the buyer's principal residence. Non-mortgage eligibility requirements include: limited origination period, the special arbitrage rules for qualified mortgage bonds, the targeted area requirement, and the mortgage subsidiary recapture provisions. An additional and important requirement is the government subsidy recapture which induces the mortgagor to rebate to the government up to 50% of the gain realized on the sale of a mortgage assisted residence if liquidated within nine years of purchase.

In evaluating single family mortgage revenue bonds, one must remember several points: (1) do not use taxable mortgage-backed valuation techniques; (2) compare insured bonds with uninsured equivalents; (3) consider alternative minimum tax implications; (4) with respect to appropriation bonds, one must consider S&P and Moody's rating concerns along with the mortgage eligibility requirements; (5) be aware that single family mortgage revenue bonds are riddled with esoteric call options which compound in complexity as a direct function of maturity serialization; and, (6) the rating effects.

The structure and the difficulties that result in analyzing the cash flows of single family mortgage revenue bonds present numerous problems. Given the number of variables involved and the intricacy of their relationships, it is easy to see why valuation of mortgage revenue bonds is still considered more of an art than a science.

APPENDIX

Example of a Call Cross Option: Department of Housing and Community Affairs Single Family Mortgage Revenue Bonds Series D and Series E

Prior Mortgage Loans

The proceeds of certain Single Family Mortgage Revenue Bonds and certain other moneys have been used to purchase Mortgage Loans (including Mortgage Certificates representing Mortgage Loans). All Mortgage Loans acquired to date under the Trust Indenture are fixed rate loans with terms not exceeding 30 years. The following table summarizes certain information regarding the Mortgage Loans (including Mortgage Certificates representing Mortgage Loans) acquired with the proceeds of the Single Family Mortgage Revenue Bonds. For a more detailed examination of the Mortgage Loans, the portfolio of Mortgage Loans, delinquent Mortgage Loans and information regarding Mortgage Loan insurance, see "APPENDIX F-1 -- DEPARTMENT'S MORTGAGE LOAN PORTFOLIO." Unless otherwise specified, all information is as of July 31, 1996.

Series	Mortgage Loan Rate	Original Amount of Mortgage Loans Purchased	Mortgage Loans Outstanding
1980 Series A	11.20%	$133,937,742	$21,816,414
1982 Series A	13.93	14,212,374	495,828
1983 Series A	10.79	216,229,754	42,579,408
1984 Series A/B	12.10/9.75	171,555,575	22,743,819
1985 Series A	9.75	118,045,235	38,379,542
1985 Series B	9.70/9.55	29,176,697	8,163,934
1985 Series C	8.20	27,726,038	13,179,728
1986 Series A	8.70	73,021,140	36,617,156
1986 Series B	7.99/7.90	81,998,265	46,549,484
1987 Series B	7.99/8.05/8.70	69,454,306	41,452,419
1995 Series A-1/B-1	6.65	34,147,391	34,074,886
Total		$969,504,517	$306,052,618

As of September 30, 1996, $38,837,260 of monies remained in the Mortgage Loan Fund relating to the 1995 Series A-1/B-1 Bonds to purchase Mortgage Certificates bearing an interest rate of 6.65%. Except for that amount reserved for targeted area loans, substantially all of such remaining moneys have been committed to the origination of Mortgage Loans for specified borrowers. In addition, $15,595,000 of lendable proceeds were deposited in the Mortgage Loan Fund relating to the 1996 Series A Bonds and 1996 Series B Bonds on October 1, 1996 and will be used to originate Mortgage Loans evidenced by Mortgage Certificates. Such funds are designated for certain limited geographic areas in the State for a period of eighteen months. Such proceeds will be used to purchase Mortgage Certificates bearing an interest rate of 6.95%. Although the Department expects that all of the remaining lendable proceeds relating to the 1995 Series A-1/B-1 Bonds and the 1996 Series A Bonds and 1996 Series B Bonds will be used to purchase Mortgage Certificates, it can give no assurance that the availability of such monies will not affect the ability of participating Mortgage Lenders to fully originate the lendable proceeds of the Series D/E Bonds. Failure to fully originate the lendable proceeds of the Series D/E Bonds could result in their early redemption at par. See "THE SERIES D/E BONDS -- Redemption Provisions."

Since the inception of the Department's Program, the Department has foreclosed on approximately 2,888 Mortgage Loans having an outstanding principal balance, at the time of foreclosure, of $149,972,948. The Department continues to hold title to property securing 23 of such Mortgage Loans. In an effort to maximize its return on real estate owned by the Department as a result of foreclosures, the Department has entered into a contract with outside contractors to manage, maintain and arrange for sales, in conjunction with real estate brokers, of such real estate owned. See APPENDIX F-1 -- DEPARTMENT'S MORTGAGE LOAN PORTFOLIO for information concerning the Department's current delinquency and foreclosure rates with respect to the Mortgage Loans.

Source: Page 16 of Official Statement

B. Credit Analysis

Chapter 12

The Default and Loss Experience of Nonagency MBS

Thomas Gillis
Managing Director
Standard and Poor's

INTRODUCTION

Private placements initially dominated the early years of the nonagency MBS market. These privately placed transactions (in the late 1970s and through the early 1980s), kept their loss experience confidential. As the public nonagency MBS market emerged, so did the reporting of loss information. Investors and analysts' appetite and demand for credit information on the loans underlying these transactions grew along with the whole loan market. Loss information, reported on only 43% of all outstanding publicly rated pools in 1994 has risen to approximately 77% in 1996.

The improvements made in the dissemination of credit information has been significant. However, further credit related disclosure is necessary and will only advance investor comfort with the product. Additional information about real estate owned (REO) would help predict future losses more accurately. A loan that goes from foreclosure to REO will have the effect of reducing reported foreclosures without increasing reported losses. These properties in REO are generally losses waiting to be incurred. Information with respect to estimated property value, location, and accrued interest to date would greatly enhance investor's ability to predict near term losses. Differences also exist in defining currently reported information. Nevertheless, the market is heading in the right direction, making more information available and accessible to the market. In this chapter, a review of loss information on 1,130 whole-loan pools selected from the Standard & Poor's data base is provided.

Since the market's inception, Standard & Poor's has rated approximately 2,600 issues, representing over $340 billion of nonagency mortgage securities. The loss analysis presented in this chapter focuses solely on pools of first-mortgage loans securing publicly issued nonagency mortgage-backed securities that were rated by Standard & Poor's. The sample was drawn from all transactions outstanding as of June 1996 and approximately 140 issues that have matured. Actual loss data are used where available. Otherwise, a loss is assumed to be the difference between the original credit support provided and the current credit support outstanding.

LOSS EXPERIENCE

CMO loss experience is a function of the foreclosure and loss experience on the loans securing the CMOs. If all of the mortgages pay, the CMO will pay. If mortgages default and losses are incurred, those losses will be covered by a third-party credit enhancement or allocated to the appropriate classes of the MBS.

Because credit protection and subordinated classes are barriers against loss to senior classes, the loss experience at the loan level can differ significantly from the loss experience of the securities supported. Since most senior classes are rated either AA or AAA, these classes receive the greatest amount of credit protection. Credit protection for senior classes rated by Standard & Poor's has averaged 9%, down from 10.5% in December 1993. Lower average loss coverage numbers reflect the high volume of lower risk mortgage pools issued as a result of the refinance boom in 1993 and 1994.

A simple rule of thumb for assessing credit protection is to convert it into the range of foreclosure and loss scenarios that it protects against. Credit protection of 9% translates into a range of potential default scenarios: from 100% of loans being foreclosed upon and incurring a 9% loss on average to a foreclosure rate of 9% and incurring a 100% loss. The typical loss incurred on a mortgage will approximate 30% to 40%. At an average loss of 40%, credit protection of 9% will guard against 22.5% of the loans in the pool being foreclosed upon.

LOSS ANALYSIS

Our analysis compares losses at the loan pool level and not the security level. Since securities often represent less than 100% of the unpaid principal balance of the loans securing the issue, the analysis would not be an accurate measure of losses at the security level. Most nonagency MBS are multi-class securities, with the subordinate class, which is in a first-loss position, generally retained by the seller.

The 1,130 pools of mortgages surveyed had approximately $254 billion in original principal amount. The pools had an average balance of $183 million. To date, losses total $1.6 billion, averaging $1,427,984 per pool, representing 63 basis points. These pools are protected with approximately $18.8 billion of credit support, an average of 9.0% per pool. Exhibit 1 provides a breakdown by year of security issuance.

Any loss analysis performed for mortgages needs to be conducted on the basis of the origination year. As Exhibit 1 indicates, mortgage losses are a function of time. The losses increase over time, with the newest pools experiencing the lowest losses. This is a normal occurrence, given the nature of mortgages. A foreclosure on average takes over a year to complete, making any losses in the first year unlikely.

Exhibit 1: Breakdown of Loan Pool Level ($ Millions)

Year	Number of Pools	Total $ Amount	Total Losses	Losses as % Initial $ Amount
1986*	91	7,474.2	91.3	1.22
1987	76	7,857.6	99.2	1.25
1988	92	8,527.2	148.3	1.74
1989	91	9,585.3	209.5	2.09
1990	71	10,180.7	294.2	2.79
1991	84	15,257.6	290.0	0.75
1992	160	53,503.1	321.7	0.54
1993	178	38,442.6	120.0	0.27
1994	199	41,090.6	30.7	0.07
1995	88	17,695.5	8.7	0.04
Total	1,130	209,614.4	1,613.6	0.64

* Includes transactions issued prior to 1986.

Exhibit 2: Residential Default Curve

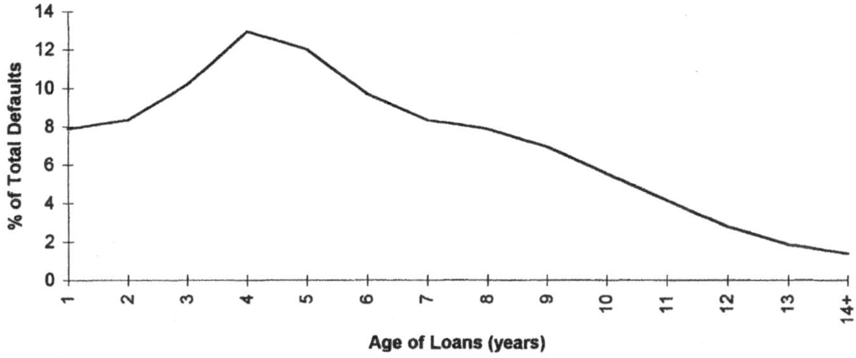

Likewise, as the mortgage amortizes, losses become more remote after a certain passage of time, generally five to seven years. This is commonly referred to as the *loss curve*. The losses, being reported in the 1995 transactions, are a result of including seasoned, and on occasion delinquent, mortgages in some of those transactions. Standard & Poor's surveillance of outstanding losses will measure a transaction's performance using as a proxy the default curve in Exhibit 2.

Using this curve, we can equate the losses experienced for pools originated over different years. If each pool's future losses follow this curve, a projection of the total losses that will be incurred over the life of these transactions can be made.

While the curve provides a useful way to compare pools originated in different years, it too has its shortcomings. Each pool has its own loss curve, which can vary substantially from another. Pools with little seasoning render the use of the curve less reliable. Likewise, the more years a pool has seasoned beyond its origination date, the more weight can be placed on the loss curve analysis. The loss curve is a conservative approach, pushing more losses out into the future than may actually occur.

Exhibit 3: Actual versus Projected Losses

Year	Actual Losses		Projected Losses	
	Dollar (000)	Percentage	Dollar (000)	Percentage
1986*	91,269	1.22	97,115	1.30
1987	99,161	1.25	117,685	1.50
1988	148,339	1.74	191,876	2.25
1989	209,520	2.09	301,728	3.15
1990	294,233	2.79	481,481	4.73
1991	290,000	0.75	564,312	3.70
1992	321,700	0.54	817,535	1.53
1993	120,000	0.27	454,718	1.18
1994	30,700	0.07	189,506	0.46
1995	8,700	0.04	110,546	0.62

* Includes transactions issued prior to 1986.

Exhibit 3 tabulates losses projected for the life of the pools sold each year, assuming all the pools follow the same pattern of loss as determined by the default curve in Exhibit 2. As Exhibit 3 indicates, losses have been and are projected to be quite volatile from origination year to origination year. Losses are projected to average 2.0% of the initial principal balance for the 10-year period, with a standard deviation of 1.4.

The impact of the rolling recession can be seen as losses from 1988 through 1991 stand out as all being higher than average. The 1994 and 1995 book of transactions is less reliable, because there has not been enough time yet to judge the ultimate performance of these transactions. The volatility of the historical loss performance demonstrates the importance of the economic cycle in determining future losses. Mortgages originated at the peak, the Northeast in 1988-1989 and California in 1990-1991, are accumulating losses at a significant pace, in spite of little relative difference in their risk profile (excluding the RTC in 1991).

Exhibit 4 provides additional information about range of loss experienced by pool within an origination year. The exhibit segregates the number of pools by dollar loss into six categories. Two thirds of all pools have experienced equal to or less than $500,000 in losses, with only 6% exceeding $5 million in losses. However, looking at the peak loss years of 1988 through 1991 the distribution of losses changes considerably. In those years, pools that have experienced zero losses occur at less than half the rate of all outstanding transactions. Nonagency MBS that have experienced losses of $5 million or more during the 1988 through 1991 time period occur at almost twice the rate of the overall population.

ABOUT THE DATA

Standard & Poor's data base, which is one of the most extensive in the industry, required some adjustments in order to produce this analysis. Reporting differences from one issuer to another and the complexity of the data make precise measurements not possible.

Exhibit 4: Pool Losses

Year	Zero	$500,000	$1 million	$5 million	$10 million	>$10 million
1986*	37	26	10	14	2	2
1987	26	17	10	17	5	1
1988	19	27	10	31	3	2
1989	22	7	13	34	13	2
1990	21	5	4	22	10	9
1991	27	28	12	16	0	1
1992	59	16	10	60	10	5
1993	93	36	22	23	2	2
1994	138	52	5	3	1	0
1995	65	22	1	0	0	0
Total	507	236	97	220	46	24
% Total	45%	21%	9%	19%	4%	2%
1988-1991	26%	20%	12%	30%	8%	4%

Header spanning: Number of Pools with Total Losses not Exceeding

* Includes transactions issued prior to 1986.

For purposes of this analysis, all loss comparisons are made on the pools backing the transactions and not the specific issues. Issuers offering one series backed by two distinctive pools of mortgages are treated as two pools. Similarly, multiple series backed by the same pool of mortgages are treated as one pool. All second mortgage and most bond insured transactions were eliminated. Other pools are eliminated because of the lack of timely information.

Precise loss data are available on only 77% of the pools. The loss data for the vast majority of the pools were as of June 1996. When actual loss information was available, an amount equal to the difference between initial and current support levels was used as a proxy. In most cases, the change in loss coverage will overstate actual losses.

Bond insured transactions were used where loss information was available, but excluded entirely from all calculations involving initial loss coverage. This adjustment was made to prevent the potential of the 100% covered bond insured transactions from skewing the data.

All losses are rounded to the nearest thousand. For senior/sub transactions, the subordinated levels are added to the certificate amounts to approximate the total pool size. The size of the sample, notwithstanding these adjustments, should be useful for analysis of the nonagency MBS market.

FACTORS INFLUENCING LOSS

Four major factors influence losses: economic, underwriting, loan to value, and payment structure. The economic factor is the most important of these as the above exhibits demonstrate. Standard & Poor's recently announced that its residential loss model will now adjust loss coverage based on the pool's exposure to local economic strength or weakness. A regional analysis is performed through the use of a proprietary index that measures an area's residential home price stability and vulnerability to future price declines.

The residential price stability index, designed by DRI/McGraw-Hill for Standard & Poor's, focuses on four main factors: housing price trends, housing affordability, migration, and industry concentration. Standard & Poor's and DRI/McGraw-Hill determined these factors to have the most predictive ability after an in-depth study of the nation's largest metropolitan areas. Depending on the location of the property, an adjustment is made to the assumed loss severity depending on characteristics unique to that location.

Within any given economic environment, additional factors will play a role in determining loss experience. Underwriting is one of the more influential factors. Conservative and diligent underwriting provides the best defense against future economic uncertainty. Loans underwritten to less stringent standards are more vulnerable to losses.

Poor underwriting standards were prevalent during the 1988-1991 peak loss years and made a significant contribution to the losses now being experienced from those origination years. Low document and accelerated underwriting programs became the norm. Originators tried to offset borrower quality with additional equity without success. The recent analysis performed by developers of automated underwriting systems indicate that borrower quality is a major explanatory variable in assessing future default probabilities. Income and employment should be verified, along with the source of the mortgagor's down payment. Credit scores and automated underwriting are relatively new tools available to the mortgage market and should have a positive impact on determining underlying credit quality of a pool's mortgagors.

Equity in the home can offset all other factors in mitigating or eliminating the loss potential of a mortgage. However, this is more theoretical than practical in that LTVs of less than 50% are necessary to mitigate losses in the most dire economic environments.

Loan pools composed of only 50% or lower LTVs are not a significant factor in our 1,130 pool sample. Certainly higher LTV mortgages can be found in our sample, and represent additional risk.

High LTV mortgages reduce the primary safety feature of a mortgage, which is asset protection. A 95% LTV provides a built-in loss feature if a mortgagor defaults before any significant appreciation occurs. The 5%, that is, equity is insufficient to cover foreclosure costs, guaranteeing a loss upon foreclosure. If it were not for the presence of primary mortgage insurance, there would be little incentive to originate these mortgages at all from a credit perspective.

Most pools will include a spattering of LTVs ranging from 95% to 60%. While concentrations of loans above 80% LTV is a definite indicator of risk, pools with weighted average LTVs of between 70% and 80% are not always useful in differentiating risk. The lower LTVs of loans originated under limited and no-document programs of the late 1980s turned out to be ineffective in deterring foreclosures.

Payment structures have a direct impact on future losses. Depending on the loan's payment structure, the chances of a default can be mitigated or increased. The traditional fixed-rate, fully amortizing mortgage is the safest payment structure.

The fully amortizing mortgage, along with insurance, was promoted by the Federal Housing Administration after the Great Depression to attract lenders who had left the market after incurring major losses on partially amortizing and interest-only mortgages. These balloon mortgages can still be found in the market today. Balloon mortgages increase the risk of loss by adding the risk of refinancing to the normal risk that a mortgagor will default.

The fixed-rate, fully-amortizing mortgage is structured ideally with respect to a mortgagor's income. Adjustable-rate and graduated-payment mortgages, while fully amortizing, add the additional risk that the borrower will not be able to maintain income growth that is commensurate with a rising mortgage payment.

Measuring all of the factors that influenced risk of loss can be a daunting task. To assist issuers, investors and analysts, Standard and Poor's recently introduced its residential analytic model "LEVELS™" to the market. Standard & Poor's LEVELS™ provides a loan by loan analysis with estimates of the necessary loss coverage for all rating categories.

ASSESSING FUTURE LOSSES

Investors have little information about a whole-loan pool to judge the numerous factors affecting loss. Credit protection, to cover potential risks, is based on rating agency risk assessments for loan pools. Credit protection puts all pools on an equal footing, reducing unnecessary concern with the risk of any individual mortgage pool. Knowledge about the risk factors and related loss experience can only enhance the quality of an investor's decision.

Exhibit 5 indicates S&P's experience of measuring loss coverage with risk. The amount of loss coverage has varied as a percentage of initial pool balances from a low of 7.5% to a high of 13.4%. Coverage for projected total losses fluctuates inversely with projected losses. The 1994 and 1995 data are too early in their life cycle to be considered reliable. The 1990 year projects the lowest level of coverage for projected losses of 1.80 times, is heavily influenced by Guardian Savings and Loan Association, Huntington Beach, CA loss experience. Guardian's losses account for 37% of all pools originated in 1990. In fact Guardian and the Resolution Trust Corp. account for only 5% of total issuance and 31% of total losses.

Exhibit 5: Measuring Loss Coverage with Risk

Year	Initial Pool Balance (Million $)	Initial $ Loss Coverage (Million $)	Initial Loss Coverage (%)	Projected Losses (Million $)	Ratio of Initial Loss Coverage to Projected Losses
1986*	7,437.8	600.5	8.1	97.12	6.18
1987	7,857.6	600.3	7.6	117.68	5.10
1988	8,527.2	753.5	8.8	191.88	3.93
1989	9,585.3	906.5	9.5	301.73	3.00
1990	10,180.7	866.7	8.5	481.48	1.80
1991	15,257.6	2,047.9	13.4	564.31	3.63
1992	53,053.0	5,198.2	9.7	817.53	6.36
1993	38,442.6	3,210.6	8.4	454.72	7.06
1994	41,090.6	3,097.1	7.5	189.51	16.34
1995	17,695.5	1,536.0	8.7	110.55	13.89

* Includes transactions issued prior to 1986.

Chapter 13

The Rating Agencies' Approach

Douglas L. Bendt
President
Mortgage Risk Assessment Corporation

Chuck Ramsey
Chief Executive Officer
Mortgage Risk Assessment Corporation

Frank J. Fabozzi, Ph.D., CFA
Adjunct Professor of Finance
School of Management
Yale University

INTRODUCTION

Credit analysis of nonagency mortgage-backed securities relies upon an unusual combination of large-scale statistical aggregate analysis and micro loan-by-loan analysis. This combination arises from knowing that out of a pool of 1,000 newly originated mortgages, it is virtually certain that at least ten will be defaulted upon and go into foreclosure, but there is no way of knowing *which* ten.

The expectation that ten or more homeowners will default is based on studies of millions of mortgages conducted by private mortgage insurers, federal agencies, and the four major credit rating agencies. But not all of these studies are relevant to the default experience of mortgages collateralizing nonagency mortgage-backed securities.

For example, studies by private mortgage companies focus only on mortgage defaults on loans with high loan-to-value (LTV) ratios, as would those done on FHA/VA mortgages. And by definition, studies of mortgages that meet Fannie Mae and Freddie Mac standards are not relevant. That leaves studies by Standard & Poor's Corporation, Moody's Investors Service, Fitch, and Duff & Phelps.[1]

---

[1] "Moody's Approach to Rating Residential Mortgage Passthroughs," *Moody's Investors Service Structured Finance and Research Commentary* (New York, NY: Moody's Investors Service, 1990; revised November 1996); Standard & Poor's Ratings Group, *Residential Mortgage Criteria* (New York: McGraw Hill, 1996); *Rating of Residential Mortgage-Backed Securities* (New York, NY: Duff & Phelps Credit Company, 1995); *Fitch Mortgage Default Model* (New York, NY: Fitch Investors Service, Inc.,1993); and, "Fitch IBCA Residential Mortgage-Backed Securities Criteria" (New York, NY: Fitch IBCA, Inc., December 1998).

Exhibit I: Assumed Default Frequencies

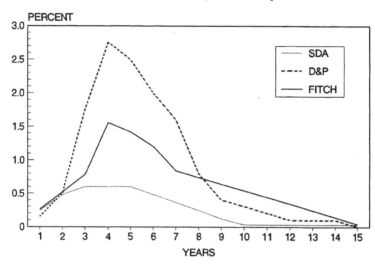

This chapter reviews the approach these agencies take in evaluating the loss potential of defaults of nonagency mortgages and presents new evidence about additional factors influencing losses. Rating agencies need to evaluate the magnitude of potential loss of a pool of loans to determine the amount of credit support the issuer is required to implement to achieve the desired credit ratings. Their approaches consist of four parts: (1) frequency of default; (2) severity of loss given default; (3) pool characteristics or the structure of the pool; and (4) credit enhancement or the structure of the security.

FREQUENCY OF DEFAULT

Most homeowners default relatively early in the life of the mortgage. Exhibit 1 shows the effect of seasoning assumed by two rating agencies and the Public Securities Association.[2] These seasoning curves are based on default experience of so-called prime loans — a 30-year fixed-rate mortgage with a 75% to 80% LTV that is fully documented for the purchase of an owner-occupied single-family detached house. These characteristics describe the most common mortgage type generally associated with the lowest default rates.

Loans with almost any other characteristic generally are assumed to have a greater frequency of default. Exhibit 2 summarizes the evaluation of these other risk characteristics among the four rating agencies.

---

[2] *Standard Formulas for the Analysis of Mortgage-Backed Securities and Other Related Securities* (New York, NY: Public Securities Association, 1990).

Exhibit 2: Effect of Required Credit Enhancement for AAA Levels

Category	Standard & Poor's	Moody's	Fitch	Duff & Phelps
Frequency of Foreclosure Loan-to-Value			FICO = 700	
100	4.50	N.A.	2.96	3.27
95	3.00	N.A.	2.21	3.05
90	1.50	1.70	1.67	2.41
85	1.00	N.A.	1.28	1.59
80	1.00	1.00	1.00	1.00
75	1.00	N.A.	0.80	0.91
70	1.00	0.63	0.67	0.77
65	1.00	N.A.	0.58	0.50
≤60	1.00	0.41	0.49	0.32
FICO Scores	Not available	Not available	LTV = 80% 820 0.42 1600 0.45 2340 0.68 3040 1.00 3700 1.62 4320 2.78 580 4.77	Not available
Seasoning	1. 50% of home price appreciation 2. 100% of depreciation 3. Variable, depending on term, mortgage type	1. Current LTV 2. 5 years 0.68	1. Adjustments for current LTV 2. Adjustments for payment history	1. Partial adjustments for current LTV 2. Affects timing of losses 3. Compare actual pool performance to expected performance

Exhibit 2 (Continued)

Category	Standard & Poor's	Moody's	Fitch	Duff & Phelps
Term				
15-year	0.73	0.65	0.75	0.80
20-year	0.88			0.88
25-year		0.76		0.95
30-year	1.00	1.00	1.00	1.00
40-year	>1.00	1.10		1.20
ARMS	1.05 - 1.70; additional 1.25 - 2.00 if pay cap is hit	1.15	1.05 - 2.00	1.15 - 1.30
Loan Purpose				
Cashout refinance	Add 5% to LTV	1.13-1.48	1.00-3.00	1.15
Rate/term refinance	1.00	1.00	1.00	0.95
New construction				1.05
Relocation				0.60
Reduced Documentation	LTV >90 2.00 - 3.00 80 - 90 1.50 - 2.00 75 - 80 1.20 - 1.50 60 - 75 1.10 - 1.50 <60 1.05 - 1.20	Limited 1.05 - 1.20 Poor/None 1.50	1.00-3.00 1.00-5.00	Alternate 1.05 Reduced 1.30 Poor reduced 1.50 None 1.75 Streamlined 1.30
Property Type				
Second Home	3.00	N.A.	1.00-1.25	1.10
Investor	3.00	1.48	1.00-2.00	1.40
Condo, Co-ops, Townhouses	Low-rise, 2-Family 1.20	1.14 - 1.28	1.00-2.20	1.25
2 - 4	Hi-rise, 3-to-4-Family 2.00	N.A.	1.00-1.50	1.40

Exhibit 2 (Continued)

Category	Standard & Poor's	Moody's	Fitch	Duff & Phelps
Credit measures	High debt ratio 1.10 Delinquencies: 2-to-5 1.10 6+ 1.20	1. WAC + 2 pts. 1.11 - 1.17 WAC − 2 pts. 0.83 - 0.89 2. "B" quality 1.18 - 1.32 "C" quality 1.49 - 1.99 3. Debt to income 25% 0.56 - 0.71 50% 1.26 - 1.60	1. Mortgage or credit scores: 10% to 30% reduction	1. Interest rate above market 2. originators "score" (A, B, C, D) 3. credit scores
Mortgage Size/ House Price	>$400,000 1.2 >$600,000 1.6 >$1,000,000 3.0	Avg/low 1.00 3 to 5 × median 2.00 6 to 9 × median 2.50 9+ × median 3.00	>$300,000 1.05[a] >$600,000 1.40[a] >$1,000,000 1.60[a]	4× median 1.22 6× median 1.34 8× median 1.48 10× median 1.63
SEVERITY OF LOSS				
Foreclosure costs	13% balance + interest	25%+/loan balance	Varies by state, coupon, and loan type; generally 23% to 28% for prime credits — higher for subprime	15% of Sale price
Market Decline	34.5%[b]	25%	21-49%; varies by region	40%[c]

Exhibit 2 (Continued)

Category	Standard & Poor's	Moody's	Fitch	Duff & Phelps
POOL CHARACTERISTICS				
Pool Size	Minimum 100 FF = Foreclosure frequency n = pool size $FF + 2.58\left(\dfrac{FF(1-FF)}{N}\right)^{1/2}$ $FF + 2.58\left(\dfrac{FF(1-FF)}{300}\right)^{1/2}$	>500 0.95 <200 1.20	If pool size (PS) < 125, $\dfrac{125 - PS}{125}$ plus factor for economic concentration	<110 1.50 110 1.30 200 1.10 300 1.00 400 0.98 500 0.95 1500 0.92 2500+ 0.90
Geography	High zipcode concentrations penalized; wider areas on a case-by-case basis	Economic diversity: 0.9 - 1.3 Foreclosure time: 0.9 - 1.2 Zipcode concentration Adjustments for regional economic conditions	0.9-1.1 by region	Volatility varies by MSA 0.80 - 1.25 Concentration factor by state, MSA, zipcode 0.90 - 1.20

a Adjustments to market value decline

b Adjusted for jumbo ~ 1.5

c Adjusted by region

Credit Scores

All of the rating agencies have revised their models recently to take the borrower's credit history into account. Freddie Mac's Loan Prospector and Fannie Mae's Desktop Underwriter paved the way for these model revisions.

Both Loan Prospector and Desktop Underwriter use a credit score derived by Fair Isaac and Company, Inc. as a summary measure of a borrower's credit history. This "FICO" score depends upon the frequency of late payments and the extent of a borrower's existing credit obligations, among other factors. (Fair Isaac does not publish the exact components of its score.) The FICO score ranks borrowers on their relative probability of defaulting on any credit obligations: people who score high have a high likelihood of not having any future delinquencies, while people who score low are more likely to have future delinquencies.

The rating agencies also use FICO scores in their own models; it is generally the most important determinant of the frequency of default. When the models were revised to take account of FICO scores, some of the other influences on the frequency of default — especially the loan-to-value ratios — became less important.

This finding makes sense because of patterns of co-variation between variables. For example, people who are able to make larger down payments generally have better credit scores while people who are scraping to put down 5% or less generally have worse credit scores. And people who take out 15-year mortgages generally have better credit scores than people who take out adjustable-rate mortgages.

Loan-to-Value Ratio/Seasoning

A mortgage's loan-to-value (LTV) ratio is the second most important determinant of its likelihood of default and therefore the amount of required credit enhancement. Rating agencies impose penalties of up to 500% on loans with LTVs above 80%. The rationale is straightforward. Homeowners with large amounts of equity in their properties are unlikely to default. They will either try to protect this equity by remaining current, or if they fail, sell the house or refinance it to unlock the equity. In any case, the lender is protected by the buyer's self-interest.

On the other hand, if the borrower has little or no equity in the property, the value of the default option is much greater. This argument is consistent with the long-held view that default rates for FHA/VA loans are much higher than for conventional loans.

Until recently, rating agencies considered the LTV only at the time of origination. Seasoning was an unalloyed good — if a loan did not default in the first three to four years, it deserved credit for making it past the hump. And many loans did not default because they were prepaid.

The recent declines in housing prices, increased volume of seasoned product, and greater emphasis on surveillance have made the *current* LTV the focus of attention. Seasoning now is as likely to be a negative for a pool as it is to be a plus. It is little comfort to own a pool of original 80% mortgages from California originated in 1990 because many of the borrowers will owe more than their houses are worth; their LTVs will exceed 100%. Moreover, the prepayment option has been taken away for these borrowers.

Mortgage Term

Amortization increases the equity a homeowner has in a property, which reduces the likelihood of default. Because amortization schedules for terms less than 30 years accumulate equity faster, all the rating agencies give a "credit" of 15% to 35% — i.e., reduced credit enhancement levels, for 15-year mortgages. Conversely, mortgages with a 40-year term are penalized up to 10%. Adjustable rate mortgages that allow negative amortization are similarly penalized.

Mortgage Type

Fixed-rate mortgages are considered "prime" because both the borrower and the lender know the monthly payment and amortization schedule with certainty. Presumably, the loan was underwritten considering this payment stream and the borrower's current income.

Both lender and borrower are uncertain about the future payment schedule for adjustable-rate mortgages (ARMs). Because most ARMs have lower initial ("teaser") rates, underwriting usually is done to ensure that the borrower will be able to meet the monthly payment assuming the rate adjusts up to the fully indexed rate at the first reset date.

Beyond that first date, however, there is uncertainty both about the future stream of payments and the borrower's ability to meet higher payments. Future payment schedules for other mortgage types such as balloons and graduated payments are known, but uncertainty about borrowers' income still exists. All non-fixed-rate mortgages carry penalties of 5% to 100% or more.

Transaction Type

Mortgages taken out for cash-out refinancings are considered riskier than mortgages taken out for purchases, chiefly because the homeowner is reducing the equity in the home. In addition, the fact that the homeowner is taking out cash may be an indication of *need*, which could indicate shakier finances, and the homeowner's monthly payment will increase. On the other hand, a no-cash refinancing — in which the rate is reduced — lowers the monthly payment and speeds the rate of amortization, so there are no penalties.

Documentation

"Full" documentation generally means that the borrower has supplied income, employment, and asset verification sufficient to meet Fannie/Freddie standards. "Low," "alternative," or "reduced" documentation means at least one form was not supplied, perhaps, for example, because the borrower is self-employed. In this case, because the income stream is likely to be more volatile, the borrower is more likely to default.

"No" documentation loans generally are made as "hard money" loans —
i.e., the value of the collateral is the most important criterion in the lending decision. Typically, lenders require larger down payments for these type loans. Guardian Savings and Loan in California — seized by the RTC for insolvency — had
been a major proponent of this type of program. Its collateral was put into RTC
91-9, which has a 40% serious delinquency rate, despite an average LTV of 65%.

Occupancy Status

Property owners obviously have a greater vested interest in not defaulting on a
mortgage on a house in which they live. Thus, mortgages for second homes or
rental property are penalized.

Property Type

Generally, single-family detached houses are the most desirable properties
because they are larger, more private, and include more land. Moreover, the supply of condominiums or townhouses is more likely to become overbuilt in a local
area with the addition of a single large project, potentially increasing the volatility of prices and the length of time needed to sell a property.

Mortgage Size/House Price

Most mortgages are sold into nonagency mortgage-backed securities because the
dollar amounts exceed the agency conforming limits (currently $203,150). The
rating agencies make the strong presumption that higher-valued properties with
larger mortgages are much riskier; they impose penalties of up to 200%.

Creditworthiness of the Borrower

Loan originators place a great deal of emphasis on the borrower's credit history
and capacity directly in addition to the information that is summarized in a FICO
credit score. For example, they look at debt-to-income ratios and the pay history
on previous mortgages (or the current mortgage if the loan is seasoned).

Originators also use underwriting matrixes that define credit quality (A, A–
, B, C, and D) in terms of discrete credit characteristics. For example, an A quality
borrower would have no mortgage delinquencies in the last 12 months; 1 30-day
mortgage delinquency in the last 12 months would drop the borrower to an A–, while
2 30-day delinquencies or 1 60-day delinquency would drop a borrower to a B.

In addition, most of the rating agencies have developed models specific to
lower credit quality borrowers. These models were necessary because the relationships between some of the variables are different between high credit quality borrowers and low credit quality borrowers. For example, among A-credit quality
borrowers, lower loan-to-value ratios are associated with higher FICO credit scores.
Among B, C, and D credit quality borrowers, lower LTV's are associated with lower
FICO credit scores because lenders try to offset the higher expected frequency of
default with lower expected loss severity because the borrower has more equity.

SEVERITY OF LOSS

In the case of default, foreclosure, and ultimate property sale, lenders incur two costs: (1) direct foreclosure costs, and (2) market decline. These costs may be mitigated to the extent there is equity in the property, i.e., lower LTVs will reduce the severity of loss.

Direct Foreclosure Costs Once a lender begins the foreclosure process — often as soon as a borrower becomes 60 days delinquent — it begins to incur significant direct costs.

Unpaid Interest The lender stops accruing interest on the mortgage as income, instead adding it to the unpaid balance of the loan.

> Cost = coupon rate of the mortgage per year

Property Taxes The lender becomes responsible for paying taxes to preserve its first lien position.

> Cost = up to 2% or more of the house price annually

Management Fees The property must be maintained so as to preserve its value for sale.

> Cost = average 6% of the house price annually

Legal Fees Variable.

Market Decline When a house is sold out of foreclosure, the lender is unlikely to obtain market value. Potential buyers know that the seller is distressed and know the size of the mortgage on the property. One common bidding strategy is to bid for the amount of the outstanding mortgage, figuring it is the seller's obligation to cover the out of pocket costs. The price received on a foreclosure sale depends greatly on local economic conditions and future housing prices, both of which are unknown at the time a rating agency is evaluating a loan. The range of assumed losses is 25% to 45%.

POOL CHARACTERISTICS

Rating agencies draw upon general portfolio theory that diversification reduces risk and concentration increases risk. They typically consider two characteristics of the overall pool composition in setting credit enhancement levels: (1) size of the pool, and (2) geographic composition/location.

Pool Size

Pools with fewer than 300 loans are penalized by three of the four rating agencies, while larger pools are credited. The rationale is that smaller pools are not sufficiently diversified to take account of (unspecified) desirable statistical properties.

Geography

The first kind of geographic consideration is again a question of diversification: "too many" loans concentrated in a single zip code or small local area. For example, a lender might finance an entire subdivision, townhouse development, or condominium project that might be exposed to a common, special risk such as a single plant closing or an environmental hazard.

The second kind of geographic consideration is generally broader in scope, such as a pool with a high concentration in Southern California that is exposed to risks not of a single plant but of a single industry. In special cases such as Boeing in Seattle, the risk is both industry- and company-specific.

CALCULATING CREDIT ENHANCEMENT LEVELS

Pool characteristic risks are cumulative; that is, if a loan has two or more adverse characteristics, the factors are multiplied to determine the relative degree of the frequency of default. Then one calculates an expected loss equal to the discounted probability of default times the expected loss severity. After performing these calculations on a loan-by-loan basis, the overall pool characteristics are taken into account.

Credit enhancement levels are determined relative to a specific rating desired for a security. Specifically, an investor in a AAA-rated security expects to have "minimal," that is to say, virtually no chance of losing any principal. For example, Standard & Poors requires credit enhancement equal to four times expected losses to obtain a AAA rating.

Lower-rated securities require less credit enhancement for four reasons. First, the loss coverage ratio is lower. Second, some of the factors may be less stringent. Third, the base case frequency of default may be lower. And fourth, the severity of loss may be less.

NEW EVIDENCE

Default rates calculated from a data set comprised of mortgages securitized by major issuers of nonagency MBS are particularly relevant in setting factors for the frequency of default. The discussion is based on analysis of more than 500,000 such non-conforming mortgages.

Exhibit 3: Delinquency Rates by Current LTV Range

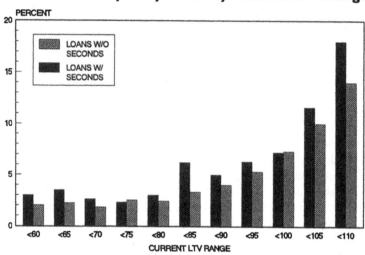

Loan-to-Value Ratio

With current LTV now the measure, assessment of risk needs to extend above 100%. Exhibit 3 shows that delinquency/default rates for mortgages with LTVs continue to rise. Approximate rates for 105% and 110% are 7.5 and 10, respectively, compared with 5 at 100%.

Exhibit 3 also shows that delinquency rates are higher for first mortgages whose borrowers have taken out second mortgages or home equity lines of credit even if their combined equity positions are identical. That is, if homeowner A has an 80% first mortgage, and homeowner B has a 65% first with the same coupon rate as A and a 15% second, homeowner B is a poorer credit risk. This heightened risk probably is a result of homeowner B's higher monthly payment.

In 1998 and 1999, high LTV lending was in and out of favor. Although there were well-publicized difficulties in this sector, some forms of these instruments are likely to stay around. Second mortgages of up to 125% LTV and first mortgages of 100% LTV are no longer rare. First mortgages with a high LTV second behind them are likely to perform even worse than the statistics in Exhibit 3 indicate. Rating agencies have separate models for high LTV seconds and if high LTV first mortgages become more popular, they undoubtedly will develop separate models for them, too.

As a special case of homeowners with seconds, consider borrowers who take out secondary financing as part of a purchase transaction. For example, the seller of the house — an individual if the house is a resale, the developer/builder if the house is new — may lend the buyer all or part of the down payment to facilitate the transaction. Exhibit 4 shows that the foreclosure rate for such transactions is nearly triple the rate of all transactions.

Exhibit 4: Delinquency Rates for Loans With and Without Silent Second Mortgages

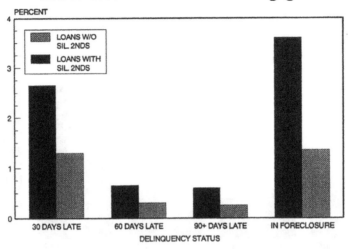

Exhibit 5: Ratio of Current Delinquencies
15-Year versus 30-Year Fixed Rate

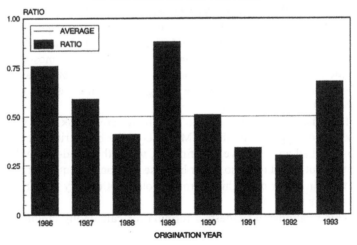

Mortgage Term

Recent experience with 15-year products has been exceptionally good, suggesting that previous credits were not generous enough. With the increasing popularity of 15-year mortgages as a liability management tool — to time the mortgage payoff either with retirement or children entering college, for example — a credit of as large as 50% seems appropriate (based on Exhibit 5) compared with the current range of 15% to 35%.

Exhibit 6: Ratio of Current Delinquencies
ARMS versus 30-Year Fixed Rate

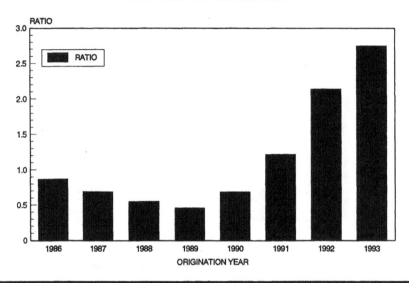

Mortgage Type/Borrower Credit

Although ARMs are considered riskier than fixed-rate mortgages, seasoning can have an adverse effect on mortgage holders and their ability to prepay. Consider homeowners who took out mortgages in 1990. A holder of the most popular ARM based on the one-year Treasury bill would have paid about 9% initially, and about 7% currently. In contrast, a fixed-rate mortgage would have cost about 10% in 1990 and about 7.75% currently.

If neither has refinanced, who's the better credit risk from this point forward? Exhibit 6 suggests that the ARM holder is the better risk because that borrower has not had an incentive to refinance, while the fixed-rate holder has had the incentive but failed to do so either because of a lack of equity or credit history deterioration. In either case, this borrower could not qualify for a new mortgage and is more of a risk.

This relationship suggests a formula for calculating credits/penalties by mortgage type:

$$\text{Fixed-rate mortgage} = \frac{\text{mortgage coupon}}{\text{current coupon}}$$

$$\text{ARM's} = \frac{\text{current rate}}{\text{initial rate}}$$

For ARM's, this formula has the additional feature of explicitly increasing the penalty as the rate rises in the future.

Exhibit 7: Ratio of Current Delinquencies
Cashout Refis versus Purchase Transactions

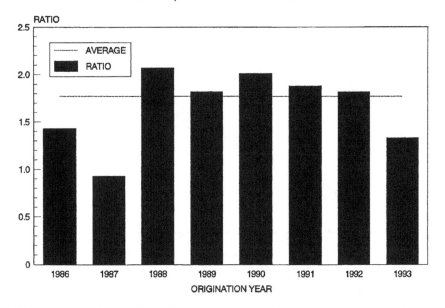

Transaction Type

Cash-out refinancings have performed abysmally in recent years, primarily because those still in existence were taken out at or near the peak in prices in California. However, there is no reason to think that the lending mistakes of California could not be repeated in other hot markets such as Seattle. Exhibit 7 indicates that the penalty for cash-out refinancings should be 100% compared with the rating agencies' maximum of 25%.

No-cash refinancings are currently not penalized by the rating agencies, although, Exhibit 8 shows significant "appraisal bias" for refinance transactions for which the appraiser has no purchase price as a guide. The extent of the bias is measured by noting that almost all the appraised values are higher than a property value estimated from indexing the previous sale price of the property to trends in property values in the same zip code; no such bias is present in Exhibit 9, which shows comparable data for purchase transactions for which the sale price is available to the appraiser.

This bias probably makes its effect felt in homeowners acting according to their "true" (read: higher) LTV. Thus, instead of penalizing refinance transactions directly, it would probably be more effective to raise the stated LTV at origination by 5% to 10% to reflect this bias. The impact on the required credit support would then be greater for relatively high LTV loans.

Exhibit 8: Evidence of Appraisal Bias
Refinance Transactions

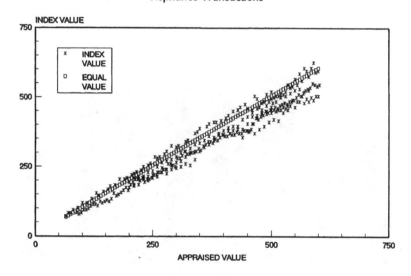

Exhibit 9: Evidence of Appraisal Bias
Purchase Transactions

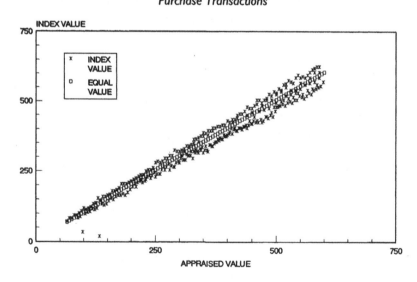

CONCLUSION

Rating agencies have moved to keep up with changes in the residential mortgage markets by revising their models approximately every three years. In the main, they have been successful. But as the pace of change accelerates, they too will have to accelerate the cycle of their revisions to every two years or even shorter.

For example, credit scores and automated underwriting models became widely accepted since 1997. Now, automated property valuations have begun to be accepted, which will require more revisions to the rating agencies' models.

Each set of revisions makes the mortgage market more efficient and lowers the costs of homeownership. The rating agencies' job is to make sure that the investors in mortgage-backed securities aren't the ones paying for these costs.

Chapter 14

The Evaluation of Excess Spread in Sub-Prime Transactions

Abner Figueroa
Vice President
Duff & Phelps Credit Rating Company

INTRODUCTION

Sub-prime mortgage loans bear an interest rate that is in excess of the amount needed to pay bondholders and cover the expenses of a securitization. This excess coupon is often referred to as excess interest cash flow or excess spread. In many transactions, the excess spread may be used to create an interest-only bond. In the case of sub-prime loans, the excess spread is large enough to use as internal credit enhancement for a securitization.

We believe that the evaluation of excess spread is crucial to determining appropriate credit enhancement levels for sub-prime securitizations. In this chapter we will describe DCR's methodology for evaluating excess spread. We will also discuss the internal credit enhancement of a typical sub-prime transaction utilizing a senior subordinated/over-collateralization structure. Finally we will present an overview of DCR's Spread Model and its role in valuing excess spread.

REVIEW OF SUB-PRIME DEAL STRUCTURE

Excess spread is the difference between (1) interest received at the weighted average interest rate on the mortgage collateral and (2) the sum of interest paid at the passthrough rate on the bonds and any monthly fees. Excess spread is generated because sub-prime mortgages bear higher interest rates than prime quality loans in order to compensate lenders for the lower credit quality of the borrowers. As a result, the typical transaction generates excess cash flow that ranges from 200 to 500 basis points (bps) per annum.

A senior-sub/over-collateralization structure is a commonly used form of internal credit enhancement for sub-prime transactions. This structure allocates excess spread to accelerate the principal paydown of the bonds. Typically, the

209

excess spread is used to pay down the principal balance of the senior bonds at a faster rate than the mezzanine or subordinate bonds. This process causes the principal balance of the mortgages to exceed the principal balance of all the bonds, which creates a cushion for losses. The loss cushion is commonly referred to as over-collateralization (OC).

Typically the most subordinate class in a transaction is rated BBB. The excess spread is the available credit enhancement to protect this class from losses. DCR will analyze the excess spread consistent with a BBB credit risk and calculate how much excess spread needs to be trapped and used to create OC to adequately protect the bonds from credit losses. The amount that is trapped is called the over-collateralization target (OC target). This target is calculated as a percentage of the original outstanding principal balance of the mortgage loans and can be established either initially or built up over time (OC buildup). Any excess spread that is not used to pay for losses or build toward the OC target is released to the residual holder in the transaction. This process is a "use it or lose it" concept.

For example, let's assume a principal balance of $100 million in mortgages with a 3% OC target. A deal can be structured initially with $97 million in bonds backed by $100 million in mortgages, thereby immediately providing the required level of OC. In the second instance, a deal can initially issue $100 million in bonds backed by $100 million in mortgages. In this case, the transaction's OC target is met by allocating monthly excess spread to accelerate the principal paydown of the bonds so that over time the required level of OC is established.

Losses are covered first by monthly excess spread, then OC buildup, and finally by the subordinated bonds. The example in Exhibit 1 will best illustrate how losses are allocated.

In month 20, there is enough excess spread to cover that month's losses. As a result, no losses are allocated to the OC Balance or the Remaining Subordination. In addition, there is sufficient Monthly Excess Spread available to distribute $30,000 to the residual holder. In month 21, the $100,000 of losses is $30,000 more than the available Monthly Excess Spread, and available over-collateralization must be used to protect the bondholders from losses. In this case, the End of Month OC Balance is reduced by $30,000. In month 22, the large amount of losses uses all of the available Monthly Excess Spread and reduces the remaining OC balance to zero. In this month, because the losses are so great, a portion of the subordinate bonds principal balance must be reduced to protect the more senior bondholders from losses.

CREDIT ENHANCEMENT AND THE IMPACT OF SPREAD VALUATION ON SUBORDINATION

As the example in Exhibit 1 illustrates, it is important that a transaction be structured with the requisite amount of credit enhancement. Credit enhancement can be derived from a variety of sources, including excess spread and subordination.

Proper valuation of each source is essential to providing adequate protection for the bonds at each rating category.

Spread Model

Several models are used to determine stress case losses and the value of excess spread at each rating category. The first step in analyzing a sub-prime pool is the application of DCR's loan level default model to generate the amount of credit enhancement (CE) necessary at each rating category. The required CE will come from two sources: subordination and excess spread (which includes the resulting OC build-up). For example, if the required CE at AAA were 18% and DCR's spread model calculates that 4% of the total CE can be provided by excess spread, then the required subordination would be 14%.

The valuation of excess spread is dependent on the interaction of the following variables:

1. Loss incidence and loss severity
2. Loss curve (timing pattern of losses)
3. Prepayment speeds
4. Relationship between the weighted average coupon and bond rates

Loss Incidence and Severity

DCR's loan level default model generates the loss incidence and severity for a pool of sub-prime collateral at each rating category. Mortgage characteristics such as loan-to-value ratios, borrower quality (e.g., A– or B grade), and the level of documentation are examples of the attributes that have an impact on the analysis.

The product of the loss incidence and severity represents the stress case level of losses expected at each rating category. There are infinite combinations of these two variables that will produce identical loss levels. Nevertheless, the relationship between these two variables plays an important role in the valuation of excess spread.

For example, let's assume $200 million in mortgage collateral, expected stress case losses of 7%, and that 2% of total losses occur in the current month. Exhibit 2 presents two distinct scenarios of 7% losses. Scenario 1 has a low loss incidence level with a high level of severity while scenario 2 has a higher loss incidence and a lower severity. In both scenarios the total level of losses is the same, 7%. The exhibit shows the impact that the different scenarios have on the remaining principal balance. In scenario 2, the higher loss incidence causes the remaining principal balance to experience a greater decline.

Exhibit 1: Illustration of Loss Allocation

Month	Monthly Losses	Monthly Excess Spread	End of Month OC Balance	Monthly Excess Spread Released	Remaining Subordination
20	$40,000	$70,000	$200,000	$30,000	$1,000,000
21	$100,000	$70,000	$170,000	$0	$1,000,000
22	$300,000	$70,000	$0	$0	$940,000

Exhibit 2: Two Scenarios of 7% Losses

Scenario	Loss Incidence	Loss Severity	Total Losses	Monthly Liquidated Principal*	Monthly Losses**	Remaining Principal Balance
1	20%	35%	7%	$800,000	$280,000	$199,200,000
2	35%	20%	7%	$1,400,000	$280,000	$198,600,000

* Monthly liquidated principal is calculated by multiplying the original principal balance of the mortgages by the loss incidence and then by the percent of total losses occurring in that month.
** Monthly losses are calculated by multiplying monthly liquidated principal by the loss severity.

Exhibit 3: DCR's Loss Curve

Period	Months	Period Losses	Cumulative Losses	Monthly Increments
1	13-24	15%	15%	1.25%
2	25-36	25%	40%	2.08%
3	37-48	25%	65%	2.08%
4	49-60	20%	85%	1.67%
5	61-72	15%	100%	1.25%

Scenario 1 provides a larger remaining principal balance of mortgages, and as a result will generate a greater amount of excess spread in the following month.

Loss Curve

Not only is the magnitude of monthly losses important but also their timing. The loss curve illustrates what percent of total losses will be realized in any month. DCR's loss curve has a 12-month grace period where no losses occur. Losses begin in month 13 and continue through month 72. Exhibit 3 shows DCR's loss curve.

The curve is divided into five periods, with each period representing 12 months. Losses occurring within a period are realized in equal monthly increments. For example, period 2 losses are realized in equal monthly increments of 2.08%.[1]

DCR's loss curve is designed to provide a stress case scenario where losses are realized every month for a period of five years. In DCR's analysis of excess spread, the dollar amount of monthly losses is maintained at a fixed level for each period, despite the level of prepayments. As a transaction pays down, monthly losses increase on a percentage basis when compared to the current principal balance of the mortgages. This percentage increase occurs because monthly losses are calculated as a percentage of the original principal balance of the mortgage pool, not the current balance.

Prepayment Speed

The speed at which one assumes the loans will prepay plays a crucial role in determining how much excess spread is generated within a transaction. At faster

---

[1] Losses realized in that period divided by 12.

speeds the principal balance of the loans pays down more quickly thereby generating less excess cash flow. DCR has developed prepayment curves that are both product and rating category specific. The curves, shown in Exhibit 4, are based on research conducted by DCR's Residential MBS rating group. The research relied upon data provided by DCR's RMBS monitoring group and several investment banks. The data covered a cross section of several major issuers and was delineated by product type.

Exhibit 4: DCR's Prepayment Curves
Fixed Rate Prepay Curves

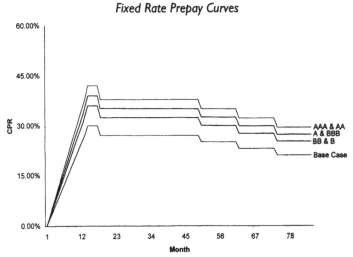

2/1 & 2/6 Prepay Curves*

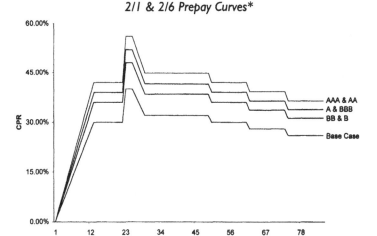

* Fixed for 2 years and then floats monthly based on 1-year CMT or 6-month Libor.

The prepayment curves used in our analysis take into account the concept of voluntary and involuntary prepayments. Voluntary prepays represents those loans that are paid off due to a refinancing or a borrower selling their home. Involuntary prepayments are caused by defaults. The sum of these components equals total prepayments. The involuntary portion of prepayments is calculated using DCR's loss curve and loss incidence projections.[2] As a result, the monthly involuntary CPR can easily be calculated. The model solves for the voluntary portion so that the sum of the two components, on a dollar basis, is equal to that month's targeted stress case CPR.

An example will best illustrate what the model is doing. Let's assume that the current month's stress case all-in prepay speed is 35 CPR, which is equivalent to $5 million in total prepayments for the month. Next, let's assume that the involuntary component is $2 million. The model will solve for the CPR that generates $3 million in voluntary prepayments.

By solving for the components individually, DCR's spread model avoids prepaying the mortgage loans faster than intended, which would underestimate the amount of excess spread being generated by the transaction.

Weighted Average Coupon/Average Bond Rate

The weighted average interest rate on the underlying mortgage collateral is the weighted average coupon (WAC) of a transaction. The bond rate is the interest rate paid to the bondholders on a monthly basis. In a deal where fixed-rate collateral backs fixed-rate certificates, the spread calculation is relatively simple. Over time some variability may occur, depending on the dispersion of coupons on the collateral or the difference in rates on senior and subordinate bonds as the bonds are paid down.

On the other hand, transactions with floating-rate-certificates or floating-rate collateral introduce the concept of basis risk into the evaluation of excess spread. Basis risk is the potential mismatch between the revenue generated by the underlying mortgage collateral and the interest due to certificate holders.

We will first describe typical floating-rate deal structures and then discuss the various scenarios where basis risk can impact the valuation of excess spread.

Review of Deal Structures One typical deal structure has securities that pay an investor 1-month LIBOR plus some spread and is backed by loans that bear interest at 6-month LIBOR plus some margin. A Net Funds Cap feature limits the interest rate payable on the securities to the net interest received from the mortgages. The loans have life and periodic caps. Life caps limit the maximum interest rate that the borrower will pay in any given period during the life of the loan (generally 6% over the teaser rate). Periodic caps limit the maximum amount the rate can change at a given reset date (generally 2% per year).

The second deal structure is one where the mortgage pool is composed of several different types of ARM product. The securities continue to pay investors as described above but the loans can bear interest at 6-month LIBOR, 1-year

---

[2] The involuntary portion of prepays is equal to the monthly liquidated principal. See footnote one.

CMT, or can be hybrid mortgages where the rate is fixed for 2 to 5 years and then floats at 6-month LIBOR. The third deal structure is where floating-rate certificates are backed by fixed-rate collateral.

Problem: Inverted Yield Curve and Rate Reset Mismatch When analyzing a transaction, DCR is concerned with identifying scenarios that cause the amount of excess spread to deteriorate. The first scenario involves an inverted yield curve where 1-month LIBOR is higher than 6-month LIBOR. The increased risk exposure in this scenario is best illustrated with an example.

Assume that 1-month and 6-month LIBOR are at 8% and 7%, respectively. In this case, the index that determines the interest rate payable on the securities is higher than the index on the underlying loans. As a result, the excess spread in the transaction is 100 basis points less than it would have been in the typical upward sloping yield curve environment. Fortunately, the 1- and 6-month LIBOR curves have been negatively sloped only twice in the last 34 years for longer than 3 months. The average duration of the inversion was five months. In view of this fact, it is important to consider this worst case scenario, but it is clear that the probability of its occurrence is quite small.

The second scenario involves the timing mismatch between when the interest rates on the securities and the underlying loans reset. An additional concern is the periodic cap that restrains the amount by which the rate on the underlying loans can change at a given reset date. Exhibit 5 best illustrates the possible risk exposure.

As the example in Exhibit 5 shows, in a rising rate environment, the excess spread is reduced every month as the index that determines the interest rate payable to the securities increases. In addition, even when the interest rate on the underlying loans does reset, it is restricted by the periodic cap (1% semiannual, 2% annual).

DCR has developed stress case scenarios, which are rating category specific, to address basis risk. These scenarios, shown in Exhibit 6, are applied to the forward curve of the index used to determine the interest rate payable to bondholders to generate a stress case path of interest rates for each rating category. This methodology allows the model to take into account the risk of spread compression caused by the timing mismatch between the indices.

Determining the OC Requirement
As discussed earlier, an OC structure creates a cushion for losses by accelerating the principal paydown of the bonds. As a result, the determination of an adequate OC target is essential to providing sufficient credit enhancement to protect the bonds from credit losses.

Exhibit 5: Spread Compression

Month		1	2	3	4	5	6
Bond Rate	1-Month LIBOR	6%	6.50%	7%	7.50%	7.75%	7.75%
Mortgage Rate	6-Month LIBOR	6.25%	6.25%	6.25%	6.25%	6.25%	7.25%
Monthly Excess Spread		400 BPS	375 BPS	325 BPS	275 BPS	250 BPS	350 BPS

Exhibit 6: DCR's Stress Case Scenarios

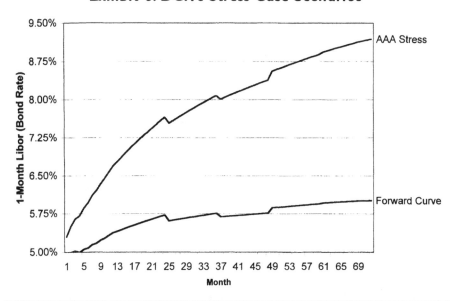

Based on the interaction of the key variables, the DCR Spread Model solves for the minimum OC target that, when combined with monthly excess cash flow, will exactly cover DCR's stress case loss scenario. If the combination of OC buildup and monthly excess cash flow is insufficient to cover DCR's loss scenario, then an initial OC amount will be required.

Over the life of a transaction the amount of over-collateralization will fluctuate as it is used to cover losses and then is replenished in future months with excess spread until it once again reaches the required OC target. Under DCR's stress case loss scenario, the OC can not be replenished. The stress case losses at each rating category are severe enough to prevent the replenishment of the OC target. This level of conservatism increases DCR's confidence in its calculated OC target.

It is important to recognize that once the monthly excess spread is released to the residual holder it can not be recalled into the deal to pay for losses. In view of this fact, it is of critical importance to determine an appropriate OC target to prevent a transaction from being structured without adequate credit enhancement.

This initially calculated OC target is the starting point for further sensitivity analysis. The DCR spread model is designed not to be a "black box" but to provide the analyst with a tool to asses the value of excess spread given various assumptions. This analysis is crucial to establishing the sensitivity of the OC target to changes in the assumptions.

CONCLUSION

The DCR spread model provides its analyst with the tools and the theoretical framework necessary to evaluate excess spread. Using this model, DCR believes that the combination of excess spread and subordination in each DCR-rated transaction is sufficient to protect bondholders at each rating category.

Chapter 15

A Credit Intensive Approach to Analyzing Whole Loan CMOs

Edward L. Toy
Managing Director
Teachers Insurance and Annuity Association

INTRODUCTION

As with most financial investments, the analysis of opportunities in the mortgage-backed securities market can be divided into two principal components: fundamental and technical. While aspects of the two components inevitably overlap at times, this chapter focuses on fundamental analysis. The fundamental side of the mortgage market equates to careful consideration of the various aspects of collateral type and quality. The bulk of this chapter will focus on differences in underlying mortgages as they may impact default frequency and loss severity. However, many of these same characteristics, and differences, also have a direct impact on prepayment experience and expectations.

For agency-backed securities, those benefiting from a guarantee by the Federal National Mortgage Corporation (FNMA or Fannie Mae), the Federal Home Loan Mortgage Corporation (FHLMC or Freddie Mac) or Government National Mortgage Corporation (GNMA or Ginnie Mae), credit analysis is very simple and straightforward. Holders of securities guaranteed by Ginnie Mae can rely on the full faith and credit support of the U.S. government. Fannie Mae and Freddie Mac supported securities are also treated by many as having the equivalent of U.S. government backing. Investors rely on provisions giving these government sponsored entities (GSEs) the ability to sell securities to the U.S. Treasury. Unlike agency-backed securities, private label securities, often also referred to as whole loan securities, whether pass-throughs or collateralized mortgage obligations (CMOs), do not benefit from any kind of government support. Investment decisions as they relate to default risk must, therefore, necessarily rely on different criteria.

WHY CREDIT ANALYSIS IS IMPORTANT

While historical experience in the mortgage market has generally been very good, it is nonetheless true that borrowers do default on their loans and losses do occur.

Without the benefit of a guarantee from FNMA, FHLMC, or GNMA to cover such losses, investors must rely on the quality of the underlying collateral and other forms of credit enhancement like subordinate securities, cash reserves, and pool insurance or guarantees. Subordinate securities represent only a small portion of the overall pool and other forms of credit enhancement rarely represent a significant percentage of the pool either. A careful fundamental approach to the analysis of the collateral will lead to a basic understanding of a mortgage pool's underlying quality and an ability to forecast its future performance on the basis of reasonably rational criteria. Alternatively, developing a basic understanding of the relevant risk areas will permit the setting of logical standards for making comparisons between competing investments or avoiding certain pools altogether.

While such a credit-intensive approach is important generally, it is critical for investors in the subordinate classes. These are the at-risk securities that have a greater likelihood of being impaired. In a senior-subordinate structure, the subordinate classes, or B-pieces, act as internal credit enhancement for the senior, or class A, securities. Depending on the quality of the collateral, the subordinate classes in total will account for between 5% and 8% of the structure.

Generally, the subordinate layer is further tranched into several subclasses. The result is very small layers with gradually smaller levels of subordination to support the given certificate. The most junior security, referred to as a first-loss piece, may be no larger than 25 basis points or 0.25% of the pool. The actual size and credit quality of the subordinate classes will be determined by the rating agencies analyzing the pool, but market acceptance of different subordination levels is also an important influence.

Analyzing a pool from the credit side is more important to B-piece investors because if the pool experiences defaults and losses on foreclosure, the subordinate classes will be allocated those losses sequentially, beginning with the lowest class, or first-loss piece. The senior bonds in any structure are allocated losses only after the subordinate classes are completely eliminated. Since the subordinate classes are allocated all of the first losses even though they represent only a small percentage of the overall structure, the subordinate classes are subject to a great deal of "negative leverage." This negative leverage will continue to be quite substantial until the pool experiences prepayments. With prepayments first allocated to the senior bonds in the typical senior-subordinate structure, gradually the subordinate classes will represent an increasing percentage of the remaining pool, thus reducing the negative leverage.

As even a relatively low level of losses can impair the value of the subordinate certificates, it is obvious that any investor considering such an investment must first develop an opinion about the likelihood of losses exceeding the level of subordination supporting the security. Even an extremely well-underwritten pool should be expected to experience some losses during its life. If the proposed investment is one of the lower classes or first-loss pieces, where little or no actual support exists in the structure, protection from losses will depend more on equity in the underlying collateral.

If one continues to assume some nominal level of losses, the emphasis shifts somewhat for these lowest classes to the timing for the losses. This is because until defaults and losses are actually experienced, even the lowest classes continue to receive a share of the interest and principal cash flow that is being generated by the pool.

A credit intensive approach to the analysis of mortgage pools will result in a strong base for estimating the likelihood and timing of losses in a pool.

THE ORIGINATOR/UNDERWRITER

The credit-intensive part of whole-loan analysis must begin with the seller of the underlying mortgages, or the entity on whose underwriting standards and abilities any investor relies. This may be the actual originator and underwriter of the mortgages. Or, it could be a conduit that is purchasing mortgages from various sources and re-underwriting those mortgages before combining them into a pool.

In this latter case, the underwriting standards of the actual originators are not relevant, because the conduit, even if it purchases packages of mortgages in bulk, will pick and choose out of that package, throwing out mortgages that do not fit its underwriting standards. The conduit will also dictate underwriting standards to its sellers so that the weeding out is not extensive. In some situations, the underwriting criteria referred to may also be underwriting guidelines of the mortgage pool insurers, to the extent a conduit program or dealer relies on pool certification by a pool insurer to package transactions. In some rare situations, the pool could involve a combination of all three. In most situations, the originator/underwriter is also the servicer or master servicer of the pool.

Historical Performance

Review of an originator begins with a basic and fairly simple quantitative approach with respect to its historical performance. Delinquency information is reviewed. Besides delinquencies, the review should include foreclosure data and segmentation of the total delinquency data into 30-, 60-, and 90-day delinquencies. Each of these should be analyzed in absolute dollar terms and as a percentage of the originator's servicing or master servicing portfolio. Generally speaking, only a fraction of 30-day delinquencies turn into unresolvable defaults. Therefore, while any delinquency may be problematic, the delinquencies of 60 to 90 days and 90 days or greater are more important.

One should view with some degree of suspicion low overall delinquency statistics, but high levels of serious delinquencies, either compared with the overall numbers or compared with other originators. This may indicate a definitional oddity that simply does not report delinquencies until they become more serious. Alternatively, a sudden increase in 30-day delinquencies, as a percentage of the overall portfolio, may be an indication of future problems. Just as for a straight corporate issuer, some degree of trend analysis can be quite revealing.

Finally, loss experience on foreclosures is also important. To the extent that an underwriter is more aggressive with respect to approving borrowers and debt-to-income levels, much of this can be offset with tighter underwriting of the collateral or enforcing tighter loan-to-value standards, resulting in lower loss levels. Of course, higher loss levels may indicate a lax underwriting approach, as opposed to just being aggressive. Housing price volatility does tend to increase with size, especially among jumbo loans. Most originators try to offset this somewhat by imposing tighter loan-to-value ratios with increased loan size, or alternatively by limiting loan size for higher loan-to-value ratios.

In looking at performance statistics, it is important to factor out distortions, both positive and negative. One factor that has led to performance statistics looking better than reality is high origination levels in a low interest rate environment. A large influx of new mortgages into a servicing portfolio will make the numbers look better than they actually are by increasing the denominator in the equation. Unless underwriting of the borrowers has been unusually weak, it would be surprising to see many newly originated mortgages going delinquent in the first year or two.

Generally speaking, one would not expect the typical mortgage pool to experience any significant defaults until the third or fourth year after origination (the "standard default curve"). Thus, in a high origination pattern, the delinquency and default numbers, which constitute the numerator in the equation, would initially stay relatively low. The easiest way to factor out this distortion is to take the current delinquency information but use the prior year's portfolio balance as a denominator, or, alternatively, use the average of the two years.

On the other side, when we see somewhat higher delinquency data, it is helpful at times to take a closer look at the reasons instead of making the automatic judgment that the underwriting is poor. For example, many originators in the late eighties were aggressive in pushing limited documentation programs to build volume. Since limited documentation loans tend to show higher defaults over time, the poor experience of these "low-doc/no-doc" mortgages may inflate the default numbers.

Current origination patterns emphasize full documentation underwriting and only permit limited documentation loans in selected situations. The shift for some originators has been from highs of 60% or 70% of originations to less than 20%. On top of this shift, today's limited documentation loans for most originators are themselves of better quality. In any case, it is only fair to note when applicable that the current profile of originations has a different breakdown and adjust historical numbers accordingly.

There are also several ways of taking a static pool approach that will reveal the true quality of the underwriting. Static pool analysis focuses on breaking down the originator's performance by origination year. The most common approach is to take the total number of loans originated in each year and determine how many loans became delinquent within 6, 12, and 18 months of origination. It can be equally informative to develop a foreclosure curve for each origination year and compare the accumulation pattern for those years. Static pool analysis is useful because overall portfolio numbers are affected by the addition of new loans and the prepayment of older loans.

Underwriting Criteria

The basic quantitative approach, of course, only gets us part of the way. Second is a thorough review of the underwriting criteria itself. While unforeseen problems can always occur, leading to a default on a mortgage, participants in the mortgage market know that certain types of loans have a higher probability of going into default. Also, loss severity can vary depending on the loan category. It would be easy simply not to make those loans, but that could also seriously limit an originator's ability to generate product. Therefore, originators set up different underwriting criteria to compensate somewhat for the additional risk of default. The task for investors is then to look at what adjustments exist for currently known risk areas.

There are four common areas of concern: documentation type, loan purpose, property type, and occupancy type. The relevant issue first is how the originator compensates for these risk areas. The most common methods are limitations on loan size or maximum loan-to-value ratios.

For example, if we accept the fact that cash-out refinancing mortgages have historically shown a higher probability of default, one would expect the maximum allowed loan-to-value to be lower, say 75%, as opposed to general restrictions for other loan types that may go as high as 90% or 95%. Also, if the usual maximum loan size is $1 million, the maximum loan size for cash-out refinancing loans might be as low as $650,000. Besides establishing specific standards to minimize known risk factors, the underwriter should also have rules that limit the possibility of loans that have cross-over risk, such as including cash-out refinancing mortgages that are also limited documentation loans. This kind of cross-over would compound the likelihood of default on the loan.

Third, and perhaps most important when reviewing originators, is the basic issue of quality control. The key is whether the establishment of underwriting criteria is a dynamic process under constant review and evaluation. The better originators will have set procedures for reassessing their approach. Many will take a regular sample of their servicing portfolio and re-underwrite the loans, looking for trends in defaults or losses.

This will likely go as far as including another appraisal. If there is a material change in the appraised value, this will be deemed suspicious, especially if the original appraisal is relatively recent. The result could be a conclusion that a given appraiser is aggressive or unreliable, and therefore no longer qualified for that originator's loan underwriting.

As discussed earlier, originators will make certain loans, notwithstanding the fact that they are recognized as having higher risk characteristics. The originator's quality control policies should include an ongoing review of the actual default rate and loss severity of such loans. If the originator concludes that the numbers are higher than expected, this should lead to adjustments for allowed loan-to-value ratios and loan sizes.

For the conduits, the statistical analysis is also key to tracking discernible patterns for defaults coming from a given mortgage originator. If a given originator shows a higher than average default pattern, that should result in the originator being put on notice, or possibly being deleted from the approved pool of originators. Generally the conduit will first look to working with the originator to determine and correct any underwriting problems.

Since in most situations the originator is also servicer or master servicer, the originator's servicing capabilities and procedures should often also be a subject of discussion during due diligence. There are several areas to focus on, such as capacity and efficiency of the servicing operation. One simple approach to getting a quick read on this is to review in some detail the mechanics of the servicing operation, specifically the procedures in place for dealing with delinquencies. For example, how quickly does the servicer react to a delinquency to get payments flowing again?

Given the substantial growth of some servicing portfolios, capacity utilization and efficiency are important issues, just as in any service-intensive industry. Many servicing operations have turned increasingly to various levels of automation to improve the effectiveness of a given group of service representatives. Just as an added level of review, it can be informative to see how and where loan files are maintained, including how much is computerized.

THE COLLATERAL

To the extent an originator/servicer passes this kind of detailed review, analyzing individual pools of collateral becomes a much more mechanical exercise. The process of reviewing individual pool characteristics can result in a sea of statistics. The easier approach is to use any anomaly as a red flag warranting further review. While it might not be possible to correct the problem by changing the constitution of the pool, any investor should at least recognize, and presumably be compensated for, pools that carry higher risk components. There are several key points that require emphasis.

Loan Type

One overall factor to be considered is loan type. The mortgage market is dominated by basic 30-year fully amortizing fixed-rate mortgages. Using that as a benchmark, there are other loan types that have tended to show different performance characteristics. Fifteen-year mortgages, another basic product type, have proven to be higher-quality collateral over time. This is because a shorter term requires higher debt service requirements. Borrowers who choose this option are, therefore, higher-income individuals who can afford to make those payments.

Also, the more rapid amortization of principal results in a faster build-up of book equity. It is also true that pools of 15-year mortgages tend to have lower loan-to-value ratios to begin with as these borrowers generally bring more equity to the transaction.

One key characteristic for both of the mortgage types is that they are fully amortizing. On the opposite extreme are balloon mortgages. While there are undoubtedly many reasons for borrowers choosing a balloon mortgage, one significant one is the inability to meet higher debt service requirements under a fully amortizing one. This lower level of financial flexibility, when combined with a slower amortization of principal, results in loans that are inherently riskier. Beyond the increased likelihood of default during the life of the loan, pools that include balloon mortgages also face the potential problems that may arise in refinancing the larger final payment. The borrower's ability to do so will depend on the actual size of the balloon, the direction of home values and interest rates during the interim, and changes in the borrower's creditworthiness.

One last major product type is adjustable-rate mortgages, or ARMs. The principal concern surrounding ARM products is the potential for "sticker shock" whenever the rate adjusts. This is particularly true with the first adjustment because the initial coupon is usually an especially low teaser rate offered to entice the borrower into choosing that option. There is also the possibility that in underwriting the loan, the originator used a lower initial debt service requirement to qualify the borrower, rather than one that is more realistic for the longer term. The risk of a substantial increase in debt service, and therefore the risk of default, however, exists whenever there is a rising interest rate environment.

Geographic Concentration

The one pool characteristic recently requiring the most attention is geographic concentration. Given the historical balance of originations, this has most often evolved into a question of California concentration. Since most whole-loan packages consist almost exclusively of jumbo products, and California accounts for a very large percentage of jumbo loan originations, many pools have also been formed with exposures to California loans of 60% to 70%, and even higher. Notwithstanding the many arguments about the size and diversification of the California economy, that kind of pool concentration in most cases is imprudent.

Some have rationalized that if an investor's overall portfolio of mortgage securities is lighter in California exposure, say, 20% on average through all the individual pools, it should be possible to take a pool that is higher because the overall portfolio concentration is still low. Even though portfolio considerations are important, this logic is faulty, because the strength or weakness of one pool has no direct impact on other pools in the portfolio.

For the logic to prove out, a certain scenario would have to be true. When one pool, because of its higher California concentration experiences some difficulties, thus weakening or expending credit enhancement levels; and other pools, given their lower concentrations, maintain their credit enhancement levels or perhaps even experience improvements with loan prepayments; the first pool would have to be able to gain access to the latter's improved positions. This is, of course, not the case, since all pools are distinct legal entities with no direct link. An indirect link might occur in the marketplace to the extent that market prices for the lower concentration pools could improve at the same time that the market prices for the higher concentration pools deteriorate. This is not a very reliable link. An analogous argument is to believe that owning an IO and PO, but of different coupon collateral, represents a perfect interest rate hedge.

Unfortunately, even the most detailed and thorough economic analysis cannot fully substitute for simple diversification. Until it actually occurred, few believed that home values in California could decline as far as they did between 1990 and 1993. And if one were to rely heavily on historical experience, one would have expected defaults in California to be only a fraction of the national average. Defaults in 1993, in California, were much closer to, and in some areas of the state exceeded the national average.

This is not to say that California is the only state to be on the watch for in terms of heavy concentrations, although the focus inevitably moves there because the state accounts for so much of the jumbo loan originations in the United States. Any concentration in any one state is not wise because that pool is vulnerable to the specific economic circumstances of that state. Over time, we have also experienced varying levels of concern about the Northeast, especially Massachusetts and the tri-state area surrounding New York City. Also, lest we forget, one of the most oft-referred to disaster scenarios is, after all, the "Texas Scenario."

Geographic dispersion goes beyond just looking on a state-by-state basis. Further limitations are important since maintaining a 10% concentration maximum in California is good only to the extent that all those California loans are not located in the same zip code. A very large percentage of California's jumbo originations come in the Los Angeles area and its surrounding counties. Rules of thumb have thus evolved in terms of concentrations within individual five-digit zip code areas, three-digit zip code areas, and county concentrations. Economics notwithstanding, it is always good to know that a large percentage of a pool's loans are not within five miles of the most recent earthquake's epicenter.

One factor that has provided some limited relief on the California factor is the divergence between northern and southern California. While both are subject to the same state government influences, the size of the state and the differences in economic drivers mitigate higher California exposures with some north-south diversification.

Of some greater difficulty is looking at cross-border concentrations. Suppose a pool has 20% of its loans in Maryland and 20% of its loans in Virginia. A 20% limit might be deemed acceptable, but this profile would mean 40% between two neighboring states, plus whatever might be located in the District of Columbia. The combination is actually a relatively small geographic area. A more detailed look might also show that in fact all 40+% of the pool is located within a very narrow geographic corridor between northern Virginia and Baltimore.

This is not to say that some exceptions could not be found with more detailed analysis. It might be possible to be more comfortable with a pool that has a somewhat higher California concentration if one finds that the loans in California were underwritten to tighter standards. Beginning in 1992, many originators in fact began to hold California underwriting to tighter standards, either by management focus or outright policy. If we could break down a pool between California loans and non-California loans, this differential might become readily apparent. In one pool, for example, we might be willing to go somewhat higher if the California loans had generally lower loan-to-value ratios, especially if the differential between the California loans and the pool in general increased with increasing loan sizes. There might also be greater comfort if a larger percentage of the California loans fell into the more attractive categories of single-family detached, owner-occupied, primary residence, rate/term refinancing mortgages with full documentation packages.

Other Collateral Characteristics

Geographic dispersion is not the only area that requires detailed analysis. Other collateral characteristics warrant careful review. These include documentation type, loan purpose, property type, and occupancy type.

Documentation Type

In documentation type, a significant difference generally exists between full documentation and different limited documentation programs. A full documentation package includes a significant amount of paperwork, verifying data that the borrower has supplied about employment history, income levels, and net worth. When an originator agrees to omit some of this documentation, the potential exists that not everything is as it appears.

There are times when some amount of flexibility in documentation requirements is warranted and does not materially change the risk profile. A simple example is requiring written employment verification from someone who is self-employed.

The one form of documentation that has proven to be critical in complete underwriting is asset verification. Most will agree that having invested a substantial amount of real equity in a home is one of the prime deterrents to borrower default. To be comfortable that some amount is actually being invested by the borrower, even if the loan includes a relatively high loan-to-value ratio, originators check to see that the borrower actually had assets equal to the downpayment for at least some period of time prior to closing. This avoids late discovery that the borrower also borrowed the down payment. In that case, not only does the borrower have little or no equity invested in the property, the debt-to-income ratio is also higher, further increasing the risk of default.

Whenever written asset verification, or some other important documentation is omitted, the loan is referred to as a limited or low documentation loan. Limited documentation loans have historically shown higher incidences of default, although the differential from full documentation loans tends to vary with the originator. This is because some originators focus on other forms of verification, at least on an oral basis to compensate for the missing documentation. When verification of facts is completed through other written means, and there is at least written asset verification, loans are categorized as alternative documentation loans. An example would be accepting W-2 forms in lieu of tax returns. Generally, alternative documentation loans are seen as performing the same as full documentation loans.

Loan Purpose

Concern about default also varies substantially depending on loan purpose. In most situations, there are only three basic categories: cash-out, or equity refinancing mortgages, rate/term refinancing mortgages, and loans to fund an actual purchase of a home.

Cash-out loans are seen as much riskier than purchase loans or rate/term refinancing mortgages. A cash-out loan is in direct conflict with a prime deterrent of default. Rather than putting real equity into a home, the borrower is taking out equity. The risks of a cash-out refinancing mortgage are especially pronounced when the borrower is self-employed. Often this could mean the borrower is starting a new business, trying to expand an existing business (both risky), or trying to shore up a failing business.

While the riskier nature of cash-out refinancing loans seems readily apparent, the differential between purchase and rate/term refinancing loans is less distinct. In a rate/term refinancing transaction, the borrower can be accomplishing any one of a number of goals. The borrower could be reducing the remaining term of the loan from a 30-year to a 15-year mortgage. This will result in an accelerated amortization of the loan, thereby increasing the book equity and reducing the loan-to-value ratio. The borrower could also be keeping the same term but reducing the interest rate and therefore the monthly debt service requirements. The reduced cash requirement should mean additional financial flexibility for the borrower, therefore reducing the chances of running into cash flow problems. It also could enable the borrower to prepay a portion of the loan with the extra cash, again reducing the loan-to-value ratio at an accelerated pace. The one counterweight to these positive traits is that the appraised value in this case is not based on an arm's-length transaction, but will depend solely on comparables.

While the bulk of the market consists of purchase mortgages, within this general category are some stratifications. The most interesting is one that focuses on relocation mortgages. The relocation market largely consists of loans created by mortgage originators that develop relationships with large corporations. Through these relationships, the mortgage originator helps facilitate management relocations. The nature of the transaction, that they generally involve higher income individuals and that the relocation is part of a corporate program, results in a higher quality profile. It is not uncommon for pools of relocation mortgage to not experience a single default during its entire life. At the same time, the nature of the transaction also often results in a much more volatile prepayment profile. In many cases, the individuals being relocated will be relocated again within a few years.

Property Type

While other factors are seen as more significant drivers for default rates on a pool, one other characteristic that can have a significant impact on recoveries when defaults do occur is property type. Property types can be broken down into very detailed categories. Generally the type recognized as cleanest is single-family detached housing. These loans are considered more desirable because they are somewhat easier to realize value on and are also less subject to loss in value due to external factors.

Second on the list is residences that are part of planned unit developments, but for which the common or shared facilities are considered de minimis. An example of not de minimis common facilities would be a golf course. In this case, the value of the residence itself is heavily dependent on the attraction of the golf course.

Miscellaneous other types are: two- to four-family homes, townhouses, condominiums, and coops. Of these, coops are considered the worst because the asset is not actually real estate, but a share ownership. There is more volatility in values for these latter categories. Loss severity can also be somewhat higher because more time may be required for resale after foreclosure, especially in a weak real estate market. During this time the servicer will in most cases advance interest on the remaining principal amount, but the servicer will then have priority for recovery of these advances from the proceeds of liquidation, thereby increasing the loss on principal to the pool.

Occupancy Type

Most properties can be defined as primary residence, secondary residence (or vacation home), or an investor-owned property. Given the overriding desire to maintain one's home, there is no question that the best occupancy type is primary residence. Vacation homes and investor-owned properties where the owner does not occupy the property for most of the year, if at all, can create difficulties because the borrower can more easily rationalize walking away from the property.

Loan-to-Value and Loan Size

Throughout the discussion of important factors that drive default rates, there has been one recurring theme — loan-to-value. This, in conjunction with loan size, is the simplest aspect of collateral analysis because these are simple numbers with little room for judgment. There is little disagreement that loan-to-value is a prime determinant of default risk. There are two reasons for this. First, a large equity investment represents a substantial incentive to continue one's mortgage payments. Second, to the extent an income problem does arise, a lower loan-to-value provides significant cushion for either the borrower or the servicer to sell the home at a price sufficient to cover the remaining principal outstanding.

For these reasons, a key consideration in any mortgage pool is the weighted average loan-to-value and the number of loans with loan-to-value ratios greater than 80%. Most pools of 30-year mortgages have weighted average loan-to-value ratios between 70% and 75%. Most pools of 15-year mortgages have weighted average loan-to-value ratios between 65% and 70%. Any pool higher than the norm should then be considered somewhat riskier.

More difficult is the extent to which the pool consists of some very low loan-to-value mortgages and some very high loan-to-value mortgages, resulting in a normal weighted average. The situation is slightly muddied by the fact that most loans with loan-to-value ratios in excess of 80% are insured down to 75% by primary mortgage insurance. While these loans are a theoretical equivalent to a 75% loan-to-value, their likelihood of default will not be driven by the existence of insurance. Therefore, investors need to decide on how comfortable they can be relying on insurers on which little if any analysis has been done.

To the extent that analyzing loan-to-value ratios is relatively straightforward, the question of loan size is also not very complicated. The simplest aspect of this factor is that the smaller the loans in a given pool, the greater the diversification for the given pool size. Larger loans, to the extent they become delinquent, will have a proportionately greater impact on the health of the overall pool. Generally speaking, higher-priced homes also tend to experience greater price volatility during cyclical swings in real estate values. The risk is also markedly greater when the price of the home is significantly above the median price for homes in the geographic area. In that case the resale process is almost certain to take significantly longer, and the likelihood of needing to accept a price that is closer to the median at resale is high.

Seasoning

One factor that can be used, on occasion, to offset some of the risk factors discussed is seasoning of the loans in the pool. The greatest likelihood of default is generally viewed to be in the early years of the loan, more specifically in years two through six. Few borrowers will default in the first twelve months of a loan. Also, after the first few years, default frequency tends to decline rapidly. This phenomenon has several explanations. The most important is the build up of book equity in the home through amortization of principal. When borrowers have more invested in the home and have more flexibility in the selling price they can accept because of their lower mortgage balance, it would be unusual for a problem to arise. A more intangible factor is the increased emotional commitment to the home.

Relying on seasoning can, however, be dangerous. To the extent an investor is considering a more seasoned pool, or a new pool that includes some more seasoned products, it is important to review in greater detail where and when those mortgages were originated. One may find that the loans were made at the peak of the market, and that home values in the area have dropped dramatically since then. This would clearly offset many of the perceived benefits of seasoning. It could also prove important to analyze the timing of the originations with changes in the originator's underwriting criteria since many originators go through cycles where underwriting standards are loosened or tightened to meet certain management objectives.

BORROWER QUALITY

The majority of this chapter so far has focused on characteristics of the mortgage loans. Basic to the work of loan underwriters is also a credit assessment of the potential borrower. Underwriters rely on information provided in the loan application and supporting documentation, as well as credit reports available from various vendors. Most loan applicants going through this process are considered "A"-quality borrowers. Although their income levels and available assets may result in differing levels of debt capacity, their credit histories do not have any significant blemishes.

Through the 1980s, individuals without clean credit records, especially those with more significant problems, found mortgage funding from different sources. Since they were considered higher risk borrowers, or borrowers that were more likely to default on their mortgages, lenders to this group generally relied more heavily, if not exclusively, on the appraised value of the home and the loan-to-value. At its extreme, lenders in this group were considered "hard-money" lenders, who underwrote the transaction almost entirely based on the quality of the asset, giving little consideration to the quality of the borrower. These lenders offset the higher risk by charging interest rates that were sometimes two or three times the more typical mortgage rate. This market was highly fragmented among relatively small lending operations. Securitization of these loans was also rare because underwriting and documentation was not standardized. This changed substantially in the 1990s. Underwriting and documentation became more standardized as the larger, more traditional originators became active in the market. With improved and standardized documentation, securitization of what has come to be called the B&C market has also grown.

Although having more finely honed categories of borrowers, from "A" to "A-minus," "B," "C," and "D," depending on the severity of their past credit problems, should be of benefit to investors, it is not without its concerns and issues. Mostly this is because while much more standardized, definitions for these categories continues to vary somewhat among originators and between rating agencies. In general, the range of quality runs from those borrowers that have had a minor number of situations where they have been late for short periods of time on credit card, or other non-mortgage related debt payments, to those who have experienced recent personal bankruptcies. The time frame in which these credit problems occurred is also considered important, with more recent occurrences being of greater concern. Also originators and rating agencies will focus on the frequency of these credit problems. On the originator's side, loan underwriters may be willing to consider reasons for these problems as mitigating factors to the extent they may be considered one-time events. Rating agencies are less likely to give credit for such considerations. These differences serve to exacerbate the confusion. A "B-quality" borrower to one originator can be a "C-quality" borrower to another. Ultimately investors in the B&C market need to understand the impact of these differences. This is especially true for investors in subordinate certificates. The easiest way to deal with this concern is through complete and adequate disclosure so that investors can make an informed decision. This disclosure should be both about the quality of the borrowers and the underwriting process.

A related issue is the occasional tendency for originators, conduits, and brokers to mix borrowers with different quality levels into a single pool. This makes it very difficult to determine appropriate assumptions for both prepayment expectations and default and loss assumptions. It will also potentially confuse matters when investors try to monitor and draw conclusions from actual loss experience as the transactions mature.

Another reason for concern is that some originators in their drive to enter this market may not put sufficient emphasis on the fact that the origination and servicing needs of the less than "A-quality" market are significantly different from what is necessary for the traditional "A-quality" loan. Underwriting due diligence should be higher. The balance between borrower credit profiles and asset coverage should be different. These borrowers also need a great deal more guidance during the servicing period to avoid the delinquency problems that put them is this position to begin with. Finally, loss mitigation techniques must be much more intense and must be applied much more quickly to limit severity.

Given these many considerations why has the B&C market gained the kind of attention that it has in a relatively short amount of time. Initially, this could be attributed to the wider spreads and higher yields that investments in this asset class offered. This was especially true before the asset class became more generally accepted. A second, more longstanding, reason is the different prepayment profile. Generally, the nature of the borrower is expected to offer a more stable near term prepayment profile. Since these borrowers have had credit problems, they have fewer options and are not expected to have as many refinancing opportunities.

MORTGAGE SCORING

While loan underwriters each have their own criteria for analyzing borrower quality, many also rely on simple grading systems, typically referred to as credit scores, that are marketed by various vendors. The use of credit scores has greatly simplified the underwriting process by narrowing down the many credit considerations into a single score that can then be compared from one borrower to another on an objective basis. Credit scores can also be used to provide the different gradations between "A-quality" borrowers and less than "A-quality" borrowers. A more recent innovation by both independent vendors and originators has been mortgage scoring systems that also take into account risk components associated with the other factors described earlier, such as loan-to-value and geographic location. Most scoring systems being introduced today are also based on very detailed, and highly robust statistical models. The parameters behind these models are based on the analysis of loan characteristics of both good and defaulted loans numbering in the hundreds of thousands originated over many years.

As scoring systems encourage standardization of underwriting, a positive trend has been developing. Oftentimes problems have resulted from errors in underwriting when certain potential risk factors are overlooked. Standardization should reduce the frequency of these problems. Nonetheless, scoring in and of itself should not be considered a panacea for several reasons.

First is that credit scoring and the credit component of a mortgage score focuses on the borrower's past credit history and current financial profile. As such it is only a near term predictor of the borrower's likelihood of default. It should not be assumed to be predictive for the entire life of the mortgage.

Second is the basic differential between credit scores and mortgage scores. Especially considering the short-term nature of the score, it is potentially dangerous to assume that a good credit score completely offsets other risk factors. While clearly an essential part, if not the most important part of the loan underwriting process, a borrower's ability to pay is only one aspect driving potential defaults. Taking that one step further, it is inappropriate to assume that good mortgage scores, even to the extent that they include other loan characteristics, are enough. Automated underwriting should not be mistaken for automatic underwriting. A good scoring system can be a very useful tool to the originator for determining the extensiveness of any further underwriting needs. By defining the two extremes, "easy passes" and "easy fails," a mortgage scoring system can make the process much more efficient, allowing the allocation of greater resources towards underwriting the large majority of applications that fall between the extremes. A mortgage scoring system can also give guidance on those specific areas that require more diligence. This diligence should still result in rejection for some loan applications, at least with respect to their appropriateness for certain pools.

From an investor's standpoint good mortgage scores should also not translate into an assumption that all risks have been mitigated. Loans considered to have higher risk characteristics continue to have those characteristics even if there are other factors that are considered lower risk. As an example, a cash-out loan with a high balance still represents a significant risk to investors even with a borrower that has a good credit history and a home in a good geographic area. It would not be too much of a stretch to see a dramatic decline in real estate values leading to a higher loss severity that can eliminate credit protection for the lower level tranches. Another way for investors to become overly comfortable with a pool of loans that are mortgage scored is to forget that a good average score for the pool may be a combination of some loans with better scores and some with lower quality scores. Just as with the other factors described here, detailed information on the mix of scores is important to gain full knowledge about the pool.

Assessing the reliability of any originator's scoring system also includes the same level of analysis that was necessary in reviewing an originator's underwriting criteria. One critical aspect of this is understanding and gaining comfort in how dynamic the guidelines are. Any standardized scoring system would quickly become stale and unpredictive if not continuously reviewed and adjusted to take new economic realties into account. It is important therefore to understand what management control systems exist for such regular quality control of the scoring system.

Given these provisos, investors should gain some comfort from the fact that a pool of loans has mortgage scores provided that there is still adequate information about the various loan characteristics that have been described here and the full range of mortgage scores that are represented in the pool.

At this time, there are also limitations on where mortgage scores can even be available. For the most part, mortgage scores cannot be created after the fact. Once a loan has been originated, many of the facts necessary to calculate a mortgage score become either unavailable or stale. Also since mortgage scores rely very heavily on historical statistical studies, there are many areas where that amount of historical background is insufficient.

SUMMARY AND CONCLUSION

The two questions of availability of information and actual benefits that can be realized inevitably must be dealt with. As to the latter issue, the potential benefits are clearly much greater for the lower rated classes in the typical senior-subordinate structure. Assuming subordination levels stay relatively robust, this level of detail has only limited value to the AAA investor. It can have some impact on potential resale prices, but only in the extreme case of an unusually constituted package will a pool actually sustain losses sufficient to impair the senior class. This may happen when there are extremely heavy state concentrations or very high levels of limited documentation loans when originators chase after market share and pure production to sustain growth in overhead.

The analysis is much more important for the subordinate classes. Especially in the early years of a pool, it does not take much in the way of delinquencies and foreclosures for stop-loss levels to be triggered. The blockage of payments, even on a temporary basis, can have a significant impact on realized yield. Further, with the very thin layers of subordination, any concentrated problem can very quickly eliminate supporting securities through allocation of actual losses in the pool.

The only way investors have of limiting this potential, since it cannot be completely eliminated, is to focus on quality of the mortgage underwriting and quality of the collateral. Alternatively, if investors are prepared to take those risks, they should be in a position to look for higher potential returns.

As to the amount of effort required, let alone the ability to access information, much of the work on originators can be done up-front in anticipation of future investment opportunities. A substantial amount can be turned into a formulaic exercise. Only where there have been substantial changes in underwriting approaches at a given originator does the process become more time-consuming.

A good collateral summary on a specific pool from a dealer will also answer the majority of questions about the characteristics of the pool, at least enough to reveal anomalies requiring further analysis. Therefore while the detail can seem daunting at first, the credit analysis side of the mortgage market is nothing that a good fundamental analyst cannot handle.

Chapter 16

Risk-Based Pricing Nonagency Mortgages and Securities

Frank Raiter
Structured Finance Ratings
Standard & Poor's

The evolution of mortgage underwriting technology and risk analyses that has occurred since mid-1995 has created a number of unique opportunities for mortgage bankers, issuers, and investors. One of the most enticing opportunities that has arisen from this technology is the ability of mortgage originators and portfolio managers to apply risk-based pricing techniques to individual loans. The developments in these techniques are a direct result of the implementation of automated underwriting systems that incorporate statistical mortgage scoring capabilities. These scoring systems have driven the refinements to analytical models that provide the information necessary for investors to gauge the relative risk of an individual loan and to establish a price or, conversely, a coupon reflecting the inherent risk.

AUTOMATED UNDERWRITING SYSTEMS

The automated underwriting systems that are currently available include GE Capital Mortgage Insurance Co.'s Omni System, MGIC's LPS, PMI's Aura, and UGI's AccuScore. These systems share the same fundamental advantages of objectivity, consistency, speed, and efficiency. In addition, each of these systems incorporates to some extent advances in technology that provide for the verification of key elements of the application such as income and employment. Several of these systems also incorporate links that provide access to advanced systems for alternative collateral assessment, mortgage insurance evaluation, and other subsystem routines that further streamline the single-family mortgage application process.

These improvements in systems design and data accumulation will all reduce the time associated with processing a mortgage application and, therefore, reduce the associated costs. However, it is the advances in statistical mortgage scoring that have been the engine that has driven the market so rapidly toward the potential of risk-based pricing and integrating risk management.

MORTGAGE SCORING

A mortgage score, by common definition, is a calculated numeric score that represents the probability of a mortgage default. Mortgage scores have a significant advantage over manual underwriting. This advantage is a result of the number and diversity of variables that a scoring model can manipulate in arriving at a conclusion as compared to a human underwriter poring through a thick paper file.

Most mortgage scoring systems address the key aspects of the mortgage file, including application data such as employment, residence, and down payment information, and borrower capacity data, including assets, reserves, income, and overall borrower liabilities. In addition, mortgage scoring systems look at borrower credit data that include previous credit performance, timing and usage of credit, and the various types of credit a borrower utilizes. Finally, scoring systems look at mortgage-specific data, including property type, financing type (first lien, second lien, or cash out/refinance), and the type of loan product (fixed-rate, adjustable, or other) that is represented by the proposed mortgage note. The scoring systems reviewed and calibrated by Standard & Poor's weighted the key variables according to their proprietary formulas, yet each provided a high degree of predictability.

The analyses and research that have been completed by the sponsors of the models and the analysts at Standard & Poor's substantiated the premise that mortgage scores are both objective and consistent. As a result of Standard & Poor's calibration process, a loan that is run through the mortgage scoring systems that have been validated and mapped by Standard & Poor's would receive the same risk grade regardless of the scoring system used. The same cannot always be said for a loan that is reviewed by five underwriters applying standard guidelines with subjective exception rules. In addition, mortgage scoring systems have proved to be highly consistent. A loan that is scored on a particular system will receive the same score two weeks later, as long as no variables have been altered.

Mortgage scores also have proved to be highly predictive of the probability of the mortgage default or loss. Therefore, these scores allow better management of credit risk than bucketing by guidelines interpreted by underwriters at the time of origination.

SETTING A NEW STANDARD

While mortgage scores were one of the critical developments in the evolution taking place in the mortgage market, the proliferation of scoring systems did not provide the industry with one easily applied standard for risk ordering loans based on the new technology. As a result, Standard & Poor's, working with the major score system sponsors, mapped the scores of these systems into a matrix that allowed a consistent system of risk grading loans to be established. These risk grades (RG1–RG7) reflect default probabilities based on mortgage scores. Therefore, they contain the same elements of objectivity and consistency that are inherent in the underlying scoring systems.

The Standard & Poor's risk grades RG1-RG7 are intended to replace the current underwriting guideline base system of A, A–, B, C, and D (see Exhibit 1). In particular, the objectivity and consistency of the mortgage scores in the jumbo and sub-prime arena provide, for the first time, a standard that can easily be applied to any new or existing loan. Regardless of the originating institution, given an adequate amount of data, including current credit information, a mortgage can be scored and assigned a Standard & Poor's risk grade reflecting the loan's current likelihood of default. While some scoring systems built into automated underwriting systems can only score a loan at origination, the algorithm incorporated in Standard & Poor's LEVELS™ model can score loans any time using a standard data tape with a current FICO score.

RISK-BASED PRICING

The standardization of risk grades tied to default probabilities provides the link to the analytical models that integrate the mortgage characteristics and pricing in the secondary market. Standard & Poor's has developed its LEVELS™ model to analyze individual mortgage loans and assign the appropriate risk grade. The LEVELS™ model uses the standard mortgage data file to compute estimated loss coverage requirements for residential mortgage loans or pools of loans based on Standard & Poor's rating criteria.

The model consists of the following six primary subroutines:

- quality control
- risk grade assignment
- foreclosure frequency adjustments
- loss severity estimation
- loss estimates
- the generation of credit enhancement levels

Exhibit 1: Standard & Poor's Risk Grades

RG1: Superior quality loans exhibiting the lowest potential of default.
RG2: Above average quality, expected to outperform the market overall.
RG3: Average quality loans exhibit default rates generally expected of loans underwritten to guidelines.
RG4: Slightly below the quality exhibited by agency underwriting.
RG5: Loans exhibiting default expectations that are considerably higher than the average loan.
RG6: Loan with default rates at significant multiples of the average quality loans.
RG7: Loan exhibiting the highest risk of default.

The quality control module checks each record in a loan data file to identify missing and/or incorrectly defined fields. The model generates output reports that identify any problems detected and, if not corrected, the reports will identify the assumptions that the model uses in order to complete the analyses. Risk grades assigned are based on the scores from validated mortgage scoring systems. If there is no validated mortgage score, the LEVELS™ model will assign a risk grade based on its internal mortgage scoring algorithm. Loan files submitted to Standard & Poor's that include FICO scores will receive mortgage scores from the LEVELS™ model. These scores then will be mapped into the risk grades. The model adjusts the foreclosure rates associated with the mortgage score based on the prime pool characteristics.

The next major calculations performed by the LEVELS™ model relate to the estimation of the expected loss severity associated with the given loan predicated on the assumed market value decline of the property in the event that foreclosure occurs. Estimates for liquidation expenses associated with foreclosure including brokerage fees, legal fees, taxes, and accrued interest payable are incorporated in these estimates. Loss severity estimates are developed as a percentage of the original loan values and converted to an estimated dollar amount. The loss estimates are then used as a basis for developing loss coverage or credit enhancement levels necessary to protect investors under different economic scenarios for different classes of rated securities. The ratings range from AAA to B. LEVELS™ then provides output for investors or for issuers pooling mortgages for securities. The output comprises the following three main elements:

- the risk grade of the associated loan
- the loss estimate of the loan
- the range of credit enhancement requirements associated with the particular loan or pool of loans

The information provided by the LEVELS™ analytics lends itself to several key risk management activities of portfolio managers, investors, and secondary market professionals. These include risk grading, which stratifies a portfolio across seven risk grades that are currently available. The information also allows gauging loan loss reserve requirements based on the loss estimates on a loan-by-loan and portfolio basis. Last but not least, the opportunities for risk-based pricing and its subsets of decision management include establishing risk-adjusted coupons at the time loans are originated and best execution analysis at origination between whole loan sale or securitization. Tools for the portfolio manager include marking portfolios to market, stratifying portfolios for liquidity, and performing best execution analyses of the whole loan and securitization options. Finally, the information provided can benefit in servicing management, as the intensity of servicing required is a function of a loan risk grade. In addition, by periodically calculating FICO scores on a portfolio of current mortgages, the complexion of the risk of a portfolio can be updated and the full range of value calculations completed for asset/liability management and interest rate risk measurement.

Exhibit 2: LEVELS™ Output

Prime Loan			Credit enhancement requirements (%)
Risk grade = RG1			
Collateral information			
Balance ($)	100,000	AAA	6.00
WAC (%)	8.0	AA	3.64
WAM (mos.)	360	A	2.55
WALA (mos.)	3	BBB	1.82
WALTV (%)	76.7	BB	0.91
Full doc. (%)	100	B	0.46
		N.R.	N.R

WALA—Weighted average loan age. N.R.—Not rated

Exhibit 3: Structuring a Synthetic Transaction

Assumed Speed: 225 PSA

| Avg. life: (yrs) | 7.0 | 7.0 | 7.0 | 7.0 | 7.0 | 7.0 | 7.0 |

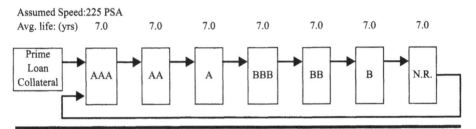

A SIMPLIFIED APPROACH TO RISK-BASED PRICING

Risk-based pricing can now be implemented at the point of origination because of the advances made in loan risk grade standardization coupled with the availability of credit enhancement requirements on a loan-by-loan basis (see Exhibit 2). The credit enhancement requirements then can be used to map an individual loan transaction into the secondary market's pricing mechanism.

This mapping can take place through structuring a synthetic transaction, as market prices are only available through specific rated bonds that have been recently sold to investors (see Exhibit 3). In the prime loan arena the predominant structure is the senior/subordinated passthrough. In the sub-prime arena the predominant structure uses the excess spread-bond insured structure, although issuers are interested in extending the senior/subordinated passthrough structure to the sub-prime market.

Using one of the readily available structuring systems the sized classes can be structured and prepayment speeds applied to determine average lives for each bond and a coupon set. In the example shown in Exhibit 4, the coupon selected is 7.5%, creating an interest-only (IO) strip of 50 basis points to cover servicing and provide some excess to the originator.

Exhibit 4: Bond Size and Pricing

Rating	Size ($)	Coupon (%)	Price	Proceeds ($)
AAA	94,000,000	7.5	100.0	94,000,000
AA	2,360,000	7.5	99.4	2,345,840
A	1,090,000	7.5	97.0	1,057,300
BBB	730,000	7.5	94.6	690,580
BB	910,000	7.5	87.0	791,700
B	460,000	7.5	64.0	294,400
N.R.	460,000	7.5	30.0	135,000
Total	100,000,000			99,314,820

N.R.—Not rated

Exhibit 5: Proceeds Analysis

Bonds proceeds		$99,314,820
IO (loan @ 8.00%)	50 bps @ $100,000,000	2,000,000
Minus		
	PV servicing	(510,000)
	Securitization fee 0.50	(500,000)
	ROE	(694,820)
		$99,610,000
Plus IO 10 bps:		390,000
Adjusted loan coupon = 8.10%		$100,000,000

In establishing a risk-based pricing mechanism, the value of a loan must be defined in its entirety so that the various pieces, including the net coupon, the servicing fees, up-front points, origination costs, securitization costs, and required rates of return on equity, must all be factored into the calculation. The market value of the risk associated with an individual loan or portfolio is established by the private-label MBS market by looking at the spreads to Treasuries for AAA through N.R. and IO strips of transactions that were recently brought to market. Establishing a synthetic securitization allows the real-time couponing of a loan against the current spreads in the market place.

In Exhibit 4, the synthetic structure has been established and each bond priced against the current Treasury curve. The gross proceeds at $99,314,820 equate to a price of 99.3 versus funding at par. A review of the proceeds analysis takes into account the other economic variables integral to appropriately sizing the loan coupon and providing for best execution comparisons (see Exhibit 5). In this example, the proceeds are augmented by the value of the IO strip and reduced by the costs associated with servicing the loan, securitizing a transaction, and providing a return to the originator's capital. After making these adjustments, the loan has achieved a value of $99,610,000. The risk-based pricing adjustment to bring the loan to break even is an additional IO strip of 10 basis points. In other words, adding 10 basis points to the coupon (raising it from 8.00% to 8.10%) provides the originator with sufficient coupon to break even on securitization, retain the servicing, and enjoy a return on capital. From a best execution perspective, should the whole loan bid be in excess of 100, the originator adds to the return originating the loan.

UNIQUE DIMENSION ADDED

Risk-based pricing can be applied to new volumes at the time applications are underwritten or adapted to risk grading and valuing seasoned portfolios for asset/liability management or whole loan trading. Because the tools now exist to periodically risk stratify a portfolio of single-family whole loans or to review the risk status and market value of the remaining loans supporting a previously issued security, a unique dimension has been added to mortgage analytics.

C. Prepayment Analysis and Valuation Modeling

Chapter 17

The Next Generation of Prepayment Models to Value Nonagency MBS

Dale Westhoff
Senior Managing Director
Bear Stearns & Co.

V.S. Srinivasan
Associate Director
Bear Stearns & Co.

INTRODUCTION

The rapid evolution of the nonagency mortgage market has necessitated the development of a new breed of mortgage prepayment model that accommodates a much wider range of loan and borrower attributes than we have seen historically. In just the last few years the nonagency sector has grown from a single market dominated by jumbo[1] loans with fairly uniform characteristics to one with several sub-sectors predicated on diverse loan features that fall outside of the scope of agency underwriting guidelines. Existing nonagency prepayment models have not kept pace with these developments, in part because of a lack of historical prepayment data on these new sub-sectors. Furthermore, despite access to a rich database of property level information in the nonagency sector, technology constraints have prevented modelers from bringing the full value of this data to investors. Today, however, three factors are serving to change the face of nonagency valuation models going forward:

1. The technology now exists to handle the massive computational requirements involved in implementing a prepayment model entirely at the property level.

---

[1] Loans that exceed GSE loan size limits.

2. The refinancing events in the first and fourth quarters of 1998 filled critical information voids in our Alternative-A and Jumbo prepayment databases.
3. The availability of detailed loan level information in the nonagency sector allows us to examine this recent refinancing experience in extensive detail.

Taken together these factors represent the foundation for what we believe will be a new era in nonagency mortgage valuation technology. For the first time we believe the precision and accuracy of these models will far surpass what is available in the agency sector where there is no disclosure of property level information. It is in this context that we introduce our new nonagency prepayment model that incorporates this new data while delivering uncompromised, loan level parametrics to the nonagency mortgage investor.

INNOVATIVE FEATURES:
A TRUE LOAN LEVEL IMPLEMENTATION

The most unique aspect of our new model is that it is implemented entirely at the property level[2] despite enormous computational requirements. In general, the precision of first generation loan level prepayment models was compromised by the need to aggregate data at run-time to reduce computational load and turnaround time. This resulted in a loss of information and precision. A full loan level implementation implies that when evaluating a particular security for a given interest rate assumption, the model preserves all loan level information by amortizing each loan individually rather than aggregating loans together. To do this, a unique vector of single monthly mortality (SMM) rates is generated for each loan in a deal conditional on the interest rate path and specific loan and borrower characteristics. Until recently, the drawback to this approach was its processing demand, particularly in an option-adjusted spread (OAS) framework where hundreds of randomly generated interest rate scenarios are evaluated in the calculation of a single OAS. For example, for a nonagency deal backed by 2,000 loans the prepayment function is invoked 648 million times to compute the option-adjusted duration of a single bond.[3] To overcome these tremendous computational requirements, we employ state-of-the-art multi-processor technology in a distributed computing user environment to deliver timely run-time executions.

Our return from this investment in technology is a level of precision in cash flow projections that was previously unattainable. This comes at a time when there is a growing demand from mortgage investors for more rigorous valuation models that address increasingly disparate loan and borrower features. It is imperative that nonagency investors have the ability to quantify the performance implications of

---

[2] No run-time aggregation is performed.

[3] $(2,000 \text{ loans}) \times (360 \text{ amortization months}) \times (300 \text{ interest rate paths}) \times (3 \text{ scenarios}) = 648$ million model evaluations.

wide distributions in loan size, coupon, and loan-to-value. Furthermore, models must be able to differentiate along secondary loan characteristics such as property type, occupancy status, loan purpose, documentation level, and borrower credit quality.

Beyond the added precision of a loan level implementation, our second generation nonagency prepayment model incorporates several unique and innovative features:

1. *Borrower specific home equity levels calculated:* A borrower's current equity position in the home is a key determinant of both refinancing and housing turnover prepayment behavior. Since loan-to-value (LTV) changes as home prices rise or fall in a particular region, we update the LTV of over 350,000 loans in our nonagency database every month using Mortgage Risk Assessment Corporation (MRAC) zip code level home price indices.

2. *Incorporation of 1998 refinancing data:* 1998 provided invaluable nonagency prepayment data, particularly in the Alternative-A sector. Our model incorporates this new data without sacrificing its fit to pre-1998 data.

3. *Borrower self-selection and burnout:* One of the intrinsic benefits of a loan level prepayment model is that it replicates the borrower self-selection or "burnout" that occurs as borrowers prepay their mortgages. By amortizing each loan individually our forecast always reflects the characteristics of the surviving population of borrowers in a pool or deal.

4. *Unique loan sectors addressed:* In addition to the standard residential mortgage types (30-year, 15-year amortization loans) our model handles several less traditional mortgage types, including: relocation mortgages, Community Reinvestment Act (CRA) loans, and prepayment penalty mortgages.

THE BEAR STEARNS NONAGENCY PREPAYMENT DATABASE

Central to the development of a robust loan-level prepayment model is having access to prepayment data that cover a wide range of interest rate environments over a diverse set of loan and borrower attributes. Our nonagency models were estimated from over 350,000 jumbo and Alternative-A nonagency loans collected from six major issuers and originated between 1990 and 1998. Actual prepayment observations cover 1990 to 1998, a period marked by a 400 basis point range in long-term interest rates and punctuated by four major refinancing events. These data represent over 70% of the outstanding nonagency MBS universe. The Alternative-A sub-universe of loans in our database is generally characterized by conforming balances but other non-standard features that prevent agency purchase. The unique characteristics of these loans will be discussed in a subsequent section.

It is important to note that most of the loans coming from the major conduits are actually purchased from broker/correspondents. Therefore, the data tend to represent a fairly diverse group of originators. This is one reason why we elected not to use issuer specific parameters in our model estimation. Issuer specific prepayment models run the risk that a change in an issuer's broker/correspondent purchasing patterns or a change in originator underwriting guidelines will disrupt historical prepayment patterns at the issuer level. That weakness also calls into question the cross-issuer applicability of models developed from a single issuer's data set. Instead, we chose to specify our model by identifying long-term relationships in loan and borrower attributes from a multiple issuer data set. We believe this approach delivers a model with the broadest application while leveraging on the richness of loan level detail.

THE IMPACT OF THE AGENCIES ON NONAGENCY PREPAYMENT BEHAVIOR

Changes in agency underwriting guidelines directly impact the prepayment behavior of nonagency securities. By definition, the nonagency sector contains loans above the agency loan size limits or outside of other underwriting criteria established by Fannie Mae and Freddie Mac. Nearly every year agency loan size limits are adjusted higher based on the observed increase in national home prices over the year.[4] In addition to changes in loan size limits, the successful implementation of automated underwriting systems has allowed the agencies to price credit risk more effectively and expand underwriting criteria to accommodate less traditional mortgagors with impaired credit or non-standard features. Clearly, the portion of the existing nonagency universe that qualifies under expanded agency guidelines is at greater risk of prepayment since borrowers can usually obtain much lower financing rates in the conforming market.

These guideline changes can sometimes wreak havoc on short-term prepayment rates in the nonagency sector. For example, at the end of 1997 the agencies raised their loan limits from $214,600 to $227,150, increasing the refinancing incentive on existing jumbo loans with balances between these levels (since they qualified for agency purchase). By isolating the post-change prepayment rates of the loans that fell between the old and new limits we can see a clear structural increase in speeds beginning in 1998 as these borrowers started to refinance into conforming loans. As Exhibit 1 illustrates, the "between limit" loans prepaid systematically faster than identical loans with balances just above the new limit. To an uninformed investor, this would seem counterintuitive since we would normally expect smaller balance loans to pay slower than their large balance equivalent.

---

[4] So far this has always been an upward revision (or the level has remained flat) since aggregate home prices have not declined.

*Exhibit I: Impact of Increase in FNMA/FHLMC Loan Size
Limit on the Nonagency Sector (GWAC = 8.25)*

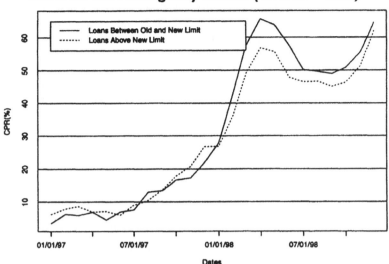

Fortunately, access to loan level information in the nonagency sector allows us to identify the nonagency mortgage population affected by such a change and adjust our models accordingly before the change is implemented.

Expanded agency underwriting criteria also impact the conforming sector where loan disclosure is limited to pool level statistics. As the agencies stretch their guidelines to accommodate less traditional mortgagors that currently fall under the Alternative-A, home equity, or B/C umbrellas, TBA pools become increasingly heterogeneous and less predictable. Without disclosure of property level information or a separate pool prefix to identify these loans, we currently have no mechanism at the agency pool level to model the impact of increased dispersion in loan characteristics. This puts agency prepayment models at a significant disadvantage versus their nonagency counterparts. Exhibit 2 summarizes the disclosure deficit that currently exists between the agency and nonagency sectors.

DEFINING THE SUB-SECTORS WITHIN THE NONAGENCY MARKET

The importance of loan size and its impact on prepayment behavior in the residential mortgage sector has been well studied and empirically documented. In the nonagency sector, loan size takes on added importance because it serves to classify loans into three sub-sectors with different levels of prepayment risk: jumbo loans, conforming balance Alternative-A loans, and jumbo balance Alternative-A loans. Exhibit 3 compares the loan characteristics of these three sub-sector classifications. The jumbo sector represents the most credit worthy and prepayment sensitive group of borrowers in the mortgage market. Loans in the jumbo sector do not qualify for agency purchase almost exclusively because the loan size exceeds the conforming limit. In contrast, the Alternative-A sector is characterized by loans below the agency conforming limit but with other features that prevent agency purchase. This usually involves limited documentation/no income verification loans, investor properties, cash-out loans or some combination of these characteristics. It should be noted that the Alternative-A sector does not imply a substantially weaker borrower credit profile as evidenced by FICO scores that average only 10 points below the average jumbo FICO score.

In 1998, a hybrid sector developed consisting of Alternative-A loans above the agency loan size limit. This sector has a lower concentration of investor properties and a heavier concentration of limited documentation loans than the traditional Alternative-A sector. A key distinction between the jumbo, conforming Alternative-A, and jumbo Alternative-A sectors is the rate premium paid by the borrowers over the prevailing prime jumbo rate. Alternative-A borrowers face a rate premium of between 20 and 150 basis points depending on their non-standard loan characteristics. A further blurring of definitions occurs between the home equity and Alternative-A sectors where the key to differentiation often lies in the lower credit quality of home equity borrowers.

We can think of the nonagency sector as a continuum of borrowers who face a range of transaction costs. At one end of the spectrum we find the jumbo borrower who is characterized by a large balance, superior credit, no rate premium, and few barriers to refinancing. At the other end of the spectrum we find small balance Alternative-A borrowers with non-standard features, high rate premiums, and significant barriers to refinancing. One important advantage of our loan level approach is that it allows us to focus entirely on the loan and borrower attributes that determine the level of transaction costs faced by individual borrowers. The model is impervious to classification distinctions such as Alternative-A, home-equity, and jumbo.

Exhibit 2: Disclosure Deficit Between the Agency and Nonagency Sectors

	Agency (Pool Level)	Nonagency
Loan Age	Weighted Average plus FHLMC quartiles	Loan Level
Loan Maturity	Weighted Average	Loan Level
Location	State Level	Zip Code Level
Loan Size	Weighted Average + FHMLC quartiles	Loan Level
LTV	None	Loan Level (original and current)
FICO	None	Loan Level
Occupancy	None	Investor/Owner
Purpose	None	Purchase/Cash-out/Refinancing
Documentation	None	Limited/EZ/Full
Rate Premium	None	Loan Level

Exhibit 3: Collateral Profiles in the Nonagency Sector 1997 and 1998 Deals

Product	Avg. Bal	LTV	FICO	Rate Premium	Documentation		Purpose			Occupancy		
					Full	Other	Purchase	Cashout	Refinance	Owner	Investor	Other
Alt-A	$96,646	74.7%	716	0.92	58.3%	41.7%	58.7%	25.6%	15.7%	51.7%	43.1%	5.2%
Jumbo Alt-A	$330,129	73.9%	714	0.65	53.3%	46.7%	44.3%	26.5%	29.2%	87.9%	6.8%	5.3%
Jumbo	$312,072	73.8%	725	0.09	80.1%	19.9%	54.2%	11.7%	34.1%	97.5%	0.0%	2.5%

In this framework our forecast is determined by where a particular loan is positioned on the nonagency borrower/transaction cost continuum. For example, a loan labeled as "Alternative-A" but with a jumbo balance, standard loan features, and a small rate premium will be treated as a standard jumbo loan.

DE-CONSTRUCTING OUR NONAGENCY PREPAYMENT FORECAST

Mortgage prepayments occur for five reasons:

1. The borrower elects to sell the home and relocate;
2. The borrower refinances the existing mortgage to lower interest costs and/or cash-out equity;
3. The borrower pays more than the scheduled monthly principal and interest payment (partial prepayment or curtailment);
4. The borrower elects to pay off the entire mortgage ahead of schedule;
5. The borrower is unable or unwilling to make scheduled payments and defaults on the mortgage.

Although identifying the reasons for a mortgage prepayment is straightforward, modeling the probability that a prepayment will occur in any particular month is a complex process that requires understanding a myriad of forces — both internal and external to the borrower — that influence the prepayment decision. The more insight we have into a borrower's current circumstances, the more likely we will be able to understand and model his behavior. Indeed, in our study of property level information in the nonagency sector, we find that what frequently appears to be an "inefficient" exercise of the prepayment option can often be explained by sound underlying economic factors that affect a borrower's transaction costs and ability to refinance.

By far, the most important type of prepayment is the refinance transaction. It is the only class of prepayment where a large number of borrowers respond, more or less in unison, to an external event (lower mortgage rates). This can drive annualized prepayment rates from below 10% CPR to above 60% CPR in just two or three months time. Equally important from the mortgage investor's perspective is that refinancing events almost always serve to negatively impact performance; that is, they shorten the duration of mortgage securities in a low interest rate environment (refinancing increases) and extend the duration of mortgage securities in a high rate environment (refinancing declines). In contrast, the other types of prepayment events tend to be much less volatile and more spread out, driven more by long-term housing fundamentals and/or a borrower's current economic situation than by interest rates.

For example, although prepayments from home resale activity account for about 10% CPR for fully seasoned jumbo securities, it is highly unlikely that a surge in activity would cause this level to change by more than just a few percent. Default and partial prepayments are even less volatile components of the overall prepayment mix, accounting for less than 1.5% CPR on a combined annual basis.[5] Since refinancing accounts for much of the volatility and negative convexity observed in historical prepayments, we will begin our discussion with the refinancing component of our model.

DEFINING THE BASELINE NONAGENCY REFINANCING PROFILE

Our refinancing sub-model is contingent on the complex interaction of multiple variables defined at the property level. To present our findings in a way that is both intuitive and transparent to the reader, we first define a baseline refinancing profile for a representative nonagency jumbo and Alternative-A borrower and then measure the relative change in this profile for different permutations of loan level characteristics. Our baseline jumbo profile (see Exhibit 4) depicts the projected prepayment rate[6] for an average jumbo borrower across a wide spectrum of refinancing incentives. For purposes of this analysis we assume that our baseline jumbo loan has the following characteristics: it is a new, full documentation, purchase loan; single family detached home, owner occupied property, with a $300,000 loan balance, 75% LTV, and no rate premium.[7] For our Alternative-A baseline we modify the jumbo profile in the following way: $150,000 loan balance, limited documentation, and 90 basis point rate premium. In addition, we choose a representative refinancing environment by assuming that mortgage rates are at a 3-year low and that the 2-year to 10-year yield curve slope is 80 basis points. For comparative purposes, Exhibit 4 also shows the baseline profiles for the agency and jumbo Alternative-A borrowers.

To understand the many nuances of refinancing behavior it is critical that we have access to historical refinancing data in a wide range of interest rate environments. Fortunately for the nonagency sector much of this important refinancing data was collected in 1998.

We chose to model a borrower's refinancing incentive as the ratio of loan rate to prevailing mortgage rate (rather than the difference) since it best approximates the dollar cost savings of the refinancing transaction. We will first address two critical aspects of refinancing behavior that are a function of the historical path and absolute level of mortgage rates.

The first of these "path dependent" behaviors is often referred to as "burnout" and occurs at the pool level as borrowers selectively prepay their mortgages. The second effect occurs at the loan level as borrowers respond with increased intensity to certain absolute levels in the prevailing mortgage rate.

---

[5] During the initial five years of the seasoning process.

[6] Expressed in terms of an annualized prepayment (CPR).

[7] The rate premium is the spread above the prevailing prime jumbo mortgage rate.

Exhibit 4: Baseline Refinancing Profiles

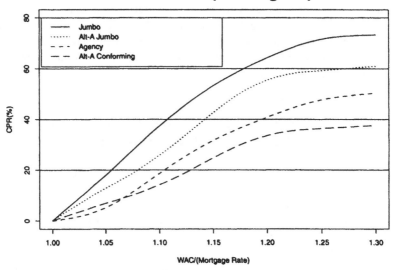

UNDERSTANDING BORROWER SELF-SELECTION AND "BURNOUT"

One of the first observations we can make regarding historical refinancing behavior is that we rarely observe the same refinancing response from the same pool of mortgagors through two different interest rate cycles. As a general rule, pool-level prepayments tend to become less interest rate sensitive over time. This occurs because of the refinancing self-selection in borrowers that takes place as they prepay their mortgages. If we think of a pool of mortgages as a continuum of borrowers with various refinancing transaction costs, then over time we would expect the borrowers with the lowest costs to refinance first, leaving the borrowers with the higher costs and slower prepayment speeds behind. In nearly all situations, the surviving borrower population at any point in time will have fundamentally different prepayment characteristics than the original pool.

We find that refinancing self selection or burnout has both permanent and transitory components. Since the largest loans with the highest rates tend to refinance first in the jumbo sector, both the loan size distribution and coupon distribution tend to shift downward, reducing the expected level and volatility of future prepayments. These are permanent structural changes at the pool or deal level that have long-term implications for our prepayment forecast. However, self-selection also takes place based on more transitory properties associated with an individual's financial status. The most common financial barriers arise from either a lack of equity in the home (caused by declining home values) or a weak credit history.

Clearly, these factors are more temporary in nature as depressed home values usually recover with cyclical housing market expansions and credit status improves with stable or rising personal incomes. Although initially a powerful component of "burnout," there is substantial empirical evidence to support the diminution of credit and equity related refinancing barriers over time. The most recent example of a dramatic shift in the transaction cost structure of a population of borrowers occurred in Southern California, where a recent recovery in home prices has unlocked significant pent-up refinancing demand as previously equity-impaired borrowers take full advantage of lower financing costs. We will discuss the California situation in more detail in a subsequent section on LTV.

Traditional agency prepayment models are at a tremendous disadvantage when it comes to modeling the complex forces that cause burnout. Having access to pool level information only, agency models have no mechanism available to them to model the actual change in borrower composition or the actual change in surviving borrower transaction costs. Instead, modelers are left to develop artificial proxies for this behavior such as a cumulative measure of historical refinancing incentives/prepayments or assumed distributions of fast/slow prepayment buckets. Many of these approaches are predicated on the assumption that borrower self-selection is a cumulative and permanent process, i.e., there is no diminution of refinancing constraints over time.[8]

One of the most powerful aspects of a model estimated and implemented entirely at the property level is that it replicates the changing composition of a pool over time. In a property-level framework we process and amortize each loan separately, insuring that our composite forecast for a pool of mortgages reflects the characteristics of the surviving borrowers. Each forward month forecast is contingent on the distribution of loan characteristics of the previous month's surviving population. We add further precision to this forecast by monitoring and dynamically updating each surviving borrower's monthly equity position using zip code level home price indices. This captures the most transitory component in an individual's financial profile that could inhibit or aid a refinancing transaction.

The profound impact that prepayments have on the distribution of loan attributes is best illustrated with an example. In Exhibit 5 we summarize the loan attributes of 1992 jumbo originations before and after the severe 1993 refinancing event. To demonstrate the ability of our model to replicate this process we also provide the same attribute statistics based only on our model projected prepayment rates over the period. Approximately 48% of the loans refinanced during this time. As Exhibit 5 clearly illustrates, the loan attribute distributions were substantially altered by the refinancing wave as borrowers with high loan rates, large loan balances, and high levels of equity refinanced out of the deal. Secondary loan attributes also shifted toward the less refinance sensitive characteristics such as limited documentation and non-purchase loans. Our model projected change in attributes mirrors the actual change that occurred.

---

[8] However, some models assume a decay constant in the definition of the burnout function.

Exhibit 5: Loan Attribute Distributions Before and After the 1993 Refinancing Event (1992 Jumbo Originations)

Loan Characteristics	Actual		Model Projected
	Jan 1993	May 1994	May 1994
WAC	8.66	8.54	8.53
Avg. Loan Size	$326,753	$300,556	$300,195
Loan Size > 300K	46.52%	38.82%	39.20%
LTV	71.29%	73.01%	72.23%
LTV > 80	9.9%	12.4%	11.8%
Limited doc	35.7%	43.5%	41.5%
Cash-Out	16.3%	17.0%	16.8%

Exhibit 6: Actual Agency Prepayment Curves

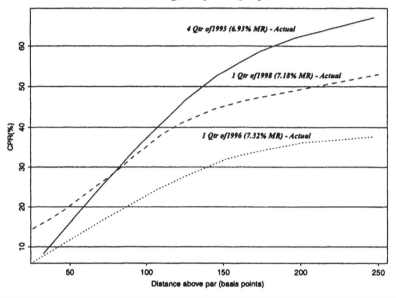

MODELING BORROWER REFINANCING INTENSITY

Even after carefully controlling for all loan characteristics, including refinancing incentive, loan age, and loan size, substantial differences emerge in refinancing behavior through different refinancing events. Consider the refinancing patterns of new conventional conforming loans in three different interest rate cycles: the fourth quarter of 1993, the first quarter of 1996, and the first quarter of 1998 as shown in Exhibit 6. In each case, whether we look at agency or nonagency prepayment data the intensity of the borrower response to the refinancing opportunity is substantially different. While some of these differences can be explained by structural efficiency gains in the refinancing process itself, we are still left with a fundamentally different borrower response in each period, particularly in 1996. Why do borrowers with nearly identical loan attributes and identical refinancing incentives sometimes exhibit very different refinancing behavior? How we reconcile this behavior is one of the most important challenges facing prepayment modelers today.

What is clear from empirical analysis is that borrowers time their refinancing transactions to lock-in a perceived low point in the mortgage rate cycle. Borrower perceptions of the relative attractiveness of the prevailing mortgage rate play a crucial role in determining the timing and intensity of a lock-in event. Panel studies suggest that these perceptions are shaped by the recent path of mortgage rates as well as the absolute level of today's rate. For example, if we are in a declining interest rate environment and similar refinancing opportunities have existed in the recent past, borrowers will often refrain from refinancing on the expectation that rates will continue to decline in the future. However, the propensity of a borrower to refinance increases sharply as the rally pushes the absolute level of mortgage rates through previous historical low points. This is usually accompanied by increasing media attention, raising the consciousness of the entire mortgage universe. The condition that ultimately triggers a simultaneous rate-lock by borrowers is usually a sudden back-up in interest rates, as was the case in the fourth quarter of 1993, or when rates match a historically significant threshold, as in the first quarter of 1998.

To model this behavior we have defined a "look-back" function that compares today's mortgage rate to all previous historical levels. This function is sensitive to both the absolute level of rates and the time since equivalent refinancing opportunities existed in the past. In this way it takes on increasing significance as the mortgage rate matches previous historical lows in rates, e.g. a 1-year low in rates takes on less significance than a 5-year low in rates. The function achieves its maximum value when mortgage rates reach an all time low as in 1993 and the fourth quarter of 1998. This framework is logical and intuitive in that it captures the pent-up demand that results when a long period of time elapses between equivalent opportunities. It also matches the data extremely well. By viewing prior refinancing events in this context the observed discrepancies in 1993, 1996, and 1998 come into focus:

- The 1996 refinancing wave was very muted because the market had experienced equivalent or better opportunities in the recent past (the fourth quarter of 1993 and the first quarter of 1994).
- The first quarter of 1998 refinancing episode was triggered when mortgage rates fell below 1996 levels, making it the best opportunity to refinance in over four years. This event was still less intense than the 1993 episode, which represented a 30-year low.
- The fourth quarter of 1998 spike in new issue prepayments almost equaled 1993 as mortgage rates approached a lifetime low.

Exhibit 7: Projected Baseline Jumbo Refinancing Profiles

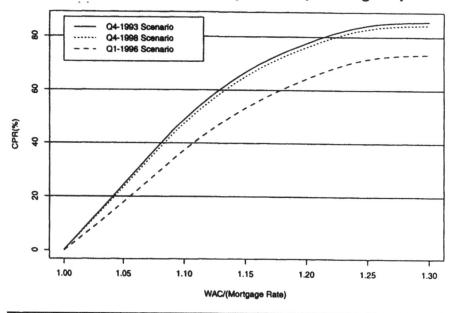

It should be noted that this function serves to steepen the refinancing profile for all mortgage products including very seasoned/burned-out issues (although the relative magnitude of prepayments between new and seasoned issues is maintained). This is consistent with recent data showing that even seasoned borrowers respond to a historic low in mortgage rates despite having passed up nearly similar opportunities in the recent past. Exhibit 7 provides our projected baseline jumbo refinancing profiles if we replicate the conditions that existed 1993, 1996, and 1998. Note that the relative magnitude of the curves is consistent with actual experience.

THE IMPACT OF LOAN SIZE ON NONAGENCY REFINANCING BEHAVIOR

Apart from refinancing incentive, loan size is the most important determinant of prepayment behavior in the nonagency sector. A small loan balance reduces the economic incentive to refinance assuming fixed transaction costs. Even if small balance borrowers amortize these costs in a "no-point" option, they still face higher effective mortgage rates since the costs are a larger percentage of the loan balance. Jumbo borrowers, on the other hand, have an increased economic incentive to refinance and are more likely to be aggressively solicited by mortgage brokers (broker commissions are commensurate with loan size).

Exhibit 8: Prepayment Profile Comparison

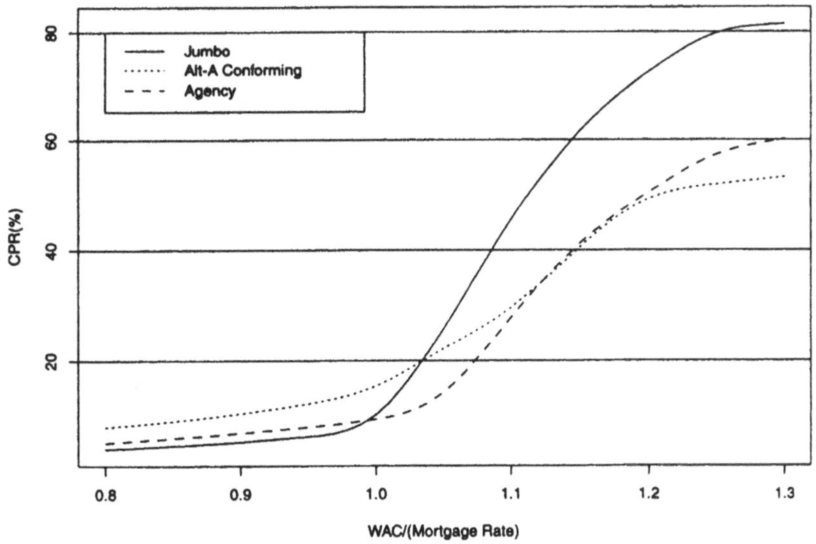

The opposite is true in a rising rate environment, when jumbo borrowers have a greater disincentive to prepay their below market mortgage rate relative to conforming balance borrowers. Rising rates also make "trading-up" in homes less attractive, forcing some borrowers to postpone a planned move. This behavior is responsible for the increased "negative convexity" often associated with the nonagency jumbo mortgage market. This is clearly evident in Exhibit 8 which contrasts the prepayment profile of our baseline jumbo borrower (average balance of $300,000) to the much flatter profiles of agency borrowers (average balance $110,000) and conforming balance Alternative-A borrowers (average balance $96,646).

Beyond the refinancing economics, borrowers with small loan balances typically represent a lower income and demographic segment of the population given that personal income is the key underwriting criteria that originators use to size a mortgage. Exhibit 9 summarizes jumbo and Alternative-A loan characteristics by loan size quartile. In general, we observe that there is a positive correlation between loan size and a borrower's income level, and credit rating. Furthermore, we observe that small balance borrowers tend to pay a higher rate premium (spread over the prime jumbo rate) than large balance borrowers. In the Alternative-A sector, we also find that investor properties make up over 40% of the loans with balances below the conforming limit. As we will show, all of these characteristics are linked to less efficient refinancing behavior in the small balance universe.

Exhibit 9: Jumbo and Alternative-A Loan Characteristics by Loan Size Quartile

Product	Quartile	Avg. Bal ($)	Avg. Prem	LTV (%)	Documentation (%)		Purpose (%)			Occupancy (%)		
					Full	Other	Purchase	Cashout	Refinance	Owner	Investor	Other
Jumbo	25%	521,776	0.04	71.5	91.7	8.3	47.8	12.4	39.8	96.9	0.0	3.1
	50%	311,523	0.05	74.4	93.1	6.9	52.5	11.5	35.9	97.8	0.0	2.2
	75%	259,058	0.08	76.2	93.6	6.4	55.9	9.8	34.3	98.0	0.0	2.0
	100%	163,904	0.21	73.0	62.1	37.9	60.3	13.2	26.5	97.2	0.0	2.7
Alt-A	25%	293,087	0.68	74.1	50.4	49.6	46.2	26.6	27.3	85.8	9.1	5.1
	50%	132,909	0.85	75.8	50.8	49.2	56.2	24.6	19.2	66.4	28.1	5.5
	75%	82,471	0.93	74.3	58.8	41.2	58.2	27.0	14.9	49.2	45.2	5.5
	100%	45,235	1.06	74.0	71.1	28.9	64.4	24.7	10.8	29.5	66.0	4.6

Exhibit 10: 1998 FHLMC LLB Actual Prepayments (CPR) (Post -1993 Originations)

Coupon	Universe (CPR)	LLB (CPR)	% Slower
7.0	17.6	8.3	−53
7.5	29.5	17.0	−42
8.0	37.3	23.9	−36
8.5	40.0	30.0	−25

It is important to note that these findings are consistent in both the agency and nonagency sectors even though we cannot observe loan-level attributes directly in the agency sector. We can, however, examine actual agency prepayment speeds conditional on the average loan size of a pool. For example, Exhibit 10 compares the 1998 prepayment speeds of FHLMC pools with average loan sizes less than or equal to $70,000 to their equivalent TBA counterparts. The low balance pools paid 25% to 53% slower than otherwise equivalent TBA pools during a period dominated by refinancing activity. The jumbo universe shows a similar separation in speeds by loan size category up to approximately the $400,000 loan balance (see Exhibit 11). Above this level there is little additional increase in prepayment sensitivity.

Another important aspect of loan size that is not fully captured by traditional prepayment models is the substantial risk associated with loan size dispersion at the deal level. Exhibit 12 shows the distribution of loan sizes by balance in the jumbo and Alternative-A sectors for deals issued in 1997 and 1998. Although the Alternative-A distribution is lower and more concentrated than the jumbo distribution, both sectors have substantial exposure to a high balance "tail" in the distribution. For example, on a balance weighted basis approximately one third of the loans in the Alternative-A sector are above the $200,000 mark while nearly 20% of the jumbo distribution is above $500,000.[9] This tends to make nonagency cash flows very "front-loaded" since the largest balance loans refinance first, generating proportion-

---

[9] On a frequency basis these numbers would be much lower. For example, the percentage of jumbo loans exceeding $500,000 drops to 6% based on frequency of occurrence.

ally larger prepayment rates (a large balance loan is a bigger percentage of the total outstanding principal of a pool/deal than a small balance loan). Therefore, a pool with a wide distribution is much more likely to exhibit a high level of prepayment volatility early in its life than a pool with the same average loan size but a narrow distribution. The additional prepayment sensitivity caused by a wide distribution in loan sizes is the primary reason that most nonagency deals are priced to a significantly faster prepayment assumption than equivalent agency deals, i.e., most nonagency deals have a portion of this distribution that is in the "refinancing window."

Exhibit 11: Loan Size Effect - Jumbo Sector

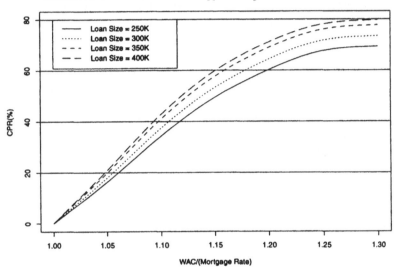

Exhibit 12: Jumbo versus Alt-A Loan Size Distribution (balance weighted)

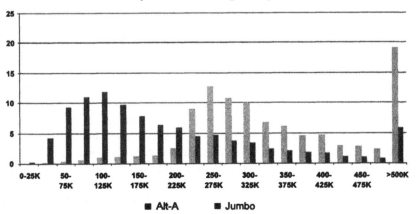

However, as pools are exposed to multiple refinancing opportunities, the distribution of loan sizes migrates rapidly toward smaller balances as the large balance portion of the deal pays off. The dramatic shift that takes place in the loan size distribution is best illustrated by an actual example. Consider PHMSC 9501, a $205 million jumbo deal issued in 1995 with an original average loan size of $249,000 (38% of the loans had balances above $300,000) and a GWAC of 8.85%.

As Exhibit 13 shows, PHMSC 9501 experienced two major refinancing events: one at the beginning of 1996 and the another at the beginning of 1998. Exhibit 13 also tracks the migration of average loan size and WAC since the deal was issued. We find that by December 1998 — at the end of the refinancing waves — the average loan size of PHMSC 9501 declined to $190,000 (a drop of nearly $60,000) with only 24% of the remaining loans in the above $300,000 category. Meanwhile the percentage of loans below $200,000 increased from 10% to 26% while the WAC decreased from 8.85% to 8.72%. Clearly the prepayment characteristics and our forecast for PHMSC 9501 have changed radically since its issue. The key to accurately modeling the powerful effects of loan size and loan coupon dispersion and the front-loaded nature of the resulting cash flows is through loan level processing. Since our model amortizes each loan individually, it predicts the migration of loan size and coupon distributions.

In the Alternative-A sector, despite very disparate loan and borrower attributes, we also find that loan size plays a central role in refinancing behavior. Exhibit 14 plots the refinancing profiles conditional on loan size category for our baseline Alternative-A borrower. The small balance universe in this sector is characterized by a heavy concentration of investment properties and large rate premiums while the large balance population is distinguished by refinancing transactions, owner occupied properties, and low rate premiums. While the overall interest rate sensitivity of this sector is lower than in the jumbo or agency sector, the familiar pattern of increasing refinancing sensitivity with increasing loan balances is clearly evident in the data. Note also the clear separation in speeds above and below the agency conforming limit of $240,000.

The distinction between the Alternative-A and jumbo sectors blurs at loan balances above the agency conforming limit. With minimal differences in credit quality, it is the non-standard features of jumbo balance Alternative-A loans that tend to increase the transaction and "hassle" costs associated with refinancing. This is evidenced by an average rate premium of 65 basis points paid by jumbo Alternative-A borrowers versus 0 to 5 basis points for regular jumbo borrowers. Over time, we would expect a large percentage of the Alternative-A jumbo borrowers to qualify for standard financing as they establish consistent income patterns or they fall within the expanded loan limits established by FNMA/FHLMC. A comparison of the refinancing profiles of our baseline jumbo borrower to an equivalent loan size Alternative-A borrower is shown in Exhibit 15. As we previously stated, our model forecast is completely independent of the Alternative-A or jumbo sector designation. The model relies solely on the type of non-standard features and the relationship of these features to historical prepayments to determine a specific loan's refinancing sensitivity.

Exhibit 13: PHMSC 9501 Loan Size and WAC Migration

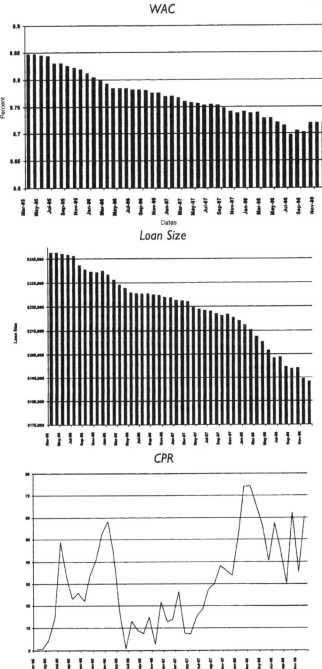

Exhibit 14: Loan Size Effect - Alternative-A Sector

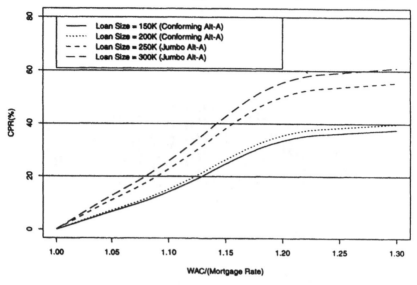

Exhibit 15: Traditional Jumbo versus Alternative-A Jumbo Refinancing Profiles

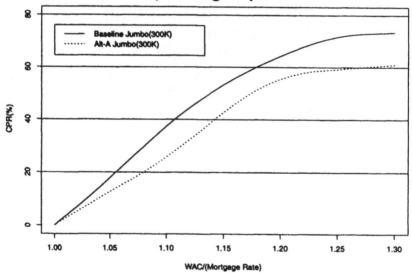

Exhibit 16: FICO Distribution (Jumbo Avg. = 725, Alt-A Avg =715)

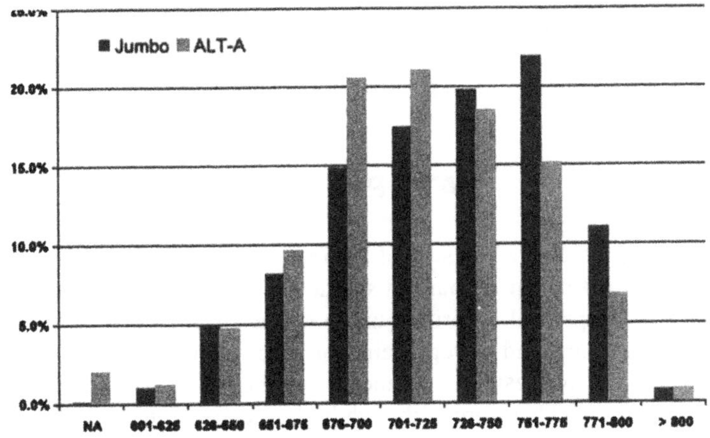

CREDIT QUALITY

Borrowers with weak credit typically receive less attractive financing rates than borrowers with strong credit because originators must compensate for the greater likelihood of default. As a result, weak credit can substantially alter prepayment behavior since, to a large extent, the borrower's evolving credit status — not interest rates — governs the prepayment decision. This accounts for the well recognized "credit cure" effect that accelerates prepayments in the B/C home equity market as borrowers in a low credit tier improve their credit and qualify for a lower financing rate in a higher credit tier.

In general, jumbo and Alternative-A residential borrowers do not exhibit credit curing since they represent the highest end of the credit spectrum (average FICO scores in both sectors usually exceed 675). Very few nonagency loans are below the agency FICO "floor" of 620. Therefore, we feel that credit does not present a significant barrier to refinancing in the nonagency sector unless there is substantial erosion in credit status after a loan is originated. However, we find this to be the exception and not the rule given that credit quality usually improves as personal incomes and property values increase over time. Exhibit 16 compares the jumbo and Alternative-A FICO distributions collected from several recently issued nonagency deals.

Within the jumbo and Alternative-A sectors we do find a weak but intuitive correlation between FICO and other loan attributes. Exhibit 17 provides summary FICO quartile statistics in the Alternative-A and jumbo sectors. In both sectors a lower FICO is associated with a higher average rate premium, a higher LTV, and a bigger percentage of cashout refinance transactions (lower percentage of purchase transactions). Not surprisingly, in the jumbo sector we find that the largest balances are associated with the highest FICO score. Finally, although the average Alternative-A borrower has a slightly lower FICO score than the average jumbo borrower by about 10 points, these findings confirm the fact that circumstances other than credit prevent agency purchase of Alternative-A loans. FICO alone did not produce statistically significant results as an explanatory variable in our nonagency prepayment model.

RATE PREMIUM

We found that an objective measure of a borrower's underwriting status could be obtained by calculating the amount of spread or "rate premium" that the individual pays above the prevailing prime jumbo rate at origination.[10] Loans with the highest rate premium tend to represent borrowers with the least standard loan characteristics, the smallest loan balances, and the lowest credit quality as measured by FICO score. Therefore, although high rate premium loans may be nominally more "in-the-money," they are intrinsically less refinanceable than low rate premium loans. This is confirmed in Exhibit 18 which shows that as the rate premium increases, the concentration of high LTV non-owner occupied properties increases while loan size decreases.

Exhibit 17: Loan Characteristics by FICO Score Quartile

Product	Fico	Quartile	Avg. Bal ($)	Avg. Prem	LTV (%)	Documentation (%)		Purpose (%)			Occupancy (%)		
						Full	Other	Purchase	Cashout	Refinance	Owner	Investor	Other
Jumbo	666	25%	304,092	0.27	75.6	91.6	8.4	39.8	13.9	46.3	99.2	0.0	0.8
	713	50%	309,807	0.19	74.5	87.4	12.6	40.5	12.3	47.2	98.9	0.0	1.1
	746	75%	325,544	0.16	72.7	89.4	10.6	43.7	10.6	45.8	99.2	0.0	0.8
	777	100%	325,760	0.13	72.2	92.7	7.3	49.2	10.4	40.4	99.3	0.0	0.7
Alt-A	664	25%	139,956	0.97	79.4	71.0	29.0	47.5	32.1	20.4	56.4	41.6	2.0
	702	50%	138,609	0.93	77.2	53.0	47.0	50.8	27.6	21.6	57.7	39.0	3.4
	732	75%	135,393	0.91	77.0	54.7	45.3	55.7	24.5	19.8	54.5	43.5	2.0
	770	100%	132,980	0.86	76.3	57.4	42.6	64.3	20.1	15.6	50.7	46.1	3.2

Exhibit 18: Alternative-A Loan Characteristics by Rate Premium Quartile

Rate Prem	Quartile	Avg. Bal ($)	LTV (%)	Documentation (%)		Purpose (%)			Occupancy (%)		
				Full	Other	Purchase	Cashout	Refinance	Owner	Investor	Other
0.19	25%	177,236	70.5	53.2	46.8	47.1	26.7	26.3	80.1	15.5	4.3
0.71	50%	150,980	73.0	49.1	50.9	52.1	27.9	20.1	70.0	24.5	5.5
1.05	75%	125,244	75.4	56.2	43.8	57.4	27.0	15.5	53.8	40.7	5.5
1.52	100%	103,938	79.4	71.2	28.8	67.6	21.6	10.8	29.3	65.2	5.5

---

[10] Given that we know when every loan in our nonagency prepayment database was originated, we can estimate its rate premium.

Exhibit 19: Fourth Quarter 1998 Prepayment Comparison (1997 Originations)

Alt-A Gross WAC	Alt-A RALI (CPR)	Alt-A RAST (CPR)	Equiv. Jumbo (CPR)	Equiv. FNMA (CPR)
7.50%	22	30	12	10
8.00%	29	34	37	25
8.50%	30	34	52	38

This suggests that the prepayment behavior of the high rate premium borrowers is likely to be closely associated with a change in their particular situation and less correlated to a change in interest rates. Often their need for alternative financing diminishes over time as they establish sufficient income history, as property values increase or as they qualify under expanded agency underwriting policies. Once an Alternative-A borrower qualifies under agency guidelines there is an immediate and significant refinancing incentive that is usually in excess of 75 basis points.

As a result, a pattern develops that is similar to "credit curing" in the B/C home equity sector: a high base level of prepayments is established by "situation curing" as former Alternative-A borrowers refinance into conforming mortgages. However, existing Alternative-A borrowers still exhibit less sensitivity to interest rates since they continue to face higher transaction costs. This was indeed the case during the major fourth quarter 1998 refinancing event summarized in Exhibit 19. The exhibit compares the actual fourth quarter prepayments of Alternative-A borrowers (all of whom paid a significant rate premium) to equivalent, rate adjusted jumbo and agency prepayments. The Alternative-A sector exhibited very little differentiation in speed across coupons while a 100 basis point differential in coupon in the jumbo and agency sector resulted in a 40 CPR and 28 CPR separation in speed, respectively. Exhibit 20 shows the impact of a 20 basis point differential in rate premium on our baseline Alternative-A refinancing profile.

One consequence of the expanded underwriting criteria implemented by both FNMA and FHLMC that specifically targets the Alternative-A and/or credit impaired borrower is that more agency pools are likely to be issued with a rate premium. We believe these self-selected pools will exhibit a more stable prepayment profile than equivalent WAC non-rate premium pools. In fact, we can isolate pre-existing cohorts of rate premium pools in our agency database to support this expectation. For example, Exhibit 21 compares the recent prepayment experience of 8.75%-9.0% gross WAC FNMA pools issued in 1996 to those issued in 1994. Since mortgage rates never exceeded 8.50% in 1996, we know that these borrowers paid a substantial rate premium, while mortgage rates averaged 8.75% in 1994 indicating that these borrowers did not pay a rate premium. Under normal circumstances, we would expect the more "burned out" 1994 pools to prepay slower than the 1996 pools. However, as Exhibit 21 clearly shows, the rate premium effect has produced exactly the opposite results.

Exhibit 20: Alternative-A Rate Premium Effect

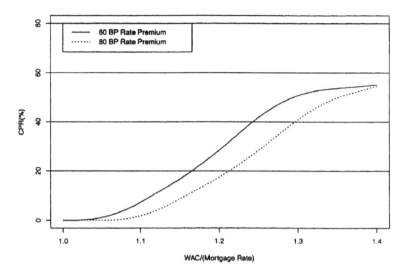

Exhibit 21: Agency "Rate Premium" Effect
1994 versus 1996 Origination 8.75% Gross WAC FNMA MBS

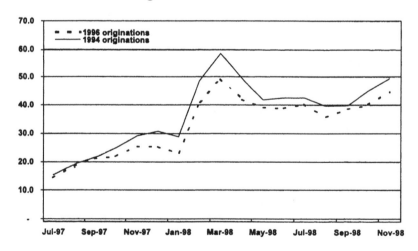

SECONDARY REFINANCING EFFECTS: DOCUMENTATION, LOAN PURPOSE, OCCUPANCY STATUS

The jumbo nonagency sector represents the most homogeneous group of borrowers in the residential mortgage market. As Exhibit 3 showed, the vast majority of jumbo mortgage transactions are characterized by borrowers with excellent credit histories, full documentation, owner occupied properties, and less than 80% LTVs. Consequently, most of the historically observed jumbo prepayment behavior can be explained by the level of mortgage rates and the interaction of four loan attributes: WAC, age, loan size, and LTV. We feel the biggest risk to investors in jumbo transactions is the implicit "front-loaded" nature of the cash flows owing to the powerful effects of coupon and loan size dispersion. As previously discussed, we believe that our loan level implementation replicates the evolution of loan size and coupon distributions.

In contrast, the hallmark of the Alternative-A sector is its heterogeneous loan and borrower composition. In this sector, secondary loan characteristics play a key role in defining the ability of a borrower to refinance today and offer insight into whether a borrower will be able to qualify for agency financing in the future. We have identified three of these attributes that, when observed in isolation, significantly alter prepayment behavior in the Alternative-A sector. They are documentation level, loan purpose, and occupancy status.

Limited Documentation versus Full Documentation

Limited documentation loans typically are obtained by borrowers who want financing without verification of income or employment. These programs are often structured so that only "stated income" levels are necessary. Many borrowers who qualify under these options are self-employed or work on commission and do not have a steady income or employment history. Under these programs, underwriting criteria highlight a borrower's credit history and ability to pay, while limiting the maximum allowable LTV. Limited documentation loans make up nearly 50% of the Alternative-A universe and often have other factors that preclude agency purchase. The higher transaction and "hassle" costs associated with qualifying under limited documentation programs have historically reduced the refinancing efficiency exhibited by these borrowers.

Exhibit 22 compares our baseline Alternative-A refinancing profiles for full and limited documentation borrowers. To the extent that a borrower establishes a consistent income pattern in the future or qualifies under expanded streamlined documentation programs implemented by FNMA and FHLMC, these barriers to prepayment may be eliminated over time. Therefore, we view limited documentation in itself as having only a moderate and transitory effect on prepayment speeds.

Exhibit 22: Alternative-A Documentation Effect

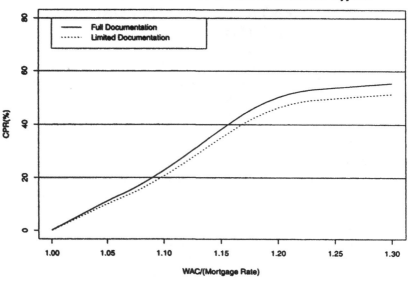

Investor versus Owner Occupied Properties

Investor properties make up approximately 36% of the total Alternative-A universe with some issuers originating much heavier concentrations than others. Investor properties typically have smaller loan balances, higher rate premiums, and somewhat higher LTVs than owner occupied properties. Prepayments differ from owner occupied properties in two important respects:

1. Housing turnover prepayments tend to be higher than in owner occupied properties.
2. Investors tend to refinance less optimally than owner occupied properties.

In the first case, we find that investors are more likely to take advantage of a housing market expansion by selling the property and locking in profits than are owner occupied properties. In the second case, investors typically face greater documentation scrutiny, increasing the "hassle" factor when refinancing. More importantly, investors tend to view their financial situation in a different context than the owner occupied population; that is, maintaining positive cash flow on a property is often more important than optimizing financing. Exhibit 23 contrasts our baseline refinancing profile for owner occupied properties to that of investor properties in the Alternative-A sector.

We observe that existing investor properties with LTVs in the 70% to 80% range are the most vulnerable to the recent expansion in agency underwriting guidelines (although it is not yet evident in actual data). To the extent that these borrowers now qualify under agency guidelines, we would expect a structural shift to faster prepayments in this segment of the Alternative-A universe as borrowers take advantage of lower agency financing rates.

Loan Purpose: Cash-Out Refinance, Rate/Term Refinance, Purchase

We find very little difference in the overall prepayment characteristics of loans originated as rate/term refinance transactions versus loans originated to purchase a home. We suspect that there may be a minor appraisal bias associated with refinancing transactions that is responsible for a slight LTV offset in our findings. For example, we observe that a 75% LTV refinancing transaction is similar to an 80% purchase transaction in terms of refinancing sensitivity. We believe the average purchase appraisal is likely to be more rigorous and conservative than the average refinancing appraisal.

Cash-out loans exhibit about 5% less sensitivity to interest rates than either rate/term refinance or purchase loans. A cash-out transaction may be indicative of a borrower with less financial capacity than other borrowers. This view is supported by our finding that FICO score is negatively correlated to cash-out levels (see Exhibit 17). Although cash-out borrowers may be predisposed to another cash-out transaction once equity levels increase sufficiently, this decision tends to be influenced more by home price appreciation and amortization than by interest rates.

Exhibit 23: Alternative-A Investor versus Owner

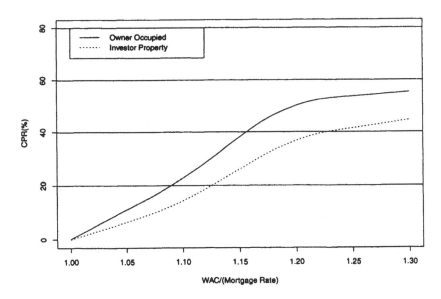

Exhibit 24: FHLMC 30-Year Mortgage Refinance Transitions

	30-year	20-year	15-year	ARM	5yr- Balloon	7yr-Balloon
	New Transition Product					
1993 Q4	58%	7%	26%	5%	2%	2%
1998 Q1	62%	7%	29%	0%	0%	1%

In every loan purpose category, we observe a period of 6 to 8 months after a loan is originated where borrowers exhibit a strong aversion to refinancing despite sometimes significant incentives. During this window new borrowers are probably reluctant to incur additional out-of-pocket expenses so soon after their last transaction.

THE YIELD CURVE AND REFINANCING TRANSITIONS

After the 1993 refinancing wave some market participants attributed the record setting prepayment speeds, in part, to a steep yield curve since it served to increase the refinancing incentive of 30-year mortgage holders into shorter maturity products like ARMs and balloons. By 1998, however, it was clear that some of the original assumptions made about the impact of the yield curve were overstated. Prepayments of new 30-year MBS in 1998 reached record levels across the entire spectrum of refinancing incentives despite a 150 basis point flattening in the yield curve since 1993. A review of 1993 and 1998 FHLMC refinancing transition data (see Exhibit 24) reveals that there was remarkably little difference in the refinancing choices of 30-year borrowers between the two periods. The most notable difference was a 9.0% transition rate from 30-year product into ARMs/balloons in 1993 compared to just 1% in 1998. We speculate, however, that for most of these "term" transition borrowers the yield curve does not preclude a refinance transaction; rather, it serves to change the optimal transition product. The important point is that in most cases a full prepayment occurs whether the yield curve is flat or steep.

We also note that the 30-year to 15-year transitions were actually higher in 1998 (29%) than in 1993 (26%) despite the fact that the 30-year to 15-year mortgage rate spread declined from 48 basis points in 1993 to 33 basis points in 1998. Here again the absolute yield curve effect is secondary to the borrower's desire to optimize his transition mortgage.

In view of these findings, we think a strong argument can be made that a steep yield curve has a localized effect on prepayment behavior that is limited to the marginal refinancer at the cusp who may not otherwise have an opportunity to refinance when the yield curve is flat. Borrowers well "in-the-money," on the other hand, are likely to refinance in either situation (although it may be into different products). Exhibit 25 shows projected refinancing prepayments conditional on the slope of the yield curve for our baseline jumbo borrower with a marginal refinancing incentive.

Exhibit 25: Refinancing Conditional on Yield Curve Slope (Borrowers with Marginal Incentive WAC/MR = 1.05)

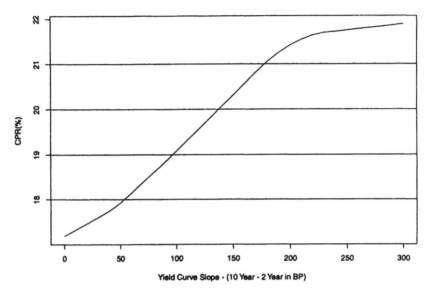

Yield Curve Slope - (10 Year - 2 Year in BP)

THE VALUE OF UPDATED LTV INFORMATION

A borrower's equity position in the home as measured by the loan-to-value ratio is a key determinant of both refinancing and housing turnover prepayments. One of the unique aspects of our modeling platform is that it incorporates real-time loan-to-value information updated every month on over 350,000 nonagency loans in our database. This is accomplished by using zip code level home price data to compute current property values across the country. Equity plays a crucial role in a borrower's financial decision-making process. Rising property values increase the likelihood that a borrower will "trade-up" to a bigger home or monetize the gain in value through an equity take-out refinance. Increasing equity also lowers a borrower's financing costs by reducing default risk to the lender and reducing or eliminating private mortgage insurance costs. Finally, it provides borrowers with financial leverage when evaluating alternative sources of financing. A high LTV ratio, on the other hand, increases refinancing transaction costs, reduces the likelihood of a cash-out transaction, and limits the ability of a borrower to trade-up.

A recent example of a dramatic shift in the transaction cost structure of a population of borrowers occurred in Southern California where jumbo borrowers experienced home price declines of up to 40% at the bottom of the California real estate cycle in 1996. In this situation, the loss of equity and rising LTVs served to increase refinancing transaction costs and slow prepayments on a large segment of our nonagency database. As a result, the impact of the housing recession in California is clearly evident in the historical prepayment behavior of nearly every seasoned jumbo deal (the typical jumbo deal has a 45% California concentration), particularly those issued in the early 1990s at the peak of the California housing market.

Consider, for example, PHMSC 9204, a 9.09% gross WAC jumbo deal issued in 1992 with a 70% California concentration and a $261,000 average loan size. Exhibit 26 plots a time series of actual prepayments for PHMSC 9204 since 1993. What is extraordinary about Exhibit 26 is the contrast between prepayments in the first quarter of 1996 and the first quarter of 1998. In 1996, despite a 130 basis point refinancing incentive, PHMSC 9204 borrowers showed virtually no reaction to the refinancing opportunity. In contrast, during the first quarter of 1998 PHMSC 9204 speeds spiked to 50 CPR despite 6 years of seasoning and only a marginally better refinancing incentive than in 1996. At this point most prepayment models would predict significant "burnout" in these loans.

What has changed since 1996 that would increase the prepayment speeds of this deal? Upon closer inspection we find that the percentage of loans with LTVs above 80% increased from 9.6% at deal issue to 46% in 1996 (70% of the loans backing PHMSC 9204 were from California). Refinancing had become pro-hibitively expensive for many of the PHMSC 9204 borrowers. By 1998, however, a home price recovery in California plus two additional years of amortization pushed equity levels into positive territory for the first time in 6 years, unlocking an explosive surge in pent-up refinancing demand.

Exhibit 26: PHMSC 9204 Actual versus Projected Prepayments

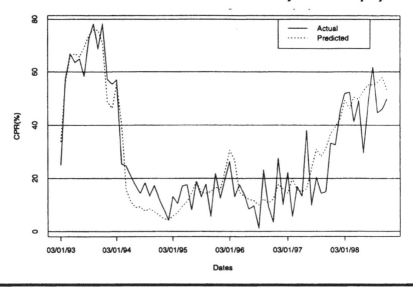

**Exhibit 27: LTV Effect - Alternative-A Sector
(Purchase Loans)**

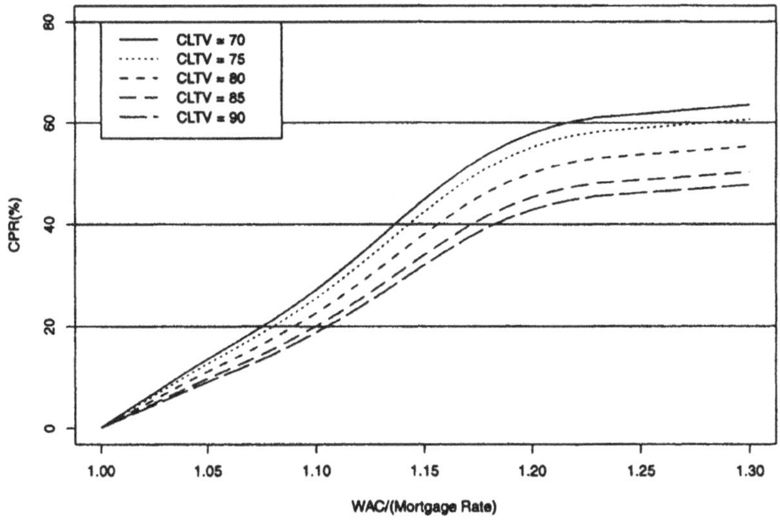

In addition to the historical prepayments of PHMSC 9204 shown in Exhibit 26, we also provide our model projections for the deal incorporating monthly updated LTV information for each of the surviving loans in the deal. The close fit of our projected deal prepayments to actual experience confirms the value of incorporating current LTV information into our model specification. LTV explained the inability of borrowers to respond to a strong nominal refinancing incentive in 1996 and the subsequent release of that pent-up demand in 1998.

Exhibit 26 also demonstrates the ability of current LTV to capture the impact of regional economic activity on prepayments, e.g. a weak regional economy will be reflected in a contracting housing market, declining real estate values, and increasing LTVs (this would tend to slow our projected prepayments for loans located in that region). Thus, LTV eliminates the need to incorporate other regional economic variables to explain this behavior. Exhibit 27 illustrates the impact of a change in LTV on our baseline Alternative-A refinancing profile for purchase loans.

HOUSING TURNOVER PREPAYMENTS:
SEASONING AND LOCK-IN

Housing turnover prepayments tend to increase as a loan ages — a reflection of the natural life-cycle of homeownership. New homeowners are less likely to move since, by definition, the property fulfills their current housing demands. Moreover, borrowers are less willing to incur moving expenses so soon after the original relocation. However, over time there is an increasing probability that a borrower will relocate, "trade-up" in homes, or monetize equity gains as real estate values increase, their financial situation improves, housing demands increase, or job status changes. In addition, there is an increasing probability that a non-economic prepayment event will occur from other factors such as divorce or death. The unique baseline seasoning pattern for each of the sectors is shown in Exhibit 28 (it plots current coupon prepayments conditional on loan age).

For jumbo loans, we find that this baseline seasoning process takes about five years. Jumbo seasoning starts out slower than that found in the agency sector but eventually overtakes agency seasoning after about 2.5 years. In the Alternative-A sector there is an added dimension to the seasoning process caused by "situation curing" (previously discussed in the Rate Premium section). Over time, there is a greater likelihood that an Alternative-A borrower will qualify for more attractive conventional financing. As shown in Exhibit 28, this accelerates the baseline seasoning function to 15 CPR over approximately 20 months, well above that found in both the agency and nonagency sectors.

Two other exogenous factors affect the seasoning process:

1. *Home values:* As previously discussed, rising home values increase the probability that a borrower will "trade-up" to a larger home or cash-out the gain in equity. Exhibit 29 illustrates the impact that a change in real estate values has on the baseline seasoning curve in the jumbo sector.

Exhibit 28: Seasoning Function

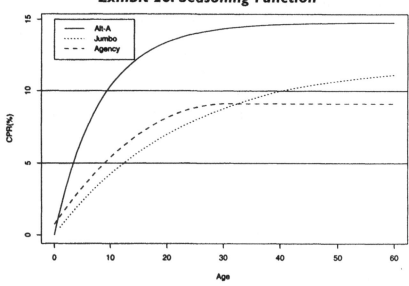

Exhibit 29: Jumbo Seasoning Function - LTV Effect

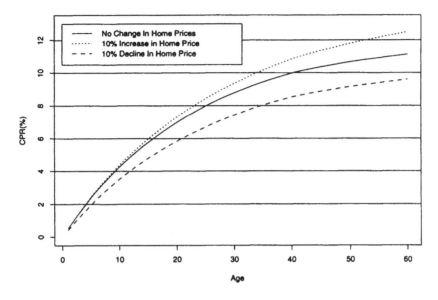

2. *The level of interest rates:* Just as borrowers have an economic incentive to prepay an above market rate mortgage, they have a financial disincentive to prepay a below market rate mortgage. This disincentive or "lock-in" effect is proportional to loan size and, consequently, has the greatest effect on the jumbo mortgage seasoning profile. Given their current funding advantage and less attractive housing affordability levels at prevailing market rates, borrowers with below market mortgages are less likely to move or cash-out equity. Exhibit 30 plots the baseline jumbo aging profile conditional on various levels of lock-in.

SEASONALITY

It has long been recognized that housing turnover prepayments are linked to the weather, vacation schedules, and the school year. Homeowners are much more likely to move in the summer when the weather is warm and their children are out of school than in the winter when the opposite is true. The seasonal patterns observed in our nonagency prepayment data (shown in Exhibit 31) are very consistent with the seasonal adjustments reported by the National Association of Realtors (NAR) and with that found in the agency sector. Housing turnover related prepayments usually peak in late spring and summer at levels that are 20% faster than the annual average and bottom in February at 26% slower than the annual average. This results in an absolute prepayment difference of approximately 5% CPR from the fastest to the slowest month for a fully seasoned, near current coupon jumbo mortgage security. Absolute seasonal variations will be proportionally less than this for newer issues. Actual versus model projected plots for low coupon jumbo loans originated in 1993 are shown in Exhibit 32. Note that the strong seasonal patterns in housing turnover were evident even when the loans were very new.

Exhibit 30: Jumbo Seasoning Function - Lock-in Effect

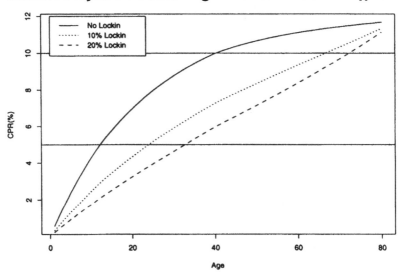

Exhibit 31: Nonagency Seasonal Adjustments

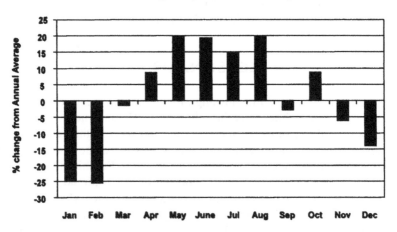

Exhibit 32: Actual versus Model Projected Seasonal Prepayments

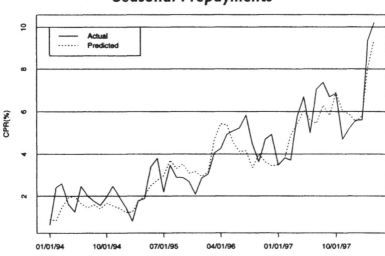

ADVERSE SELECTION IN HOUSING TURNOVER PREPAYMENTS

The model also captures a more subtle version of borrower self-selection that takes place on a regional basis from housing turnover prepayments. As properties located in high growth areas prepay out of a pool, we are left with an increasing share of properties in areas of the country experiencing lower growth rates or a housing contraction. The key difference between refinancing and housing turnover adverse selection is the time it takes to develop. In general, it takes several years for housing turnover related prepayments to significantly alter the composition of a pool versus just several months for a refinancing cycle. In addition, the adverse selection in LTV is often wiped out by amortization and the general trend of rising home prices across the country. Nevertheless, we capture all forms of "burnout" in an identical way: by modeling the evolution in the distribution of loan attributes over time.

This discussion highlights our previous observation that the vast majority of the prepayment volatility and negative convexity observed in the mortgage market comes from refinancing activity rather than housing resale activity. Indeed, because housing resale related prepayments occur throughout the year and are more correlated to where an individual is in the homeownership cycle than to interest rates, we will never see a refinancing-like spike take place because of an increase in housing activity. Consequently, MBS valuation results based on simulated interest rates tend to be dominated by the refinancing component in economic prepayment models.

Exhibit 33: Jumbo Defaults Conditional on Loan Age

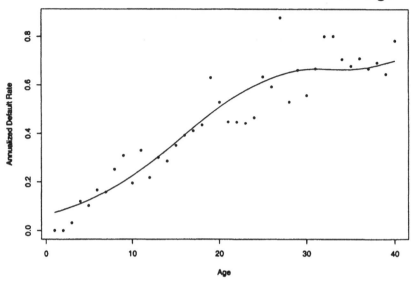

INVOLUNTARY PREPAYMENTS AND CURTAILMENTS

Two other types of prepayments that affect the observed seasoning patterns in all mortgage-backed securities are involuntary prepayments (defaults) and curtailments. In the nonagency universe the combined contribution of these two components occurs at a rate that is usually less that 1.5% CPR during the first 5 years of the seasoning process; however, both types of prepayments tend to increase as a loan seasons after origination.

The foreclosure and liquidation of a property (default) always results in a full prepayment of the mortgage. We find that the probability of default is influenced by two factors:

1. The level of equity a borrower has in a property;
2. An individual's ability to meet debt obligations.

We find that it is usually a combination of events rather than a single factor that triggers a default. For example, declining real estate values accompanied by sudden financial distress (e.g. job loss, income disruption or unexpected debt) greatly increases the likelihood of a default. Consequently, current LTV and FICO score are often used contemporaneously to explain the propensity of a borrower to default. Since nonagency borrowers represent the top of the FICO spectrum and the low end of the LTV spectrum, defaults have historically played a relatively minor role in the seasoning process (see Exhibit 33).

Exhibit 34: Jumbo Curtailments Conditional on Loan Age

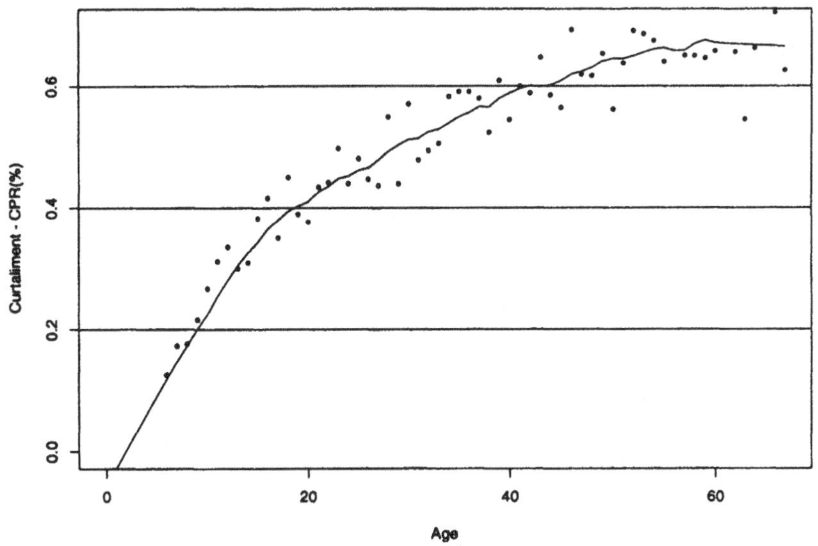

A similar profile emerges when we isolate curtailments or partial prepayments as a function of loan age. Borrowers often send in payments that exceed scheduled principal and interest as a way to increase their equity position in a property and reduce the time it takes to pay-off their mortgage debt. As a loan seasons and a borrower's financial status improves over time, partial prepayments tend to increase. In addition, when a loan amortizes to a very small balance, borrowers will often increase their curtailment rate to accelerate retirement of the debt and avoid the fixed transaction costs associated with a refinance transaction. Exhibit 34 plots partial prepayments conditional on loan age in the jumbo sector.

REFINANCING EFFICIENCY: THE NEXT FRONTIER

We believe the next frontier for efficiency gains in the refinancing process is likely to come from the internet as mortgage service providers work toward a vertically integrated origination process. It is clear that the internet is changing the way Americans refinance their mortgages. Although it is estimated that less than 10% of the refinance transactions in 1998 were executed over the internet, a far greater number of borrowers used it to shop for competitive rates. Furthermore, the success of internet based mortgage companies such as E-loan, Homeshark, and Keystone plus a proliferation of sites from virtually every major originator is a testament to the viability of the internet as a delivery mechanism for mortgage services.

The burgeoning use of the internet is resulting in a democratization in mortgage service providers, as smaller lenders find that they can compete and market effectively on the internet. However, further automation and integration of the origination process is needed, particularly in the area of title search processing. With 50% of American households now having access to internet services we believe the number of transactions completed over the internet is likely to explode in coming years (some estimates suggest that within 5 years 75% of all refinancing transactions will be completed on the internet). The remarkable growth of E-commerce in 1998 reflects a growing consumer confidence in the viability and security of the internet as a means of commerce. We believe the natural evolution of E-commerce will take consumers up the product/service spectrum leading them to mortgage-related services.

This end-to-end integration of mortgage services will be facilitated by the automated underwriting systems already put in place by the agencies and other venders. These risk-based pricing systems include automated credit and appraisal evaluations, providing lenders with a near instantaneous assessment of where a loan fits on the credit continuum and whether or not a loan qualifies for agency purchase.

Therefore, it seems inevitable that electronic refinancing is destined to become the gold standard in the mortgage industry. This will continue to put pressure on transaction costs, shorten processing times, and increase the number of "marginal" refinance transactions — all trends that were clearly evident in the 1998 refinancing prepayment data. More than anything else, this sweeping transformation in refinancing behavior will minimize the "hassle costs" involved with refinancing, allowing borrowers to respond more "efficiently" and frequently to refinancing opportunities. Consequently, we would expect the refinancing elbow to shift even lower in the future.

MODELING THE MORTGAGE RATE PROCESS

Since 1993, the spread between jumbo and conforming mortgage rates has been as narrow as 10 basis points and as wide as 50 basis points. This has important implications in terms of the relative prepayment risk faced by agency and nonagency securities. For example, as Exhibit 35 clearly illustrates, there was a convergence in prepayment speeds between the jumbo and conforming sectors in 1998-jumbo prepayment speeds were the same or slower in 1998 than in 1993 while the opposite was true for agency prepayments.[11] We attribute most of this convergence to the widening spread between jumbo and conforming mortgage rates.

In general, jumbo borrowers found much less attractive refinancing opportunities as jumbo rates lagged the rally in conforming rates. This occurred

---

[11] Burnout also played a role in slowing high premium jumbo prepayments in 1998.

because global credit events caused subordinate spreads to widen dramatically (doubling spreads in many cases), making the economics of securitization much less attractive to issuers which in turn negatively impacted conduit pricing of mortgage purchases. In addition, the flat yield curve mitigated the additional arbitrage gained from faster prepayment assumptions on jumbo product. In contrast, nearly opposite conditions prevailed in 1993 as a steep yield curve and fast prepayment assumptions improved deal arbitrage. At the same time subordinate pricing remained competitive. All of these factors served to compress the jumbo to conforming mortgage rate spread in 1993.

Exhibit 35: Convergence Trend Between Jumbo and Conforming Prepayments

Jumbo Refinancing Curves

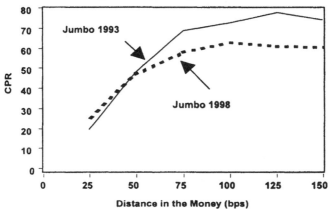

Agency Refinancing Curves

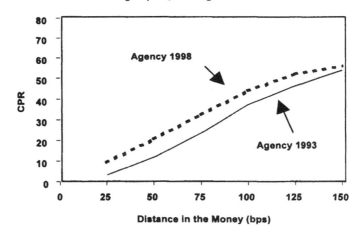

To calculate current nonagency mortgage rates in our modeling framework, we closely monitor mortgage rate spreads between the conforming, jumbo, and Alternative-A sectors. For jumbos we add the appropriate spread to our conforming rate consistent with today's pricing of jumbo mortgages. Since there is very little uniformity in the Alternative-A sector, we must calculate an appropriate spread for each individual loan, and apply this spread to our current prime jumbo rate. To the extent that today's jumbo to conforming spread is above/below historical averages, we allow for a mean reversion in this spread when forecasting.

MODEL TESTING

The production version of our nonagency prepayment model was evaluated using both in-sample and out-of-sample testing to assess forecast error. It was particularly important that the model explain certain key aspects of the data that we felt provided unusually valuable insights into nonagency prepayment behavior. These include:

- The muted refinancing response of new issues during the first quarter of 1996 despite substantial economic incentives to refinance.
- The impact of the contraction and expansion phases of the California housing cycle from 1990 to 1998.
- The relative magnitude of the refinancing spikes in 1993, 1996, the first quarter of 1998, and the fourth quarter of 1998.
- The unique seasoning and refinancing patterns associated with the Alternative-A sector.

We relied heavily on deterministic variables defined at origination such as loan size, LTV, rate premium, and documentation type to explain nonagency prepayments. We avoided using artificially constructed variables that, although correlated to historical prepayment data, are often less reliable predictors of future prepayment behavior. It was important that each model variable explain a fundamental aspect of prepayment behavior that could be observed consistently over time and that would likely persist in the future. The model also handles three less standard mortgage types that are not addressed in this chapter: prepayment penalty mortgages, Community Reinvestment Act (CRA) loans,[12] and relocation mortgages.

In the appendix to this chapter we provide both in-sample and out-of-sample, actual versus model predicted results for the jumbo and Alternative-A sectors across all major origination years. An out-of-sample test provides a "real world" check on the model specification given that it measures the accuracy of the model against data that was not part of the estimation. In our test, we first esti-

---

[12] See Chapter 10.

mated on data through June of 1998 and then measured the accuracy of our model forecast versus post-June 1998 data (the out-of-sample test) as well as pre-June 1998 data (the in-sample test). Of course the production version of our model was estimated from the complete data set. The representative deals shown in the appendix were selected on the basis of deal size (to minimize the noise in the data) and collateral profile.

The appendix is intended to be only a representative sample of our results not an exhaustive review of the fits (a comprehensive series of both in-sample and out-of-sample model fits is available upon request). The results demonstrate that the model explains much of the monthly variation observed in nonagency prepayment data since 1990. Moreover, we believe the results satisfy our "key aspects" criteria outlined above.

Nevertheless, a good fit to the data is only the first step in the successful implementation of a model. We must be cognizant of potential structural changes in the nonagency market that could erode model performance going forward. These may include additional modifications to current agency underwriting guidelines, the introduction of an alternative or competing mortgage product, or a significant change in transaction costs.

CONCLUSION

We have presented a new and innovative prepayment model for the valuation of nonagency mortgage-backed securities. We believe the union of new processing technology, new prepayment information, and the availability of extensive property level data will usher in a new generation of nonagency prepayment models whose accuracy and precision will surpass that of existing agency models where no loan level data are available. Central to our effort is a full property-level implementation of the model that captures the powerful effects of WAC and loan size dispersion on the expected future prepayments of nonagency issues. Also unique to our model is the incorporation of current housing price and LTV data as key determinants of both refinancing and housing turnover prepayments. In addition, the model accounts for the influence of secondary loan characteristics such as loan purpose, occupancy status, documentation type, and rate premium. We find that this specification performs well in rigorous in-sample and out-of-sample tests on actual deal level prepayments in both the jumbo and Alternative-A mortgage sectors. The end result is a model that, we believe, provides nonagency mortgage investors with a powerful new valuation tool that can be used to accurately model portfolio cash flows, make informed cross-sector relative value decisions, and enhance hedging capabilities.

APPENDIX

Model Projected versus Actual Results for Representative Deals

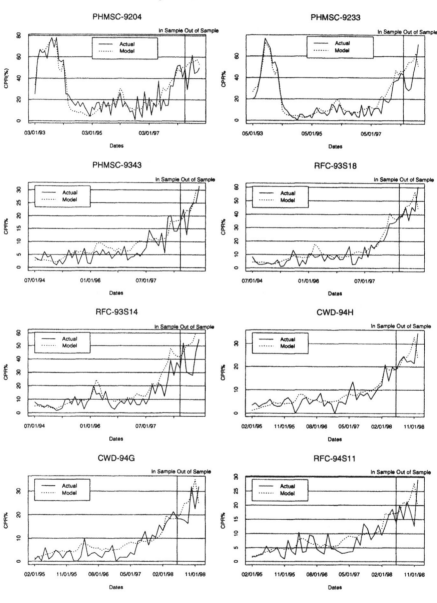

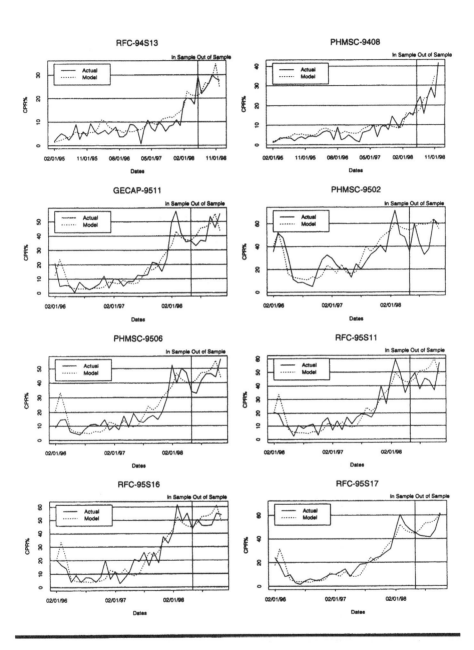

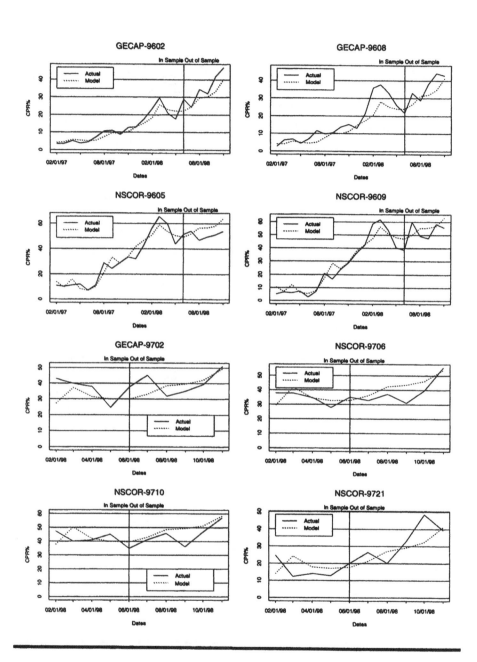

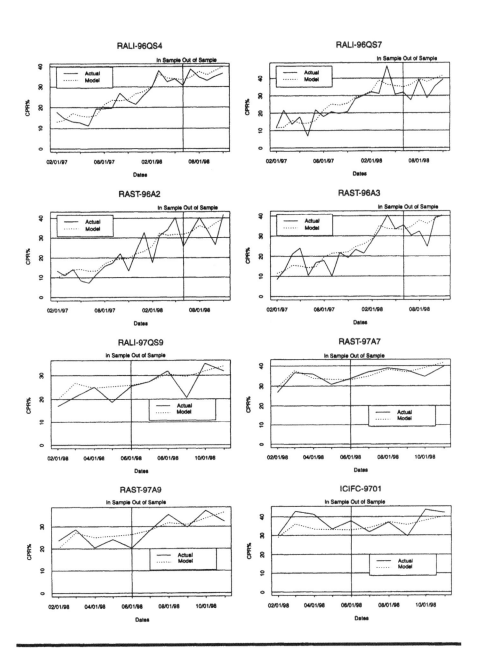

Chapter 18

Prepayment Modeling and Valuation of Home Equity Loan Securities

Dale Westhoff
Senior Managing Director
Financial Analytics & Structured Transactions Group
Bear, Stearns & Co., Inc.

Mark Feldman
Managing Director
Financial Analytics & Structured Transactions Group
Bear, Stearns & Co., Inc.

INTRODUCTION

Understanding and valuing prepayment risk is a fundamental concern for most investors in the rapidly expanding home equity securities market. Yet conducting even a rudimentary prepayment analysis can be a difficult task because of the diversity of loan and borrower attributes at the deal level. In addition, there is often little historical prepayment information available to investors on new deals or on deals with similar collateral profiles. While the current market prepayment convention centered on issuer specific prepayment curves (similar to the PSA curve) is useful in establishing a static pricing speed assumption, it lends little insight into the underlying causes of home equity prepayments and is generally inadequate as a valuation tool. In this chapter we present a home equity prepayment model developed from historical observations on nearly 300,000 individual loans provided by leading issuers of home equity securities. The multi-issuer database used is unique in both the breadth of its coverage and in its loan-level detail, which includes information on a borrower's credit status. For the first time,

The authors would like to thank the issuers listed in Exhibit 1 for their cooperation in providing data for this study.

the underlying forces that govern home equity loan prepayments can be analyzed and statistically measured, all at the loan level. Our model, developed entirely from this new data, incorporates several innovative features:

- Given that borrowers of different credit quality exhibit fundamentally different prepayment behavior, our model is constructed as a composite forecast from three functionally independent sub-models, each representing a distinct level of borrower credit.
- Each model was estimated on a loan by loan basis using a discrete choice estimation to preserve all loan and borrower attributes (no data aggregation was performed).
- The borrower's current equity position, a key determinant of home equity prepayment behavior, is dynamically updated and measured using proprietary regional home price indices.
- Users have the ability to assess the joint effects of changes in home prices and interest rates on home equity loan prepayments.
- Borrower adverse selection, responsible for "burnout" and other path dependent prepayment behavior, is implicitly accounted for by the loan-level specification and sub-model structure of our forecasting framework.

THE LOAN-LEVEL HOME EQUITY DATABASE

A prepayment model is only as good as the data set employed in its estimation. In contrast to pool-specific data like that from FNMA/FHLMC and GNMA, loan-level information greatly enhances the precision and scope of variables available to the modeler. Bear Stearns has assembled one of the largest and most comprehensive loan-level home equity databases in the asset-backed industry. The database targets finance company fixed rate, closed-end home equity issuers and incorporates statistics on a borrower's credit status, property location, original combined loan-to-value ratio (CLTV), updated CLTV, lien position, loan size, rate, and term. The database contains ten years of historical prepayment information, including the important prepayment experience from the 1992 and 1993 prepayment cycles.

In general, there is a high level of dispersion in the loan attributes of finance company issues since the loans are made to a broad spectrum of borrowers (most with lower than A credit ratings). Home equity securities from different issuers can exhibit very different prepayment behavior owing to disparities in the credit quality of the underlying borrowers and the specific underwriting criteria imposed by an issuer. To date, most home equity prepayment studies have focused on data from a single issuer and are applicable to a relatively small universe of securities with similar collateral characteristics. By drawing our database from a representative cross-section of issuers we can minimize issuer specific effects and isolate the common loan and borrower characteristics that are responsible for the observed differences in prepayments across issuers and deals. This is particularly important given that several issuers have recently altered their product mix for strategic reasons or in response to current market opportunities. A model constructed from this data is more robust and can be applied to a wider array of securities than a model based on data from a single issuer.

The disparity in loan attributes at the issuer level is evident in the summarized issuer data shown in Exhibit 1. For example, issuers originating a greater portion of loans to higher credit quality borrowers tend to have much lower average loan rates and higher average combined loan-to-value ratios. Two observations can be made regarding the data in Exhibit 1.

First, a traditional analysis based on a stratification of home equity securities by weighted average coupon (WAC) may produce very misleading results because it ignores the substantial credit premium associated with lower credit borrowers. A high WAC often indicates the presence of credit impaired borrowers who exhibit prepayment behavior that is fundamentally different from borrowers with better credit ratings. Second, to the extent that an issuer targets loan production to a particular segment of borrowers, the prepayments of that issuer will be subject to any prepayment patterns that are unique to that sub-population.

THE DETERMINANTS OF HOME EQUITY PREPAYMENTS: IDENTIFYING THE RISKS

From the investor's perspective, the most attractive feature of home equity securities is that they are less negatively convex[1] when compared to securities backed by conventional purchase money mortgages. Indeed, historical observations indicate that finance company home-equity borrowers are relatively insensitive to changes in interest rates. For example, during the severe 1992 and 1993 refinancing cycles, most home equity securities experienced prepayments that were considerably slower (rarely above 35 CPR for more than one period) than similar mortgage-backed securities (MBS). Conversely, home equity securities did not extend as much as MBS when interest rates rose in 1994. This pattern is clearly evident in Exhibit 2, a comparison of historical prepayments between the 1990 issue FNMA 9.0% 15-year MBS and a typical B/C home equity deal (Fleet Finance 90-1). Given this experience, investors have embraced home equity issues as an attractive alternative to traditional mortgage securities since they have the advantage of limited call and extension risk. In addition, investors have found that home equity securities make a reasonable substitute for short average life CMOs since they offer PAC-like average life stability without the premium paid for a CMO structure.

---

[1] Negatively convex securities tend to shorten in duration when interest rates fall and increase in duration when rates rise.

Exhibit 1: The Bear Stearns Home Equity Database

Contributing Issuer	Number of Loans	Average Loan Rate	Average Loan Size	Credit Distributions			Lien Position		OLTV Distribution			
				A	B	C	First	Second	<= 60%	60%-70%	70%-80%	> 80%
GE	55,832	10.54	54,968	88%	12%	0%	49%	51%	26%	18%	42%	14%
Conti	47,037	11.66	55,276	57%	29%	14%	66%	34%	31%	21%	42%	6%
Equicredit	101,709	12.30	39,306	46%	35%	19%	57%	43%	20%	18%	50%	12%
Advanta	69,200	13.39	33,710	49%	41%	10%	39%	61%	24%	14%	32%	30%
Alliance Funding	32,504	14.04	51,104	15%	40%	45%	47%	53%	67%	26%	6%	1%
Totals	306,282	12.31	44,601	53%	30%	17%	53%	47%	29%	18%	39%	14%

Exhibit 2: Historical MBS and Home Equity Prepayments

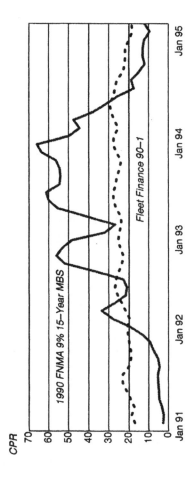

Exhibit 3: Home Equity Pricing Speeds Versus Actual Prepayments*

Date	Issuer	Pricing Speed	Actual CPR 3 Months	Actual CPR 6 Months
21-Feb-91	ADVANTA 91-1	18	21.00	20.30
31-Jul-91	AFC 91-3	20	29.40	22.20
10-Sep-91	ADVANTA 91-3	22	20.80	18.10
25-Oct-91	AFC 91-4	20	23.20	24.00
29-Jan-92	AFC 92-1	20	28.60	25.90
13-Mar-92	ADVANTA 92-1	22	19.40	17.20
26-Mar-92	OSCC 92-1	21	25.70	22.90
5-Jun-92	OSCC 92-2	25	19.90	18.70
16-Jun-92	TMS 92B	22	22.20	19.10
18-Jun-92	AFC 92-3	20	24.40	20.70
11-Sep-92	ADVANTA 92-3(14)	23	23.90	20.60
17-Sep-92	AFC 92-4	20	24.70	25.40
26-Oct-92	OSCC 92-4	25	21.50	18.80
4-Dec-92	TMS 92D	23	16.30	N/A
16-Dec-92	AFC 92-5	20	22.00	23.70
2-Mar-93	ADVANTA 93-1	23	12.30	12.30
12-Mar-93	TMS 93A	23	15.00	14.30
27-May-93	ADVANTA 93-2	23	17.90	16.20
10-Jun-93	TMS 93B	23	10.70	9.90
28-Jul-93	TMS 93C	23	14.70	N/A
16-Nov-93	First Alliance 93-2	25	29.80	22.90
16-Feb-94	TMS 94A	23	10.70	10.30
3-Mar-94	ADVANTA 94-1	23	15.60	12.20
10-Mar-94	Equicon 94-1	23	20.00	19.70
24-May-94	TMS 94B	22	13.50	11.80
25-May-94	EQCC 94-2	25	22.60	19.10
8-Jun-94	ADVANTA 94-2	22	18.90	14.90
20-Jun-94	Contimortgage 94-3 (16)	26	18.30	14.30
9-Sep-94	ADVANTA 94-3	23	20.30	16.30
13-Sep-94	EQCC 94-3	24	26.90	22.80
18-Oct-94	Equicon 94-2	23	29.00	19.30
2-Dec-94	Contimortgage 94-5	20	20.70	16.20
8-Dec-94	ADVANTA 94-4	20	12.40	9.90
8-Mar-95	ADVANTA 95-1	20	10.60	8.20

* Actual prepayments as of September 1995.
Source: Moody's Asset Credit Evaluations Report

With broad investor acceptance there has been little differentiation in deal pricing speeds. The vast majority of deals have been priced to a long term speed of between 20 and 25 CPR with various permutations on the seasoning ramp. However, a comparison of the pricing speed assumptions to actual 6-month prepayments (see Exhibit 3) suggests that more deal differentiation is needed. Key loan and borrower attributes, like borrower credit quality, that influence the seasoning ramp and long-term level of home equity prepayments must be identified and accounted for at pricing. No single ramp standard (or ramp multiple) can explain the disparity evident across deal prepayments.

More importantly, within the home equity universe investors must be compensated for securities whose prepayments are more likely to be correlated to changes in interest rates. Although the market may be justified in pricing two deals to similar static long term prepayment speeds, there may still exist substantial differences in the negative convexity of the securities. Consider the extreme case of First Interstate Bank of California (FICAL) 90-1, GE 91-1 and Fleet Finance 90-1. Although all three deals were priced between 20 and 23 CPR, actual prepayments through the 1992 and 1993 interest rate cycles proved to be radically different. For example, during the period from January 1992 to December 1993 the three deals peaked at 62 CPR, 42 CPR and 30 CPR, respectively. Obviously, not all home equity securities are created equal. Nevertheless, the task of identifying deals that are more vulnerable to interest rate swings has been onerous due to the heterogeneous mix of borrower and loan attributes. In addition, the trend by finance companies to originate home equity first lien mortgages has clouded the distinction between a traditional purchase money mortgage[2] and a home equity loan. For instance, should we expect a home equity security backed by A credit borrowers with large balance, first lien loans to exhibit the same prepayment behavior as a deal backed by C credit borrowers with small balance, second mortgages? Clearly, the answer is no; however, until now valuing the impact of these disparities has been virtually impossible.

The Bear Stearns home equity model addresses the need for a prepayment forecast consistent with the underlying mix of borrower and loan characteristics present in a deal. The model inputs include six loan attributes and two exogenous variables whose independent and joint effects explain home equity loan prepayment behavior. Each of these parameters and their values as they relate to increasing prepayment risk is provided in Exhibit 4. A more detailed discussion of our findings with respect to each of these parameters follows.

Exhibit 4: Model Inputs and Prepayment Risk

Model Input	Lower Prepayment Risk (more prepayment stable)	Higher Prepayment Risk (more prepayment sensitive)
Borrower Credit Status	C Borrower	A Borrower
Borrower Credit Premium	High	Low
Loan Age	Seasoned Loans	New Loans
Combined Loan-to-Value	High CLTV	Low CLTV
Lien Position	Second Lien	First Lien
Loan Size	Small	Large
Level of Interest Rates (Exogenous)	Neutral	Declining
Level of Home Prices (Exogenous)	Stable/Declining	Rising

---

[2] A purchase money mortgage is used exclusively to finance the initial purchase of a home.

Exhibit 5: Representative Finance Company Home Equity Obligor

Age	40-45 years
Employment	8-10 years; Blue collar/light-white collar
Residence	8-10 years
Income	$40K
Credit	5-6 cards
Home Value	$100-$125K

STRUCTURAL CONSIDERATIONS

There are three structural factors that suppress the interest rate sensitivity of finance company fixed rate home equity loan securities: small loan sizes, short amortization schedules, and below A borrower credit quality. First, smaller average loan sizes greatly reduce the economic benefit of a refinancing opportunity. In our sample, the average loan balance was $45,000 compared to $124,000 for a standard purchase money mortgage. As a rule of thumb, interest rates must fall two to four times further in the home equity market before the interest cost savings of a refinance breaks even to the interest cost savings realized from a standard purchase money refinance. It should be noted, however, that this effect is partially negated for second lien home equity loans because second liens are subject to the full refinancing risk of the underlying first mortgage.

Second, the 10-year to 15-year amortization schedule of most home equity loans limits the average life variability and price sensitivity of HEL securities. For example, a 10 CPR increase in prepayments will shorten the average life of a 30-year security by approximately 4.7 years compared to only 2.2 years for a 15-year security.[3] Third, credit impaired home equity borrowers tend to be cash-strapped and, consequently, more payment sensitive (less interest rate sensitive) than purchase money borrowers. Exhibit 5 profiles a representative finance company home equity obligor. The combination of these three factors produces a return profile that is intrinsically more stable and less interest rate sensitive than that of a standard purchase money mortgage security. Nevertheless, within the home equity universe, there still exist significant disparities in the rate of seasoning, long-term level, and interest rate sensitivity of prepayments.

BORROWER CREDIT QUALITY IS THE MOST IMPORTANT DETERMINANT OF HOME EQUITY LOAN PREPAYMENTS

Different levels of borrower credit quality expose investors to different levels of prepayment risk. The typical home equity security is backed by borrowers across a broad spectrum of credit ratings. Intuitively, the A credit borrowers are the most likely to prepay their loans when interest rates fall because they can usually qualify for a new

---

[3] Assuming a 9.0% gross coupon and an initial base speed of 8% CPR.

loan and are more likely to be in a financial position to pay transaction costs. Less credit worthy borrowers are less likely to refinance because they are less financially "able" to pay transaction costs and usually have fewer refinancing alternatives available to them. Lenders will generally underwrite lower credit borrowers at higher spreads and with more points and fees to offset their increased exposure to default. Moreover, during a refinancing cycle, lenders will target better credit borrowers with large balance loans before lower credit borrowers. Thus, the refinancing economics for B/C rated borrowers are usually much less attractive than for A borrowers. In effect, these constraints act as a prepayment penalty imposed on low credit borrowers.

Historical observations confirm the "credit effect" on prepayments. For example, Exhibit 6 tracks the historical prepayment experience of four separate deals, each selected to represent a different level of borrower credit quality. The highest credit borrowers populate the bank issue (FICAL 90-1) followed by A- borrowers (GE Capital 91-1), B/C borrowers (Fleet Finance 90-1), and finally D borrowers (Goldome Credit 90-1). During the refinancing waves of 1992-93, the range of prepayments across these different issues of home equity securities was extraordinary. The bank issue exhibited refinancing levels that rivaled any security in the conventional MBS market while the finance company issues, populated by more credit impaired borrowers, exhibited a much more restrained response to lower interest rates.

The degree to which prepayments were unresponsive to lower rates can be linked directly to the level of borrower credit. In the case of the Goldome issue (D borrowers) prepayments were completely uncorrelated to changes in interest rates. Moving up the credit spectrum, the Fleet Finance issue (B/C borrowers) exhibited a modest correlation to interest rates while the GE issue (A- borrowers) spiked above 35 CPR on three separate occasions; each spike was coincident with a new low in interest rates. The strong relationship between borrower credit status and prepayments was again evident in 1994 when interest rates moved higher, only this time prepayments slowed and securities extended. In the absence of a refinancing incentive, the bank home equity security became the slowest paying issue, followed by GE and then Fleet Finance. Once again, Goldome showed no response to the movement in interest rates.

Exhibit 6: Historical Prepayments on Selected Home Equity Issues

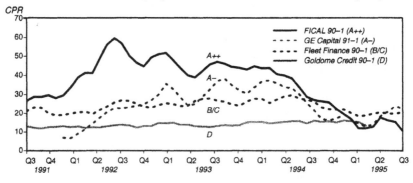

The greater contraction and extension risk exhibited in securities backed by higher credit quality borrowers makes them more negatively convex than securities backed by credit impaired borrowers. Indeed, securities backed by the lowest credit borrowers remained positively convex through the prepayment cycles of 1992 and 1993. The radically different prepayment behavior evident across different credit "domains" underscores the importance of developing a sound methodology to model the influence of credit on home equity prepayments. We have accomplished this by constructing our model as a composite forecast from three independent, credit based sub-models. Loans are first stratified by credit designation, then directed to the appropriate sub-model where a separate forecast is made based on loan-level attributes. The individual forecasts are then re-combined to form the final aggregate projection. We found that this approach produced the most accurate aggregate projection for securities that are often backed by a diverse collection of borrowers. The first step in this process, however, is to identify the level of credit.

TWO MEASURES OF BORROWER CREDIT QUALITY: ISSUER RATING AND CREDIT PREMIUM

A reliable measure of credit quality is essential for an accurate prepayment forecast in the home equity sector. Unfortunately, generating a consistent measure of a borrower's credit quality can be problematic because of the lack of standardized underwriting criteria for each credit designation among issuers. To overcome this problem, each loan in our database is indexed in two ways: first by its credit designation (supplied by the issuer) and second by a measure based on a "credit premium" paid by the borrower at origination. Despite differences in underwriting guidelines, we found that the credit history criteria applied to a particular credit designation were relatively uniform. Therefore, in lieu of discarding the issuer supplied credit rating we use it as a broad indication of a borrower's recent credit standing, and account for differences in issuer underwriting limits for CLTV, loan size, etc., by directly measuring them at the loan level. Exhibit 7 summarizes the most common credit history criteria applied to each of the classifications.

Within a given credit class we further stratify the loans by calculating a credit premium. It is based on the spread between the prevailing conforming rate (we use the FHLMC commitment rate) and the home equity contract rate on the day that each loan was originated. While this measure ignores the possibility that a borrower "buys" the rate down, it has proven to be strongly correlated to the actual credit quality of each borrower, i.e., the higher the credit premium, the lower the credit quality of the borrower. Exhibit 8 conclusively shows that in our loan sample the average credit premium is substantially higher for lower credit classes.

Exhibit 7: Finance Company Issuer Credit Ratings

Classification	Meaning
A	Good to excellent credit
	Maximum of 2 30-day delinquencies in past 12 months
	No bankruptcies in past 5 years
B	Satisfactory credit
	Maximum of 3 30-day delinquencies in past 12 months
	No bankruptcies in past 3 years
C	Fair/poor credit
	Maximum of 4 30-day and 1 60-day delinquencies in past 12 months
	No bankruptcies in past 2 years

Exhibit 8: Home Equity Credit Premiums

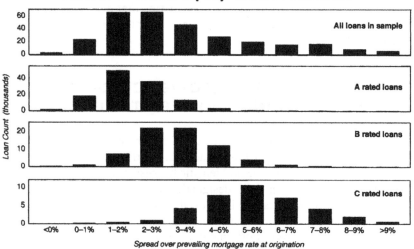

For example, the average credit premium for all A, B, and C designated loans is 1.89%, 3.32% and 5.68%, respectively. In addition, the variation in premium within a credit class, particularly the C's, indicates numerous sub-levels of credit. The credit premium provides a mechanism to statistically measure the various gradations of credit quality within a credit class. Estimation results validate the credit premium as an explanatory variable; after loan age it was the most statistically significant variable in our sub-models.

THE SEASONING OF HOME EQUITY LOANS OCCURS IN TWO PHASES

One of the most important aspects of home equity loan prepayments is how rapidly prepayments increase or "season" with loan age. Given that prepayments are less correlated to interest rates, the most common mistake at pricing is a mis-specification of the slope and leveling point of the seasoning ramp. In general, the seasoning period for home equity loans is much shorter than that exhibited in the purchase money market (measured to be 30 months by the PSA standard). Home equity deals can season in as little as 10 months or as many as 30 months depending on the credit mix of the borrowers and the loan attributes of the deal. Moreover, we have found that the aging process actually consists of two distinct phases: an initial period that is characterized by rapid seasoning and an eventual plateau in prepayments, followed by a longer second period of steadily declining prepayments.

Phase 1: Rapid Seasoning and the "Credit Cure" Effect

Our research indicates that in a neutral interest rate environment, lower credit quality loans tend to season much more rapidly and plateau at a higher level than better credit loans, all else equal (see Exhibit 9). For example, in a no-change interest rate scenario A loans season in approximately 30 months, leveling between 18 and 20 CPR; B loans season in 15 to 18 months leveling near 24 CPR; and C loans season in 12 to 15 months leveling near 30 CPR. It should be noted that the actual aging profiles shown in Exhibit 9 are conditional on age only and, thus, independent of interest rate levels. Consequently, there is some distortion in the A profile since prepayments are heavily influenced by interest rates. This will be addressed in more detail in the next section. In contrast, there is minimal interest rate distortion in the B/C aging profiles shown in Exhibit 9, since there is less correlation to interest rates. We have identified several factors that contribute to Phase 1 of the seasoning process (in order of significance):

Exhibit 9: Historical Prepayments Conditional on Loan Age and Credit Domain (All Issuers, 1988-Present)

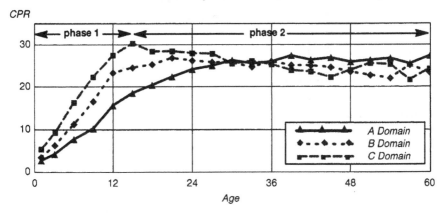

The "Credit Cure" Effect

As some of the lower credit borrowers improve the timeliness of their payments, they become eligible for a lower rate loan in a higher credit domain. Many brokers monitor the status of low credit home equity borrowers and solicit a refinance when their credit status improves. We have seen previously that there is a substantial difference in credit premium between adjacent credit domains. For example, a C rated borrower will reduce his rate by an average of 2.36% simply by qualifying for a B rated loan, while a B rated borrower will improve his rate by only 1.43% by qualifying for an A rated loan. Therefore, the lower the credit quality of borrowers in a deal, the greater the potential for a "credit cure" effect and the steeper the seasoning ramp. Furthermore, we found that once borrowers attain an A rating, credit curing is much less pronounced. The lack of a credit cure effect in the A credit domain causes a seasoning pattern that is more akin to the purchase money market (a 30 month seasoning ramp like the PSA curve). While A rated borrowers as a group remain more sensitive to interest rates, they will season at a substantially slower rate than lower credit loans when there is no incentive to refinance.

Higher Margin Loans Attract More Broker Competition

With brokers often working to originate loans 7 to 8 points above the FHLMC commitment rate, there is naturally more latitude for competition in the lower credit sector. In addition, lenders often try to offset declines in refinancing volumes by competing more aggressively in the B/C sector.

Higher Default Rates On Lower Credit Loans

While this is a marginal contribution to overall prepayments (a maximum of 2 or 3 CPR in the early months of the seasoning process), low credit domain loans experience higher default rates.

Phase 2: The "Credit Inertia" Effect

We also found that after lower credit domain loans reach their peak speed in the 10th to 20th month after origination (depending on the joint effects of credit premium, CLTV, and other factors), there is a pronounced slowdown in prepayments lasting 3 to 4 years. We believe this effect can be explained by a self-selection among borrowers in the lower credit groups. The "credit cure" effect quickly eliminates the borrowers that have the ability to improve their credit status, leaving borrowers that are more likely to remain credit impaired in the future. These borrowers have a demonstrated history of delinquency behavior that prevents them from improving their status. Unless they change this behavior there is little chance of qualifying for a better rate. The probability of a "cure" decays as a function of time so that in a period of three to four years most of the remaining borrowers are either habitually delinquent or have some other constraint (such as equity) that prevents a prepayment. We call this process the "credit inertia" effect because it characterizes the growing inability of the remaining borrowers in the population to change their status, improve their rate, or take out more equity. This puts a downward pressure on prepayments that is clearly visible in Exhibit 9 (in the B/C credit domain). The A credit domain, on the other hand, exhibits little credit inertia.

PURE INTEREST RATE EFFECTS: WHAT THE DATA TELL US

To analyze pure interest rate effects on home equity prepayments one must adjust for the higher credit premium imposed on lower credit borrowers. One common mistake made by market participants is to perform a simple WAC stratification of historical prepayments to assess the sensitivity to interest rates. Although commonly used in the MBS market, this approach can have very misleading results in the home equity market because it masks the true sensitivity to interest rates. Indeed, we often find that home equity securities behave in a manner exactly opposite to that of securities backed by conforming purchase money mortgages, i.e., prepayments from the highest WAC home equity deals are the least sensitive to low interest rates. Stratifying historical prepayments by WAC alone with no adjustment for credit premium tends to produce a flat prepayment profile and a false picture of call protection. To correct for the credit premium, Exhibit 10 plots actual home equity prepayment rates partitioned by credit domain and conditional on how much rates have risen or fallen since each loan was originated. Once these adjustments are made a more reliable picture of pure interest rate effects emerges.

Exhibit 10: Historical Prepayments Conditional on Changes in Interest Rates, and Credit Domain

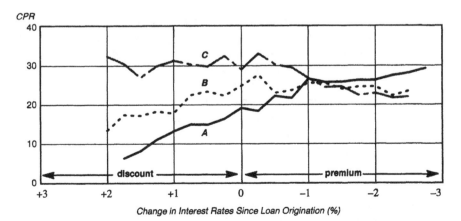

Change in Interest Rates Since Loan Origination (%)

Each point on a curve in Exhibit 10 represents the average prepayment rate for only seasoned[4] loans that map to a specific credit domain and change in rates. Several well-defined trends emerge from the prepayment curves shown in Exhibit 10.

- Prepayments of A domain loans are highly correlated to the level of refinancing incentive. Loans that are deeply out-of-the money prepay on average slightly less than 10 CPR (only 2 to 3 CPR faster than the baseline level of a discount conventional MBS) while loans with the largest refinancing incentive have an average prepayment rate that is approximately 30 CPR.
- B domain loans are less correlated to interest rate changes than A loans, increasing from approximately 14 CPR on loans well out-of-the-money and leveling at around 25 CPR for loans well in-the-money.
- C domain loans range between 22 and 32 CPR but exhibit little correlation to interest rates. In fact, C loans with a positive refinancing incentive have historically prepaid modestly slower than loans with no incentive.

The curves shown in Exhibit 10 are average prepayment rates across all periods and loans within each credit domain. Actual prepayments at the deal level may be faster or slower than shown in the exhibit depending on specific loan attributes. The slightly inverted C domain profile can be explained by recent competitive forces in the B/C sector that have accelerated the discount prepayment observations in Exhibit 10. For example, in 1994 the B and C domains displayed a rapid acceleration in prepayments despite rising interest rates. A closer examination of the data in the exhibit confirms that the discount region (left side of the horizontal axis) is dominated by observations from the 1994/95 backup in interest rates, while the premium observations are more dispersed across time with burnout helping to suppress the speeds in the highest premium regions. Recent notable entrants include Residential Funding Corporation under its Alternet A program and Option One Mortgage offering adjustable rate home equity loans. In addition, when interest rates rise, refinancing business dries up and existing lenders look to other areas, like B and C loans, to offset the drop in loan production.

Another view of pure interest rate effects in A credit loans is shown in Exhibit 11. It stratifies the A credit domain by current, premium, or discount[5] and plots historical prepayments conditional on loan age. Once again, the data confirms a clear segmentation by rate incentive. Loans in the current coupon region ramp to just under 20 CPR in approximately 30 months, while the premium loans ramp to 30 CPR and the discounts to just above 10 CPR.

---

[4] For this analysis, seasoned loans in the A, B and C domains constitute loans older than 18, 15, and 12 months, respectively.

[5] The "current" sector is defined as loans with rates within 50 basis points of the actual current coupon; "premium" designates all loans with rates at least 50 basis points above current; "discount" designates all loans with rates at least 50 basis points below current coupon.

Exhibit 11: "A" Credit Home Equity Prepayments Partioned by Current, Premium, And Discount Loans

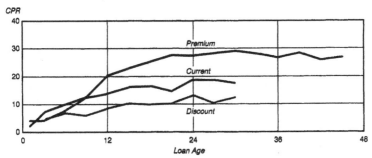

Exhibit 12: Home Equity Originations by Loan Purpose

Purpose	Percentage
Debt Consolidation	39%
Refinance	44%
Purchase Money	2%
Other	15%

A final stratification of our database by loan purpose reveals the substantial contribution to prepayments caused by either changing interest rates or credit curing. Although the population and definition of the loan purpose field varied from issuer to issuer, the general breakdown provided in Exhibit 12 confirms that home equity loans are often used to consolidate debt. However, an even higher percentage of existing loans is refinanced as a result of normal credit curing or rate and term refinancing.

COMBINED LOAN-TO-VALUE AND GEOGRAPHIC EFFECTS

After credit domain and loan age, the combined loan-to-value (CLTV)[6] ratio is the most important explanatory variable in our model. An inverse relationship exists between the CLTV and home equity loan prepayments. A low CLTV increases the probability of a prepayment for the following reasons:

- Existing home equity borrowers with substantial equity remaining in their homes are much more likely to take out additional equity in the future, whether on their own or through broker solicitation. These borrowers not only possess the necessary equity to take out a new loan but also have a demonstrated willingness to borrow against their equity.

---

[6] The CLTV is calculated by adding the balances of the first and second liens and dividing the total by the value of the house.

Exhibit 13: Common CLTV Underwriting Limits

Credit Domain	Maximum Allowable CLTV	CLTV Threshold
A	≈ 85%	75%
B	≈ 80%	70%
C	≈ 75%	60%

- Borrowers that use home equity loans to consolidate debt are predisposed to another consolidation if their debt levels continue to increase.
- A low CLTV ratio increases the likelihood that a borrower will trade-up to a new home.
- A low CLTV improves a borrower's ability to refinance.

Although a low CLTV also reduces the probability of a default, any potential decline in prepayments from lower default rates is overwhelmed by the four factors cited above. Naturally, the strength of a regional economy can have a significant impact on prepayment behavior because it changes a borrower's equity position. For example, a vigorous local economy tends to increase borrower mobility and strengthen home prices, lowering CLTVs and increasing prepayments. Conversely, a sluggish local economy lowers mobility and weakens home prices, slowing prepayments. Consider California, once the fastest prepayment state in the country, where a housing recession has severely eroded home prices and slowed prepayments to a level that is currently 15% below the national average. In general, investors should prefer geographically disperse collateral because it reduces exposure to regional economic volatility.

To account for regional loan concentrations, we dynamically update CLTVs in our home equity database by applying our proprietary regional home price indices to the original CLTV supplied by the issuer. In this way prepayment forecasts remain consistent with current home price trends across the nation. In addition, by modifying our baseline appreciation assumption, investors can assess the joint effects of changes in home prices and interest rates on the prepayment and return profile of their portfolios.

We also found that the CLTV threshold that suppresses prepayments in the home equity sector varies by credit domain. Exhibit 13 shows common CLTV underwriting limits for each credit domain followed by the approximate CLTV threshold where there is a measurable impact on prepayments. Loans with CLTVs above the thresholds listed in Exhibit 13 tended to be slower than identical loans with lower CLTVs. Bear in mind that there has been a recent trend towards relaxing CLTV standards as lenders struggle to maintain market share. It is not uncommon today for lenders to underwrite loans with CLTVs even higher than those listed in Exhibit 13. In the short term, this will put an upward pressure on prepayments as brokers canvas the existing universe of equity-rich borrowers to take out additional equity. However, the trend will ultimately slow prepayments (but increase defaults) as new limits are reached and borrowers are left with lower overall levels of equity.

CHANGES IN THE UNDERLYING BORROWER MIX AFFECT FUTURE PREPAYMENT BEHAVIOR

The unique seasoning and refinancing patterns evident in each of the borrower credit domains implies that, over time, the underlying composition of the borrowers will also change. This can have a profound impact on the future prepayment behavior of home equity securities. For example, one type of altered behavior results when lower interest rates remove the most rate sensitive borrowers from a pool of mortgages. Widely referred to as burnout, this particular type of evolution in the mix of borrowers tends to temper interest rate related prepayments in the future. From a broader perspective, the mix of borrowers at any point in time is a function of the prior interest rate path and the prepayment experience along that path. We believe home equity securities are particularly vulnerable to the "path dependent" aspect of prepayments because of the diverse mix of borrower credit quality and refinancing abilities present in most deals.

Path dependency is often the most challenging aspect of mortgage prepayment modeling owing to the complex processes at work. In the absence of loan-level data, there is no mechanism available to keep track of the remaining borrowers in a pool (modelers are forced to treat an entire pool of loans as if it were one mortgage); consequently, proxies[7] for path dependent behavior must be developed. One of the remarkable features of a loan-level model is that it automatically accounts for the borrower self-selection that is responsible for "burnout" and many other path dependent changes in prepayment behavior. Having access to loan level data allows us to model actual borrower behavior, and avoid the need to develop variables to "simulate" this behavior. We believe a loan-level model produces a superior forecast because it directly models the fundamental cause of path dependent prepayment behavior, i.e., a change in the composition of the underlying borrowers.

To the extent that borrowers are self-selected over time, our composite forecast will begin to take on the prepayment characteristics of the surviving borrowers. For example, an initially disperse credit base will shift toward B/C borrowers and more stable prepayments after a low interest rate cycle since A borrowers are much more likely to refinance out of a pool (our A domain submodel will forecast a very fast prepayment rate, eroding the A component of the pool). Conversely, the concentration will shift toward A borrowers and more interest rate sensitive prepayments in a neutral to high interest rate cycle since B/C borrowers tend to pay faster than A borrowers in a non-refinancing environment.

LIEN POSITION AND LOAN SIZE

A significant percentage of recent home equity originations have been first liens. This trend tends to be correlated with interest rates, i.e., during low interest rate

---

[7] Often survivorship (the percentage of a pool that has not prepaid) is used to measure the degree of burnout.

cycles many home equity borrowers prefer to refinance all of their debt (including their first mortgage) at the more attractive prevailing rate. Conversely, in a rising rate environment homeowners preserve the low rate on their first mortgage by opting to take out a second lien home equity loan. A comparison of prepayments between first lien and second lien home equity loans indicates that second liens tend to prepay systematically faster than first liens in the high credit domains. Exhibits 14, 15, and 16 compare historical first and second lien prepayments in the A domain for the discount, current and premium sectors, respectively.

An important distinction between first and second lien home equity loans is that second liens are subject to the full prepayment risk of the underlying first mortgage. A second lien must always be refinanced when the first is refinanced to avoid subordination of the new first lien to the old second lien. Therefore, if homeowners elect to refinance their first mortgages when interest rates fall, second liens will exhibit a matching increase in prepayments. In addition, a borrower may elect to refinance his second lien independently of his first lien at any time.

For credit worthy second lien borrowers, the relative ease of refinancing the underlying purchase mortgage in the era of "frictionless" refinancing may have contributed to the speed differential exhibited in Exhibits 14, 15, and 16. Indeed, as Exhibit 6 illustrated, second lien borrowers with no credit impairment (represented by the FICAL issue) prepaid as fast as comparable MBS through the 1992/1993 prepayment cycle.

Exhibits 14, 15, and 16 illustrate several key differences between first and second lien prepayments.

- The prepayment difference is most pronounced in the discount sector, where second lien prepayments may be accelerated by higher turnover levels and some additional refinancing of the underlying first mortgage (which may itself be in the money).
- The prepayment difference narrows in the premium sector.
- There is more extension risk in first lien home equity loans.

Although on the surface first lien home equity loans "look" more like traditional purchase money mortgages, we found that they do not prepay like them if (1) the borrowers have a lower than A credit rating, (2) equity is taken out of the transaction, and (3) average balances remain below standard purchase money levels. One benefit of first lien home equity transactions is that investors have complete information to determine refinancing risk. There is generally no information on the attributes of the underlying first mortgage in a second lien transaction. Our models explicitly account for the observed differences in prepayment behavior between first and second lien home equity securities. In the lower credit domains there was little systematic divergence between first and second lien home equity prepayments. Less credit worthy borrowers were probably less able and less willing to take advantage of refinancing opportunities, whether they held a first lien or a second lien home equity loan.

Exhibit 14: Discount Sector Home Equity Prepayments
Conditional on Age and Lien Position

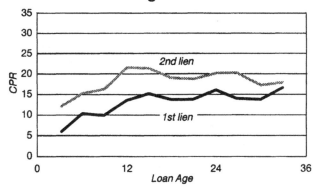

Exhibit 15: Current Sector Home Equity Prepayments
Conditional on Age and Lien Position

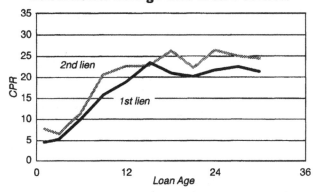

Exhibit 16: Premium Sector Home Equity Prepayments
Conditional on Age and Lien Position

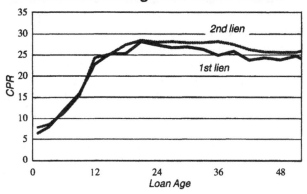

Exhibit 17: Historical Prepayments Conditional on Changes in Interest Rates and Original Amount

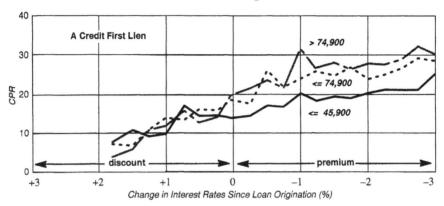

Exhibit 18: Historical Prepayments Conditional on Changes in Interest Rates and Original Amount

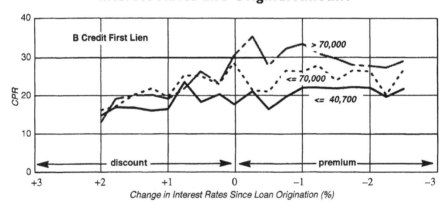

We also found a statistically significant relationship between loan balance and prepayments, i.e., with a positive refinancing incentive large balance loans tended to prepay consistently faster than small balance loans. The influence of loan size was most apparent in A and B domain first lien loans. Second lien loans were uniformly small with an average balance of just $35,100, restricting any economic incentives to refinance. Exhibits 17 and 18 plot historical prepayments for seasoned A and B domain first lien loans conditional on loan amount and changes in interest rates. The clear segmentation evident by loan amount in Exhibits 17 and 18 reflects the greater dollar cost savings of refinancing large balance loans. In addition to the economic benefits, credit worthy borrowers with large loans are the most likely targets of broker solicitations to refinance when interest rates decline.

Exhibit 19: The Default Contribution to CPR by Credit Domain

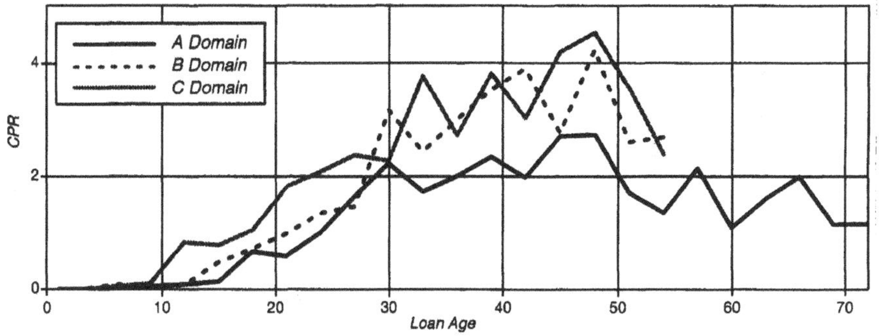

PARTIAL PREPAYMENTS AND DEFAULTS

We found that curtailments (partial prepayments) and defaults play a relatively minor role in home equity loan prepayments. Low curtailments may seem counter-intuitive given that home equity loan rates are so much higher than purchase money rates. Clearly, borrowers have an economic incentive to reduce their home equity debt service. However, by definition many of the finance company home equity borrowers are cash-strapped and unable or unwilling to make payments above the scheduled amount. This may have contributed to curtailments that were uniformly low, averaging about 1% CPR. Nevertheless, as a borrower's economic situation improves over time, we would expect higher curtailment rates to reflect a greater capacity to pay down debt over time.

Similarly, the default contribution to prepayments was relatively small but increased over time, with the maximum impact occurring between months 30 and 50 and then declining thereafter (see Exhibit 19). Lower credit domain loans experienced a higher default rate that peaked at approximately 4.5 CPR between month 40 and month 50. "A" credit domain loans exhibited a similar pattern but peaked at only 2.5 CPR. Despite these relatively low default levels, we anticipate that defaults will play a larger role in the future as increased competition pushes CLTV limits higher.

STATISTICAL ESTIMATION AND MODEL STRUCTURE

Each sub-model was developed entirely from loan level data; no data aggregation was performed. Direct measurements of WAC, age, credit rating, CLTV, and balance were available from the issuer data on a loan by loan basis. A discrete choice estimation was selected because it utilizes all loan level information, modeling the probability that a given home equity borrower will either prepay or not prepay his loan in any given period. We assumed that the probability of prepayment was a non-linear function of the independent variables with a probability distribution that follows a modified logistic curve. Prepayments were explained by the individual and joint effects of the independent variables listed in Exhibit 20.

Exhibit 20: Independent Variables

> • Borrower credit rating
> • Borrower credit premium
> • Loan age
> • Original combined loan-to-value
> • Updated CLTV
> • Refinancing incentive
> • Loan size
> • Lien position
>
> *Assuming that:*
> the probability of prepayment = C * exp(beta) / [1 = exp(beta)]
> *where:*
> C = Constant
> beta = sum (coefficient[i] * Independent variable[i])

As previously mentioned, the impact of borrower adverse selection is implicitly accounted for by the loan level specification and sub-model structure of our forecast. Having access to loan level data allows us to model behavior at the borrower level and eliminate the need to develop variables that "simulate" behavior at the aggregate level. There are other potential variables that could be added to our home equity model; however, it is our experience that a more parsimonious approach focusing on the correct identification and specification of the key determinants of prepayments, leads to a more robust and predictive model. Furthermore, while adding variables always improves the fit, it often increases the complexity of a model with little improvement in predictive power.

The implementation of our model is straightforward, as shown in Exhibit 21. Loan level data are direct inputs and can originate from either actual deal data or hypothetical user inputs. Once loan attributes have been supplied, cash flows can be generated for various interest rate scenarios.

Projections

Exhibit 22 shows our flat rate scenario forecast for representative loans in each credit domain. Baseline loan attribute assumptions are shown in the accompanying box in Exhibit 22. As discussed earlier, under neutral interest rate conditions the forecasts exhibit seasoning profiles that are unique to each credit class. To the extent that loan attributes deviate from our baseline loan assumptions, actual forecasts may be faster or slower than those shown in Exhibit 22. In addition, the higher the concentration of A domain loans backing a given home equity security, the more sensitive it will be to a change in the interest rate assumption. For example, Exhibit 23 shows our forecasts under plus and minus 300 basis point interest rate shocks (in 100 bp increments) assuming a 100% A domain concentration. The prepayment variation caused by these extreme interest rate shocks totals approximately 26 CPR (low extreme to high extreme) in the A domain and 18 CPR in the B domain for seasoned loans with baseline attributes.

Exhibit 21: Prepayment Model Structure

```
                    ┌─────────────────────────────────┐
                    │        Loan Level Inputs        │
                    ├─────────────────────────────────┤
                    │  – loan rate      – location     │
                    │  – loan age       – credit rating│
                    │  – lien position  – credit premium│
                    │  – loan size      – original CLTV│
                    └─────────────────────────────────┘
                                    │
                                    ▼
                         ┌──────────────────┐
                         │   Credit Filter  │
                         └──────────────────┘
                                    │
                                    ▼
                         ┌──────────────────┐
                         │ Exogenous Inputs │
                         ├──────────────────┤
                         │ – Interest rate scenario│
                         │ – Home price scenario   │
                         └──────────────────┘
              ┌─────────────────┼─────────────────┐
              ▼                 ▼                 ▼
    ┌──────────────────┐ ┌──────────────────┐ ┌──────────────────┐
    │ A Credit Domain  │ │ B Credit Domain  │ │  C/Lower Credit  │
    │    Sub–Model     │ │    Sub–Model     │ │ Domain Sub–Model │
    └──────────────────┘ └──────────────────┘ └──────────────────┘
              └─────────────────┼─────────────────┘
                                ▼
                      ┌──────────────────┐
                      │ Composite Forecast│
                      └──────────────────┘
```

Exhibit 22: Baseline Forecasts for A, B, and C Domain Home Equity Loans

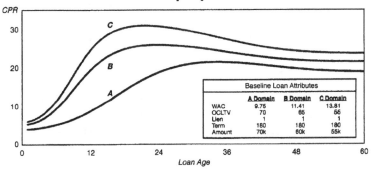

Baseline Loan Attributes			
	A Domain	B Domain	C Domain
WAC	9.75	11.41	13.81
OCLTV	70	65	55
Lien	1	1	1
Term	180	180	180
Amount	70k	60k	55k

Exhibit 23: Interest Rate Sensitivity Forecast for A Domain Home Equity Loans

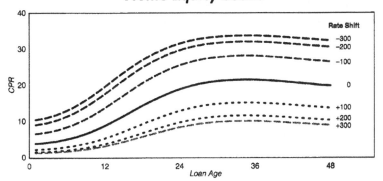

Valuation

In general, home equity securities have been priced and traded on an average life spread basis. This approach calculates a cash flow yield using a static prepayment assumption and then measures the yield spread differential to the equivalent average life point on the Treasury yield curve. The obvious disadvantage of this approach is that it does not adjust for the value of the prepayment option. A well-specified prepayment model in conjunction with an option based pricing methodology allows investors to determine the expected reduction in the static yield spread as a result of prepayment volatility. The option adjusted spread (OAS), derived from a random sample of interest rate paths, measures the expected spread over the entire Treasury curve adjusted for future interest rate and prepayment uncertainty. The value of the prepayment option, usually referred to as the "convexity cost," is measured as the difference between the static cash flow spread (0% volatility OAS) and the OAS assuming market volatilities. OAS analysis has generally proved to be the best framework to value a bond with interest rate contingent cash flows, improving the accuracy of duration, convexity and return measures.

We present two sets of complete option adjusted spread valuations in Exhibit 24 (synthetic deals) and Exhibit 25 (actual deals). In both tables, the reduction in the static cash flow spread (0% volatility OAS) measured by the convexity cost column is primarily a function of the loan and borrower-level inputs to the prepayment model and the volatility assumption used in the OAS model. Our results confirm that home equity securities have less negative convexity (lower convexity costs) than comparable agency MBS, but are more negatively convex than credit cards and autos.

In Exhibit 24 and 26, we quantify the influence of credit quality on valuation results using three hypothetical deals with identical sequential structures but with different credit distributions. We assume Synthetic Deal #1 is comprised of 100% A credit domain loans; Synthetic Deal #2 is equally distributed across A/B/C credits; and Synthetic Deal #3 is an equal split between B/C credits with 0% A concentration. Once again we assume baseline loan attributes for each credit domain. Exhibit 26 illustrates the flattening in the projected prepayment profile caused by a heavy concentration of B and C loans. Note that each point on a curve in Exhibit 26 represents the constant life speed that corresponds to the projected monthly vector of speeds at that specific interest rate assumption. In the no change scenario, Synthetic Deals #2 and #3 accelerate above Deal #1 because of the "credit cure" effect. However, Deal #1 is faster in the down 200 and 300 basis point scenarios because of additional rate refinancing.

OAS results from our synthetic deal analysis (see Exhibit 24) are intuitive and support our empirical findings. Several important observations can be made regarding the results shown in Exhibit 24:

Exhibit 24: Home Equity Valuation Results (Synthetic Deals)

Security				Prepayment Forecast (CPR)					Static Analysis							Option Adjusted Spread		
				−200	−100	0	+100	+200	Tranche	Price	Yield	Avg Life	A.L. Sprd	Dur.	Convex.	Cash Flow Sprd	OAS	Convex. Cost
Synthetic Deal #1				26.26	23.40	18.31	12.67	9.13	A1	99.821	5.99	1.30	84.72	1.19	−0.20	81.75	63.69	18.05
Collateral:	Credit	lien	%	WAC	age	rtrm	size	oltv	A2	99.815	6.21	3.23	93.71	3.43	−0.32	91.05	45.15	45.89
	A	1	100.0	9.75	0	180	70K	70	A3	99.733	6.54	4.92	110.76	5.19	−0.23	105.78	49.26	56.52
									A4	99.226	7.00	6.65	145.93	6.23	−0.20	145.94	87.96	47.98
									A5	98.788	7.40	10.83	163.34	7.73	0.20	158.72	134.16	24.55
Synthetic Deal #2				25.70	24.43	21.54	17.44	14.62	A1	99.816	5.98	1.21	84.01	.89	−0.07	77.47	72.22	5.25
Collateral:	Credit	lien	%	WAC	age	rtrm	size	oltv	A2	99.948	6.15	2.89	90.86	2.66	−0.16	89.83	66.56	23.27
	A	1	33.3	9.75	0	180	70K	70	A3	99.714	6.54	4.28	116.74	4.45	−0.22	114.10	80.92	33.18
	B	1	33.3	11.41	0	180	60K	65	A4	100.318	6.77	5.73	128.67	5.71	−0.09	122.27	86.73	35.54
	C	1	33.3	13.81	0	180	55K	55	A5	98.915	7.39	9.56	166.80	7.74	0.25	160.20	140.00	20.21
Synthetic Deal #3				25.44	24.94	23.31	20.28	18.06	A1	99.808	5.98	1.16	84.16	.82	−0.06	76.78	74.16	2.63
Collateral:	Credit	lien	%	WAC	age	rtrm	size	oltv	A2	99.929	6.15	2.73	92.27	2.33	−0.08	91.56	78.09	13.47
	B	1	50.0	11.41	0	180	60K	65	A3	99.869	6.49	3.98	114.73	3.92	−0.11	113.94	93.77	20.17
	C	1	50.0	13.81	0	180	55K	55	A4	100.747	6.66	5.29	120.42	5.26	−0.04	116.63	93.29	23.34
									A5	99.072	7.37	8.85	169.23	7.58	0.25	160.47	144.77	15.70

Exhibit 25: Valuation Results For Selected Home Equity Deals

AAMES 95C

Prepayment Forecast (CPR)				
-200	-100	0	+100	+200
21.63	21.08	19.64	17.02	14.65

Collateral:

Credit	lien	%	WAC	age	rtrm	size	oltv
A	1	20.1	10.2	2	303	90K	66
	2	5.0	12.0	2	232	38K	60
B	1	17.8	10.8	2	335	86K	62
	2	3.0	12.2	2	208	27K	64
C	1	49.7	12.3	2	351	85K	62
	2	4.4	13.5	2	222	31K	61

Historical CPR speeds: 1 Mo 4.9, 3 Mo NA

Tranche	Static Analysis						Option Adjusted Spread		
	Price	Yield	Avg Life	A.L. Sprd	Dur.	Convex.	Cash Flow Sprd	OAS	Convex. Cost
AA	100.688	6.16	2.18	97.80	1.56	-0.14	80.65	64.14	16.52
AB	100.953	6.66	5.21	121.24	4.62	-0.27	123.00	89.08	33.91
AC	100.828	7.29	9.03	159.87	7.11	0.05	159.24	131.00	28.24

FNMA 95W1

Prepayment Forecast (CPR)				
-200	-100	0	+100	+200
29.62	27.49	23.10	17.06	11.90

Collateral:

Credit	lien	%	WAC	age	rtrm	size	oltv
A	1	51.6	10.0	13	172	61K	69
	2	35.7	10.2	21	159	34K	67
B	1	8.6	10.6	17	170	64K	67
	2	4.1	10.9	19	161	32K	65

Historical CPR speeds: 1 Mo 20.1, 3 Mo 18.2

Tranche	Static Analysis						Option Adjusted Spread		
	Price	Yield	Avg Life	A.L. Sprd	Dur.	Convex.	Cash Flow Sprd	OAS	Convex. Cost
A2	101.891	6.18	1.21	103.95	0.59	-0.13	69.57	65.73	3.84
A3	103.047	6.19	1.97	102.81	1.40	-0.34	87.63	70.42	17.21
A4	103.750	6.36	2.72	113.66	2.15	-0.32	112.40	78.11	34.29
A5	104.422	6.49	3.48	119.75	3.03	-0.62	126.03	84.36	41.67
A6	105.312	6.82	5.06	137.87	4.50	-0.36	146.61	95.19	51.42
A7	105.249	7.45	9.42	173.59	6.90	0.03	179.47	145.75	33.72

FNMA 95W4

Prepayment Forecast (CPR)				
-200	-100	0	+100	+200
27.59	25.86	22.08	16.22	10.92

Collateral:

Credit	lien	%	WAC	age	rtrm	size	oltv
A	1	60.7	9.9	6	187	70K	71
	2	28.3	10.7	12	170	31K	68
B	1	8.1	10.7	10	184	68K	70
	2	2.9	11.4	12	170	31K	67

Historical CPR speeds: 1 Mo 22.3, 3 Mo 17.5

Tranche	Static Analysis						Option Adjusted Spread		
	Price	Yield	Avg Life	A.L. Sprd	Dur.	Convex.	Cash Flow Sprd	OAS	Convex. Cost
A2	101.625	6.19	1.81	103.00	1.51	-0.29	87.20	67.39	19.81
A3	102.031	6.33	2.88	108.58	2.88	-0.37	107.08	61.43	45.66
A4	102.609	6.43	4.11	136.04	4.40	-0.47	110.09	50.05	60.04
A5	102.641	6.87	6.10	136.04	6.00	-0.35	136.27	78.37	57.90
A6	100.949	7.40	9.66	167.02	7.64	0.21	165.15	132.67	32.49

Exhibit 25 (Continued)

Security	Prepayment Forecast (CPR)					Tranche	Price	Yield	Avg Life	A.L. Sprd	Dur.	Convex.	Cash Flow Sprd	OAS	Convex. Cost
	−200	−100	0	+100	+200			Static Analysis					Option Adjusted Spread		
FNMA 95W5	23.80	21.27	15.53	10.97	7.33	A1	100.250	5.94	1.95	77.31	1.98	−0.32	71.73	31.21	40.52
						A2	100.359	6.18	3.77	85.25	4.37	−0.65	85.03	20.07	64.96
						A3	100.141	6.45	5.51	98.16	5.81	−0.44	91.55	24.53	67.02
						A4	99.844	6.85	7.89	122.89	7.27	−0.03	113.06	58.29	54.77
						A5	99.062	7.25	11.29	147.20	8.05	0.12	140.61	110.79	29.83

Collateral:

Credit	lien	%	WAC	age	rtrm	size	oltv
A	1	82.6	9.0	2	199	76K	72
	2	17.4	10.0	4	180	29K	71

Historical CPR speeds: NA, newly issued deal

Security	Prepayment Forecast (CPR)					Tranche	Price	Yield	Avg Life	A.L. Sprd	Dur.	Convex.	Cash Flow Sprd	OAS	Convex. Cost
GEHEL 951	26.61	24.13	19.38	13.59	9.39	A1	100.422	6.17	1.02	103.46	0.65	−0.14	74.22	67.48	6.73
						A2	101.125	6.34	2.71	111.73	2.47	−0.39	104.74	64.84	39.90
						A3	101.250	6.65	4.46	125.75	4.52	−0.47	126.38	65.13	61.26
						A4	101.271	7.05	6.18	153.90	5.74	−0.39	151.49	91.59	59.90
						A5	101.270	7.40	10.09	164.72	7.42	0.09	164.72	129.50	35.21

Collateral:

Credit	lien	%	WAC	age	rtrm	size*	oltv
A	1	66.7	9.2	10	180	77K	72
	2	23.5	10.4	13	171	50K	70
B	1	8.1	10.1	9	183	77K	70
	2	1.7	11.0	12	180	39K	70

* Non balloons only

Historical CPR speeds: 1 Mo 18.3, 3 Mo 12.1

Definitions and Assumptions:

CPR: Average Life equivalent prepayment speed projected by Bear Stearns' Econometric Prepayment Model.

Yield: Bond Equivalent Yield calculated using projected CPR.

Average Life: Weighted average time to principal return, in years, using projected prepayment speed.

Average Life Spread: Yield spread of security to interpolated Treasury with equal average life.

Duration: Price sensitivity of the security, expressed as the percentage price change, given a 100 basis point move in interest rates.

Convexity: A measure of the sensitivity of duration to changes in interest rates.

Cash Flow Spread: 0% volatility OAS.

Convexity Cost: Difference between OAS at 0% volatility and OAS with observed volatility.

Volatility: Volatility is calculated by first pricing an at the money 10 year libor cap and then solving for the implied volatility that gives the same cap price. Our implied volatility assumption is 19.8%. The volatility is *internally* translated for calculations using mean reversion. At 5% mean reversion the equivalent mortgage rate volatility is approximately 12.77%

Pricing: Bid side as of 1/12/96

Yield Curve:	3 mo	6 mo	12 mo	2 yr	3 yr	5 yr	7 yr	10 yr	30 yr
	5.18	5.18	5.13	5.16	5.25	5.44	5.56	5.75	6.16

Exhibit 26: Projected Life Prepayment Speeds

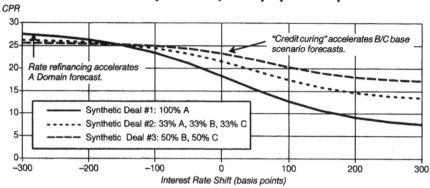

- Synthetic Deal #1 (100% A credit) has inherently more volatile prepayments than the other synthetic deals, as evidenced by substantially higher levels of convexity cost across all average life points on the Treasury curve. In the most sensitive tranche, prepayment volatility reduces the static yield spread by over 55 basis points.
- Synthetic Deal #3, backed by the most credit-impaired borrowers (50/50 B/C split), was the least negatively convex security. Convexity cost levels remained below 25 basis points even in the most volatile tranches.
- In general, finance company securities backed by the highest credit quality borrowers are two to three times more negatively convex than deals backed by the lowest credit borrowers (as measured by convexity cost). For the average deal with a relatively disperse credit profile, investors should be compensated an additional 20 to 40 basis points for prepayment uncertainty depending on the average life of the security.
- In the long average life sector, risk/reward favors the last tranche where convexity costs are lowered by the additional call protection of preceding tranches, less overall extension risk, and more stable long-dated cash flows. Convexity costs tended to drop by 30% to 40% in these issues. The most volatile tranches (highest convexity costs) tended to be concentrated in the 4 to 6 year average life sector of the curve.

We also present full option adjusted spread analytics in Exhibit 25 for 25 actual home equity securities from 5 recently issued deals. Note that differences in projected base case speeds can be explained by either a difference in seasoning or a difference in credit quality. For example, the FNMA-95W5 issue has a slower base speed than FNMA-95W1 or FNMA-95W2 since it is at the beginning of its seasoning ramp. In addition, projections for the 95W1 and 95W4 issues are propped up by today's lower interest rates (relative to when they were issued). The results in Exhibit 25 are consistent with our findings from the synthetic deal analysis presented in Exhibit 24. The reduction in static yield spread due to pre-payment volatility ranged from just several basis points in the shortest average life securities to well over 60 basis points in the 5 to 7 year average life securities backed by A credit borrowers. The most notable drop in convexity cost was evident in the AAMES issue, a result of the heavy concentration of B/C loans. In contrast, FNMA-95W5 was penalized by the heavy concentration of A domain loans and the newness of the issue. Once again, risk/reward favored the long dated tranches where convexity costs were cut by 30% to 40% relative to preceding tranches.

CONCLUSION

To address the need for a more sophisticated and robust valuation framework, we have presented the results of a comprehensive prepayment study derived from borrower level information on over 300,000 home equity loans. The result of our efforts is a prepayment model that accounts for the key determinants of home equity prepayment behavior. Linked to our option adjusted spread model, our prepayment model allows investors to differentiate and value the prepayment uncertainty inherent in home equity securities with very disperse loan and borrower attributes. Using this technology, investors can make informed and reliable cross-sector relative value decisions as well as anticipate the market response to changing interest rates and home prices. It also provides the basis for superior hedging capabilities, including option adjusted duration and convexity measurements.

Chapter 19

Identifying Relative Value in Home Equity Loan and Manufactured Housing Securities Using OAS Analysis

Akiva Dickstein
Vice President
Lehman Brothers

INTRODUCTION

The introduction of OAS into the ABS market represents a significant advance and is a logical extension of the effort by market participants to understand prepayment behavior in the home equity loan and manufactured housing sectors. The use of OAS will help investors to identify relative value within a sector and to compare securities across a range of product types. Although OAS is not the only measure of value and should generally be supplemented by scenario analyses and views on interest rates, it is the best single measure of the prepayment risk-adjusted spread on a security.

We first describe prepayments in the MH and HEL sectors and address several factors that affect prepayment risk for structured securities. Then we calculate OAS for current coupon, premium, and discount securities, and make relative value comparisons. Finally, we stress our findings by using a modified model in which prepayments are more sensitive to interest rates than they have been historically.

PREPAYMENTS ON HOME EQUITY LOAN AND MANUFACTURED HOUSING COLLATERAL

Prepayments on both MH and HELs are less sensitive to interest rates than conventional agency mortgages, with home equity loans more sensitive than manufactured housing. Exhibit 1 shows the projections of the Lehman Brothers manufactured housing and agency mortgage models along with projections of home equity loan prepayments. We focus here on finance company home equity loans.

Exhibit 1: Sensitivity of Prepayments to Interest Rates* (% CPR)

Asset Class	Interest Rate Move (bp from current coupon)							
	−300	−200	−100	0	+100	+200	+300	Range
Manufactured Housing	17.0	14.4	11.7	9.2	7.4	6.6	6.0	11.0
Home Equity Loans	35.0	32.0	28.0	23.0	17.5	13.0	10.0	25.0
30-yr FNMA Mortgages	62.1	48.3	20.2	8.3	6.8	5.7	4.9	57.2

* We use a single CPR that equates the outstanding balance at the end of three years to the projection of the Lehman Brothers prepayment model. For HELs and MH, the loans are assumed to be fully seasoned (12 months for HELs and 24 months for MH).

The relative stability of interest rates for both HELs and MH is due to a number of factors. Both finance company home equity and manufactured housing loans are characterized by relatively small loan sizes (averages are about $35,000 on MH and about $55,000 on HELs) and higher loan rates (currently averaging about 10% to 11%) than in the agency mortgage market. Both of these factors contribute to the relative insensitivity of prepayments for these sectors. First, smaller loans have a lower dollar incentive to refinance for a given movement in interest rates, and mortgage brokers have less incentive to refinance smaller loans. Indeed, the smaller MH loans are less sensitive than the HELs to interest rate movements. Second, in both markets the high rate paradoxically indicates that fewer refinancing opportunities exist because defaults on finance company HELs and MH have historically been higher than on conforming mortgages; fewer lenders are willing and able to originate and service these loans. In addition, the borrower base is somewhat less sophisticated in terms of refinancing.

The prepayment projections shown in Exhibit 1 are based on typical securitized home equity and manufactured housing transactions. Our research indicates that additional factors such as credit quality, loan size, prepayment penalties (on HELs), loan-to-value (LTV) ratios, and burnout also affect the prepayment behavior of these loans. All these factors are incorporated into the Lehman Brothers MH and HEL models.

PREPAYMENT RISK IN STRUCTURED SECURITIES

Almost all recent home equity and manufactured housing transactions have been structured with several bond classes of various average lives. As a result, it is important to understand not only the prepayment behavior of the underlying collateral, but also the effect of such behavior on particular classes within a structure.

One way to observe the prepayment risk of a given class is to examine its change in average life over a range of interest rates. The response of a security's average life to interest rates may be affected by a number of factors: the sensitivity of borrowers to interest rates; loan characteristics such as WAM, range of loan maturities, and percentage of balloon loans; and, structural features such as clean-up calls.

Exhibit 2: Sensitivity of Average Life to Interest Rates for Selected Collateral Types

Bond	Collateral	Interest Rate Scenario (bp)							
		−300	−200	−100	0	+100	+200	+300	Range
Green Tree 1996-1 A-3	Manufactured Housing	3.6 yrs	4.4 yrs	5.5 yrs	6.7 yrs	7.6 yrs	8.2 yrs	8.5 yrs	4.9 yrs
EquiCredit 1995-4 A-4	Home Equity Loans	5.7	6.1	6.7	7.6	8.6	10.2	11.5	5.8
FNR 1994-31 B	Agency Mtgs. (7s of 94)	1.5	1.9	4.1	7.7	9.0	10.2	11.2	9.7

Interest Rate Sensitivity of Collateral

Securities backed by collateral with lower interest rate sensitivity will have a more stable average life profile. Exhibit 2 shows three securities with similar average lives in the base case and their average life profiles as a function of interest rates using the prepayment projections shown in Exhibit 1. The agency CMO shows the greatest average life drift, while the MH security is the most stable. This HEL security's average life is only slightly more sensitive to rates than the MH security.

Loan Amortization Characteristics

Even securities with identical prepayment sensitivities to interest rates may react differently in terms of average life drift due to different loan amortization characteristics. For example, we looked at two home equity loan securities with similar average lives, EquiCredit 1995-4 A-4 and Conti 1996-1 A-6. While the two securities behave similarly in falling rate environments, the EquiCredit transaction has significantly less extension risk than the Conti transaction if prepayments slow (Exhibit 3). The reason for this is directly related to the WAM of the two transactions: the shorter WAM on the EquiCredit transaction results in less extension of the security in a rising interest rate environment (low prepayment rates) due to the faster amortization of the underlying loans. Consequently, the EquiCredit security has less prepayment risk than the comparable Conti security. This difference would be further accentuated if the securities became discounts, with a greater possibility of a slowdown in prepayments.

In addition to WAM, other collateral characteristics affect prepayment risk in more subtle ways. For instance, a high proportion of balloons can cause more extension risk because the scheduled amortization of the loans is less than that of comparable maturity level-pay mortgages. In addition, a dispersion of WAM may have the effect of reducing extension on short classes that benefit from the shorter WAM collateral, while increasing extension risk on longer classes that are disproportionately backed by the longer WAM collateral.

Structure

Another influence on prepayment risk is the structure of the transaction. Short securities generally have less prepayment risk, since their average lives and durations are less likely to experience extreme changes due to a large move in interest rates. Very long classes also have somewhat less prepayment risk because burnout reduces call risk in the long run and scheduled amortization is a more significant portion of principal payments. However, the last class in most HEL and MH transactions is usually subject to the effects of a 10% clean-up call that gives the issuer the option to call the transaction and pay off the remaining securities at par once the outstanding balance has dropped below 10% of the original balance. Because one must assume that the issuer will call the security only in an environment where the loans could be resecuritized at a lower rate (i.e., in a low rate environment), the investor is essentially short a call option that must be valued appropriately.

USING OAS TO MEASURE PREPAYMENT RISK IN STRUCTURED MH AND HEL SECURITIES

To quantify the effect of prepayment risk in structured securities beyond simple scenario analysis, we use a full option-based framework. The traditional OAS methodology divides the nominal spread on a security with embedded options such as prepayments into a component that represents compensation for prepayment risk (the convexity or option cost) from the spread that investors receive for credit risk and liquidity. Using an OAS perspective allows us to compare relative value across various classes of MH and HEL securities as well as across ABS and mortgage sectors. We begin with an explanation of the zero-volatility spread and OAS.

Zero-Volatility Spreads

The most basic approach to valuing any security is to compare its yield with the yield of a comparable average life Treasury security; the difference is known as the *nominal spread*. However, for an amortizing security, this may not be an appropriate measure even in the absence of prepayment risk. Because the principal is paid down over a period of time, the appropriate alternative Treasury investment is not a bullet maturity bond matched to its average life, but rather a portfolio of Treasury securities with cash flows that replicate the cash flows of that security. To capture this effect, a zero-volatility (ZV) spread is used.

Exhibit 3: Effect of WAM on Extension Risk in Home Equity Loans

Bond	WAM	CPR (%)							Range
		35	32	28	23	18	13	10	
EquiCredit 1995-4 A-4	172 mo	5.0 yr	5.6 yr	6.3 yr	7.3 yr	8.8 yr	10.7 yr	12.1 yr	7.1 yr
Conti 1996-1 A-6	205	4.5	5.0	5.8	7.2	9.2	12.2	14.1	9.6

WAM = Weighted average maturity.

To a first approximation, the ZV spread is a weighted average of the spread to the par-priced zero coupon Treasury curve over the period in which the investor receives cash flows. Technically, the ZV spread is calculated using the forward curve to project a series of 1-month Treasury rates to find the spread that must be added to these rates when discounting the cash flows in order to match the current price of the security. The ZV spread gets its name from the fact that with no volatility the forward curve would have to be the realized spot curve to prevent arbitrage. The forward curve and the corresponding implied future interest rates are calculated using off-the-run Treasury securities, and ZV spreads are therefore quoted to the off-the-run Treasury curve.

The cash flows that are discounted when calculating the ZV spread are determined by a prepayment model along the path of interest rates implied by the forward curve. However, because the ABS market has grown up without prepayment models for the most part, ZV spreads have been calculated using a single prepayment assumption for the life of the security. These two approaches can produce different results since the forward path of interest rates rises when the yield curve is upward-sloping, which causes prepayments to slow along this path for many securities. In this chapter, we use the technically correct approach, allowing the model to determine prepayment rates along the ZV path.

Option-Adjusted Spreads

Although the ZV spread is an improvement over the nominal spread, it does not capture the prepayment risk inherent in a security whose cash flows may be significantly changed by the interest rate scenario. In practice, the interest rate path implied by the forward curve is only one of many possible paths that may be observed. In OAS analysis, a wide range of potential future interest rate paths is considered. The set of paths is generated using a model for the term structure of interest rates; the volatility in this model is calibrated to a robust set of options of various maturities. Along each path, a prepayment model is used to determine the response of the collateral to these interest rates and to determine cash flows. The OAS is defined as the spread that must be added to Treasury spreads so that when these cash flows are discounted to their present value, the average present value across all interest rate paths is equal to the actual price of the security today.

Mathematically,

nominal spread = zero volatility spread (ZV) + yield curve compensation

ZV spread = OAS + convexity cost (or option cost)

OAS is the compensation investors receive for credit risk, liquidity, and prepayment model risk.

Exhibit 4: OAS Analysis of Current Coupon HELs and MH

Avg. Life @ Model (years)	Home Equity Loans (bp)				Manufactured Housing (bp)				Agency PACs OAS	Credit Card ZV
	Nominal Sprd[a]	ZV Sprd[b]	Option Cost	OAS	Nominal Sprd	ZV Sprd	Option Cost	OAS		
1	65	58	21	37	50	41	11	30	30	30
3	85	79	38	41	50	46	18	28	35	30
5	102	95	33	62	55	52	21	31	40	34
7	125	117	33	84	73	63	20	43	45	42
10/11	150	121	40[c]	81	93	80	17	63	50	42
16	NA	NA	NA	NA	145	97	17[c]	80	50	NA

[a] Nominal spreads are quoted to the Treasury with the same maturity as the average life predicted by the model. In practice, the prepayment assumptions used in actual pricing may have a significant effect on the OAS, although option costs are not significantly affected by these assumptions.
[b] ZV spreads throughout this report are calculated using prepayment model projections along the zero volatility path. They therefore may differ from ZV spreads which assume a fixed prepayment rate.
[c] Option costs on the last classes include the cost of the optional clean-up call.

OAS Evaluation of Current Coupon Securities: Longer Classes Offer Value

In both the HEL and MH sectors, nominal spreads rise significantly as the average life of the securities increases. This is principally due to two factors: a narrower investor base in the longer part of the curve and a perception that prepayment risk increases as the duration of the class rises. OAS analysis allows us to quantify the prepayment risk on various classes and reveals that the longer classes offer the most attractive option-adjusted as well as nominal spreads.

We have selected two relatively recent transactions, EquiCredit 1995-4 and Green Tree 1996-1 as representative transactions for OAS analysis (Exhibit 4).[1] The manufactured housing security has less option cost than the home equity loan due to the more stable prepayments. In both securities, with the exception of the last class, option costs tend to be highest in the 3- to 7-year sector. Securities with shorter average lives have less call risk since there is a limit to how much they may shorten, while securities in the back end of the curve have lower convexity cost because of collateral burnout and the relatively large contribution of scheduled principal payments to total principal payments. The last class in both of these examples, however, has additional option cost due to the 10% optional clean-up call. We estimate that this feature contributes 5 bp in option cost on the Green Tree transaction and 18 bp on the EquiCredit transaction.[2]

---

[1] To ensure that the bonds were priced at par for our analysis, we adjusted the coupons on our securities from the actual security. In all other respects the bonds used were identical to EquiCredit 1995-4 and Green Tree 1996-1. In addition, because Green Tree 1996-1 did not include 1- and 3-year securities, we adjusted the structure of the security by splitting the 2-year class into a 1- and a 3-year.

[2] In calculating the option cost due to the clean-up call, we took into account the rate at which the loans could be resecuritized if called as well as the step-up in coupon on the floating rate class if the EquiCredit transaction is not called.

Exhibit 5: OAS Values in Home Equity Loans Depend on WAM of the Collateral

Average Life (years)	Longer WAM (Conti 1996-1), 205 months (bp)	Shorter WAM (EquiCredit 1995-4), 175 months (bp)
5	46	62
7	74	84

Because nominal spreads are higher on longer average life classes while convexity costs are generally lower, the highest OAS are located in the longer securities. For example, the 7-year HEL offers an OAS of 84 bp, about 40 bp wider than agency PACs and credit cards. The 16-year MH security has an OAS roughly 30 bp wider than PACs. In contrast, the OAS on the 3-year ABS securities are not significantly wider than PACs, and any difference is warranted due to credit spread, as PACs have agency guarantees while the asset-backed securities examined here are rated triple A.

HEL securities backed by different WAM collateral may have significantly different OAS values. For example, ContiMortgage 1996-1 has a WAM of 205 months, compared to only 175 months for EquiCredit 1995-4. As a result, the Conti security will extend more if prepayments slow (see Exhibit 3), resulting in higher convexity costs and lower OAS values even though the two securities have the same nominal spreads (Exhibit 5).

Premium Securities: Higher Nominal Spreads More Than Compensate for Prepayment Risk

Premium HEL and MH securities are generally priced at considerably wider spreads than current coupon par-priced bonds since these bonds are perceived to have higher prepayment risk and are less liquid because some investors do not buy premium-priced securities in the secondary market. However, OAS analysis indicates that the extra spread more than compensates for the increased risk, especially in the home equity loan sector.

Using the same securities (EquiCredit 1995-4 and Green Tree 1996-1), we constructed a scenario where interest rates drop 100 bp so that the same securities would be trading at a premium.[3] The results are shown in Exhibits 6 and 7.

In both the HEL and MH sectors, the relationship between prepayments and interest rates is fairly linear, in sharp contrast to the refinancing curve for agency and nonagency residential mortgages which steepens dramatically for cusp coupons relative to current coupons (see Exhibit 1). Therefore, although convexity costs on agency premiums are higher from those on current coupons by about 25 bp, convexity costs for premium HEL and MH securities are roughly similar to those for current coupons. For example, convexity costs are 27 bp on the 4.6-year

---

[3] We used the same securities in order to avoid complications arising from different structures with different collateral characteristics.

premium HEL class and 33 bp on the 5.4-year par-priced security. In the MH sector, convexity costs are slightly higher on the premium securities, by about 4-8 bp.

Premium securities also benefit from smaller differences between the nominal spread and the ZV spread (this difference is commonly referred to as the "ZV drop"). This is because prepayments in the ZV case are based on the rising interest rate path implied by the forward curve, which tends to slow prepayments and benefit premiums. Thus, the ZV drop in the current coupon case for the 7-year current coupon HEL is 8 bp but only 1 bp for the premium.

Because the nominal spread increases on premium securities while the ZV drop falls and convexity costs remain similar, the OAS on premium HEL and MH securities are significantly higher than on current coupons. For example, in the 5-year sector, the premium HEL class offers an OAS of 100 bp, a pick-up of 38 bp in OAS over the current coupon. In manufactured housing, the pick-up is usually smaller but still significant: the 8-year premium has an OAS of 83 bp compared to 63 bp for a current coupon 9.5-year security.

Discount Securities: Convexity Costs are Related to Extension Risk

Similar to our illustration of premium securities, we analyzed discounts by examining the same HEL and MH securities (EquiCredit 1995-4 and Green Tree 1996-1) in a scenario where interest rates have risen by 100 bp.

Exhibit 6: OAS Analysis of a Premium HEL Security

Class	Avg.Life (@ Model)	Approx. Price	Nominal Spread (bp)	ZV Spread (bp)	Convexity Costs (bp)	OAS (bp)	OAS Pickup vs. Current Coupon (bp)
A-1	0.9	$101	65	62	10	52	15
A-2	2.8	102	105	106	26	80	39
A-3	4.8	103	132	127	27	100	38
A-4	6.7	104	160	159	25	134	50
A-5	6.9	105	175	162	51	111	30
	(to call)						

Exhibit 7: OAS Analysis of a Premium Manufactured Housing Security

Class	Avg.Life (@ Model)	Approx. Price	Nominal Spread (bp)	ZV Spread (bp)	Convexity Costs (bp)	OAS (bp)	OAS Pickup vs. Current Coupon (bp)
A-1a	0.9 yrs	$101	55	51	10	41	11
A-1b	2.7	102	60	61	18	43	15
A-2	3.8	103	70	73	25	48	15
A-3	5.5	105	85	85	28	57	14
A-4	7.9	106	110	108	25	83	20
A-5	13.5	106	175	142	23	119	39
	(to call)						

Exhibit 8: OAS Analysis of a Discount HEL Security

Class	Avg. Life (years)	Approx. Price	Nominal Spread (bp)	ZV Spread (bp)	Convexity Costs (bp)	OAS (bp)	OAS Pickup vs. Current Coupon (bp)
A-1	1.3	99	65	48	35	16	-21
A-2	3.9	97	85	64	42	22	-19
A-3	6.5	94	120	102	36	66	+4
A-4	8.5	93	135	112	31	81	-3
A-5	12.4	92	155	114	26	88	+7
	(to maturity)						

Exhibit 9: OAS Analysis of a Discount MH Security

Class	Avg. Life (years)	Approx. Price	Nominal Spread (bp)	ZV Spread (bp)	Convexity Costs (bp)	OAS (bp)	OAS Pickup vs. Current Coupon (bp)
A-1a	1.2	99	50	39	8	31	+11
A-1b	3.6	97	50	42	12	30	+2
A-2	5.2	96	55	41	13	28	0
A-3	7.6	94	73	59	10	48	+5
A-4	10.7	93	93	65	11	54	-9
A-5	18.2	91	150	94	11	83	+3
	(to maturity)						

Nominal spreads on discount HELs and MH are not substantially different from those on current coupon securities. However, on MH securities convexity costs fall in the discount sector because extension is limited. In HELs, a 100 bp rise in rates results in prepayments of about 17% to 18% CPR. Because HEL prepayments may continue to fall as rates rise, these securities still have extension risk; therefore, convexity costs are about the same as for current coupons (see Exhibits 1 and 2).

In both cases, the ZV drop is higher for a discount security, as slower prepayments along the forward path of rates tend to extend the security and cause the yield to decline. Thus, the ZV drop on the home equity loan A-3 class is 7 bp in the par case and 18 bp in the discount case.

The net result is that OAS levels on discount HEL securities are often lower than on current coupon securities while in MH the OAS on discount securities are often slightly higher than on current coupon securities (Exhibits 8 and 9).

Discount securities also are not immediately subject to the spread widening that occurs on par-priced securities when interest rates rally. This will have a positive impact on realized total return for discounts relative to current coupon securities as long premium securities trade at wider OAS.

SENSITIVITY TO PREPAYMENT MODEL ASSUMPTIONS

Our OAS analysis is based on prepayment assumptions we believe are reasonable, but we also considered potential changes in prepayment behavior in the HEL and

MH markets. Our home equity loan data extend as far back as 1988, but the market is becoming more competitive, which could change prepayment behavior. Our MH data are extensive, reaching back to the early 1970s, but changing loan characteristics, such as increasing loan size and improved borrower credit as well as increased competition, may result in prepayment responses that differ from historical experience.

In this section, we consider two types of changes in prepayment behavior: increases in "turnover" (i.e., a general rise in prepayments across all interest rate scenarios) and increases in the slope of the refinancing function. In each case, we illustrate the effect of such a prepayment change on the OAS of a 7-year security in the discount, current coupon, and premium sectors.

Increased Turnover

Over the last year, prepayments on current coupon Green Tree collateral have been higher then the historical levels of 100% MHP.[4] Prepayments on fully seasoned current coupon collateral rose to 150% MHP and pools with a weighted average coupon 100 bp lower than the prevailing Green Tree rate prepaid at about 120% MHP.[5] We have incorporated this change into our analysis above, but such a trend could continue if borrower mobility continues to improve or competition increases. For this reason, we have calculated OAS on the above securities using a variant of the prepayment model in which all speeds are higher by about 1% CPR (see Exhibit 10).

Exhibit 10: Higher Turnover Scenario in Manufactured Housing

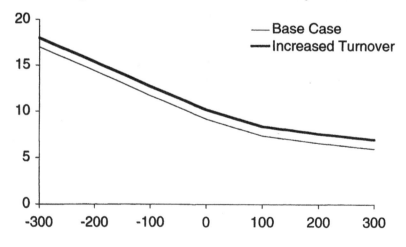

---

[4] MHP is the manufactured housing prepayment curve and is generally used as the standard in the manufactured housing market. It runs from 3.7% CPR in month 1 to 6% CPR in month 24 and is flat thereafter.

[5] See the Lehman Brothers report, *Manufactured Housing Prepayments in 1995*, January 19, 1996.

Exhibit 11: Higher Turnover Scenario in Home Equity Loans

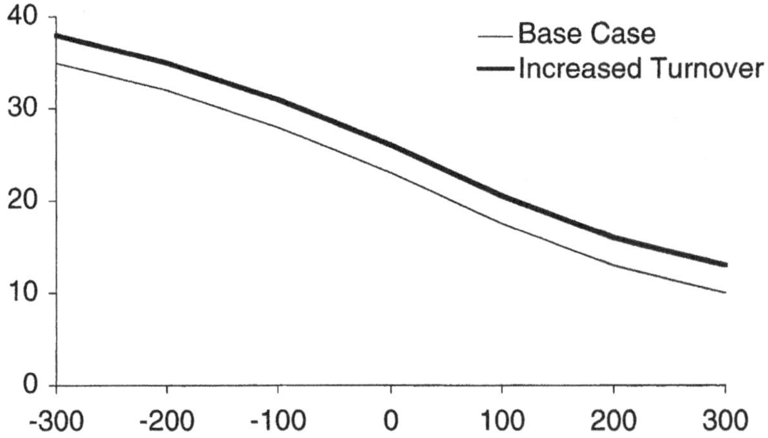

Legend: —— Base Case, —— Increased Turnover

Exhibit 12: Effect of Higher Turnover on HEL and MH OAS

Security	Type	Base Case		Higher Turnover		OAS
		Average Life (years)	OAS (bp)	Average Life (years)	OAS (bp)	Change (bp)
Par	MH	6.7	43	6.1	50	+7
Premium	MH	5.5	57	5.0	56	−1
Discount	MH	7.6	48	7.0	62	+14
Par	HEL	7.5	84	6.9	100	+16
Premium	HEL	6.7	134	6.1	138	+4
Discount	HEL	8.6	76	7.9	99	+23

In the home equity market, we are not concerned with increasing mobility, but increasing competition among originators for new loans or a significant rise in housing prices could result in higher prepayments and easier refinancing for all home equity loans. Exhibit 11 shows a scenario in which home equity loan prepayments increase by 3% CPR. (We increased prepayments by 3% CPR in this market so that the percentage change in prepayments in the MH and HEL markets would be similar.)

Exhibit 12 shows the effect of the higher turnover on 7-year average life MH and HEL securities. In general, convexity costs are unaffected by a uniform shift in prepayments. Current coupon securities appear more attractive because the average lives of the bonds shorten, widening the spread to the comparable average life Treasury given the upward slope of the yield curve. The discount looks even more attractive since the yield on the bond rises when prepayments are higher. The premium bond appears slightly less attractive relative to the par and discount securities under this scenario due to the decline in yield when prepayments are fast. Even at these stressed levels of prepayments, however, the premium bond offers OAS values considerably wider than the current coupon security.

Exhibit 13: Increased Interest Rate Sensitivity Scenario in Manufactured Housing

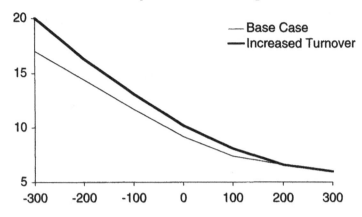

Exhibit 14: Increased Interest Rate Sensitivity Scenario in Home Equity Loans

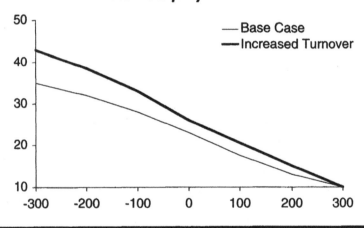

Increased Sensitivity to Interest Rates

Unlike increases in turnover, heightened sensitivity to interest rates directly affects convexity costs. We have stressed the above manufactured housing and home equity securities using a prepayment assumption with more sensitivity to interest rates, as shown in Exhibits 13 and 14. In both cases, we assume that the entire prepayment curve steepens significantly, so that current coupon prepayments are higher than the base case and premium prepayments increase even more. If we were to see increased competition in these markets, this is the type of change we believe would occur because increased competition would probably stimulate refinancing for current coupons as well as for premiums.

Exhibit 15: Effect of Higher Interest Rate Sensitivity on HEL and MH OAS

		Base Case		High Sensitivity Model		
Security	Type	Average Life (years)	OAS (bp)	Average Life (years)	OAS (bp)	OAS Change (bp)
Par	MH	6.7	43	6.2	37	−6
Premium	MH	5.5	57	4.9	49	−8
Discount	MH	7.6	48	7.3	41	−7
Par	HEL	7.5	84	6.8	82	−2
Premium	HEL	6.7	134	5.8	128	−6
Discount	HEL	8.5	81	7.8	80	−1

Applying these stresses will naturally generate higher convexity costs and lower OAS values. In the manufactured housing market, OAS values drop by 6-8 bp; in the home equity market, OAS values drop similarly by up to 6 bp. However, the premium securities again retain their value relative to the par-priced securities (see Exhibit 15).

CONCLUSION

Although the mortgage market has made significant strides in pricing convexity risk, the ABS market is only starting to use this methodology. This approach can reveal inefficiencies in the market in terms of OAS, and thereby suggest relative value opportunities. These opportunities may diminish, however, as market participants start relying on valuation models to price prepayment risk on the basis of convexity cost and prepayment model risk.

Chapter 20

Home Equity Loan Prepayment Model and OAS Implications

Charles Schorin

Principal

Director of ABS Research

Morgan Stanley Dean Witter

Steven Weinreich

Associate

Morgan Stanley Dean Witter

Oliver Hsiang

Analyst

Morgan Stanley Dean Witter

INTRODUCTION

The market environment since 1998 has created a conundrum for investors in mortgage-related products. In 1998, conventional mortgage-backed securities experienced their largest prepayment surge since the 1991-1994 period, and market participants had been divided over the impact of the market rally on home equity loan prepayments. The evidence from 1998 convinced most investors that home equity loans are markedly less interest rate sensitive than conventional mortgages. Now that the market has traded off, and conventional mortgage-backed prepayments have fallen, the question has arisen about the prepayment rate sensitivity of home equity loans in a bear market. Therefore, the issue of the extent of the prepayment response remains an open question. The need for a model to quantitatively depict prepayments on home equity loan asset-backed securities and to value the bonds' embedded prepayment option has become all the more necessary.

To meet this need, we have developed a statistically estimated model to project prepayments on ABS backed by fixed rate home equity loans. The model can be used to derive

• prepayment projections on HEL ABS for given interest rate scenarios

337

- option costs and option adjusted spreads of HEL ABS over numerous interest rate diffusion paths
- hedge ratios for HEL ABS
- relative value of HEL ABS versus conventional MBS and CMOs.

As with other existing home equity loan prepayment models, our model relies on the credit quality of the borrower as a fundamental input to prepayment behavior. There are, however, two primary advantages of our model over existing products:

- Even though the model was estimated using the data from one home equity loan issuer, the model generalizes across issuers. Rather than simply use the credit grade assigned by a lender, we impute the credit quality of borrowers from their loan note rate relative to Treasuries and statistically transform the distribution of credit quality from the estimated data to the transaction being considered.
- Not only does the model employ the distribution of borrower credit quality at inception, the model dynamically adjusts the borrower credit quality distribution as it projects prepayments along a rate scenario. This means that borrower credit quality and, therefore, prepayment risk evolve over time as the model prepayment projections amortize the security balance.

This chapter begins by discussing the estimation process. We then describe the implementation of the model, which translates the statistical analysis to a usable analytical tool. Given the development and implementation backdrop, we turn to the model's projections under given static interest rate scenarios. Finally, we examine the use of the model as an analytical tool by showing results of our option-adjusted spread (OAS) analysis and comparing the OAS and interest rate optionality of home equity loan ABS relative to conventional mortgages and CMOs.

ESTIMATION

To discuss the estimation process, we consider in turn the model structure, data, explanatory variables, and statistical methods. We then discuss our analysis of the results of the estimation process.

Structure

The Morgan Stanley Home Equity Loan prepayment model predicts the probability of a home equity loan's prepayment as a function of various explanatory variables. The prepayment projections will therefore vary depending upon the distribution of the explanatory variables in the composition of the pool of mortgages. In addition, as the model projects prepayments along an interest rate path, the distribution of borrower credit quality dynamically evolves based upon the projected amortization of the loan pool.

Exhibit 1: Morgan Stanley HEL Prepayment Model Structure

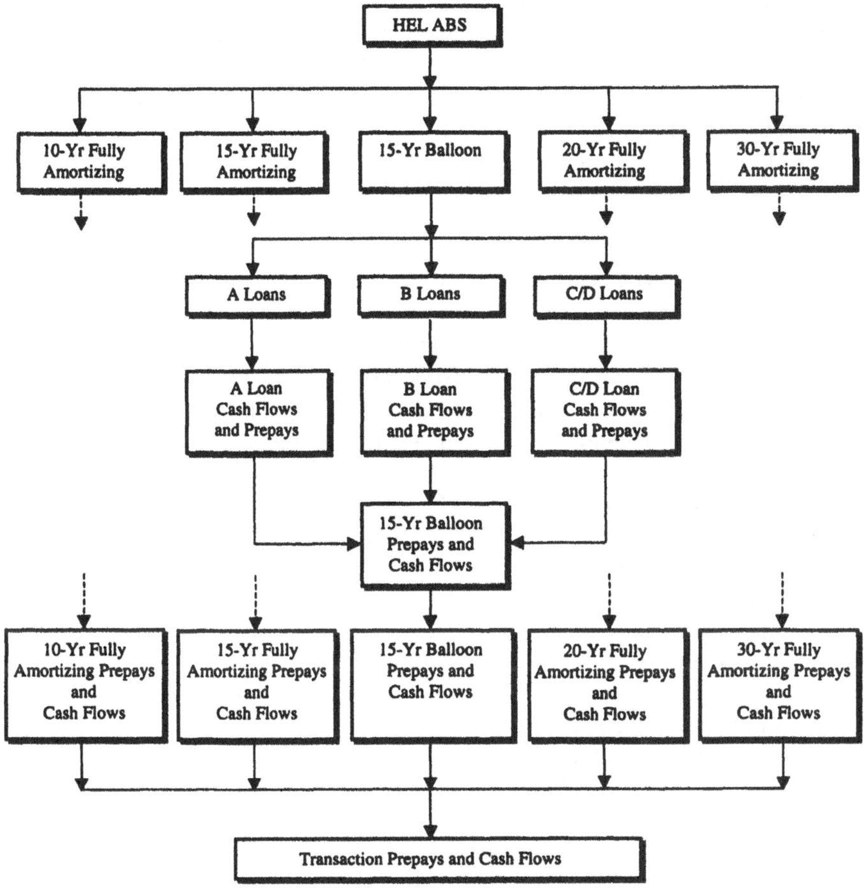

Source: Morgan Stanley

The prepayment model is really a system of sub-models: one for each loan product type (e.g., 15-year fully amortizing, 15-year balloon, etc.); within each product type sub-model, there are further sub-models, one for each of credit grades A, B and C/D. This is described schematically in Exhibit 1.

Rather than simply categorize borrowers by the same letter credit grade assigned by their respective lender, the prepayment model standardizes credit grades across issuers: borrowers were divided into credit categories, based upon the spread to Treasuries of the mortgage note rate relative to the distribution of home equity loan spreads originated over the history of our data set. The greater the spread, the more likely is the lower the quality of the borrower. Deriving credit grades in this manner, rather than merely using the A, B, C, D categories of specific lenders, makes the model more robust across issuers. Therefore, even though the model was an in-depth estimation employing data from one issuer — ContiMortgage — the model generalizes across the spectrum of home equity issuers. The statistical method for making these credit inferences is discussed below.

Within each borrower credit grade, sub-models for prepayment behavior were estimated. The model employs a non-linear, non-parametric maximum likelihood estimation technique. The model is a generalized additive model, where projected SMM is the sum of $SMM_{voluntary}$ and $SMM_{involuntary}$. The functional form is

$$SMM = [1 + \exp\{-\Sigma_i f_i(x_i)\}]^{-1}$$

where $\{f_i\}$ are nonparametric functions of the input variables $\{x_i\}$.

Data Framework

ContiMortgage provided Morgan Stanley with loan level information on more than 100,000 home equity loans it had originated. Each loan record contained data on the various attributes of the loan. These data fields include, among others:

- Origination date
- Loan type and term (10-, 15-, 20-, and 30-year fully amortizing loans, plus 15-year balloons)
- Note rate
- Borrower credit grade
- Lien position
- Owner occupancy
- Prepayment penalty
- Documentation level
- Original loan-to-value ratio
- Current balance
- Loan purpose
- Loan termination date
- Loan termination type (prepayment, default or maturation)

Based upon the loan termination date, we know the balance that remained when the loan either prepaid, defaulted or matured. We then applied the estimation technique to the data set, deriving coefficients for each of the explanatory variables.

Explanatory Variables Defined

Below we define the variables used in the prepayment model.

Credit Grade

Within each loan type and term, the credit grade is the most important predictive variable in the model. There are separate sub-models for the A, B and C/D credit grades. To actually implement the model and use it for estimation, we need to determine the credit grade of the borrowers in the pool.

The pool collateral is summarized in what are termed "replines" (for representational lines of collateral). These can be found in the transaction prospectus. A typical home equity transaction may have from six to 12 replines. For each repline, the distribution of credit grade is estimated from a base distribution and the difference between the gross mortgage note rate and the 5-year CMT at the time of origination. The average spread — used in combination with the distribution of the Conti data set — is used to determine a distribution of spreads, from which a distribution of credit grades is derived. This means that the spread over the 5-year CMT is taken to be the determining factor in estimating the credit quality of the borrower.

This method allows us to put borrowers on an equal footing across issuers, where the borrower's "true" credit grade is given by the interest rate charged on his mortgage. This is an improvement over using simply a lender's assigned credit grade, as there is no uniformity among issuers on credit grades: a borrower may be classified as an A credit by one lender and as a B credit by another.

Mortgage Rate and Refinancing Incentive

We defined the interest rate refinancing incentive as the change in the 5-year CMT (with weights of 0.25, 0.50 and 0.25 on lags three, two, and one months) since origination. If m_{t-i} is the 5-year CMT in period t–i, then the relevant interest rate M_t used in the model is given by

$$M_t = 0.25m_{t-1} + 0.50m_{t-2} + 0.25m_{t-3}$$

and the interest rate refinancing incentive R_t is given by the change in the relevant interest rate since origination, or

$$R_t = M_0 - M_t$$

where M_0 is the relevant interest rate at loan origination. We use the change in the CMT to depict refinancing incentives, rather than the difference between the loan rate at origination and prevailing mortgage loan rates, which is the typical formulation in a conventional mortgage prepayment model. The reason is because with the various credit grade borrowers in the home equity sector, it is impossible to point to *the* current market rate. We instead use the change in the Treasury to which the home equity loan is spread.

An alternative formulation of the refinancing incentive would be to take the relative change in rates since origination M_0/M_t, although the practical difference in the results between the relative and additive difference in rates was small due to the fairly low interest rate environment over which data are available. The absolute difference, however, was a marginally better predictor of prepayment behavior than the relative change.

Refinance Burnout

Refinance burnout, though it was determined to be not statistically significant in explaining interest rate refinancing, was defined as the cumulative sum of the positive refinancing incentives since origination times the current refinancing incentive, if positive. Refinance burnout B_t was taken to be relevant only after the first 12 months.

$$B_t = (\Sigma_{t=13,\ldots,t-1} \max \{R_t, 0\}) \times \max \{R_t, 0\}$$

Default Burnout

Even though refinance burnout was not statistically significant, prior refinancing opportunity actually was statistically significant in terms of predicting default related prepayments. It turns out that the higher the prepayments experienced by the pool, the higher the conditional default rate (CDR) by the remaining pool. This is because for a given dollar amount of defaulted loans in a pool, faster prepayments in the pool reduce the balance remaining — the denominator in the CDR calculation — and lead to higher CDRs. For the purposes of default burnout, we define

$$D_t = \Sigma_{t=13,\ldots,t-1} \max\{R_t, 0\}$$

Note that this term is similar to the refinancing burnout term B_t except that it does not include the extent to which loans are currently in-the-money, since that would not explain the higher CDRs that result from previously experienced prepayments.

Loan Age

The loan age used in the model is the WALA, or weighted average loan age. This is defined as the number of months since loan origination.

Original LTV

There are four LTV categories used in the implementation of the model: <60%, 60-70%, >70-80%, >80%.

Statistical Methods

The model was estimated using a non-linear non-parametric maximum likelihood technique. An inverse logit function of the explanatory variables was used to estimate separately voluntary and involuntary prepayment functions, which were combined.

The $SMM_{voluntary}$ was estimated as an inverse logit function of the explanatory variables:

• loan age (WALA)

- change in interest rates since origination
- original LTV and
- refinance burnout.

The $SMM_{involuntary}$ was estimated as an inverse logit function of the explanatory variables:

- loan age (WALA)
- original LTV
- default burnout.

Other variables were included in the initial estimation, but were determined to be either not statistically significant (such as refinance burnout) or impractical to include (for e.g., full versus limited documentation loans and prepayment penalties) because of the lack of information uniformity across transactions.

The projected SMM is then converted to CPR, using the standard annualization formula. We determined the statistical significance of the explanatory variables by examining the estimated functional relationship between each respective variable and the CPR, and the standard errors around the fit. Relationships with extremely large standard errors, such as refinance burnout as a determinant of voluntary prepayments, were removed from the final version of the model.

Analysis of Results

For a given credit grade, the most important variable in explaining prepayment behavior is the interest rate incentive, defined as the change in the 5-year CMT (with lags) since origination. The loan age also was very important in terms of a seasoning pattern. We found that, all else equal, home equity loans season over a period of about 16 months, reach their peak and then decline smoothly — albeit modestly — thereafter (see Exhibit 5 in Chapter 5).

Loan-to-value ratios also were an important explainer of prepayment behavior, with higher LTVs implying slower prepayment rates. As indicated above, refinance burnout was not a statistically significant explanatory variable.

Other variables, however, did display statistically significant results, although incomplete and differential information across transactions would make incorporation of these other factors impractical to implement in an option pricing, or OAS, model. These factors include lien position, documentation level, loan balance, owner occupancy, prepayment penalties and loan purpose. The influence of these factors on home equity collateral prepayments is discussed as well in Chapter 5.

In addition to voluntary prepayments, securitized transactions may also see involuntary prepayments as the result of defaults. After a borrower defaults, his loan is essentially "bought out" from the pool, either by the monoline insurer or by the internal credit enhancement.

Similar to the effects of loan attributes on voluntary prepayments, we can examine the affect of various loan characteristics — such as lien position, documentation level, original loan-to-value ratio and the marginal credit quality — on defaults, or involuntary prepayments. The influence of these factors on home equity loan default-related prepayments is discussed at length in Chapter 5.

IMPLEMENTATION

The key to the home equity loan prepayment model is that it projects prepayments based upon various important loan characteristics such as borrower credit grade, as well as exogenous factors such as market interest rates. Since the prepayment estimates depend upon features of the underlying loans, the prepayment projections for a pool of home equity loans will necessarily depend upon the representation in the pool of these loan characteristics. The distribution of the borrower credit grade in the pool evolves over time as the securities amortize. We describe here an algorithm for projecting prepayment rates for a loan pool without complete information on each of the loans in the pool. The procedure here utilizes only summary statistics at the pool level — repline information — to make statistically valid projections.

There are fixed-rate prepayment models for each of the following types of collateral:

- 15-year fully amortizing
- 30-year fully amortizing
- 20-year fully amortizing
- 10-year fully amortizing
- 15-year balloons (amortizing on a 30-year schedule)

Within each of these collateral types, there are sub-models for credit grades A, B and C/D. In addition, a prepayment curve is assumed for ARMs that is a function of loan age and is invariant to any other exogenous factors. This is needed for those transactions that have ARMs collateral that impacts fixed rate tranches in the same deal.

The collateral is described for each deal by replines that provide indicative information on subsets of the collateral. The subsets are broken down first into product type, such as fully amortizing versus balloon, and then into term buckets. Each repline contains the following information about the collateral group: principal balance, gross note rate, net note rate, original term to maturity, remaining term to maturity, original amortization term and amortization method.

The three basic steps to implementing the model and projecting prepayments are the following:

- Begin with the repline description format of the collateral sub-groups used by Morgan Stanley's CARVE structuring system.

- Calculate the scheduled amortization and prepayments for each sub-repline. (Repline expansion into sub-replines is described below.)
- Combine the cash flows for each sub-repline into repline cash flows, and then combine the repline cash flows into deal cash flows.

Repline Expansion

Each repline is expanded to 12 sub-replines based upon the three separate credit grades (A, B, C/D) and four LTV (<60%, 60-70%, >70-80%, >80%) categories. For example, for a repline of 15-year balloon mortgages, one sub-repline would correspond to A quality borrowers with LTV less than 60%. For each of these 12 credit grade/LTV cells, we compute the joint probability of occurrence p_{ij}, for $i=1,...,3$ and $j=1,...,4$, where i represents credit grade and j denotes LTV categories.

We derive the balance for each of the sub-replines as the pro rata share of the principal balance of the original repline. For each of the sub-replines, the model would project a prepayment vector for a given interest rate scenario, based upon the loan collateral type (for e.g., 15-year balloons). The prepayments for each sub-repline are then aggregated, with each sub-repline's prepayment rates weighted by current balance, to derive a prepayment vector for the original repline. This prepayment vector for the original repline is the input to the CARVE structuring model. The algorithm to expand the replines follows.

Credit Distributions

We infer the credit quality of the borrowers from the relation between the average borrower's mortgage note rate and the 5-year CMT at the time of loan origination. The greater the spread to the CMT relative to the average loan originated in the same month, the worse in probability we assume to be the credit quality of the borrower. The spread distribution of the Conti data set is used as a benchmark.

The spread distribution of the repline is derived by multiplicatively scaling the distribution of Conti spreads so that the mean of the scaled Conti distribution equals the repline gross mortgage rate minus the 5-year CMT at origination. Therefore, the repline is imputed to have the same spread distribution (up to a Jacobian scaling) as the Conti data set, with the distribution centered around the repline spread.

In going from spread to credit distribution for a repline, we assume the distribution of credit, given the spread, in the Conti data set. The proportion of a given credit quality borrower in a repline is taken to be the sum (or integral) over the spreads of the product of the probability that a borrower is a particular credit grade, given the spread, times the probability of the given spread. For example, the proportion of A credit grade borrowers in a repline is given by

$$\Pr(\text{Credit} = A) = \int \Pr(\text{credit} = A \mid \text{spread})\, p(\text{spread})\, d(\text{spread})$$

The integral is evaluated numerically.

Exhibit 2: Joint and Marginal Probabilities of Credit Grade and LTV

		\<60	60-70	>70-80	>80	Marginal Probability of Credit Grade	
Credit	A	p_{11}	p_{12}	p_{13}	p_{14}	p_{1i}	p_{1i}^{new}
	B	p_{21}	p_{22}	p_{23}	p_{24}	p_{2i}	p_{2i}^{new}
	C/D	p_{31}	p_{32}	p_{33}	p_{34}	p_{3i}	p_{3i}^{new}
	Marginal Probability of LTV	p_{i1} p_{i1}^{new}	p_{i2} p_{i2}^{new}	p_{i3} p_{i3}^{new}	p_{i4} p_{i4}^{new}		

Source: Morgan Stanley

Credit Grade and LTV Distributions

The distribution of credit grade and LTV for the expanded replines is based upon the distribution within the Conti data set across credit grades of the four LTV categories for the product type: <60%, 60-70%, >70-80% and >80%. An example of credit grade/LTV proportions is given in Exhibit 2.

In order to generalize from the Conti data to other issuers, we use a procedure called raking so that the proportions in the inner cells of the table are consistent with the marginal LTV and marginal credit proportions of the issuer we are examining. The raking procedure works as follows:

The basic idea is to iteratively multiply the cells in each row and then in each column of the table by constants so that the joint probabilities given by the cells is consistent with the new marginal probabilities. For example, consider the borrower credit grade and LTV and their joint probability distribution shown in Exhibit 2. With credit grades A, B and C/D and LTV categories <60%, 60-70%, >70-80% and >80%, we get the matrix in Exhibit 2 indicating the joint probability of each of the 12 potential combinations of credit grade and LTV. We have the new marginal proportions p_{1i}^{new}, p_{2i}^{new} and p_{3i}^{new}. We need to update the old proportions p_{ij} so that the following sums hold:

$$p_{11}^{new} + p_{12}^{new} + p_{13}^{new} + p_{14}^{new} = p_{1i}^{new}$$

$$p_{21}^{new} + p_{22}^{new} + p_{23}^{new} + p_{24}^{new} = p_{2i}^{new}$$

$$p_{31}^{new} + p_{32}^{new} + p_{33}^{new} + p_{34}^{new} = p_{3i}^{new}$$

This is accomplished by multiplying the elements in the first row of the matrix by p_{1i}^{new}/p_{1i}. The elements in the second row are multiplied by p_{2i}^{new}/p_{2i}, and those in the third row are multiplied by $(1 - p_{1i}^{new} - p_{2i}^{new})/(1 - p_{1i} - p_{2i})$. A similar procedure is then applied to each of the columns of the matrix sequentially, and then again to the rows, until the probabilities converge. This usually takes between one and three iterations.

Exhibit 3: Projected Prepayment Rate Paths for Indicated Interest Rate Shifts: B Quality Borrowers

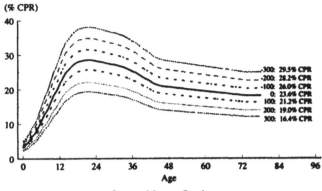

Source: Morgan Stanley

Exhibit 4: Higher Quality Borrowers Display Greater Interest Rate Sensitivity Than Weaker Borrowers

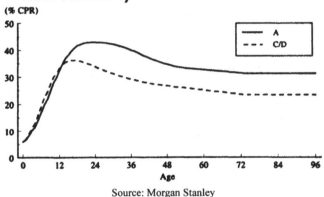

Source: Morgan Stanley

PREPAYMENT MODEL PROJECTIONS

We consider here projections from the Morgan Stanley Home Equity Loan Prepayment Model. First, we examine the manner in which borrowers respond to interest rate movements. Exhibit 3 shows projected prepayment paths for B quality borrowers under interest rate shifts of up and down 300 bp. Listed next to each prepayment path is the rate scenario and the long term, or average life equivalent, CPR.[1]

Exhibit 4 compares the projected prepayment paths for A and C quality borrowers in a 200 bp rally scenario. The higher quality borrowers display greater interest rate sensitivity.

---

[1] The long-term, or average life equivalent, CPR is the single CPR that, if it were to occur every month, would result in the same average life as the projected month-by-month vector of CPRs.

Exhibit 5: Prepayment Model Projections for Various HEL ABS

Deal Name	Group	Base Case Projected CPR* (%)	Projected CPR for Indicated Scenario* (%)									WAC (%)	WAM
			-300	-200	-100	-50	Base	+50	+100	+200	+300		
Advanta 97-2	Fixed	28.8	40.0	40.0	35.0	31.2	28.8	26.9	25.0	21.6	17.5	10.81	242
Advanta 98-1	Fixed	25.6	37.5	35.0	30.0	27.5	25.6	24.4	22.5	19.4	15.0	10.54	247
Amresco 96-5	Fixed	28.8	37.5	37.5	33.8	31.2	28.8	26.9	25.0	22.2	18.8	11.03	306
Amresco 97-1	Fixed	28.1	40.0	40.0	35.0	31.2	28.1	25.6	23.8	20.6	16.9	10.06	318
Amresco 98-1	Fixed	28.1	40.0	40.0	33.1	30.0	28.1	25.6	24.1	20.6	16.6	10.43	317
Conti 95-2	Fixed	33.8	38.8	38.8	37.5	36.2	33.8	32.5	30.0	27.5	25.0	12.16	167
Conti 96-4	Fixed	35.0	43.4	43.4	40.0	37.5	35.0	33.1	31.2	28.8	24.4	11.68	194
Conti 97-3	Fixed	36.2	45.0	45.0	41.9	38.8	36.2	33.8	32.5	28.8	24.4	11.44	210
Conti 98-1	Fixed	32.5	41.9	41.1	36.2	35.0	32.5	31.2	29.4	26.2	20.9	10.54	244
IMC 97-5	Fixed	31.2	38.8	38.8	36.2	33.8	31.2	28.8	27.5	23.8	20.6	11.45	215
IMC 98-3	Fixed	25.6	35.0	33.1	28.0	26.9	25.6	23.8	22.5	19.4	15.3	10.83	257

* Projected CPR is the long term average life-equivalent CPR. This is the single CPR that results in the same average life as that given by the projected vector of CPRs until maturity. Projections are based upon the Treasury yield curve as of 9/15/98.

Source: Morgan Stanley

Now we turn to prepayment projections for some actual home equity loan transactions, under interest rate shift scenarios of up and down 300 bp (Exhibit 5). Projections differ among the transactions depending upon the characteristics of the borrowers. Some deals have faster base case speeds, but less of a response to rate shifts, whereas others may project slower speeds in the base case, but with more of a prepayment response to rate movements.

OAS IMPLICATIONS OF HEL PREPAYMENT MODEL

In this section, we extend our discussion from prepayment projections under a given interest rate scenario to analysis of the embedded optionality of home equity loan ABS. We analyze home equity loan securities through the same option pricing, or OAS, model that we employ for valuing conventional mortgage backed securities. This way, both HEL and MBS are valued against the same metric, giving us the ability to make a direct comparison between the two types of securities.

Before turning to specific securities, we first consider the affect of the borrower credit grade on the OAS and option cost of home equity loan ABS. We modeled generic home equity loan transactions, with a senior/subordinate credit structure, a series of sequential senior tranches and a NAS bond. The only difference in the transactions was the assumptions that we made regarding the credit quality of the underlying borrowers: one transaction is assumed to consist entirely of A quality borrowers; the second consists of a combination of A, B and C/D borrowers with each category making up one-third of the deal; and the third comprises one-half B borrowers and one-half C/D borrowers. The results are shown in Exhibit 6.

Exhibit 6: Higher Quality Borrowers Give a Transaction More Interest Rate Optionality

Borrowers: 100% A

Tranche	Type	Price	Pricing Spread/AL@CPR	Proj CPR	Proj AL	Mod Dur	Effective Duration	Effective Convexity	OAS (bp)	Option Cost (bp)
A-1	Seq	99.88	80/0.18 yr @ 25 CPR	10.9	0.46	0.17	0.41	-0.07	122	1
A-2	Seq	100.06	85/0.62 yr @ 25 CPR	16.4	1.04	0.59	0.98	-0.20	98	4
A-3	Seq	100.30	90/1.52 yr @ 25 CPR	21.9	1.80	1.41	1.84	-0.56	76	13
A-4	Seq	100.58	105/2.45 yr @ 25 CPR	24.1	2.58	2.22	2.90	-1.19	73	23
A-5	Seq	100.89	118/3.41 yr @ 25 CPR	24.6	3.48	2.99	3.97	-1.63	71	35
A-6	Seq	100.87	128/4.43 yr @ 25 CPR	24.6	4.49	3.77	4.96	-1.91	70	42
A-7	Seq	100.80	145/6.12 yr @ 25 CPR	24.1	6.57	4.93	6.44	-1.82	84	42
A-8	Seq	98.45	180/11.78 yr @ 25 CPR	22.7	12.80	7.93	8.76	-0.14	128	20
A-9	NAS	101.74	111/6.13 yr @ 25 CPR	23.0	6.32	4.96	5.39	-0.20	78	16
M-1	Mezz	99.98	170/4.94 yr @ 25 CPR	24.1	5.13	4.06	5.27	-1.05	118	28
M-2	Mezz	99.49	210/5.16 yr @ 25 CPR	24.1	5.40	4.13	5.31	-0.92	154	28
B-1	Sub	96.56	350/4.43 yr @ 25 CPR	24.6	4.54	3.60	5.13	-1.15	288	30

Borrowers: 33% A, 33% B, 33% C/D

Tranche	Type	Price	Pricing Spread/AL@CPR	Proj CPR	Proj AL	Mod Dur	Effective Duration	Effective Convexity	OAS (bp)	Option Cost (bp)
A-1	Seq	99.88	80/0.18 yr @ 25 CPR	13.1	0.41	0.17	0.38	-0.03	120	0
A-2	Seq	100.06	85/0.62 yr @ 25 CPR	18.6	0.91	0.59	0.85	-0.07	97	2
A-3	Seq	100.30	90/1.52 yr @ 25 CPR	24.1	1.55	1.41	1.46	-0.20	79	6
A-4	Seq	100.58	105/2.45 yr @ 25 CPR	27.3	2.23	2.22	2.18	-0.42	81	9
A-5	Seq	100.89	118/3.41 yr @ 25 CPR	27.9	2.77	2.99	2.85	-0.70	80	18
A-6	Seq	100.87	128/4.43 yr @ 25 CPR	28.2	3.75	3.77	3.66	-1.22	85	23
A-7	Seq	100.80	145/6.12 yr @ 25 CPR	27.9	5.12	4.93	5.29	-1.37	97	29
A-8	Seq	98.45	180/11.78 yr @ 25 CPR	26.2	11.18	7.93	8.31	-0.14	133	23
A-9	NAS	101.74	111/6.13 yr @ 25 CPR	26.8	5.88	4.96	5.10	-0.21	81	13
M-1	Mezz	99.98	170/4.94 yr @ 25 CPR	27.3	4.52	4.06	4.40	-0.54	133	15
M-2	Mezz	99.49	210/5.16 yr @ 25 CPR	27.3	4.72	4.13	4.49	-0.50	169	17
B-1	Sub	96.56	350/4.43 yr @ 25 CPR	27.9	3.97	3.60	4.10	-0.55	314	16

Exhibit 6 (Continued)

Borrowers: 50% B, 50% C/D

Tranche	Type	Price	Pricing Spread/AL@CPR	Proj CPR	Proj AL	Mod Dur	Effective Duration	Effective Convexity	OAS (bp)	Option Cost (bp)
A-1	Seq	99.88	80/0.18 yr @ 25 CPR	13.1	0.40	0.17	0.38	-0.01	119	0
A-2	Seq	100.06	85/0.62 yr @ 25 CPR	19.7	0.88	0.59	0.83	-0.03	97	1
A-3	Seq	100.30	90/1.52 yr @ 25 CPR	25.2	1.49	1.41	1.39	-0.08	80	3
A-4	Seq	100.58	105/2.45 yr @ 25 CPR	27.9	2.15	2.22	2.00	-0.15	84	5
A-5	Seq	100.89	118/3.41 yr @ 25 CPR	29.0	2.59	2.99	2.53	-0.31	86	9
A-6	Seq	100.87	128/4.43 yr @ 25 CPR	29.0	3.53	3.77	3.15	-0.48	92	14
A-7	Seq	100.80	145/6.12 yr @ 25 CPR	29.3	4.72	4.93	4.44	-0.50	113	12
A-8	Seq	98.45	180/11.78 yr @ 25 CPR	29.1	9.57	7.93	7.65	-0.10	150	16
A-9	NAS	101.74	111/6.13 yr @ 25 CPR	29.5	5.55	4.96	4.82	0.05	86	7
M-1	Mezz	99.93	170/5.41 yr @ 25 CPR	35.0	4.72	4.31	4.18	-0.08	140	8
M-2	Mezz	99.49	210/5.16 yr @ 25 CPR	29.5	4.45	4.13	3.99	-0.12	180	8
B-1	Sub	96.56	350/4.43 yr @ 25 CPR	29.5	3.81	3.60	3.55	-0.15	327	7

Pricing and volatility as of 9/15/98.

Projected CPR is the average life equivalent CPR for the particular tranche. The average life equivalent CPR is defined in footnote 1.

Source: Morgan Stanley

Not surprisingly, the higher the percentage of better quality borrowers in the transaction, the greater the interest rate sensitivity of the collateral. This means that deals with better quality borrowers result in bond classes that, all else equal, are more negatively convex and have higher option cost. For a given nominal spread, the higher option cost translates into a lower OAS.

We now consider actual home equity loan ABS, and compare them to conventional mortgages and CMOs. Exhibit 7 reports the results for several tranches of various HEL transactions, conventional 30- and 15-year pass-throughs and assorted CMOs backed by conventional mortgage collateral.

The home equity loan ABS clearly and unequivocally demonstrate less interest rate sensitivity than the conventional mortgages. This is seen in lower option costs and effective convexities in the HELs.

The results in Exhibit 7 show that the home equity loan ABS are cheap relative to conventional CMOs, as of the pricing date for the analysis in the table. The reason is that the relatively minimal option cost on the home equities more than compensates for any structural advantages of the CMOs and provides the HELs with value relative to the CMOs.

Spreads on mortgage pass-throughs widened significantly with the market rally that pushed the 10-year Treasury yield below 5%. Pass-throughs may be rich or cheap relative to HELs on a case-by-case basis, depending upon the specific coupon and maturity.

Exhibit 7: OAS Comparison of HEL ABS to MBS and CMOs

Tranche	Type	Price	Pricing Spread/AL@CPR	Proj CPR	Proj AL	Mod Dur	Effective Duration	Effective Convexity	OAS (bp)	Option Cost (bp)
Home Equity Loans										
Advanta 1997-3 A-2	Seq	100.09	120/0.79 yr @ 30 CPR	30.6	0.75	0.75	0.64	-0.16	113	3
Advanta 1997-3 A-3	Seq	100.83	105/1.41 yr @ 30 CPR	31.7	1.32	1.31	1.10	-0.34	87	7
Advanta 1997-3 A-4	Seq	101.38	115/1.84 yr @ 30 CPR	31.7	1.74	1.69	1.58	-0.73	89	12
Advanta 1997-3 A-5	Seq	102.24	126/2.76 yr @ 30 CPR	31.2	2.48	2.45	1.92	-1.00	79	27
Advanta 1997-3 A-6	Seq	104.10	150/4.43 yr @ 30 CPR	30.6	4.31	3.69	3.18	-1.54	109	24
Advanta 1997-3 A-7	NAS	103.33	139/4.76 yr @ 30 CPR	30.6	4.64	3.96	4.03	-0.20	109	11
Amresco 1996-5 A-2	Seq	99.67	120/0.26 yr @ 25 CPR	35.0	0.19	0.25	0.18	-0.02	108	1
Amresco 1996-5 A-3	Seq	99.97	120/0.86 yr @ 25 CPR	35.0	0.59	0.81	0.49	-0.14	96	2
Amresco 1996-5 A-4	Seq	100.91	112/1.82 yr @ 25 CPR	32.8	1.31	1.67	1.07	-0.33	69	7
Amresco 1996-5 A-5	Seq	101.76	126/3.01 yr @ 25 CPR	31.7	2.29	2.66	1.95	-0.61	79	13
Amresco 1996-5 A-6	Seq	103.06	146/4.74 yr @ 25 CPR	31.7	3.64	3.95	3.02	-0.45	98	11
Amresco 1996-5 A-7	Seq	100.52	220/5.51 yr @ 25 CPR	32.8	4.01	4.43	3.50	-0.06	195	6
Conti 1997-5 A-3	PAC	101.00	118/2.35 yr @ 30 CPR	35.0	2.32	2.12	1.97	-0.22	97	9
Conti 1997-5 A-4	PAC	101.75	127/3.27 yr @ 30 CPR	35.0	3.32	2.87	2.80	-0.22	104	10
Conti 1997-5 A-5	PAC	102.17	138/4.36 yr @ 30 CPR	35.0	4.55	3.69	3.78	-0.10	111	13
Conti 1997-5 A-6	PAC	101.99	177/5.58 yr @ 30 CPR	35.0	4.83	4.51	4.33	-0.58	139	15
IMC 1997-7 A-2	Seq	100.52	107/1.19 yr @ 25 CPR	30.6	0.90	1.12	0.76	-0.18	78	3
IMC 1997-7 A-3	Seq	101.00	122/2.15 yr @ 25 CPR	32.8	1.58	1.95	1.38	-0.37	82	8
IMC 1997-7 A-4	Seq	101.72	135/3.10 yr @ 25 CPR	31.7	2.25	2.73	2.00	-0.63	85	13
IMC 1997-7 A-5	Seq	101.87	152/4.05 yr @ 25 CPR	31.7	3.05	3.45	2.80	-0.88	103	17
IMC 1997-7 A-6	Seq	101.31	187/5.92 yr @ 25 CPR	30.1	4.56	4.73	4.50	-1.20	138	25
IMC 1997-7 A-7	Seq	100.53	220/7.08 yr @ 25 CPR	28.4	6.15	5.42	5.54	-0.96	179	24
IMC 1997-7 A-8	NAS	101.35	160/5.41 yr @ 25 CPR	28.4	5.06	4.38	4.37	-0.36	132	15

Exhibit 7 (Continued)

Tranche	Type	Price	Pricing Spread/AL@CPR	Proj CPR	Proj AL	Mod Dur	Effective Duration	Effective Convexity	OAS (bp)	Option Cost (bp)
Mortgage Pass-Throughs										
FNMA 30yr 6.5	MBS	100.91	N/A	13.1	6.29	5.65	3.84	-2.03	68	53
FNMA 30yr 7.0	MBS	102.09	N/A	18.9	4.51	4.91	2.80	-2.08	78	57
FNMA 30yr 7.5	MBS	102.75	N/A	24.8	3.45	3.74	2.12	-1.70	96	50
FNMA 30yr 8.0	MBS	103.66	N/A	28.9	2.96	2.71	1.73	-1.09	105	40
FNMA 30yr 8.5	MBS	104.19	N/A	30.4	2.81	2.39	1.63	-0.79	129	33
FNMA 30yr 9.0	MBS	105.31	N/A	30.6	2.76	2.49	1.48	-0.52	129	30
FNMA 15yr 5.5	MBS	98.73	N/A	8.4	5.67	4.66	4.24	-0.86	57	21
FNMA 15yr 6.0	MBS	100.30	N/A	10.2	5.25	4.59	3.62	-1.18	64	31
FNMA 15yr 6.5	MBS	101.55	N/A	13.9	4.51	4.21	3.00	-1.31	74	37
FNMA 15yr 7.0	MBS	102.28	N/A	19.5	3.61	3.64	2.45	-1.19	90	37
FNMA 15yr 7.5	MBS	102.80	N/A	24.6	2.92	2.79	1.99	-0.77	110	27
FNMA 15yr 8.0	MBS	102.67	N/A	24.9	2.70	2.28	2.03	-0.36	165	15
CMOs										
FHLMC 1297 I	Broken PAC	105.70	165/4.76 yr @ 345 PSA	24.9	4.27	4.55	2.63	-2.55	75	50
FHLMC 1970 M	Seq	103.87	90/3.82 yr @ 35 CPR	37.6	3.65	3.27	2.05	-1.87	40	38
FNMA 92-132 C	AD	105.68	135/3.43 yr @ 400 PSA	28.4	3.06	2.93	1.72	-0.90	79	28
FNMA 98-39 GD	Seq	104.81	150/9.74 yr @ 215 PSA	20.0	6.43	6.93	4.02	-3.02	74	55
FHLMC 1513 L	PAC	102.36	124/4.64 yr @ 207 PSA	16.5	4.64	3.90	3.00	-0.88	88	18
FHLMC 1070 H	Z	103.87	19/1.70 yr @ 340 PSA	26.0	2.69	1.55	1.93	-0.61	72	27
FHLMC 1343 K	PAC	103.88	58/1.96 yr @ 335 PSA	26.5	2.25	1.78	1.24	-1.56	57	25
FHLMC 1513 AC	Scheduled	102.57	64/2.52 yr @ 215 PSA	16.5	2.33	2.27	1.71	-0.80	35	9

Exhibit 7 (Continued)

Tranche	Type	Price	Pricing Spread/AL@CPR	Proj CPR	Proj AL	Mod Dur	Effective Duration	Effective Convexity	OAS (bp)	Option Cost (bp)
CMOs (Continued)										
FHLMC 2055 OB	PAC	101.68	86/4.20 yr @ 185 PSA	12.5	4.20	3.63	2.13	-1.24	33	38
FHLMC 2064 PT	PAC	101.88	87/3.68 yr @ 166 PSA	12.0	3.68	3.19	1.63	-1.57	35	38
FHLMC 1784 PG	PAC	104.04	30/1.52 yr @ 445 PSA	28.8	2.14	1.40	0.97	-1.51	88	25
FHLMC 1903 D	Seq	102.47	50/1.86 yr @ 50 CPR	42.8	2.23	1.69	1.14	-1.43	42	29
FNMA 96-48 M	Seq	102.27	50/1.86 yr @ 50 CPR	42.5	2.24	1.69	1.18	-1.41	43	29
FNMA 96-53 PD	PAC	103.48	85/4.18 yr @ 280 PSA	8.8	4.18	3.58	2.31	-1.25	41	29
Residential Funding 93-S7 A8	Broken PAC	101.10	150/1.29 yr @ 40 CPR	21.9	2.28	1.19	1.90	-0.58	178	17
Union Planters 98-1 A1	Seq	100.31	110/2.03 yr @ 12 CPR	30.6	0.80	1.82	0.68	-0.24	60	7

Pricing as of 9/15/98.

Source: Morgan Stanley

SUMMARY

The Morgan Stanley Home Equity Loan Prepayment Model incorporates borrower credit quality as a fundamental determinant of home equity loan prepayments. Lower quality borrowers prepay at a faster base speed, but with less interest rate sensitivity, than higher quality borrowers. Most importantly, this model provides two fundamental advances over other products. In particular, the model:

- generalizes across issuers, and
- dynamically adjusts the borrower credit quality distribution as it projects prepayments along a rate scenario.

The former means that the model is not restricted to be used for the issuer — ContiMortgage — that provided us with data for estimating the model. The latter means that the model embodies changing borrower credit quality and, therefore, prepayment risk over time as its projections amortize the security balance.

To compare home equity loan ABS to conventional mortgage-backed pass-throughs and CMOs requires analyzing all of these securities within the same option pricing model. The implication of our OAS analysis is that the home equities have lower option costs and better convexity characteristics than conventional mortgage product. This means that HELs provide value relative to conventional mortgages if HELs have a wider nominal spread, and in many cases will also provide value relative to conventional mortgages even when the HELs have tighter nominal spreads.

Chapter 21

A Risk-Return Framework for Evaluating Non-Investment-Grade Subordinated MBS

Laurie Goodman, Ph.D.
Managing Director
Mortgage Strategy Group
PaineWebber, Inc.

Linda Lowell
Director
Mortgage Research
Credit Suisse First Boston

INTRODUCTION

Investors in non-investment-grade subordinated mortgage-backed securities (MBS) often focus exclusively on the delinquency history of an issuer in evaluating their holdings. In fact, however, this subordinated paper is more appropriately judged in a risk-return framework that looks at the price paid for the security in conjunction with its anticipated losses. Although delinquencies are highly correlated with mortgage defaults, they are not at all the same measure. But the attention given to delinquencies sometimes obscures the importance of other factors critical to analyzing this paper. Three we consider essential are: (1) the actual loss generated by each foreclosure (commonly known as the loss severity), (2) the timing of the defaults, and (3) the price paid for the security.

In this chapter, we demonstrate how to incorporate both defaults and loss severities into a yield analysis of non-investment-grade subordinated MBS. We compare relative value between different subordinated classes and take a close look at how home-price appreciation affects loss severity. We show that during a period of even very modest increases in housing prices, subordinated mortgage paper can withstand a substantial increase in defaults and still maintain yield.

This chapter was originally written when Linda Lowell was a senior vice president in the mortgage strategy Group at PaineWebber.

Delinquencies Do Not Equate to Losses
On Credit Tranches

An important point mortgage-backed securities investors should bear in mind in evaluating subordinated issues: The vulnerability to *loss* of credit support tranches is not simply a function of delinquencies. Most mortgage delinquencies are cured before the loan is foreclosed. For example, in the first quarter of 1998, the MBA reported that 30-day delinquencies amounted to 2.16% of conventional loans; in the following quarter, the second quarter of 1998, 60-day delinquencies were a much smaller 0.44% of conventional loans. This makes sense. Mortgage borrowers have powerful incentives to avoid foreclosure: The home provides shelter and is the center of family life; in addition, equity in the home represents, if not the largest, a major investment for most households. Along with the down payment and regular amortization, home-price appreciation builds equity; borrowers in extreme circumstances who have equity to protect are far more likely to sell the house rather than allow the servicer to foreclose. (We are ignoring the value, as well, of good credit to most households.)

Owner's equity also serves as a buffer against loss to the investor if the loan does go into foreclosure. As a result, not every foreclosure need result in a loss. Once the servicer liquidates the property, proceeds are applied first to satisfy amounts owed to the servicer for advances, servicing compensation, foreclosure expenses and so forth; then to any accrued interest payable but not advanced to bondholders; and third to the outstanding principal balance of the loan. The realized loss is the remaining loan balance. Loss severity expresses the loss as a fraction or percentage of the outstanding loan amount. (Alternatively, we can speak of "recovery rate," or the fraction that is recovered. A loss severity of 20% would be equivalent to a recovery rate of 80%.)

Clearly, loss severity is a function (1) of the length of time from default to liquidation — this variable largely determines the amount of the servicers' advances and other foreclosure expenses — and (2) of the owner's equity. Owner's equity, in turn, is a function of the original down payment, or original LTV ratio, and the amount of home-price appreciation. The higher the rate of home-price appreciation, the lower the severity of any loss.

We can make this concrete with a simple example. Assume a borrower defaults on a remaining balance of $85,000 on a house originally purchased at $100,000, and the servicer incurs expenses of $17,000 — including advances to investors — in the course of foreclosing and liquidating the property (in other words, expenses amount to 20% of the remaining loan amount, an assumption slightly more conservative than the mid-point by state[1]). To break even, then, liquidation proceeds must amount to $102,000. If the property's market value remains unchanged, a loss of $2,000 will be realized. That equates to a loss sever-

---

[1] Clearly this is an artificial example for A-quality whole loan collateral. Private mortgage insurance (PMI) is required on loans with LTVs greater than 80%.

ity of 2%. On the other hand, if the house has appreciated by 5%, liquidation proceeds are $105,000 and no loss is realized. We would argue, in fact, that the homeowner would endeavor to liquidate (and thus prepay) before foreclosure to limit his own loss. Any home-price *depreciation,* on the other hand, would clearly *increase* the loss severity. For instance, 5% depreciation would result in a loss of $7,000, or a loss severity of 7%.

As a matter of fact, most housing markets performed very well in 1997-1998. This was the fourth consecutive year of robust home price appreciation. Exhibit 1 details, by state, rates of home-price appreciation as calculated by Freddie Mac from the joint Freddie Mac-FNMA Repeat Sales database for the period extending from third quarter 1997 to third quarter 1998. For the United States as a whole, home prices appreciated 5.0% over the period. Moreover, the increases were very broad-based, ranging from a low of 1.78% in Nevada to 8.72% in California. Jumbo mortgages are concentrated in California and the Northeast, both areas of robust home price appreciation.

Exhibit 1: Annual House-Price Appreciation Rates, Third Quarter 1997 to Third Quarter 1998

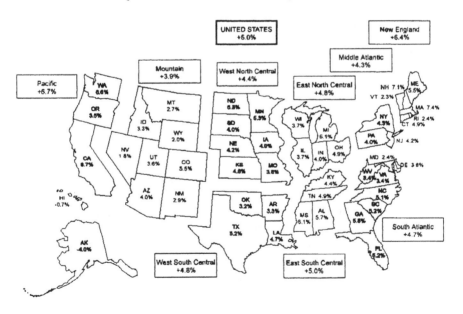

* Data not available due to inadequate repeat transactions.
Source: Conventional Mortgage Home-Price Index (national, regional levels); Freddie Mac; Weighted Repeat Sales Index (state level)

Exhibit 2: SDA Curve

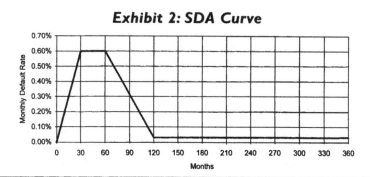

SDA: Incorporating Defaults and Loss Severities into Yield Analysis

Clearly, the yield on lower rated or unrated credit tranches is subject to a number of factors, including default rates, loss severity, and the timing of the losses. To reflect these various parameters in cash-flow analyses of credit tranches in a consistent, standardized manner, the Public Securities Association adopted the Standard Default Assumption (SDA) in May 1993. The SDA provides for monthly default rates to rise (in linear fashion, by even steps) from 0 to a peak of 0.6% per month (annual rate) over the first 30 months. They remain at that peak rate for the next 30 months (month 30 to month 60). After month 60, defaults decline to a "tail" value of 0.03% per month over the next 60 months (month 61 to month 120). They remain constant at the tail value until the last month of the remaining life of the pool, when the default rate drops to 0. Default rates for a specific cash-flow calculation are expressed as a multiple of SDA — 245% SDA, for example — just as with the PSA prepayment standard. Exhibit 2, depicts 100% SDA. (Most readers familiar with the credit analysis of mortgage pools will recognize that this pattern is roughly analogous to the default assumptions made by the rating agencies. The agencies have determined that at least 80% of defaults occur in the first seven years of the life of a mortgage loan. In Moody's model, losses are concentrated in years 4 and 5; S&P assumes that defaults occur in the second through fourth years of the transaction.)

The SDA methodology requires that three additional factors be specified in order to incorporate loss-experience assumptions into cash-flow analysis: loss severity, time to liquidation, and whether principal and interest are advanced to the subordinate in question. Clearly, regardless of the assumptions made about these inputs, the number of defaults registered as losses will also depend on the prepayment experience of the pool (given a constant rate of default, if no loans prepay, the absolute number of loans). The SDA was intended to be used in conjunction with the PSA's prepayment standard. For example, assuming a loss severity of 20%, 12 months to liquidation, and advancing at 200% PSA, 100% SDA generates 2.5% cumulative defaults on new 30-year mortgages with a 7.5% gross WAC. Cumulative losses equate to cumulative defaults multiplied by the loss severity. For example, if 2.5% of the pool defaults, with a severity of 20%, then the loss rate is 0.5% ($0.025 \times 0.2 = 0.005$).

Exhibit 3: Details of Subordinate Tranches
in a Representative Structure
($500mm, 7.5% Coupon, 200% PSA)

Tranche	Rating	Amount ($mm)	Percent of Deal	Pricing
Senior	AAA	471.21	94.25	
Mezz	AA	11.26	2.25	
B1	A	6.26	1.25	
B2	BBB	5.51	1.10	
B3	BB	2.75	0.55	+500/10yr., Px = 71:10
B4	B	1.00	0.20	+1000/10yr., Px = 53:14
B5	Unrated	2.00	0.40	Px = 24:00
Total		500.00	100.00	

SDA Analysis of an Example Deal

To assess the relative impact on subordinate tranches of delinquency rates on the one hand and recovery rates on the other, we structured the simple deal shown in Exhibit 3. As can be seen, the senior bonds make up 94.25% of the deal and subordinate tranches the remaining 5.75%. The three investment-grade classes, mezzanine, B1 and B2, comprise 4.6% of the deal. The non-investment-grade classes B3, B4, and B5 — double-B, single-B, and unrated, respectively — comprise the remaining 1.15% of the deal. Tranche B3 is assumed to be priced at 500 basis points over the 10-year, corresponding to a dollar price of 71:10. (Pricing levels are as of June 26, 1996.) Class B4 is priced at 1,000 basis points over the 10-year, corresponding to a dollar price of 53:14. Class B5, the unrated first-loss piece, is assumed to be offered at a dollar price of 24:00. Note that the market prices assume no defaults and are based on the pricing speed of 200% PSA, for loans with a 7.90% gross WAC.

Yield/cumulative loss profiles for classes B3, B4 and B5, given various prepayment (PSA) and default (SDA) assumptions, are shown in Exhibits 4, 5, and 6 respectively. When applying the SDA, we assume a recovery rate of 80%, equivalent to a loss severity of 20%. (Later, we will examine the effect of different recovery rates.) We also assume a period of 12 months between default and liquidation, commonly referred to as the "lag." When a borrower is seriously delinquent on a loan (typically more than 90 days), the servicer will move to foreclose. At this point, the borrower gives over the deed, or the property is repossessed; this is the event that defines a *default*. The legal foreclosure process differs state by state; it lasts from three to six months in some states to over two years in others, after which the servicer can liquidate the property. The common reasonable assumption is of a 1-year lag between default and liquidation. A longer lag would raise the yield on the subordinated tranches, a shorter lag would lower it. We also assume that the servicer continues to advance delinquent principal and interest payments through foreclosure. In nearly all deals, this is the case.

Exhibit 4: Tranche B3 Default/Yield Matrix*
Price: 71.31

% PSA	Percent SDA									
	0	20	50	75	100	150	200	250	300	350
100										
Yield	11.46	11.47	11.52	11.28	10.65	5.58	−9.14	−16.43	−22.32	−27.34
Cumulative Loss	0.00	0.12	0.31	0.46	0.62	0.92	1.21	1.51	1.79	2.07
150										
Yield	11.71	11.72	11.76	11.78	11.61	7.52	−5.98	−14.27	−20.36	−25.53
Cumulative Loss	0.00	0.11	0.28	0.42	0.55	0.83	1.09	1.36	1.62	1.87
200										
Yield	11.93	11.94	11.97	12.00	12.01	9.04	2.38	−11.89	−18.31	−23.65
Cumulative Loss	0.00	0.10	0.25	0.38	0.50	0.75	0.99	1.23	1.46	1.70
250										
Yield	12.12	12.14	12.16	12.19	12.21	10.58	5.28	−9.07	−16.12	−21.67
Cumulative Loss	0.00	0.09	0.23	0.34	0.46	0.68	0.90	1.12	1.33	1.54
300										
Yield	12.30	12.31	12.33	12.36	12.37	11.71	7.33	−0.45	−13.72	−19.59
Cumulative Loss	0.00	0.08	0.21	0.31	0.42	0.62	0.82	1.02	1.22	1.41

* Recovery rate of 80%, lag of 12 months.

Exhibit 5: Tranche B4 Default/Yield Matrix*
Price: 53.44

% PSA	Percent SDA									
	0	20	50	75	100	150	200	250	300	350
100										
Yield	16.09	16.11	15.27	12.78	1.54	−10.06	−18.57	−25.31	−30.77	−35.35
Cumulative Loss	0.00	0.12	0.31	0.46	0.62	0.92	1.21	1.51	1.79	2.07
150										
Yield	16.54	16.56	16.63	14.42	5.93	−8.38	−17.13	−24.11	−29.78	−34.60
Cumulative Loss	0.00	0.11	0.28	0.42	0.55	0.83	1.09	1.36	1.62	1.87
200										
Yield	16.93	16.95	17.02	16.22	10.58	−6.58	−15.65	−22.82	−28.69	−33.63
Cumulative Loss	0.00	0.10	0.25	0.38	0.50	0.75	0.99	1.23	1.46	1.70
250										
Yield	17.27	17.30	17.34	17.40	13.33	−4.59	−14.05	−21.44	−27.46	−32.62
Cumulative Loss	0.00	0.09	0.23	0.34	0.46	0.68	0.90	1.12	1.33	1.54
300										
Yield	17.58	17.60	17.65	17.70	16.25	−2.28	−12.36	−20.00	−26.21	−31.43
Cumulative Loss	0.00	0.08	0.21	0.31	0.42	0.62	0.82	1.02	1.22	1.41

* Recovery rate of 80%, lag of 12 months.

Exhibit 6: Tranche B5 Default/Yield Matrix*
Price: 24.00

% PSA	0	20	50	75	100	150	200	250	300	350
100										
Yield	36.26	32.89	24.72	16.18	9.88	0.13	−7.17	13.00	−17.86	−22.12
Cumulative Loss	0.00	0.12	0.31	0.46	0.62	0.92	1.21	1.51	1.79	2.07
150										
Yield	36.98	33.89	25.81	17.36	10.83	0.85	−6.65	−12.60	−17.57	−21.83
Cumulative Loss	0.00	0.11	0.28	0.42	0.55	0.83	1.09	1.36	1.62	1.87
200										
Yield	37.63	34.70	27.54	18.89	11.87	1.62	−6.07	−12.18	−17.25	−21.57
Cumulative Loss	0.00	0.10	0.25	0.38	0.50	0.75	0.99	1.23	1.46	1.70
250										
Yield	38.20	35.43	29.94	21.13	13.01	2.44	−5.42	−11.66	−16.90	−21.30
Cumulative Loss	0.00	0.09	0.23	0.34	0.46	0.68	0.90	1.12	1.33	1.54
300										
Yield	38.72	36.10	31.10	23.60	14.31	3.35	−4.72	−11.12	−16.41	−20.99
Cumulative Loss	0.00	0.08	0.21	0.31	0.42	0.62	0.82	1.02	1.22	1.41

Column header spanning all numeric columns: Percent SDA

* Recovery rate of 80%, lag of 12 months.

An SDA yield table is a matrix, with varying PSA assumptions on one dimension (the vertical on Exhibits 4, 5, and 6) and SDA assumptions on the other. For every PSA/SDA combination, two numbers appear in the cell. The top number is the yield and the bottom number is the cumulative losses to final maturity on the collateral, given the various assumptions. Thus, at 100% SDA and 200% PSA, Class B3 yields 12.01%, reflecting cumulative losses of 0.50%. Note the yield is approximately the same in this case as that of 0% SDA because the principal of this tranche is not hit. Instead, lower-rated tranches B4 and B5, representing 0.60% of the deal absorb the losses.[2]

Now let us look at what happens when defaults do begin to erode the principal of B3. At 150% SDA and 200% PSA, B3 yields 9.04%, given cumulative losses to the collateral of 0.75%, which eat into its principal. At 200% PSA and 200% SDA, the bond yields 2.38%, with cumulative losses of 0.99%, cutting deep into its principal. That is, cumulative losses of 0.99% take out more than half of B3's share of the principal; the first 0.60% would come from B4 and B5 and the remaining 0.39% from B3, which comprises 0.55% of the total deal. Thus, 70.8% (0.39/0.55) of B3's principal would be lost and only 29.1% would eventually be returned to investors.

There are several characteristics of SDA analysis investors should note. First, the faster the collateral prepays, the higher the yield for any given SDA default rate. For example, at 100% SDA and 200% PSA, Class B3 yields 12.01%.

---

[2] Actually, the yield will be marginally higher at 100% SDA, 12.01%, than at 0% SDA, 11.93%, because if there are no principal losses on the B3 piece, the cash flows will be received a bit earlier at higher SDAs.

At the same SDA and 300% PSA, the bond yields 12.37%. In general, the higher the prepayment rate for a given default frequency, the lower the cumulative defaults and hence losses. This occurs because faster prepayments reduce the principal balance faster; so that the same default rate is applied to smaller remaining balances to generate smaller dollar amounts of defaults.

Second, investors should notice how well the yields hold up as the bonds begin to absorb losses. For example, there is no combination of speeds between 100% and 300% PSA and defaults between 0% SDA and 100% SDA that can eliminate the 0.60% of the support below B3 (noted in Exhibit 3) and result in actual principal losses to B3. In the 150% SDA scenarios, the losses are high enough to take out a portion of B3's principal. As we pointed out above, at 200% SDA, B3 loses more than half its principal return.

What might surprise a number of readers is that despite the negative yield in scenarios in which a large portion or all of the tranche is eliminated by losses, the total rate of return may still be close to zero or positive. In the case of B3, at 200% SDA and 200% PSA, the total rate of return is 2.38%. The explanation lies in the timing of the losses. The bond pays a coupon of 7.5%. However, the coupon is based on the nominal, or face amount. The actual price of the security is 71.312 (71:10) so that the current yield on the security is 10.52%.[3] In other words, the investor earns 10.52% current yield on the bond until losses are realized (plus the difference between 71:10 and par as any principal is returned by regular amortization).

Timing of losses is even more significant in the case of B5, the first-loss piece (Exhibit 6). At 100% SDA and 200% PSA, cumulative loses of 0.50% on the collateral wipe out the bond's principal. However, the yield is still 11.87%. In effect, the investors earn a 7.5% coupon on the nominal amount, but that is returned against a purchase price of 24. The total return would reflect the fact that, while the entire principal was lost, the coupon payments still were more than sufficient to deliver a positive return. This can be seen intuitively by considering that, if the collateral has no losses for 3.2 years, while the bond pays a coupon of 7.5%, and then the tranche is wiped out, the return is effectively zero (7.5/24).

Relative Value Relationships
Between the Subordinated Classes

The relationship *between* the classes is quite interesting, as well, particularly in relative value terms. Exhibit 7 compares yields as a function of SDA, assuming 200% PSA, for Classes B3, B4 and B5. (The 200% PSA rows from Exhibits 4, 5, and 6, respectively). The first thing that stands out in the figure is that Class B3, rated BB, and in the third-loss position, has, generally speaking, less yield variability than B5, the unrated first-loss piece; when defaults are low, B3 yields less, when defaults are high, B3 yields more. Investors should conclude that if they expect losses to be lower, the unrated first-loss piece will perform better. In other

---

[3] Current yield is coupon/price.

words, at low SDAs, the first-loss piece is obviously more attractive. As the SDAs increase, Class B3 starts to look better than the first-loss piece; given prepayments speeds of 200% PSA, the crossover point is between 75% and 100% SDA. (Note that at very high default rates, there is another crossover point, between 250% and 300% SDA. At this point, cumulative loses are such that Classes B3, B4, and B5 are all wiped out. No investor who expected this kind of losses would consider this paper.) Ultimately, making a choice between B3 and B5 depends on what investors believe the cumulative losses will be. If lower SDAs are anticipated, the first-loss piece is preferable; if there is more uncertainty about the prospects for default, B3 is the better choice.

Interestingly, as Exhibit 7 demonstrates, Class B4, the B-rated second-loss piece looks extremely unattractive relative to the credit tranches on either side of it on the loss ladder. It is always dominated by B5 (assuming 200% PSA). It is easy to see intuitively why this is the least attractive bond of the three. It has little more protection than the first-loss piece. The first-loss piece absorbs the first 40 basis points of losses and this one the next 20 basis points. However, the dollar price of this piece is more than twice that of the first-loss piece — 53:14 versus 24:00. Quite frankly, we think that, at that price, investors are paying a great deal for little additional protection.

Investors who buy single-B paper — and who don't want to buy unrated paper — instead, may wish to consider a combination of unrated paper and BB-paper. A portfolio invested in 50% unrated paper and 50% in BB-rated paper actually provides more loss protection, a lower dollar price ((1/2 (71:10 + 24) = 47:21 versus 53:14 on the B4 tranche) and a considerably higher yield in all scenarios than the B-rated bonds. This comparison is illustrated in Exhibit 8. While a yield of 1,000 basis points over the 10-year may sound like a lot of yield, using small amounts of unrated paper in combination with more highly rated paper is a better strategy. During the time we were evaluating these securities, we did not believe that B-rated subordinates could tighten any further without the unrated paper doing even better.

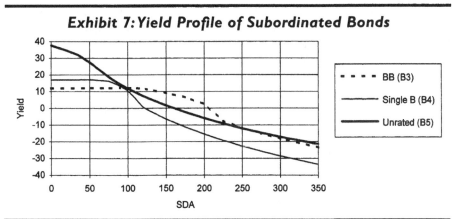

Exhibit 7: Yield Profile of Subordinated Bonds

Exhibit 8: Yield Profile on Combination of BB and Unrated Tranche versus Single B

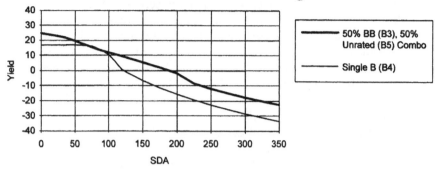

Exhibit 9: Yield Profile of BB (B3) Bond

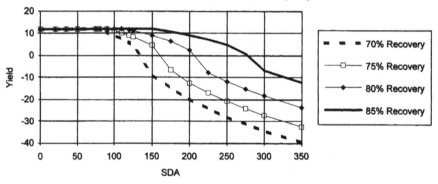

The Effect of Home-Price Appreciation

Assumptions about the recovery rate, or loss severity, have a major impact on the yield profiles of credit tranches. Home-price appreciation, as we have discussed, raises the recovery rate. Exhibits 9, 10, and 11 show the effects of various recovery rates on yield at 200% PSA for various SDA assumptions on Classes B3, B4, and B5 from our model transaction. There are two ways to look at the effect of an increase in the recovery rate. We can first look at the increase in yield as the recovery rate increases. For example, at 100% SDA, raising the recovery rate from 75% to 80% on B3 (the BB-rated tranche) increases the yield from 11.22% to 12.01%. The same change in recovery rate raises tranche B4's yield from −1.14% to 10.57%, and raises B5's yield from 6.05% to 11.86%. Readers can read the increase for other SDAs off Exhibits 9, 10, and 11.

These yield changes are quite significant. In fact, even if these increases in the recovery rate were simultaneously associated with increases in default rates, the investor might still be better off. This can be seen by simply drawing a horizontal line in Exhibits 9, 10, and 11 from one recovery curve to the next. We illustrate this procedure using B5, the unrated first-loss piece, in Exhibit 11. We initially pick a point, such as 100% SDA on the 70% recovery curve. The corresponding yield is 1.17%. We then drawn a horizontal line at this yield through the other recovery curves. From this, we determine, that, if the recovery rate were to improve to 75%, the SDA could be 121% in order to yield the same 1.17%. That is, this "breakeven SDA" is the intersection of the horizontal line in Exhibit 11 and the 75% recovery curve. Thus, raising the recovery rate from 70% to 75% raises the "break-even SDA" to 121% — a sizable increase. Raising the recovery rate from 75% to 80% means the collateral can default at a rate of 153% SDA and still yield the same 1.17%. These breakeven SDAs are shown in Exhibit 12 for all three tranches.

It is clear from the Exhibit 12 that, for given recovery rates, the breakeven SDAs are relatively similar across the three non-investment-grade tranches. In particular, an increase in the recovery rate on B5 from 75% to 80% would increase the breakeven SDA from 121% to 153%, similar to B3, where the breakeven SDA increases from 121% to 157%, and B4, where the break-even SDA increases from 121% to 154%.

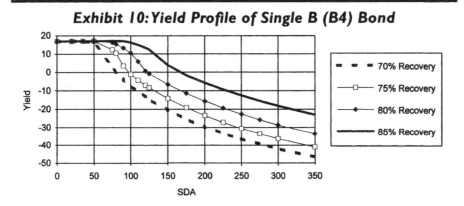

Exhibit 10: Yield Profile of Single B (B4) Bond

Exhibit 11: Yield Profile of Unrated (B5) Bond

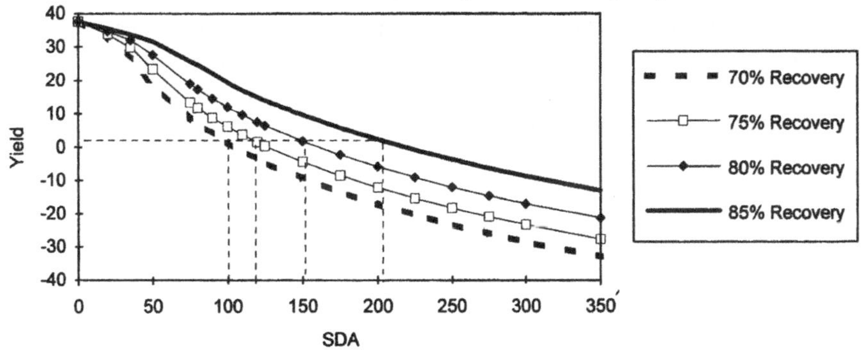

Exhibit 12: Breakeven Yield SDAs at Various Recovery Rates

Bond	Yield (%)	SDA	Recovery Rate (%)	Cumulative Defaults
BB (B3)	8.98	100	70	2.51%
BB (B3)	8.98	121	75	3.03%
BB (B3)	8.98	157	80	3.91%
BB (B3)	8.98	184	85	4.56%
Single B (B4)	−7.40	100	70	2.51%
Single B (B4)	−7.40	121	75	3.03%
Single B (B4)	−7.40	154	80	3.83%
Single B (B4)	−7.40	211	85	5.21%
Unrated (B5)	1.17	100	70	2.51%
Unrated (B5)	1.17	121	75	3.03%
Unrated (B5)	1.17	153	80	3.81%
Unrated (B5)	1.17	207	85	5.12%

For most investors, saying the break-even SDA can increase from 121% to 153% doesn't mean much. We can easily translate this number into cumulative defaults, also shown in Exhibit 12. (For each recovery rate, we know the yield and cumulative losses. Cumulative defaults are simply the cumulative losses divided by the loss severity.) Thus, for example, on B5, a 70% recovery rate corresponds to a cumulative default rate of 2.51%, a recovery rate of 75% corresponds to a cumulative default rate of 3.03%, and a recovery rate of 80% corresponds to a cumulative default rate of 3.81%. The critical point is how much higher a default or loss rate can produce the same yield with a 5% increase in the recovery rate. Our point is that home-price appreciation has lifted the recovery rate, and this effect on non-investment credit tranches is far greater than any increase in delinquencies could have — especially on highest quality collateral.

Consequences for Investment Decisions

To recap, there is one important point for investors considering subordinated mortgage tranches to bear in mind. Nationally, home-price appreciation has been healthy. Even in those areas of the country where jumbo mortgages represent a more significant share of the market, home prices have enjoyed moderate appreciation. A rise in home prices raises the recovery rate. And even a modest increase in the recovery rate will offset major hikes in the default rate — hikes far larger than anything we have experienced thus far.

Chapter 22

Prepayments on Jumbo Loans

Laurie Goodman, Ph.D.
Managing Director
Mortgage Strategy Group
PaineWebber, Inc.

INTRODUCTION

In this chapter we discuss the differences between prepayment experience for jumbo collateral during 1993 and 1998. An understanding of the prepayment characteristics of jumbo loans is important for understanding the convexity characteristics of securities backed by these loans and consequently the total return performance of these securities.

EVIDENCE FROM 1992 PRODUCTION

Most of the market continues to believe that jumbo collateral is far more negatively convex than agency product (as was the case in 1993). However evidence indicates otherwise. Jumbo collateral is still more negatively convex than agency paper, but that gap is much smaller now.

This can be seen in Exhibit 1, where we graph the prepayment profile of 1992-originated FNMA 7s versus 1992-originated jumbos with gross WACs of 7.50-7.99. We have chosen this pairing methodology because the gross WAC behind a 7.0% mortgage is just a bit over 7.5%. The spread between a conforming size loan and a jumbo loan is 25 basis points. Thus, 1992-originated jumbos with gross WACs of 7.50-7.99 indeed captures loans originated in the same environment. For this and our two additional exhibits presented later, we display 3-month CPRs, as it eliminates month-to-month noise and allows patterns to be seen more easily.

As can be seen from the Exhibit 1, 1992-originated FNMA 7s are actually faster in 1998 than they were at the height of the 1993 rally, even though mortgage rates were slightly lower then. Note that prepayments on jumbo mortgages with coupons of 7.50%-7.99% are much slower. One way to evaluate this is to look at the ratio on jumbos against agencies when speeds were at their peak in 1993 versus that ratio in May 1998. A second methodology is to look at the CPR differential. We did both.

Exhibit 1: 1992 Issue FNMA 7.0 versus Jumbo 7.50-7.99

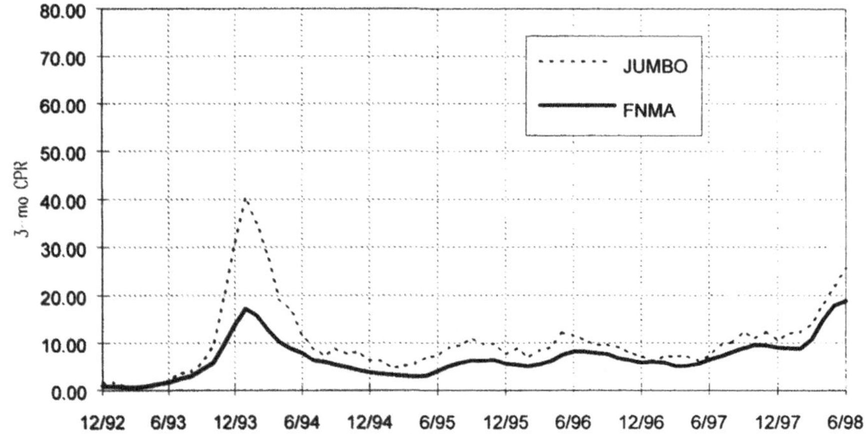

Exhibit 2: Agency versus Jumbo Prepays

		Review Date	Ratio	CPR Diff	Review Date	Ratio	CPR Diff
1992	FN 7.0s vs Jumbo 7.50-7.99	12/93	2.35	23.2	5/98	1.36	6.7
	FN 7.5s vs Jumbo 8.00-8.49	12/93	1.85	32.0	5/98	1.46	14.0
	FN 8.0s vs Jumbo 8.50-8.99	12/93	1.30	17.6	5/98	1.22	8.8
1996	FN 7.0s vs Jumbo 7.50-7.99				5/98	1.26	4.7
	FN 7.5s vs Jumbo 8.00-8.49				5/98	1.43	15.2
	FN 8.0s vs Jumbo 8.50-8.99				5/98	1.29	13.2

The 3-month CPRs peaked for most mortgages during October, November, and December of 1993 (with the data released in January of 1994). The ratio between FNMA 7s and jumbos with a gross WAC of 7.50-7.99 was 2.35 in 1993 versus the current level of 1.36. (That is, for the last quarter of 1993, the jumbo speed was 40.4 CPR and the agency speed was 17.2 CPR (40.4/17.2 = 2.35). The May 1998 number reflects a jumbo speed of 25.5 CPR and an agency speed of 18.8 CPR (25.5/18.8 = 1.36). The absolute CPR differential was 23.2 (40.4 – 17.2) at the end of 1993, versus 6.7 (25.5 – 18.8) in 1998. The ratios and CPR differentials are shown in Exhibit 2.

Exhibit 3 evidences a similar pattern for 1992-issued FNMA 7.5s versus jumbos with coupons of 8.00-8.49. The agency collateral is slightly slower in mid-1998, while jumbos are much slower. The ratio in December of 1993 was 1.85; it is 1.46 in mid-1998 (Exhibit 2). The absolute differential was 32.0 CPR at the end of 1993 versus 14.0 in mid-1998. Exhibit 4 shows prepayment speeds on 1992-originated FNMA 8s versus jumbos with gross WACs of 8.50-8.99. For this coupon, note that both agencies and jumbos are much slower than they were at the 1993 peaks. However, in 1993 there was a much larger differential between jumbos and agencies than in mid-1998. Again, this can be seen by simply looking at the ratios of jumbo speeds to agency speeds, as shown in Exhibit 2. In December of 1993, that ratio was 1.30, and the May 1998 value was 1.22. The absolute CPR differential was 17.6 at the end of 1993, versus 8.8 in mid-1998.

EVIDENCE FROM 1996 PRODUCTION

One might think that the results for the 1992 production could simply be a function of burnout. The factor was so much lower on the whole loans, as a result of dramatically higher prepayments in 1993, that the more responsive borrowers have already responded.

Exhibit 3: 1992 Issue FNMA 7.5 versus Jumbo 8.00-8.49

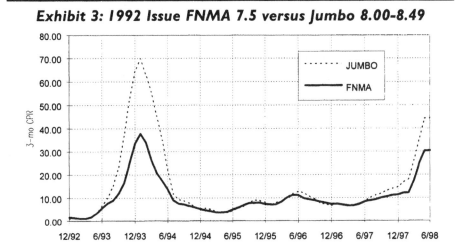

Exhibit 4: 1992 Issue FNMA 8.0 versus Jumbo 8.50-8.99

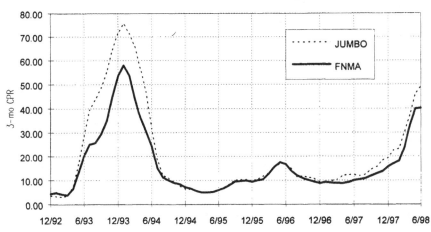

Exhibit 5: 1996 Issue FNMA 7.0 versus Jumbo 7.50-7.99

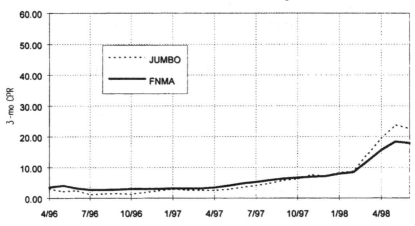

We can easily test this possibility by looking at how prepays on 1996 origination during 1998 compared to those on 1992 origination during late 1993. Prepayment behavior of 1996-originated FNMA 7s and jumbos with gross WACs of 7.50-7.99 is shown in Exhibit 5. As can be seen, the jumbos are more rapid than the agency collateral, but again, the difference is reasonable. The ratio of the jumbo prepays to agency prepays is 1.26 — less than the May 1998 ratio on the 1992 production, and much less than the ratio on 1992 production at the end of 1993 (results of which are also summarized in Exhibit 2). In absolute terms, the mid-1998 differential is 4.7 CPR, which is very muted relative to the 1993 experience.

For completeness, we depicted 1996-originated FNMA 7.5s (Exhibit 6) and 8s (Exhibit 7) versus their originated-matched jumbo siblings (gross WACs of 8.00-8.49 and gross WACs of 8.50-8.99, respectively). For the former, the May 1998 CPR differential is 15.2 CPR, and the ratio of the two prepayment speeds is 1.43. This contrasts sharply to behavior of 1992 production in late 1993, when the absolute difference was 32 CPR and the ratio was 1.85. Results are, in fact, nearly identical to the behavior of 1992 production in the first half of 1998. Exhibit 6 shows the May 1998 13.2 CPR differential between jumbos and agencies, which is less than the 17.6 CPR differential at the end of 1993.

Tapping Home Equity Value

Why is there a difference? It seems that the mortgage market's most important trend is the leveraging of home equity. We've seen that in a number of forms. First, the 125% LTV market is testament to this phenomenon. Second, one of the reasons that speeds on 7% and 7.5% agency coupons in the first half of 1998 have been comparable to or higher than 1993 levels, despite higher mortgage rates, is that cash-out refis appear to be behind much of the refinancing. Jumbo borrowers have both less of a need and are more constrained in leveraging their home equity.

Exhibit 6: 1996 Issue FNMA 7.5 versus Jumbo 8.00-8.49

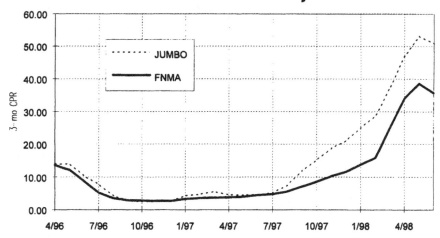

Exhibit 7: 1996 Issue FNMA 8.0 versus Jumbo 8.50-8.99

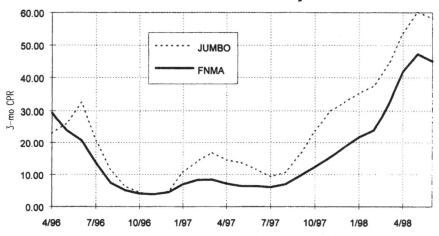

We have repeatedly hypothesized that investors were refinancing for less of an incentive than in 1993 due to (1) the increased efficiency of the refinancing process, as well as (2) the desire to leverage home equity. The latter incentive is very powerful. With the robust home price appreciation during 1994-1997, the cheapest way to borrow money was a cash-out refi. Exhibit 8 details an example of an investor who, in early 1995, bought a $125,000 house with 20% down and a $100,000 mortgage at 8%. We also assumed that over the next three years, the homeowner-cum-investor has racked up $12,500 in credit card debt. The value of the home has appreciated, on average, by 14.11% (5.2% appreciation in 1995,

3.6% in 1996, and 4.7% in 1997) and after 3 years, equals $142,637. If the investors taps into that by taking out a new loan sufficiently large to cover the remaining principal balance on the existing loan, the credit card debt, plus $3,000 in refinancing fees, then over $400 is saved in monthly payments. Without a cash-out refi, the drop in monthly payments would be much more muted, about $50 a month.

Data from Freddie Mac confirm the attractiveness of cash-out refis. In 1997 (the latest data available) 59% of the refis were for a loan amount more than 5% higher than the remaining balance on the existing loan. (And this had followed several years of robust home price appreciation.) In 1993, only 34% of the mortgages were cash-out refis. We believe that the refinancing surge was driven, in large part, by the fact that a cash-out refi was, by far, the most cost effective way to consolidate debt.

Cash-Out Refis: Less Common in Jumbos

We would expect jumbos to be faster than conforming-sized mortgages, as the typically more well-heeled home buyers taking out jumbos tend to be more efficient at refinancing. They are usually more educated and aware of their options. Plus with larger loan balances, they have more to save. And their friendly mortgage bankers (compensated based on the percent of principal balance) are more apt to solicit these home buyers. For all these reasons, we expect jumbo home buyers to be more responsive to prepayments than their conforming loan brethren.

Exhibit 8: Cash Out Refis: The Impact

- Assume: In early 1995, borrower moved into a $125,000 house, put down 20%, and took out a $100,000 mortgage.
    - Interest rate: 8.0%
    - Payment: $728.91
    - Remaining principal balance: $97,280
- Credit card debt: $12,500
    - Interest rate: 18%
    - 2% principal repayment per month
    - Payment: $437.50
- Total payments: $1,166.41
    - Value of home is $142,637, assuming 5.2% appreciation in 1995, 3.6% in 1996, and 4.7% in 1997 (total appreciation of 14.11%)
- Consolidated:
    - $97,280 current mortgage
    - $12,500 credit card debt
    - $3,000 refinancing fees
    - Total new loan size: $112,780
    - Interest rate: 7.25%
    - Payments: $764.74
    - Over $400 in savings!
- Without cash-out, payments drop from
    - $728.91 to $679.97 (not much of a difference)

However, with the greater importance of cash-out refis in the agency universe, we would have expected jumbo and agency prepays to have converged at least a bit since 1993 — as has been the case. Jumbo borrowers are, by and large, more affluent and hence less apt to have credit card debt to consolidate. Thus they have less need to tap their home equity, and hence are less apt to refinance motivated primarily by the desire to take out dollars.

Additionally, cash-out criteria are generally more stringent on a jumbo-sized mortgage. On a cash-out refi, agencies have no problem insuring a loan up to 80% of principal. But for a jumbo loan, the cash-out refi limit is generally capped at 75% LTV. Thus, homeowners starting with an 80% LTV first are able to pull less of the appreciation out of a jumbo mortgage than an agency mortgage.

Another quite important component of cash-out refis is the group of investors who took out an 80% LTV first mortgage and simultaneously, a 10%-15% second mortgage at a higher rate. The latter is oftentimes called a "piggyback" mortgage. With robust home price appreciation, it is now economic to consolidate the two into a new 80% first. But Jumbo universe piggybacks are much less common than within conforming product. Additionally, since the maximum jumbo cash-out refi LTV is 75%, more appreciation is needed to make this transaction possible. Thus, the refinancing gap between jumbos and agency product is shrinking due to the lesser importance of cash-out refis in the jumbo world.

CONCLUSION

Reviewing prepayment behavior on jumbo collateral during the first half of 1998, we find that it is still more negatively convex than agency paper. However, the difference between jumbo and agency collateral during 1998 is far less than what it was during 1993. We believe this results from jumbo mortgage homeowners' reduced need to leverage their home equity, as well as the additional constraints against doing so.

Section II

Commercial Mortgage-Backed Securities

Chapter 23

Introduction to Commercial Mortgage-Backed Securities

Brian P. Lancaster
Managing Director
Bear Stearns & Co. Inc.

INTRODUCTION

While CMBS existed as early as the late 1980s and 1990 mostly in the form of private placements, it was the Resolution Trust Corporation (RTC) that in 1991 and 1992 jumpstarted the market from a sleepy backwater to a respectable bond sector. Commercial mortgage-backed securities (CMBS) are securitizations of mortgage loans backed by commercial real estate. Investors were interested in the new sector's generous spreads and prepayment protection while issuers were looking for new financing outlets. But it was really the RTC that created models or templates for future transactions. It was the volume of RTC issuance and the attractive pricing of their deals that increased investor awareness, stimulated demand and provided pricing benchmarks. However, as RTC issuance faded in the ensuing years, the market continued to grow as Wall Street conduits, led by the now defunct Capital Company of America, stepped in to fill the void left by traditional bank and portfolio lenders.

By 1998, annual issuance had grown by 37% per year to hit $80 billion. Currently about $250 billion of CMBS are outstanding (see Exhibit 1) or about 25% of U.S. commercial real estate debt. The U.S. CMBS market is almost the same size as the non-agency market and about 40% of the size of the ABS market (see Exhibit 1). However, 1998 was far more than an issuance watershed. In late August, a default in Russia triggered a bond market panic that stifled trading in nearly all U.S. bond sectors. With fewer and more leveraged investors than other sectors, the CMBS market was hit harder than most. Liquidity almost completely dried up and one of the few key leveraged investors in the critical subordinate sector, CRIIMI Mae, filed for bankruptcy protection.

Exhibit 1: CMBS versus Other Securitized Markets

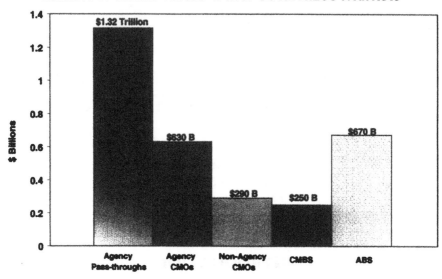

Which leaves us where we are today — a market in transition. The dislocations of 1998 shook out a number of weaker leveraged players, sobered up all participants to the risks of the sector and created opportunity for newer ones. While trading and spreads in higher rated tranches, such as triple-As, have tightened, they still remain about 40% greater than their average spread in the previous year. In the lower rated sectors, such as double-Bs, spreads still remain close to their historic wides although new funds are being set up each month to invest in the sector. With real estate prices in most areas still appreciating and spreads still wide, opportunities abound for the savvy investor. This chapter is designed to provide an introduction to the opportunities in the triple-A CMBS sector. The appendix to this chapter provides summaries of the various rating agencies' approach to the CMBS rating process.

WHAT ARE COMMERCIAL MORTGAGE-BACKED SECURITIES?

Commercial mortgage-backed securities are securitizations of mortgage loans backed by commercial real estate. These securities are typically structured as sequential-pay bonds and receive credit ratings from AAA through the lower credit grades (AA through B-/CCC/Not Rated). Sequential pay simply means that after each tranche is paid off, starting with the highest rated tranche, the next lower rated tranche begins to receive principal and so forth in sequential order until all tranches in the deal are paid off (see Exhibit 2). Unlike the sequential-pay structure in the residential mortgage security market, CMBS sequential-pay structures often have only a 5-year and a 10-year tranche due to the maturities of the underlying loans. Due to the need to protect outstanding higher rated tranches, most subordinate tranches have average lives of 10 years or greater.

At issuance, about 70% to 75% of the deal's securities typically receive a AAA rating. AAA rated securities represent the bondholders' first claim on receipt of principal and interest from the underlying collateral. The remaining 25% to 30% of the deal consists of lower rated subordinate tranches which credit enhance higher rated tranches. In contrast, residential mortgage security subordination levels range between 4% and 5%. Thus if a loss occurs on the underlying collateral, the lowest rated or unrated tranche's principal is "hit" or reduced by the amount of the loss. If the loss is greater than the unrated tranche then the next higher rated tranche's principal is reduced and so forth (see Exhibit 2).

A common misconception in the market is that AAA tranches of CMBS deals with higher percentages of subordination are "better." On the contrary, at issuance higher subordination levels are a sign of lower credit quality collateral since the rating agencies require greater subordination to make up for any deficiencies in the collateral. This as we shall see has negative implications for the stability of the cash flows.

Exhibit 2: CMBS Paydown and Loan Schedule

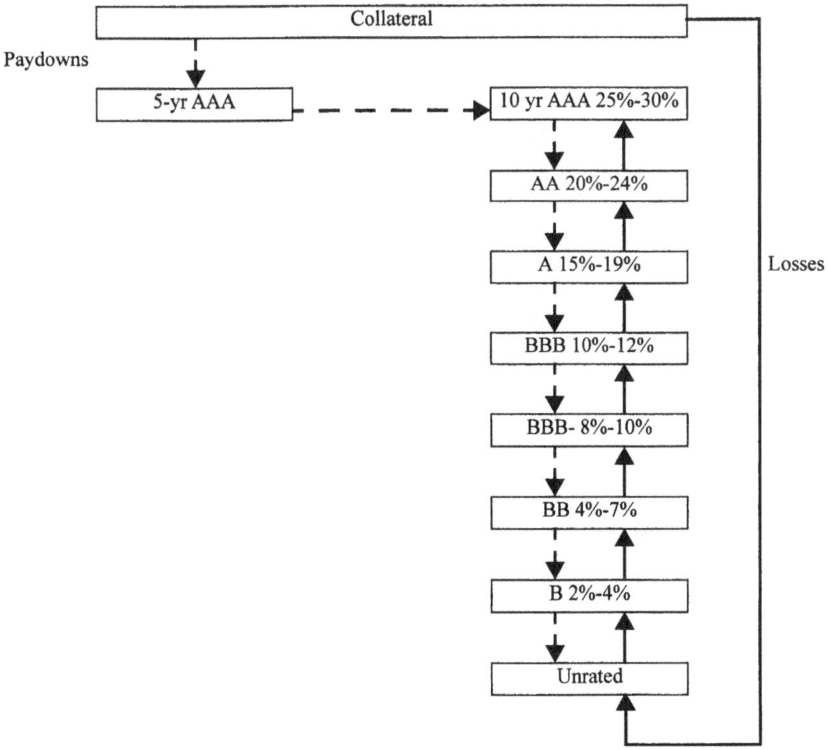

THE CHARACTERISTICS OF COMMERCIAL REAL ESTATE LOANS

The loans that serve as CMBS collateral commonly are secured by commercial real estate such as apartment buildings, shopping or strip malls, warehouse facilities, etc. Unlike most residential mortgage loans, these loans often do not provide recourse to the borrower[1] nor any form of guarantee. Lenders and investors look to the collateral, not the borrower, for ultimate repayment. Thus analysis of the cash flows generated by the underlying properties as well as their value is critical. Residential mortgage securities also typically consist of thousands of small loans versus hundreds for commercial mortgage securities.[2] The larger number of loans allows for greater diversification. Also, unlike most residential loans, commercial mortgage loans typically have excellent call protection and average life stability. Commercial mortgage loans may or may not amortize but most do, typically over a 20- to 30-year period.[3] However, they usually balloon after 10 or 15 years and must be paid in full. Amortization of principal helps to reduce risk as it reduces the loan to value ratio of the property over time and increases the borrower's equity in the property assuming stable or increased property values.

Because of the balloon feature of most commercial loans as well as the lack of borrower recourse, refinancing of the loan at the balloon date is critical. A rise in interest rates, which significantly increases the debt servicing requirements of a floating rate loan or the refinancing requirements for a fixed rate balloon loan, could significantly alter its economics increasing the risk of default. More commonly, terms may be renegotiated between the lender, here represented by the special servicer,[4] and the borrower, which could result in an extension of the loan term and the average life of the commercial mortgage security.

Of course the loan could also be paid down at or before the balloon date whereby the deal would "deleverage" (i.e., the ratio of the subordinates to the senior tranches could increase). This can result in an upgrade of some of the remaining tranches in the deal. Declining interest rate and rising commercial property price environments, such as those experienced between 1990 and 1999, can result in the deleveraging and upgrading of CMBS deals. Falling property prices and rising rates may have the opposite effect.

---

[1] Lack of borrower recourse is common in the U.S. but not in other countries, such as Japan where borrower recourse is typical. Commercial loans are sometimes cross collateralized to mitigate the risk of borrower default. Cross collateralization means that if a borrower defaults on one property it is effectively treated as a default on all properties.

[2] Residential mortgage loan sizes often range from $100,000 to $400,000 per loan whereas commercial mortgage loans are usually ten times as large or greater.

[3] Agency commercial loans may amortize over a 40-year period but this is atypical. A number of commercial loans also have only an interest only period followed by a balloon date but these are less common.

[4] The master servicer typically handles routine administrative tasks while the special servicer usually handles workouts and delinquencies. Special servicers often invest in the lower rated tranches of CMBS so their interests are typically aligned with those of the investor.

ANALYZING AND VALUING CMBS: WHAT TO LOOK FOR

Given the relative youth of the CMBS market, newer investors approach the market with a variety of different perspectives and backgrounds. Some are "bond people" with backgrounds in corporate bonds or residential MBS; others are "real estate people." The following section provides a basic framework which investors with either background may use when analyzing CMBS transactions. All deals require some subjective assessment, but using the following methodology should be an effective approach to compare and contrast various CMBS transactions and to make relative value decisions regarding specific bonds.

Credit Indicators: DSCR and LTV

Two of the most important indicators of the credit quality of the collateral backing a CMBS deal are the debt service coverage ratio (DSCR) and the loan to value ratio (LTV). The primary indicator of the credit quality (default and loss risk) of a commercial mortgage is the loan's debt service coverage ratio (DSCR). The DSCR is considered most important because it is more precise than LTV. The DSCR is based on current debt service and current net operating income. The LTV is viewed as less reliable as the value of the property will change significantly depending on the capitalization rate assumed (the discounting term for the cash flows generated by the property).

The debt service coverage ratio which equals "net operating income" divided by "mortgage payment" quantifies how much cash flow a property is generating versus required loan payments. As the DSCR rises, default risk declines. Investors look at the DSCR to assess how much of a downturn a borrower can withstand and still be able to make loan payments.

It is important to consider not only the weighted average DSCR but also the dispersion or range of DSCRs for the loans in a pool. Thus investors should ask what is the weighted average DSCR as well as the range of DSCRs for a deal. Acceptable levels of DSCRs vary depending on the property type, loan type, rating level and credit enhancement features. However, most conduit transactions' weighted average DSCRs fall in the range of 1.35 and 1.45. The percent of loans in a deal with DSCRs below 1.25× should raise a red flag since these are loans with greater default risk. If the percent is under "10%" this would generally be considered acceptable. Under 5% would be "good." (Exhibit 3 summarizes a number of quality indicators for CMBS deals.) It is important for the AAA holder to consider the DSCRs as defaults will likely translate into prepayments at par.[5] A triple-A rating addresses timely payment of interest and ultimate repayment of principal. It does not address the issue of prepayments due to liquidations.

---

[5] Legally borrowers are supposed to pay yield maintenance and/or other prepayment penalties on default, however there is rarely sufficient cash left over to do so.

Exhibit 3: A Quick Guide to CMBS Quality

Average DSCR	Good	Fair	Poor	
	1.45	1.45-1.35	1.35	

% of Deal with DSCRs below 1.25	Good	Fair	Poor	
	Under 5%	10%	>10%	

Average LTV	Very Good	Good	Fair	Poor
	<65%	65%	75%	>75%

% of Deal with LTVs >75%	Excellent	Very Good	Good	Fair
	<5%	6%-10%	11%-15%	>16%-20%

Prepayment Protections	Excellent	Very Good	Good	Fair
	Treasury Defeasance - Lock-out	Yield Maintenance	Prepayment Penalty Points	

Geographic Concentration	Acceptable	High
	<40% in one State	40% or greater in one State

Property Type Concentration	Acceptable	High
	<40% in one Property Type	40% or greater in one Property Type

This exhibit is designed to serve as a rough guide to quality in the CMBS market. There are of course, exceptions to these basic indicators. As such each deal should be analyzed on its own merits.

The loan to value ratio (LTV) is used in conjunction with the DSCR to determine how much a property is leveraged. A common way of calculating property value is to apply a capitalization rate to projected net operating income (NOI).[6] The problem is what capitalization rate to use. This potential subjective element can diminish the effectiveness of the LTV as an indicator of the credit quality of a commercial property.

Here too the investor should ask what is the weighted average LTV and the range of LTVs for a deal. Most conduit transaction weighted average LTVs fall in the range of 65% to 73%. The percent of loans in a deal with LTVs greater than 75% should be considered because these loans have greater default risk due to higher leverage. The lower the percent the better. Under 15% is good, under 10% is very good and under 5% is exceptional. The percent of a deal with LTVs greater than 75% is probably more important than the weighted average LTV.[7,8]

---

[6] Net operating income (NOI) equals the gross revenues of a property less cash expenses. i.e., does not include non-cash expenses such as depreciation.

[7] Credit lease deals can skew the above mentioned percentages because most credit lease deals are done with high LTVs and 1.00× to 1.10× DSCRs because they are more corporate credit deals than real estate deals. Credit lease deals could be removed from the pool analysis to arrive at more standardized numbers. For a useful analysis of credit tenant leases see, Moody's Investor Service special report, October 2, 1998, *CMBS: Moody's Approach to Rating Credit Tenant lease (CTL) Backed Transactions*.

[8] Shorter amortization schedules can also skew the LTVs since a higher LTV loan which rapidly amortizes causing the LTV to fall may be just as good or better than a lower LTV loan which slowly amortizes or does not amortize at all.

Exhibit 4: Default Rate*

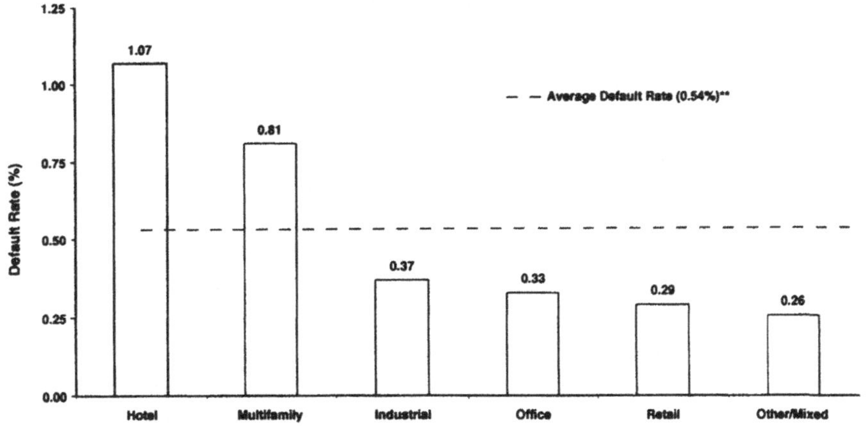

* Default rate equals number of defaults by type divided by the number of loans by type.
** Average default rates equals number of total defaults divided by number of total loans.
Source: Fitch IBCA

Property Location and Types

A dispersion of properties geographically is desirable in securitizations since changes in real estate values tend to be primarily influenced by local economies. Geographic diversification can reduce credit risk and is recognized by the rating agencies as doing so. A concentration of 40% or higher in any single state is generally considered a significant concentration.

The investor should consider the diversity of property types backing the loans in a CMBS deal. Diversification by property type is desirable in securitizations. There is no ideal percentage mix by property type, however a concentration greater than 40% to 50% is considered a large concentration. While there are several characteristics of commercial mortgage loans that are common to all property types, there are also a tremendous number of issues that are specific to different property types. Default rates for several property types are shown in Exhibit 4.

Good quality commercial real estate meets two standards: many different tenants can use the property, and the property can be leased or managed by many different operators. These characteristics reduce the risk that a mortgage loan ultimately depends on a single tenant or landlord.

Multifamily loans are generally considered to be most desirable because their short-term leases allow revenues to rise with expenses. Multifamily properties have strong historic credit experience, limited leasing risk, relatively transparent financial reporting and represent a large market-about 34.5% of total outstanding commercial real estate loans (see Exhibit 5). In addition, the universe of potential new tenants is larger than for other property types. However, the short-term nature of the leases also make multifamily loans susceptible to economic downturns. Multifamily properties also tend to have higher LTVs than other types. Fitch IBCA in a recent study found multifamily loans had the second highest default rate of various loan types (see Exhibit 4). Financing for multifamily properties tends to be widely available and highly competitive as Freddie Mac and Fannie Mae compete for loans along with conduits and portfolio lenders. Freddie Mac, Fannie Mae and the Federal Home Loan banks also have a mandate to purchase CMBS tranches backed by high concentrations of multifamily loans (usually 35% or greater).

Retail properties range from regional malls to community strip centers. The critical qualitative consideration in evaluating these properties is the quality of the tenant roster combined with the fundamental aspects of the real estate and the relationship of the lease rents to market rent. Whether a retail property is "anchored" (e.g., a shopping center with a supermarket) or "unanchored" is an important distinction. Retail properties that are anchored have traditionally been perceived to be less risky. A strong anchor can be a stabilizing influence on a property. Retail properties can be adversely affected by the presence of such retailers as dry cleaners, which may present hazardous waste problems.

A wide range of office property types exist, with different considerations for each. A common view is to differentiate properties within a central business district versus suburban office properties. For both, an assessment of quality centers on tenancy and location. An analysis of lease structures and roll over risk and the relationship of the lease rents to market rents is essential.

Office properties have longer-term leases than other property types — which can provide steady cash flow, but pose substantial risks at lease expiration. The cost of attracting new tenants can be high as offices, lobbies etc. must be tailored to the needs of new occupants. For example, given the increasing technology needs of financial institutions expenses can be high to reoutfit buildings to accommodate new wiring schemes, air conditioning systems, power systems etc. Office loans are often large — most loans are under $10 million, but many exceed $100 million, which creates "lumpy" pools diminishing diversification.

Exhibit 5: Breakdown of CMBS Issued from 1996 to 1998 by Property Type*

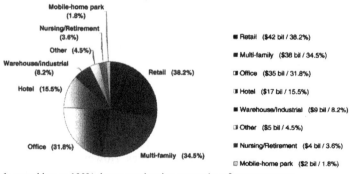

* Numbers do not add up to 100% due to overlapping categories of property types.

Source: *Commercial Mortgage Alert*

Exhibit 6: Commercial Delinquency Rates by Property Types (1998)

Property Type	Delinquency Rate	Yearly Change	4th Quarter Change
Apartment	0.21	−0.14	−0.01
Retail	0.49	−0.39	−0.17
Office Buildings	0.72	−0.51	−0.06
Industrial	0.28	−0.26	−0.03
Hotels	0.78	−0.17	0.66
Other Commercial	0.21	−0.04	−0.24
Commercial, Total	0.48	−0.42	−0.09

Source: American Council of Life Insurance

Major tenants are critical to an office property. Longer-term leases defer rollover risk and also offer some protection against inflation with partial passthroughs[9] of expenses and consumer price index rent escalators in many cases.

Industrial properties have strong historic credit experience and short leases, but require underwriting expertise for specialized uses. Concerns with industrial properties are potential limitations on alternative uses for the property should the tenant decide to vacate and environmental problems. Many lenders stick to warehouses and distribution facilities. A qualitative review of industrial property focuses on site characteristics including clearance heights, column spacing, number of bays and bay depths, divisibility, truck turning radius and overall functionality and accessibility. Of equal importance is the property's access to the local labor pool, proximity to supply sources and customers, and accessibility to major highways, rail lines and airports. A thorough analysis of lease structure and roll over risk and the relationship of lease rent to market rent is important.

Hospitality properties require a separate underwriting discipline. Many investors contend that these are as much operating businesses as they are commercial real estate. The market distinguishes between limited service properties which can be subject to stiff competition and low barriers to entry and luxury or destination properties which may possess unique attributes. One obvious risk: the leases last for 24 hours. Occupancy rates in certain locations can be volatile and highly dependent on the vagaries of the economy and consumer travel budgets, a discretionary expenditure.

Health care and related properties are also largely operating businesses and are subject to regulations (and, often, price controls). Some CMBS include a small exposure to health care, although the trend is to exclude this property type. Special purpose properties are introduced reluctantly. Properties such as cold-storage facilities or car washes may be highly creditworthy, but even given excellent credit, educating the market presents a substantial barrier. Other property types include self-storage facilities and theaters. Current delinquency rates by property types are shown in Exhibit 6.

---

[9] Passthroughs are expenses, such as real estate taxes, utilities, insurance, upkeep of common areas, which are passed through to the tenant.

Loan Size/Concentration

Within the universe of CMBS, the underlying loans have some obvious differences: balances can vary from under $1 million to over $500 million. While smaller loans typically allow for greater diversification of collateral in a CMBS deal and hence a reduction in the credit risk of an overall transaction,[10] it is more difficult for an investor to analyze the credit quality of many small loans. Here the investor has to rely more on the rating agencies and diversification as well as updates of loan level information provided by the servicer and third party information sources, such as Conquest.[11] A deal consisting of a few larger loans on the other hand allows the investor to analyze the properties more readily and thoroughly in a cost-effective manner.

Different investors continue to favor different deal types. Large loan deals tend to be purchased by "buy and hold" accounts such as insurance companies and pension funds which have real estate expertise and typically are not actively traded. On the other hand, smaller loan conduit deal investors tend to consist of more total return, "mark to market" accounts. As such liquidity is generally better. While each deal must be analyzed individually, in general large loan deals can be analyzed more easily since only a few loans have to be scrutinized in great detail. However, while conduit deals have the significant benefit of diversification, it is more difficult to analyze the real estate individually. While one can argue the merits of each type of deal, we expect the market to favor more diversified conduit deals in the immediate future given the market's ongoing liquidity concerns.

The investor should ask what percent of the collateral pool is represented by the largest loan. In the past the rule of thumb used to be that the rating agencies liked to see that no single loan exceeded 5% of the pool. However, we are now beginning to see this "rule of thumb" broken more frequently with the advent of "hybrid" or "fusion" deals. These are deals that combine smaller "conduit style" loans with large or "mega" loans. Unless an investor can become comfortable with the credit of the particular property backing the largest loan, it is generally desirable not to have too large an exposure to any single property. The investor should also determine what percent of the collateral pool the three largest loans make up — and then the 10 largest loans.

The rating agencies also note that even if no loan makes up more than 5% of a pool, the pool may still be concentrated. For example, a pool consisting of 20 or 30 loans with each accounting for less than 5% of the pool could still be highly concentrated. Concentration is important because it is sometimes difficult for the rating agencies to predict which commercial loans will default and why. For example, a major competitor could move in next to a property or a major tenant could leave. With greater diversity, deterioration in any one cash flow will have less impact on the overall deal.

---

[10] This is recognized by the major rating agencies that give a "credit" for sufficient diversification.

[11] Conquest, an on-line service, currently provides loan level data on most commercial mortgage securities.

Consider credit support (subordination) of 28%. This would protect against a 70% frequency of default and 40% loss severity.[12] If there are 100 loans each making up 1% of the pool, it is highly unlikely that 70 separate loans will each experience a 1% default rate to achieve the 70% default rate. However, if there are 20 or 30 loans that make up 3% or 4% of a pool, it would be more likely for these 20 or 30 loans to experience a 1% default rate.

Loan Types

Coupon rates of commercial loans may be either fixed or floating. Commercial loans with floating coupons of course can be more risky as the debt service coverage ratio will change along with interest rates, improving as rates fall, deteriorating as rates rise. Medium and long-term commercial mortgage loans (5+ years) are generally fixed rate. Short-term loans or interim financing may have an adjustable rate. About 86% of CMBS issued since 1996 have fixed rate coupons with the balance floating-rate coupons.

Fixed-rate loans are typically level pay, amortizing on a 20-year to 30-year schedule. Most loan terms are 7 to 10 years. Unamortized principal is payable as a "balloon balance" at the loan's due date. The need to finance balloon payments introduces refinancing risk (sometimes called "balloon extension risk").

Loan Underwriting Standards

The investor should always consider (1) who underwrote a particular CMBS transaction and (2) who originated the underlying loans. Some conduits originate the mortgages directly, while others use brokers to originate. In both cases, the issuer most of the time "re-underwrites" the loans to assure quality control.[13] Some deals have collateral contributed from multiple originators (four to five); other deals have collateral from only a few originators (one to three); neither one is necessarily better or worse. It depends most importantly on the quality of the originator and the underwriting process.

Loan underwriting standards vary substantially between lenders and it is important to have a "feel" for which issuers have a good name in the market and which ones don't. One of the easiest ways to distinguish among underwriters is to talk to the rating agencies and ask them specific questions regarding the conduits.In addition, one can usually examine the historic credit quality of underwriters' deals for high and/or rising delinquency rates, defaults or special servicing.

All real estate lenders balance two basic underwriting decisions: loan proceeds and coupon rates. Proceeds-driven lenders tend to offer maximum loan proceeds, while charging relatively high interest rates. These lenders contend that extra rate more than compensates for additional credit risk. Rating agencies gen-

---

[12] Loss severity is the percent of a mortgage that is lost after a loan is liquidated.

[13] Some issuers such as Fannie Mae do not reunderwrite the loan but rather delegate the underwriting and servicing to a third party, hence the Fannie Mae delegated underwriting and servicing program (DUS).

erally require higher subordination levels to support AAA ratings — sometimes over 31%. Coupon-driven lenders tend to offer a minimum loan coupon while providing more modest levels of loan proceeds. These lenders put a premium on minimizing credit exposure, and contend that borrowers who choose lower rates and proceeds are more likely to repay their loans. Rating agencies respond with lower subordination levels to support AAA ratings — sometimes under 25%.

Prepayment Terms/Call Protection

Call or prepayment protection is the key structural component of a CMBS transaction as call protection is the primary reason investors buy CMBS. Most commercial mortgage loans have several forms of call protection. Many are "locked out" for the first two to five years, after which there is a "yield maintenance period" which continues up until several months before maturity. This short period at the end of the loan lasting a few months is called the free period since there is usually no prepayment penalty. These and other principal types of call protection in the CMBS market are described below.

Lockout
Prepayment lockouts explicitly prohibit prepayments for a specified period of time. As such it provides complete protection against voluntary or optional prepayments. Lock-outs usually only cover the first few years of a loan and are often used in combination with other forms of prepayment protection.

Defeasance
One of the best types of call protection is defeasance. The borrower must purchase a portfolio of Treasuries or Treasury equivalents, which replicates future cash flows of the mortgage to defease future payments. The cost to borrowers is similar to the cost of yield premiums discounted by Treasuries flat. Investors see no change in their bond payments (i.e., it is as if the mortgages were locked out for the entire term). Thus unlike yield maintenance agreements there is no issue of how to allocate prepayment penalty proceeds among various tranches in the deal.

The replacement of mortgages with Treasuries or other high quality securities[14] also improves the credit quality of the deal possibly leading to upgrades. Also the investor is not required to pay additional taxes since no prepayment penalties are distributed. Commercial mortgages are typically locked out for 3-4 years after which time the borrower can then defease the loan.

Yield Maintenance Agreement
The yield maintenance penalty is designed to compensate the lender for the early retirement of principal. If prevailing interest rates are lower than when the loan was originated, prepayment will cause the investor to reinvest at a lower rate and lose interest income. The yield maintenance penalty calculates the present value of this

---

[14] Fannie Mae allows borrowers to defease FNMA DUS MBS with FNMA debentures.

lost income, and imposes this amount as a prepayment disincentive to the borrower and protection to the investor. If current interest rates are higher than when the loan was originated, there is generally no penalty and the investor is not worse off because he can reinvest at higher rates. In many cases, the yield maintenance penalty equals the present value of the future cash flows of the commercial loan discounted by the yield of the Treasury with an average life equal to the remaining term of the commercial loan. In this case yield maintenance is truly a prepayment penalty since the lender or investor receives more than the present value of the lost income.

One of the most important issues concerning yield maintenance is the allocation of proceeds to the various tranches in a commercial mortgage deal. Depending on the formula or methodology all tranches may not be made whole. The simplest way to understand this is to realize that the average yield of all of the bonds in a CMBS deal is unlikely to be the same as the coupon on the loan that is being prepaid. The shape of the Treasury yield curve typically changes so that short and long bond yields as well as the yields of the underlying loans will all be different after origination when prepayments occur requiring different levels of compensation. Since the yield maintenance penalty is designed to generate sufficient cash flow to compensate for the foregone interest of the prepaid loan, not the foregone average yield of all the bonds in a deal, the proceeds of the penalty may be more or less than necessary to compensate all bondholders.

There are a number of methods that try to distribute the penalty in the most equitable fashion, but most favor one bond class or another under various circumstances. The three most common ones are the principal allocation method, the base interest fraction method and bond side yield maintenance.[15]

Prepayment Penalty Points

The least common type of call protection, the prepayment penalty points method is often expressed as a percentage of the mortgage balance. Unlike the yield maintenance penalty, it is unrelated to prevailing interest rates, and is expressed as a fixed percentage of the prepaid balance. There are many variations in the magnitude and schedule of prepayment penalty points. Typically, the prepayment penalty points decline with loan age, and goes to zero after a certain point. A common type of percentage premium is the 5-4-3-2-1-% each year for five years after the loan lock-out ends. Prepayment penalty points are generally regarded as a weak form of prepayment protection, due to their short time frame and the fact that the amount of the penalty is usually much less than if it were calculated using most yield maintenance methods. However, they may be superior in rising rate environments. For example, the prepayment penalty resulting from yield maintenance could be zero if rates rise high enough, whereas it would still be significant if the penalty were calculated as a percentage of the mortgage balance.

---

[15] Principal allocation percentage method considered the simplest method, allocates the yield maintenance penalty in proportion to the amount of prepayment principal that each bond receives. These methods are explained in Chapter 24.

Lockout and defeasance are the most desirable form of call protection; yield maintenance is slightly less desirable; percent penalties are generally the least desirable form of call protection. Investors should get a breakdown of the collateral pool by type of call protection and take note as to how large the average open prepay window is (the period between the expiration of call protection and loan maturity).

The simplest way to get a quick sense for how call protected a deal is, is to look at yield tables that show prepay speeds of 0 CPR to 100 CPR applying the speeds on a loan level basis after any lockout, defeasance, or yield maintenance period expires. How the average life of the bond changes will give a good indication of how well protected the collateral of a pool is. As a general rule, a change in average life of less than one half year when speeds range from 0 CPR to 100 CPR would indicate "decent" call protection.

Call protection provided by commercial mortgages varies widely. In older CMBS pools, the underlying loans may include all sorts of call protection. In newer transactions, a given pool's call protection tends to be more consistent. Prepayment terms may include combinations of lock-outs, penalties, or Treasury defeasance.

Finally the investor should be aware that in a strong real estate market and falling rate environment, loans with anything but lockouts and defeasance might be prepaid even with very large prepayment penalties. There are a number of reasons for this. The prepayment penalty is tax deductible for the borrower which reduces its "sting". The penalty may be financed such that the loan payments on the new borrowed amount even including the penalty may be lower than the original payments. Finally and most importantly if the borrower, often a real estate developer, can cash out a significant amount of equity from a property through refinancing he will do so regardless of the penalty.

Imagine the case where a developer pays $5 million for a property and borrows $3 million to finance it. Several years later rents rise, rates fall, the property's value increases to $8 million and the prepayment penalty is $500,000. If the borrower can get a new loan for $5 million, he can pay off the old loan ($3 million), finance the penalty ($500,000) and take out $1.5 million which would give him a 75% return on his equity investment. In addition, he can get a tax deduction for $500,000. He can then take the $1.5 million, borrow more money, develop another property and start all over again. If rates have fallen enough, the increase in his monthly loan payments may easily be supported by higher rents. For example if rates fell from 8.5% to 6%, annual interest payments on the old mortgage would be $255,000 ($3,000,000 × 8.5%) versus $300,000 ($5,000,000 × 6%) on the new larger loan.

HOW CMBS TRADE

Because of their excellent prepayment protection and sensitivity to credit risk, highest quality investment grade CMBS (AAAs through As) tend to trade more like corporate bonds than residential MBS. In general they tend to be more sensitive to changes in swap levels (which tend to reflect A/AA rated corporates) and credit spreads than interest rate levels. Most Wall Street firms, conduits and many investors in the sector use swaps to hedge their positions. The relationship between swap levels and CMBS spreads is apparent in Exhibit 7. During the bond market panic between August and November of 1998, due to the difficulty in pricing deals over Treasuries, a number of new issues were priced at a spread to swaps.

However, investment grade CMBS tend to widen more than non-callable corporate bonds as their price increases over par. The reason is investor concern over a default-induced prepayment. Unlike a regular prepayment, which is either forbidden due to lock out or compensated for in the case of prepayment penalties, yield maintenance or Treasury defeasance, the CMBS investor usually receives his cash back at par without compensation if the prepayment was caused by a default (assuming the cash is available). For example, in early May 1999, a high quality 10 year AAA CMBS (one with low subordination at origination) would trade 2 bps wider if it had a 103 "handle"[16] than if it had a par "handle." The spread would widen by about another 2 bps/point until a 105 "handle" after which the spread would widen by about 3 bps per point.

For lower quality triple As (ones with higher subordination levels at origination), the widening would be greater due to the greater probability of a default induced prepayment. In contrast, single A and higher rated 10 year non-callable corporate bonds typically would not experience widening until their handles hit 110 in which case the spread might widen one or two basis points. Residential MBS (RMBS) of course experience far greater widening than CMBS. For example in early May, the spread between a par GNMA passthrough and a GNMA pass through with a 103 handle was about 28 bps.

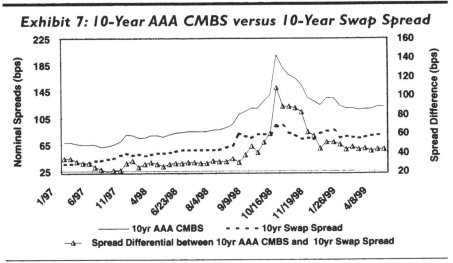

Exhibit 7: 10-Year AAA CMBS versus 10-Year Swap Spread

————— 10yr AAA CMBS   - - - - 10yr Swap Spread
—△— Spread Differential between 10yr AAA CMBS and 10yr Swap Spread

---

[16] For real estate participants that are new to the bond market, "handle" refers to that part of a bond's price that is valued in points. For example, a bond priced at 102:16 would have a 102 "handle." A bond priced at 100:12 would have a "par handle."

Exhibit 8: 10-Year AAA CMBS versus 10-Year A Corporates and 10-Year Swaps

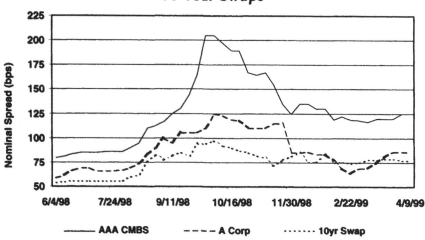

In addition, CMBS average lives can extend if the borrower cannot make his balloon payment and has to work out an arrangement with the servicer. It is important to note however that in both cases CMBS are not nearly as negatively convex as RMBS as either event is not necessarily correlated with a change in interest rates.

Because of this average life and price risk, CMBS tend to trade at wider spreads than same rated and same average life corporate bonds (see Exhibit 8). In addition, the nature of CMBS collateral can pose a greater analytical challenge than corporate debt. Although detailed property information is now readily available[17] because conduit CMBS tend to be collateralized by a hundred and often more property loans, investors have to rely more on agency ratings rather than analyzing in detail the different properties. In contrast, the financial statements of corporations can be more easily analyzed.

Although the multiple loans of CMBS deals can pose a greater analytical challenge, they can offer the advantage over corporates of "slow motion" credit deterioration. The large number of loans in a deal often offers the investor the time to act if one or two start to become delinquent. With corporate bonds event risk can suddenly trigger a rating downgrade. In addition, the paydown of individual loans can result in the deleveraging of a deal so that subordination increases and a tranche is upgraded.

Spread differences between corporate bullet bonds and CMBS can also arise due to the presence of amortizing loans in a CMBS. The market currently tends to calculate spreads in both the CMBS and corporate bond markets on the

---

[17] For example, Charter Research's Conquest allows investors to look at the loan level detail in each deal.

same basis (the difference between the yield of the security and the yield of the nearest equivalent average life Treasury benchmark). However, while calculation of the spread of the bullet corporate versus one point on the Treasury curve is reasonable since the bulk of the corporate bond's cash flow occurs on the bullet date, amortizing CMBS cash flows are spread out along the Treasury curve. Calculating their spread to one point on the Treasury curve can be misleading. Because some of the cash flows occur after the average life of the CMBS bond and some before, these cash flows should be compared with corresponding equivalent maturity Treasury cash flows. The best method to compare bullet and amortizing security spreads is to compare their cash flow spread or Z spread.[18] Thus, it may be important to compare the cash flow spread (or zero volatility OAS) of CMBS and corporate bonds, particularly in a steep yield curve environment.

CMBS also tend to trade differently than corporates for a number of technical reasons. For example, while liquidity was limited in other bond markets between August and December 1998, the situation was exacerbated in the CMBS market by two factors.

First, unlike corporates, CMBS dealers warehouse collateral originated by their conduits. A CMBS dealer can be exposed to a billion dollars or more of commercial mortgages for 3 to 6 months which have to be warehoused until there is sufficient size to do a securitization. If spreads begin to widen, this collateral can represent a significant exposure to the sector. In the fall, many dealers already had substantial exposure to the sector when investors had to liquidate securities. In contrast, corporate dealers are not long collateral. They are more able to provide liquidity in a crunch. New issuance in the corporate market is underwritten on an agency basis, not as a principal. Today, this is less of a problem in the CMBS market as dealers more carefully manage their loan inventories through faster and smaller deal issuance. This keeps the gestation period and inventory for deals at lower levels thereby enabling dealers to provide more liquidity to the market.

Second, short-term leverage hampered some substantial investors in both investment grade and non-investment grade CMBS. Highly leveraged hedge funds played a significant role in the AAA CMBS sector, while mortgage REITs, also leveraged players, had an even more dominant role in the non-investment grade sector. In fact, most mortgage REITS used repo debt to lever their holdings, effectively lending long and borrowing short. As spreads widened, margin calls pulled these positions apart. The below investment grade market spiraled downward, as falling values and margin calls reinforced each other. Less leveraged sectors were not as susceptible. This situation while still present in CMBS, is gradually improving as newer, less leveraged investors enter both the investment and non-investment grade CMBS sectors.

---

[18] Also called the zero-volatility option-adjusted spread (OAS). This cash flow spread is that spread which when added to all of the Treasury spot rates corresponding to the cash flows of the CMBS, discount the CMBS cash flows back to the present value of the CMBS.

Exhibit 9: Selected Triple-A CMBS Bonds

Deal	Offer (4/26/99)	% Subordination at Orig/Now	Coupon	WAL/ Window	Bid/Offer
BSCMS 1999-C1 A2	110/Cur	22.5/22.535	6.02	9.63(5/08-2/09)	2 bps
MSC 1999-WF1 A2	111/Cur	23.0/23.035	6.21	9.31(4/08-9/08)	2 bps
CHASE 1998-1 A2	114/Cur	27.0/27.245	6.56	8.81(12/06-5/08)	3 bps
JPMC 1998-C6 A3	120/Cur	29.0/29.389	6.61	8.65(7/07-1/08)	3 bps
DLJCM 1998-CF1 A1B	120/Cur	29.5/29.816	6.59	8.89(2/08-2/08)	3 bps
MSC 1998-XL1 A3	125/Cur	27.5/27.718	6.48	8.73(4/07-5/08)	4 bps
MCFI 1998-MC3 A2	124/Cur	30.5/31.09	6.34	9.03(9/07-7/08)	4 bps
GSMS 1998-C1 A2	128/Cur	30.5/30.65	6.62	9.09(7/07-10/08)	4 bps
CMAT 1999-C1 A3	130/Cur	28.5/28.5	6.56	9.88(7/08-9/10)	5 bps

Within the CMBS sector, similarly rated CMBS with similar average life can trade at spreads as different as 20 bps. As shown in Exhibit 9, 10-year AAA bonds traded as tight as 110 bps (Bear Stearns 1999-C1 A2s) to as wide as 130 bps (Commercial Mortgage Asset Trust 1999-C1 A3s). For example, AAA bonds that at issue have lower subordination because of the strong credit quality of the collateral, such as bank names,[19] trade between 5 bps and 20 bps tighter than other names. The reason for this is the concern of a default-induced prepayment. The rating agencies AAA rating certifies only an expectation that the investor in the AAA will get his money back not when. Therefore the market is more concerned about a default-induced prepayment if the collateral is of such low quality that high subordination levels are required.

Liquidity concerns can also cause spread tiering. Given the experiences of many last fall, liquidity concerns are still understandably paramount in the minds of many. For example, 10-year AAA tranches of Nomura (Capital Company of America-CMAT 1999-C1 A3) at this writing trade 10 to 20 bps wider than other paper because of the firm's exit from the CMBS market and market concerns that there will be less support for secondary trading activity in the paper. These concerns have increasingly lead to joint issuer deals to reassure investors that several firms will make markets in a deal after it is issued.

While liquidity is critical and bonds with tighter bid/offer spreads tend to trade at tighter offer spreads, this certainly doesn't explain all of the extra spread the market currently demands for certain bonds. For example, the difference between the bid/offer spread of MSC 1999-WF1A2s (2 bps) and that of GSMS 1998-C1A2s (4 bps) is only 2 bps, yet the latter is offered 17 bps wider. Clearly liquidity alone as represented by bid/offer spreads does not explain the large spread differentials.

How well a "name" trades and has traded versus other "names," currently seems to be as important or more important than fundamental value. For example, the current market "wisdom" is that bank issues should trade better than

---

[19] Bank names currently tend to trade tighter than many conduit names because there is a perception that banks have more of a "credit culture" than conduits.

many issues generated by Wall Street conduits or some investment banks, on the theory that commercial banks have more of a "credit culture."

While we would argue and agree that 10 year AAAs backed by high quality collateral should trade tighter than AAAs backed by lower quality collateral due to cash flow uncertainty this is not always the case in the market. While Bear Stearns, BSCMS 1999 C1 A2s justifiably trade tighter than Chase and First Union due to the high quality of the collateral (see Exhibit 9), bank deals do tend to trade tighter than investment bank conduit deals. For example, Chase and First Union AAA bonds tend to trade at the tight end of the spectrum while those at the wide end are all investment bank deals, with Nomura's trading the widest.

However whether all bank deals are of better quality is questionable. For example, 1.04% of NLFC 98-1, a deal originated by NationsBank, is either 30 or 60 days delinquent, an additional 0.29% is 90 days or more delinquent and 2.73% of the deal is being specially serviced. Using the "percent subordination at origination" as an objective indicator of the credit quality of the underlying collateral, Chase 1998-1 A2 and JPMC 1998-C6 A3 had about the same or greater subordination at origination as compared with DLJCM 1998-CF1 A1Bs and MSC 1998 XL1 A3s (see Exhibit 9). Yet they trade as much as 11 bps tighter. Even the window of MSC 1998-XL1 A3s is about the same as the bank deals and the DLJ tranche has a bullet window, which is narrower. For investors willing to break out of the herd mentality and look through the name and to the fundamental credit quality of a deal, there is significant value to be found.

WHO SHOULD INVEST IN TRIPLE -A CMBS

A wide variety of investors should consider investing in CMBS including corporate bond buyers, insurance companies, pension funds, and state funds, money managers versus an index, as well as banks. CMBS offer significantly greater spread than lower rated corporate bonds yet can have excellent call protection and average life stability. In addition, they can help diversify portfolio risk. While insurance companies and banks were initially the largest investors in higher rated CMBS, money managers are becoming increasingly important. And with the entry of the Lehman CMBS index into its Aggregate index we expect more pension funds and state funds to increase their current investments as well. Finally, U.S. CMBS can offer non-U.S. investors significant opportunity. Commercial loan capitalization rates in the U.S are typically higher than those in Europe. As such U.S. CMBS may offer better rates of return than those available in Europe.

ERISA Eligibility

ERISA is the Employee Retirement Income Security Act of 1974, the federal law that regulates private-sector employee benefit plans, including pension plans. Various funds may be subject to ERISA or to parallel provisions in Section 4975 of the Internal Revenue Code, including:

- any employee benefit plan or other retirement plan or arrangement, including individual retirement accounts and annuities, Keogh plans, and collective investment funds;
- insurance company separate accounts and (in some cases) insurance company general accounts in which such plans, accounts or arrangements are invested; and
- any entity the assets of which include assets of such a plan.

Persons with discretionary authority over such plans and accounts should carefully review with their legal advisors whether the purchase and holding of Commercial Mortgage Pass-Through Certificates is permitted under ERISA, the Internal Revenue Code and applicable guidelines. In general ERISA imposes certain restrictions and may prohibit certain transactions between employee benefit plans and "parties-in-interest" which may include the service providers in a securitization. Generally, these prohibited transaction rules may apply to the purchase of CMBS and to the operation of the asset pool backing such Commercial Mortgage Pass-Through Certificates.

Certain employee benefit plans, such as governmental and church plans, may not be subject to ERISA restrictions. State and local government plans, however, may be subject to similar restrictions under applicable State laws.

Exemptions granted by the U.S. Department of Labor permit ERISA plans to purchase certain certificates and relieve the operation of the underlying asset pool from application of the prohibited transaction rules of ERISA. The principal exemption applicable to the Commercial Mortgage Pass-Through Certificates is the Underwriter Exemption, which makes ERISA-eligible the senior-most Certificates of a series of Commercial Mortgage Pass-Through Certificates as long as certain conditions are met, including that these Certificates are rated in one of the three highest rating categories by a rating agency.

Subordinate classes of Certificates generally are not ERISA-eligible. Insurance company general accounts, however, may be permitted to purchase subordinate Certificates. Under an amendment to ERISA adopted in 1996, after the Supreme Court's Harris Trust decision, insurance company general accounts are generally exempt from ERISA's plan asset and prohibited transaction rules pending issuance of final regulations by the U.S. Department of Labor. Regulations regarding the application of ERISA to insurance company general accounts have been proposed but are not yet final. Insurance company general accounts may be permitted to purchase subordinate Commercial Mortgage Pass-Through Certificates if they meet the requirements of Prohibited Transaction Class Exemption 95-60. Insurance companies should review these requirements with their legal advisors.

SMMEA Eligibility

A mortgage-backed security is SMMEA eligible if it qualifies as a "mortgage related security" under the Secondary Mortgage Market Enhancement Act of

1984 (as amended by Section 347 of the Riegle Community Development and Regulatory Act of 1994 "SMMEA"). SMMEA amends several federal banking laws and securities laws with respect to mortgage related securities to, among other things, (1) relax the margin requirements previously imposed by the Securities Exchange Act of 1934, (2) remove restrictions on investment in private mortgage-backed securities by federally-chartered depository institutions, savings and loan associations and credit unions previously subject to regulatory limitations and (3) preempt state legal investment laws and blue sky laws which previously limited investment in private mortgage-backed securities by state-chartered financial institutions and required registration under the various state securities laws.

The 1994 Amendment to SMMEA, which became effective on December 31, 1996, added securities backed by mortgages secured by commercial structures to the definition of securities subject to SMMEA eligibility. In order to qualify as a mortgage related security, the security must be rated in one of the two highest rating categories by at least one nationally recognized credit-rating agency (i.e., Duff & Phelps, Fitch IBCA, Moody's or S&P) and the mortgage loans backing the security must meet certain criteria.

In general, (1) the related mortgage note (or similar instrument) must be secured by a first lien on (A) a single parcel of real estate, in the case of property on which is located residential structure or (B) one or more parcels of real estate, in the case of property on which is located multifamily or commercial structures and (2) the mortgage loan must be originated by an institution supervised and examined by federal or state authority or by a mortgage lender approved by the secretary of the Department of Housing and Urban Development (HUD). The staff of the Division of Market Regulation of the Securities and Exchange Commission (SEC) has issued several no-action letters discussing the requirements a mortgage-backed security must meet in order to be considered SMMEA eligible.

THE LEHMAN CMBS INDEX: IMPACT ON THE MARKET

The introduction of the Lehman CMBS index on January 1, 1999 should benefit the CMBS market. The index provides a measurable benchmark against which all industry participants may be judged and may impose greater discipline on portfolio lenders. To the extent that both CMBS investors and portfolio lenders are benched against the index, this creates greater efficiency and transparency between these two major groups of lenders.

To the extent market participants can short the index to hedge positions, this will help reduce risk for conduits warehousing loans. Lehman Bros. swap group is reportedly working on developing a swap based on their new index. While there is the risk that many market participants will all want to go one way (i.e. shorting the index), Lehman Bros. noted that they have seen two way interest. Some investors who do not have the manpower to analyze each individual

CMBS sector may want to go long with respect to it in order to beat the Lehman Aggregate Fixed Income Index.

Lehman Brothers will also include part of the CMBS index in their Aggregate index on July 1, 1999. This should be a plus as it will bring in a number of investors that have not invested in CMBS before but need to be weighted in the sector. We expect that this could bring in another $3 billion to $5 billion of new money primarily from pension funds which often use the aggregate index as a performance measure. Initially, CMBS will make up only about 1% of the Aggregate Index, however given the long average maturities of CMBS this percentage should grow significantly over time.

The Lehman CMBS Index: Description

The Lehman CMBS index actually consists of three independent indices: a CMBS investment grade index which includes CMBS classes rated Baa3 or higher,[20] a CMBS high yield index which includes classes rated Ba1 or lower and NR classes as well as private certificates; and a CMBS IO index which includes all ratings and private certificates. A combination of all three indices comprises the commercial whole loan index. The size and number of classes in each index are shown in Exhibit 10.

To be included in the indices, classes must be denominated in U.S. dollars, have an average life of at least one year, be from a deal with an original size of at least $500 million and a current deal balance of at least $300 million. Conduit, fusion and large loan deals are included while agency deals, floaters and residual classes are excluded. All certificates must be fixed, capped WAC or WAC bonds.

Exhibit 10: Lehman Bros. CMBS Index*

Rating	Number of Classes	Market Value ($ mm)	% of Total
Investment Grade			
AAA	158	$53,405	79.8%
AA	63	$4,094	6.1%
A	66	$4,182	6.2%
BBB	117	$5,269	7.9%
Total	404	$66,949	100.0%
High Yield			
BB	134	$3,188	67.8%
B	119	$1,199	25.5%
NR	79	$315	6.7%
Total	332	$4,702	100.0%
I/O Classes			
Total	90	$4421	100>%

[20] Moody's will be the primary rating agency. If the bonds are unrated by Moody's, Lehman will look first to Standard and Poor's, then Fitch and Duff and Phelps. Private certificates are excluded.

Month to date index returns calculated using Lehman's models consist of price return, coupon return, paydown return, and prepayment premium return and will be calculated weekly and at month end. Pricing will occur on Friday at 3:00 PM using a pricing speed of 0. If the market begins pricing deals with a speed then that speed will be used.

SUMMARY

The CMBS market is currently in transition. The dislocations caused by spread widening last year while unsettling to some have set the market up for what we believe will be a favorable year. The market is young and growing pains are to be expected. New investors continue to enter the sector searching for the investment opportunities brought about by the dislocations, the ability to diversify their bond portfolios or because CMBS are now a part of the Lehman Aggregate index. Whatever the reason, we hope this chapter will serve as a useful point of entry and framework to discover the opportunities in the AAA sector.

APPENDIX

GENERAL OVERVIEW OF RATING AGENCY APPROACHES

DCR's Approach to Rating Commercial Mortgage-Backed Securities[21]

Duff and Phelps Credit Rating Co. (DCR) has been rating commercial mortgage-backed securities (CMBS) since the mid-1980s. What follows is an overview of our methodology for assigning CMBS ratings.

Typically, the rating process begins with a preliminary analysis of the loan pool. DCR provides preliminary feedback on an anticipated mortgage loan pool based upon the quantitative and qualitative characteristics of the pool. Quantitative characteristics include the debt service coverage (DSCR) and the loan-to-value (LTV) ratios of the loans. Qualitative factors include the strength of the originator's policies and procedures, number of loans, structure of the borrowers, diversification by property type, location, borrower and loan size, property age and loan seasoning.

Depending on the type of CMBS transaction (e.g., conduit, seasoned loan, credit-tenant lease, large loan), we have specific approaches through which the quantitative and qualitative characteristics of a pool can be analyzed. In a preliminary analysis, we will reduce the cash flows and estimate values by applying selected capitalization rates by property type. The reductions in cash flows are based on either past experience with the originator, when available, or 5%.

Once DCR is selected to rate the transaction, the analysis of the pool begins. Following are highlights of the steps taken in the rating process.

Sample

A representative sample of loans from the pool is selected to be inspected and analyzed. If the transaction is a large loan deal, DCR inspects and analyzes the cash flows and values of substantially all of the properties in the pool. For conduit transactions, the sample is dependent on the number of loans and the mortgage loan balance of the transaction. Typically, between 75-120 properties are inspected, resulting in a sample of approximately 50-65% of the pool by mortgage loan balance.

DCR's sample includes the 10 largest loans, with the remainder being a representative sample based on property type, geographic distribution and loan balance. Small loans are included in the sample to ensure that the same underwriting standards are applied regardless of loan size. Lastly, if the deal contains loans from more than one contributor, a representative sample is chosen from each. The sample composition will closely mirror the composition of the total pool.

---

[21] Duff and Phelp's contributed this section.

Travel/Site Inspections

After the sample is chosen, site inspections are performed to provide a better understanding of a property and the market in which it is located. Focus is placed on the quality and competitiveness of the property, the expertise of management, the surrounding neighborhood and new construction or vacant land in the area. Based on the site inspection, DCR scores the property. The quality score is a component used in determining the capitalization rate that will be applied to DCR's cash flow to derive value. Also, the scores provide an indication of the property quality of the overall pool.

Management Meetings

For large loan transactions, single borrower transactions and significant borrower concentrations within a conduit, DCR conducts meetings with the senior management of the borrower. The purpose of these meetings is to explore management's experience, operating style, business plan for the asset(s) in the pool, historical financial trends for the company and future growth plans. The management meetings allow us to achieve a better understanding of the current tenant profile, tenant leasing status and strategies, and rent default issues.

Third-Party Reports

Third-party due diligence materials, including the appraisal, environmental, engineering and seismic reports, are reviewed. In the appraisal review, DCR focuses on the market analysis of the property as well as the trade area. Emphasis is placed on historical and future trends impacting the property and its competitiveness relative to comparable properties. The appraisal provides market income and expense data including historical and budgeted operating statements, income and expense comparables, rent estimates, tenant improvement allowances and leasing commissions. DCR looks to comparable sales data in selecting the appropriate capitalization rate and in determining value.

The environmental reports or summaries on all of the properties are reviewed to assess whether there are issues that would adversely impact the property. It is expected that Phase I reports will follow ASTM guidelines with an additional level of review to include asbestos-containing materials, lead-based paint and radon. To the extent the engineer makes recommendations to resolve any environmental conditions, we will review those recommendations and confirm that the proposals are being implemented. If DCR is uncomfortable with the environmental situation, either the cap rate will be increased or we will estimate an increased loss severity for the loan.

The property condition report is reviewed to assess the adequacy of the utilities and the structural condition and soundness of the heating, ventilating and air conditioning, as well as fire, life and safety systems. DCR also examines compliance with zoning and building codes and other appropriate governmental requirements, flood plain status and an overall evaluation of the construction quality, design and appearance. The report should contain estimates of both the immediate repair and replacement costs for these items and a summary of the repair or replacement costs that will be needed over the next 12 years (assuming a 10-year loan term) on an inflationary basis. DCR uses the evaluation of capital improvements planned, expected or needed to determine the appropriate capital reserve requirement.

Finally, we examine the seismic reports to identify properties with significant seismic exposure. The probable maximum loss (PML) should be calculated based on a 10% likelihood of occurrence over the next 50 years based on a 475-year lookback period. We address the risk of having a PML in excess of 20% on properties without earthquake insurance by reducing DCR's value by the amount in excess of 20%.

Originator Review

As part of the qualitative aspects of the rating process, DCR conducts a review of each originator and examines, among other issues, the originator's borrower due diligence and credit reviews, cash flow verification process, lease reviews, policy and procedures manuals, training of employees, third-party selections and review process and employee incentive compensations. In addition, the review will be updated for each new transaction to determine whether there have been any changes to the originator's policies and procedures.

Determination of NCF and Value

Once the data gathering/field work is completed, DCR analyzes the cash flows and values of the properties in the sample. Our net cash flow (NCF) is determined by analyzing the historical performance of each sampled property using the DCR Underwriting Guidelines matrix (for a copy, call (312) 368-3198 or visit the DCR Web site at http://www.dcrco.com.)

For properties with short-term leases, such as multifamily and self storage, trailing 12-month revenue is used to determine an appropriate income amount. For properties with longer-term leases, such as office, retail and industrial, DCR looks to contractual rents in place for tenants in occupancy and marks rents to market on a lease-by-lease basis.

Vacancy deductions are generally the higher of actual, market or the DCR minimum vacancy parameter by property type. Vacancy will be further increased to take into account new construction. Management fees are generally the higher of DCR parameters, market or actual. Leasing commissions and tenant improvement allowances are generally the higher of DCR parameters or market. Value is determined by applying an appropriate capitalization rate to DCR's adjusted NCF. The average NCF and value variances from our analysis are then applied to the nonsampled assets by property type and contributor, if applicable.

Additionally, in determining the appropriate debt service for the property, DCR shortens the amortization schedules of the loans to reflect the age and estimated remaining economic life of the properties. These amortization adjustments artificially stress the DSCR of the properties with the greatest likelihood of obsolescence.

Determination of Credit Enhancement Levels

Once a normalized NCF and value are determined for each property in the pool, the cash flows and values are run through the appropriate model, which sizes each loan based on the more constraining of its DSCR and LTV.

For floating-rate transactions, DCR generally stresses the debt constant on the underlying mortgages up to the interest rate lifetime caps. The level of stress is dependent on the rating category and loan term.

Large loan transactions and micro loan transactions (i.e., loans less than $1 million) are analyzed differently. Large loan transactions are sized like typical conduits but with adjustments for lower diversification because each loan typically comprises a greater percentage of the total pool. The larger the loan concentration, the greater the single event risk and, therefore, the greater the concentration penalty.

Micro loan transactions benefit from total diversification but are typically penalized due to the reduced level of third-party due diligence, lesser quality of information in the asset summaries and lack of impounds, cash controls and borrower structure.

In addition, DCR stratifies the pool across several different statistics including, but not limited to, DSCR, LTV, loan size, geographic locations and property type. Particular focus is placed on the percentage of the pool that is less than 1.20X DSCR and more than an 80% LTV. The stratification analysis results help us to better evaluate the pool by identifying both positive and negative concentrations.

Parties to the Transaction

The performance of the certificates is dependent, to an extent, on the performance of certain parties: the master servicer, special servicer and trustee. DCR does not rate these parties but approves them on a transaction-specific basis. We believe this is the most efficient way to ensure that a particular party has the expertise needed for a specific transaction and has adequate personnel in place for each new deal.

Legal Documents

DCR reviews the relevant legal documents for each rated transaction to understand, among other issues, the distribution of cash flow, the relative responsibilities of the parties to the transaction and the strength of the representation and warranties of the mortgage loan seller. The legal documents typically include the Prospectus and/or Private Placement Memorandum, the True Sale Opinion, the Mortgage Loan Purchase Agreement and the Pooling and Servicing Agreement.

Final Committee

Once the pool analysis and legal review are completed, the transaction is presented to credit committee to determine final ratings. The presentation provides an overview of the collateral and the deal structure.

Publications

Prior to Transaction Closing

• Investor Call

To describe our analysis, DCR hosts a conference call for all interested potential investors. The call gives investors an opportunity to gain a better understanding of our rating approach on the transaction and to obtain additional insight into some of the larger loans.

• Preliminary Financing Report

The Preliminary Financing Report (PFR), gives a written description of DCR's analysis. The PFR describes the parties to the transaction, summarizes key statistics such as DCR's DSCR and LTV, and the geographic, property type and other relevant concentrations. It also describes the largest loans in the pool and discusses our approach to analyzing them. Lastly, it provides a summary of strengths and weaknesses/risks of the transaction and mitigants to these concerns. The PFR is available for distribution on the day of the investor call and is available on DCR's web site at www.dcrco.com.

Post Transaction Closing

• Press Release

DCR announces the rating of the transaction through a press release on the day the deal closes. The press release provides investors with the rating and subordination level associated with each class and also gives an abbreviated description of our analysis.

• Financing Report

The Financing Report (FR) is a final version of the PFR, including any changes that may have occurred subsequent to its initial release. Once the FR is published, it replaces the PFR on DCR's web site.

Fitch IBCA's Approach to Rating Commercial Mortgage Securities

Commercial mortgage-backed securities (CMBS) enable an issuer to aggregate cash flow from numerous loans secured by diverse commercial properties, structure the priority of payments, and sell bonds with ratings that match investor risk tolerance. The formation of a rating is a statistical analysis of credit risk. Subordination of various tranches or classes is the most common and often the only form of credit enhancement.

CMBS can be composed of either new loans originated for the purpose of securitization (conduits) or seasoned loans from an existing portfolio. Recent CMBS polled transaction ranged from $100 million to almost $4 billion.

Fitch IBCA's credit analysis includes a reunderwriting of real estate assets and stressing of loan terms to refinance constants. The rating incorporates a review of the quantitative aspects of the collateral, as well as an assessment of the financial and legal structure of the CMBS transaction. This report outlines Fitch IBCA's methodology for rating transactions backed by pools of performing commercial mortgages. It also summarizes data requirements, the due diligence process, and the legal and structural issues considered in a transaction.

Fitch IBCA Model Overview

Fitch IBCA's performing loan model is predicated on research indicating that debt service coverage ratios (DSCRs) are the best indicators of loan default and that a loan with a high DSCR is less likely to default than a loan with a DSCR below 1.00 times (×). Fitch IBCA begins its modeling analysis by calculating DSCRs assuming an "A" stress environment. The default probability and loss severity assumptions based on the DSCR for each loan are adjusted based on certain property and loan features to determine credit enhancement based on individual loan characteristics. Next, the composition of the pool is analyzed to identify any concentration risks. Finally, the transaction structure is evaluated and incorporated into the ratings. The results are further adjusted to reflect various stresses from "AAA" to "B." The final credit enhancement levels for a transaction equal the sum of the loan-by-loan expected loss based on DSCR analysis plus or minus adjustments (add-ons) for particular asset characteristics, pool concentration issues, and deal structure requirements.[22] A sample credit enhancement is shown below:

I. Base Credit Enhancement
    Aggregate Loan Level Expected Loss
        Based on Fitch IBCA Stressed DSCR   14
II. Adjustments (Plus or Minus)
        Asset Analysis   2

---

[22] This section is excepted from Fitch IBCA's 9/18/98 report, *Performing Loan Securitization*, which contains a more complete review of their approach.

Moody's Approach to Rating
Commercial Mortgage Securities[23]

For most structured transactions, Moody's seeks to ensure that the credit support protects bond holders from levels of default frequency and loss severity consistent with a given rating. Moody's approach to establishing the credit support level for commercial real estate is by necessity, somewhat more qualitative than for other structured finance assets. Only a limited amount of dependable long-term performance data is available, and the data that is available is seldom on point with the facts of the transaction being rated.

To demonstrate the order of magnitude of commercial real estate (CRE) credit support, a pool of seasoned life insurance company quality loans might require a 25% credit support to receive a Aa rating. This would protect an investor from a scenario in which 50% of the loans defaulted and in which the defaulting loans lost 50% of their value. In contrast, an Resolution Trust Co. (RTC) commercial real estate pool may require credit support as high as 45% to achieve a Aa rating, which would protect an investor from default rates as high as 90% combined with 50% losses on the defaulting loans.

Moody's approach to developing credit support for a pool is to first assign a credit support level consistent with the highest requested rating to each property in the pool and then to take the weighted-average credit support of all the properties and adjust it for portfolio factors. The credit support that we assign to each loan is a function of Moody's assessment of the probability of default and severity of loss for a given property. Loans with high debt service coverages and low LTVs require little credit support, as some is already built into the loan in the form of borrower's equity.

Moody's also adjusts credit support to reflect our opinion of the relative quality of a given asset within its class, with the closest scrutiny given to individual assets and to smaller pools. Among our concerns are:

• Location,
• Creditworthiness of tenants.
• Terms of the tenants in occupancy,
• Physical condition.

As part of the review process, Moody's verifies physical condition through inspection reports, site visits, and engineering studies.

Default Frequency
The key factor in Moody's assessment of potential frequency of default is the debt service coverage (DSC) of a loan. Loans with debt service coverage ratios below 1.00 are expected to have a high frequency of default, as borrowers cannot be expected to fund losses indefinitely.

---

[23] This section was contributed by Moody's Investor Services.

Loans with debt service coverage ratios above 1.00 have a lower likelihood of default because they have a built-in excess cash flow buffer available which would have to erode before the borrower would experience losses and consider defaulting. For example, a property with a 1.20 DSC should be able to withstand a decline in gross income of 10% before hitting break-even, assuming that its expenses are 40% of income.

Loss Severity

The key determinant of severity of loss is the potential for decline in the value of the property securing a given loan. Moody's studied data from most of the major US markets since 1980, which helped us determine how far rents can fall and vacancies can rise in order to establish potential severity ceilings. With this data, we've created sample proformas that we use to size the resulting declines in net income and value from the peak of the market to the trough.

However, a mitigating factor in our assessment of potential severity is the current LTV ratio of a given loan, because part of any potential decline can be absorbed by built-in overcollateralization.

Another mitigating factor is our assessment of the strength of a specific market and its potential for declines. In most cases, we are not using the full potential peak-to-trough decline as a severity adjustment, giving some credit for the substantial declines that have already taken place. We generally do not lower the severity adjustment to minimal levels, however, because we like to have protection against false bottoms and other unforeseen circumstances.

The Role of NOI

The net operating income (NOI) of a property is what drives debt service coverage and LTV; therefore, we are extremely sensitive to the quality of the NOI that the issuer/underwriter supplies for a transaction. The optimal situation is to have audited historic NOIs for each property in a pool, together with a mark-to-market scenario that indicates the NOIs potential for rising or falling in the near term.

These data are not always available for each transaction that Moody's rates, and we make conservative assumptions when it is missing. When the transaction involves a single property or a small pool, we give each income statement additional scrutiny and make additional deductions for items such as vacancy, management fees, and capital expenditures. We place little or no reliance on "annualized" or projected income estimates.

The Risk Continuum

Moody's views on credit support are shaped by our opinions on the inherent risk of each asset class. We believe that the stability of asset values of the major property types, ranked in order from best to worst, is as follows: regional malls, multifamily, anchored community retail, industrial, office, and hotel.

Standard and Poor's Rating Process for CMBS Transactions[24]

Standard & Poor's rating process begins when an issuer, or an investment banker representing the issuer requests our analysis of the credit quality of a single commercial mortgage or a pool of commercial mortgages. For a first time issuer this usually entails a meeting to discuss S&P's criteria and overall analytical approach. After the initial meetings, Standard & Poor's will perform a preliminary analysis of the collateral to determine the indicative credit support requirements. If the issuer accepts these indicative levels, after a formal engagement, Standard & Poor's begins the official rating process.

Standard & Poor's breaks down CMBS transactions into two major categories-property specific and pool transactions.

1. The property specific analysis is used for the following transactions:

- single-loan backed by a single asset;
- single-loan backed by multiple assets,
- multiple properties with multiple loans to a single-borrower,
- or small pools of less than 50 borrowers.

The property specific transaction is an in-depth analysis of the asset/assets and all of the related engineering, appraisal, and environmental reports. Among the major considerations are the asset's construction quality, location, tenancy, lease structures, historical performance, market position, current and anticipated competition, lien status, and overall loan structure. A very important aspect of this analysis is S&P's evaluation of the borrower/sponsor and its management capabilities based on an in-depth meeting with the corporate and on-site management teams and visit to the assets. Even more important are the legal considerations regarding the borrowing entity and the overall deal structure, the absence or presence of bankruptcy-remote borrowing entities, the borrowers and its affiliates credit history, the borrower's ability to incur additional debt and the form of additional debt that can be incurred.

2. A pool analysis consists of a combination of asset-specific analysis and some statistical sampling. This approach is applied to pools that consist of loans to 50 or more separate, unaffiliated borrowers. Fusion transactions are analyzed differently i.e; the large loans are analyzed and credit support is determined based on property specific standards, the conduit loans are analyzed using the combination pool treatment, and credit tenant leases are analyzed based on the credit tenant approach. The credit support requirements for each component are derived separately, weighted, then pooled to determine the ultimate transaction credit support.

S&P's evaluation of a CMBS transaction can be divided into three major areas: (1) the real estate analysis and (2) pooling and credit support determina-

---

[24] This section was contributed by Standard & Poor's.

tion, and (3) the legal and financial analysis of the transaction. It is the integration of the results of these analyses that will determine the ultimate credit support requirements and the final ratings for the transaction.

S&P begins with the evaluation of the underlying real estate. S&P reviews the due diligence file that is provided by the issuer. Our analysts visit the assets, evaluate the tenancy, and re-underwrite the property cashflows to incorporate adjustments to reflect market and economic expectations. S&P typically visits 60% of the pool, but the number of assets that are visited will depend on property types, geographic concentration, loan skewness, borrower concentration, and the number of loans in the pool. S&P also will sample and re-underwrite additional loans and property types to arrive at a true representative sample of the pool in order to extrapolate the results to the rest of the unseen assets.

Cashflow adjustments typically include marking rents down to market, increasing vacancy assumptions, increasing expenses to reflect a normalized level, as well as deducting the expenses related to future tenant rollover and leasing costs, and ongoing capital expenditure requirements. These adjustments (haircuts) are made to the property's in-place, current cashflow to derive an S&P stabilized cashflow and the resulting debt service coverage ratio (DSCR). S&P then applies a capitalization rate to this adjusted cashflow to determine an appropriate value for the property and the resulting LTV for the loan. S&P's analysts also read the related environmental, engineering, and appraisal reports as part of the real estate evaluation of the assets. S&P views the "bricks and mortars approach" as the foundation of any analysis of CMBS pools, since it is important to ensure that the properties can maintain their ability to generate cashflow throughout the life of the transaction.

The cashflows resulting from this loan-by-loan analysis are stressed at each rating category and aggregated to determine the credit support required for the overall pool. The absence of special hazard coverage, such as earthquake and windstorm insurance requirements and unresolved environmental issues can result in increased credit support requirements.

Overlaying the real estate analysis are the legal and financial issues that govern the transaction structure, and these issues play a critical role in determining the final credit support levels for the transaction. This analysis focuses on the strengths and weaknesses of the deal; the structure of the borrowing entities, the representations and warranties provided by the mortgage sellers, and the legal opinions governing the transfer (true sale) of the assets from the seller to the depositor. Other issues that are considered include the flow of funds within the transaction and any additional liquidity that may be required to prevent an interruption of payments to the bondholders, priority of payments to the rated tranches, the Servicing and Trustee roles, including their required Rankings and ratings, and the ratings of the providers of hazard insurance coverage.

Chapter 24

Understanding Prepayments in CMBS Deals

Da Cheng
Vice President, Software Development
Wall Street Analytics, Inc.

Adrian R. Cooper, Ph.D.
President
Wall Street Analytics, Inc.

Jason Huang
Vice President, Structured Finance
Wall Street Analytics, Inc.

INTRODUCTION

One of the most important and least understood aspects of CMBS deals is their behavior under prepayments. In residential deals the bondholders are protected against prepayments solely by the cash flow distribution structure. For commercial deals, call protection at the loan level leads to a greater cash flow certainty, and this has led some investors to grossly misprice CMBS tranches by ignoring the allocation of prepayment risk. Within a declining rate environment, which is often coupled with a booming real estate market, a thorough analysis of the prepayment risks become especially important.

The prepayment protection in commercial deals comes from both the call protection available at the loan level, and also from the CMBS structure. The call protection is provided by a combination of prepayment lockouts, prepayment penalties, and yield maintenance, so it is important to understand the way that these interact with the structure of the deal. The purpose of this chapter is to provide a comprehensive catalog of the methods commonly used for prepayment protection in CMBS deals.

Exhibit 1: Static Penalty Schedule

Year after lockout	Prepayment Penalty
1	5% of prepayment amount
2	4%
3	3%
4	2%
5	1%
6 and after	no penalty

LOCKOUTS AND PREPAYMENT PENALTIES

The simplest method of affording call protection is to require that for some period after the loan is originated, no prepayments be allowed to occur. This is known as a *lockout*, and has the advantage that it is simple to model and provides complete protection against prepayments. A lockout typically only covers the first few years of a loan, and CMBS deals that use them almost invariably combine them with at least one other method.

The next simplest form of call protection is a *prepayment penalty*. This represents an additional penalty that the borrower must pay when he chooses to prepay the loan. It is expressed as a percentage of the prepayment amount, and generally declines over time. Prepayment premiums are often substantial, and may be used in conjunction with lockouts. A commonly used schedule is shown in Exhibit 1.

In a typical CMBS deal, the prepayment penalties will be distributed separately from other funds. The rules by which they are allocated are obviously crucial for assessing the risk exposure of various bonds. There is a common misconception amongst investors that prepayment premiums are a relatively ineffective means of providing call protection. However, as we will see below, in a rising rate environment they may significantly outperform yield maintenance.

YIELD MAINTENANCE

In addition to lockouts and prepayment premiums, most CMBS deals also use a far more complex form of call protection. This is known as *yield maintenance* (YM), and perhaps represents the most misunderstood aspect of commercial deals. At the current time there is a peculiar stratification of the CMBS marketplace. On the one hand, since yield maintenance is generally too complex to be modeled on spreadsheets, many buyers are forced to ignore it. Those with more sophisticated systems, however, are able correctly price even the most volatile tranches, giving them a significant investing advantage. More surprisingly, perhaps, even issuers are finding that their in-house systems are able to handle only the simplest methods of yield maintenance. In fact, one major investment bank was recently embarrassed when they discovered that the language in their prospectus didn't agree with their own yield maintenance model. At this point — long after issuing the deal — they were forced to invent a new type of yield maintenance to match the prospectus, and to acquire a new analytical system that allowed them to model it.

Yield Maintenance Defined

The basic concept behind yield maintenance is quite simple: When a borrower prepays his loan, he must pay the lender an additional *yield maintenance charge* (or *make-whole charge*). The amount of the charge is calculated so that the lender becomes indifferent to prepayments. So the question is, what is a fair compensation to the lender for receiving a prepayment?

To illustrate this point, imagine that we make a loan in January with a maturity date in May. The first couple of months go by without event and we receive our principal and interest payments as scheduled. Suddenly in March the borrower informs us that he wishes to prepay. How much should we charge him for this privilege? A fair approach would be to require that the total check that we receive in March be equal to the value of all the remaining payments we were due to receive in order to "make us whole." In other words, he must pay us a yield maintenance charge given by

YM charge = Value of future scheduled payments − Amount prepaid

Our intention is that by reinvesting the prepayment amount and the yield maintenance charge, we could reproduce the future cash flow that we'd been scheduled to receive from the original loan. At this level, the concept of yield maintenance is very simple. The complexity comes from determining exactly how the value of future scheduled payments should be computed, or equivalently from deciding how the prepayment proceeds can be reinvested. In the following sections we shall explore the rather daunting variety of yield maintenance methods in the marketplace today. These have generally evolved from differing assumptions about the available reinvestment options, although some of their variants have arisen as mere historical accidents.

Having decided on the YM penalty that should be paid by the borrower, a further complication arises when we realize that the prepaying loan is part of a CMBS deal. Even after the YM charge has been computed, the question remains as to how it should be distributed amongst the bondholders. We shall discuss the various allocation methods that are currently used, and describe in particular how *bond yield maintenance* is used to make whole the individual tranche holders.

The Importance of Analyzing Yield Maintenance

Before discussing the details of yield maintenance, we give a brief example of the magnitude of its effects. These will generally be most significant for an IO strip.

To illustrate this, we take an actual CMBS deal and plot the yield of the IO against prepayment speed both with and without the effects of yield maintenance. The results are shown in Exhibit 2.

It is important to stress that the beneficial effects of yield maintenance to the bondholder may be either less than or greater than those of a simple prepayment lockout, depending on the precise form of YM used and the scenario under consideration.

YIELD MAINTENANCE FOR COMMERCIAL LOANS

In the following, as is typical in CMBS deals, we assume that when a loan prepays it prepays completely, so that *prepaid amount* is equal to the outstanding balance of the loan at the date of prepayment. It is a simple matter to allow partial prepayment of loans instead. The basic philosophy behind all the methods is to compare the value of the cash flow that would have occurred in absence of prepayments to the value of the cash flow after the prepayment has occurred. Although the details of many of the methods may seem rather convoluted and artificial, they have all been used in actual CMBS transactions, and so must be understood and modeled by anyone wishing to accurately price commercial deals.

The Simple Model

The most straightforward form of yield maintenance (generally referred to as the *simple model*) estimates the value of future scheduled cash flows by adding up future scheduled payments. The YM charge then becomes

$$\sum \text{Future scheduled payments} - \text{Prepaid amount}$$

or equivalently

$$\sum \text{Future scheduled interest payments}$$

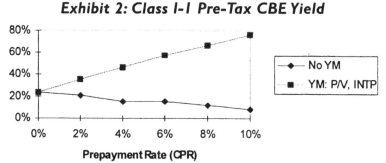

Exhibit 2: Class I-I Pre-Tax CBE Yield

From Mortgage Capital Funding, Inc., Multifamily/Commercial Mortgage Pass-Through Certificates, Series 1994-MC1

The lender in this case will clearly be overcompensated since there is no discounting of the future value of cash flows. For this reason it is not commonly used in today's loans.

The Bullet Model

A slightly more complex variant of the previous method is the *bullet model*. For this, the YM charge is given by

$$\text{Prepaid amount} \times \text{Remaining Term} \times (\text{Loan coupon} - \text{YM Coupon})$$

where *Loan coupon* represents the coupon of the loan at origination, and *YM coupon* is a prevailing interest rate at the prepayment date. The interpretation behind this is that at the date of prepayment we pretend that the loan represented a single bullet that would come due on its maturity date, and in the meantime paid interest at the loan coupon rate. We next assume that the prepaid amount can be invested in a similar bullet bond, bought at par, and paying interest at YM coupon. As in the case of the simple model, we ignore discounting and take the difference between the two cash streams to give the YM charge.

This method ignores both the loan amortization and the discounting of future cash flows. For loans with a short balloon period, this assumption will be less inaccurate.

The Single Discount Factor Model

The *single discount factor model* is a little more sophisticated and gives the YM charge as

$$\sum \frac{\text{Future scheduled payment}_t}{(1 + \text{YM yield})^t} - \text{Prepaid amount}$$

where the summation index t represents the number of months after the prepayment date. The model computes the net present value of the future scheduled cash flows discounted back at a constant rate of *YM yield*. This rate will typically be chosen as the yield of a Treasury of comparable maturity, plus some hand-picked spread. If there were no spread, then the YM charge would allow the lender to exactly reproduce the future scheduled cash flow with a risk-free Treasury portfolio, which is clearly an overcompensation.

The Multiple Discount Factor Model

The *multiple discount factor model* is similar to the single discount factor model, but the discounting of future cash flows is taken with respect to the Treasury spot curve and gives the YM charge as:

$$\sum \frac{\text{Future scheduled payment}}{(1 + \text{Treasury spot rate}_t + \text{YM spread})^t} - \text{Prepaid amount}$$

Again the summation index t represents the number of months after the prepayment date. With *YM spread* set to zero, this model is known as *Treasury flat yield maintenance*, and provides a sufficient charge for the lender to reproduce the future scheduled cash flow by purchasing a Treasury portfolio. This is clearly an overcompensation, since a Treasury portfolio would be risk free. With a non-zero value of *YM spread*, the charge would be sufficient to allow the lender to reproduce the scheduled cash flow by purchasing a portfolio of investments with a YM spread over the Treasury curve. Its value is therefore chosen to represent the expected spread of bonds with a similar risk profile to the original loan. With YM spread of 150 basis points, this model is generally known as a "T+150" yield maintenance premium.

In many ways this model represents the most sensible definition of yield maintenance, and the others described here can be thought of as approximations to it.

The Interest Difference Model

For the *interest difference model*, the YM charge is given as the present value of the difference between the scheduled interest payments, and the scheduled interest payments that would have been due with the same amortization schedule but with the coupon of the loan replaced by the coupon of a Treasury bond of comparable maturity. More precisely it is

$$\sum_t \frac{\text{Scheduled interest}_t - \text{Scheduled interest at YM yield}_t}{(1 + \text{Treasury spot rate}_t)^t}$$

where *YM yield* is chosen as the yield of a Treasury bond of comparable maturity to the loan, plus a possible hand-picked spread. The justifying assumption behind this approach is that upon receiving the prepayment, the lender can reissue bonds with an identical amortization schedule. The (fixed) coupon of these new loans will equal some spread over a comparable Treasury. The difference between the present value of the two cash flows produces the YM charge.

As a slight variant of this method, YM yield is occasionally based upon the yield of a Treasury bond whose maturity is comparable to the remaining average life of the loan at the prepayment date, rather than its remaining term. In another variation, the Treasury spot rate in the denominator is replaced by a single discount factor.

The Truncated Interest Difference Model

Unfortunately, the preceding model has spawned a rather confusing mutation in which the YM charge is given by

$$\sum_t \frac{\text{Max}(\text{Scheduled interest}_t - \text{Prepaid amount} \times \text{YM yield}, 0)}{(1 + \text{YM yield})^t}$$

where again *YM yield* is chosen as the yield of a Treasury bond of comparable maturity to the loan, plus a possible hand-picked spread. Roughly speaking, the assumption behind this is that the prepayment can be reinvested in a non-amortizing bond that pays YM yield for some period of time. (However, the duration of this period has no sensible interpretation.) The resulting cash flows are discounted at a single rate of YM yield. Exhibit 3 illustrates how this method is calculated. The portion of interest higher than prepayment × yield is the cash flows used to calculate the discounted present value.

Yield Maintenance Floors

For most of the methods described above, the YM charges will decrease in a rising interest rate environment. In order to provide additional protection to lenders, they are often supplemented with *yield maintenance floors*. These impose a minimum value for the YM charge as follows:

$$YM \text{ charge} = \text{Max (Model YM charge, Prepaid amount} \times YM \text{ floor rate)}$$

where *Model YM charge* represents the charge before the floor is taken into account.

ALLOCATION OF YIELD MAINTENANCE CHARGES

In the previous sections we have discussed various methods of implementing yield maintenance on the commercial loans. It is now necessary to consider how the resulting YM charges will be allocated amongst the bondholders of a CMBS deal.

Exhibit 3: The Truncated Interest Difference Method

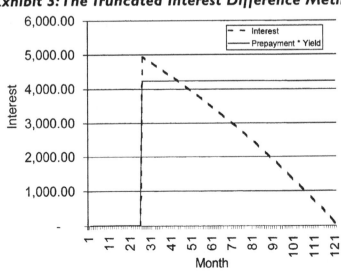

Exhibit 4: Different YM Allocation Rules

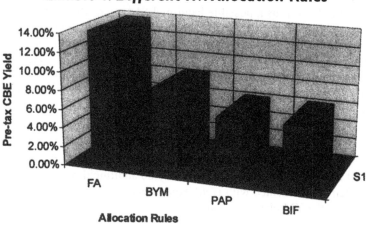

Statistical results generated by the *Structured Financing Workstation* by Wall Street Analytics, Inc. This IO certificate is part of the *Nationslink Funding Corporation, Commercial Mortgage Pass-Through Certificates, Series 1996-1*. Price 3% excludes accrued interests. All mortgage loans balloon 60 month from the cut-off date.

FA   Full allocation of yield maintenance to IO certificate
BYM Bond yield maintenance method
PAP Principal allocation method
BIF Base interest fraction method

It is important to realize that under many circumstances, even though the YM charge is computed so as to protect the whole loan against prepayments, it may be insufficient to protect all of the bonds. In other words the sum of the make-whole amounts for the bonds will not equal the make-whole amount for the collateral. Given this discrepancy, it is obviously extremely important to model the allocation of the YM charges completely. To further illustrate this point, Exhibit 4 shows how switching between some commonly used allocation methods (discussed below) may dramatically affect the yield of a bond.

The Principal Allocation Percentage Method

The simplest method used for the allocation of the YM charge is the *principal allocation percentage method*. For this, the YM charge is paid to the bonds in proportion to the amount of prepayment principal that they receive. Specifically, a bond X receives as its share of the YM charge

$$\frac{\text{Prepayment paid to X}}{\text{Total prepaid amount}} \times \text{YM charge}$$

This method has the advantage that it is simple to implement, although it tends to undercompensate the holders of bonds that are structurally locked out. Moreover, a discount bond would tend to be overcompensated since it would generally benefit from a prepayment, while the converse would be true of a bond bought at a premium. As an extreme example of this consider the case of a PO strip. If the entire collateral prepaid one month after the deal had been issued, then the PO holder would obviously be delighted. There is obviously no reason to compensate him further with a portion of the YM charge.

The Base Interest Method

The *base interest method* provides a far more complex, though somewhat arbitrary means of distributing the YM charge. When a mortgage M prepays, the amount of the resulting YM charge distributed to a bond X is given by

$$\frac{\text{Principal paid to X}}{\text{Total principal paid}} \times \frac{\text{Max(Coupon of X} - \text{YM coupon, 0)}}{\text{Gross coupon of M} - \text{YM coupon}} \times \text{YM charge}$$

with all excess YM charge being distributed to the IO strip. This has an advantage over the previous method in that it treats premium and discount bonds more fairly. In particular, a PO strip will receive no portion of the YM charge. A complete analysis of the deal would be required to tell whether a particular bond was fairly compensated.

Bond Yield Maintenance Method

Perhaps the most logical method for allocating the YM charge is to use *bond yield maintenance*. This is somewhat analogous to the process of calculating collateral yield maintenance. The concept is that a bondholder should be "made whole" for the disruption in cash flow that he suffers for receiving a prepayment. For a particular bond, the fair value for this is

$$\text{Bond YM amount} = \sum_t \frac{\text{Scheduled bond payment}_t - \text{Actual bond payment}_t}{(1 + \text{Bond YM yield})^t}$$

where *Scheduled bond payment$_t$* represents the total payment that the bond would receive at time *t* if the prepayment had not occurred, and *Actual bond payment$_t$* is the total payment that the bond would receive at time *t* after taking into account the effects of the prepayment (but ignoring any YM distributions). *Bond YM yield* is set equal to the Treasury spot rate for a maturity comparable to the bond, plus a spread. This spread may be the same as the current bond spread at the time of prepayment. Alternatively, if it is expected that the bond will be upgraded, a lesser spread might be used. (This will generate a higher Bond YM amount, which is obviously reasonable if the bond has become more valuable.)

As an extension to this method, if the prepayment has the effect of changing the bond's risk profile, then different discount spreads may be used for computing the two present values. In other words,

$$\text{Bond YM amount} = \sum_t \frac{\text{Scheduled bond payment}_t}{(1 + \text{Bond YM yield}_1)^t} - \frac{\text{Actual bond payment}_t}{(1 + \text{Bond YM yield}_2)^t}$$

where *Bond YM yield*$_1$ is the Treasury rate corresponding to the scheduled maturity (or average life) of the bond, plus a spread appropriate to the scheduled term and risk profile. Similarly, *Bond YM yield*$_2$ is the Treasury rate corresponding to the scheduled maturity of the bond after taking into account the prepayment, plus a spread appropriate to this term and risk profile. The exact values of these spreads will be negotiated between issuer and buyer.

The Bond YM amount computed above would give the bondholder a fair compensation for receiving a prepayment. However, as we have mentioned before, there is no guarantee that the total YM charge collected from the borrowers will be sufficient to pay each of the bondholders their fair bond YM amount. Instead, a bond X will receive as its share of the YM charge an amount equal to

$$\frac{\text{Bond YM amount for X}}{\sum_{\text{all tranches}} \text{Bond YM amounts}} \times \text{YM charge}$$

This is effectively the "best that we can do" with the available YM charge.

From a purely practical standpoint, the correct modeling of bond yield maintenance can prove extremely difficult. For a scenario with n prepayments, the deal must be run $n+1$ separate times. However, a good structuring or modeling tool should be able to perform these calculations automatically.

PV Yield Loss Method

Due to the complexity and execution time of applying the previous method, a simplified version is used in the markets. It's called the *PV yield loss method*. The method involves calculating the interest losses due to prepayment for each of the bondholders. The amount is equal to the present value of a series of monthly payments, each equal to the amount, if any, by which the bond interest rate exceeds the applicable reinvestment rate on the Treasuries, multiplied by the amount of such prepayment that is payable in reduction of such bond. The monthly payments are from each of the subsequent payments dates after the prepayment to the earlier of (1) the final distribution date for such bond and (2) the stated maturity for such mortgage loan. The assumption is that the bondholders will take the prepayment and reinvest it in a Treasury bill/note matching the term stated earlier in (1) and (2). This amount is calculated on a loan-by-loan basis and the total amount from all of the loans will be paid pro-rata to the related bondholders according to the availability of the yield maintenance/premium amount.

The following formula illustrates the calculation of this method

$$\sum_{\text{all mortgage loans}} \text{NPV}\{\text{Prepayment amount for X(Coupon for X} - \text{Treasury yields)}\}$$

For notional certificates, it will replace the formula by specified "stripped" coupons from each of the entitled classes and the prepayment amount will be the principal amount in reduction of the notional balance from the related classes.

In terms of pro-rata allocation to each of the classes entitled to get yield maintenance, it will follow the same formula as discussed earlier

$$\frac{\text{Bond YM amount for X}}{\sum_{\text{all tranches}} \text{Bond YM amounts}} \times \text{YM charge}$$

This design usually maximizes the amount of yield maintenance/premium paid to the entitled classes. By overstating the PV losses amount of each of the entitled certificates and paying pro-rata, they will obtain the maximum amount from the yield maintenance/premium available from the underlying mortgage loans. As described in the formula above, the amount of interest under the "no prepayment" scenario is overstated because no amortization is assumed, the losses compared to the yields on Treasuries are overstated, too. The available yield maintenance/premium amount will be then allocated pro-rata based on each certificate's PV yield loss amounts. Since this method is usually applied to senior certificates, the yields on these certificates are maintained.

Defeasance

For completeness, we should also mention the most precise form of call protection. This is known as *defeasance*. From the point of view of the borrower, it is equivalent to Treasury-flat yield maintenance. However, the proceeds generated from the YM charges are not distributed directly to the bondholders, but are instead invested by the servicer in a Treasury portfolio. By design, this generates the same future cash flows that would have been obtained in absence of prepayments, and these are distributed to the bondholders as if no prepayments had occurred. This has the advantage of imposing no extra taxes due to the distribution of YM charges, and also maintains a higher level of credit on the remaining assets.

SPECIAL CONSIDERATIONS FOR IOS

While prepayment considerations are important for all bonds in a CMBS deal, their most dramatic effect can generally be seen on the IO. In this section we briefly review the necessity of the IO strips, and discuss their risk profiles in more detail.

Typically, a CMBS deal will contain collateral with a wide range of coupons. Since different loans will amortize at different rates, and some may prepay or default, the weighted average coupon for the collateral will tend to change over time. The presence of this *coupon dispersion* obviously makes it impossible to structure a deal with only fixed-rate bonds. Sometimes this is dealt with by creating one or more *WAC bonds* whose coupon changes with the collateral. In effect, the dispersion is passed through to the bondholders. An alternative approach is to allocate any excess interest payments over some specified cutoff to an IO strip, thus giving the collateral a constant effective passthrough rate. This strip may be taken either directly from the collateral, in which case the technique is referred to as *ratio stripping*, or it can be taken from the bonds.

An IO that has been stripped directly from the underlying loans will obviously be influenced the most by high coupon loans. These loans will have higher coupons either because they were originated when rates were higher, or because they are loans on riskier asset types. The former type will be particularly subject to prepayment risk, while the latter will be subject to credit risk, so it may seem that such an IO would be at high risk from both defaults and prepayments. In a well structured deal, however, the allocation of prepayment premiums will protect it against calls. Moreover, since the servicer is generally required to advance principal and interest, the IO holder will normally receive several months scheduled payments before the defaulted loan is liquidated.

In contrast, an IO that has been stripped from a senior bond will be affected very differently by prepayments and defaults. Because of the subordination structure, it will be relatively insensitive to default risk. However, the same subordination structure will cause it to be highly sensitive to prepayment risk.

When investing in IOs, it is especially important to realize that a deal using yield maintenance does not always provide the best call protection. For many of the methods discussed in this chapter, the YM charge may be reduced to zero in an upward rate environment. A prepayment could then cause the IO to disappear, without any distribution of YM charges to compensate. In contrast, a lockout or prepayment premium would provide far better protection. This highlights the point that when analyzing an IO, there is no substitute for thoroughly modeling the entire yield maintenance provisions of the deal, and performing analysis runs for multiple scenarios.

CONCLUSION

In this chapter we have provided a catalog of the different methods that are used to provide prepayment protection in CMBS deals, and have illustrated the dramatic effect that they can have on the risk-return profile of bonds. This emphasizes the importance to investors of completely modeling the prepayments of a CMBS deal and performing analyses under several scenarios.

Within residential CMOs, it is the payment structure of the deal that protects some of the tranches against prepayments. This is often achieved with considerable complexity and may involve multiple layers of PAC classes and accrual bonds. In contrast, CMBS deals typically have a far simpler bond structure. They instead achieve call protection by imposing various prepayment lockouts and fees on the collateral, the most complex of which is yield maintenance. In this, a borrower who chooses to prepay is subject to an additional charge that is intended to fairly compensate the lender for any loss of yield in his investment. This penalty is then distributed to the bondholders in such a way as to render them indifferent to the prepayment. We have examined the different ways in which the yield maintenance charge may be defined, and have also listed the current methods for allocating it among tranches.

As the market evolves, it seems inevitable that the methods of CMBS call protection discussed in this chapter will become supplemented by some of the methods used in residential deals. In this case we can look forward to deals that combine PAC bonds, Z bonds, and bond yield maintenance within a single structure. It is obviously important that anyone building a CMBS structuring or analysis model designs it with enough flexibility to allow for this future expansion.

Chapter 25

Credit-Driven Prepayment and Default Analysis

Michael A. Ervolini
President & CEO
Charter Research Corporation

Harold J. A. Haig
Head of Marketing & Sales
Charter Research Corporation

Michael A. Megliola
Vice President
Bear Stearns & Co.

INTRODUCTION

To date, default and prepayment analyses for commercial mortgage-backed securities (CMBS) have borrowed heavily from residential MBS. The result has been both positive and limiting. Traditional MBS analyses succeed in basic mathematics that are sound and rigorously defined. Familiar and widely accepted, these analytics allowed investors to jump-start the CMBS market. However, these analytics fail to reflect fully the credit risk embedded in these assets:

- *Credit risk.* CMBS assets are generally non-recourse loans secured by income-producing property. These loans exhibit substantial *credit risk* — the likelihood that each may prepay or default depending upon changes in the credit quality of the underlying property. Existing analytics focus on interest rates; commercial loan performance is driven by the *combination* of interest rates and credit quality.

- *Credit-related disclosure.* CMBS financial reporting typically includes quarterly or annual disclosure of each underlying property's income statement. Existing analytics offer no direct mechanism to incorporate this information into bond pricing.

425

Credit-driven analysis is a set of rules that retain the underlying mechanics of traditional prepayment and default analyses, but extend these analyses to take full account of the credit risk of commercial mortgage loans. Credit-driven analyses directly incorporate the credit-related disclosure that is available for many CMBS transactions.

THE BASIS OF CREDIT-DRIVEN ANALYSIS

Traditional conditional prepayment rates (CPR) and credit default rates (CDR) organize assets into pools. Within a pool, each loan is projected to prepay or default in equal proportions over time.

Prepayments or defaults occur at specified periodic rates, or "speeds." For example, a traditional prepayment analysis might specify that during each period, 1% of the then outstanding loans prepay. A default analysis might specify that 1% of the loans default, and that each defaulted loan bears a certain specified loss "severity," perhaps 30% of the loan's defaulted balance. A combined prepay/default analysis applies both behaviors simultaneously. Which loan prepays or defaults is immaterial — all loans within a pool are treated equally.

Credit-driven analysis is based on the idea that prepayment or default assumptions should be applied to each loan, individually, depending upon that loan's projected credit quality.

Currently, investors and traders perform this function through intuition — they group loans that have similar characteristics, then apply appropriate "speeds" and "severity" for each analysis. Loans with high coupons might be grouped together and subjected to a higher rate of prepayment, while loans in a given geographic region might be subjected to higher rates of default.

Credit-driven analysis offers a mechanism to codify this intuition. The goal of credit-driven analysis is to guarantee that changes in interest rates or credit quality are equally reflected across loans within a given analysis, and likewise equally reflected from one analysis to the next.

Credit-driven analyses *modulate* the rate of prepayment or default on a loan-by-loan, month-by-month basis. A loan prepays or defaults at a specified rate during only those projection periods when that loan meets certain *conditions*:

- *Prepayments*. Credit-driven prepayments occur when (a) prepayment is permitted under the terms of the loan, and (b) refinancing the loan results in some specified level of net new proceeds to the borrower (after paying any required prepayment premium).

- *Defaults*. Credit-driven defaults occur when the underlying property's net income is insufficient to cover debt service. Following a specified delay, the severity of loss is computed to reflect the underlying property's performance and financeability.

By introducing these mechanics, credit-driven analyses change the nature of the assertion that underlies a given analysis. A traditional analysis may assert that "this group of loans will prepay at 5% per year," while a credit-driven analysis might assert that "highly financeable loans will prepay at 25% per year, given the following interest rate and property market assumptions..." The traditional analysis would prepay all loans equally; a credit-driven analysis prepays the loans that satisfy certain criteria.

The power of credit-driven analysis lies in its ability to connect the dots. Which loans in a 3-year-old pool could be refinanced now at twice their original balance? What if interest rates fall but property markets weaken? Credit-driven analytics provide the mechanical support to allow investors or traders to examine these questions directly.

DEFINITIONS

A detailed discussion of credit-driven analytics requires certain defined terms:

> *Horizon Yield Curve:* A prospective yield curve that represents the assumed yields on various U.S. Treasury obligations. For purposes of creating a cash flow projection, the horizon yield curve is employed in any calculation that depends upon market interest rates (e.g., a yield maintenance calculation), while the actual yield curve is employed to express bond yields (e.g., "70bp over the curve").
>
> *Recent NOI:* The most recently reported net operating income (NOI) for the property that serves as collateral for a commercial mortgage loan. At a transaction's cut-off date, Recent NOI equals the NOI listed in the offering (or implied by the debt-service coverage ratio listed in the offering). Following cut-off, Recent NOI is updated when reported to the trustee (typically on a quarterly basis).
>
> *Recent Value:* The most recently reported appraised property value for the property that serves as collateral for a commercial mortgage loan. At a transaction's cut-off date, Recent Value equals the value listed in the offering (or implied by the loan-to-value ratio listed in the offering). Following cut-off, Recent Value is updated when reported to the trustee (generally not more often than annually; in some cases only as a result of affirmative action by the servicer).
>
> *Growth:* Along with interest rates, one of the two key economic assumptions that drive a credit-driven analysis. Growth is the rate at which Recent NOI and Recent Value are projected to grow over time. Growth can vary over the course of a projection. For example, a simple analysis may specify "today's yield curve and 2% growth," while an analysis anticipating a recession could call for "interest rates up 150bp and growth of negative

5% for two years, flat for two years, then 3%." The combination of Recent NOI, Recent Value, and Growth allow credit-driven analyses to project a property's NOI and value during any projection period.

Loan Underwriting Standards: A set of prospective loan-level underwriting standards, including a debt-service coverage ratio (DSCR), amortization schedule, pricing mechanism (a loan coupon's spread to a specified treasury rate), and an optional loan-to-value ratio (LTV). Because projected property values are not tied directly to interest rates, inclusion of an LTV ratio could generate results that do not fully reflect movements in interest rates.

Financeable Balance: The prospective estimate of the gross proceeds of financing a new loan secured by a first mortgage on a given property. Calculating Financeable Balance begins with projected NOI and value, applies Loan Underwriting Standards (pricing the new loan off the Horizon Yield Curve), and arrives at projected gross proceeds.

Proceeds-to-Balance (PTB): The ratio of Financeable Balance to scheduled outstanding balance. For example, during the 60*th* month of a projection, an asset may have a scheduled outstanding balance of $4.0 million, and a calculated Financeable Balance of $5.6 million. For that period, that asset's PTB would be $5.6 million / $4.0 million = 140%. PTB is a basic credit-driven measure of an asset's propensity to either prepay or default. A PTB of over 100% suggests that prepayment may result in proceeds to the borrower, while a PTB of under 100% suggests that a balloon payment may not be paid when due.

Net New Proceeds: The excess of the Financeable Balance minus the sum of (i) the scheduled outstanding loan balance and (ii) any required prepayment premium. Net New Proceeds represent the amount of proceeds available to a borrower to cover the costs of a new financing and to retain as proceeds from a new financing.

For example, if, in a given projection period, a loan had a scheduled outstanding balance of $6.2 million and required a prepayment premium of $0.4 million, a Financeable Balance of $7.5 million would result in Net New Proceeds of $7.5 million – ($6.2 million + $0.4 million) = $0.9 million.

Excess Proceeds: The minimum level of Net New Proceeds required to a cause specified prepayment to occur (at a specified prepayment rate), expressed as a percentage of the scheduled outstanding loan balance. Excess Proceeds represent the notion that a borrower will not have sufficient incentive to refinance a property until the level of Net New Proceeds reaches some amount that is material, given the size of the loan.

For example, Excess Proceeds of 30% specifies that a loan with a scheduled outstanding balance of $3.0 million will not prepay unless Net New Proceeds is at least 30% of $3.0 million, or $0.9 million.

Exhibit 1: CMBS Pool: Loan Characteristic

Loan type:	Fixed-rate, level-pay, with balloon
Property value:	$5,300,000
Net Operating Income	400,000
Loan Balance	4,000,000
Coupon Rate	8.50%
Amortization schedule	360 months
Annual principal & interest	352,207
Scheduled balloon date	10 years
Scheduled balloon balance	3,508,988
Prepayment lock-out	3 years
Prepayment permitted with yield maintenance	6 years
Prepayment permitted, no penalty	1 year

Debt Service Shortfall: The monthly amount by which the scheduled loan payment exceeds projected monthly NOI. Any Debt Service Shortfall causes a specified default to occur (at a specified default rate and delay). For example, a loan with a projected monthly NOI of $200,000 and a scheduled loan payment of $240,000 has a Debt Service Shortfall of $200,000 – $240,000 = ($40,000) per month.

Balloon Shortfall: The amount by which the scheduled loan balance exceeds the Financeable Balance. For example, a loan with a Financeable Balance of $3.8 million and a scheduled balance of $4.2 million has a Balloon Shortfall of $3.8 million – $4.2 million = ($0.4 million).

Calculated Severity: The sum of (i) cumulative Debt Service Shortfall over the course of a specified delay and (ii) Balloon Shortfall at the end of the specified delay. For example, a loan that has a cumulative Debt Service Shortfall of $0.5 million over the course of an 18-month delay, and a Balloon Shortfall of $0.9 million at the end of the 18-month delay, has a Calculated Severity of $0.5 million + $0.9 million = $1.4 million.

AN EXAMPLE OF A CREDIT-DRIVEN ANALYSIS

We can illustrate credit-driven analysis assuming a CMBS pool consists of the one loan shown in Exhibit 1. How does this loan perform if interest rates rise or fall, and if property performance improves or declines? The results are summaraized in Exhibit 2. The assumptions are discussed below.

Projections assume that the Horizon Yield Curve shifts up or down by 200bp, based upon an actual yield curve from February 1998. Projections assume that Growth equals +2% or –2% per year, respectively. This Growth assumption is deliberately simplified for purposes of presentation. A more likely Growth assumption would probably vary over time, such as "3% for two years, then – 15%, then 2% thereafter."

Exhibit 2: Summary of Results when Rates Change

(yield % / WAL yrs)	Interest Rates: Up	Interest Rates: Down
Base case	8.58% / 9.6yr	8.58% / 9.6yr
Prepayment: Positive growth	8.62% / 9.1yr	12.21% / 5.0yr
Prepayment: Negative growth	8.58% / 9.6yr	8.80% / 9.0yr
Default: Positive growth	8.58% / 9.6yr	8.58% / 9.6yr
Default: Negative growth	6.77% / 7.2yr	8.57% / 7.2yr

For simplicity, Loan Underwriting Standards are assumed to remain constant at a DSCR of 1.15×, a 360-month amortization schedule, and a coupon of the 10-year Treasury plus 170bp. An actual set of Loan Underwriting Standards would probably segregate loans by property type, then apply differing standards to each set of loans.

Prepayment and Default

On a loan-by-loan basis, prepayments are projected to occur at a specified periodic rate (or "speed"), but only during those periods that meet two conditions: (i) prepayment is permitted, and (ii) Excess Proceeds equal or exceed a specified percentage of the then scheduled loan balance. Projected prepayments always adhere to a loan's stated terms. For example, no prepayment is ever projected to occur during a loan's lock-out period, and any stated prepayment premium is always calculated. For this example, the credit-driven prepayment assumption is "prepay at 40% CPR when Excess Proceeds are at least 10%."

On a loan-by-loan basis, defaults are projected to occur at a specified speed, but only during those periods for which a loan has a Debt Service Shortfall. Any default is subject to a specified delay (in months), during which loan payments are assumed to be advanced in full, and at the end of which the loan bears loss equal to the Calculated Severity. For this example, the credit-driven default assumption is "default at 30% with a delay of 12 months." A complete default analysis would include possible balloon defaults or loan extensions. These mechanics are not part of traditional MBS analysis and therefore fall outside of the scope of this chapter.

Prepayment Conditions

Interest Rates Rise and Growth is Positive Following the loan's look-out period:

- Higher interest rates decrease Financeable Balance (borrowing new money is more expensive), but also decrease yield maintenance premiums.
- Positive Growth drives projected NOI/value and projected property value upward, increasing Financeable Balance.

- Net New Proceeds are effectively driven in two directions — downward, owing to the increased cost of new financing, and upward, owing to a diminished yield maintenance premium and to an increasing projected NOI/value.
- *If Growth is sufficient to overwhelm increased financing costs, prepayments occur.*

Interest Rates Rise and Growth is Negative Following the loan's lock-out period:

- Higher interest rates decrease Financeable Balance (borrowing new money is more expensive), but also decrease yield maintenance premiums.
- Negative Growth drives projected NOI/value and projected property value downward, decreasing Financeable Balance.
- Net New Proceeds are effectively driven downward — owing to both the increased cost of new financing and decreasing projected NOI/value. The offsetting effect of decreasing prepayment premiums in unlikely to ever trigger a prepayment.
- *Prepayments do not occur.*

Interest Rates Fall and Growth is Positive Following the loan's lock-out period:

- Lower interest rates increase Financeable Balance (borrowing new money is cheaper), but also increase yield maintenance premiums. These effects may roughly offset each other, depending upon the remaining life of the loan and the slope of the Horizon Yield Curve. Yield maintenance premiums diminish as remaining life diminishes, but are typically computed using a shortening-maturity Treasury rate, which increases prepayment premium with a positively-sloped yield curve.
- Positive Growth drives projected NOI/value and projected property value upward, increasing Financeable Balance.
- Net New Proceeds are effectively driven upward — owing to both the decreased cost of new financing and increasing projected NOI/value. The offsetting effect of increasing prepayment premiums is unlikely to prevent a prepayment.
- *When cumulative Growth (helped along by lower interest rates) is sufficient to drive Net New Proceeds to a specified level, prepayments occur. The yield maintenance premium dampens but does not prevent prepayment.*

Interest Rates Fall and Growth is Negative Following the loan's lock-out period:

- Lower interest rates increase Financeable Balance (borrowing new money is cheaper), but also increase yield maintenance premiums. These effects may roughly offset each other, depending upon the remaining life of the loan and the slope of the Horizon Yield Curve. Yield maintenance premiums diminish as remaining life diminishes, but are typically computed using a shortening-maturity Treasury rate, which increases premium [???] with a positively-sloped yield curve.

- Negative Growth drives projected NOI/value and projected property value downward, decreasing Financeable Balance.
- Net New Proceeds are effectively driven in two directions — upward, owing to the decreased cost of new financing, and downward, owing to an increased yield maintenance premium and to a decreasing projected NOI/value.
- *The combined dampening effect of lower NOI/value plus an increased yield maintenance premium likely overwhelm the benefit of decreased borrowing costs; prepayments are prevented or substantially curtailed.*

Default Conditions

Interest Rates Rise and Growth is Positive Starting at the outset of the projection:

- For fixed-payment loans, higher interest rates do not affect the incidence of default (Debt Service Shortfall is independent of interest rates). Higher interest rates do decrease Financeable Balance, increasing Balloon Shortfall, and therefore increasing Calculated Severity. Note that for adjustable-rate/adjustable payment loans, higher interest rates would affect Debt Service Shortfall.
- Positive Growth drives projected NOI upward, guaranteeing no Debt Service Shortfall.
- *Because NOI is always sufficient to cover scheduled loan payments, no defaults occur.*

Interest Rates Rise and Growth is Negative Starting at the outset of the projection:

- For fixed-payment loans, higher interest rates do not affect the incidence of default (Debt Service Shortfall is independent of interest rates). Higher interest rates do decrease Financeable Balance, increasing Balloon Shortfall, and therefore increasing Calculated Severity. Note that for adjustable-rate/adjustable payment loans, higher interest rates would affect Debt Service Shortfall.
- Negative Growth drives projected NOI downward, eventually causing Debt Service Shortfall and triggering defaults. Diminishing NOI increases Calculated Severity, both by increasing cumulative Debt Service Shortfall over the course of a specified delay and by decreasing Financeable Balance.

- *Diminishing NOI causes defaults to occur; diminishing NOI and higher interest rates each increase Calculated Severity; defaults occur and losses are severe.*

Interest Rates Fall and Growth is Positive Starting at the outset of the projection:

- For fixed-payment loans, lower interest rates do not affect the incidence of default (Debt Service Shortfall is independent of interest rates). Lower interest rates do increase Financeable Balance, decreasing Balloon Shortfall, and therefore decreasing Calculated Severity. Note that for adjustable-rate/adjustable payment loans, lower interest rates would affect Debt Service Shortfall.
- Positive Growth drives projected NOI upward, guaranteeing no Debt Service Shortfall.
- *Because NOI is always sufficient to cover scheduled loan payments, no defaults occur.*

Interest Rates Fall and Growth is Negative Starting at the outset of the projection:

- For fixed-payment loans, lower interest rates do not affect the incidence of default (Debt Service Shortfall is independent of interest rates). Lower interest rates do increase Financeable Balance, decreasing Balloon Shortfall, and therefore decreasing Calculated Severity. Note that for adjustable-rate/adjustable payment loans, lower interest rates would affect Debt Service Shortfall
- Negative Growth drives projected NOI downward, eventually causing Debt Service Shortfall and triggering defaults. Diminishing NOI also contributes to Calculated Severity, in the form of cumulative Debt Service Shortfall over the course of a specified delay.
- *Diminishing NOI causes defaults to occur; diminishing increases Calculated Severity but cheaper borrowing reduces Calculated Severity; defaults occur, losses are mitigated by lower interest rates.*

IMPLICATIONS

The implications of the credit-driven analysis presented in this chapter are as follows:

Option-Adjusted Spreads: Credit-driven analyses fully reflect changes in interest rates — whether through an asset's stated terms (e.g., an adjustable-rate loan) or by modeling rational borrower behavior (e.g., the inability to finance a non-recourse balloon payment). Credit-driven analysis offers the underpinning for OAS analysis of CMBS bonds.

Fundamental Property Market Research: Credit-driven analysis offers an obvious means to incorporate fundamental property-market research into CMBS pricing. The future growth in property income is a key independent variable that determines credit-driven results. Better estimates of growth (whether by geography and property type or on a property-by-property basis) will produce more accurate bond prices.

Increased Dependence on Property-Level Reporting: Credit driven analysis directly incorporates reported property-level financial information, and therefore depends upon accurate and timely reporting of property operating results. Credit-driven analysis will likely compel investors to demand more and better property-level reporting.

Differentiation of CBMS Transactions: Credit-driven analysis allows investors to differentiate risks more clearly within CMBS transactions. Differences in the character of a given asset pool (coupon rates, loan terms, performance of underlying collateral) are immediately expressed as differences in bond prices. As transactions age, these differences will become more distinct. If broadly employed, credit-driven analysis will cause greater price differentiation among CMBS bonds.

Chapter 26

An Empirical Framework for Estimating CMBS Defaults

Dale Westhoff
Senior Managing Director
Bear Stearns & Co.

V.S. Srinivasan
Associate Director
Bear Stearns & Co.

Mark Feldman
Managing Director
Bear Stearns & Co.

INTRODUCTION

Ideally, an expected default rate for a given set of commercial or residential loans is derived from a complete history of default frequencies on identical collateral through multiple real estate cycles. In reality, historical default information is often very limited in scope and not reflective of current underwriting standards or regional economic trends. This leaves investors with few alternatives beyond static scenario analysis to assess the default risk of a commercial mortgage portfolio.

To address the need for a more rigorous, empirical framework for default analysis, Bear Stearns has developed a powerful new approach based on the rich historical data available on actual commercial real estate values and rents. This data set consists of 13 years of property value and rent data on four different property categories (apartments, industrial/warehouse, office, and retail) in 38 regions. The breadth of this data allows us to dynamically simulate future property values and rents in a manner consistent with that observed historically, accounting for both regional and property type variations in the data. In this framework, we can ascertain financial solvency for individual properties across thousands of randomly generated property value/rent paths to derive an expected periodic default rate. By aggregating these individual results, we can then derive an "expected" default curve for any given set of commercial properties. The key to this approach is that the simulations are calibrated to match the observed volatility and serial correlation in actual real estate values at the regional level. Once this is done, it is a simple matter to track an individual loan's performance along each simulated path given its property type, initial debt service coverage ratio (DSCR), and initial loan-to-value (LTV). Furthermore, this framework allows investors to perform more rigorous and sophisticated scenario analysis that is rooted in actual historical experience. For example:

1. Investors can modify the property value/rent volatility assumption to measure the sensitivity of a security to real estate cycles that are, on average, more severe or less severe than what we have seen historically.
2. Investors can impose a long-term price or rent trend on the simulation process.
3. Investors can define a specific price/rent scenario if they have a strong view on where we are in the current commercial real estate cycle.

The advantage of this statistical framework is that it does not rely on historical default information which is often limited in scope, biased by inconsistent underwriting standards, and linked to specific periods in regional economic cycles. These data problems tend to make traditional default analysis more subjective in nature. Using simulation, we eliminate these problems while still accounting for the intrinsic characteristics of the loans and the regional and property specific influences on commercial default behavior. Furthermore, we believe this approach is particularly well suited to large, diversified commercial loan portfolios where extensive loan-level due diligence may be difficult to perform.

THE PRICE AND RENT DATA

Our historical price and rent data come from the National Real Estate Index which is owned and operated by CB Commercial. This organization publishes property value and rent indices on four different property types (apartments, offices, warehouse/industrial, and retail) in 38 regions. The indices span 13 years including the severe commercial real estate recession from the late 1980s through the early 1990s. The property value index is derived from actual sales prices on 50,000 properties reported by brokers, title companies, REITs, and appraisers. The rent price indices are derived from quarterly surveys of asking rents for the same properties.

THE SIMULATION PROCESS

Just as we sample alternative interest rate paths in an option-adjusted spread framework, we can simulate real estate price and rent paths in the commercial market to determine the probability of default in any given period. However, in this case we sample from actual historical price and rent data using a statistical method known as "bootstrapping."

In this procedure, for a given property type and region, we repeatedly sample its historical price and rent data series to construct a simulation that is consistent with actual price and rent volatility and serial correlation[1] observed at the regional real estate market level. By simply repeating this procedure, we can generate thousands of random paths over which we can evaluate individual loan performance. For example, once price and rent simulations are constructed we can track DSCRs and LTVs along every path to determine if default conditions are met. The probability of default for an individual loan in any given period is simply the ratio of the predicted default occurrences across all paths divided by the number of paths. The "expected" default rate for a collection of commercial loans is calculated as the weighted average of the individual probabilities. This analysis can be further stratified by region, property type, or loan attribute to define areas of concentrated default risk.

Conditions that Trigger a Default

We assume a mortgage will default when the following two conditions are met:

1. the net operating income (NOI) is less than the scheduled mortgage payment (i.e., the DSCR is less than one), and
2. the market value of the property is less than the outstanding value of the debt (i.e., the LTV ratio is greater than 1).

Both conditions must be met before a default occurs. For example, if the DSCR is less than 1 but the LTV is also less than 1, we assume the owner would attempt to sell before defaulting. Conversely, if the LTV is greater than 1 but the DSCR is also greater than 1, the owner is unlikely to default unless forced to sell.

Simulating the Debt Service Coverage Ratio

DSCR is defined as (Revenue − Operating Expenses)/Debt Service and is a critical measure of a borrower's ability to meet debt obligations. The probability of a default is inversely correlated to DSCR and values below 1.0 indicate insufficient income to meet debt payments. We simulate DSCR by assuming revenue is directly proportional to simulated property rents while operating expenses are assumed to grow at the inflation rate. Although expense ratios vary by location, property class, type of lease, services, etc., we assume the conservative initial expense ratios for the various property categories shown in Exhibit 1.

Finally, simulated revenue cash flows must be adjusted to account for the average lease term for a given property type. For example, a change in rents today

---

[1] To replicate the serial correlation observed in the data, each sample iteration selects 3-year sequences rather than a single data point.

will immediately impact hotel revenues since "leases" are typically for one night only. In contrast, a change in office rents today will have a lagged effect on revenues since the average office lease is approximately five years. In our simulation process, we account for this relationship by assuming the average lease terms and average roll times for each property category in Exhibit 2.

Simulating Loan-to-Value Ratios

LTV is another important measure used to assess the likelihood of default as well as the potential loss severity after foreclosure and liquidation. LTV is the current loan amount divided by the market value of the property. Highly leveraged transactions (high LTV ratios) provide less equity cushion against default and tend to increase loss severity when a default occurs. Simulated property values are calibrated to the volatility observed in actual property values for a given region and property type. The second condition of our default trigger is met when the LTV ratio exceeds 1.0 at any point in the simulation process.

CONSERVATIVE ASSUMPTIONS

We view the results from this statistical framework as conservative for the following reasons:

1. If trigger conditions are met, we assume a ruthless and immediate default occurs. In reality, if the DSCR falls below 1, owners will sometimes carry the property in an effort to resolve a temporary shortfall in revenue.

Exhibit 1: Expense Ratios by Property Category

	Expense Ratios (Operating Expenses/Revenues)
Industrial	10%
Retail	20%
Multifamily	35%
Office	45%
Hotel	70%

Exhibit 2: Assumed Average Lease Term and Time to Roll by Property Category

Property Category	Average Term of Lease	Average Time to Roll
Industrial	3.0 years	1.5 years
Apartments	1.0 years	0.5 years
Office	5.0 years	2.5 years
Retail	4.0 years	2.0 years
Hotels	Overnight	Instantaneous

Exhibit 3: Long-Term Growth Rates by Property Type

Property Type		Growth Rate
Apartment	Price	3.7%
	Rent	2.9%
Industrial	Price	1.8%
	Rent	1.9%
Office	Price	1.0%
	Rent	0.7%
Retail	Price	1.3%
	Rent	1.9%
Aggregate		1.9%

Source: CB Commercial 1984-1998

2. In general, to derive our baseline "expected" default curves, we center the simulation process around a 1% long-term growth rate in property values and rents. Historical data from the 15-year period 1984-1998 suggest that over long periods of time, rents and property values increase by an average of about 1.9% per year. Exhibit 3 provides observed price and rent long-term growth rates for each property category.

3. The highly leveraged transactions of the 1980s amplified the correction in commercial real estate values seen in the late 1980s and early 1990s beyond what would be expected in a "normal" real estate cycle. Nevertheless, our simulation framework includes unadjusted data from this entire period despite the fact that a similar scenario seems highly unlikely in the near future.

APPLICATION OF THE CMBS DEFAULT MODEL

Our simulation-based default model is particularly useful in comparing the relative default risk of multiple commercial deals with diverse loan characteristics. For example, Exhibit 4 provides projected cumulative defaults in basis points for six representative CMBS deals. The projections were generated assuming actual property value and rent volatilities derived from the property type and location of each loan backing the deals. We also calibrated the model to a long-term growth rate in property values and rents of 1%. It is important to note that although a change in the long-term growth rate assumption changes the absolute level of projected defaults, it does not affect the relative performance of the deals. The projected cumulative defaults shown in Exhibit 4 are consistent with the risk profile of the loans backing each deal. For example, projected defaults are highest in GMAC 97-C1 reflecting the large percentage of loans with DSCRs < 1.25. In contrast, BSCMS 98-C1 has the lowest projected cumulative defaults at 168 basis points, which is consistent with the absence of loans with DSCRs < 1.25 and the very low percentage of loans with LTVs > 75%.

Exhibit 4: Projected Defaults for Representative CMBS Deals

Deal	Projected Cumulative Defaults (in basis points)	Actual CMBS Data			
		% of Loans DSCR< 1.25x	% of Loan LTV > 75%	% of Loan Office	% of Loan CA
Chase 98-1	321	9.70%	25.60%	21.30%	15.70%
FULB 98-C2	305	7.70%	36.60%	20.40%	11.80%
BSCMS 98-C1	168	0.00%	7.50%	17.20%	27.40%
GMAC 97-C1	613	28.12%	27.16%	18.07%	17.30%
GMAC 98-C1	394	8.00%	38.30%	11.00%	9.00%
MCFI 98-MC2	553	21.00%	52.00%	34.00%	12.00%

Exhibit 5: Expected and Worst Case Defaults from Model Simulation: MSCI 1998 - HF2

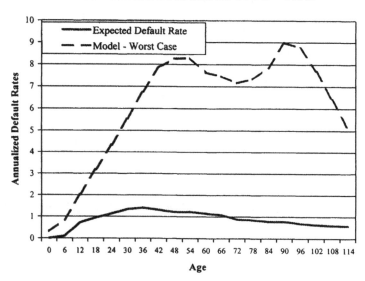

The simulation approach also provides a framework for analyzing the impact of defaults on individual tranches within a structure. For example, Exhibit 5 shows our expected default curve for a representative CMBS deal — MSCI 1998-HF2. If the losses implied by the expected curve shown in Exhibit 5 are applied to the deal structure, we find that all of the tranches down to the B-rated bond remain intact.[2] However, the unrated and CCC rated tranches are completely wiped out while 17% of the principal of the B-rated tranche is eroded (see Exhibit 6).

---

[2] We assume a loss severity of 30%.

Exhibit 6: Projected Cumulative Losses by Tranche for MSCI 1998 - HF2 Using Expected Defaults Curve

Tranche	Size of Tranche ($ mill)	Cumulative Loss ($ mill)	Cumulative Loss As a %of Original Bal.
AAA (10yr)	547.80	0	0
AA	52.90	0	0
A	52.90	0	0
BBB	58.20	0	0
BBB–	21.20	0	0
BB	18.50	0	0
B	10.60	0	0
B–	15.90	2.7	17
CCC	10.60	10.6	100
Unrated	10.60	10.6	100

Assumptions: 30% severity; 18 month lag to recovery

Exhibit 7: Projected Cumulative Losses by Tranche for MSCI 1998 - HF2 Using Worse Case Scenario

Tranche	Size of Tranche ($ mill)	Cumulative Loss ($ mill)	Cumulative Loss As a %of Original Bal.
AAA (10yr)	547.80	0	0
AA	52.90	0	0
A	52.90	0	0
BBB	58.20	0	0
BBB–	21.20	9.1	43
BB	18.50	18.5	100
B	10.60	10.6	100
B–	15.90	15.9	17
CCC	10.60	10.6	100
Unrated	10.60	10.6	100

Assumptions: 30% severity; 18 month lag to recovery

We can further stress the deal by selecting the single worst case scenario from all of the random scenarios generated during the simulation. This vector, also shown in Exhibit 5, peaks at an 9.0% CDR, over six times the peak CDR of the expected case and well above the highest CDR registered by commercial loans held by insurance companies since 1990. If we apply losses from the worst case scenario we find that all of the investment grade tranches remain intact; 43% of the BBB– tranche is eroded; and all of the BB and lower rated tranches are completely wiped out (see Exhibit 7). Although not done here, we can further assess the risk profile of a particular deal by again using our simulation results to define confidence intervals around our expected default curve.

Michael Youngblood, Ph.D.
Managing Director
Banc of America Securities LLC

INTRODUCTION

The market for multifamily and commercial mortgage securities has grown dramatically in the 1990s, from a meager $5.7 billion in 1990 to $170.7 billion in the first quarter of 1999. Such vigorous issuance has provided investors with a wide range of opportunities, spanning virtually all investment grades (from AAA rated to unrated), intermediate and long maturities, fixed and floating interest rates, and property types. In addition, it has enlarged the secondary market for multifamily and commercial mortgage securities. Nevertheless, the proliferation of multifamily and commercial mortgage securities should not obscure the risks to which they expose investors. Greater liquidity does not necessarily mean lower risk, as the markets for high-yield securities and syndicated bank loans attest. The primary risks facing investors are prepayment or default of one or more of the underlying mortgage loans. These events could result in reinvestment of principal at lower interest rates and or in outright loss of expected interest or principal, or both. Even if a subordinated class or cash reserve fund should absorb any loss, the elevated cash flow variability or the reduction in available credit enhancement could widen yield spreads and undermine performance. These are, obviously, the primary risks of single-family mortgage securities as well, although the much larger size of the underlying loans and the much smaller number of them magnify these risks for multifamily and commercial mortgage securities.

Consider the most salient examples of the risk of prepayment and default of these securities in recent years:

- One $122 million privately-placed floating-rate multifamily security, issued in June 1993 and maturing in August 1998, was refinanced two years later. Ironically, the borrower used the same collateral to support a new $125 million fixed-rate security, maturing in 2015, in July 1996.

- Cumulative losses have exhausted the $122.2 million reserve fund of Resolution Trust Corporation, Series 1991-M2, leaving a single $51.9 million subordinated class to protect $151.6 million of senior classes from future losses (as of the July 1996 remittance report). In light of the vulnerability of the senior classes, Moody's Investors Service and Standard & Poor's Rating Group have sliced the original ratings from Aa1/AA or Aa2/AA to Baa3/B.

- The first two non-RTC multifamily securities issued in the 1990s have effectively failed. The rating of very first security tumbled from AA in 1991 to D (Standard & Poor's) in July 1996, as the most senior class incurred losses of $1.7 million, or 3.1% of the unpaid principal balance, after the utter depletion of the subordinated classes. To forestall potentially huge investor losses, the issuer of the second non-agency security of 1991 repurchased all of its senior classes in 1994. The ratings on this security and one other, which was also repurchased, were withdrawn before they could be cut.

The poor performance of these landmark issues, three of which contributed prominently to re-establishing the non-agency multifamily market in 1991, after its virtual dissolution in the late 1980s, highlights the risks inherent in multifamily and commercial securities.

    We can evaluate the risks of prepayment and default of multifamily mortgage loans and securities through the same option-theoretic approach that has evolved to evaluate them for single-family mortgage loans and securities. This approach has evolved from the seminal work of Black and Scholes,[1] Merton,[2] and Cox, Ingersoll, and Ross,[3] and from continuous refinements by Fabozzi and practitioners over the past decade. In this chapter, we focus exclusively on multifamily loans and securities to illustrate the approach. We focus here on prepayment and default of multifamily mortgage loans rather than securities because the former necessarily leads to the latter. And the operation of non-agency credit enhancement in absorbing losses on the loans underlying multifamily securities requires no explanation to institutional investors. While using a common option-theoretic approach, we need to adjust for certain fundamental differences between multifamily and residential loans, borrowers, and properties. By adjusting for these differences, we can specify the multifamily (and, without loss of generality, commercial) prepayment and default functions that allow optional valuation under Monte Carlo or binomial simulation of an interest rate process.

---

[1] Fischer Black and Myron Scholes, "The Pricing of Options and Corporate Liabilities," *Journal of Political Economy*, 81 (1972), pp. 637-54.

[2] Robert Merton, "Theory of Rational Option Pricing," *Bell Journal of Economics and Management Science*, 4 (1973), pp. 141-83.

[3] J.C. Cox, J.E. Ingersoll Jr., and S.A. Ross, "A Theory of the Term Structure of Interest Rates," *Econometrica*, 53 (1985), pp. 385-407.

CONSTRAINTS ON PREPAYMENT

Multifamily and residential mortgage loans differ fundamentally in their terms and conditions. Multifamily mortgage loans generally amortize over terms of 240 to 360 months, with a final balloon payment of principal due in 60 to 240 months. Some loans amortize fully over terms of 300 to 360 months, with no balloon payment. Some loans do not amortize at all, but pay only interest until the final maturity date. Most loans have significant constraints on prepayment before maturity, which can take many forms:

- lock-out periods, which absolutely prohibit prepayment and which may be succeeded by further constraints.
- yield maintenance premiums that require the borrower to pay the present value of the change in the yield of a specified Treasury note between closing date and prepayment date, depriving him or her of any pure interest-rate incentive to refinance; variations in calculating these premiums may reduce the borrower's disincentive.
- prepayment penalties, expressed as a percentage of the unpaid principal balance of the loan, which typically decline as the loan approaches maturity.
- defeasance provisions, which do not permit prepayment of the underlying mortgage loan until its scheduled balloon or maturity date, but which allow the borrower to substitute a portfolio of U.S. Treasuries which match the scheduled payments of principal and interest.

Loans that do allow the borrower to prepay, subject to constraints like these, usually require payment in full and explicitly prohibit partial payment. In contrast, the huge majority of single-family mortgage loans, whether fixed-rate or adjustable-rate, amortize over 15- or 30-year terms. (Of course, the comparatively small number of residential balloon loans amortize over 360 months, with final payments of principal due in five or seven years.) Single-family loans generally permit prepayment in full or in part at any time without penalty.

RATIONAL EXERCISE OF OPTIONS

The multifamily borrower has invested equity in and raised debt on the security of the apartment property solely to obtain the after-tax real financial returns that it generates, in the form of periodic income and ultimate proceeds from sale. In maximizing the return on equity, the borrower, who is rarely an individual and usually a partnership or corporation, will act rationally to prepay or to default on the mortgage loan. In contrast, residential borrowers usually derive housing services as well as financial returns from the equity and debt invested in a house; the physical or emotional value of housing services may outweigh the investment returns. Hence, the residential borrower may not act rationally to maximize return on investment. Moreover, individuals generally lack access to the full information about alternative returns from investment or costs of debt that institutional borrowers generally possess, which ignorance may contribute to evidently irrational actions.

The multifamily borrower will generally prepay the mortgage loan, subject to the constraints set forth in the related note or deed of trust, when the present value of the scheduled payments exceeds the present value of payments on a new loan under whatever terms may prevail in the future, plus transaction and other costs. If the borrower seeks to prepay when yield maintenance or prepayment penalties are required by the note, then these payments will effectively increase the present value of the alternative loan. Similarly, the borrower will incur substantial upfront costs in refinancing a multifamily mortgage loan, which will overtly increase the present value of the alternative loan. These expenses include:

- the fees to the commercial loan broker who located the lender of the new loan (1% to 3% of the new loan amount)
- commitment fees and other "inducements" to the lender (1% to 5%)
- the title insurance policy or its equivalent (1%)
- fees for a FFIEC-eligible appraisal, engineering report, and Phase I environment assessment
- legal fees, including those for recordation

The last two typically represent 0.50% of the new loan amount. It is estimated that borrowers incur transactions costs, on average, of 5% of the new loan amount. These average transaction costs are roughly equivalent to an additional 1% on the annual interest rate of a 10-year non-amortizing balloon mortgage loan. In sharp contrast, residential borrowers can obtain new loans for average points and fees of 1.50%, or less, of the loan amount.

Furthermore, the engineering report and Phase I environment assessment may reveal deferred maintenance, or violations of building codes, or environmental hazards. These may range from the innocuous, i.e., potholes in the parking lot, to the pathological, i.e., friable "popcorn" asbestos sprayed on a significant proportion of the interior surface of an apartment building. If these conditions impair the current or future value of the building, then the lender will routinely require the borrower to cure these conditions. The lender will always require cure of building code violations, without which the borrower cannot obtain a certificate of occupancy. The lender may not agree to advance any or all of the funds needed to cure these conditions, which would present the borrower with additional upfront expenditures, further inflating the present value of alternative credit. Together, prepayment penalties, transactions costs, and deferred maintenance expenditures set a high threshold on prepayment that can deter the borrower from prepayment.

Prepayment Function

In light of these considerations, we can define the *prepayment function* as the relationship between the present value of the existing loan under the terms set forth in the mortgage note, and the present value of an alternative mortgage loan under whatever terms lenders may offer in the future. The prepayment function discounts the principal and interest payments scheduled under the original loan by current interest rates, plus the average risk premium or yield spread that lenders currently charge for comparable loans as expressed mathematically below:

$$\Pi_0 = \sum_{i=0}^{T} (P_i + I_i)\left(1 + \frac{r_0 + s}{2}\right)^{-2t_i} \tag{1}$$

where

$$\begin{aligned}
\Pi_0 &= \text{the original loan amount} \\
P_i &= \text{the scheduled principal payment of period } i \\
I_i &= \text{the scheduled interest payment of period } i \\
T &= \text{the final period} \\
r_0 &= \text{the base rate at origination (month 0)} \\
t_i &= \text{the time to receive principal and inters payments of period } i \\
s &= \text{the risk premium}
\end{aligned}$$

It also discounts the principal and interest payments scheduled under the alternative loan by the interest rates that prevail in the future, plus the same risk premium, and then adds prepayment penalties, transaction costs, and deferred maintenance expenditures as expressed below:

$$\sum_{i=0}^{T} (P_i + I_i)\left(1 + \frac{r_{i_0} + s}{2}\right)^{-2(t_i - t_{i_0})} = \Pi_{i_0} + PP_{i_0} + PTC_0 + DM_0 \tag{2}$$

where:

$$\begin{aligned}
&T, t_i, s, P_i, \text{ and } I_i \text{ are the same as above} \\
r_i &= \text{the discount rate at } i_0 \\
&= \text{the alternative loan amount at } i_0 \\
PP_{i_0} &= \text{the prepayment penalty at } i_0 \\
PTC_0 &= \text{the prepayment transaction cost} \\
DM_0 &= \text{deferred maintenance expenditures}
\end{aligned}$$

If the value of first term of the inequality, the existing loan, exceeds that of the second term, the alternative loan, then the borrower should prepay, presumably in the following month.

The rationality of the borrower simplifies this part of the valuation of multifamily loans relative to that of residential loans. One does not need to introduce an econometric model to estimate the likelihood or rate of non-rational prepayment as one does with residential loans. One needs only to solve the prepayment function in conjunction with an appropriate interest-rate process.

UNDERSTANDING THE BORROWER'S DECISION

Unlike the residential borrower who acquires a house as a shelter and as an investment, the multifamily borrower acquires an apartment property only as an investment. He or she acquires the property, with a mixture of equity and debt, in order to receive the monthly *net operating income* and the proceeds from eventual sale that it will generate. Net operating income is the cash that remains after deducting the opportunity cost of vacant units and the operating expenses of a property from its gross possible income.[4] It does not include deductions for accounting depreciation or debt service payments. Most real estate investors calculate the expected return on equity and debt from net operating income and sale proceeds, using one of the many forms of the *discounted cash flow approach*.

However, the borrower does not receive net operating income, but rather the residual cash that remains after payment of scheduled principal and interest and of escrows for property taxes, insurance premiums, replacement reserves, and other impounds. Indeed, multifamily loans sometimes require the apartment manager to remit all rents, late payment penalties, deposit forfeitures, and other collections directly to a lock box, which the lender controls. The lender will remit to the borrower only the residual amount that remains after payment of all amounts due. Similarly, the borrower does not receive all of the proceeds from the eventual sale of the property, but rather the residual cash after repaying the unamortized loan amount. No lender will release the title on sale of a property until payment of the remaining loan amount, any interest accrued but not yet paid, and any late payment penalties outstanding.

Therefore, the borrower should expect to receive the present values of the monthly net income from the property and the net proceeds from sale. The present values of the net income and the net proceeds will jointly determine the borrower's decision each month over the life of the mortgage loan either to make principal and interest payments, and other mandatory payments, or to default. Understanding this monthly decision is essential to the analysis that follows: the valuation of the borrower's option to default depends on both the net income and the net proceeds. Unless net income falls below zero (when net operating income is less than principal and interest payments), the borrower will not default, even if the present value of net proceeds is negative (when the market value of the property is less than the loan amount). Monthly net income must fall below zero *and* the market value of the property must fall below that of the loan balance.

---

[4] See Charles Wurtzebach and Mike Miles, *Modern Real Estate*, 4th ed. (New York: John Wiley, 1991), pp. 206-211.

Furthermore, the borrower will include transaction costs in the monthly decision to pay or to default on the loan. Whereas one can quantify the transaction costs incurred in prepayment, one cannot precisely quantify those incurred in default because they include three components that vary widely among borrowers:

- decreased availability and increased cost of future debt and equity
- lender recourse to the borrower
- federal income tax liability

First, some lenders do not extend credit to real estate borrowers with a history of uncured defaults. Those who do extend credit to such borrowers routinely impose more stringent terms; these terms may become onerous for borrowers with a history of opportunistic default. Second, fewer loans originated in the 1990s than heretofore allow recourse to the borrower in the event of default. The declining popularity of recourse provisions belongs, in part, to fierce competition from conduits and other non-traditional lenders and, in part, to the legal form of many borrowers. If the borrower takes the legal form of a limited partnership or a special purpose corporation, the mortgaged property may be the only asset. Where recourse provisions exist, the borrower must weigh the likelihood of the loss of other assets in addition to those explicitly pledged in the mortgage note. One cannot measure the value of these assets, or the lender's ability to locate and attach them. Third, the borrower will incur a federal income tax liability equal to the difference between the loan amount and the property value. The value of this difference to the borrower depends upon his or her marginal income tax rate and other considerations, which one does not know.

Nevertheless, one can estimate the loss of operating funds, the forfeiture of property, and certain expenses:

- operating income from the property until definitive foreclosure
- working capital, accounts receivable, and escrows
- furniture, fixtures, and equipment used to furnish or manage the property
- management fees for operating the property
- legal fees, which increase if the borrower also files for bankruptcy

Offsetting these costs, the borrower may retain rents, late payment fees, and other miscellaneous income collected over several months, until the lender can accelerate the mortgage note and take control of the property. We estimate that these transaction costs average 7.0% of the loan amount.

Default Function

In light of these considerations, one can define the *default function* from two simultaneous relationships:

- monthly net operating income less scheduled principal and interest, and other payments over the term of the *loan*

- the present value of monthly net operating income over the life of the *property*, plus transaction costs, less the present value of scheduled principal (including the final balloon) and interest, and other payments over the term of the loan

As long as the first relationship remains positive, the borrower will not default. He or she has sufficient income to pay monthly debt service, and, bolstered by the endemic optimism of real estate investors, will continue to make scheduled payments even if the second relationship has turned negative. As long as the second relationship remains positive, the borrower will not default. He or she retains the excess of the property value over the loan amount, or positive equity. If the first relationship turns negative, then he or she can sell the property, repay the outstanding loan, thereby avoiding default, and realize the amount of positive equity. This relationship reveals an important aspect of the default option on mortgage loans: the loan amount represents the price at which the borrower can sell, in effect, the property to the lender at any time in the future, should equity become negative. When the first and second relationships turn negative, the borrower will default. He or she lacks the income to pay scheduled monthly principal and interest, while the future value of the property, plus transaction costs, has fallen below the loan amount, leaving negative equity.

Rents, Vacancies, and Operating Expenses

The default function of the first relationship compares net operating income to scheduled payments of principal and interest, and escrows. Hence, it requires projection of net operating income as the sum of gross possible rents, the opportunity cost of vacant units, and operating expenses, for each month over the term of the loan. We project future rents as a function of employment growth, income growth, population growth, household formation, housing affordability, net change in the stock of apartments, the natural vacancy rate — all from the housing sub-market in which the property is located — and future 10-year Treasury rates. We estimate the opportunity cost of vacant units from the *natural vacancy rate*, as developed by Rosen and Smith[5] as an equilibrium function of historical rents and operating expenses. Last, we project future operating expenses from their historical correlation with rents. Like the prepayment function, the default function discounts the scheduled principal and interest payments, and other payments, on the loan by the interest rates that prevail in the future, plus the initial risk premium or spread charged by the lender. Therefore, we can project both the net operating income from the property, over the life of the property, and the scheduled payments, over the term of the loan, given an interest rate process.

Similarly, the default function of the second relationship discounts monthly net operating income over the life of the property by the interest rates

---

[5] Kenneth Rosen and Lawrence B. Smith, "The Price-Adjustment Process for Rental Housing and the Natural Vacancy Rate," *American Economic Review*, vol. 73 (1983), pp. 779-786, and Lawrence B. Smith, "A Note on the Price Adjustment Mechanism for Rental Housing," *American Economic Review*, vol. 64 (1974), pp. 478-481.

that prevail in the future, plus the multifamily risk premium. We project net operating income as before over the expected *economic life* of the property, which we obtain the from the mandatory FFIEC-eligible appraisal or engineering report. A new apartment property has an expected economic life of 50 years, assuming that rehabilitation does not extend it, but most of the apartment properties underlying multifamily (and mixed-property commercial) securities are not new, which reduces the term over which they can generate net operating income.

The default function of the second relationship discounts the net operating income by the interest rates expected to prevail in the future, plus a multifamily risk premium. The multifamily risk premium is the entrepreneurial return that the borrower requires for investing equity and debt in the apartment property. We measure it by the spread between the *yield capitalization rate* of the property and the interest rates that prevailed at origination of the mortgage loan. The yield capitalization rate is the internal rate of return that equated the appraised or sales value of the apartment property, at the time of the origination of the mortgage loan, to the future net operating income that it may generate over its economic life, assuming no rehabilitation.[6]

Therefore, default occurs in any month i_0 over the term of the mortgage loan, if both of the following relationships are satisfied:

$$NOI_{i_0} < P_{i_0} + I_{i_0} + E_{i_0} \tag{3}$$

$$\sum_{i = i0}^{EL} NOI_i \left(1 + \frac{r_{i_0} + ycr}{2} \right)^{-2(t_i - t_0)} + DTC_0$$

$$- \sum_{i = i_0}^{T - 1} (P_i + I_i + E_i) \left(1 + \frac{r_{i_0} + s}{2} \right)^{-2(t_i - t_0)} < 0 \tag{4}$$

where:

NOI_{i_0} = a (future) payment of net operating income, from the rent process, at period i

r_{i_0} = the discount rate at period i_0

ycr = the discount mortgage risk premium

P_i = the scheduled principal payment of period i

I_i = the scheduled interest payment of period i

T = the final period in the term of the mortgage loan

EL = the final period in the economic life of the property

r_0 = the base rate at origination (month 0)

t_i = the time to receive principal and inters payments of period i

s = the risk premium

DTC_i = default transactions costs at period i

---

[6] See Kenneth M. Lusht and Jeffrey D. Fisher, "Anticipated Growth and the Specification of Debt in Real Estate Value Models," *AREUEA Journal*, vol. 12 (1984), pp. 1-11.

Alternatively, we can re-write equation (4) such that default occurs if the following inequality obtains:

$$\frac{\sum_{i=i0}^{EL} NOI_i\left(1 + \frac{r_{i_0} + ycr}{2}\right)^{-2(t_i - t_0)} + DTC_0}{\sum_{i=i_0}^{T-1}(P_i + I_i + E_i)\left(1 + \frac{r_{i_0} + s}{2}\right)^{-2(t_i - t_0)}} < 1 \tag{5}$$

If the ratio of present value of the property, plus default transaction costs, to the present value of the mortgage loan falls below 1 and if the relationship in equation (3) is less than zero, then the borrower will default.

INTEGRATING PREPAYMENT AND DEFAULT EXPERIENCE

The default and prepayment functions assume the same interest rate process, which generates the future interest rates that discount both the principal and interest payments of the mortgage loan and the net operating income of the apartment property. For the interest rate process, we employ a proprietary multifactor model of the term structure. We begin with the discount rate of the on-the-run 1-month Treasury bill and generate a series of 1-month arbitrage-free forward rates that extend over the entire Treasury yield curve, i.e., over 360 months. We calibrate these rates so that they recover, or produce the exact prices of, the on-the-run Treasury coupon curve. These are the future interest rates described in the two previous sections. Generating these rates requires the on-the-run Treasury yield curve and a measure of interest-rate volatility for each of the 360 months. To provide the monthly volatilities, we interpolate the term structure of volatility from the series of average implied volatilities of puts and calls on (U.S. dollar) interest rate swaps, which range from one week to 10 years in term. Furthermore, we can generate a full path of 360 arbitrage-free riskless discount rates for any sequence of 360 monthly volatilities that we may produce with Monte Carlo or other methods.[7]

By applying the default and prepayment functions simultaneously to the path of forward discount rates generated by this process, we can simulate the borrower's decision to default on or prepay any multifamily loan in the present or any future month. Indeed, we can value the borrower's options to default and to prepay by simulating these decisions over all possible paths of forward discount rates. While this comprehensive simulation would require infinite calculations, we can achieve equivalent valuation of the borrower's options by simulating a finite

---

[7] See Frank J. Fabozzi, *Valuation of Fixed Income Securities and Derivatives* (New Hope, PA: Frank J. Fabozzi Associates, 1995), pp. 131-154.

set of paths of forward discount rates that achieves a normal distribution, using established tests with appropriate size and power for the normal distribution.

To value the options to default and to prepay, we simulate the borrower's rational decisions over a sufficiently large set of discount rate paths in the following sequence:

- Decompose the loan amount into its scheduled monthly payments of principal and interest over months (t) of its remaining term, and its balloon payment, if any, at term (T).
- Re-price the loan, using the appropriate on-the-run Treasury note, plus a risk premium, which is the average yield spread charged by lenders on comparable loans for the same term.
- Solve for the Z-spread of the loan, using current forward discount rates.
- Calculate the present value of the loan over every month in its term with the associated forward discount rate plus the Z-spread.
- Over every path, calculate the present value of the loan over every month with the associated forward discount rate plus the Z-spread.
- Compare the present value of the loan, obtained using current rates, with the present value of the loan (plus prepayment penalties, prepayment transaction costs, and deferred maintenance expenditures) in each path, using path-specific rates; if the conditions of equation (1) obtain in any month in any path, prepay the unamortized principal balance.
- Decompose the property value into its projected net operating income over months (t) of its expected economic life (EL).
- Solve for the yield capitalization rate and the related Z-spread of the mortgaged property, using the contemporary appraised value or sales price, and current forward discount rates.
- Calculate the present value of the property over every month with the associated forward discount rate plus the Z-spread.
- Compare the present value of the property, obtained using current rates (plus default transaction costs) with the present value of the loan in each path, using path-specific rates; if the conditions of equations (3) and (4) or (3) and (5) obtain in any month in any path, default the mortgage loan.
- Integrate the principal and interest payments over every month and every path; then solve for that risk-adjusted spread to the discount rates in every path that produces an average loan price equal to price of the loan.

CREDIT RISK OPTION-ADJUSTED SPREAD

This approach to the simultaneous valuation of the borrower's options to prepay and default enables us to solve for the option-adjusted spread (OAS) or, more precisely, the credit risk option-adjusted spread (CROAS) of a multifamily mortgage loan. Solution of CROAS requires only two steps, assuming the prior simulation of arbitrage-free forward discount rates along a sufficiently large number of paths. First, we integrate the principal and interest payments that result from allowing rational prepayment and default in every month over the term of the loan and over every path of forward discount rates. One series of payments, from origination to termination of the loan, corresponds to each path of discount rates. Second, we solve iteratively (by trial and error) for the spread, that added to the forward rates along each path, will discount each series of monthly payments to its present value, the average of which equals the current price of the loan (plus accrued interest). The semi-annual bond-equivalent of this spread is the CROAS in the equation below:

$$P + I = \sum_{i=0}^{N} \sum_{j=0}^{T} (PF_{i,j} + IF_{i,j}) \times D_i \times \prod_{i=d}^{i+d} \left(1 + \frac{r_{i,j} + s'}{12}\right) \tag{6}$$

$$s = 2 \times \left[\left(1 + \frac{y' + s'}{12}\right)^6 - \left(1 + \frac{y}{2}\right)\right]$$

where

P	=	the price
I	=	the accrued interest
N	=	the number of paths
T	=	the number of months to maturity
$PF_{i,j}$	=	the principal cash flow in ith path and jth month
$IF_{i,j}$	=	the interest cash flow in ith path and jth month
D_i	=	the extra discount factor in ith path due to fractional month of the cash flow's timing
$r_{i,j}$	=	the 1-month Treasury rate (30/360) in ith path and jth month
y'	=	the mortgage-equivalent 10-year
s'	=	the CROAS expressed in mortgage equivalent term (12 month compounding)
y	=	the bond-equivalent 10-year Treasury yield
s	=	the CROAS expressed in bond equivalent term (semi-annual compounding)

This CROAS is directly comparable to the OAS of any mortgage or non-mortgage security evaluated using the same interest rate process.

Furthermore, we can calculate the first and second derivatives of the price and CROAS of the multifamily loan with respect to the term structures of interest rates and volatility: *effective duration, convexity, volatility sensitivity, volatility convexity,* and so on. We calculate these additional parameters of value by numerical methods, changing the term structures of interest rates or of (average implied swaption) volatility. For *effective duration,* we increase the term structure of discount rates by any arbitrary magnitude, for example, 25 basis points, for all paths and solve for the average price that results. We then decrease the term structure by the same magnitude for all paths and solve for the average price that results. The difference between the two average prices that result, scaled by the change in basis points and the current price, is the effective duration of the mortgage loan as shown in equation (7).

$$D = \frac{\Delta P}{2P\Delta y} = \frac{P_+ - P_-}{2P\Delta y} \tag{7}$$

where

$\quad D \;=\;$ the duration
$\quad C \;=\;$ the convexity
$\quad P \;=\;$ the current price
$\quad P_+ \;=\;$ the projected price when the yield curve is up by Δy
$\quad P_- \;=\;$ the projected price when the yield curve is down by Δy

Equation (7) measures the sensitivity of the price of the loan to a change in the term structure of interest rates, unlike the modified duration of an option-free securities, which measures the sensitivity of the price to a change in yield. The second derivative of price with respect to the term structure of interest rates, *convexity*, follows directly from this calculation. It is the effective duration scaled by the current price multiplied by the square of the same change in interest rates as shown in equation (8).[8]

$$C = \frac{\Delta^2 P}{100P\Delta y^2} = \frac{P_+ - 2P + P_-}{100P\Delta y^2} \tag{8}$$

We calculate the volatility sensitivity and the volatility convexity of the mortgage loan in the same way.

A MULTIFAMILY EXAMPLE

Consider the example of a representative multifamily mortgage loan, which was underwritten to FNMA DUS standards and originated in August 1996. FNMA's underwriting standards for the DUS program are representative of those employed by most institutional lenders; indeed, most conduit lenders have openly embraced these standards for their multifamily programs for the expedient reason that the rating agencies and institutional investors generally accept them. The lender furnished the following limited information about the loan and the related property:

---

[8] Andrew Kalotay, George Williams, and Frank J. Fabozzi, "A Model for Valuing Bonds and Embedded Options," *Financial Analysts Journal* (May-June 1993), pp. 35-46, and Fabozzi, *Valuation of Fixed Income Securities and Derivatives*, pp. 93-130.

Property city, state, and zip code:	Houston, TX 77077
Principal balance amount:	$8,000,000
Mortgage interest rate:	8.42%
Maturity date:	8/1/2006
Original amortization term:	30 years
Prepayment premium option:	Yield maintenance
Yield maintenance period:	7.0 years
U.S. Treasury yield rate:	5.625%
Security due date:	2/1/2006
Total number of units:	436
Annual net operating income:	$951,904
Loan-to-value ratio:	79.21%
Appraised value:	$10,100,000
Occupancy:	92%
Debt service coverage ratio:	1.29×

From our own analysis of the Briar Forest sub-market, in which this property is located, and our econometric models of the apartment market in metropolitan Houston, we add the following to FNMA's information:

Risk premium of DUS Tier II loans:	1.67%
Yield capitalization rate:	13.00
Long-term rent growth rate:	3.26
Long-term rent volatility:	6.86
Natural vacancy rate:	11.20
Prepayment transaction costs:	5.00
Default transaction costs:	7.00

From this information and our projections of rent growth, rent volatility, and the natural vacancy rate for the apartment property, we calculate the following parameters of risk and value:

Frequency of prepayments:	11.3%
Average months to prepayment:	83
Average prepayment price:	107-04 (32s)
Option Cost:	9 b.p.
Frequency of defaults:	20.7%
Average months to default:	82
Average loss severity:	27.1%
Option cost:	45 b.p.
Z-spread:	166 b.p.
Prepayment and default option cost:	54 b.p.
CROAS:	112 b.p.
Effective duration:	6.08 years
Convexity:	0.30

This multifamily mortgage loan has an 11.3% probability of prepaying and a 20.7% probability of defaulting over its 10-year term. The probabilities of prepayment and default combine to reduce the nominal and Z-spreads of this mortgage loan by 54 basis points to a CROAS of 112 basis points. Similarly, the effective duration of the loan, which reflects the combined risks, is 6.08 years, whereas the modified duration of the loan, which assumes neither prepayment nor default, is somewhat longer, 6.25 years.

It is striking that the frequency of default and the average severity of loss projected on this multifamily loan, which was underwritten to common institutional standards, fall within the ranges of default and loss experienced historically by mainstream institutional lenders. From his most recent study of the historical performance of commercial mortgage loans originated by life insurance companies in the years 1972-1991, Synderman finds an aggregate lifetime rate of default of 13.8%.[9] However, Synderman concedes that the historical default rate is artificially low, because many of the loans in the insurance company sample remain outstanding — they have yet to default or mature. After adjustment, he projects an 18.3% lifetime default rate. Similarly, on reviewing Synderman's first two studies, Fitch Investors Service noticed that the widespread restructuring of loans by life companies reduced the frequency of default.[10] Based on this review and a separate study of the commercial mortgage portfolios of 11 life companies, Fitch projects a much higher lifetime default rate of 30%. This level forms the baseline for its rating of commercial mortgage securities. It is also consistent with the default rate projected on the representative multifamily mortgage loan.

In addition, Synderman finds that the severity of loss of commercial mortgage loans (measured as a percentage of the unpaid principal balance) varies widely by the origination year, from a low of −7% in 1972 to a high of 96% in 1984. He concludes that the severity of loss averaged 33% in the 1970s and 45% in the 1980s; the average yield cost of default was 50 basis points. Fitch adopts the average loss severity of the 1980s, projecting a loss factor of 40% to 50% for defaulted commercial mortgage loans. As with default frequency, the loss severity projected on the representative multifamily loan is consistent with the historical experience of mainstream commercial lenders. Indeed, Synderman's estimate of the yield cost of default of 50 basis points is virtually the same as the yield cost of default of 45 basis points on this multifamily loan.

MODEL SENSITIVITIES

We can explore the risks of this multifamily mortgage loan in greater depth by calculating the sensitivity of the CROAS to its salient parameters: *loan-to-value ratio, debt service coverage ratio, term to maturity of the loan, long-term rent growth rate, long-term rent volatility*, and *natural vacancy rate*. By exploring the partial derivatives of these parameters to CROAS, we expose the influence on the likelihood of prepayment and default of the underwriting criteria, the terms and conditions of the loan itself, and the local property market (see Exhibit 1). Accordingly, we vary each parameter across a wide, but arbitrary range of values

---

[9] Mark Snyderman, "Update on Commercial Mortgage Defaults," *Real Estate Finance Journal* (Summer 1994), pp. 22-32.
[10] Fitch Investors Service, Inc., "Commercial Mortgage Stress Test," *Structured Finance* (June 8, 1992), pp. 1-12.

and record the CROAS that results, in the form of basis points and price; we hold all other parameters and the price of the loan constant.

- Increases in the loan-to-value ratio (LTV), by diminishing the borrower's equity and increasing his or her leverage, decrease CROAS modestly. A decline in LTV from 79.8% to 55% increases CROAS from 112 basis points to 136 basis points. Decreases in LTV increase CROAS symmetrically.
- Increases in the debt service coverage ratio (DSCR) increase CROAS slightly less than the given changes in LTV. An increase from 1.29× to 2.5× DSCR would increase CROAS from 112 basis points to 131 basis points. Decreases in DSCR also affect CROAS symmetrically.
- Term to maturity affects CROAS inversely: the longer the term of the loan, the lower CROAS. This inverse relationship reflects the operation of volatility; the longer a loan remains outstanding, the broader the range of rental growth rates, including negative rates, that may occur. Term to maturity affects most options in this fashion, especially the short-term exchange-traded financial options that the Black-Scholes or Black futures models evaluate accurately. Indeed, given the unambiguously positive influence that shorter terms have on CROAS, it is paradoxical that the four rating agencies penalize loans with them, requiring more credit enhancement than for otherwise identical loans with longer terms.

Exhibit 1: Sensitivity of Parameters and Terms of Multifamily Mortgage Loan Expressed as CROAS (in basis points and price in 32s)

The influence of these parameters on CROAS reveals its acute vulnerability to the initial equity and leverage of the borrower, and to the conditions of the local market. Investors will need to scrutinize carefully loans with LTVs above 85% or DSCRs below 1.2%, and loans with underlying properties located in volatile real estate markets.

					Base					
LTV (%)	100	95	90	85	79.8	75	70	65	60	55
CROAS (b.p.)	83	91	99	106	112	120	125	129	133	136
CROAS (32s)	4-24	4-10	3-27	3-15	3-05	2-21+	2-14	2-05	1-30+	1-25
DSCR	0.90	1.00	1.10	1.20	1.29	1.40	1.50	1.75	2.00	2.50
CROAS (b.p.)	94	102	109	110	112	116	117	122	126	131
CROAS (32s)	4-02+	3-21	3-09	3-07	3-05	2-30	2-27	2-19	2-12	2-03+
Term (Years)	30	25	20	15	10	7	5	3	2	1
CROAS (b.p.)	52	54	59	76	112	128	130	143	184	229
CROAS (32s)	5-24+	5-21+	5-11	4-18+	3-05	2-17+	2-11	1-19	0-23+	0-08+
Rent Growth (%)	−1.0	0.0	1.0	2.0	3.3	4.0	4.5	5.0	5.5	6.0
CROAS (b.p.)	42	64	81	98	112	123	127	131	134	137
CROAS (32s)	15-28+	5-20+	4-25+	3-28	3-05	2-16	2-08+	2-02	1-29	1-22+
Rent Vol (%)	25.0	20.0	15.0	10.0	6.9	5.9	4.9	3.9	2.9	1.9
CROAS (b.p.)	−83	−35	11	77	112	128	137	144	150	154
CROAS (32s)	12-21	10-14	8-08	5-00	3-05	2-07+	1-23+	1-10+	0-29+	0-23+

Exhibit 2: Structure of Evans Withycombe Finance Trust, August 1994 (Dollars in Millions)

Class	Amount	Coupon (%)	Maturity	Call Date
A-1 (Senior)	102.0	7.98	8/1/2001	3/1/2001
A-2 (Sub.)	15.0	7.98	8/1/2001	3/1/2001
A-3 (Sub.)	9.0	7.98	8/1/2001	3/1/2001
A-4 (Sub.)	5.0	7.98	8/1/2001	3/1/2001

- The long-term rent growth rate affects CROAS strongly and asymmetrically. An increase from 3.26% to 6.0% increases CROAS from 112 basis points to 137 basis points, but a decrease to −1% drops CROAS to 42 basis points. It is noteworthy that the rent growth rate crosses a threshold of sensitivity below 2%. From 2% to 0%, the rent growth rate cannot overcome the influence of the projected 6.9% volatility, which propagates enough simulated negative growth rates to render CROAS consistently negative. Of course, below 0%, negative growth rates predominate with commensurate effects on CROAS.
- Long-term rent volatility affects CROAS even more strongly than the rent growth rate. It governs the range of potential growth rates associated with the simulated forward discount rates, in effect, raising or lowering the influence of interest rates on rents. High levels of volatility will propagate over time broader ranges of rent growth rates, including negative rates, that ultimately turn CROAS negative.
- The natural vacancy rate acts asymmetrically on CROAS. Increasing vacancy rates diminish CROAS more than increasing ones inflate CROAS. It is particularly striking that CROAS declines very rapidly once the vacancy rate exceed 25%.

APPLYING THE MODEL: AN EXAMPLE

The analysis of this representative multifamily mortgage loan leads directly to that of non-agency multifamily and, by extension, commercial mortgage securities. It enables one to quantify the risks of prepayment and default of the underlying mortgage loans, and to measure the adequacy of the credit enhancement provided by the security. Consider a truly exemplary multifamily mortgage security, the Evans Withycombe Finance Trust, which was issued in August 1994 by a special purpose Delaware limited partnership, which is, in turn, wholly-owned by a publicly-held real estate investment trust. The multifamily security consists of four classes, one senior (A-1) and three subordinate (A-2, A-3, and A-4), all totaling $131 million (see Exhibit 2). The three subordinated classes, which total $29 million and represent 22.1% of the principal balance, protect the senior class against loss from default on the underlying mortgage notes. Each class receives payment of interest sequentially at a 7.98% annualized rate; class A-1 receives interest, then A-2, and so on. The securities do not amortize and mature in August 2001; they cannot be prepaid in whole or in part until March 2001. Unusually, the servicer has no obligation to advance interest in the event that the borrower fails to pay on any due date.

The underlying collateral consists of 22 apartment properties, which are located in the Phoenix and Tucson metropolitan areas. They incorporate 5,380 apartments units, with 4.88 million square feet of rentable space; the average apartment size is roughly 907 square feet. The borrower describes the properties as "oriented to upscale residents seeking high levels of amenities, such as clubhouses, exercise rooms, tennis courts, swimming pools, therapy pools, and covered parking." The units rented for an average of $606 a month in the 12 months ending May 31, 1994, subject to a 92% economic occupancy rate. The apartments units were constructed between 1984 and 1990, leaving little scope for economic or functional obsolescence. A subsidiary of the public REIT manages the properties on behalf of the special purpose partnership. The underwriters estimated a debt service coverage ratio of 1.68× and a loan-to-value ratio of 54% at issuance of the security. After updating this information for current apartment market conditions in Phoenix and Tucson, we project a long-term rental growth rate of 2.3% on these properties, a long-term volatility of the rental growth rate of 4.3%, and a natural vacancy rate of 10%.

Assuming that dealers would offer the senior class A-1 at a nominal spread of 75 basis points over an interpolated Treasury note with a 4.7-year maturity, we calculate a CROAS of 74 basis points (see Exhibit 3). We estimate a zero probability of prepayment, given the absolute prohibition against it until March 2001, and a zero probability of default, given the high DSCR, low LTV, and favorable rental growth and volatility rates of the properties. Arbitrarily reducing the initial DSCR to 1.20× and raising the initial LTV to 80% would produce a 17.7% probability of default, and an 11% expected loss rate; the CROAS of class A-1 falls by six basis points to 68 basis points. Under this scenario, losses of 1.95% of the principal balance of the mortgage notes, or $2.55 million, would result. Losses of this magnitude would eliminate 51% of the A-4 subordinated class, but leave classes A-2 and A-3 intact. Arbitrarily reducing the initial DSCR to 1.0× and raising the initial LTV to 100% would produce a 47.5% probability of default and a 12.3% expected loss rate; the CROAS of class A-1 would fall by 106 basis points to −32 basis points. Under this scenario, losses of 5.84% of the principal balance of the mortgage notes, or $7.65 million, would result. Losses of this magnitude would eliminate the A-4 subordinated class entirely, and 29.5% of the A-3 class, but leave the A-2 class intact. The senior class would not suffer actual loss, but rather an erosion of relative value such that it would yield substantially less than a comparable Treasury note. Since extreme conditions must occur to undermine the performance of class A-1 to such an extent, we conclude that the credit enhancement for class A-1 more than compensates for the likely risk of default and may render class A-1 a candidate for upgrading from AA by Standard and Poor's.

Exhibit 3: Scenario Performance of Evans Withycombe Finance Trust, Class A-1

Scenario (DSCR / LTV)	Nominal Spread	CROAS	Loss Frequency (%)	Loss Severity (%)
1.68/54	75	74	0.0	0.0
1.20/80	75	68	17.7	11.0
1.00/100	75	-32	45.7	12.3

ADVANTAGES OF THE MODEL

The approach to joint valuation of the prepayment and default options of multi-family loans that we developed in this chapter offers the following important advantages over other approaches:

- It unifies the valuation of multifamily and commercial mortgage loans and securities with that of single-family mortgage loans and securities, by means of a common interest rate process. The simulation of arbitrage-free forward discount rates using the term structure of (average implied swaption) volatility along a sufficiently large number of paths by Monte Carlo methods provides the framework for discounting all monthly (or other periodic) future cash flows, whatever their source, commercial or residential, by appropriate risk premia. Hence, one can directly compare the usual first and second derivatives of price, rate, and volatility across the various types of loans and securities.

- It unifies the valuation of the mortgage loan and the related apartment property, by a more complex application of the common interest rate process. It discounts all future monthly cash flows, from loan or from property, by the same set of forward discount rates, plus respective risk premia. It offers thereby a framework capable of valuing a wide variety of financial instruments, not only mortgage loans and securities. Furthermore, it simulates the future net operating income from an apartment property as a function of economic and demographic variables, drawn from the local real estate sub-market, and the yield of the 10-year Treasury note. It thereby creates a direct link to forward 10-year discount rates and an indirect link through dynamic covariance coefficients for each economic and demographic variable to the 10-year rate. These coefficients will vary in size, sign, and lag. Hence, we can simulate the future net operating income for a property consistently with the simulation of future interest payments on alternative mortgage loans, which could lead to prepayment. In contrast, most other approaches simulate the value of the loan separately from the value of the property, using distinct stochastic processes. Accordingly, they may randomly associate future states of the property with future discount rates, propagating potentially aberrant relationships; one could find a very high growth rate or high variability of property price inflation associated with a very low discount rate.

- It estimates the value of the property by the function described above for each month of the term of the related loan, including the final balloon payment. Thus, it avoids recourse to an externally specified value of the property at maturity of the loan. The continuous internal determination of property value overcomes a critical weakness in the discounted cash flow approach that many lenders, borrowers, and appraisers use to value multifamily loans and properties: the arbitrary choice of the value of the property at maturity of the loan. Amid its countless variations, the discounted cash flow approach generally applies a constant discount rate, usually the yield of a comparable Treasury note plus a risk premium, to the projected annual net operating income and to the final sale price or market value of property, as of the maturity of the loan. This value is determined by capitalizing the projected net operating income in the last year at a projected rate. The projected capitalization rate is seldom derived by any methodology; rather, appraisers and others often use a rule of thumb, adding 1% or more to the initial capitalization rate, which is itself an average of capitalization rates sampled from recent sales or loans. Thus, the discounted cash flow method, thus, founders at a critical point in any valuation by arbitrary, if not randomly, selecting terminal property value.

- The continuous internal determination of the value of a specific property overcomes another critical weakness in the valuation of multifamily properties: the arbitrary choice of the rate of return or "building-payout rate." Those who evaluate the property by a pure stochastic process often assume that it will offer the same rate of return as did equity real estate investment trusts (REITs), i.e., 8%, over some arbitrary period of time such as 1980-1987. This choice of rate of return invites numerous objections. REITs provide investors with valuable liquidity, which permits a higher valuation and lower rate of return on the properties that they own. REITs represent many different property types, so that any average return will not reflect a return specific to apartment properties. REITs own different types of properties in different markets, allowing a smoothing of return by the natural covariance of returns across property types and markets, which again leads to imprecision in valuing an individual apartment property. REITs typically use much less debt than other real estate investors; lower leverage implies lower risk and, appropriately, lower returns to investors. Also, REITS provide professional management of income-producing properties that small apartment properties (36 units or less) may not, which would motivate investors generally to require higher returns and expect higher variance of returns from them. In contrast, our approach infers the yield capitalization rate of a specific property and the risk premium to current interest rates implied by this rate. It then adds the property-specific risk premium to the forward discount rates across all paths, which produces a different series of capitalization rates for each path. Therefore, our approach provides greater specificity as well as greater flexibility in the valuation of mortgaged properties.

- It estimates the incidence of default and loss on foreclosure by the same function. Default occurs when the two conditions of the default function occur simultaneously. The number of paths on which default occurs automatically furnishes the frequency of default. The delay between default and final foreclosure and sale, which we obtain by random draws from a normal distribution that assumes an average of 24 months and variance of five months, permits calculation of the accrued interest foregone. (To the accrued interest, we add additional foreclosure costs of 5% the loan balance, and deduct net operating income received from the property over the foreclosure period.) The loss on foreclosure of the property derives from the difference between the property value, 24 months or so after default, and the unpaid principal balance of the loan. Hence, the magnitude of loss arises from the internal operation of our approach to value. Of course, one can compare the incidence of default and severity of loss projected on any loan to the historical experience of comparable loans originated by life insurance companies, RTC-administered financial institutions, or agency multifamily portfolios.

- Finally, our approach offers a compromise in the persistent debate on the subject of *ruthless* versus *non-ruthless* default. Some contend that a borrower will rationally default on a property whenever its present value falls below that of the related mortgage loan, without consideration of transaction costs; hence, ruthless default. Any delay by the borrower in defaulting on the loan arises from his or her unwillingness to forego the persistent value of the option to default in the future, since the property value may continue to decline. (This decline magnifies the borrower's implicit gain and the lender's loss, because the loan amount fixes the strike price or tacit sales price of the property to the lender.) However, others contend that a borrower will rationally default on a property whenever its present value falls below that of the related loan, but will include transaction costs in assessing its value; hence, non-ruthless default. The borrower will not default as soon as the present value of the property falls bellow that of the loan, eliminating equity, but waits until negative equity should accumulate to the amount of observable and unobservable transaction costs.

- While our approach clearly incorporates transaction costs in anticipating the borrower's rational decision, it also tenders a compromise to the opponents in the debate. We contend that the borrower should default in any month when two conditions occur: when net operating income falls below scheduled debt payments and when property value falls below loan amount, eliminating the borrower's equity. In practice, the second condition occurs before the first. The present value of expected net operating income falls below the present value of scheduled mortgage payments before income falls below scheduled payments. Property value declines faster than loan value, in part, because net operating income is discounted with a much higher risk premium than is the mortgage payment. Accordingly, the borrower may have sufficient cash flow to make scheduled payments even though the property value has fallen below the loan amount, plus transactions costs. He or she will rationally delay default as long as net operating income continues to exceed scheduled monthly payments, even though equity is negative. Therefore, the future option to default consists only of the option to default before these cash flows decline to zero. Our approach conflates the value of the present and future options to default.

- Furthermore, those who conclude that the borrower has an option to default in the present and in the future must ignore the presence of the lender, who should act as rationally as the borrower. While few mortgage notes give the lender the ability to act unilaterally when the borrower's equity turns negative, all lenders have the legal right to accelerate the note and begin foreclosure as soon as the borrower fails to pay. The separate assignment of rents enhances the lender's ability to collect rents as soon as default occurs. Indeed, the lender will attempt to take possession of the property in order to forestall the borrower from optimizing the value of the option to default! The lender endeavors to obtain the property before its value falls below that of the loan, minimizing the value of default to the borrower. In most states, within three months of the first failure to pay scheduled principal and interest, the lender can obtain possession of, if not title to, the property and begin to receive net operating income. In conclusion, if a value to default in the future does exist, it consists either of the option to receive cash flow until it turns negative, or an option on property value from the month that cash flow turns negative until the lender assumes control of the property. These options have little time or intrinsic value, and we already incorporate them within our approach to valuation.

Chapter 28

An Options Approach to Commercial Mortgages and CMBS Valuation and Risk Analysis

David P. Jacob
Managing Director
Director Global Capital Markets
Capital America

Ted C.H. Hong
Director
Capital America

Laurence H. Lee
Warburg Dillon Reed LLC

INTRODUCTION

Investment in commercial mortgages and commercial mortgage-backed securities (CMBS) has received increased attention from mainstream fixed-income investors. Yet, much of the quantitative technology that has been developed for analyzing relative value in such areas as residential mortgage-backed securities (MBS) and corporate bonds has not been applied to commercial mortgages. Investors in agency mortgage-backed securities and callable corporate bonds, for example, have used option pricing to determine fair value for securities whose cash flows are uncertain due to the possibility of an early call. Commercial mortgages typically have greater call protection than residential MBS and corporate bonds, although they still have some callability. Most commercial mortgages have lock-out periods followed by a period during which a penalty is applied to premature principal payments, followed in turn by a free period. The technology applied to

---

Laurence H. Lee was employed by Nomura Securities International, Inc. when he contributed to this chapter.

other fixed-income instruments to value these features could be used for assessing risk and relative value in commercial mortgages and CMBS.

In addition to the risk of early principal payment, commercial mortgages, like corporate bonds, are subject to the risk of losses in a foreclosure following a default. Pricing methodology described in academic journals has been applied to this risk for corporate bonds, but for a variety of reasons it has not proven to be practical.[1] The analysis and valuation of this risk for commercial mortgages using similar quantitative analysis, while discussed in the academic world, has not been applied in the market for commercial mortgages.[2]

The need for improved tools has increased with the introduction of securitization, where the most popular method of credit enhancement is the senior-subordinated structure. Whole loans, which are typically of BB quality, are aggregated and their cash flows are then allocated to create securities with credit ratings from AAA down to B and unrated. As a result, the risk of loss due to default is leveraged up in the junior classes and leveraged down in the senior classes. The analogy in the residential MBS area is the creation of planned amortization class (PAC) bonds and support tranches where the PAC bond has leveraged down prepayment risk and the support bond has leveraged up prepayment risk. Moreover, the senior subordinated structure requires that recoveries from foreclosures first be used to pay senior bondholders. From the perspective of these bondholders a prepayment event has occurred, even though the unscheduled cash flow came about due to a credit event. Nevertheless, it must be considered in the valuation and risk of these AAA rated securities.

When an investor looks at a CMBS deal it would be useful to know whether or not the AAA class at 90 basis points over Treasuries is a better value than the B class at a +600 basis point spread. How should one compare the risk of a bullet loan with one that amortizes? How does the risk of default affect the value of a security trading at a premium? What is the fair value of an interest-only strip when the loans underlying the deal have percentage penalties versus yield maintenance, versus lockout. This chapter describes a two-factor contingent-claims theoretic framework and applies option pricing methodology to commercial mortgages to answer these questions.

In the next section we outline the elements of valuation and the basic analytic approach to pricing commercial mortgages. Following this, we apply the

---

[1] The complexity of the capital structure of a corporation and the possibility of a leveraged buyout make the application of the option approach less practical for corporate bonds. For more details on the option approach to pricing default risk in high yield bonds, see Richard Bookstabber and David P. Jacob, "Controlling Interest Rate Risk," Chapter 8 in *The Composite Hedge: Controlling the Credit Risk of High-Yield Bonds* (New York: John Wiley & Sons, 1986).

[2] There has been some work published in this area. See Chapter 12 and Patrick J. Corcoran "Commercial Mortgages: Measuring Risk and Return," *Journal of Portfolio Management* (Fall 1989);Sheridan Titman and Walter Torous, "Valuing Commercial Mortgages: An Empirical Investigation of the Contingent Claims Approach to Pricing Risky Debt," *Journal of Finance* (June 1989); and, Paul D. Childs, Steven H. Ott, and Timothy J. Riddiough, "The Pricing of Multi-Class Commercial Mortgage-Backed Securities," Working Paper (December 1994).

approach to commercial whole loans and show the effects of each factor on the value of the mortgage. Next, a multi-class senior-subordinated deal is evaluated. We then use the model to look at the relative risk of different securities. Finally, we draw some conclusions, discuss practical issues relating to the model, and propose some future applications. In the appendix we show some of the mathematics behind the model.

THE ELEMENTS OF VALUATION

The value of all real estate securities is contingent upon the value of the underlying real estate asset since they each have a claim on this asset. For example, the equity holder has a residual claim on the income stream after the debt holder is paid. If the income from the real estate asset is insufficient to meet the debt obligation and a default results, the debt holder has a claim on the real estate. Usually, the equity holder defaults only when the value of the real estate is less than the value of the loan and when income is insufficient to pay debt service. The debt holder, in this case, will receive the smaller of the debt payment or the value of the real estate and the equity holder receives nothing.

The analytic approach we use is to view the owner (lender/investor) of a commercial mortgage as having a long position in a credit risk-free, non-callable mortgage, a short call option, and a short put option. The commercial mortgage investor/lender (debt holder) has written an option to the borrower (equity holder) to call (prepay) the debt, and an option to put (default) the real estate to the debt holder. That is,

Commercial mortgage = (Default-free and non-callable mortgage)
 – (Call option) – (Put option)
 PREPAYMENT   DEFAULT

As compensation for writing these options the debt holder receives a spread over the yield on Treasury bonds usually in the form of a higher coupon. Therefore, in order to value the commercial mortgage, one can value the risk-free cash flows and the associated call (prepayment) and put (default) options. To properly value the options, the default and prepayment options need to be analyzed *simultaneously* since as we will show they are interrelated.

To value the options we need to define what circumstances would cause the property owner to exercise his options.

Prepayment option — triggering conditions: Prepayment is triggered for two reasons:

    a. economic benefit from refinancing which occurs if
      1. the general level of interest rates drop.

or

> 2. the property value increases, thus allowing the borrower to refinance at a tighter spread to Treasuries.

or

> b. Owner wants to sell property and the mortgage is not assumable.

For condition *a* to be viable, net operating income (NOI) must be sufficiently greater than the scheduled payments required under the new rate, since otherwise the borrower would not qualify for the loan. If the borrower does qualify, he will refinance so long as the present value of the future promised payments minus the value of the options (fair market value of the debt including its embedded options) is greater than the face value of the remaining debt plus refinancing costs such as prepayment penalties. Thus, as interest rates drop (for newly originated fixed-rate mortgages) and as the quality of the property improves the likelihood of refinancing increases since under these circumstances the market value of the debt increases.

In addition, property owners sometimes want to realize the return on their properties particularly as the tax benefits of ownership decline through time. If the mortgage is assumable or a substitution of collateral is permitted, the owner could sell the property with the loan remaining intact. Otherwise the owner would have to prepay the mortgage. Another situation that could occur that would lead to prepayment even in a rising rate environment is if the property appreciates in value, and the owner desires to re-leverage the property. If the mortgage note prohibits additional financing (this almost always the case for CMBS), then the borrower must first repay his loan.

Empirical evidence on commercial mortgage prepayments by Abraham and Theobald reported in Chapter 3 of the first edition of this book suggests that when it is economic for commercial property owners to prepay, they do so at an even faster rate then owners of residential properties. Moreover, turnover rates in property ownership indicate that even if refinancing is uneconomic property owners sell their properties to realize profits. For example, Abraham and Theobald found that the cumulative prepayment rate for low coupon mortgages that were outstanding for 10 years was 82.4%. [3]

Default option-triggering conditions: For the property owner to exercise his default option there are two necessary conditions.

> i) Net operating income is less than the current period's scheduled mortgage payment[4]
> and

---

[3] This is one reason why interest strips from CMBS deals that have lockout provisions as opposed to simply yield maintenance are far less risky and should trade at tighter spreads.

[4] Net cash flow might be more appropriate, but here we use NOI for simplicity.

ii) The market value of the property is less than the market value of the debt.[5]

For a non-callable mortgage, default will never be necessary for a rational borrower if the NOI is enough to cover debt payment. Default starts to occur when the NOI is insufficient to meet the debt service. When that happens and the property value is also less than the value of the debt, the default option would be exercised. Both conditions are necessary because if the property value is greater than the value of the debt, but the NOI is insufficient to pay the debt service, the property owner would attempt to sell the property and payoff the debt rather than go through foreclosure.

Default as a method of prepayment — triggering conditions: Sometimes the property owner may try to use a default as a method of prepaying so as to avoid the prepayment penalty and/or lock-out feature.[6] In this case, the triggering conditions for default are more complicated. The conditions would be triggered to default as follows:

i) The NOI has to be greater than the payments that would be required at the time if the loan were to be refinanced.

and

ii) the present value of the future promised payments minus the value of the options (fair market value of the debt including its embedded options) is greater than the face value of the remaining debt plus foreclosure expenses.

If these two conditions hold the borrower can default, go through foreclosure, pay off the face value of the debt with the proceeds, and then refinance. This situation can arise when interest rates drop and property value and NOI increase, but the loan is either locked-out or there is a stiff prepayment penalty. In this case if the foreclosure expenses are not too onerous, the borrower has an incentive to default. It is unclear, however, how the courts would treat this situation. It is possible that the bankruptcy judge would force the borrower to compensate the lender.

The Combined Default and Prepayment

Since the call and put options are embedded in the mortgage debt, the call option and the put option cannot actually be separated. The incentive to prepay as we have discussed is linked not just to the general level of interest rates, but to the ever changing level of operating income of the property and the resulting avail-

---

[5] The market value of the debt is the present value of the future promised payments plus the current payment that is due minus the value of the options.

[6] Experts in bankruptcy law feel that in a true default, prepayment penalties could be construed by the judge as usury and therefore disallowed.

able refinancing spread. Thus, the value of the prepayment option is related to factors that affect the value of the default option. Similarly the incentive to default is related to the level of interest rates which in turn affects the value of the prepayment option. Moreover, borrowers who either prepay or default terminate the contract of the mortgage. This results in the termination of both options. Our triggering conditions, thus, do not work independently, but need to be evaluated simultaneously.

To visualize the triggering process for the prepayment option, look at Exhibit 1. The horizontal axis measures time. The vertical axis tracks interest rates which in turn determines the present value of the promised payments. As time passes, interest rates can move up or down. As interest rates drop, the market value of the debt increases above the face value making it economically worthwhile for the borrower to refinance.

A lock-out or penalty reduces the value of the call option since it lessens the likelihood of the option being exercised. In general, the longer the term to maturity and the more volatile the interest rate, the more valuable the prepayment option since the likelihood of exercise increases.

In order to visualize the triggering process for a loan default, we make use of the metaphor of a drunk person walking along the edge of a cliff trying to go from point A to point B. The closer he is to the edge when he begins his walk, the more erratic his walk, and the longer the distance from point A to point B, the more likely he will fall off the cliff before reaching point B. Similarly, in the case of an income generating property, the more volatile the NOI, the greater the initial loan-to-value (LTV), the lower the debt service coverage ratio (DSCR), and the longer the maturity of the debt, the higher probability of default prior to maturity. In Exhibit 2 the horizontal axis measures time to maturity. The vertical axis measures the level of NOI and LTV. As time passes NOI and LTV can move up or down. If NOI/LTV moves down/up sufficiently, the property owner will default and hand the keys of the property to the lender.

Exhibit 1: Prepayment Option of a Commercial Mortgage

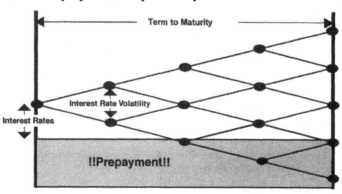

Exhibit 2: Default Option of a Commercial Mortgage

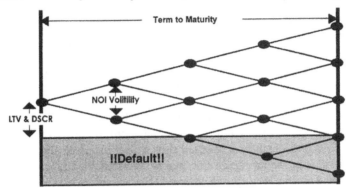

Determinants of Option Values

Now that we have defined the conditions that lead to the exercise of the options, we need to identify the determinants of the options' values. The value of the embedded options depends upon many factors. The direct determinants are

1. Current balance of mortgage
2. Term to maturity of mortgage
3. Mortgage payments including interest and principal, and the amortization schedule
4. Prepayment terms and penalties
5. Net operating income from the collateral property
6. Volatility of net operating income
7. Terms of default and foreclosure costs
8. Interest rates
9. Volatility of interest rates
10. Correlation between interest rates and net operating income

The first four items specify the information necessary to calculate the promised cash flows of the underlying mortgage. This information in conjunction with current and the potential future interest rates are necessary for calculating the value of the prepayment option. Items 5, 6, and 7 which relate to the property are essential for valuing the default option. The last three items are critical for valuing all assets, including the mortgage, the real estate, and the options.

The Valuation Process

The process of interest rates and net operating income determine the entire valuation procedure of the commercial mortgage and its embedded options. In our framework, we assume that interest rates and NOI are the two underlying building blocks. The property value which is the present value of all future NOI's can be calculated from interest rates and NOI. To solve for the option values, a two-dimensional binomial tree or pyramid is constructed (by combining Exhibit 1 and Exhibit 2) based on the assumptions of the process and volatility governing future NOI and interest rates.[7]

For every path of interest rates there is a whole set of possible paths of NOI. The tree will specify the future cash flows of the mortgage under the full range of interest rates and NOI scenarios. Once the pyramid is created, the value of the property can be calculated at each node of the pyramid.[8] Similarly other relevant variables such as LTV and DSCR can be calculated as well. At each node, the action taken by the borrower (prepayment, default, or scheduled payment) determines the cash flow that the debt holder receives. The option values and the fair value of the mortgage can then be calculated by discounting the cash flows backward in time through the pyramid. The values are equal to the expected discounted value of the cash flows through the pyramid. The theoretical or fair value of the commercial mortgage can be obtained by combining these terms.

Option-Adjusted Spread

Since the market value or market price of a financial security may differ from its fair value, the fixed-income market has developed the concept of *option-adjusted spread* (OAS).

OAS is a spread relative to the Treasury curve, quoted in basis points, which is used for measuring the relative value of securities with a series of uncertain cash flows. The OAS can be obtained by calibrating the theoretical present value to the current market price. The theoretical present value takes all possible cash flow streams discounted by the corresponding discount rates and weighted by assumed probabilities. The OAS, thus, is a constant spread added to the risk-free interest rate and is used as the discount rate for the corresponding cash flows. The procedure involves solving for the spread which equates the price obtained via discounting the cash flows to the market price.

The larger or more positive the OAS, the cheaper the security is relative to its theoretical value. The OAS can be thought of as the risk premium which the investor would earn if he repurchased or hedged, at fair value, the options that he has implicitly shorted by owning the security. The concept of OAS was originally introduced to analyze relative value in residential mortgage-backed securities and callable corporate bonds, where the borrower's prepayment option substantially negatively

---

[7] When a multi-class commercial mortgage-backed security is evaluated, the path-independent condition for the remaining balances of the bond classes does not necessarily hold. Fortunately, so long as the underlying loans satisfy the path-independent condition, Monte Carlo simulations which randomly select a finite number of paths from a virtually infinite number of paths can be utilized to calculate the option values. Since a huge path selection process is involved, variance reduction techniques turn out to be very important to improve the sampling method.

[8] In our model we specify a term which indicates the growth rate, if any, in the NOI. We define the property value to be equal to $NOI/(R - R \times G)$ where R equals prevailing interest rates, NOI is net operating income, and $R \times G$ is the growth rate in NOI. $R - R \times G$ equals the traditional cap rate.

impacts the value of these securities. If the OAS is positive/negative, then the investor is receiving more/less than he should have for shorting the embedded options.

Parameter Estimation and Practical Considerations

Like all option models, a number of parameters need to be estimated and assumptions need to be made regarding the process governing the random variables. In our case, we need to have an estimate for the volatility of NOI for the property, the volatility of interest rates, and the correlation between these. If the loan or a security is backed by a number of properties, then we also need the correlation matrix of NOI of all the properties.

Regarding interest rates there is a voluminous body of literature which addresses the interest rate process necessary to properly price fixed-income income options and to satisfy the arbitrage-free condition for the term structure of interest rates.[9] In this chapter, we use the Black, Derman, and Toy model and its binomial tree to calibrate the interest rate lattice to the initial yield curve.

To empirically estimate the NOI volatility, we first used the Russell/NCREIF Property Index (RNPI) despite all of its drawbacks.[10] The RNPI index is the most widely quoted index for real estate property performance. It provides data such as net operating income and appraisal value of commercial buildings by region and by property type on quarterly basis. We also used the RNPI series to estimate the correlation between interest rates and net operating income. The 6% volatility of NOI that was estimated from the large and diversified pool of properties that underlie the RNPI series greatly understates the true NOI volatility of individual properties. Based on our own data we expect the volatility of NOI to range between 9% and 16%. There are differences by property type. As we would expect multi-family properties have lower NOI volatilities and hotels tend to have higher volatilities. In practice one needs to estimate the volatility for the property in question.[11]

---

[9] Ho and Lee used a binomial tree to create an arbitrage-free interest rate model. See Thomas S.Y. Ho and S.B. Lee, "Term Structure Movements and Pricing of Interest Rate Contingent Claims," *Journal of Finance* (December 1986). Black, Derman, and Toy also constructed a binomial tree model and, furthermore, allowed various volatilities for the entire term structure. See Fischer Black, Emanuel Derman, and William Toy, "A One-Factor Model of Interest Rates and its Application to Treasury Bond Options," *Financial Analysts Journal* (January-February 1990). Hull and White created a trinomial tree and provided a closed form solution for arbitrage-free model in continuous time. See John Hull and Alan White, "One-Factor Interest-Rate Models and the Valuation of Interest-Rate Derivative Securities," *Journal of Financial and Quantitative Analysis*, (June 1993). Both Jamshidian and Chan assumed a variety of interest rate process to calibrate to the term structure. See Farshid Jamshidian, "Forward Induction and Construction of Yield Curve Diffusion Models," *Merrill Lynch Research* (March 1991); and, Y.K. Chan, "Term Structure as a Second Order Dynamical System, and Pricing of Derivative Securities," *Bear Stearns Research*, 1992.

[10] The Russell/NCREIF property index is an appraisal-based index of property returns and values. This index represents data collected from the Voting Members of the National Council of Real Estate Investment Fiduciaries. Many researchers feel that the appraisal process causes the data to significantly understate the price volatility. The volatility of the income component, on the other hand, might be representative for a large pool of assets.

[11] Specific features such as cross-collateralization, which would lower NOI volatility need to be modeled.

Exhibit 3: Average Cumulative Default Rates for Corporate Bonds

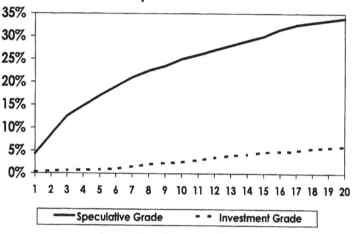

Source: Moody's Investors Service.

One way to calibrate the NOI volatility assumption is to see what pattern and level of defaults is produced using the parameter assumptions. In Exhibit 3 we show the actual average cumulative default rates for investment grade and speculative grade corporate bonds as a function of time as computed by Moody's Investors Service for the years 1970- 1994. One can see that for the high quality debt the marginal default rate starts out low and increases over time. On the other hand, the marginal default rate (as measured by the slope of the curve) for the speculative grade debt declines over time. The reason for this is that lower quality debt that survives the early years has a decreasing probability of defaulting. Whereas, high quality debt has an increasing (or at least non-decreasing) chance of defaulting as time passes.

In Exhibit 4 we show the marginal default rates for high quality (low LTV) and low quality (high LTV) loans that are implied by our model using an assumption of 16% volatility of NOI. In Exhibit 5 we show the implied cumulative default rates. The pattern is very consistent with the Moody's data and demonstrates the ability of the model to differentiate the default pattern associated with different quality loans. Moreover, the level of defaults, while higher than what Moody's found for corporate bonds, in our view represents a reasonable level of defaults.[12]

Aside from parameter estimation, there are some practical considerations when implementing the model that differ from the theory. The theory assumes the following conditions: (1) liquidity, (2) symmetry of market information, (3) optimal exercise, and (4) refinancing ability.

---

[12] The cumulative default level after 10 years implied the by the model for a 70% LTV loan with an initial DSCR of 1.5× using a 16% NOI volatility is about 26%. Moreover, the implied loss severity is about 19%, both of these statistics exceed the levels found with the historical data. We feel that our standard of 16% NOI volatility is reasonable.

Exhibit 4: Implied Marginal Default Rates for Commercial Mortgages

50% LTV

90% LTV

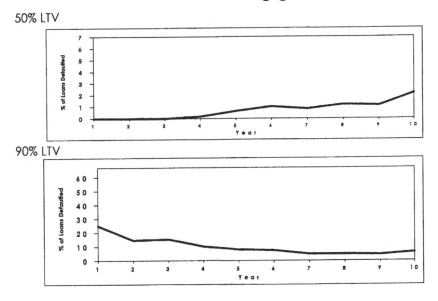

Exhibit 5: Implied Cumulative Default Rates for Commercial Mortgages

50% LTV

90% LTV

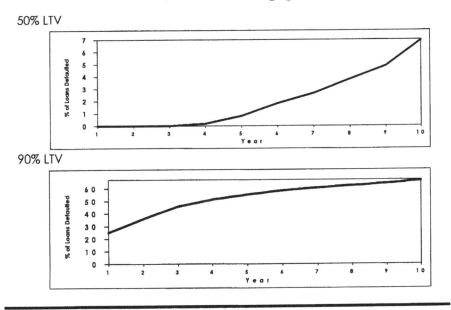

Liquidity refers to how easy it is to buy or sell real estate and commercial mortgages in the secondary market. The theoretical model assumes that transactions costs are low and that the markets are very liquid. Symmetry of market information refers to whether borrowers and investors have the same information. Optimal exercise refers to how efficiently the borrower exercises his options if arbitrage opportunities emerge. Refinancing ability refers to the fact that financing is based solely on the property consideration irrespective of the borrower. Even though many of these conditions do not hold in practice, the model provides value by incorporating in a single framework the primary factors driving the value of the mortgage. As a result it becomes useful as a relative value tool and for comparing risk.

COMPARATIVE ANALYSIS

In this section we use OAS as the measure to analyze the factors that affect the value of a commercial mortgage. In the next section, we apply the framework to a multiclass CMBS structure. In order to use the model to analyze the factors affecting the value of a commercial mortgage, we could either keep the spread constant (OAS), and see how the price varies as we change each of the factors. Or, we could keep the price constant and see how the factors affect the OAS as we change each of the factors. We adopt the latter approach since the market sets the price.

Since the OAS is considered compensation for shorting options, the OAS decreases for a fixed mortgage price as the default or prepayment risks increase. The degree of risk exposure depends upon the characteristics of the mortgage debt, the performance of underlying collateral as well as the economic factors such as interest rates. We analyze default risk with respect to four factors — DSCR, LTV, volatility of NOI, and mortgage maturity date. These factors are the usual measures of risk quoted in real estate markets for analyzing default risk.

In this section we use as an example, a commercial mortgage with a 10-year maturity (9.4 year weighted-average life), 7% coupon, initial DSCR of 1.30x, initial LTV of 70%, initial 10-year Treasury at 4.76%, and volatility of 11% and 16% for interest rates and NOI, respectively.[13] The initial spread of the loan is +226 bp over the 9.4-year interpolated Treasury. A correlation of 0.2 between interest rates and NOI is used. We assume that the loan follows a 30 year amortization schedule and pays a balloon payment at the end of year 10. *Initially, we assume that the mortgage is non-prepayable.*

Debt Service Coverage Ratio (DSCR)

The debt service coverage ratio (DSCR) is defined as the annual NOI divided by annual cost of debt service including principal payments. Normally, as DSCR gets larger, the probability of default and a resulting loss decreases. Thus, as

---

[13] To reduce the number of calculations we assumed a semi-annual pay mortgage.

DSCR increases the value of the default option decreases. As a result, for a fixed price the OAS increases as DSCR decreases. This can be seen in Exhibit 6 for a wide range of initial DSCR. Moreover, as DSCR gets very large, further increases do not result in a higher OAS.[14] For lower initial values of DSCR, the OAS is lower, indicating that the investor is really getting on average something less than +226 bp implied by his coupon. For example, at a DSCR of 2.50× the OAS is 188 bp, or equivalently the default option is worth +38 bp.

As one would expect the model shows that the OAS line for a bullet loan always lies below the line for the amortizing loan, since the amortizing loan has a built-in risk reduction mechanism. Even though both loans start with the same LTV, the LTV of the amortizing loan decreases through time, thus reducing its risk. The model computes the value of the amortization to be worth 30-40bp.

Loan-To-Value Ratio (LTV)

The loan-to-value ratio (LTV) is defined as the ratio of loan amount to the value of the collateral property. This ratio is frequently used as a measure of leverage to assess the level of protection from default. A lower LTV loan is considered more credit worthy due to its better default protection. In terms of OAS, the OAS should increase as the initial LTV drops since the probability of a default and a loss decreases. This can be seen in Exhibit 7. When the LTV is sufficiently low, the loan is so default-protected that the OAS will start to level off. Lower initial LTVs do not lead to further increases in OAS. At this point the probability of default is near zero and the OAS equals the nominal spread of +226 bp.

Exhibit 6: OAS versus DSCR: Default Option

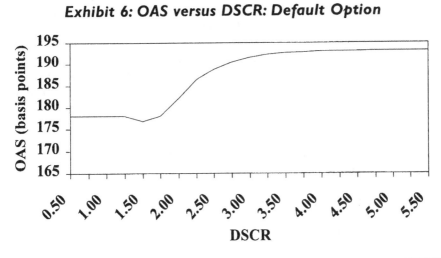

---

[14] Since we kept initial LTV constant at 70%, the OAS does not increase much above 195 bp. Thus, the probability of default does not go to zero. In reality LTV would likely go lower and the OAS would go to +226 bp. Similarly, as the DSCR gets lower, LTV should get lower and lead to lower OAS.

Exhibit 7: OAS versus LTV: Default Option

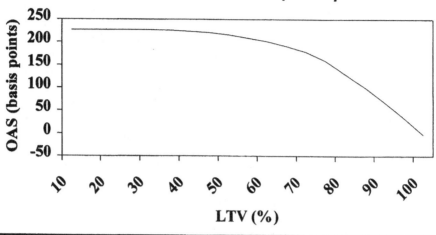

The impact on OAS due to change of LTV is more significant for bullet loans than amortizing loans.[15] This is because, as we stated earlier, the amortizing loan has a built-in LTV decreasing mechanism to automatically reduce default risk over time.

Volatility of Net Operating Income

The more volatile a property's income stream, the greater the probability of default. From the model's perspective volatility of NOI affects value because with greater volatility there will be more paths under which income will be insufficient to pay the debt service and under which the value of the property declines below the value of the debt (see Exhibit 2). Thus, given a mortgage price, the corresponding OAS decreases as the volatility increases. Exhibit 8 clearly indicates this result: the greater the volatility of NOI, the lower the OAS. It should be clear from the graph that at a 70% initial LTV, the volatility of NOI has a profound influence on the value of the loan.[16]

This parameter enables investors to estimate the required excess spread for different property types. For example, mortgages on hotels or other property types with relatively high operating margins should offer higher spreads than mortgages on property types such as multi-family which tends to have a more stable income stream, assuming the same initial LTV and NOI. In practice, loans and CMBS backed by hotel or office properties tend to have lower initial LTVs (in the case of CMBS greater subordination which translates into a lower effective LTV) and therefore the difference is not reflected in the spread.

---

[15] A bullet loan pays no principal until the maturity and then the entire principal amount is fully paid. The amortizing loan pays principal according to its amortization schedule until the maturity and then the remaining principal amount is fully paid.

[16] Note that for sufficiently high LTV, as NOI volatility increases to a certain level, the OAS levels off.

Exhibit 8: OAS versus Volatility of NOI: Default Option

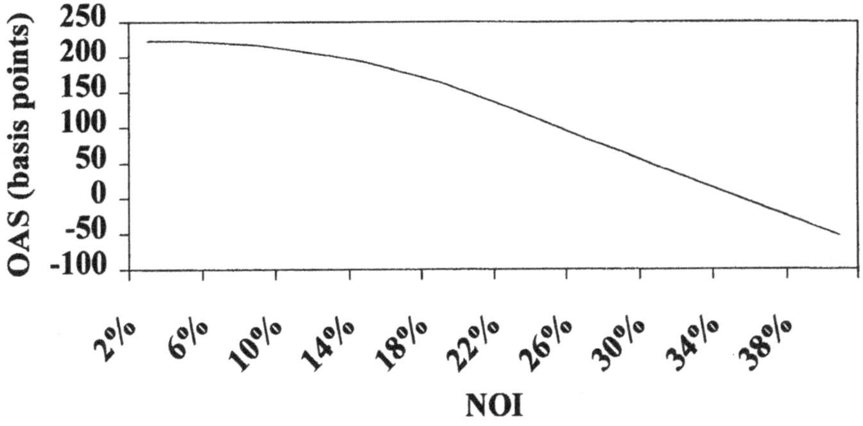

Term to Maturity

As previously shown in Exhibit 2, the longer the term to maturity, the higher default risk is. This is because there is more time for things to go bad. The cumulative probability of default increases as the term to maturity lengthens. As a result, the OAS should decrease as the term to maturity lengthens. Our model shows that OAS decreases as term to maturity increases, particularly for the higher quality loan (see Exhibit 9). On the other hand, when the loan starts out as a lower quality loan, increasing the maturity of the debt can actually lead to increasing OAS indicating increasing value. At first this seems strange, since the probability of default should increase with time. There are two reasons for the odd result. First, even though the cumulative probability of default increases, with a longer term to maturity the time to default is pushed further into the future.[17] Second, when a loan is really at risk of default, additional time gives the property owner some chance of getting the property back on track. An analogy can be made to a sporting event. Suppose a team is down by seven runs. It would far prefer it to be the first inning instead of the ninth, whereas the team that is ahead by seven runs would prefer that it be the bottom of the ninth inning.

Another interesting phenomenon is that even for the higher quality loan, after a certain point the OAS stops declining and even rises a bit until it levels off. This happens because even though the probability of default increases, on a present value basis, this added risk of default does not add much to the expected loss. The result is interesting in that it shows that longer term to maturity does not necessarily mean greater risk.

---

[17] This is similar to the results found in Robert Merton, "On the Pricing of Corporate Debt: The Risk Structure of Interest Rates," *Journal of Finance* (May 1974).

Exhibit 9: OAS versus Term to Maturity: Default Option
(at different LTVs)

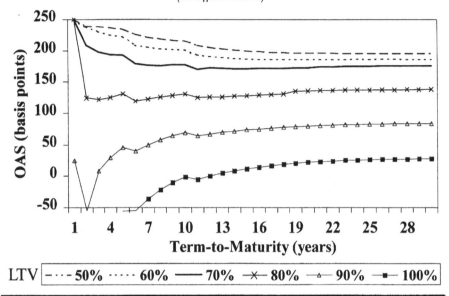

Valuing the Prepayment Option

Thus far we have assumed that the commercial mortgage was completely non-callable. In reality, while most commercial mortgages are more call-protected than residential mortgages, many have free periods. For example, the borrower in a 10-year balloon mortgage may be locked-out from prepayment for five years, and then is permitted to prepay. In addition, many commercial mortgages do not have lock-out provisions, but instead prepayment penalties which come in a variety of forms. The investor in the mortgage needs an ability to place a value on the lock-out and/or penalties in order to properly compare investment alternatives.

In order to analyze the effects of callability we continue with our example where we assumed a commercial mortgage with a 10-year maturity, 7% coupon, initial DSCR of 1.30x, initial LTV of 70%, initial 10-year Treasury at 4.76%, interest rate volatility of 11%, and NOI volatility of 16%. We assume that the loan follows a 30-year amortization schedule and has a balloon payment at the end of year 10 (which implies a 9.4-year weighted-average life). In addition, we assume that the loan is fully callable after 5 years without penalty at par. (This is obviously very favorable for the borrower. In practice, there would likely be some sort of penalty structure following the lock-out period.)

Naturally, if the loan is also callable, the investment is less attractive. As a result, the OAS is lower as can be seen in Exhibits 10, 11, and 12. It is interesting to note that the difference gets larger for lower quality loans. This is because the option to call-in lower quality debt is even more valuable.

Exhibit 10: OAS versus DSCR: Refinance and Default Options

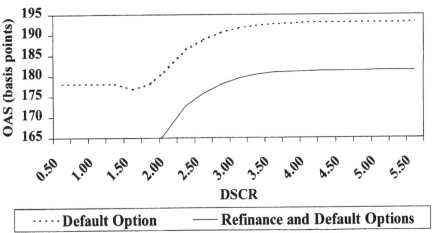

Exhibit 11: OAS versus LTV: Refinance and Default Options

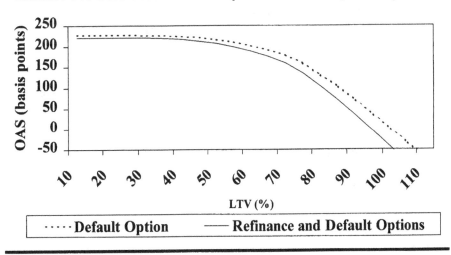

In addition to the issues of callability there are factors which, while not discussed here, have an impact on value and show up in the OAS. These include the particular penalty structure; what happens in a default, extension, and modification provision in a balloon default; the price of the loan (assumed in all of the above analysis to be priced at par[18]); the shape of the yield curve; etc. All of these can be analyzed by the model.

---

[18] If the investor purchased the loan at a deep discount, a default could be a favorable event if the proceeds from the foreclosure are sufficient. Similarly, a loan purchased at a premium will suffer if there is a default even if the foreclosure process only recovers the par amount

Exhibit 12: OAS versus Volatility of NOI: Refinance and Default Options

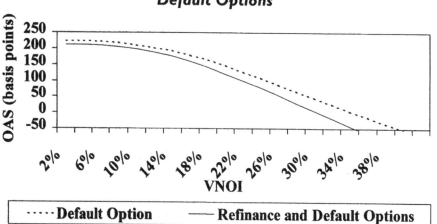

VALUING MULTI-CLASS COMMERCIAL MORTGAGE-BACKED SECURITIES[19]

Thus far, we have applied the model to the valuation of a commercial mortgage. In this section we use the model to analyze multi-class commercial mortgage-backed securities. Securitization is the process of converting financial assets that produce cash flows into securities that trade in the financial markets. The cash flows from the loans are used to pay the certificate holders. Often many loans are pooled together in the securitization. A single class of bondholders can be created or there can be numerous classes. In addition to creating liquidity, the securitization process can be used to alter credit quality through various means of credit enhancements. These credit enhancements can take the form of guarantees, over collateralization, or senior-subordination. Today, senior-subordination is used almost exclusively. By creating a credit and payment prioritization, credit risk is reallocated among the bond classes. Typically, all principal payments that are made by the borrower(s) are used to pay off the most senior outstanding bond class, whereas losses are allocated to the most junior outstanding class. This process effectively decreases the LTV of the most senior bond class.

Because the losses are mostly absorbed by the junior classes, the senior class has more credit protection than its underlying collateral. By utilizing subordination, one can create securities which have higher credit ratings than the underlying collateral. The rating agencies set the effective LTV and DSCR requirements in each deal in order to achieve the desired bond ratings.

---

[19] Note that there will be some differences in the valuation results since in this section we use Monte Carlo simulation rather than obtaining an exact solution from the binomial tree.

Exhibit 13: An Example of a Sequential Structure of CMBS: Default Option (10 Loans)

Class	Size ($mm)	WAL	Price	Yield Spread	OAS Vol. 6%	Vol. 9%	Vol. 16%	Vol. 20%	Vol. 30%
Collateral	200.0	9.40	100.00	226	217	202	140	96	-18
AAA Short	24.5	5.14	101.50	138	134	131	117	112	105
AAA Long	119.5	9.99	101.50	146	150	150	149	149	141
AA	12.0	10.00	100.00	176	179	176	165	165	10
A	11.0	10.00	100.00	201	203	192	160	121	-286
BBB	9.0	10.00	96.05	281	275	253	166	31	-744
BBB-	3.0	10.00	89.60	381	364	330	170	-75	-1147
BB+	8.5	10.00	77.31	600	566	514	205	-224	-1495
BB	2.0	10.00	76.05	625	567	488	-71	-715	-2009
BB-	2.0	10.00	67.96	800	724	621	-60	-782	-2050
B+	3.5	10.00	63.86	900	789	648	-294	-1125	-2263
B	1.0	10.00	61.93	950	799	599	-617	-1604	-2324
B-	1.5	10.00	56.61	1100	925	641	-772	-1692	-2220
N/R	2.5	10.00	29.20	2424	2201	1767	-18	-677	-1181
IO	200.0	5.07	2.75	500	434	350	194	168	148

A Simple Sequential CMBS Structure

The question which investors would like to be answered is: Which has better value — the AAA bond at +85 bp or the BBB bond at +190 bp? Our model can be used to help answer this type of question. We use the following example to demonstrate the application of the model.

We start with the same type of loan as in the prior section, i.e. a 7% coupon, 10-year balloon loan with a 30-year amortization schedule, 10-year Treasury rates at 4.76%, NOI volatility of 16%, interest rate volatility of 11%, and a correlation of 20% between interest rates and NOI. For analytic purposes we assume that instead of a single loan, we have a pool of ten $20 million loans with LTVs ranging from 61.6% to 81.1% (weighted average 70%) and DSCRs ranging from 1.48× to 1.12× (weighted average 1.30×).

Exhibit 13 depicts a typical CMBS deal.[20] In the deal, the N/R (unrated) class is structured as the most junior tranche. There are two AAA classes, one short maturity and one long maturity. The other classes range from AA to B–. In addition there is an IO class stripped from the AAA through the A rated classes.

As was the case with the unstructured commercial mortgage, when the NOI volatility is low, the OAS is almost equal to the stated yield spread.[21] At higher levels of NOI volatility, the OAS declines. As expected, the largest declines take place in the most junior classes since they are the first to absorb losses caused by defaults. Interestingly, the OAS also declines substantially for

---

[20] In this example, the spreads are reasonably representative of the market as of the first quarter of 1999.

[21] Since the Treasury curve is positively sloped the OAS would still be below the stated yield spread due to the dispersion of the cash flows.

the most senior class. This is because the recoveries from defaults are used to pay the most senior classes first. Since, in this example, the senior classes are priced at a premium, the premature receipt of principal at par leads to a degradation in the bond's yield. In Exhibits 14 and 15 we show the OAS versus NOI volatility for the senior bonds.

Exhibit 14: OAS versus Volatility of NOI for Senior Tranches: Default Option

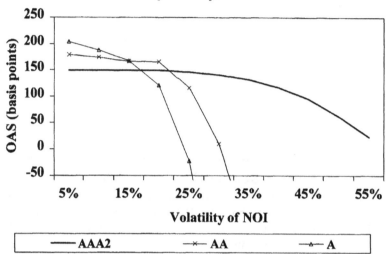

Exhibit 15: OAS versus Volatility of NOI for Senior Tranches: Refinance and Default Options

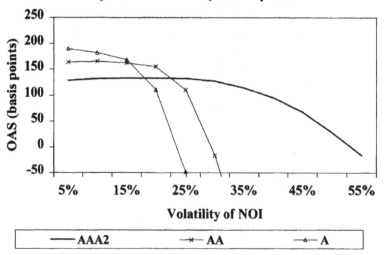

Exhibit 16: An Example of a Sequential Structure of CMBS: Refinance and Default Options (10 Loans)

Class	Size ($mm)	WAL	Price	Yield Spread	OAS Vol. 6%	Vol. 9%	Vol. 16%	Vol. 20%	Vol. 30%
Collateral	200.0	9.40	100.00	226	202	185	111	58	−79
AAA Short	24.5	5.14	101.50	138	129	130	122	116	107
AAA Long	119.5	9.99	101.50	146	130	131	133	133	127
AA	12.0	10.00	100.00	176	164	166	159	155	−17
A	11.0	10.00	100.00	201	189	184	159	111	−322
BBB	9.0	10.00	96.05	281	273	257	160	16	−821
BBB−	3.0	10.00	89.60	381	377	346	157	−99	−1267
BB+	8.5	10.00	77.31	600	600	539	171	−310	−1637
BB	2.0	10.00	76.05	625	596	506	−139	−836	−2159
BB−	2.0	10.00	67.96	800	771	657	−124	−858	−2293
B+	3.5	10.00	63.86	900	840	656	−375	−1209	−2626
B	1.0	10.00	61.93	950	845	547	−779	−1886	−2681
B−	1.5	10.00	56.61	1100	971	551	−986	−1874	−2585
N/R	2.5	10.00	29.20	2424	2395	1738	−46	−650	−1374
IO	200.0	5.07	2.75	500	−248	−353	−515	−543	−471

There are several other points worth noting. First, the most protected classes are the long AAA and the AA. Their OAS changes the least as a function of NOI volatility since they are not the first to absorb losses or recoveries. Second, the A rated CMBS appears to be a better value than the underlying loan if the two are offered at the same stated spread for a wide range of NOI volatilities. Finally, the lowest rated classes appear to be the cheapest for low levels of NOI volatility.

In Exhibit 16, we allow the loans to be callable after 5 years without penalty. This substantially hurts the value of the collateral and the long AAA. The greatest damage is to the IO class. This is why a complete prepayment lockout or at least a substantial yield maintenance allocation to these classes is so important and valuable. The subordinate classes can actually benefit as shown by the improvement in their OAS because they are priced at a discount.

Subordinate Bonds

The subordinate bond classes (B-pieces) in a CMBS deal are usually priced at a discount. Our analysis shows that the OAS of the B-pieces remains wide compared to the senior tranches when a volatility as high as 9% is assumed for the NOI. (See Exhibits 17 and 18.)

Interest-Only Strips

As we noted earlier, since senior bonds are priced with lower yields than the collateral, they would have prices substantially above par if they had the same coupon. Since many investors do not want to purchase premium bonds, interest is stripped off and interest-only (IO) classes are created.[22] Interest is usually

---

[22] This can be done either at the loan level or the bond class level.

stripped in order to price the senior class close to par or at low premium in the CMBS deal. It is in the interest of the issuer to create the strip class if the proceeds from the strip class and the par bond is greater than the proceeds from a premium bond. Since the price of an IO strip is more sensitive than its principal bond with the same credit rating, it is traded at a much wider spread.

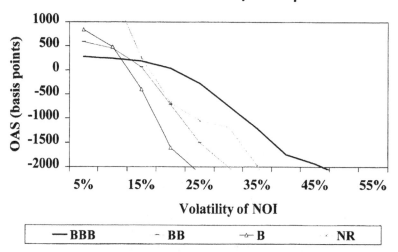

Exhibit 17: OAS versus Volatility of NOI for Subordinate Tranches: Default Options

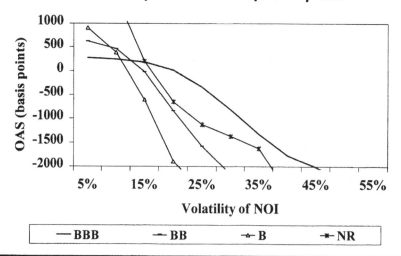

Exhibit 18: OAS versus Volatility of NOI for Subordinate Tranches: Refinance and Default Options

IO strip classes have special characteristics, which make the use of an OAS model in their valuation extremely useful. Since interest is paid only when the notional principal is outstanding, when the notional principal upon which the IOs payments are based is reduced, the amount of interest paid to the IO holder declines. There are two ways in which the erosion of notional principal can occur. The reduction in principal takes place due to either losses or due to principal payments. In the case of a loss, the senior-subordinated structure requires that the loss be allocated to the most junior outstanding class. Thus, IOs which are stripped from the AAA bond are relatively insulated from erosion of principal due to the allocation of losses. On the other hand, erosion of principal also occurs due to principal payments. The senior-subordinated structure requires that the most senior outstanding class receive principal payments. Thus, even a minor amount of prepayments leads to the erosion of principal associated with the IO stripped from the AAA bond. Principal payments can be either voluntary or involuntary. Voluntary prepayments are related to refinancing or the selling of the property. The IO holder, thus, derives considerable protection from prepayment protection features.[23]

Involuntary principal payment is a slightly more subtle concept. It arises from recoveries from foreclosure proceedings. These recoveries also must go to the most senior outstanding class. Thus, high defaults with a high rate of recovery also can erode the principal of the IO stripped from the most senior bond. The senior IO holder is in the odd position in the case of a default of hoping for zero recovery.

Exhibit 19 shows that the OAS for the IO class remains high at relatively high levels of NOI volatility, whereas Exhibit 13 shows how poorly the IO performs when the loans are prepayable. Investors should be willing to pay up substantially for IO's that are backed by well call protected loans. Note that while we assumed immediate foreclosure, the foreclosure process on average takes about a year. This would substantially improve the value of the IO classes.

DISPERSION OF LOAN QUALITY

Investors need to give serious consideration to the diversity of the loans backing the bond classes in a CMBS deal. In the prior CMBS examples, we assumed there were ten loans with a range of LTVs and DSCRs. While the average LTV was 70% and the average DSCR was 1.3×, the dispersion in quality generally has a negative impact on the bond classes. In Exhibits 20 and 21 we compare the OAS versus NOI volatility for the AAA bond and the B rated class assuming a ten loan

---

[23] Lockout, however, provides better protection than yield maintenance for two reasons. First, while yield maintenance serves as a disincentive, it is possible that in the event of prepayment the IO holder may not be allocated his fair share. More importantly, as we mentioned earlier property owners may want to prepay even when interest rates rise. In this in instance there may be no yield maintenance to distribute.

portfolio and a single loan portfolio. One can see that the dispersion lowers the OAS for the B rated class. As a junior class, it suffers the downside of the lower quality loans without an equal benefit from the higher quality loans. The AAA bond on the other hand gets the benefit of the diversity, because the lower quality loans default, and the remaining pool consists of much higher quality loans.

Exhibit 19: OAS versus Volatility of NOI for Interest-Only Strip: Default Option

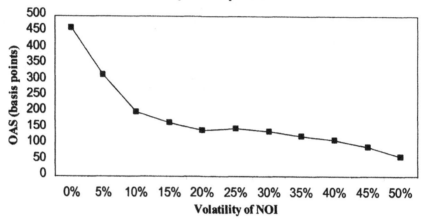

Exhibit 20: Effect of Loan Quality Dispersion: AAA CMBS Bond Class

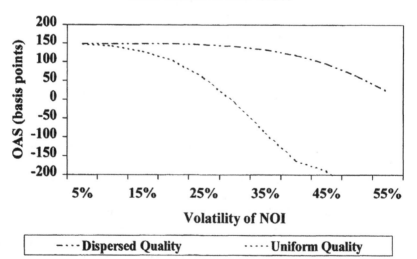

Exhibit 21: Effect of Loan Quality Dispersion: B CMBS Bond Class

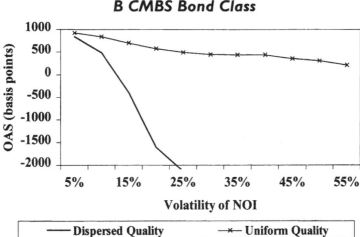

RELATIVE RISK OF CMBS BOND CLASSES

Up to this point we have used OAS model mostly as a tool for pricing and assessing relative value. The model, because it is based on the evaluation of the securities in the probability space, can also be used to determine relative risk. We use the prices that are obtained from the price distribution. One would expect that the price variation for the less risky securities be smaller (as a percent of the security's price) than for the more risky securities. This is generally the case. In Exhibits 22, 23, and 24 we show the price distribution resulting from the model assuming NOI volatility of 16%. To focus on the credit risk we held interest rates constant. Notice how much tighter the price range is for the AAA bond than for the collateral; look how wide the range is for the B rated class.

In Exhibit 25 we summarize the statistics of the distributions for each of the bond classes. In general, the lower rated classes have the highest risk as measured by the coefficient of variation.[24]

If we use the coefficient of variation as our risk measure, and OAS as our measure of relative value, we can construct the "efficient frontier" for investment analysis. Certain bonds lie on the boundary of the efficient frontier. This suggests that portfolios consisting of these bonds can be formed to outperform combinations of the other bonds. Perhaps investors should take the ratio of OAS to the coefficient of variation as the measure of relative value, much like the Sharpe ratio in stock analysis.[25]

---

[24] The coefficient of variation normalizes the risk by looking at the ratio of standard deviation to the mean.

[25] William F. Sharpe, "Mutual Fund Performance," *Journal of Business* (January 1966).

Exhibit 22: Price Distribution of Loan

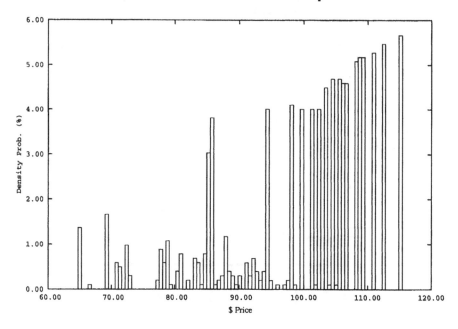

Exhibit 23: Price Distribution of CMBS — AAA

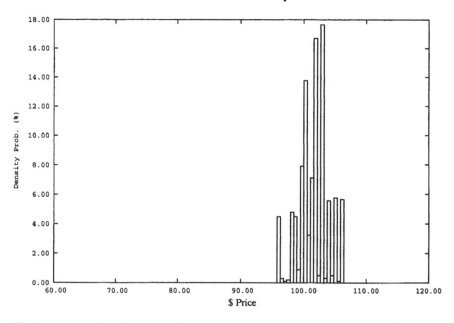

Exhibit 24: Price Distribution of CMBS — B- Class

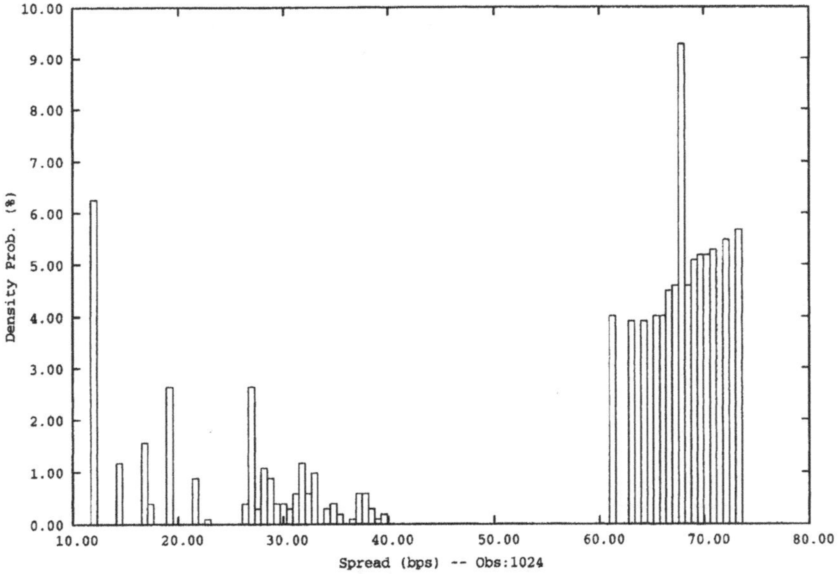

Spread (bps) -- Obs:1024

Exhibit 25: CMBS Summary Statistics

	Mean	Standard Deviation	OAS	Coefficient of Variation
Col	100.00	12.27	150.00	12.27
AAA1	101.50	2.36	134.46	2.32
AAA2	101.50	7.97	133.22	7.85
AA	100.00	26.67	49.34	26.67
A	100.00	33.49	−2.72	33.49
BBB1	96.05	39.86	3.53	41.50
BBB2	89.60	36.69	100.96	40.95
BB1	77.31	30.51	315.69	39.47
BB2	76.05	30.00	338.14	39.44
BB3	67.96	25.92	511.94	38.14
B1	63.86	23.87	611.32	37.38
B2	61.93	22.91	661.03	37.00
B3	56.61	20.29	810.24	35.85
NR	28.72	7.36	2,172.75	25.64
IO	2.75	0.70	218.81	25.57

Finally in Exhibit 26 we present the same information as in Exhibit 25 but instead of using one loan or (uniform quality) portfolio, we use a portfolio with the same *average* quality but with dispersion among the loans. One can clearly see how the diversity lowers the standard deviation of the AAA bond, but dramatically raises it for the lower rated classes.

Exhibit 26: CMBS Summary Statistics (Diverse Pool)

	Mean	Standard Deviation	OAS	Coefficient of Variation
Col	100.00	8.64	140.00	8.64
AAA1	101.50	1.51	116.65	1.49
AAA2	101.50	5.16	148.85	5.09
AA	100.00	9.99	165.04	9.99
A	100.00	15.40	159.77	15.40
BBB1	96.05	23.62	165.93	24.59
BBB2	89.60	30.49	170.44	34.03
BB1	77.31	33.52	204.60	43.36
BB2	76.05	49.31	−70.72	64.84
BB3	67.96	48.77	−60.19	71.76
B1	63.86	56.87	−294.44	89.07
B2	61.93	72.34	−617.27	116.81
B3	56.61	75.67	−771.63	133.68
NR	29.20	34.44	−17.95	117.95
IO	2.75	0.28	193.81	10.09

CONCLUSION

In this chapter we introduced a model which uses the borrower's behavior to construct a decision payoff matrix for exercising default and prepayment options and utilizes option theory to value these options. The model employs interest rates and the net operating income of the mortgaged property as the two underlying factors. Based upon the model, the option values can be assessed. We then derived an option-adjusted spread (OAS) to measure the relative value of commercial mortgages and commercial mortgage-backed securities. Given a market price, the OAS decreases as the risk exposure increases. The model serves as a unifying framework, bringing real estate valuation, fixed-income pricing, and option theory together. Factors affecting the real estate, mortgages, and structure are evaluated simultaneously across a wide range of scenarios. This analysis helps reveal hidden weaknesses in the structure and enables the analyst to compare deals.

APPENDIX: MODEL SPECIFICATION

The embedded options of commercial mortgages are American options which can be exercised at any time prior to expiration. Given state variables — interest rate and net operating income — we denote the rest of the variables as follows:

r = default-free one-period spot rate

N = net operating income

S = the expected present value of the future promised payments

C = the value of the prepayment option

D = the value of the default option

H = the total embedded option value which is equal to C plus D

G = the expected present value of the next period H

W = the market value of the underlying loan which is equal to S minus G

B = the market value of the collateral property

M = the scheduled mortgage payment

M^* = the potential refinancing scheduled mortgage payment

U = the face amount of mortgage remaining balance

Δ_d = foreclosure expense

Δ_c = prepayment penalty

We assume the process of r and N in discrete time as follows:

$$\log r_t = \alpha_t + \log r_{t-1} + \varepsilon_t$$

$$\log N_t = a_t + \log N_{t-1} + \zeta_t$$

where t is time index and, for any given t, ε and ζ have constant variances, σ^2 and s^2 respectively, and is correlated with correlation coefficient ρ.

To satisfy the above conditions, instead of generating ε and ζ directly, we generate ε and ζ and assume a relationship between ζ, ε, and ξ as follows:

$$E\left[\varepsilon^2\right] = \sigma^2$$

$$E\left[\xi^2\right] = (1-\rho)s^2$$

$$\zeta = b\varepsilon + \xi$$

where

$$E[\xi] = E[\varepsilon\xi] = 0,$$

$$b = (\rho s)/\sigma$$

Then we have

$$E[\varepsilon] = E[\zeta] = 0$$

$$E[\varepsilon\zeta] = \rho s \sigma$$

$$E\left[\zeta^2\right] = s^2$$

To obtain property value B, we assume $B=N/(r-rg)$ where g is constant through time. The property value B can be interpreted as the present value of an infinite series of prevailing net operating income with a growth rate g multiplied by r and discounted by the prevailing interest rate r. Since r, B, and N are known initially, g can be obtained through the equation. The value of $(r-rg)$, in essence, is the capitalization rate of the property.

Triggering Conditions

The prepayment triggering conditions:

(i) $N > M^*$
(ii) $G + \Delta_c < S - U$

The default triggering conditions:

(i) $N < M$
(ii) $G < S + M - B$

The default-as-a-method-of-prepayment triggering conditions:

(i) $N > M^*$
(ii) $G + \Delta_d < S - U$

Exhibit 27 provides an arbitrage table for decision support.

Implementation of the Options Calculation

Based on the stochastic processes of N and r, as well as generic mortgage debt information, we are able to generate r, N, B, M, M^*, U, and S to span the whole solid binomial pyramid.

    Starting from the maturity date of the mortgage debt, the option value G can be calculated backward in time.

At maturity date of period T:
Given r, N, B, M, and $S=U$, based on the default and prepayment trigger condition:

$$H = \begin{cases} U + M - B \text{ (default)} \\ 0 \text{ (otherwise) and } G = 0 \end{cases}$$

Exhibit 27: Arbitrage Table for Decision Support

Triggering Condition				Action Code	H value	
I	II	III	IV		$t < T$	T
$I-M = \text{Min}[B-M, U+\Delta_d, U+\Delta_c] < S\text{-}G$	$N<M$			1	$S+M-B$	$U+M-B$
	$N>M$	$U+\Delta_d = \text{Min}[U+\Delta_d,U+\Delta_c] < S\text{-}G$	$N>M^*$	2	$S-U-\Delta_d$	0
			$N<M^*$	0	G	0
		$U+\Delta_c = \text{Min}[U+\Delta_d,U+\Delta_c] < S\text{-}G$	$N>M^*$	3	$S-U-\Delta_c$	0
			$N<M^*$	0	G	0
$U+\Delta_d = \text{Min}[B-M, U+\Delta_d,U+\Delta_c] < S\text{-}G$	$N>M^*$			2	$S-U-\Delta_d$	0
	$N<M^*$	$B > S+M\text{-}G$		0	G	0
		$B < S+M\text{-}G$	$N>M$	0	G	0
			$N<M$	1	$S+M-B$	$U+M-B$
$U+\Delta_c = \text{Min}[B-M, U+\Delta_d,U+\Delta_c] < S\text{-}G$	$N>M^*$			3	$I-U-\Delta_c$	0
	$N<M^*$	$B > S+M\text{-}G$		0	G	0
		$B < S+M\text{-}G$	$N>M$	0	G	0
			$N<M$	1	$S+M-B$	$U+M-B$
$\text{Min}[B-M, U+\Delta_d,U+\Delta_c] \geq S\text{-}G$				0	G	0

Note: numbers 0,1,2, and 3 in Action column denote to "no action," "default," "default-as-a-method-of-prepayment," and "prepay" respectively.

At time t where $t < T$:
Given r, N, B, M, M^*, U and S, based on the default and prepayment trigger condition:

$$H = \begin{cases} S + M - B \text{ (default)} \\ S - U - \Delta_d \text{ (default as involuntary prepayment)} \\ S - U - \Delta_c \text{ (prepay)} \\ G \text{ (otherwise)} \end{cases}$$

and then G can be calculated from next-step H by discounting the interest rates with weighted probabilities.

Index

497

Banc of America Securities

The Vision of a Leader

The real estate industry is built on vision.
It takes vision to see the hidden potential for
new homes in a depressed area, to imagine
a sophisticated mixed-use development in a
sea of cornfields, to build an office structure
that reaches higher than anyone ever dreamed.

At Bank of America, we share that vision.

Our ability to provide well-designed,
comprehensive financial structures that turn
visions into realities has made us the largest
real estate capital provider in the world.

Commitment to clients.

Global capabilities.

Market insights.

Results.

Printed and bound by CPI Group (UK) Ltd, Croydon, CR0 4YY

23/04/2025

14661010-0002